Reflections on Uneven De

Reflections on Uneven Democracies

The Legacy of Guillermo O'Donnell

EDITED BY
DANIEL BRINKS, MARCELO LEIRAS,
AND SCOTT MAINWARING

Johns Hopkins University Press
Baltimore

The Eugene and Helen Conley Professorship of Political Science at the University of Notre Dame helped support the publication of this volume.

Johns Hopkins University Press
2715 North Charles Street
Baltimore, Maryland 21218-4363
www.press.jhu.edu

Library of Congress Cataloging-in-Publication Data

Reflections on uneven democracies : the legacy of Guillermo O'Donnell / edited by Daniel Brinks, Marcelo Leiras, and Scott Mainwaring.
pages cm
Includes bibliographical references and index.
ISBN 978-1-4214-1459-1 (hardcover : alk. paper)—ISBN 978-1-4214-1460-7 (pbk. : alk. paper)—ISBN 978-1-4214-1461-4 (electronic)—ISBN 1-4214-1459-7 (hardcover : alk. paper)—ISBN 1-4214-1460-0 (pbk. : alk. paper)—ISBN 1-4214-1461-9 (electronic) 1. Democracy—Latin America. 2. Democratization—Latin America. 3. Political culture—Latin America. 4. Latin America—Politics and government—1948–1980. 5. Latin America—Politics and government—1980– 6. O'Donnell, Guillermo A. I. Brinks, Daniel M., 1961– , author, editor of compilation. II. Leiras, Marcelo, author, editor of compilation. III. Mainwaring, Scott, 1954– , author, editor of compilation.
JL966.R38318 2014
320.98—dc23 2013048641

A catalog record for this book is available from the British Library.

Special discounts are available for bulk purchases of this book. For more information, please contact Special Sales at 410-516-6936 or specialsales@press.jhu.edu.

Johns Hopkins University Press uses environmentally friendly book materials, including recycled text paper that is composed of at least 30 percent post-consumer waste, whenever possible.

CONTENTS

This volume honors the legacy of Guillermo O'Donnell by advancing debates related to his work on democracy. The volume includes chapters by two of O'Donnell's closest collaborators, Philippe Schmitter and Laurence Whitehead, his coeditors of the iconic *Transitions from Authoritarian Rule,* published in 1986 by Johns Hopkins University Press. It also includes chapters by midcareer scholars who were inspired by O'Donnell's work, and a rich combination of European, US, and Latin American scholars—reflecting the broad range of influences that O'Donnell had in the scholarly world.

The book title's reference to "uneven" democracies can be understood in multiple ways, all of which are central to analyzing democracy in contemporary Latin America. First, these democracies (and semi-democracies) are uneven in the sense that they have registered some important achievements but most also have notable shortcomings. Foremost among the achievements is the fact that they have survived. Since 1990, openly authoritarian regimes have been rare, marking the first time in Latin American history in which stable democracies have dominated the region for such an extended period of time. In recent years there has been only one exception, Cuba. While celebrating this achievement, O'Donnell devoted the last two decades of his scholarly career (1991–2011) to advancing a democratic critique of democracy, calling attention to many deficits. Second, as O'Donnell (1993) noted, these democracies and semi-democracies are territorially uneven within countries. Some "green" areas have high-level democracies, whereas some states and provinces in the same countries have "brown" areas, with hybrid subnational political regimes that fall short of being democratic. Likewise, the rule of law is uneven across different parts of national territories. Third, Latin America has long been the region of the world with the highest inequalities. O'Donnell (1992) called attention to the multiple ways in which these profound social inequalities undermined the evenness of citizenship.

This book goes beyond recapitulating O'Donnell's contributions to thinking about the continuing implications of his work for the study of democracies everywhere. The contributions catalogue the unevenness of democracy, drawing on his fecund conceptual innovations. The authors sometimes confirm and other times disagree with O'Donnell's arguments. The result is a tribute to his insights and knowledge and also a volume for thinking about enduring puzzles and continuing challenges in research on democracy and democratization.

In March 2012, we organized a conference in Buenos Aires to honor O'Donnell, with the thought of subsequently producing this volume. We thank the Kellogg Institute for International Studies of the University of Notre Dame, the Ford Foundation, and the Fundación OSDE for the generous financial support that made the conference possible. The Kellogg Institute, the Universidad de Buenos Aires, the Universidad de San Andrés, the Universidad Nacional de San Martín, the Asociación Nacional de Politólogos, the Sociedad Argentina de Análisis Político, and the Latin American Program of the Woodrow Wilson International Center for Scholars cosponsored the conference and a series of other events to honor O'Donnell. We are grateful for their support.

The conference drew an international cast of luminaries in democratization studies. Their participation enriched the conference and made our few days in Buenos Aires special. A partial list includes Carlos Acuña, Cynthia Arnson, Ernest Bartell, CSC, Paola Bergallo, Pablo Bulcourf, Isidoro Cheresky, David Collier, Michael Coppedge, Martín D'Alessandro, Miguel De Luca, Gustavo Dufour, Alberto Föhrig, Alejandro Foxley, Manuel Antonio Garretón, José María Ghio, Evelyne Huber, David Lehmann, Abraham Lowenthal, Gerardo Munck, Gabriela Ippolito-O'Donnell, María Matilde Ollier, Oscar Oszlak, Timothy Scully, CSC, Ximena Simpson, Catalina Smulovitz, Alfred Stepan, Luis Tonelli, María Gloria Trocello, Eduardo Viola, Francisco Weffort, and Rodrigo Zarazaga, SJ.

Special thanks to Gabriela Ippolito-O'Donnell for her encouragement and help in organizing the conference and the other events to commemorate O'Donnell's life and work.

The staff of the Kellogg Institute provided support for the conference and the tributes to O'Donnell. Thanks to Therese Hanlon, Peg Hartman, Elizabeth Rankin, Steve Reifenberg, and Sharon Schierling. María Victoria De Negri helped with the tribute to Guillermo O'Donnell and in the editing and indexing of this volume. Michele Callaghan of Johns Hopkins University Press did the copy editing.

Finally, thanks to our editor, Suzanne Flinchbaugh, for her enthusiasm, helpful ideas, and advice. It was a great pleasure to work with her. It is especially fitting that we publish this book with Johns Hopkins University Press for two related reasons: its long history of excellence in democratization studies and its association with Guillermo O'Donnell through publication of *Transitions from Authoritarian Rule*. Serendipitously, Johns Hopkins recently reissued *Tentative Conclusions about Uncertain Democracies*, the book that O'Donnell and Schmitter published in 1986 as volume 4 of *Transitions from Authoritarian Rule*.

Reflections on Uneven Democracies

Guillermo O'Donnell and the Study of Democracy

DANIEL BRINKS, MARCELO LEIRAS, AND SCOTT MAINWARING

This book advances the research agenda on democratization by building on the legacy of Guillermo O'Donnell (1936–2011) to analyze some of the fundamental ongoing questions in this field. O'Donnell made enormous contributions to the study of breakdowns of democracy, transitions to democracy, and the nature of the ensuing democratic regimes. We take his contributions as a starting point and push them forward to think about crucial contemporary theoretical and empirical issues in the study of democratization. The result simultaneously honors the dominant figure in the study of Latin American politics since the early 1970s and advances knowledge on key themes related to democratization.

In this introduction, we outline some features of O'Donnell's contributions, draw out the common themes in the various chapters as well as the major points of contention, and sketch some basic questions in the ongoing research agenda in democracy studies. O'Donnell's work spawned many of the most important current debates about democratization. Three basic themes in his writings frame much of the work on democratization and the functioning of democratic regimes. First are the questions of regime change he addressed in *Modernization and Bureaucratic-Authoritarianism* (1973) and in *Transitions from Authoritarian Rule* (O'Donnell and Schmitter 1986): what leads to the breakdown of democratic regimes and what leads to transitions to democracy? The second major area of inquiry draws attention to the political economy of democracy: what is the connection between a society's economic structure and the key features of its democratic regime? The third relates to the nature and quality of the resulting regime: how are contemporary post-transition democracies functioning, and how do the features of these regimes push us to revise democratic theory? Is a different kind of regime being institutionalized—one that is low on horizontal accountability and shares the features of what O'Donnell (1994) called delegative democracy?

These themes remain central to the global comparative literature. The first two themes are classic issues about which an important theoretical debate is ongoing. The third, on the nature and quality of democracy, the rule of law, and institutional performance, involves some the most pressing issues in much of the world today, from Latin America to the post-Soviet countries and much of Africa, Asia, and the Middle East. All are at the core of current debates in social science.

Parts I and II of this volume deal with the first two themes. Parts III and IV build on ODonnell's work on post-transition democracies and his late career emphasis on human agency. In the fifth and final part, we turn in a more methodological direction to address the contemporary and future implications of how O'Donnell approached political science.

Part I: Democratic Survival, Breakdowns, and Transitions

Democratic breakdown was the central topic of O'Donnell's classic 1973 book, *Modernization and Bureaucratic-Authoritarianism*. His analysis focused on why democracies were breaking down in Latin America's most developed countries. *Modernization and Bureaucratic-Authoritarianism* was a seminal work in understanding the origins of modern authoritarianism in Latin America. His argument prompted a critical rethinking of modernization theory, which posited that more developed countries are more likely to be democratic. The analysis of why democracies break down or survive continues to be a cutting-edge issue in comparative politics. This issue is relevant not only to understanding Latin America's past but also to analyzing prospects for democratization in other parts of the world and to contemplating the possibilities of an erosion in democracy in contemporary Latin America.

Much of this literature focuses on the relationship between the level of economic development and democracy. O'Donnell (1973) was an early skeptic of the modernization argument that economic development leads to more democracy. Some more recent quantitative analyses have suggested that, whatever its effect on the stability of democracy, economic development has not led to democratization (Przeworski et al. 2000). Others have questioned this conclusion, arguing that development does have an independent effect on transitions to democracy, although that effect might be felt more at low levels of development and democracy (Boix 2011; Brinks and Coppedge 2006: 481; Epstein et al. 2006) and might be conditional on other factors (Boix 2011). Still others argue that the relationship between democracy and development is an artifact of other factors, including, for example, the influence of Western missionaries on education (Woodberry 2012) and literacy rates in former colonies (Acemoglu et al. 2008). The question remains unsettled.

Part I of this book takes up this question anew. Chapter 1 begins with a quantitative regional analysis, and chapter 2 offers a close analysis of Argentina, the case that first motivated O'Donnell's insights.

In chapter 1, Aníbal Pérez-Liñán and Scott Mainwaring examine why democracies survive or break down, with an empirical focus on Latin America from 1945 to 2005. Their argument deviates from the quantitative literature and a good part of the qualitative literature on democratic survival and breakdown. They show that structural variables such as the level of development have *not* shaped prospects for democratic survival in Latin America, supporting O'Donnell's skepticism about modernization theory for this region.

Pérez-Liñán and Mainwaring introduce a novel strategy for studying regime breakdown and survival, namely, the use of an actor-based approach on a large enough scale that it is possible to do quantitative analysis. They analyze 1,460 political actors in 290 presidential administrations from 1944 to 2010 for the twenty Latin American countries, coding these actors according to their policy radicalism or moderation and their normative views toward democracy and dictatorship. Previous quantitative approaches to the study of democratic survival did not indicate who the key actors are, and they did not test propositions about regime survival and breakdown based on the observed properties of real political actors.

Pérez-Liñán and Mainwaring argue that actors' policy moderation or radicalism has an important impact on the survival or breakdown of competitive regimes. The presence of radical actors makes competitive regimes more vulnerable to breakdown. Actors' normative commitment to democracy in the third wave has helped buffer competitive regimes from breakdown even in the face of dramatic economic challenges. The findings suggest that a key variable has been missing in these analyses and offer a way forward for democratization studies that seek to incorporate key actors and agency into structural approaches. Along with some of the chapters analyzed below, this chapter suggests new directions for the study of democratization processes —here, a focus on actors and their preferences—and provides a new reference for analyses that seek to go beyond structural models.

In chapter 2, Carlos Gervasoni seeks to understand what has changed for Argentina since O'Donnell's 1973 classic. His fundamental question is why Argentina went from being a chronic democratic underachiever until 1983 to being a consistent overachiever since then, relative to its level of development. Argentina long defied modernization theory. It combined a high level of development and five breakdowns of democracy between 1930 and 1976. Since 1983 it has remained democratic despite several profound economic and political crises.

Consistent with Pérez-Liñán and Mainwaring's account, Gervasoni finds that decreasing levels of political violence and radicalism and increasing levels of elite democratic preferences are among the few existing explanatory factors that can account for Argentina´s regime turnaround. Classic structural factors such as modernization, inequality, or class structure are partially or totally inconsistent with Argentina´s regime trajectory. He also agrees with Pérez-Liñán and Mainwaring that the changed international political environment with the end of the Cold War and changes in U.S. foreign policy have helped support democracy. Gervasoni's analysis calls into question many of the dominant theories of democratization, briefly summarizes his own pathbreaking analysis of subnational democracy, and challenges future researchers to pay more attention to agency and political action than to constructed political identities and interests.

Together chapters 1 and 2 offer two important lessons. First, many quantitative, national-level studies of democratization miss a large part of what has produced the stable set of democracies present in the world today. These studies focus on "objective," easily quantifiable variables, usually available off the shelf. Most of them assume that actors support or oppose regimes according to the material benefits they expect to reap under democracy or dictatorship. Relying on the available indicators and building upon materialistic models of political action, not even the most recent contributions —for example, Boix (2011) or Woodberry (2012)—can account for variations within Latin America or the stability of democracy in countries that had long been showcases for political instability and the breakdown of democracy. In light of the increasingly contested importance of economic development or inequality as explanatory variables (Ahlquist and Wibbels 2012), scholars must pay more attention to the complex genesis of preferences over regime type—a process in which distributive concerns are just one ingredient—and to the behavior inspired by those preferences. This requires supplementing the abundant information about social structure and institutional environments with information about political actors—as do Pérez-Liñán and Mainwaring—and delving into particular cases, as Gervasoni does, in order to probe more deeply into the roots of democratization. Future scholars will have to develop new measures and refine theories and methods to explore more agency-based accounts of democratization. And, equally important, they will have to continue exploring subnational variation in levels of democracy, both because it is important in its own right and because it offers additional analytic leverage in exploring the causes of democratization.

By revisiting well-known cases and regions decades after O'Donnell's 1973 analysis, chapters 1 and 2 prompt a broader examination of Latin America's apparent exceptionalism. They call into question a simplistic association between the level of development and democracy in and beyond Latin America. Yet this finding for Latin America does not refute the broader, global empirical association between higher per capita income and democracy. Why has Latin America not conformed to the broader finding that more economically developed countries are less likely to experience democratic breakdowns? Given both that empirical association and the finding that actors' preferences are crucial to democratic stability and breakdown, is there a connection, for much of the world but not for Latin America, between development and these preferences? Why does modernization theory appear to work for other parts of the world but not for Latin America?

In chapter 3, Philippe C. Schmitter reflects on "transitology"—the study of transitions to democracy—more than a quarter of a century after the publication of the seminal O'Donnell and Schmitter (1986) volume on transitions. O'Donnell and Schmitter opened a new research question that was hugely important both for political science and political sociology and in the "real" world.

This chapter reflects on the initial O'Donnell and Schmitter (1986) contribution and on what needs to be revised in light of subsequent developments. Schmitter notes the stunning and wholly unanticipated number of transitions that took place after the early ones that he and O'Donnell analyzed. He argues that the two key assumptions of their 1986 volume—an emphasis on uncertainty and agency—were correct. The fact that a higher level of development has only a modest effect on the probability of a transition from authoritarianism to a competitive regime empirically substantiates O'Donnell and Schmitter's original emphasis on agency (Epstein et al. 2006).[1] Schmitter recognizes, however, that uncertainty about outcomes and the space for agency (i.e., for crafting the outcome) vary over time and that on average uncertainty and agency have declined in importance as the third wave of democratization progressed.

In earlier waves of democratization, many new competitive regimes quickly broke down and were replaced by new dictatorships. In contrast, among the cases the O'Donnell/Schmitter/Whitehead volumes considered, Schmitter notes that in the third wave "not a single one has (yet) suffered a manifest or sudden regression to autocracy." This argument is consistent with the data in Pérez-Liñán and Mainwaring on the dramatic decline in the breakdown rate of competitive regimes in Latin America since 1978. But, argues Schmitter, the "dirty secret" behind the infrequency of breakdowns is that few cases of democratization since 1974 have led to profound policy and substantive change—a contrast to many earlier cases. Schmitter's observation vindicates the well-known assertion by Przeworski (1986) that democratic stability may be purchased at the expense of policy moderation. It is also consistent with the sharp decline Pérez-Liñán and Mainwaring report in radicalism among Latin American political actors in the 1990s (see also Weyland 2005).

O'Donnell and Schmitter viewed transitions as games among domestic actors and largely downplayed international influences. Schmitter in chapter 3 notes that "contrary to our expectations, the relevance of the international context increased monotonically with each successive demise of autocracy and attempt to establish democracy." No modern account of democratic stability or of the likely outcome of a regime transition can neglect international influences. Schmitter's reflections show what has changed in the real world and in democratization studies since his agenda-setting work with O'Donnell, motivating a call for more precise and more theoretical work on the relationship between democracy and pressures for redistribution (and vice versa) and on the nature of the relationship between global forces and domestic processes.

Part II: The Political Economy of Authoritarianism and Democracy

Here the chapters return economic structures to center stage. O'Donnell's *Modernization and Bureaucratic-Authoritarianism* and his works on political regimes in Argentina from 1955 to 1976 (O'Donnell 1978a, 1978b, 1978c, 1982) adopted a political economy approach to studying authoritarianism and democracy. As noted above, the ways in which class and distributional conflict shape prospects for democracy and authoritarianism remain key issues in political science and political sociology (Acemoglu and Robinson 2006; Boix 2003; Haggard and Kaufman 1995). They also remain contentious issues. Two chapters in this volume advance this debate. Chapter 4 by Sebastián Mazzuca deploys a historical analysis to analyze contemporary Latin America, and chapter 5, by Robert M. Fishman, evaluates the role of global financial actors in the partial erosion of some of Europe's contemporary democracies.

Mazzuca examines some troubling developments in Latin America that may not be reducible to forms of democracy or even to regime type. He identifies four countries—Argentina, Bolivia, Ecuador, and Venezuela—that in his view are radical cases of the "Left Turn" within the region, suffering from deficiencies along two dimensions. Madisonian checks and balances, which O'Donnell (1999a) famously identified as mechanisms of horizontal accountability, are weak and weakening, and Weberian rational-bureaucratic states are being supplanted by more patrimonial patterns. These countries vary in the extent to which democratic institutions that relate to elections and alternation in office are still healthy. He argues that separate causal processes may account for regime and state features that relate to access to power, as opposed to those that relate to the exercise of power.

Crucial in his account is the way in which the commodity boom of the 2000s made possible the emergence of "rentier populism," a new type of political coalition based on the economic incorporation of the informal sector and funded by windfall gains from exports of natural resources. Based on a new fiscal structure, rentier populism fostered the intensification of plebiscitarian mechanisms of electoral accountability and diminished horizontal accountability. Mazzuca explores the conditions under which the commodity boom of 2003–8 spread across Latin America with differential coalitional effects in different countries. He also delineates the mechanisms that link the rentier populism coalition to the emergence of plebiscitarian presidents with hegemonic aspirations, or "super-presidents."

In chapter 5, Robert Fishman's "Democracy and Markets: Notes on a Twenty-First Century Paradox" takes these theoretical tools to twenty-first-century Europe for an examination of the impact of globalization on what seemed to be mature, well established democracies. Fishman argues that the winds of global change have been widely seen to favor the simultaneous advance of both democracy and markets for almost three decades—indeed since O'Donnell and Schmitter (1986) wrote their pioneering work on democratic transitions. The assumption that markets and democracy necessarily march together has long been subject to debate and qualification, but Fishman calls special attention to the way in which market actors have sharply reduced the space for democratic decision making. Drawing inspiration from O'Donnell's (1973) path-opening work, which theorized reasons why capitalist economic development and democracy are not *necessarily* mutually reinforcing, and from his later work (e.g., 1993, 2010a) on the state and legal infrastructure required for democratic resilience, Fishman examines recent episodes in the erosion of democracy in Europe and offers tentative theoretical lessons for future analyses.

Reading these chapters together suggests a research agenda that expands on the insights of the rentier state literature, which focuses on how dependence on "rents" from natural resources such as oil affects political regimes. Mazzuca's chapter, as well as Peruzzotti's, discussed below, argues that high natural resource rents may well contribute to a domestic democratic deficit. Rents—arising from and changing the domestic political economy—affect not only democracy but also other features of the state and the government. They fund and encourage the sort of plebiscitarian populism we see emerging in many nominally democratic regimes that exaggerate the role of personalistic leaders and permit a relatively deinstitutionalized, direct connection between those leaders and mass publics. In contrast, Fishman shows that financial pressures in the context of the global crisis can remove the most important questions of economic and welfare policy from domestic politics, tie the hands of elected policy makers, and proscribe a whole range of policy options that can be at the very core of domestic popular demands, thus deepening the democratic deficit. Natural resource rents might offer an important buffer for domestic policy makers against the pressures of international financial actors or they may insulate dominant executives from democratic accountability.

The first five chapters show a complex role for and interrelationship between global capital and domestic rents, generating an interesting tension for the analysis of twenty-first-century democracy. On the one hand, global financial pressures can leave a country with a limited version of democracy in which elected representatives face severe constraints stemming from the demands of international financial actors. One way out of this bind is through reliance on natural resource rents, as they can alter the balance of power between global capital and domestic policy makers, freeing governments to pursue their preferred policies in response to domestic politics. On the other hand, this global disciplining pressure may moderate the demands of the left and reassure the right that its interests are secure, thus making stable democracy possible. Moreover, natural resource wealth has often proven perilous for democracy: easy access to resource rents may provide public officials with significant but volatile financial leeway, compromising republican checks and civil liberties while building state power on shaky ground. The complex interaction between global and domestic forces changes the political economy of democracy in ways that were unimaginable when O'Donnell and Schmitter published *Transitions from Authoritarian Rule*.

Terry Karl's chapter analyzes the deleterious impact of social and economic inequalities on democracy in the United States, echoing O'Donnell's concern with this same issue in Latin America. She examines the political roots of the dramatic growth of inequality in the United States. Global and domestic structures may empower or weaken social actors, but it is political strategies, inspired by ideas and crystallized in institutions, that drive financial regulations and social policies, which in turn shape the distribution of income and wealth. Distributive patterns rooted in deep-seated historical factors are stable, but economic crises, such as the global crisis that began in 2008, may pave the way for political coalitions that can decisively alter policy, thus leading to sharp reductions or increases in levels of inequality.

Karl's theoretical lessons draw on a contrast between the evolution of distributive patterns in Latin American countries and the United States. In Latin America at the turn of the twenty-first century, disillusionment with the social and economic impact of free market policies led to significant electoral changes and policy shifts. The new incumbent coalitions tightened labor market regulations and used part of the rents from the commodity boom to finance transfers to the poor. These changes brought about an unprecedented reduction in levels of inequality. In the United States, in contrast, the stagflation of the late 1970s paved the way for a coalition intent on reducing top marginal tax rates and weakening regulations of labor markets and financial transactions. Beneficiaries of these changes deployed financial and political resources to keep supply side policies in place and make electoral politics more open to the influence of money. In Karl's account, supply side policies account for the significant increase in the concentration of income and wealth experienced in the United States since 1980, and the ideas and institutions that buttress the ascendancy of conservative sectors explain the resilience of these policies.

Leiras's chapter explores the mediating role of political competition on political regimes. His analysis of democratic breakdowns and coup attempts in Latin America since 1945 finds that economic performance has had less of an impact on the survival of competitive regimes than on the stability of authoritarian governments. When political competition is not institutionalized or when it is blocked, bad economic performance provides elites intent on replacing incumbents with a sign of government incompetence and an excuse for intervention. Institutionalized competition, in turn, facilitates the replacement of both incompetent leaders and failed policies. According to Leiras, this is why competitive regimes proved to be more resilient to economic outcomes in Latin America.

The contrast between this finding and the expectations of most of the literature motivates a discussion of two significant theoretical problems: the correspondence between economic regimes and particular policies and the significance of policy safeguards for the survival of competitive regimes. Leiras contends, first, that the contrast between the policies that democratic and nondemocratic regimes implement is not as sharp as some political economy literature assumes and not as relevant to regime stability as these contributions hold. Second, he argues that, when the expectation of leadership turnover is sufficiently firm, policy guarantees are not as relevant as a device to neutralize distributive conflicts; they could be counterproductive, because competitive regimes address distributive conflicts by making the replacement of undesirable policies more likely. In this sense, the survival of democracies in Latin America after the third wave may be interpreted as a combination of reinforcing dynamics: globalization-induced policy moderation and institutionalized political competition that facilitates policy change.

Part III: Weak Formal Institutions, Rule of Law, and Delegative Democracy

Part III of our volume analyzes theoretical and empirical aspects of democratization in the areas of the world with what O'Donnell called "delegative democracies" and weak "horizontal accountability." O'Donnell argued, and the authors in Part III all agree, that the competitive regimes that have emerged in much of Latin America and other regions in the third and fourth waves of democratization differ from democracies in early waves. How can we fruitfully analyze these differences? Building on O'Donnell's work, Part III advances the ongoing research agenda about how to build better democracies in much of the world, including Latin America, and about how to theorize democracy and politics in light of the democratic deficiencies of many competitive regimes in the world.

O'Donnell reexamined democratic theory and named many important concepts that remain at the core of analyses of contemporary democracy. His essays and books opened new theoretical and empirical research fields on weak formal institutions, citizenship, the weakness of the rule of law, "horizontal accountability," and "delegative democracy." Chapters 8 to 10 in Part III explore this conceptual terrain, using and adding to O'Donnell's theories.

As Timothy J. Power shows in chapter 8, this new agenda grew out of a recognition that many Latin American political regimes fulfilled minimalist procedural definitions of democracy but had grave deficiencies along what O'Donnell called the "horizontal" dimension of accountability. Power examines O'Donnell's changing research agenda between the mid-1980s and the mid-1990s. In 1985, O'Donnell initiated the first major comparative research project on democratic consolidation. Yet by the early 1990s O'Donnell was signaling a change of theoretical course, and in 1996 his essay "Illusions about Consolidation" advocated a complete rethinking of the dynamics of postauthoritarian regimes (1996a). Why did this shift occur? Power argues that the evolution of O'Donnell's thinking was driven by changing regional dynamics in Latin America, by the expansion of the third wave of democratization to new cases, and by trends in comparative political analysis. Over time O'Donnell's concern moved from the possibility of democratic breakdown to visible shortcomings in democratic quality, such as delegative democracy.

Power highlights the link between concepts and empirical and normative assumptions. Social scientists underplay the significance of the concepts and labels they use when they argue that, as long as they are clear and transparent in their definitions, they can define concepts as they choose.[2] Like Peruzzotti in chapter 12 and McGuire in chapter 13, Power suggests that embracing a particular definition of a concept or label for a phenomenon can open our eyes to some dynamics and blind us to others. It is not that it is impossible to embrace a research agenda that goes beyond founding elections if we adopt the "transition/consolidation" frame. The rich literature that emerged out of a concern for consolidation proves this. But choosing a certain definition, an evocative metaphor, or a catchy label can guide research in ways of which we are not fully conscious. By the same token, a normatively prompted concern for a particular reality can drive us to search for labels and concepts, when the existing literature does not seem to be paying attention. This is one hallmark of O'Donnell's legacy: an awareness of an understudied and troubling reality led him to coin the many phrases that came to define an entire generation of studies of democracy.

In the 1980s and 1990s, a "new institutionalism" emerged in political science (Hall and Taylor 1996; March and Olsen 1984; Thelen and Steinmo 1992) and economics (North 1990). As Levitsky and Murillo argue in chapter 9, a common assumption in much of this work was that the formal institutions actually govern actors' behavior. More than any other person, O'Donnell set an alternative research agenda that simultaneously emphasized the importance of institutions while challenging arguments that focused exclusively on the formal rules of the game (see also Helmke and Levitsky

2006a; Levitsky and Murillo 2005a; Weyland 2002). At the core of his new research agenda was a quest to understand which institutions really influence actors and how democracies in Latin America really function.[3]

In their chapter, Levitsky and Murillo examine institutional change in a weak institutional environment (i.e., where rules are unstable and weakly enforced), using the experience of Latin America to refine theories of institutional change developed for advanced democracies. Their chapter draws on the insights that O'Donnell developed in the 1990s (1993, 1994, 1996a, 1999b, 1999c) about the weakness of formal institutions and the prevalence of informal institutions in much of Latin America.

Levitsky and Murillo challenge Thelen's important work on institutional change. Thelen (2004) and Mahoney and Thelen (2010) posited two models of institutional change: rapid but infrequent change leading to a new equilibrium ("punctuated equilibrium") or gradual change. Levitsky and Murillo argue that in much of Latin America institutional change resembles neither standard punctuated equilibrium models nor gradual change but instead follows a pattern of "serial replacement," in which change is both frequent and rapid. Variation in enforcement affects institutional change. In contexts of weak formal institutions, the enforcement of the formal rules of the game cannot be taken for granted. Rather, it varies across space and time. Intuitively, it would seem that enforcement of the formal rules is a source of stability. Levitsky and Murillo argue, however, that in contexts of weak formal institutions, nonenforcement can be a source of stability and that changing levels of enforcement often induce important institutional change.

Levitsky and Murillo use the Latin American cases to challenge the dominant theoretical paradigms about institutions. Formal institutions do not function the same way when they are strong (as many are in the advanced industrial democracies) as when they are weak (as many are in much of Latin America). The chapter authors ask new questions and present important advances in our thinking about institutional change and stability in the Latin American context. Their pioneering arguments are relevant for understanding institutional change and how institutions function in the vast parts of the world in which formal institutions are not strong.

Chapter 10, Daniel Brinks and Sandra Botero's "Inequality and the Rule of Law: Ineffective Rights in Latin American Democracies," continues these themes, exploring the social and structural underpinnings of weak rights regimes. O'Donnell had a great deal to say about the legal dimension of the state, discussing its scope and definition, its constitutive relationship to democracy and democratic citizenship, and its empirical relationship to inequality and poverty (O'Donnell 1999c, 2004a, 2010a). But some of those empirical observations require updating in light of intervening events. The chapter discusses the extent to which, and the reasons why, after thirty years of democracy in some countries, the legal assignment of rights has made significant progress at a formal level and yet lags for some groups in some contexts in terms of its effectiveness. Their analysis locates the origin of the state's inability to enforce formal rights regimes not in the state itself but in the social actors who seek to exercise those rights.

Brinks and Botero build on two fundamental insights. The first is that law constitutes both equal and unequal social relationships. Legal change, and in particular the institutionalization of new rights, is likely to be the site of deep political and social struggles. The second recognizes the sometimes productive tension between "merely formal" rights and their imperfect realization. While there is a long tradition of describing formal rights as a dead letter in Latin America, there is a growing story to be told of subordinate groups taking hold of new or long-dormant formal rights to aid in political struggles for their realization. In Levitsky and Murillo's terms, this is institutional change through the activation of long-dormant rules. The chapter analyzes what is required to go from the "merely formal" to the effective and chronicles this evolution with a few examples of selected rights regimes. They argue that even the "low-intensity citizenship" that characterizes very unequal democracies (O'Donnell 1993) lends itself to important advances in terms of formal rights. But without important material or coalitional resources, the intended rights bearers will have great difficulties in developing the requisite institutional infrastructure that could support their attempts to make these rights effective.

Both of these chapters locate the origin of much institutional weakness not primarily in a shortcoming of the state—the lack of resources or qualified personnel for enforcement, or some other state attribute—but rather in a mismatch between the institutional arrangements and the actual distribution of power and interests in society. Various characteristics of Latin American (and other) democracies—frequent transitions, social inequality, changes in electoral rules, and so on—create a gap between the distribution of power at the rule-making stage and the distribution of power at the implementation and enforcement stage. When one group dominates rule making and another dominates implementation and enforcement, the rules are likely to remain "merely formal."

These contributions suggest that explanations of state weakness—understood as the failure of the rule of law, or institutional weakness, or failure to enforce state legality —are partially misdirected if they focus solely on the lack of coercive capacity of the state. Instead, the focus ought to be, first, on the political decisions to develop and deploy that capacity and, second, on the de facto powers that resist the formal rules, what Giraudy and Luna (2012) have called the challengers. The core claim of the institutionalist research agenda is that "institutions matter." However, weak formal institutions do not always guide how individuals and organizations actually behave and do not always matter in the same ways, and they often matter less in the developing world. But we still have a shortage of middle range theories to tell us when and how institutions matter. Chapters 9 and 10 help build a new research agenda on this issue.

Reexamining Delegative Democracy

In a paper that was first published in Portuguese in 1991, O'Donnell (1994) coined the term "delegative democracy"—a political regime characterized by free and fair elections but very weak mechanisms of "horizontal accountability" and hypertrophied presidential power (also O'Donnell 2011). The president presents himself (or herself) as the incarnation of the people. Horizontal accountability refers to "the existence of state agencies that are legally enabled and empowered, and factually willing and able, to take actions that span from routine oversight to criminal sanctions or impeachment in relation to actions or omissions by other agents or agencies of the state that may be qualified as unlawful" (O'Donnell 1999b: 38; also O'Donnell 2003a).[4]

O'Donnell contrasted delegative democracies to representative democracies with stronger mechanisms of horizontal accountability (O'Donnell 1994: 61; O'Donnell 2011). His work sparked many debates in contemporary political science. How should we characterize the regimes that have emerged in much of the developing world that have (reasonably) freely and fairly elected presidents but without solid mechanisms of horizontal accountability? To what degree is delegative democracy a " 'new species,' a type of existing democracies that has yet to be theorized" (O'Donnell 1994: 55)? What cases can fruitfully be considered delegative democracies? If delegative democracy is a new phenomenon, what accounts for its emergence? Lucas González and Enrique Peruzzotti reexamine these issues, first from the perspective of innovative empirical measurement and testing of O'Donnell's arguments (chapter 11), then from the normative perspective of a democratic theorist committed, like O'Donnell, to thinking about how to deepen democracy (chapter 12). Together, the two chapters open new research agendas exploring the concept and empirics of delegative democracy.[5]

Chapter 11 by Lucas González presents the first attempt to operationalize and empirically test the causes of delegative democracy. He uses an expert survey to score various countries on the attributes O'Donnell ascribed to delegative democracies and then explores the causes of that type of political regime. Based on the different dimensions in the definition, González provides an empirical classification of Latin American cases. He shows that there is large variation across country cases and across time within countries. Whereas O'Donnell initially saw some *countries* as delegative democracies and others as representative democracies, González notes that a few cases (Brazil and Peru) have shifted from delegative democracy to representative democracy while others (Venezuela, Bolivia, and to a lesser degree Paraguay) have moved in the opposite direction.

González identifies some factors that help explain variance over time and space in the degree to which competitive political regimes are delegative democracies. Consistent with O'Donnell's analysis, González finds that a weakly institutionalized party system fosters delegative democracy. Also consistent with O'Donnell, he finds that stronger citizen support for democracy increases the likelihood that democracy will be institutionalized and representative. Counterintuitively, for this sample of countries, González's empirical results only weakly support O'Donnell's hypothesis that economic crisis is favorable to delegative democracy. This analysis suggests that a key mechanism of horizontal accountability—the party system, and even the executive's own party—may be undertheorized.

González shows a high degree of within-country change in the extent to which countries experience delegative modes of governing. If countries can cycle back and forth and change from one president to the next, it is worth asking whether delegative democracy is sufficiently stable to warrant classification as a regime type, or whether we should understand it as an attribute of a particular leader or even as a phase in certain electoral cycles preceded by strong crises. Moreover, both some democracies and some authoritarian regimes (such as Peru between 1992 and 1995) have been marked by a delegative form of government. Should we then theorize it separately from democracy itself?

Enrique Peruzzotti's normative starting point in chapter 12 is the quest to develop "a critical democratic theory that could help us reflect about the pending tasks of democratic deepening in Latin America and elsewhere." He agrees with O'Donnell that delegative democracies fall far short in horizontal accountability. However, he argues that O'Donnell neglected nonelectoral vertical forms of accountability. By vertical accountability, O'Donnell referred *primarily* to electoral accountability.[6] Elections are an important but infrequent and blunt mechanism of control (Przeworski et al. 1999). Peruzzotti argues for the inclusion of forms of accountability exercised through societal and public organizations such as private and public interest groups, forms of institutionalized participation such as communal councils, and an autonomous and pluralistic public sphere (see also Smulovitz and Peruzzotti 2003). He develops the concept of "mediated politics" to refer to the interaction between these organizations and state institutions. The chapter argues for the need to consider this other accountability deficit of contemporary delegative democracies.

Peruzzotti does not specify exactly how the "newly created policy councils, communal councils, indigenous councils, and other arenas of institutionalized participation" interact with national level politics, thus opening up a new research agenda. Perhaps the central claim of the chapter—that the "active and independent field of mediated politics is a crucial asset in the promotion of more inclusive, public, and deliberative political processes"—cries out for a more detailed account of how these interactions are conducted, who participates and who is left out, what are the opportunities for participation and transparency, and so on. Peruzzotti's conceptualization suggests that the legal dimension on which O'Donnell focused and "mediated politics" are largely mutually exclusive. But courts too have begun to intrude in social policy debates at the urging of civil society groups that find electoral politics too infrequent and too clumsy for fine-tuning government responses. If this is the case, then the boundary between courts and mediated politics is somewhat permeable. An important and unresolved question is when these mechanisms for mediated politics become instruments for privileged groups to capture the government's attention, and when they truly enhance the quality of representation, responsiveness, and governance in a democracy.

Part IV: Human Agency and the Quality of Democracy

Beginning in the late 1990s, O'Donnell devoted himself to articulating the ethical foundation of his democratic critique of democracies. The notion of agency lies at the center of this theoretical endeavor. Citizenship rights and the right to share in the responsibility of making collectively binding decisions entail a recognition of agency, that is, of individuals' capacity to make choices and to respond for their consequences (O'Donnell 2001: 17). O'Donnell judged contemporary democracies through the prism of agency—that is, with a view to determining the extent to which they offered their citizens equal opportunities to live as autonomous, responsible beings. Informal institutions, feeble legal protection, and delegative tendencies are objectionable because they prevent some citizens from exercising autonomous, responsible choice. James McGuire in chapter 13 and Jorge Vargas Cullell in chapter 14 carry this critical exercise forward.

McGuire argues that democracy is valuable mainly because it offers a propitious environment for the reflective formation of political preferences and the exercise of practical reason. A firm commitment to this stance should make us more sensitive to the nature and extent of any serious compromise to the exercise of autonomous choice, not only in political arenas but also in legal and social realms. McGuire contends that descriptive endeavors should be consistent with this normative conviction. Thus, classifications of political regimes should place more stringent demands to extend the label "democratic" to any particular case, both in our time and in previous periods. This, in turn, requires replacing the more frequent classifications of regimes in two or three categories with systems with four or more discrete categories. McGuire illustrates his critique by examining existing regime classifications and observations about Latin American cases over the second half of the twentieth century. His reflection alerts us to the need to carry substantive concerns beyond the conceptual drawing board all the way to operationalization, coding, and inference, and it illustrates how a healthy democratic critique of democracy may inspire not only the assessment of results but also the exploration of causes and mechanisms.

Drawing also on O'Donnell's later work on agency, Vargas Cullell argues in favor of a multidimensional notion of democracy—one that refers to the nature of the political regime as well as to state structures and societal organizations that facilitate or hinder citizen agency. From this point of view, democratization entails more than a particular organization of the access and exercise of public authority: the removal of all obstacles, public or private, to the exercise of citizen rights. These obstacles may be of a different nature in different times or places. Democratization is an open-ended process that calls for the adoption of an equally open-ended set of concepts to describe it.

Vargas Cullell analyzes the challenges that adopting a set of broader concepts to study democratization entails. There is, first, the risk of losing conceptual distinctiveness when democracy refers to elements other than the political regime. While acknowledging this risk, Vargas Cullell holds that attributes of the state that prevent public authorities from encroaching on citizen rights are not merely facilitating conditions of democracy defined as a political regime but constitutive aspects of democracy conceived of as a political phenomenon as well. Second, the multidimensional and open-ended nature of democratization as a political process complicates both description and explanation. Vargas Cullell recognizes this difficulty but holds that the recognition of the state and societal dimensions of democratization that O'Donnell's later work makes possible is an indispensable step forward in understanding democracy once participation and competition are fully institutionalized.

Part V: Guillermo O'Donnell and the Study of Politics

Laurence Whitehead's chapter discusses some features that made O'Donnell's contributions so remarkable. Whitehead reflects on the fecundity of concepts that O'Donnell abstracted—with aspirations to illuminate more than specific cases—from particular experiences with which he was intimately familiar. What could have been inaccurate generalizations from the "most familiar case" instead have informed analyses of regimes from Africa to Asia. O'Donnell's theories were always grounded in a deep understanding and engagement with Latin American politics. This grounding revealed the ethnocentrism of some analyses coming out of the global Northwest. Whitehead argues that some of O'Donnell's insights were grounded in and bounded by his normative aspirations for the governments of Latin America—his transitions analysis in particular partook to some extent of what Lowenthal called "thoughtful wishing" (1986: viii).

Whitehead's recounting gives us reason to reevaluate the benefits of some research tools that most contemporary scholarship deemphasizes—intuitive leaps, close readings of local conditions, the contributions of scholars from the global South, and, most importantly, strong normative convictions. O'Donnell deployed all these as he built a theoretical and conceptual legacy that is virtually unparalleled in the study of regimes, transitions, and democratic practices around the world. The result is a call to open up our research agendas and theoretical tools to the normative concerns and theoretical insights of scholars "from the periphery" not out of a sense of obligation or condescension but rather to improve our understanding of the world.

In our conclusion, we discuss some fundamental philosophical, methodological, and normative debates about social science that Guillermo O'Donnell's scholarship pose for research today. We analyze five hallmarks of O'Donnell's scholarship in relation to contemporary debates about the study of politics.

First, O'Donnell always studied some of the most important issues of the day. His passion for examining these issues raises the potential trade-offs between methodological rigor and a focus on grand themes. At a time when political science is increasingly focused on methodological rigor, there must be ongoing space for addressing big issues. Second, O'Donnell's scholarship raises important questions about the relationship between scholars' value positions and their academic work. O'Donnell forcefully advocated for his own normative positions as part of his scholarship. We endorse the argument by Munck and Snyder (2007: 11–14) that much excellent work in political science revolves around issues about which scholars feel passionate and Weber's (1946: 129–56) position that social scientists should study work that is of deep interest to them, including matters on which they have strong normative positions.

Third, O'Donnell's work poses fascinating questions about how universalistic theories in political science should attempt to be. He combined great theoretical ambitions with skepticism about universalizing theories. This combination of theoretical innovation, ambition, and depth coupled with skepticism about universal theories has much to offer. Fourth, O'Donnell evinced a salutary capacity to change his mind. Future generations of social scientists can learn from his combination of deep convictions and open mindedness. Finally, O'Donnell's work suggests important questions about the relationship between case knowledge and broader theoretical questions. He used his deep knowledge of Argentina, Brazil, and Latin America to pose new theoretical questions whose importance transcended those geographic boundaries. On this count, too, he serves as an inspiration to future generations.

We hope that this volume inspires further advances in studies about democracy and authoritarianism, just as Guillermo O'Donnell's work did over the course of forty years.

NOTES

1. Likewise, Mainwaring and Pérez-Liñán (2013) show that for the Latin American cases from 1945 to 2005, per capita GDP had no influence on the probability of a transition from authoritarianism to a competitive regime.

2. See Sartori (1987: 4) for an elaboration of this point.

3. Scholars of Africa have likewise insisted on the importance of studying informal institutions. See Bratton and van de Walle (1997: 43–45, 61–96) and Riedl (2014).

4. For debates about "horizontal accountability," see Kenney (2003), Mainwaring (2003), Moreno et al. (2003), O'Donnell (1999d, 2003a), and Schmitter (1999).

5. On delegative democracy, see O'Donnell, Iazzetta, and Quiroga (2011).

6. O'Donnell (2003a: 47–49) embraced Smulovitz and Peruzzotti's (2003) notion of "societal accountability" and agreed with them that "it would be wrong to limit the concept of vertical accountability to elections" (47).

PART I

DEMOCRATIC BREAKDOWNS, SURVIVAL, AND TRANSITIONS

CHAPTER I

Democratic Breakdown and Survival in Latin America, 1945–2005

ANÍBAL PÉREZ-LIÑÁN AND SCOTT MAINWARING

Why do democracies survive or break down? In this chapter, we return to this classic question with an empirical focus on Latin America from 1945 to 2005. We pursue a new research strategy to address this question. Following a rich and extensive qualitative literature, we understand regime dynamics in terms of concrete historic actors. The survival or fall of competitive regimes depends on what political leaders, political parties, militaries, and other key actors do. These actions are shaped but not determined by structural forces and cultural patterns. But this qualitative literature has faced limitations in broadly testing arguments and theories because of the difficulty of scaling up from case studies. Following another rich and extensive literature on political regimes, therefore, the analysis in this chapter is primarily quantitative so that we can assess the generalizability of some key ideas found in some of the qualitative literature.

We argue that the level of development has not directly shaped prospects for democratic survival in Latin America. Nor, contrary to findings in some of the literature, has economic performance affected the survival of competitive regimes. Instead, we focus on the regional political environment and on actors' normative preferences about democracy and their policy radicalism or moderation. Democracies are more likely to survive when political actors have a strong normative preference for democracy and when they embrace policy moderation. The evidence also shows that democratic regimes are less vulnerable to breakdown when the regional environment facilitates the proliferation of those values domestically.

Our chapter builds on three important insights by Guillermo O'Donnell. First, in 1973, O'Donnell published his famous *Modernization and Bureaucratic-Authoritarianism*, which criticized modernization theory for positing too linear a relationship between the level of development and political regimes. For a longer time span and broader set of Latin American countries, we replicate O'Donnell's argument that the level of development has not had a straightforward impact on the survival of competitive regimes in Latin America.

Second, in *Modernization and Bureaucratic-Authoritarianism* as well as in several other works he published in the 1970s and early 1980s, O'Donnell argued that the "threat" that popular-sector mobilization posed to dominant elites (especially capitalists) was an important trigger of democratic breakdowns in Latin America (O'Donnell 1978c). We build a related argument by claiming that actors' policy moderation or radicalism has an important impact on the survival or breakdown of competitive regimes.

After focusing on democratic breakdowns early in his career, in the 1980s O'Donnell wrote on transitions to democracy, culminating in the famous work he wrote with Philippe Schmitter (1986). This work emphasized the role of political elites, their commitments, and their strategic choices. In the "Introduction to the Latin American Cases," in the *Transitions* volume, O'Donnell first laid out some daunting obstacles to stable democracy in the region. But—and this is the third insight upon which we draw—he then argued

> My hopes are rooted in a subtle, but potentially powerful, factor. . . . In most Latin
> American countries . . . there has emerged a new element. Largely as a consequence
> of the painful learning induced by the failures of those (authoritarian) regimes and
> their unprecedented repression and violence, most political and cultural forces of
> any weight now attribute high intrinsic value to the achievement and consolidation
> of political democracy. This is indeed a novelty. (O'Donnell 1986: 15)

Other scholars including Berman (1998), Lamounier (1981), Ollier (2009), and Weffort (1984) have also suggested that actors' attitudes about democracy and dictatorship help explain democratic survival and breakdown. Building on O'Donnell's insight and on related work, we argue that whether actors normatively (i.e., intrinsically) value democracy as a political regime affects its prospects for survival. We test this argument in a new way.

In this chapter, we provide an explanation for the stability or breakdown of competitive regimes from 1945 to 2005.[1] During this era the twenty Latin American countries collectively experienced 644 years under competitive systems. For simplicity and to avoid repetition we occasionally refer to those cases as "democratic" but our study includes semi-democratic cases as well (we clarify this distinction in the next section). These 644 regime-years suffered twenty-six breakdowns. Our analysis explores why (and when) competitive regimes broke down or, conversely, what factors favored their survival.

Classifying Political Regimes in Latin America, 1945 to 2010

We classify political regimes in Latin America using a simple trichotomous scale that we developed with Daniel Brinks (Mainwaring et al. 2001, 2007): democratic, semi-democratic, and authoritarian. In this chapter, we lump together democratic and semi-democratic regimes into a broader category of "competitive regimes."

Our classification of political regimes begins with a definition of democracy that revolves around four dimensions. First, the head of government and the legislature must be chosen through open and fair competitive elections.[2] Elections must offer the possibility of alternation in power even if, as occurred for decades in Japan, no actual alternation occurs for an extended time.

Second, today the franchise must include the great majority of the adult population. This means something approximating universal adult suffrage for citizens in the contemporary period.

Third, democracies must protect political and civil rights such as freedom of the press, freedom of speech, freedom to organize, and the right to habeas corpus. Even if the government is chosen in free and fair elections with a broad suffrage, in the absence of an effective guarantee of civil and political rights, the regime is not democratic. A liberal component—the protection of individual liberties—is a necessary element of contemporary democracy.

Fourth, the elected authorities must exercise real governing power, as opposed to a situation in which elected officials are overshadowed by the military or by a non-elected shadow figure (J. S. Valenzuela 1992). If elections are free and fair but produce a government that cannot control major policy arenas because the military or some other force does, then the government is not a democracy.

Based on these four dimensions, we classify governments as competitive (democratic or semi-democratic) or authoritarian using a simple aggregation rule. When governments commit no significant violations of any of the four criteria, we code them as democratic. If they incur in partial but not flagrant violations to any of those principles, we treat them as semi-democratic. They rank as authoritarian if they present one or more flagrant violations of those principles. In other terms, we employ the minimum score of the four dimensions to determine the overall level of democracy (full, partial, or none).

Waves of Democratization in Latin America, 1945 to 2010

Using this classification of political regimes, figure 1.1 shows the evolution of democratization in Latin America since 1945. The figure documents an abrupt decline in the number of competitive regimes in the mid-1960s, which partly motivated O'Donnell's early work on bureaucratic-authoritarianism, and the extraordinary surge in the number of competitive regimes after 1978, which motivated his work on transitions from authoritarian rule.

An important transformation underpins the historical cycles depicted in figure 1.1. Competitive regimes were brittle until 1978 but they became much more resilient afterward. Most Latin American countries experienced at least one period of

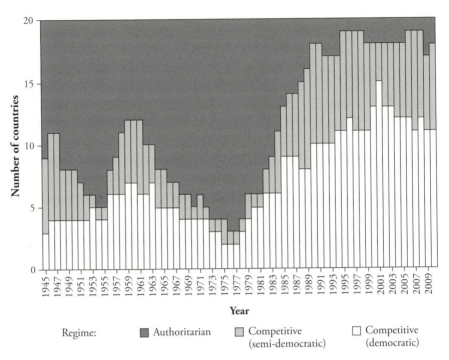

Figure 1.1. Evolution of political regimes in Latin America, 1945–2010.

democracy or semi-democracy before the 1970s, but many such regimes collapsed shortly after their establishment. Starting in 1978, however, the newly established democracies survived important challenges and the cumulative number of competitive regimes increased as new transitions took place. By 1991, the cumulative trend had stabilized, and eighteen of the twenty countries in the region enjoyed competitive politics. This transformation occurred primarily because the breakdown rate of competitive regimes (i.e., the number of breakdowns divided by the number of years of competitive) plummeted from 9.3% in 1945–77 to 0.8% in 1978–2005 (the third wave of democratization).

Actors' Policy Radicalism and Normative Preferences for Democracy

Because the survival or breakdown of democracies depends on concrete historical actors, we focus on how actors' preferences and attitudes affect regime survival. In contrast to structural theories, we argue that two relatively proximate causes affect whether competitive regimes remain in power or fall: whether actors have radical policy preferences and whether they have what we call a normative preference for democracy.

Actors develop policy preferences that run from moderate to radical. Some actors also develop a normative preference for democracy. Policy radicalism and normative preferences about the political regime are key, reasonably specific, and measurable components of actors' political beliefs. Actors do not respond automatically to their environments; rather, their beliefs shape their behavior in a given environment. Actors form their policy preferences and their normative preferences about the regime in an interactive historical context. These preferences are not historically fixed, but as Berman (1998) argued, they *usually* tend to be fairly stable.[3]

Actors are *radical* when their policy goals are located toward one pole of the policy spectrum (e.g., toward the left or right if the policy space is one-dimensional) and when they express an urgency to achieve those goals (in countries where they do not represent the status quo) or an intransigent defense of these positions (where these positions represent the status quo). Radical policy preferences need not be on the extreme left or extreme right, but they must be far enough from the preferences of other relevant actors to create polarization. They are intense preferences; radical actors are unwilling to bargain or to wait in order to achieve their policy goals.

We hypothesize that the presence of powerful radical actors will make it more difficult to sustain competitive regimes. The level of radicalization and the power of the radical players affect how threatened entrenched actors feel by the establishment or maintenance of democratic politics. To protect their interests in cases of considerable radicalization, either on the part of the government and its allies or of opposition actors, some powerful actors are more likely to try to subvert a competitive regime.

This argument also applies to the government itself. Where actors fear that a competitive regime can lead to their destruction or to major losses because the government has a radical agenda—whether this agenda is transformative or reactionary— the costs of tolerating the existing regime increase. These actors' willingness to abide by democratic rules of the game is likely to diminish, and the regime's likelihood of survival decreases. Conversely, where most powerful actors believe that a competitive regime is unlikely to impose major permanent losses, they are far more likely to accept democratic politics. Where uncertainty about the consequences of competitive regimes is great and the perceived costs of playing competitive politics might be high because of radical actors, the likelihood that such regimes can survive diminishes (Bermeo 1997; Figueiredo 1993; D. Levine 1973).

A normative *preference for democracy* means that an actor values democracy intrinsically, that is, above any policy outcomes. The actor has an ideological commitment to democracy as the best kind of political regime. It is expressed in the willingness of political actors to incur policy costs in order to defend the competitive regime. Many scholars have claimed that democracy has intrinsic value (Dahl 1971: 17–32, 1989; Lamounier 1981; O'Donnell 2010a; Przeworski 1999; Weffort 1984, 1989). If scholars believe that democracy has inherent value, political leaders and other actors can also value democracy on intrinsic grounds. A normative preference for democracy is different from strategic, situational, or opportunistic behavior in which an actor's support for the regime is contingent on policy results.

When candidates acknowledge their defeat in an election instead of challenging the adverse results, they signal commitment to the principles of the democratic regime. When government leaders accept a congressional defeat on an important issue, even if they could manipulate procedural rules to impose their preferred legislation, they signal commitment to existing procedures. These signals are credible to others because they are costly. Such behaviors are consistent with what Max Weber called "value rationality."

We hypothesize that a strong normative preference for democracy among political forces will make competitive regimes more resilient. Strong normative preferences for democracy limit how actors pursue their policy goals. If actors value the regime on intrinsic grounds, they are more willing to endure policies that hurt their interests because they perceive them as legitimate binding decisions. Conversely, they may be willing to reject beneficial policies because they are not adopted by a legitimate regime.

Our emphasis on actors' normative attitudes toward democracy draws on multiple traditions in political science and sociology. Lipset (1959) underscored the importance of legitimacy for the survival of democracy. Democratic legitimacy means that actors have a normative (intrinsic) preference for democracy; they value democracy for its own sake. Linz's (1978a, 1978b) distinctions between the loyal, semi-loyal, and disloyal oppositions revolve around differences in attitudes toward the regime. Loyal oppositions always play by democratic rules of the game; they accept and value democracy. In his work, these differences in attitudes toward the regime have an important impact on actors' behavior and therefore on regime dynamics and outcomes. Several other works have also underscored the effect of actors' attitudes toward democracy and dictatorship on regime outcomes (Berman 1998; Dahl 1971: 124–88; O'Donnell 1986: 15–18; Ollier 2009; Stepan 1971: 153–87; Walker 1990; Weffort 1984).

Although many works have staked a claim about the importance of actors' normative regime preferences, empirically demonstrating this point is difficult for a large set of countries over a long period of time. No previous quantitative analysis has undertaken such an endeavor because of problems of conceptualization, measurement, data gathering, and endogeneity.

Coding Radicalism and Preferences for Democracy

One of the critical challenges we faced in testing our hypotheses was that of data collection and measurement. We needed a combination of quantitative testing to examine the generalizability of arguments for twenty countries over a long period of time and of qualitative case studies to probe the causal mechanisms in a deeper way. The challenge for the quantitative work was figuring out a way to determine the most important actors in the twenty countries and code their policy radicalism and their normative regime preferences.

We engaged a team of nineteen research assistants to do this work. They undertook extensive research to prepare lengthy country reports that followed detailed coding rules.[4] The research team identified major books and articles dealing with the political history of the country, and the reports described the main political actors during each presidential administration between 1944 and 2010. One researcher (occasionally two or three) covered each of the twenty countries under study (some researchers coded more than one country). The reports identified a parsimonious set of actors (usually three to seven per administration) that were most prominent in the historiography of each period. Actors were included in the list if they were individuals, organizations, or movements that controlled enough political resources to exercise strong influence in the competition for power. Together, the reports discussed 1,460 political actors for 290 administrations. The president was almost always identified as a powerful actor (with the exception of a few puppet presidents). Political parties ($n = 573$), militaries (175), business associations (82), guerrilla groups (56), civil society and popular organizations (53), and trade unions and federations (52) were also commonly among the most important actors.

Researchers followed detailed coding rules to detect instances of radicalism and normative preferences for democracy. This team did not code the trichotomous regime scale to avoid contamination between the coding of the dependent and the independent variables in our study.

The researchers coded political actors as *radical* when they met any of the following conditions: (1) the actor expressed an uncompromising preference to achieve leftist or rightist policy positions in the short run or to preserve extreme positions where they were already in place or (2) expressed willingness to subvert the law in order to achieve some policy goals. The government was also coded as radical if (3) it implemented polarizing policies that deliberately imposed substantial costs to other actors (e.g., expropriations without compensation; labor-repressive regulations to increase labor supply). Nongovernmental actors were coded as radical if (4) they undertook violent acts aimed at imposing or preventing significant policy change. If actors were divided or ambiguous about these positions, they were coded as "somewhat" radical; otherwise they were coded as not radical.

Most political actors pay lip service to democracy, so the research team primarily documented the *absence* of a *normative preference for democracy*. Actors were coded as not holding a preference for democracy if they displayed at least one of the following characteristics: (1) expressed ambivalence or questioned "bourgeois," "liberal," or "formal" democracy; (2) expressed hostility toward democratic institutions (parties, legis-latures, courts, electoral bodies) instead of challenging their decisions; (3) questioned the validity of democratic procedures because they produced unfavorable results; (4) claimed to be the sole representatives of the people; (5) questioned the legitimacy of any opposition outside an encompassing national movement; or (6) consistently dismissed peaceful opponents as enemies of the people or the country.

Government officials were also coded as lacking a normative preference for democ-racy when they (7) introduced programs of partisan indoctrination into the public school system or the military and when they (8) manipulated institutional rules fre-quently in order to gain political advantage. Nongovernmental actors were treated as lacking strong preferences for democracy when they (9) expressed willingness to subvert the constitution or (10) accepted the use of fraud, political exclusions, or violence for political purposes.

Political actors were coded as having a strong normative preference for democracy if they did not manifest any of the ten hostile orientations; as "fairly strong but not entirely consistent" in their normative support if they exhibited ambiguity in any of these ten indicators; and as lacking a normative preference for democracy if they decisively met any of the criteria.

These rules provided a common protocol to generate comparable information for twenty countries over a long historical period. They are constructed so that the coding of both variables is conceptually independent of the coding for the political regime; actors' positions on policy radicalism and normative preference for democracy do not intrinsically affect a regime's classification. They are also intended to screen out instrumental, insincere deployment of democratic discourse. The coding rules are based on behaviors and discourse that are observable and documentable rather than strictly subjective evaluations. The indicators used to code radicalism and normative preferences for democracy do not eliminate the need for historical judgments about actors' preferences, but they put the judgments on a firmer ground.

We aggregated the information in a simple way. Actors were given a score of 1 (radical), 0.5 (somewhat radical), and 0 (not radical) for the first variable; and of 1 (a consistent and strong normative preference for democracy), 0.5 (a fairly strong but not entirely consistent preference), and 0 (inconsistent, ambivalent, or hostile views about liberal democracy on intrinsic grounds) for the second variable. We then estimated the average value of each of the variables for every country-year. Thus, our variable *radicalism* can be roughly interpreted as the proportion of powerful politi-cal actors with radical policy preferences, and our variable *normative preference for democracy* can be roughly interpreted as the proportion of actors with a normative commitment to democracy in each country between 1945 and 2010.

An argument that actors' normative preferences affect the survival rates of democ-

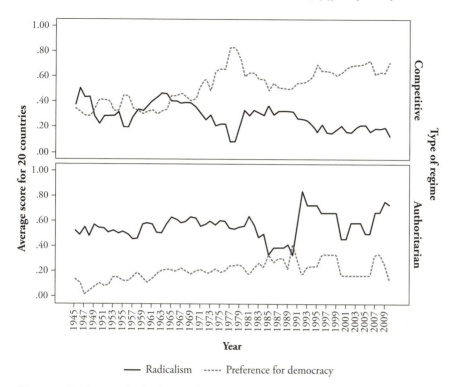

Figure 1.2. Evolution of radicalism and normative support for democracy, 1945–2010.

racy is not intrinsically tautological. At the conceptual level, normative preferences refer to actors' beliefs or world views; the way in which beliefs affect outcomes is an empirical question. Some actors might have normative preferences, but they might be overpowered by other actors. Also, many actors do not prefer a particular political regime on intrinsic grounds but join a regime coalition based on instrumental logic. The coding rules for normative preferences are designed to distinguish between instrumental and normative reasons for supporting a political regime.

Figure 1.2 depicts the historical evolution of the means for the two variables for the Latin American countries. The top panel summarizes the scores for country-years under competitive regimes (the focus of this chapter). The bottom panel, presented for comparison, summarizes the information for authoritarian cases. Among competitive regimes, radicalism showed a sustained—although by no means monotonic—decline during the second half of the twentieth century. By contrast, normative support for democracy tended to increase over time. The gap between the two series stabilized by the mid-2000s. No equivalent trend is visible among the authoritarian cases.

A careful reading of the top panel in figure 1.2 hints at the relevance of policy radicalism and normative regime preferences for democratic survival. In 1977, seventeen of the twenty countries in Latin America had dictatorships; only Colombia, Costa Rica, and Venezuela enjoyed competitive regimes. Around this point in time, the series for the competitive regimes displays the lowest levels of radicalism and the highest levels of normative democratic commitment for the whole period. This pattern suggests that in a hostile international environment, competitive regimes survived only in countries where political actors were consistently moderate and wedded to a democratic imaginary.

Comparison of the two panels in figure 1.2 also underscores an important self-reinforcing mechanism. Powerful actors in competitive regimes display on average lower levels of radicalism and higher levels of normative preference for democracy than actors in authoritarian systems. This difference is hardly surprising, not only because of the selection effects described in the previous paragraph but also because political regimes employ state capacity to protect their values and suppress potential threats. While authoritarian systems may simply repress most forms of dissent, competitive regimes may regulate the activities of radical groups and invest resources in policies intended to promote democratic values. As a result, the nature of the incumbent regime often reinforces the orientation of dominant political actors.

Alternative Explanations of Democratic Survival and Breakdown

Theories of democratic stability and breakdown have addressed a large number of alternative explanations. Accordingly, in addition to our main independent variables, we consider three theoretical clusters of explanatory variables: structural factors (economic development, class structures, dependence on primary exports) and economic performance, institutional design (party system fragmentation, presidential powers), and international conditions (the level of democracy in the rest of the region, US policies toward Latin America).

Level of development. One of the most consistent findings in the democratization literature has been that the level of modernization has a major impact on the likelihood of democracy (Diamond 1992; Lipset 1959; Przeworski et al. 2000; Rueschemeyer, Stephens, and Stephens 1992). We measure the level of development using per capita GDP in thousands of 2000 US dollars based on World Development Indicators (World Bank 2012) and Penn World Tables (Heston, Summers, and Aten 2009) and employ a quadratic specification to capture nonlinear effects.

Class structure. Diamond (1992), Lipset (1959), Moore (1966), and Rueschemeyer et al. (1992), among others, see the prospects for democracy as resting significantly on the nature of the class structure. Rueschemeyer et al. argued that "capitalist development is associated with democracy because it transforms the class structure, strengthening the working and middle classes and weakening the landed upper class"

(7). We use the percentage of labor force in manufacturing as a gross indicator of the numerical leverage of the working class.

Resource dependence. Because several scholars have argued that countries that dependence on natural resources such as oil is detrimental to democracy (Karl 1997; Ross 2001), we include a dichotomous measure of natural resource dependence, coded as 1 if exports of oil and minerals typically represented more than 10% of the gross national income. In Latin America, the cases of dependence on natural resources are Bolivia, Chile, and Venezuela from 1945 to 2005 and Ecuador since 1973 (computed from the World Development Indicators [World Bank 2012]).

Economic performance. Several scholars (Diamond 1999a: 77–93; Diamond and Linz 1989: 44–46; Gasiorowski 1995; Geddes 1999; Haggard and Kaufman 1995; Lipset et al. 1993; Przeworski et al. 2000) have argued that competitive regimes are more likely to break down if their economic performance is poor. We used change in per capita income (i.e., the rate of economic growth, based on our per capita GDP figures) to assess economic performance.

Party system fragmentation. An extensive literature has emphasized the role of institutional design in creating stable conditions for democracy. One such argument has centered on the nature of presidential regimes. Linz (1994), Mainwaring (1993), and Stepan and Skach (1994) argued that presidential regimes with fragmented party systems are more prone to breakdown. Cheibub (2002) challenged this analysis, stating that there is no significant relationship between party system fragmentation and democratic survival in presidential systems. In presidential systems, party system fragmentation might help explain the *stability* of democratic and semi-democratic regimes. We created a dichotomous variable coded as 1 if the effective number of parties in the lower (or only) chamber was equal or greater than 3.0 in a given year.[5] We employ a dichotomous indicator for theoretical reasons and because of missing data on the precise number of parties for Ecuador in the 1950s and Peru in the mid-1940s.

Presidential powers. Shugart and Carey (1992) argued that presidentialism functions more effectively with weaker constitutional presidential powers. A high concentration of power in presidential hands encourages the executive branch to bypass Congress and promotes institutional tensions in the regime. In order to assess this line of thinking, we employ Shugart and Carey's (1992) measure of presidential powers.

Regional political environment. Until the 1990s, research on political regimes focused heavily on domestic factors (for an exception, see Whitehead 1986). Since the 1990s, however, scholars have paid more attention to international factors in regime change and stability (Brown 2000; Gleditsch 2002; Levitsky and Way 2010; Pevehouse 2005; Whitehead 1986, 1996). A favorable international environment might enhance chances for democracy, while an unpropitious environment might work against democracy. To explore this possibility, we included a variable (*Region*) to assess the impact of Latin America's regional political context on the likelihood of regime durability and change. We measured the regional political environment as the proportion of democratic countries in the region every year, excluding the country in question. The coding for this independent variable was based on our trichotomous measure of democracy (with semi-democratic countries counting as half). The values can theoretically range from 0, if none of the other nineteen countries in the region were democratic in a given year, to 1 if the other nineteen countries were democratic in that year.

US foreign policy. As a hegemonic power in the Americas, the United States can affect the likelihood of transitions to competitive regimes and of regime breakdowns. We created a continuous scale to assess the orientation of US administrations toward democracy in Latin America. Using historical sources, we answered eight dichotomous questions about US policy. Four captured policies and attitudes harmful to democracy,[6] while four others addressed behaviors intended to support democracy in Latin America.[7] The first set of questions was coded −1 when the answer was affirmative, and the second set was coded +1 when the answer was affirmative. The resulting scores for each administration (from −4 to 4) were rescaled to create a continuous index called *US policy*, ranging between 0 and 1 (where 1 indicates maximum support for democracy).

Estimation and Results

We estimated the risk of democratic breakdown using a discrete-time survival model. The dependent variable is a dichotomous indicator coded as 1 for years if the competitive regime broke down and was replaced by an authoritarian system and 0 if it survived that year. Accordingly, a positive coefficient in the regression results signals a greater likelihood that a competitive regime would break down given a higher value for a given independent variable. In addition to our main independent variables, *Radicalism* and *Preference for democracy*, the equation includes eight predictors reflecting the three clusters of variables described in the previous section (structural factors and economic performance, institutional design, and international political conditions).

Following Carter and Signorino (2010) we also controlled for duration dependence using a cubic transformation of the regime's age (measured in years). This factor is relevant for econometric as well as for substantive reasons. Rustow (1970) argued that following a regime transition, the "habituation" phase is critical to establish the long-term survival of the regime. The cubic transformation of age allows us to assess whether the hazard rate for democracies changes over time and whether they truly "consolidate" in the long run.

Logistic regression survival estimates are presented in table 1.1. Model 1.1 excludes

TABLE I.I.
Survival models for competitive regimes, 1945–2005

Variable	Model 1.1 Estimate	(Standard error)	Model 1.2 Estimate	(Standard error)
Radicalism			3.047*	(1.140)
Preference for democracy			−3.686*	(1.534)
Per capita GDP, $t-1$	−1.071	(0.568)	−0.043	(0.670)
Per capita GDP^2	0.133	(0.078)	0.040	(0.091)
Growth, $t-1$	4.990	(6.203)	2.663	(6.185)
Industrial labor force, $t-1$	−0.011	(0.035)	0.026	(0.039)
Oil and mineral exports	−0.673	(0.676)	−0.884	(0.669)
Multipartism, t	0.102	(0.462)	−0.325	(0.519)
Presidential powers	−0.216*	(0.074)	−0.228*	(0.090)
Region, $t-1$	−4.307*	(1.502)	−4.901*	(1.929)
US policy, t	−0.795	(0.768)	−0.256	(0.865)
Age of the regime	0.049	(0.127)	0.328*	(0.158)
Age of regime^2	−0.002	(0.007)	−0.015	(0.009)
Age of regime^3	0.000	(0.000)	0.000	(0.000)
Constant	3.667*	(1.801)	−0.055	(2.279)
N (regime-years)	644		644	
Pseudo R	0.16		0.31	

Note: Entries are logistic regression coefficients.
*significant at the .05 level

our main independent variables, so that we can verify whether structural and economic performance variables affect democratic survival before we add the variables
for radicalism and normative preference for democracy. Only two control variables
present significant effects: a more democratic regional environment considerably reduces the risk of democratic breakdown, while—against theoretical expectations—
greater presidential powers also tend to reduce the risk of instability.[8] Consistent with
O'Donnell's *Modernization and Bureaucratic-Authoritarianism*, per capita income had
no impact on the survival prospects of competitive regimes in Latin America from
1945 to 2005. None of the other structural variables has a direct impact on democratic
survival. *Multipartism* and *US policy* exercise influence in the expected direction, but
their coefficients are also statistically insignificant. The rate of economic growth did
not affect the likelihood of regime survival; many competitive regimes survived in the
third wave despite abysmal economic performance, and before 1978 some broke down
despite respectable economic performance.

These findings remain consistent in model 1.2, which includes our measures of radicalism and normative preferences for democracy. Five results in model 1.2 deserve comment. First, actors' policy radicalism has a big impact on the capacity of competitive regimes to survive. Radical actors raise the stake of competitive politics. If radical actors win state power, they can impose very high costs on other actors, making it tempting for the losers to resort to coups as a way of preventing major and extremely difficult-to-reverse costs. For example, the radical policies of Salvador Allende's government in Chile (1970–73) and of the far left pushed the dominant faction of the Christian Democrats, the Conservatives, and the military toward supporting the 1973 coup. They feared that the consequences of allowing the Popular Unity government to remain in power might be disastrous.[9] Although this specific example invokes the fear that leftist radicalism created during the height of the Cold War, the same logic applies to rightist radicalism. Conversely, the Chilean Socialist Party's moderation after the reestablishment of democracy in 1990 made it easier for the democratic regime to survive.

This finding is consistent with O'Donnell's (1973) work on the level of threat as an impetus to democratic breakdowns, with W. Santos's (1986) analysis of the impact of radicalism on the democratic breakdown in Brazil in 1964, and with Berman's (1998) analysis of the impact of social democratic parties' radicalism or moderation on their behavior and indirectly on democratic survival or breakdown in Sweden and Germany in the 1930s.

Second, if actors have a normative preference for democracy, competitive regimes are far more likely to survive. Although this finding is hardly surprising, it indicates that O'Donnell (1986: 15–18) was prescient to argue that actors' normative preferences could go a long way toward offsetting many liabilities, including a high level of inequality, lack of a democratic political culture in most Latin American countries, and severe economic challenges. Linz (1978b) emphasized a similar idea with his notion of democratic legitimacy; legitimacy enables a regime to offset performance problems.

Many social scientists analyze outcomes based entirely on actors' instrumental (especially material) goals and are leery of claims based on normative preferences. However, a large body of work in economics, psychology, sociology, and political science has shown that individuals value procedural fairness and transparency independently of outcomes (Frey et al. 2004; Gangl 2003; Levi et al. 2009; Tyler 1990). As Hofferbert and Klingemann (1999) noted, protestors in Central and Eastern Europe took to the streets in 1989 and 1991 "for freedom, not for a stereo, fresh broccoli, or a new car." Organizations such as political parties, churches, human rights organizations, and militaries can also have normative preferences about the political regime.

Argentina is an example of how actors' normative preference for democracy can make a positive difference for regime survival (see also Carlos Gervasoni's discussion in the next chapter). From the late 1920s until 1976, few actors in Argentina valued democracy on normative grounds. Earlier works including Dahl (1971: 129–40), O'Donnell (1973, 1978a), Potter (1981), Rouquié (1982a, 1982b), P. Smith (1978), Viola (1982), and Waisman (1987, 1989) agreed on this point. As Rouquié (1982b: 341) noted, "All political forces preferred winning over the adversary in power to safeguarding the institutions."[10] Competitive regimes never enjoyed the steadfast support of powerful actors, so they were vulnerable to breakdown when actors did not get what they wanted instrumentally. In 1930, the Conservatives, the Socialists, the military, and even parts of his own party conspired against President Yrigoyen.

From 1946 until 1973, both of the main political parties (the Radicals and Peronists) and the powerful labor unions were quick to defect from the democratic coalition. In 1955, the Radicals supported a successful coup against Perón, and from then until 1969 they backed his proscription. In 1966, the Peronists and labor unions supported a coup against a Radical president in the hope that they would be able to regain state power by ending the electoral proscription against Perón. During those decades, powerful actors tolerated competitive politics only if it brought desirable policy results.

After 1976, the key actors accepted democratic competition as the legitimate route to winning political office. This reorientation toward a normative preference for democracy allowed the regime to survive despite severe economic crises in the 1980s and in 2001–2, hyperinflation in the 1989–91 period, a steep rise in inequalities, and bad average economic performance from 1983 until 2003. When there were serious threats to democracy in the late 1980s, the unions and the main parties mobilized to protect it. Organized labor supported the regime despite a 35% drop in average real wages and a 73% decline in real urban minimum wages from 1984 to 1992 (United Nations Economic Commission for Latin America and the Caribbean [ECLAC] 1992: 44–45), a sharp increase in urban unemployment from 5.9% in 1987 to 18.6% in 1995 and 19.7% in 2002 (ECLAC 1995: 50; 2009: 237), hyperinflation, and a stunning increase in the poverty rate. Business, which had frequently conspired against competitive regimes until 1976 (Acuña 1995), supported democracy after 1983 even during terrible times such as 1988–91 and 2000–2002, when the stock market plunged by 65% (ECLAC 2006: table A.20). Actors' self-interested instrumental logic suffices to explain the frequent breakdowns of democracy before 1983, but it does not explain the durability of democracy since then.

To illustrate the huge substantive effect of policy moderation and normative preferences for democracy on regime survival, consider the following estimates. Holding all other variables at their means, a competitive regime in which all actors are radical and in which no one has a normative preference for democracy would be expected to last for about a year. If all actors abandon their radical positions, the expected duration of the regime would increase to six years. And if, in addition, all actors embrace a normative commitment to democracy, the predicted lifetime for the regime would be more than 200 years.[11]

Third, a more democratic regional political environment considerably reduces the probability that competitive regimes will break down. This result meshes with the robust literature that has emerged since 1986 on international influences on democratization. A more democratic regional political environment fosters the diffusion of ideals about what is possible and desirable in politics, and it led to the establishment of legal norms in the Organization of American States intended to safeguard competitive regimes. The end of the civil war, the peace agreement of 1992, and the establishment of a competitive political regime in El Salvador helped inspire similar developments in Guatemala a few years later. Conversely, before the third wave, some authoritarian regimes served as inspirations for coups and authoritarian populists elsewhere in the region. For example, the establishment in Brazil in 1964 of a military regime that promoted the "economic miracle" from 1967 to 1974, and the military's ability to quickly defeat the revolutionary left and contain the broader left helped fuel confidence in Southern Cone militaries and rightists that the armed forces in their countries could also govern successfully.

Fourth, table 1.1 also underscores that structural factors had no direct consequences for democratic stability in Latin America. Structural predictors fail to achieve conventional levels of significance even in model 1.1 excluding the more proximate causes of regime breakdown tapped by our variables for policy radicalism and normative preferences for democracy. O'Donnell (1973) was right to be skeptical about the impact of modernization on the survival of competitive regimes in Latin America. The finding for a broader sample of countries that higher per capita income lowers the likelihood of democratic breakdown (Epstein et al. 2006; Przeworski et al. 2000) does not hold for Latin America.[12]

Fifth, counterintuitively, and also against some findings about a broader range of countries, economic performance as measured by per capita GDP growth had no impact on the likelihood of democratic survival or breakdown in Latin America from 1945 to 2005. Competitive regimes survived in Latin America in the face of grinding recessions, increasing inequalities, and hyperinflation in the 1980s and 1990s. Argentina, Bolivia, Brazil, and Nicaragua all had quadruple or quintuple digit inflation rates in the 1980s, with no breakdown of their competitive regimes. The region endured two decades of anemic average growth rates (1982–2002) even as the probability of democratic breakdowns plummeted.

Model 1.2 also suggests that the baseline hazard changes over time, but the results work *against* the idea of consolidation: the coefficient for *age* is positive and significant, revealing a progressive increase in the risk of breakdown. This effect is nonlinear: although every additional year elapsed increases the level of risk, this happens at a declining rate. Beyond year 10, the effect of regime age on the hazard rate is insignificant at the 0.05 level. In sum, the results in table 1.1 indicate that democratic survival is mostly driven by (the absence of) radical policy preferences, by strong normative preferences for democracy, and by a favorable regional political context (reflected in the presence of other democratic countries in the region but not necessarily in US policies).

The regression results are open to an obvious concern of endogeneity: if a competitive regime is in crisis, it could push some actors toward more radical policy positions or depress normative preferences toward democracy. Spatial constraints prevent a full econometric treatment of this problem here, but an examination of historical cases shows many examples in which actors' policy radicalism and their normative preferences help explain the regime outcomes and in which the regime outcome is clearly historically subsequent to, and hence cannot explain, actors' positions toward the political regime. In Argentina, for example, deep change in some actors' normative preferences occurred after the 1976 military coup but before the 1983 transition to democracy; in such a case, because change in normative preferences preceded the stabilization of democracy after 1983, we cannot explain change in actors' beliefs merely as a strategic response to democratic survival. The effect of normative regime preferences and policy radicalism does not simply stem from reverse causation.

Class, Modernization, and Contingent Action Approaches

In this section, as a way of highlighting what is distinctive in our analysis, we briefly outline class, modernization, and strategic contingent action approaches to understanding the survival and breakdown of competitive regimes and signal how we build on and diverge from these approaches. In our approach, democracies break down when powerful actors mobilize against them and overpower the regime's supporters. They survive when the constellation of forces that support democracy is more powerful than those that mobilize against them.

Although class approaches, strategic actor approaches, and our approach to political regimes agree on this broad formulation about why democracies survive or break down, in other ways they diverge. Class approaches assume a tight relationship between actors' structural positions and their preferences about the political regime. In this perspective, some classes strongly tend to be prodemocratic; others strongly tend to be proauthoritarian.

For example, Boix (2003) posited that, when democracy is feasible, the working class will always prefer it because democracy distributes income to the poor. Conversely, when a stable authoritarian regime is feasible, the wealthy prefer it except perhaps under conditions of high capital mobility, which attenuates the cost to the wealthy of tolerating democracy.[13] Likewise, Rueschemeyer, Stephens, and Stephens

(1992) argued that the working class consistently prefers democracy and the dominant classes oppose it, again based on the assumption that democracy distributes income to the poor.

In contrast, strategic actor approaches such as Linz (1978b), O'Donnell and Schmitter (1986), and ours, assume that class position has a weaker influence on whether actors support democracy or authoritarianism. To the extent to which social classes overcome collective action problems and constitute coherent actors, their decisions to support democracy or dictatorship are historically contingent (Bellin 2000; R. Collier 1999). Specific social classes do not always prefer democracy or dictatorship but rather support a regime or its alternative depending on the advantages and disadvantages the regime offers at a given moment in history. For example, in contrast to the prediction of class approaches to democracy, the Argentine union movement supported the authoritarian regime of Juan Perón (1951–55) because of the material, organizational, and symbolic and cultural benefits Perón bestowed on Argentine workers.[14] Until 1983, the Argentine labor movement opposed right-wing dictatorships but worked to undermine semi-democratic regimes not associated with Perón (1958–62 and 1963–66) and even initially embraced the military dictatorship of Juan Carlos Onganía, which overthrew the semi-democratic regime headed by Arturo Illia (1963–66).

Any theory that infers actors' preferences about the political regime from their class position (e.g., as local landowners, transnational capitalists, or industrial workers), or their class position conditional on how open the national economy is (Boix 2003) reduces important empirical questions—if, how, and to what extent structural forces drive actors' orientations towards democracy—to a convenient but often misleading theoretical assumption. Class approaches neglect the conditional formation of actors' regime preferences in a given historical context.

Our theoretical approach also stands in contrast to modernization theory, which was famously formulated by Lipset (1959, 1960: 27–63). Modernization theory claims that more economically developed countries are more likely to be democratic. Many authors have demonstrated that higher levels of development are strongly associated with a greater likelihood of democracy. Other work has convincingly demonstrated that the likelihood of democratic breakdowns diminishes at higher per capita income (Epstein et al. 2006; Przeworski et al. 2000).

However, the seemingly robust association between income and democracy does not hold for Latin America for the lengthy period from 1945 until 2005. As O'Donnell (1973) anticipated, the level of development does not predict survival or breakdown of competitive regimes for Latin America (see also Mainwaring and Pérez-Liñán 2005). During this period, competitive regimes were as vulnerable to breakdown at a higher level of development as at lower levels. Competitive political regimes have often survived at relatively low levels of development, and, as the experience of Latin America since 1978 shows, they have also often survived despite high inequality.

We do not claim that modernization theory is empirically wrong in general but rather that the relationship between the level of development and democracy is far from determinate until a high level of development makes breakdowns extremely unlikely. Modernization theory typically neglects concrete historical actors in favor of macro level quantitative work; most variants of modernization theory are actorless. The fact that the findings of modernization theory have not held up for Latin America raises questions about why this is the case. One fruitful way of addressing this question is to look at the political actors that endeavor to establish, preserve, or overthrow democracy.

If we accept the premise that political actors determine whether regimes survive or fall, then it necessarily follows that structural factors including the level of development do not operate *directly* on the stability of competitive regimes. Structural factors instead influence the formation of political actors, their resources, and their preferences and strategic choices.

Our understanding of the breakdown or survival of competitive regimes draws on contingent action approaches such as Linz (1978b), O'Donnell and Schmitter (1986), and Przeworski (1986, 1991). Like these earlier scholars, we emphasize the strategic interactions among different actors. However, our approach differs in some ways in relation to these contingent action approaches. These works focused on the regime coalitions that supported or opposed the incumbent democracy or dictatorship without analyzing the actors that underpinned those coalitions. Specific historic actors such as presidents and organizations such as political parties, labor unions, owners' associations, and the military form the core of our approach. These (mainly organizational) actors underpin the regime coalitions. This is a difference in the unit of analysis, not a theoretical conflict.

O'Donnell and Schmitter underscored the indeterminate nature of actors' regime preferences in situations of high uncertainty. Our perspective sits between theirs and that of Berman (1998), who argued that organizational interests and identities (in her lexicon, their programmatic preferences), and therefore how parties position themselves in battles over political regimes, tend to be very stable over time. We share Berman's view that even in moments of flux and high uncertainty, actors' identities and preferences—specifically their policy radicalism and their normative attitudes about the political regime—shape their behavior. In other words, we emphasize the constraining effects of organizational actors. However, we agree with O'Donnell and Schmitter that, at moments of deep crisis and possible regime change, actors' positions are more subject to change than is ordinarily the case. We also share their view that leaders have real choices and that regime outcomes are often indeterminate (Linz 1978b; Stepan 1978).

By emphasizing the role of contingent action and political agreements, this literature argued—against modernization and cultural approaches—that neither structural preconditions nor specific cultural traditions were necessary to build new democracies or to prevent their demise. For Rustow (1970) as well as for O'Donnell and Schmitter (1986), democracy was established as a result of strategic equilibriums between rival actors. For Linz (1978b) the loyalty of the opposition was more relevant to understand the breakdown of democracy than any policy problems facing the regime. We have shown that actors' normative beliefs and policy preferences are critical to explain the survival of competitive regimes. Even though these orientations are relatively stable in the medium run, actors' preferences cannot be reduced to fixed cultural traits or to rigid class interests.

In sum, we do not deny the role of structural forces (the level of economic development, patterns of dependence, class structures, or social inequality) in the constitution of political regimes. But the effect of such variables is contingent and diffuse; it ultimately manifests itself in the organization of political actors, in the relative distribution of their political resources, and in the normative regime preferences and policy moderation or radicalism of these actors. Any explanation of democratic stability that omits an independent assessment of political actors' values and orientations may overestimate the relevance of structural forces such as the level of economic development or income inequality.

Conclusions

We have introduced a novel strategy for the study of regime breakdown and survival, namely, the use of an actor-based approach on a large enough scale that it is possible to do quantitative analysis. Previous quantitative approaches to the study of democratic survival did not indicate who the key actors are and did not test propositions about regime survival and breakdown based on the observed properties of real political actors. Most variants of modernization theory do not explicitly specify actors or causal mechanisms, so the reasons for the linkage between a higher level of development and a greater probability of democracy are not clear. Boix (2003) and Acemoglu and Robinson (2006) assume that the poor, middle class, and rich determine the nature of political regimes, but they do not establish that these broad income categories actually overcome collective action problems and become cohesive political actors. Inglehart and Welzel's (2005) cultural theory argues that mass political culture determines political regimes, but it does not clearly specify who the actors are and what the causal mechanisms are by which mass political culture influences actual political actors. Because battles about political regimes involve specific actors whose preferences about the regime are not easily predictable on the basis of structural or cultural variables, we advocate historically grounded, actor-based approaches to studying regimes. Also against their cultural theory, we argue that political factors—regime failures and successes, repression, traumatic experiences, and international influences—more than modernization per se account for changes in actors' preferences.

As opposed to this "actorless" tradition in the study of political regimes, another lineage that includes the iconic works on democratic breakdowns by Linz (1978b) and on transitions from authoritarian rule by O'Donnell and Schmitter (1986), as well as many rich qualitative case studies (Berman 1998; Figueiredo 1993; Hagopian 1996; D. Levine 1973; Stepan 1971; A. Valenzuela 1978; Viola 1982) has focused on coalitions of actors or on concrete historic actors. The best work in this tradition has greatly enriched our understanding of why democracies emerge and stabilize or break down, and our core hypotheses flow out of this previous qualitative work. However, the generalizability of the findings from this tradition has been uncertain because of the limited number of observations. Our approach builds on insights from those qualitative studies but, for the first time, extends an actor-based approach to a broad range of countries over a long period of time.

We emphasize three substantive findings, which expand Guillermo O'Donnell's seminal contributions. First, the level of development did not affect the likelihood of breakdown of competitive regimes in Latin America during the long time span from 1945 to 2005. This null result confirms Guillermo O'Donnell's analysis in *Modernization and Bureaucratic-Authoritarianism*.

Second, actors' policy radicalism makes it more difficult to sustain competitive political regimes. When many radical forces compete for political power, the chances that some actors will find the cost of tolerating democratic politics too high increases. Radical threats encourage defection from competitive regimes. Conversely, pervasive policy moderation lowers the stake of democratic politics.

Third, along with Berman (1998), Dahl (1971), Linz (1978b), O'Donnell (1986: 15–18), Ollier (2009), Walker (1990), and Weffort (1984), we believe that actors' normative attitudes about the political regime have a large impact on whether competitive regimes endure or break down. Some actors intrinsically value democracy. Democracy can withstand severe crises and protracted bad performance if most actors are normatively committed to the regime. Conversely, it is highly vulnerable to breakdown in bad times if most powerful actors are indifferent to the intrinsic value of liberal democracy. Actors' normative preferences about the regime are not reducible to their structural position or to broad societal cultural patterns.

Measuring actors' policy radicalism and normative preferences about the political regime is a huge challenge, and it would be fatuous to claim that we have solved all of the difficulties. However, if policy radicalism and actors' normative preferences about the political regime are important variables that are not reducible to structural factors or broad societal cultural patterns, social scientists need to incorporate them into the analysis. Previous scholars have done so qualitatively; we believe it is important to also study these issues quantitatively.

NOTES

We are grateful to Stephen Kaplan, Cynthia McClintock, and Alfred Stepan for comments and to María Victoria De Negri for research assistance. This chapter draws on our Cambridge University Press book, *Democracies and Dictatorships in Latin America: Emergence, Survival and Fall* (2013). Some materials are used with permission from Cambridge University Press.

1. Although we code regimes in a trichotomous manner, in this chapter we focus on the breakdown of competitive regimes (democracies and semi-democracies) into authoritarianism rather than on erosions from democracy to semi-democracy.

2. The election of the head of government is indirect in all parliamentary systems and in presidential systems that have electoral colleges.

3. In our dataset of 1,460 actors, actors' normative preference for democracy at time t is correlated at .84 with their normative preference at $t + 1$. Their score for policy radicalism at time t is correlated at .75 with their score at $t + 1$. Because of our coding rules about what constitutes the same actor in time t and $t + 1$, this is a conservative (i.e., low) estimate of stability. To provide one example, if successive presidents came from the same party, we treated this as being the same actor.

4. The reports were on average 83 single-spaced pages, and the mean number of references used to generate the reports was 50.

5. The formula for the effective number of parties is $1/\text{sum}(p^2)$, where p is the proportion of seats obtained by each party (Laakso and Taagepera 1979).

6. Whether US leaders (1) supported coups or armed rebellions against competitive regimes; (2) limited the sovereignty (and hence democracy) of Latin American countries through military interventions; (3) clearly supported authoritarian regimes; or (4) expressed the view that Latin American countries could not be democracies because of cultural dispositions.

7. Whether US leaders (1) expressed a preference for democracy even when there were trade-offs with US economic or security interests, (2) promoted the democratization of authoritarian regimes or made efforts to bolster democracies under threat, (3) criticized authoritarian regimes that were not leftist, and (4) practiced a policy of nonrecognition when a military coup overthrew a competitive regime.

8. At least in part, this result may be an artifact of historical timing: trends in constitutional law drove constitution makers to write more explicit powers for the executive branch in recent decades. Thus, there was a coincidence between the wave of democratization and the powers of the president established in the new charters.

9. This is reminiscent of Przeworski's (1986) argument that the cost of democracy is willingness to respect capitalists' bottom-line interests.

10. In a converging opinion, Portantiero (1987: 281–82) wrote that "both Radicalism in its Yrigoyen faction and even more so Peronism did not see themselves as *parts* of a system, but rather

as a totality that expressed the nation and the people. The learning of loyal competition between government and opposition was never seriously undertaken in Argentina." See also Dahl (1971: 130–40); Gómez and Viola (1984).

11. The predicted probabilities of breakdown for the three configurations are 0.796, 0.156, and 0.005, respectively. Estimates are based on model 1.2, treating insignificant coefficients as zero.

12. The marginal effect of per capita GDP in model 1.2, given by the first derivative of the quadratic function (i.e., 0.08(GDP) – 0.04) is insignificant for the whole income range observed in the sample.

13. For a recent penetrating critique, see Haggard and Kaufman 2012.

14. Perón assumed the presidency in 1946. We code his regime as authoritarian from 1951 on.

CHAPTER 2

Argentina's Democracy Four Decades after
Modernization and Bureaucratic-Authoritarianism

CARLOS GERVASONI

However, there is *one blatant exception.* By any standards, Argentina's position in the political dimension is significantly different from what would be expected on the basis of the paradigm, considering its comparatively high level of socioeconomic development.

—Guillermo O'Donnell, *Modernization and Bureaucratic-Authoritarianism*

Indeed, no democracy has ever been subverted, not during the period we studied, nor even before or after, regardless of everything else, in a country with a per capita income higher than that of Argentina in 1975: $6055.

—Adam Przeworski, Michael E. Alvarez, Jose Antonio Cheibub, and Fernando Limongi, "What Makes Democracies Endure?"

Lipset was right in thinking that the richer the country, the more likely it is to sustain democracy, *except in Argentina.*

—Adam Przeworski and Fernando Limongi, "Modernization: Theory and Facts"

This chapter draws on O'Donnell's *Modernization and Bureaucratic-Authoritarianism* (1973) and on the more recent theoretical and methodological advances in the study of political regimes to analyze the trajectory of Argentina's regime from the anomalously undemocratic (in terms of modernization theory) decades before 1983 through a "normalization" over the past thirty years. I document this peculiar trajectory in comparative perspective, showing how and when it deviates from world and regional trends and from the predictions of the modernization paradigm. I also analyze the country's national and provincial democratic institutions since 1983 and rely on the growing body of research on the causes of political regimes to account for Argentina's post-1983 "normalization." Modernization and related socioeconomic structural approaches do not appear to adequately explain this drastic change. The country's

TABLE 2.1.
Transitions to dictatorship by per capita income, 1951–1990 (highest to lowest)

Country	Year	GDP per capita[a]
Argentina	1976	6,055
Argentina	1966	5,011
Argentina	1962	4,790
Uruguay	1973	4,034
Argentina	1955	3,989
Suriname	1980	3,923
Chile	1973	3,857
Greece	1967	3,176
Turkey	1980	2,957
Peru	1968	2,694

Source: Based on Przeworski, Alvarez, Cheibub, and Limongi (2000).
[a] Real GDP per capita in 1985 constant purchasing power parity (PPP) dollar; Penn World Tables.

transition to a long-lasting democratic regime, however, is consistent with explanations that emphasize (1) an international context much more favorable to democracy and (2) decreasing levels of elite radicalization and political violence after the bloody 1970s.

The quotes above stress that Argentina was, a few decades ago, a stark deviant case in terms of modernization theory. O'Donnell's *Modernization and Bureaucratic-Authoritarianism* interpreted Argentina's reluctance to behave as expected as a symptom of a more general disease. In a nutshell, under certain economic, social, and international circumstances—for example, the end of easy income substitution industrialization (ISI), fast political activation, and the "Cuban threat"—modernization may, contrary to Lipset's "optimistic equation" (O'Donnell 1973: 4), lead to (bureaucratic) authoritarianism. Przeworski and his coauthors, in contrast, see Argentina as downwardly weird, as their words above make sufficiently clear. The figures in table 2.1 stress the country's penchant for anomaly even more convincingly.

That is, four of the five instances of democratic breakdown at highest levels of income per capita during 1951–90 (the period studied by Przeworski et al. 2000) happened, of all places, in Argentina. Notice, however, that six of the cases in this table are consistent with O'Donnell's hypothesis: All the Argentine breakdowns plus those of Uruguay and Chile (which occurred after writing his book, as did the 1976 coup in Argentina) took place in modern, politically activated South American nations that were implementing ISI policies.

Argentina's "weirdness," however, precedes the exhaustion of ISI. Competitive regimes collapsed five times between 1930 and 1976,[1] indeed a world record: Table 2.2

TABLE 2.2.
Transitions to and from democracy, 1951–1990

Number of transitions	N	Examples
0 (Democracies)	33	Canada, Costa Rica, USA, India, Italy, Japan, New Zealand
0 (Authoritarianisms)	67	Cuba, China, Egypt, Haiti, Iran, Liberia, Mexico, Syria, USSR
1 (to Democracy)	12	Colombia, El Salvador, Spain, Nicaragua, Poland, Venezuela
1 (to Authoritarianism)	5	Congo, Sierra Leone, Somalia, Sri Lanka
2	9	Brazil, Chile, Ecuador, Indonesia, Uruguay
3	8	Bolivia, South Korea, Nigeria, Thailand, Turkey
4	2	Ghana and Pakistan
5	2	Sudan and Honduras
6	2	Guatemala and Peru
7	0	
8	1	Argentina (1955, 1958, 1962, 1963, 1966, 1973, 1976, 1983)
Total	141	Mean: 0.68 transitions; Median: 0 transitions

Source: Based on Przeworski, Alvarez, Cheibub, and Limongi (2000).

shows how, in the four decades studied by Przeworski et al., the country is by far the one with most transitions (from and to democracy). Argentina's eight transitions make all other Latin American nations (and the sample mean of 0.68 transitions) pale by comparison. Democracy (and authoritarianism) in O'Donnell's country had been unstable since 1930. What was different after the mid-1960s was the nature of the new authoritarian regimes. Argentina, then, seems to have been a difficult country for the survival of democracy even before the exhaustion of ISI and the emergence of bureaucratic-authoritarianism. Things changed drastically after 1983, however. In the following three decades Argentina experienced zero transitions.

Learning from Argentina: Why Has the Poster Child Been Stubbornly Democratic since 1983?

If Argentina was until the 1970s a deviant case in terms of modernization theory, since 1983 it has been another sort of deviant: a country that has remained stubbornly (if imperfectly) democratic despite its own precedents and despite undergoing several economic and political earthquakes. The same country that for decades was characterized by brittle, collapse-prone, stints of democracy, has sustained over the past three decades a democratic regime that was never in real danger of dying despite military upheavals (in 1987, 1988, and 1990), two of the harshest economic crises in recent world history (1989 and 2001–2), and four political crises that resulted in the resignation of the president or the vice president (in 1989, 2000, 2001, and 2002–3). Surprisingly for a country with Argentina's political history, not only did democracy endure these daunting challenges, but an authoritarian "solution" was not in the agenda even in the chaotic days of July 1989 and December 2001.

In methodological terms, then, Argentina gives us lots of interesting longitudinal variance on the dependent variable. In substantive terms, the case under study is an excellent opportunity to learn both about the country and about theories of democracy. In personal terms, it allows us to keep studying Guillermo's homeland (and my own), in the hope that learning about its regime evolution will give us tools to understand more fully our troubled past and to construct a better future.

In the next section I provide a quantitative description of Argentina's political regime since the mid-twentieth century in absolute terms, in comparison with Latin America and the world, and in relation to the expectations of modernization theory. Section three is a critical assessment of the country's national and subnational democratic institutions during the current democratic period, emphasizing both their resiliency and their weaknesses. In section four, I draw from the growing body of theories of political regimes to account for the sharp change in Argentina's regime trajectory since 1983.

Argentina's Democracy since 1946 in Comparative and Theoretical Perspective

First the facts: how has Argentina's regime evolved over time in absolute terms and in comparison to its region and the world? Figure 2.1, which displays the historical trends of the classic Polity IV democracy-autocracy scale (Marshall, Jaggers, and Gurr 2010) for Argentina, Latin America and the whole world, provides an initial answer to this question.[2]

The solid line (corresponding to Argentina) shows its well-known pre-1983 regime instability, but also the lesser known fact that during those years the country was generally below the world and regional mean. That is, despite its comparatively high level of development, educated population, Western culture, and other allegedly prodemocratic characteristics, Argentina was a democratic underperformer both with respect to the world as a whole and to its own region. O'Donnell's point of departure was indeed very real.

In spite of its popularity, the Polity index contains significant measurement error. A case in point: Even those of us who judge the first two Perón presidencies as rather authoritarian would hesitate to score them with a –9, a figure equal to that of North

Figure 2.1. Democracy 1946–2011: Argentina, Latin America, and World. LA = Latin America.

Korea and Oman today and worse than the –7 currently assigned to Cuba, China, or Syria.[3] Recent methodological advances in the measurement of democracy allow for a more accurate operationalization of regimes in Argentina and other countries. In figure 2.2 below I resort to the index of contestation developed by Michael Coppedge, Ángel Álvarez, and Claudia Maldonado (2008)—which summarizes many existing measures in an aggregate one through principal components analysis—to provide a more rigorous version of figure 2.1, at the cost of dropping some years from the analysis (the Coppedge et al. data are available only for 1950–2000).

Argentina looks a little better (especially during the above-mentioned Perón years), but the general picture does not change: with the exception of the short-lived democratic stints of 1958–62 (Frondizi), 1963–66 (Illia), and 1973–76 (Cámpora, Perón, and Isabel Perón), the country lagged behind the region and the world until 1983. Since then, both figures agree, Argentina has been much more democratic than the world average and somewhat more democratic than that of Latin America (although this is largely due to an authoritarian outlier, Cuba, which depresses the regional mean).

What about Argentina's regime with respect to the predictions of modernization theory? Figures 2.1 and 2.2 show absolute levels of democracy. Below, I analyze democracy conditioned on level of development or, in other words, the deviation of Ar-

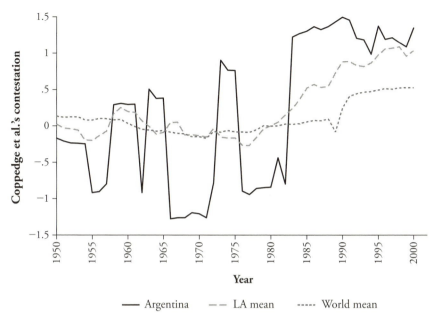

Figure 2.2. Democracy 1950–2000: Argentina, Latin America, and World (Contestation).

gentina's democracy scores with respect to the predicted values of a regression model of democracy on development (using all the countries in the world for which data are available). I do have two caveats:

First, as is standard in the literature, I use GDP per capita as a measure of development or modernization.[4] This is convenient because this indicator, unlike its alternatives, is available for most countries and for many decades. However, it has significant validity problems (see Teorell 2010). O'Donnell himself had misgivings regarding the use GDP per capita or any other average per capita indicator as a measure of modernization (see O'Donnell 1973: 15–22). One (but not the only) issue is the impact of oil wealth on sparsely populated countries. Many of the "most developed" country-years in the dataset (i.e., those with the highest per capita GDP figures) correspond to Brunei, Qatar, and the United Arab Emirates. The analysis I present below would be more rigorous if we had a more valid measure of development with wide temporal and geographic coverage. It would also be more theoretically informative if it were clear what the relationship between modernization and development is and which of the two (if different) is the expected causal factor.[5]

Second, development seems to be losing explanatory power over time (Boix, Miller and Rosato 2013; Coppedge 2012), basically because more and more less-developed

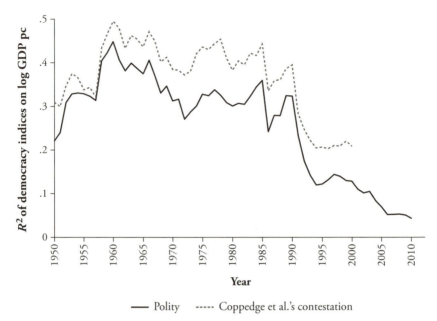

Figure 2.3. R^2 of democracy on development, 1950–2010. Polity = Polity index; GDPpc = Gross Domestic Product per capita. Coppedge, Alvarez, and Maldonado (2008).

countries are becoming democratic (such as Ghana, Mongolia, and Bolivia). Figure 2.3 shows the proportion of the Coppedge, Alvarez, and Maldonado (2008) Contestation and Polity indices explained by the log of GDP per capita in cross-sectional simple regressions since 1950. Clearly modernization by itself is a much weaker predictor of democracy in recent years than when Lipset (1959) proposed his thesis (as the figure shows, he did so at the heyday of the modernization-democracy correlation).

If we take the modernization benchmark, that is, the regime expected on the grounds of the level of development, we can observe not just the absolute level of democracy in a given country or region but also the extent to which it conforms to that prediction. Some countries are clearly underpredicted (e.g., Mongolia) while a few others are grossly overpredicted (e.g., Qatar). What about Argentina? To answer this question, I calculated the country's absolute residuals for every year available in the Coppedge et al. Contestation data (1950–2000) and plotted them (figure 2.4). The dashed horizontal line represents the model's prediction (that is, the level of democracy expected for Argentina based on its GDP per capita in each year). Negative (positive) residuals occur when the solid line is below (above) the dashed one.

From the 1950s to the early 1980s, Argentina struggled to reach its "predicted" (high) level of democracy, a goal only briefly achieved in 1973–75. That is, the coun-

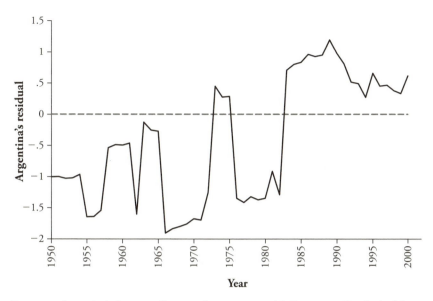

Figure 2.4. Argentina's deviation from modernization model. Regression Residual of Contestation on Log of GDP per capita. Coppedge, Alvarez, and Maldonado (2008).

try was a clear (negative) deviant case for many years before (and after) O'Donnell thought up his bureaucratic-authoritarian model. Since 1983, however, the country has been somewhat more democratic than expected, with a tendency to converge with its predicted level of democracy since 1990 (i.e., the solid line starts to decline toward the dashed line around that year). In other words, Argentina seems to have become an "on-the-line" case (Lieberman 2005); that is, a case that is close to the position expected on the grounds of its values in the hypothesized explanatory variables.

Of course, one should not exaggerate the explanatory powers of a single variable or, more generally, of structural factors. As figure 2.3 showed, GDP per capita never explains (statistically) more than 50% of regime variance, and in the past two decades the figure has been much lower than that. Multivariate, cross-national models predicting *change* in democracy levels also leave most variance unexplained: "even over the long haul, some countries deviate far from their structurally predicted long-run equilibrium levels of democracy" (Teorell 2010: 13). As Mainwaring and Pérez-Liñán (2003) have documented, the explanatory power of modernization indicators is especially weak (and nonlinear) for Latin America. A ubiquitous fact of social science research is also present here: it is often the case that "even a long list of variables does not do a good job of explaining individual cases well" (Coppedge 2012: 217).

Argentina was for most of the period from 1950 to 1983 a clear instance of a country that "deviates far" from theoretical expectations. *Modernization and Bureaucratic-Authoritarianism* presented a sophisticated and compelling theoretical account for such anomaly: even if not all the specificities of O'Donnell's bureaucratic-authoritarian model held up well to empirical scrutiny,[6] its broad contours provided a very plausible explanation for the regime peculiarities of Argentina and the Southern Cone. The post-1983 question is, precisely, about the "normalization" of Argentina: why has the deviant case that gave rise to O'Donnell's theorization finally adopted the regime predicted by structural factors?

Argentina since 1983: A Robust but Imperfect (National and Subnational) Democracy

By "robust" I mean that Argentina's democracy has proved resilient in the face of major challenges. By "imperfect" I mean that important aspects of the regime remain less than democratic.

Undoubtedly, something important has changed in the country since 1983. Having endured the political and economic earthquakes summarized above, the survival of the current democratic regime has been nevertheless beyond doubt. Underneath this solid foundation, however, political and institutional instability continues to plague Argentina. Evidence of such instability is abundant. For example, only two of the six presidential terms since 1983 lasted the six (until 1994) or four years established by the national constitution (those of Carlos Menem, 1995–99, and Cristina Fernández de Kirchner, 2007–11). That three out of six presidents resigned before finishing their terms (Alfonsín, De la Rúa, and Duhalde) is striking and very unusual in comparative perspective. A recent analysis of fifty-two third wave presidential democracies (Kim and Bahry 2008) found that from 1974 to 2003, there were only twenty-two presidential interruptions (due to resignation or impeachment) in eighteen countries, most of them in sub-Saharan Africa and Latin America. Argentina is one of the four countries (along with Bolivia, Ecuador, and the Dominican Republic) that suffered two such interruptions.[7]

Vice presidents were problematic too. Two of the six during this period resigned (Eduardo Duhalde in 1991 and Carlos Álvarez in 2000), two more went through major political conflicts with their running mates (Daniel Scioli with Néstor Kirchner and Julio Cobos with Cristina Kirchner), and the current one (Amado Boudou) is judicially and politically cornered because of very credible allegations of influence peddling. Political parties have gone through an acute process of deinstitutionalization, which is manifested, especially after the 2001 crisis, in increasing levels of party system fragmentation, party system denationalization, and extrasystem electoral volatility.[8]

As of the writing of this chapter, very little remains of the relatively institutionalized party system organized around the Peronist-Radical cleavage that characterized the country in the first years of the current democratic period (Mainwaring and Scully 1995).

What about democracy itself? Has it been healthy since 1983? It has, in the sense that no significant political actor has explicitly sought to overthrow the democratic regime (as many did in the 1930–83 period). The military revolts of colonels Rico and Seineldín in 1987–90 were serious and sometimes violent but were not aimed at taking power. The ultimate goals of the attack on the La Tablada barracks by the leftist Movimiento Todos por la Patria in 1989 is less clear, but this bloody episode was by no means a serious threat to the survival of democracy. During the 1990s there were no such incidents, and the only potential threat to democracy came from the government itself, when it tried to force a second reelection for President Menem through illegal means (the constitution forbade him from running again, so he tried to use friendly judges appointed by himself to force a convenient interpretation of the constitution). Tensions were high, but they were resolved institutionally. Menem did not run and the opposition won the presidential elections of 1999.

Notably, neither the economic, social, and political crisis of 1989 (marked by hyperinflation and the resignation of President Raúl Alfonsín) nor the even worse 2001 collapse (associated with the fall of President Fernando De la Rúa, the mega-devaluation of the peso, and the default on the public debt) led any significant political actor to consider a nondemocratic alternative. There were chaos and confusion, there were presidents who did not complete their terms, there were even riots and deaths, but the basic democratic institutions endured both episodes rather well.

Since 2002–3 Argentina has been free from both organized instances of political violence and economic collapses. True, there has not been rotation of parties in power (which did occur electorally in 1989 and 1999, and through a congressional decision in 2001), but there is no doubt that the Peronists victories in the 2003, 2007, and 2011 presidential elections were legitimately won in reasonably fair elections.

Many analysts (Guillermo O'Donnell and myself included), however, have worried about efforts to undermine democracy "from within" during the presidencies of Néstor and Cristina Kirchner. O'Donnell understood the post-2003 period in Argentina as a case of "delegative democracy," warned in his public appearances against an "authoritarian risk," and reminded his compatriots that "democracy can also die slowly, not any longer through abrupt military coups but through a succession of measures, hardly spectacular but cumulatively lethal."[9] The most clear instances of such tendencies have been the official harassment of the independent and critical media; the blatant use of many supposedly public media outlets for the private ends of the rulers; the "soft" punishment of journalists, business people, union leaders, intellectuals, and artists who express criticisms of the government; the noncompliance with Supreme Court rulings; the systematic refusal to disclose public information; the use of intelligence agencies for politically motivated spying; the neutralization of all "agencies of horizontal accountability" (O'Donnell 1999b); and, more recently, a worrying increase in instances of repression of protesters. As this chapter was being written, specific instances of authoritarianism were openly displayed by the executive branch with increasing frequency, for example selective tax inspections of business-men who expressed negative opinions of the economic policy or punishment of con-sultancies and NGOs that provided alternative (higher) estimates of the inflation rate (the official national consumer prices index has been blatantly underestimated since January 2007).

Despite these serious shortcomings, Argentina's national regime has remained es-sentially democratic, in the (minimalist) sense that there is real electoral contestation, real political parties that oppose the government and that are represented in Congress, and important alternative sources of information. If at its barest "democracy is a system in which parties lose elections" (Przeworski 1991: 10), Argentina would surely qualify: most analysts would agree that the incumbent government can lose (and in fact lost the 2009 and 2013 midterm) elections and step down as a consequence.

This apparent contradiction between a regime that is essentially (if minimally) democratic but that, at the same time, is being undermined from within, is reflected in figure 2.5. The classic Polity[10] and Freedom House (2012a) indices (normalized from 0 to 10 to facilitate comparison) remain in the upper part of the figure through-out the nine years of *kirchnerismo*, at levels similar to those of the earlier democratic years. A fourth measure, Freedom House's Press Freedom Index, however, does show a clear deterioration of democracy: starting in the mid-1990s (during Menem's admin-istration), the index began a declining trend, which was reversed during De la Rúa's short stint in office, only to turn back down at the beginning of Néstor Kirchner's administration. By 2012 the Press Freedom Index was more than two points under its 1994 level and clearly below other democracies in the region such as Uruguay and Chile (and to a lesser extent Brazil and Peru).[11] "Whether due to violence by criminal groups, as in Mexico and Honduras, or government hostility to media criticism, as in Venezuela, Argentina, and Bolivia, media freedom is on the defensive in much of Central and South America" (Freedom House 2012b: 2). In the 2013 release of its World Press Freedom Index, Reporters Without Borders assigned Argentina its lowest score since the creation of the index in 2002.[12]

To summarize, Argentina's national democratic regime now seems immune to its previous fatal disease, military coups, but it is still vulnerable to milder and more gradual pathogens, those that arise from within the regime. If from 1946 to 1955 the

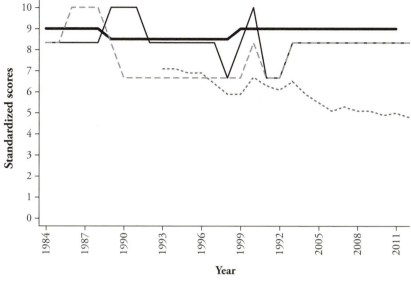

Figure 2.5. Democracy, political rights, civil liberties, and press freedom, Argentina 1984–2012. Polity = Polity index; FH = Freedom House. Freedom House (2012a, 2012b) and Marshall and Jaggers (2010).

elected and very popular administration of Colonel Perón (a former coup leader) significantly curtailed democratic freedoms, his most prominent Peronist successors in the presidency, Carlos Menem and the Kirchners, have showed milder and subtler, but still worrying, undemocratic tendencies. However, nothing they have done has moved the country far back enough as to doubt its (minimally) democratic status.

The following question sets the stage for the next section on subnational democracy: is it casual or causal that both Menem and Néstor Kirchner were previously governors of two of the least democratic provinces of Argentina?

The Subnational Picture

As national democracy became established after the 1983 transition, political analysts (journalistic before academic) started to notice the dubiously democratic features of some provincial regimes. The titles of a few books written by investigative journalists constitute a good summary: they used words such as "feudal," "tyrant," "fascism," and "terror" (Carreras 2004; Morandini 1991; Wiñazki 1995, 2002). Not surprisingly,

Guillermo O' Donnell's broad research agenda on democracy was among the first to pay attention to this issue in the academic world. He wondered "how one conceptualizes a polyarchical regime that may contain regional regimes that are not at all polyarchical" and pointed to "abundant journalistic information and reports of human rights organizations, that some of these regions function in a less than polyarchical way" (O'Donnell 1999c: 315). His hunch was right: wherever researchers following his hint looked, they found "illiberal peripheries" (Snyder 2001: 101–2) in new national democracies.[13] An early work on Mexico's subnational regimes, for example, called attention to the "survival and even strengthening of subnational authoritarian enclaves in states like Puebla, Tabasco, Guerrero, Chiapas, Oaxaca, Campeche, and Yucatán" (Cornelius 1999: 3–4). Likewise, evidence from Argentina shows that those who oppose provincial governments have faced nontrivial costs in places such as Formosa, La Rioja, San Luis, Santiago del Estero and Santa Cruz.

Should we worry about deficiencies in subnational democracy?[14] Yes, for at least two reasons. First, even though provincial governments are less autonomous than their national counterparts, they are not necessarily less important. In Argentina almost half of all public sector expenditures are executed by provinces, which also concentrate almost two thirds of all public employees (about 80% if we add municipal employees). The teachers, doctors, nurses, policemen, and judicial officials that so critically affect people's lives are largely provincial employees in Argentina.

Second, weaknesses in subnational democracy impact on the national regime in several ways (Fox 1994). The bosses of less-democratic provinces are influential in national politics, not only as governors, senators, and ministers but frequently also as presidents. Argentine politics has to a large extent been dominated by two figures since 1983, the Peronists Carlos Menem (1989–99) and Néstor Kirchner (who ruled, as president or as "first gentleman" in his wife's administration from 2003 until his death in 2010), both of whom had previously governed demographically minuscule provinces (La Rioja and Santa Cruz, respectively). There are many reasons to believe that this unlikely domination has something to do with the fact that these districts are among the country's least democratic[15] and also many to believe that the notorious "delegative" practices that characterized both presidents were imports from their provincial administrations.

I have developed two alternative indices of subnational democracy in Argentina, one based on objective institutional and electoral indicators (Gervasoni 2010a) and another based on the judgments of experts on the politics of each province (Gervasoni 2010b). I do not have space here to discuss the characteristics of each operationalization strategy, their comparative advantages and disadvantages, and their detailed results.[16] The resulting indices, however, do produce a few clear "not guilty" provinces and a few that are "guilty beyond reasonable doubt." That is, some provinces are consistently low or high in both types of measures. On the one hand, the Federal Capital and Mendoza always appear among the most democratic provinces, and Buenos Aires, Córdoba, Entre Ríos, Santa Fe and Tierra del Fuego can also be acquitted with confidence. Formosa, San Luis, Santa Cruz, and Santiago del Estero, on the other hand, are portrayed as very imperfectly democratic by both measurement strategies, followed by Jujuy, La Rioja, Misiones, and Salta.

Not even these least democratic provinces are strictly authoritarian, however. They are clear instances of "hybrid regimes" (Karl 1995) and their conceptual cousins, "illiberal democracies" (Zakaria 1997), "competitive authoritarianisms" (Levitsky and Way 2002), "semi-authoritarianisms" (Ottaway 2003), and "electoral authoritarianisms" (Schedler 2006). The electoral institutions all provinces have are not meaningless, but in some of them the game is so biased in favor of incumbents that one doubts whether there is a chance that incumbent parties lose elections. In fact, in seven provinces the same party has won the eight gubernatorial elections since 1983: Formosa, Jujuy, La Pampa, La Rioja, Neuquén, San Luis, and Santa Cruz. All have been under Peronist control except Neuquén (ruled by the local Movimiento Popular Neuquino).[17] One obvious, prominent and consequential way in which the dice are loaded in favor of the incumbent is media control: the local scholars and journalists consulted in the Survey of Experts on Provincial Politics (Gervasoni 2010b) say (and any attentive traveler can confirm) that the provincial media are heavily biased in favor of incumbent campaigns in San Luis, Jujuy, Santa Cruz, and Formosa. At the same time, the experts on provinces such as Córdoba, Santa Fe or the Federal Capital report almost no media bias. Checks and balances are also notoriously weak in many provinces: legislatures, judiciaries, and agencies of horizontal accountability exist in all of them, but they are often weak and totally unable or unwilling to control the power of the executive in provinces such as Formosa, San Luis, and Santiago del Estero. Only in the Federal Capital and Mendoza do these institutions appear to function reasonably well. Instances of open repression—media censorship, political incarcerations, police violence against demonstrations—are rare, but in some provinces authorities spy on opponents, discriminate against critical public employees and, in general, impose "soft" costs on those who express opposition. To be concise, there are no provincial Cubas, North Koreas, or Saudi Arabias in Argentina, but there are several subnational Malaysias, Russias, and Venezuelas.

In sum, the essential and minimal elements of democracy have been strong at the national level, but incumbents have attempted to undermine democratic institutions that bothered them, such as agencies of horizontal accountability, the judiciary, and the independent media. Democracy is even more imperfect in a few provinces, which although demographically small, are politically overrepresented not only in Congress but also in the Casa Rosada.

What Do Theories of Democracy Say about Argentina? (And What Does Argentina Say about Theories of Democracy?)

In this section I provide my own systematization of theories of democracy and put them in dialogue with the evidence provided by the Argentine case in longitudinal perspective, that is, during the period under study. I attempt "intensive testing" in two senses: as a way to reveal "which of several competing explanations best explains a specific outcome in a single case" (Coppedge 2012: 194), and as a way to draw some (admittedly limited) inferences about theories of democracy from the ample variance provided by the Argentine case.

The debate about the causes of democracy and authoritarianism is as lively as ever. Modernization theory has recently been refined (Przeworski et al. 2000), reinterpreted (Boix 2003), challenged (Acemoglu et al. 2008), and reasserted (Boix 2011; Epstein et al. 2006; Teorell 2010). Even those who support modernization, however, admit that its explanatory power has been declining over time (as shown in figure 2.3; see Boix, Miller, and Rosato 2013, and Coppedge 2012). Moreover, several new and exciting theoretical perspectives have entered the fray over the past couple of decades. The so-called curse of natural resources had a large impact on the field (Aslaksen 2010; Dunning 2008; Jensen and Wantchekon 2004; Ross 2001, 2012; B. Smith 2004; Ulfelder 2007) and gave rise to a related literature trying to expand the main "rentier insight" to other nontax resources with similar characteristics such as foreign aid (Morrison 2009; A. Smith 2008) and federal transfers to subnational units (Gervasoni 2010a). Despite dissenting voices (e.g., Haber and Menaldo 2011), most of the evidence points in the direction of a significant negative causal effect of resource rents on democracy.

A second, relatively novel theory of political regimes is diffusion. Diffusion approaches had been used before for other purposes, and the relatively old idea that democracies come in "waves" was to a large extent due to alleged diffusion effects (Huntington 1991; Starr 1991; Whitehead 1986). The theory was later developed in detail (Whitehead 1996) and more recently empirically tested (Brinks and Coppedge 2006; Gleditsch and Ward 2006).

Some of the authors mentioned above in the context of the debate about modernization theory also proposed new theoretical insights that have enlivened the field, for example the idea that democracy has something to do with capital mobility (Boix 2003; Acemoglu and Robinson 2006) or that what really drives regimes is the "institutional package" with which countries came into existence, often in the distant past (Acemoglu et al. 2008).

These and other rich ideas and debates on the causes of political regimes have led to at least two very recent works of theoretical integration, the books *Determinants of Democratization* (Teorell 2010) and *Democratization and Research Methods* (Coppedge 2012). Drawing on them and on the contributions briefly reviewed above, I provide a systematization of theories of political regimes, identify the main explanatory variable associated with each theory (and a representative citation), state in which direction these variables have moved in Argentina during the period under analysis (1945–2012), and indicate whether such changes are consistent or not with the behavior of the dependent variable, that is, the clear democratization of Argentina's regime after 1983 (table 2.3). The list of theories in the table is not exhaustive, but it identifies most of the main plausible and nonidiosyncratic factors that have been proposed in the literature and that have found at least some measure of empirical support.

In rather standard fashion, I classify theoretical approaches, first, as structural or agency based. This distinction is not as clear-cut as it is sometimes presented. I consider structural anything that is largely out of the control of the relevant political actors, from the level of modernization to political culture to the prevalence of democracies in the world (note that this is a broad definition of "structural factors," which are often limited only to economic and social-class variables). Agency-related factors are about the strategies and preferences of actors: they may not be able to do anything about the regime in neighboring countries, but they may use the transition to democracy in one of them as a model to follow and as an inspiration to mobilize public support. Agency-based approaches are then simply divided in those focusing on the elites and those that stress the masses or the general public. Structural approaches, much more numerous, are divided, first, into domestic and international, and then into economic, political, cultural, and institutional. I do not provide the classification criteria I use to assign each explanatory variable to each "grand approach," "dimension," and "subdimension" in the table (and cannot guarantee that the proposed categories are exhaustive and exclusive), but common sense and the approach, dimension, and subdimension to which each explanatory variable belongs should provide readers with enough information about them. Some of the explanatory variables may legitimately be seen as belonging to more than one category and some may be seen as causes of other causes (e.g., the level of political violence is probably causally related to the ratio of soft liners to hard liners). These and other issues make the classification no more than a rough attempt to put some order in the otherwise complex and diverse world of theories of democracy, with the ultimate goal of learning what type of factors seem to be (or not be) candidates to explain Argentina's regime trajectory over the past few decades.

One can easily discard from the analysis many independent variables that have changed little or nothing during the period under analysis (the equals sign in the next-

TABLE 2.3.

Classification of theories of democracy and their performance in explaining Argentina's regime trajectory

Grand approach	Dimension	Subdimension	Explanatory variable (representative author/s)	Temporal change in Argentina	Case confirms theory?
Structural	Domestic	Economic	Modernization (Lipset 1959)	+ & –	Ambiguous
			Capitalism (Moore 1966)	=	Uninformative
			Statism (Bellin 2000)	=	Uninformative
			Balance of class power (Rueschemeyer, Stephens, and Stephens 1992)	–	No
			Inequality (Muller 1988)	++	No
			Capital mobility (Boix 2003)	+	**Yes**
			Natural-resource rentierism (Ross 2001)	=	Uninformative
			Non-tax revenues (Morrison 2009)	=	Uninformative
			Economic growth (Gasiorowski 1995)	–	No
		Political	**Political violence (Finkel, Pérez-Liñán, and Seligson 2007)**	–	**Yes**
		Cultural	Ethnolinguistic heterogeneity (Dahl 1971)	=	Uninformative
			Colonial legacy (Bernhard, Reenock, and Nordstrom 2004)	=	Uninformative
			Postmaterialistic values (Inglehart and Welzel 2005)	+	**Yes**
			Dominant Religion (Fish 2002)	=	Uninformative

		Explanatory variable		Consistent
	Institutional	Presidentialism (Linz 1994)	=	Uninformative
		Type of authoritarianism (Linz and Stepan 1996)	=	Uninformative
		Colonial institutions (Acemoglu et al. 2008)	=	Uninformative
International	Economic	Dependency (Bollen 1983)	=	Uninformative
	Political	**Hegemon's support of democracy (Whitehead 1996)**	+	**Yes**
		International polarization/Cold War (Huntington 1991)	–	**Yes**
	Cultural	**International legitimacy of democracy (Diamond 2008)**	+	**Yes**
		International diffusion (Starr 1991)	+	**Yes**
		Regional diffusion (Brinks and Coppedge 2006)	++	**Yes**
	Institutional	**Membership in regional international organizations (Pevehouse 2002)**	+	**Yes**
Agency-based	Elites	**Ratio of soft- to hard-liners (O'Donnell and Schmitter 1986)**	+	**Yes**
		Policy radicalism (Pérez-Liñán and Mainwaring; this volume)	–	**Yes**
		Normative regime preferences (Pérez-Liñán and Mainwaring; this volume)	+	**Yes**
	Masses	**Peaceful demonstrations (Teorell 2010)**	+	**Yes**

Note: Hypotheses consistent with Argentina's regime trajectory before and after 1983 are in bold. The level of the explanatory variable over time can increase (+), strongly increase (++), decline (–), strongly decline (– –) or stay approximately constant (=).

to-last column in table 2.3). For example, factors such as the country's level of rentier-ism or ethnolinguistic heterogeneity or the nature of its presidential system remained essentially unchanged for decades. These factors, then, cannot account for Argentina's regime turnaround, which is not the same as saying that they are not causally relevant: for example, one could speculate (following the "political resource curse" literature) that if Argentina had become an oil-based rentier state during the 1970s, a transition to democracy would have been less likely in the subsequent decades. What the empirical evidence at hand says is that these factors did not change significantly over time, and therefore cannot account for the portion of regime variance under analysis, that is, Argentina's longitudinal variability since the mid-twentieth century. It is in this sense that the last column indicates that the case is "uninformative" with respect to these explanations: we do not know what impact they would have had on the country's regime if they had changed significantly during the period under analysis.

Conclusions regarding variables that did change over time are possible but inevitably quite uncertain given the limited empirical base: we count on just some longitudinal variance to evaluate many potential explanations for Argentina's regime turnaround. It is possible, for example, that explanatory factor X did have the expected causal effect, but that it was swamped by many other factors pushing the country in the opposite direction. In such a situation, one would tend to (wrongly) conclude that X did not have the expected impact. The conclusions spelled out below, then, should be interpreted cautiously.

The case turns up significant evidence against two proposed explanatory variables: inequality and the balance of class power. Argentina's reasonable level of socioeconomic equality from the 1940s to the 1960s started to decline in the 1970s. In fact, the current democratic regime came about and consolidated during years in which inequality increased sharply, allegedly because of labor repression (under the military), economic volatility (1974–2002), high inflation (throughout the period except 1992–2001), structural economic reforms (1989–95), and global economic and technological developments. Argentina does not seem to be alone in providing this kind of evidence: many countries with high levels of inequality (such as Bolivia, Brazil, Chile, Paraguay, and South Africa) successfully democratized during the third wave (Coppedge 2012). Argentina's deteriorating social situation during the 1970s and 1980s is also inconsistent with the "relative class power" argument articulated by Rueschemeyer, Stephens, and Stephens (1992): the transition to and consolidation of democracy happened when the country's traditionally strong middle and working classes had been decimated by stagflation, external oil and debt shocks, and deindustrialization.

There is also (weaker) evidence against the economic growth/crisis thesis: the growth performance of Argentina was reasonable (though volatile and comparatively low) until 1974 but very poor during the first years of the new democracy (1983–90). The evidence here, however, does not speak so clearly: the last military regime also suffered from bad growth performance (which very likely contributed to its demise), whereas in several democratic periods the economy did quite well (1991–94, 1996–98, 2003–8). What is clear, and contrary to the economic growth thesis, is that Argentina's democracy survived two devastating economic crises (1988–90 and 1999–2002).

Interestingly—and fittingly, given O'Donnell's ideas on the matter—the standard modernization hypothesis (which associates political regimes to levels of education, urbanization, industrialization, and media penetration) turns up ambiguous results. In many ways and in the long run, Argentina did modernize during the period. However, the picture is not so clear for the 1974–89 subperiod, which contains the transition years. Economic performance was so poor during those fifteen years (one of the worst in the world in terms of growth and inflation), that one could not easily say whether Argentina was more or less modern in 1990 than in 1973. On the one hand, urbanization, average years of schooling, and media penetration were higher in 1990. On the other hand, GDP per capita, the industrial share of GDP (an indicator closer to O'Donnell's focus on industrialization), and the proportion of workers in the formal sector were higher in 1973. In sum, in a long-term perspective one could argue that the consolidation of the democratic regime after 1983 had something to do with the accumulated increases in modernization leading up to that year (and with those occurring after 1990). This positive change in modernization, however, was not as significant as that taking place in most other developing countries during the same period (in part because of Argentina's high starting level and partly because of its ulterior poor performance) and in many ways receded during 1974–89. Modernization, then, is unlikely to have been causally central in explaining the post-1983 "normalization" (and, according to Pérez-Liñán and Mainwaring, has not directly affected democracy in the region as a whole; see chapter 1 in this volume).

Several hypotheses are consistent with Argentina's trajectory after 1983 (bolded in table 2.3). Two of them are somehow related to modernization: capital mobility and postmaterialistic values. Both variables are posited (by Boix 2003 and Inglehart and Welzel 2005, respectively) to be effects of modernization and causes of democracy, that is, mediating factors between changes in a country's socioeconomic structure and its political regime. As modernization advances, capital moves from fixed economic activities such as mining and agriculture to more mobile undertakings such as industrial production, information technologies, services, and finance. Likewise, citizens in more modern societies are less worried about survival values and more concerned with self-expression values. As in many other parts of the world, capital became more mobile and people more postmaterialistic in Argentina between the 1960s and the 1990s. However, detailed case evidence does not suggest that these factors were especially relevant: fixed-capital owners were never seriously threatened by democracy in Argentina (as they were in Bolivia or Chile), and people's values do not appear to have been the main drivers of democracy's weakness before 1983. These factors seem, at best, to have contributed marginally to Argentina's regime turnaround.

The evolution of several other variables is also consistent with the temporal variance in the dependent variable. Most of them can be reasonably grouped in two categories: those related to international influences and those related to declining levels of domestic political conflict (or to the wane of "hard-liners" on all sides).[18] These two groups broadly coincide with the factors highlighted in recent research by Aníbal Pérez-Liñán and Scott Mainwaring (see their chapter in this volume and their 2013 book): in their words, democracy's chances of survival in Latin America (the empirical domain of their research) have been a function of the "regional political environment" and of the level of "policy radicalism" and "normative preferences for democracy." These two sets of factors were in all likelihood causally connected, with the causal arrow going mainly from the international to the domestic arena: the end of the Cold War (and the collapse of its authoritarian contender), the emergence of a global democratic consensus, and the spread of polyarchies around the world (and especially in Latin America) surely contributed to the moderation of domestic political actors, who eventually became less radical, less prone to violence, and more committed to democracy.

In the international arena, Argentina's transition to and consolidation of democracy coincided with the following developments: (1) a prodemocratic turn in the foreign policy of the global and regional hegemon (with Carter and, after 1982, Reagan); (2) a change in the bipolar global balance of power (Cold War) in favor of the democratic pole; (3) a global increase in the normative acceptance of democracy as the only legitimate principle of government; (4) a worldwide wave of democratization; (5) a (very strong) regional wave of democratization in Latin America; and (6) new memberships in regional organizations that promote democracy. In sum, the international context was politically, culturally, and institutionally more favorable to democracy in the 1980s than in the 1970s, and it has become increasingly more supportive of democracy since then. The decline and eventual collapse of the Soviet Union was contemporaneous with Argentina's transition to democracy. If the installation of the Cold War in Latin America by means of the Cuban revolution had dire consequences for democracy in Latin America (a fact very much recognized by O'Donnell in *Modernization and Bureaucratic-Authoritarianism*, see pages 69–70), its termination contributed decisively to the moderation of both international and domestic radicals and hard-liners. If it was always clear that Argentina's transition was triggered by an international cause—the defeat in the Malvinas/Falklands war (Huntington 1991)—it has probably not been equally clear to what extent the international environment contributed to make the country's new democracy strong and durable. In sum, Argentina's post-1983 turnaround appears to be partially explainable by the variables highlighted by the substantial body of academic research on the international causes of democratization produced over the past quarter century (Boix 2011; Brinks and Coppedge 2006; Gleditsch and Ward 2006; Levitsky and Way 2010; Mainwaring and Pérez-Liñán 2013; Narizny 2012; Pevehouse 2002; Starr 1991; Starr and Lindborg 2003; Wejnert 2005; Whitehead 1986, 1996).

Domestically, political conflict was not processed through violent means in Argentina in the same scale as it was, for example, in several Central American countries. In spite of this, political polarization and violence started to increase in the last half of the twentieth century, first around the Peronist-Antiperonist cleavage and later around the left-right cleavage, especially when guerrilla attacks and state repression become significant features of the political landscape in the 1970s.[19] By the mid-1970s different factions of the Peronist party were killing each other, with the most prominent roles occupied by the Montoneros guerrillas and the right-wing, paramilitary Alianza Anticomunista Argentina led by Juan and Isabel Perón's right hand, José López Rega. Hundreds of Argentines were kidnapped, wounded, tortured, and/or killed by these groups. Montoneros and the (non-Peronist) Ejército Revolucionario del Pueblo even launched full-blown attacks against military barracks during the 1973–76 democratic period. The subsequent coup only brought much higher levels of state repression, including thousands of people incarcerated, tortured and killed. In other words, Argentina was in the 1960s and 1970s teeming with hard-line, radical, violence-prone actors who saw democracy as an impediment to "more important" ends, from order and investment to redistribution and socialism. By comparison, the post-1983 years have been very moderate and peaceful. A few instances of political violence (some of them mentioned above) have been the exception. Radical, left-, or right-wing organizations have been politically and electorally very weak and have hardly ever resorted to violence. Political conflict has been to a large extent processed institutionally, through elections, negotiations, congressional and judicial decisions, and even instances of direct democracy. Although demonstrations, strikes, blockades, and *cacerolazos* have been common since 1983, they have been essentially peaceful.

These two sets of explanatory factors stand in stark contrast to a recent and influential theoretical perspective emphasizing the *economic interests* of *domestic* actors, as opposed to the *political preferences* of domestic *and international* actors. In the parsimonious models of Boix (2003) and Acemoglu and Robinson (2006), the relevant actors are the rich/elites and the poor/people, and the critical considerations are their material interests. Such actors and interests are seen as structural: "Democracy is usually not given by the elite because its values have changed. It is demanded by the disenfranchised as a way to obtain political power and thus secure a larger share of the economic benefits of the system" (Acemoglu and Robinson 2006: 29). In contrast to this interpretation, the explanations summarized above emphasize not only domestic but also international agents who have *political* preferences that are not structurally fixed and that actually change over time (see chapter 1 by Pérez-Liñán and Mainwaring). In other words, these theories (and the supporting evidence from Argentina) indicate a more constructivist and international view of democratization than that suggested by structuralist approaches, including recent explanations based on inequality and capital mobility.

It could be argued that these factors are "too close to the dependent variable" to be causally informative and that we should instead ask "why did violence and radicalism decline after 1983?" Many explanations come to mind (e.g., learning, the political or military defeat of hard-liners, the end of the Cold War and consequent decline of ideological conflict throughout the world, etc.). I would first question the notion that these factors are "too close to the dependent variable." Democracy has survived in the midst of significant domestic armed conflict (e.g., Colombia, El Salvador, the Philippines) and has died in peaceful times (for example in Argentina in 1930 and 1966). Second, I would point out that decisions about causal distance are necessarily arbitrary and that learning about causes at different degrees of separation from the effects adds to our understanding or reality. Finally, a close cause can also be seen as a causal mechanism through which explanatory factors farther back exert their influence. The social sciences have been developing a consensus regarding the importance of causal mechanisms (however conceptually fuzzy; see Gerring 2008) to build a more solid discipline, so "close" causes should not be lightly disregarded.

Conclusion

I finish with a quick note on two other explanations that the regime trajectory of Argentina suggests are important and that are not clearly captured by any of the theoretical frameworks in table 2.3.

First, the performance of the previous authoritarian regime: conventional wisdom holds that the utter failure of the military in fixing the economy and in the Malvinas/Falklands war, coupled with its atrocious human rights violations, convinced both civilian elites and the public that authoritarianism (or at least the military kind) was far from guaranteeing better results than democracy. The military itself learned hard lessons about the institutional risks and legitimacy costs of assuming government and of exercising authoritarian rule. This explanatory factor can also be framed in terms of learning: the same business, political, intellectual, and union elites that used to think of the military as a solution became convinced that it was in fact a problem. Although not the most important aspect of the book, *Modernization and*

Bureaucratic-Authoritarianism takes learning seriously and at several points indicates that the structural factors it highlights may be eventually overturned by purposive political action: "politics is crucially affected by the capacity to learn," wrote O'Donnell with a grain of optimism in his otherwise gloomy 1979 postscript. The changes in the identity and preferences of actors highlighted by O'Donnell and Schmitter (1986) and Pérez-Liñán and Mainwaring (this volume) are, in the case of Argentina, probably in part a function of the appalling performance in government of the country's most powerful nondemocratic actor. Likewise, the moderation of the former radical and armed left is likely to have been a consequence of the conclusions it drew from its military and political defeats in the 1970s (Ollier 2009).

Second, and more in line with the theme of O'Donnell's *Modernization and Bureaucratic-Authoritarianism*, the constraints associated with "ISI deepening" are not there anymore. The deep global economic transformations that took place between the 1970s oil crises and the liberalizing 1990s changed the game radically. Industry lost, in Argentina and most of the middle and high-income world, its role as the dynamic core of the economy, while import substitution went out of fashion, both intellectually and in practice.[20] The contrast between the inward-oriented and stagnant Latin American economies (and other similar economies in other regions, such as India) and the export-oriented "miracles" of the Asian tigers (and Chile) suggested alternative pathways to development.

Foreign exchange constraints and the difficulties of industrial deepening—central to the economic syndrome that according to O'Donnell gave rise to bureaucratic-authoritarianism—were eventually eased by the wide availability of foreign investment, both real and financial, and the increasing development opportunities available in non "heavy-industry" and export-oriented sectors such as tourism, services, value-added foods, and information technology. Moreover, the wave of privatizations in Argentina and much of the developing world brought in billions in foreign capital, further reducing current account and real investment bottlenecks. Against initial expectations, stabilization, free-market, and export-oriented policies that took advantage of the opportunities afforded by the world economy were often rewarded by the electorates of the new Latin American democracies (Gervasoni 1999).

More recently, the boom in the price of commodities has provided a new source of hard currency for food-, oil-, and mineral-exporting countries such as Argentina. Even though its economic structure has not changed much in some important respects (it still has a relatively inefficient, import-intensive industrial sector along a very competitive agricultural sector that provides most of the foreign exchange), the global context has changed in dramatic ways. In fact, that democracy thrived in Argentina after the economic constraints stressed by the bureaucratic-authoritarian thesis receded may be interpreted as a confirmation of O'Donnell's insights. If he was right in positing a tension between the imperatives of capitalistic development in the 1960s and those of democracy, the new realities of globalized capitalism in the 1980s, 1990s, and 2000s may call for a reinterpretation of that relationship. O'Donnell's hypotheses may not be applicable anymore in their literal meaning, but the need for a theoretical understanding of the subtleties and nonlinearities of modernization and of the complex relationship between the global context, the domestic economic structure, and the political regime is as pressing as it was when he wrote his pathbreaking *Modernization and Bureaucratic-Authoritarianism.*

It is fitting that the factors suggested by the Argentine case represent two typical modes of explanation in political science: those based on free agents that construct their preferences in dynamic and contingent processes of social interaction and learning and those based on rather predictable actors that rationally maximize material interests within a given set of structural constraints. O'Donnell did not disregard either mode (as I suspect no good social scientist does). Even if *Modernization and Bureaucratic-Authoritarianism* is largely a book in the structuralist tradition, it also reminds readers of the power of agency and of learning, foreshadowing O'Donnell's later work with Schmitter (1986). They thought it "almost impossible to specify *ex ante* which classes, sectors, institutions, and other groups will take what role, opt for which issues, or support what alternative" and highlighted the explanatory relevance of actors' "*fortuna*" and "*virtù*," of their "confusion about motives and interests," and of the "plasticity, and even indefinition" of their political identities (4–5).

Perhaps the new structure of the global economy, the easier access that countries such as Argentina have to capital and foreign exchange, and even the protection that an increasing mobile capital affords to economic elites wary of redistributive electorates are helping Argentina stay democratic. Maybe the global legitimacy of democracy, the liberal nature of the reigning hegemon, and the very democratic region that surrounds Argentina constitute a solid safeguard against authoritarian regressions. But when political freedom and equality are at stake, one would like to believe that the conscious choices of leaders and citizens who have learned from past mistakes and who have more sincerely embraced democratic values make a difference. A significant piece of evidence that constitutes ground for optimism is that from 1983 through 2014, even at the country's darkest moments, not only did democracy survive but no significant political actor proposed an alternative. If, as suggested above, the main threat to democracy in Argentina since the end of the last military regime has been the hegemonic ambitions of democratically elected leaders (both national and subnational), accompanied recently by an intellectual discourse favoring a vague concept of "populist democracy" over the liberal democracy enshrined in the Constitution, the main task ahead is to remind ourselves and share with our fellow citizens that "democracy can also die slowly, not any longer through abrupt military coups but through a succession of measures, hardly spectacular but cumulatively lethal." In characterizing both the years of *menemismo* and *kirchnerismo* as delegative democracies, Guillermo O'Donnell saw through the policy and rhetorical differences between these variants of Peronism to highlight their political similarities and was one of the few scholars who criticized both at the peak of their popularities. He surely understood the structural forces behind these delegative episodes, but he undoubtedly thought that purposive political action (his own included) can help protect democracy from threats that come from within.

NOTES

I thank Daniel Brinks, Benjamín García Holgado, Scott Mainwaring, Sybil Rhodes, and Eduardo Viola for their useful comments.

Epigraphs. Przeworski et al. 2000: 98; O'Donnell 1973: 12 (my emphasis); Przeworski and Limongi 1997: 171 (my emphasis).

1. In all cases through military coups: 1930, 1955, 1962, 1966, and 1976. The 1943 coup overthrew an "elected" and civilian government (headed first by President Roberto Ortiz and, after he fell ill, by his vice president Ramón Castillo), but one that came to power through rigged elections. Although the 1955 coup is often seen as the end of a democratic period, an alternative view is that the civilian and elected administration of Juan Perón (1946–55) had become fully authoritarian by 1951 (Mainwaring, Brinks, and Pérez-Liñán 2001; Mainwaring and Pérez-Liñán 2013), so that the 1955 coup marks only the replacement of one authoritarian regime by another.

2. Data for these and the following figures come from the Quality of Government Standard dataset (Teorell et al. 2011).

3. Mainwaring, Brinks, and Pérez-Liñán (2001) code Argentina as semi-democratic for most of Perón's first term (1946–50) and as authoritarian for the remaining of his first term and his truncated second term (1951–55).

4. I use the natural logarithm of real GDP per capita (Constant Prices: Chain series) from the Penn World Table (Heston, Summers, and Aten 2009), which I took from the Quality of Government Standard dataset (Teorell et al. 2011).

5. Although modernization and development are generally understood as closely related notions, they are strictly speaking quite different phenomena. O'Donnell (1973: 27, 69) emphasized the need not to conflate them.

6. For example, several authors have found little evidence that the Southern Cone military regimes of the 1960s and 1970s were especially concerned with industrial "deepening," a central element in O'Donnell's model (Hirschman 1979; Serra 1979).

7. The study does not include the Duhalde case.

8. Extrasystem electoral volatility is defined as the vote share of new parties, that is, of parties that never competed before (Mainwaring, Gervasoni, and España-Nájera 2010).

9. "La Democracia Delegativa." *La Nación*, December 4, 2011 (*Enfoques* supplement, page 5); my translation.

10. Available at http://www.systemicpeace.org/polity/polity4.htm.

11. It is somewhat strange that this deterioration in press freedom has not been reflected in the

overall Freedom House ratings; it is likely that the weight of this particular freedom is not large enough to produce a sizeable impact in a context in which other freedoms do not decline.

12. Available at http://en.rsf.org/spip.php?page=classement&id_rubrique=1054.

13. That authorities below the national level can be nondemocratic in very significant ways even where the national regime is clearly democratic was demonstrated by the famous example of racial disenfranchisement and segregation in the US South until the 1960s.

14. In this and the next paragraph I follow Gervasoni 2011b.

15. The Rodríguez Saá brothers, from the also small and not-very-democratic San Luis, have run several times for president, and one of them, Adolfo, was briefly president (elected by Congress) during the 2001 crisis.

16. This information can be found in Gervasoni 2011a, chapters 4 and 5.

17. Santiago del Estero has not seen an incumbent defeated at the polls either. However, alternation in power did take place after a federal intervention removed the Peronist government in 2004 and convoked an election that was won by a coalition led by the opposition Radical party.

18. The shift of political culture from materialistic to postmaterialistic values does not clearly fit either of these categories, although it may be somehow related to the more peaceful and moderate political environment stressed by the second one.

19. Violence was present earlier, for example in the incarceration of opposition leaders during the first two Perón administrations, and, more cruelly, in the execution of several Peronist countercoup participants by the military government led by General Aramburu in 1956.

20. The current haphazard set of restrictions on imports applied by the Cristina Kirchner administration is generally seen much more as improvised response to the overvaluation of the peso and to capital flight than as a development strategy based on import substitution.

CHAPTER 3

Reflections on "Transitology"
Before and After

PHILIPPE C. SCHMITTER

We did not invent the concept of "transitology," but Guillermo O'Donnell and I have been repeatedly associated with it and even blamed for its existence. When we wrote *Transitions from Authoritarian Rule: Tentative Conclusion about Uncertain Democracies* in 1986, we had virtually no existing literature to draw upon. Books and articles on how REDs—"real-existing" democracies—functioned and managed to survive constituted a sizeable library. Those on how these regimes came to be democratic might have filled a few shelves—and most of them consisted of historical descriptions of single cases.[1] For the most part, we ransacked the case studies produced by the other participants in the Woodrow Wilson Center project, but both of us also reached back to the classics of political thought. I personally found a lot of inspiration in the work of Niccolò Machiavelli who, I discovered, had been grappling some time ago with regime change in the opposite direction, that is, from "republican" to "princely" rule. My hunch is that Guillermo reached similar conclusions based on his critical reading of the contemporary work on established liberal democracies that assumed the prior need for a lengthy list of requisite conditions and, hence, the virtual impossibility for any newcomers to enter this select and privileged group of about twenty regimes (Dahl 1971: 22).

Neither of us could imagine that the fledgling efforts we were observing in Southern Europe and Latin America in the early 1980s would be followed by seventy-five other regime transformations in almost all regions of the world.[2] In each case, the declared (and publicly supported) objective was to become democratic—more or less according to the norms and practices of those twenty or so forerunners in Western Europe, North America, and Oceania. These surprise events, especially the ones in Eastern Europe and the former Soviet Union, presented us with an extraordinary scientific opportunity and intellectual risk—not to mention a lot normative satisfaction. Could the concepts, assumptions, hypotheses, and "tentative conclusions" that we had derived from the early cases be stretched to fit a much larger set of countries with very different starting points in terms of prior regimes, historical experiences, and cultural norms? Needless to say, the Arab Spring that began in 2011 offers an even greater challenge to transitologists, since these countries have so often been declared "beyond the Pale" of democracy for cultural or religious reasons.

The pretense of this neo- and, perhaps, pseudo-science is that it can explain and, hopefully, guide the way from one regime to another or, more specifically in the present context, from an autocracy to a democracy. Its subject matter consists of a period of time—a liminal one of varying length—that begins with the demise of one more or less established (and more or less legitimate) set of rules for the exercise of power and ends with the consolidation of another set of rules. Its intrinsic value rests on the assumption that choices made during this period will have an enduring effect upon the eventual outcome—either upon the type of regime that ensues and/or the quality of its performance.

Its founder and patron saint, if it has one, should be Niccolò Machiavelli. For the "wily Florentine" was the first great political theorist not only to treat political outcomes as the artifactual and contingent product of human action, but also to recognize the specific problematics and dynamics of regime change.

Machiavelli ([1535] 1985) gave to transitology its two fundamental principles. *Uncertainty* (he called it *fortuna*) was the first and most important one: "There is nothing more difficult to execute, nor more dubious of success, nor more dangerous to administer than to introduce a new system of things." Furthermore, he warned us that its potential contribution would always be modest. According to his estimate, "in female times," meaning during periods when actors behaved capriciously, immorally, without benefit of shared rules, and relatively free from physical constraints (*necessità*), only 50% of political events were potentially understandable. The other half was due to unpredictable events of *fortuna*.

Agency (he called it *virtù*) was the second. When the behavior of political actors was so uncertain due to the absence of reliable institutions or practices and so underdetermined by structural constraints, the outcome would depend to an unusual extent upon the willingness of actors to take risks, the acuity with which they could assess the situation, and the decisiveness with which they could would carry through their decisions. Machiavelli attributed these qualities to the actions of a single person (hence, the title of his masterwork, *The Prince*). Today, we would probably assign this task to some collectivity—a party, a cabal, a junta—given the greater volume and complexity of the decisions that have to be taken.

Hence, transitology was born in Renaissance Florence (and promptly forgotten) with limited scientific pretensions and marked practical concerns. At best, it was doomed to become an obscure and complex mixture of rules of contingent political behavior and maxims for prudential political choice—when it was revived almost 450 years later.

Initial Assumptions cum Hypotheses

Virtually all of the following assumptions or hypotheses can be derived from its basic principles of unusual high levels of practical uncertainty and potential agency. These are present—although not always stately so explicitly—in the concluding *Transitions* volume.

The immediate situation. During the early stages of regime transformation, an exaggerated form of "political causality" tends to predominate in a situation of rapid and unpredictable change, high risk, shifting interests, and indeterminate strategic reactions. Actors believe that they are engaged in a "war of movement," (Gramsci 1971) where dramatic options are available and the outcome depends critically on their choices. They find it difficult to specify ex ante which classes, sectors, institutions, or groups will support their efforts—indeed, most of these social collectivities are likely to be divided or hesitant about what to do. Once this heady and dangerous moment has passed, some of the actors begin to "settle into the trenches" or, as the contemporary jargon calls it, to "consolidate a new regime."[3] Hopefully, these actors will be compelled to recognize and respect mutually agreed upon rules, organize their internal structures more predictably, consult their constituencies more regularly, mobilize their resource bases more reliably, and consider the long-term consequences of their actions more seriously. In so doing, they will inevitably experience the constraints imposed by deeply rooted material deficiencies and normative habits—most of which will not have changed that much with the fall of the *ancien régime*.

The possible outcomes. Transitions *from* autocratic or authoritarian regimes (as opposed to the more deterministic notion of transitions *to* democratic ones) can lead to diverse outcomes. Based solely on historical experience, the first and most probable would seem to be a reversion to the same or a different form of autocracy.[4] Few countries reached democracy on their first try or by strictly linear and incremental means. Most had to revert to some version of the *statu quo ante* or to pass through periods of rule by sheer force before becoming democratic. Some countries became notorious for the number of their attempts and failures (e.g., Spain and Portugal in Europe, Ecuador and Bolivia in South America, Turkey in the Middle East, Thailand in Asia, Nigeria in Africa), but eventually even they managed to consolidate something like a democracy. The second possible outcome is the formation of a hybrid regime that does not satisfy the minimal procedural criteria for political democracy, but that does not regress to the *statu quo ante*. These "dictablandas" and "democraduras," as we called them, probably do not constitute a stable and enduring solution to the generic problems of government, but they may be useful improvisations in order to gain time—either for a regression to autocracy or an eventual progression to democracy. A third logical outcome (which we did not explicitly entertain) may be the most insidious. Terry Karl and I subsequently called it "unconsolidated democracy" (Karl and Schmitter 1991). Polities trapped in this category are, in a sense, condemned to democracy without enjoying the consequences and advantages that it offers. They are stuck in a situation in which all the minimal procedural criteria for democracy are respected but without mutually acceptable rules of the game to regulate the competition between political forces. Whatever formal rules are enunciated in the constitution or basic statutes are treated as contingent arrangements to be bent or dismissed when the opportunity presents itself. The fourth possible outcome is the one we most obviously desired, namely, a democracy consolidated by means of mutually acceptable rules and broadly valued institutions of civic freedom and equality, political tolerance, and fair competition among its major actors. Defining the precise moment when this occurs or measuring accurately the extent to which this has been accomplished, we knew would not be an easy task. Indeed, insisting upon too much of it would mean a contradiction in terms since democracies are never completely consolidated. They are unique among regime types in their presumed capability for self-transformation and in the degree to which they incorporate uncertainty into their normal functioning.

The available agents. Antonio Gramsci had already updated Machiavelli's thoughts about agency for us when he argued that under modern conditions, the Prince could not be an individual capable of assessing the situation and taking "virtuous" risks on his own but had to be a party capable of offering a plausible alternative view of the future and capturing the allegiance of a critical mass of followers (Gramsci 1971). Granted that democracy is supposed to be produced (and re-produced) by citizens, it is only when they are assembled into a collectivity large enough to win elections or influence the formation of governments that they become capable of contributing to regime transformation. Like most political scientists, Guillermo and I took this maxim for granted.[5] We observed that political parties rarely contributed much to the demise of autocratic regimes, but as soon as a transition had become credible and, especially, after elections of uncertain outcome had been convoked, they immediately moved in and displaced the various associations, movements, and heroic individuals that had contributed so much more. By not stating it explicitly, we missed the opportunity to give early transitology one of its most stirring slogans: "Get the Parties Right!"[6] Orthodox liberal economists (who knew much less than we did about the distinctiveness of transitions) unhesitatingly proclaimed that all that was needed was to "Get the Prices Right!" and all of the other features of a functioning capitalist system would fall into place. We were probably inhibited from making such a proclamation by the fact that our own work had focused more extensively on organizations of civil society and by the suspicion that we did not know what constituted a "right" party system. The literature on "real-existing" democracies tended to assume that a system with only two effective governing parties was superior to all others, but that seemed an unrealistic and potentially perverse outcome in polities we were studying, especially those in Southern Europe. We also were aware that several of them had had historically relatively well-entrenched party systems, such as Uruguay, Chile, and Greece, that had proven incapable of preventing takeovers by autocratic rulers.

The potential modes of transition. My colleague and coauthor, Terry Karl, has advanced the hypothesis that the type and quality of democracy will depend significantly (but not exclusively) on the mode of transition from autocracy (Karl 1990). It is during this period that actors choose most of the arrangements that are going to govern their future cooperation and competition. Most important, the mode of transition influences the identity of relevant actors and the power relations between them. Also, depending on the mode, they may be compelled to make choices in a great hurry, with imperfect information about the available alternatives and without much reflection about longer-term consequences. Their fleeting arrangements, temporary pacts, and improvised accommodations to crises tend to accumulate and to set precedents. Some may find their way into more formal, even constitutional, norms. It is, therefore, useful to consider the possibility of "birth defects" in the democratization process that are due, not just to structural features long present in the society but also to conjunctural circumstances that surround the moment of regime change itself. Together, Terry Karl and I delineated four generic modes of transition depending on the presence or absence of large-scale violence and the dominance of elite or mass actors and labeled them (1) reform, (2) revolution, (3) pacted, and (4) imposed (Karl and Schmitter 1991). The first two had been the most prominent historically, but the latter two seemed even then to have become more frequent. In short, efforts at democratization from below seemed to be giving way to efforts from above—from within or in negotiation with the *ancien régime.* Each of the four seemed generically to "push" toward a different outcome.

The prevailing international context. Guillermo and I were convinced from the cases we were then comparing that democratization was (and even should be) a fundamentally endogenous process—in two senses. The exogenous structural context—precisely those features of international dependency that we both had argued were so important in the advent of autocracy during the previous two decades in Latin America—seemed too diverse and too remote from the motivations of the agents of change to have played an analogous role in the inverse process of regime transformation we were observing. The exogenous conjuncture of intentional action also seemed unfavorable—again for the countries that interested us. "Real-existing" democracies had long proclaimed their support for democracy elsewhere, but they had done little to accomplish this. Indeed, for alleged reasons of national security, they had sometimes actively encouraged and/or often passively tolerated the autocracies that emerged and persisted in both "Southern" regions. We also observed that precisely due to the uncertainty of the process and to the enhanced agency of the actors involved in making their choices about rules, outsiders seemed to be unprepared concerning when and how to act and, even if they did intervene, their actions were not likely to have a predictable and effectual impact.[7] We were, of course, aware that neodemocracies would inevitably attempt to adopt and adapt the practices of previous democracies that they considered successful, but we were confident that, since they would not be able to repeat these prior paths to democracy, the outcome of such efforts would be diverse—if not perverse. This "unrepeatability" of the democratization process has incalculable secondary consequences, all connected with profound changes both in the domestic and international contexts and with the nature of already established democracies. In other words, scholars or pundits who simply extrapolate from quantitative data or extract qualitative "lessons" based on the experiences of their predecessors are likely to make serious errors in their estimation of present outcomes.[8] In the *Transitions* volume, we carefully avoided drawing inferences about the future of our cases from past patterns of regime change—although we did not explicitly develop the notion of distinctive "waves" of democratization.

The presumed unit of government. In one key aspect, our revival of transitology differed significantly from the original version. Machiavelli's attention was focused less on the distribution and use of political power and more on the founding of the unit within which that power would be exercised. In contemporary terms, he was primarily interested in *state building*, not *regime building*. We implicitly took for granted what he regarded as most problematic, namely, the identity and boundaries of the territorial units we were studying. And yet these have to be agreed upon and effective in order for any legitimate form of rule to persist—all the more so if that form is to be democratic since the freedom to contest the unit's identity and boundaries is much greater than in autocracies. Moreover (and most embarrassing), there is no democratic mechanism for subsequently resolving these issues. The plebiscites that have sometimes been used for this purpose are a fraud since their outcome depends upon who is previously declared to be eligible to vote in them—and that usually determines the outcome. Almost all "real-existing" democracies came into being within territorial units that were formed historically by nondemocratic forces, usually war but also the fortunes of royal dynasties and their marriages.[9] In the modern period, these units were presumed to be "nation-states," that is, to have a single or at least a predominant national identity and a reliable monopoly of the use of armed violence over a specific and unique territory. With the partial exception of Spain—at least initially—the countries we were studying in Southern Europe and Latin America seemed to have already acquired these properties and the freedoms of collective expression and political competition that came with democratization did not seem likely to call them into question.

Subsequent Observations cum Lessons

Both of transitology's initial assumptions *cum* hypotheses seem to have been justified. Uncertainty and agency do combine to make this liminal period an abnormal one and, hence, to justify its being treated as a distinctive form of politics. However, with the benefit of over twenty-five years of hindsight, I have learned that some of its derivative assumptions *cum* hypotheses need to be revised and restated.

The revised situation. The extent of uncertainty and agency has varied much more across the cases than expected. It was much greater at the beginning—and nowhere more so than in Portugal after its 1974 Revolução—but tended to diminish over time.[10] One hypothesis is that something like a process of political learning set in by which a few initial, successful cases, such as Spain, served as models for those starting later. With so many cases of transition occurring within the same timeframe, the diffusion of techniques (and even of diffuse confidence) would seem inevitable—even across large cultural and geographic distances. A second hypothesis is that this decline in uncertainty and agency can be explained by the gradual ascendance of the two modes of transition that had been so rare in the past. Both "pacted" and "imposed" transitions insert important elements of greater assurance with regard to the emerging rules of the game and lesser room for autonomous action by incumbent politicians. The former does so because the negotiations between moderates within the former regime and moderates in the opposition tend to involve agreements on such things as the conduct of elections, the status of parties, and the form of executive power. The latter does so because the autocratic rulers (or at least a dominant faction among them) are sufficiently in control that they can dictate both the content and the pace of events during the transition. Another unexpected element (which will be discussed below) has been the growing role of external actors, especially regional ones. These governmental and nongovernmental organizations have been surprisingly successful in altering the incentives of domestic actors, both by rewarding prodemocratic behavior and especially by punishing those threatening a reversion to autocracy. Needless to say, this was most present among those polities that were potential members of the European Union, but the Organization of American States and MERCOSUR also played a significant role in preventing backsliding. Elsewhere, regional organizations (or global ones) were much less relevant—*vide* the African Union or ASEAN.

The eventual outcomes. The odds concerning which type of regime would emerge from an attempted transition to democracy seem to have shifted dramatically. Considering only the cases we were examining, not a single one has (yet) suffered a manifest or sudden regression to autocracy, although several spent a long time in transition, some did have close calls, and more than a few have developed symptoms of gradual deterioration. This is all the more astonishing when one considers that many of the factors that theorists had claimed facilitate (if not act as prerequisites for) "real-existing" democracy were not present in many, if not most, of these cases. Economic growth and employment rates have not always been consistently higher than under autocracy; social equality and income distribution did not always improve rapidly; trust in rulers often deteriorated; critical items measuring the "civic culture" of mass publics have declined—and still the minimal institutions of "real-existing" democracies have not been displaced. They have survived, if not always been respected and enjoyed by their citizens.

The "dirty secret" seems to be that democratic outcomes may have been more frequent, but they have also been less consequential than in the past. Considering not only the expectations of those struggling for democracy but also those of academics trying to understand the consequences of such a transition, one would have expected—based largely on the consequences of previous efforts at democratization—that such a regime change would have brought about much more significant changes in power relations, property rights, policy entitlements, economic equality, and social status. This is not to claim that "nothing changed." In the realm of respect for human rights, more decent treatment by authorities and a sense of greater personal freedom, significant changes did occur and they are appreciated by citizens (even if they are often rapidly "discounted"). But in terms of those factors that are most likely to influence the longer term distribution of power and influence within the polity, recent democratizations have accomplished much less than in the past (Karl and Schmitter forthcoming; see also Terry Karl's discussion in chapter 6 of this volume). Most important, they have proven to be much less threatening to the propertied and privileged groups that had previously supported autocracy. Once they realized that their class, sectoral, and even corporate interests were protected as well, if not better, by a democratic government than an autocratic one, a major incentive for reversion was removed.

The "real-existing" agents. We were unaware of it then, but something was already happening to both the nature and role of political parties in prior "real-existing" democracies, just about the same time that our countries began experimenting with their "just-emerging" democracies.[11] In Western Europe, since the early 1980s, established parties had been losing members and voluntary contributions of money and labor. Voters were less and less inclined to identify with them or to vote for them consistently in successive elections—at the same time that fewer and fewer voters were even bothering to go to the polls. Hence, electoral outcomes were becoming less

democracy,[12] but it was usually sporadic or ineffectual. The actual transition really began when elites—incumbents with or without challengers—decided to initiate it, admittedly, often in fear of greater future mobilization from below. Needless to say, in the *Transitions* volume, we may have applauded the possibility of pacted and even imposed transitions, but we did not predict their increase (nor did we harbor any illusions about our capacity to promote them). In retrospect the shift in mode seems reasonable. For one thing, incumbent autocrats have become more capable of physically suppressing revolutionary threats or even of diverting reformist challenges.[13] What they cannot prevent is factionalism within their ranks. And this, depending on the relative balances of power—not to mention how their policies may have satisfied or alienated key support groups in the economy and society—is usually what leads to one faction's either taking the initiative to impose a (carefully controlled) change in regime or to enter into a (cautious and contingent) negotiation with moderate elements in the opposition. To this structural potentiality, one should add two more conjunctural factors: (1) the early, unexpected, and well-publicized success of pacted transition in the Spanish case that encouraged imitation as far away as Uruguay, Poland, Hungary, and South Africa and (2) the accumulated wisdom among conservative supporters of autocracy that democratization in the contemporary context was not such a threat to their property, privileges, or capacity to compete politically.

The new international context. At the time that Guillermo and I were writing, the international context was "passively" tolerant of democratization on the periphery, but only if it did not threaten to upset the balance of power between the Western and Eastern blocs. Except for some activism by the Carter administration with regard to human rights, neither the United States nor its allies had agencies that were actively promoting democracy.[14] However, once the magnitude and spread of regime transformations had become apparent by the mid-1980s and, even more important, once the collapse of the Soviet Union in 1989–90 had removed the global security issue, the Western democracies rapidly equipped themselves with new government agencies and/or redirected existing "foreign aid" agencies for the business of "democracy promotion." Contrary to our expectations, the relevance of the international context increased monotonically with each successive demise of autocracy and attempt to establish democracy. The later a polity enters into this process, the more it is destined to benefit (or suffer) from the external intervention of already existing democratic governments. And this is by no means limited to government organizations. Each successive case of democratization seems to have contributed to the development of more nongovernmental organizations and networks for the promotion of human rights, the protection of ethnic minorities, the supervision of elections, the provision of political and economic advice, the drafting of constitutions, and the exchange of professional contacts. By now, there is not a country in the world that, even as it begins experimenting with democracy, is not literally invaded by a multitude of associations, movements, party and private foundations, consultancies, and even illustrious personalities from the international environment. Whether this intertwined network of governmental (GOs) and nongovernmental organizations (NGOs) has made some contribution to the fact that there have been so few overt regressions to autocracy is at least debatable.[15]

The very existence of such an embryonic "transnational civil society" also seems to have influenced the diplomatic behavior of donor democracies. Those governments whose citizens have most supported these pro-democratic, pro-human rights NGOs find themselves obligated to support officially and more resolutely efforts at democratization in ways that go beyond normal calculations of "national interest." Traditional protestations of "noninterference in domestic affairs" have become less and less compelling; the distinctiveness between the realms of national and international politics has been more-and-more eroded. Even more significant in the long run may be the increased reliance upon multilateral diplomacy and international organizations to bring pressures to bear on remaining autocracies or recidivist democracies. "Political conditionality" has taken its place alongside the "economic conditionality" practiced so long by the International Monetary Fund and the International Bank for Reconstruction and Development. Global and regional organizations explicitly link the concession of credits, the negotiation of commercial agreements, the entry into the ranks of their memberships, and so forth to specific demands that receiving polities take measures to reform political institutions, hold honest elections, respect human rights, and protect the physical safety and culture of ethnic or religious minorities. In extreme cases, the different levels of bilateral and multilateral conditionality combine in such a fashion as to restrict considerably the margin for maneuvering of new democratic leaders. Even more peculiar has been the spectacle of these leaders literally demanding to be subjected to international conditionality so that they can tell their respective populations that they had no choice but to take certain unpopular decisions!

The European Union, with its multiple levels and diverse incentives, was of considerable (but not sufficient) importance in the successful consolidation of democracy in Southern Europe.[16] Its role was much more significant in Eastern Europe, where the conditions imposed for membership were much more specific and comprehensive than in the case of the Southern enlargement. No other region of the world has an institutional infrastructure as complex and resourceful as Western Europe's. The Organization of American States and the Organization of African Unity have both taken some steps toward providing collective security for new democracies and have relaxed to some extent their traditional inhibitions against interfering in the domestic affairs of their members. The Arab League and the Association of Southeast Asian Nations have been conspicuously less vocal on the issue. What seems to be important—independent of the role of specific transnational organizations—are situations in which a region becomes so saturated with this mode of domination that all countries have mostly democratic neighbors. This seems to mount pressures on the few remaining autocracies and upon potential recidivists to conform to the regional norm, although the cases of Cuba and Haiti in Latin America demonstrate that the effect is hardly sufficient.

The problematic unit of government. Democracy, or at least democracy as we have known it, has developed historically within the sovereign nation-state. Granted that this has always been a bit of a fiction, in that many of these political units have strong and multiple identities within them, have not always had an effective monopoly over the use of organized violence within their boundaries, and are often subject to intensive economic and political dependencies upon foreign states, but the association has been so strong that many scholars cannot seem to imagine that democracy within any other unit is possible.[17] No one can doubt that it is preferable that national identity, territorial limits, and sovereign authority be established before introducing reforms in political institutions.[18] Moreover, there is no democratic way of subsequently deciding what should be the effective political unit. Self-determination of peoples or nations is an appealing phrase, but it tells us nothing about how this determination is to be made—especially in the course of a transition to democracy.

Several features of the regional and global context within which contemporary democratization is occurring have made this "fit" between unit and regime much more problematic than we imagined. In cases such as Spain, Czechoslovakia, Yugoslavia, and the Soviet Union, the historic imposition of centralized government had left a deep sense of resentment on the part of linguistic and ethnic minorities that was virtually programmed to resurface once democratic freedoms of expression and competition were tolerated. Here, contrary to our initial assumptions, "the national question" far outweighed "the social question" or "the military question" in importance during the transition, although it should be noted that, eventually and even after a great deal of violent conflict, solutions ranging from asymmetric federalism to negotiated secession were found. What was less expected was that even much more culturally homogeneous and politically unified units experienced novel problems of the "goodness of fit" between their national borders and external powers. Some of this was benevolent to the extent that membership (or prospective membership) in a regional supranational polity such as the EU that was itself a proponent of democracy (if not a practitioner of it) imposed serious limits on the institutional choices of national politicians.[19] More problematic, however, have been the constraints imposed by global financial institutions and multinational enterprises that have left newly established democratic governments without the capacity to respond to the expectations of their citizens. These "democracies without choice" have had to cope with unusually high levels of *desencanto*. Some of this helps to account for the prevalent disparity in public opinion between generic support for democracy as the best form of government and disaffection with the de facto government as insufficiently democratic. One of the most surprising and pervasive *lacunae* in new democracies has been the slow and erratic development of what was supposed to be a prerequisite for their survival, namely, a supportive political culture. As far as one can judge from the data, their citizens have been more cynical than civic in their declared attitudes and this may be due as much to the impotence of the unit as to the efforts of the government.

Conclusion

I return where Guillermo and I began. We knew that democracy is not a functional or an ethical necessity. It is a collective and contingent choice. Transitions to it are different from those to autocracy. The latter can be accomplished by a small, compact and hierarchically structured group (typically these days, a military junta); whereas, the former depend on a complex process of cooperation and competition involving a large number of independent agents. Moreover, immediately after it establishes formal equality in the limited political role of citizenship, a democracy must confront the informal inequality of the national and global socioeconomic systems into which it is inserted. And these inequalities are growing. Not only do they threaten the viability of democracy itself, but they are also antithetic to the very unit within which it is practiced.[20]

To our surprise, over seventy democratizations have been attempted across the globe since 1974. Fewer than we expected have failed outright, although many remain in an uncertain transitional status and some could eventually regress to the *status quo ante*. The main reason for this, I am convinced, is that the neodemocracies of the past four decades have been much less threatening to established interests than previously experienced or expected at the time. Many of the beneficiaries of the *ancien régime*—civilian and military, private and public—have survived (even thrived) and come to play an important role in the subsequent one. Whether this is a development to be praised or condemned is a matter for normative judgment. All I can say is that this was not an assumption or even a remote suspicion in our initial effort at transitology.[21]

Moreover, in polities that have not undergone a change in regime since 1974, autocratic rulers seem to have learned from these experiences and become more skillful and confident at making concessions. These hybrid regimes increasingly tolerate the presence of formal democratic institutions but deprive citizens of the crucial capacity to hold their rulers accountable. And there are still many remaining unreformed autocracies, although recent developments in the Middle East and North Africa suggest that they may not be as culturally or religiously immune from the threat of democracy as had been supposed.

It will not take long for the newly emancipated citizens produced by these "successful" transitions to discover that liberal, representative, constitutional democracy does not resolve many of their problems or satisfy many of their expectations. We are still far from reaching "the end of history" at which citizens will have become so settled in their institutions and approving of their politicians that they can no longer imagine improving them. To the contrary, I believe that, once democracy has become such a widely established norm of government and no longer has in front of it a rival regime type that is so markedly inferior, then and only then are disenchanted citizens going to demand that their leaders explain why their practices are so far removed from the ideals of democracy. Why is it that it is an increasingly remote, professionalized cast of politicians who rule and not the people? I suspect that democracy consecrated will become democracy contested—that the triumph of democracy in the last decades of the twentieth century will lead to a renewed criticism of democracy well into the twenty-first century.

NOTES

1. A notable exception was the seminal article by Dankwart Rustow (1970). It was very instrumental, reaffirming our conviction that transitions from democracy to autocracy are different from the inverse. The former are relatively predetermined by structural factors; the timing and nature of the latter are much less predictable and involve much more complex coordination problems among a greater number of collective actors.

2. The most reliable and comprehensive quantitative assessment of regime transformation lists 75 attempts at democratization and 53 cases of cases of continued autocracy (Bertelsmann Stiftung 2012).

3. The contrast between the politics of movement and that of the trenches comes from Antonio Gramsci (1971).

4. Based on my crude calculations at the beginning of the Woodrow Wilson Center project, I estimated that two out of every three attempts at democratization in Latin America since 1900 had ended in a return to autocracy.

5. Which was not the case with those transitologists *avant la lettre* in the 1960s and 1970s who analyzed "the transfer of institutions" from colonial powers to their newly independent, former colonies. David Apter, a mentor to both Guillermo and me, placed a great emphasis on the role of charisma, the (allegedly) exceptional powers of individual leaders during this crucial period. According to his neo-Weberian analysis of the Gold Coast/Ghana, Kwame Nkrumah was the forerunner of a series of "Princes" who were expected to bring parliamentary democracy to postcolonial Africa. The fact that they did not do so, and that they did not even manage to put together a viable hegemonic party, would not have surprised Gramsci (see Apter 1963, 1965).

6. He did not use the expression, but Giuseppe di Palma made this the major theme of his *To Craft Democracies* (1990).

7. An obvious historical exception was when, in the aftermath of war, the victors occupied physically the territory of the vanquished and imposed by force their preferred regime type. And even then, when the victors were democratic regimes, the success of the effort depended on a protracted and consistent intervention in favor of democracy. Witness, for example, the dramatic difference between the cases of Germany and Japan and that of Palestine under Israeli occupation.

8. Robert Dahl has long been an exception in the discipline with his repeated emphasis on the successive "revolutions" that have transformed the actual practice of democracy (1971: 248). For an updating of this notion of democracy as a "moving target," see my *The Future of "Real-Existing" Democracy* (Schmitter 2011). Bernard Manin (1991) also stresses this theme with regard to political parties, elections, and legislatures.

9. The closest exceptions would seem to be those states that came into being by means of a violent revolution or peaceful reform movement led by self-proclaimed democratic forces—usually in the context of liberation from imperial rule or in the aftermath of defeat in war. While in retrospect no one would question the bona fides of the founders of the United States, Canada, Australia, New Zealand, Norway, Ireland, and Finland, elsewhere liberators such as these either failed to create sustainable democracies or turned out to have autocratic propensities.

10. The attempted transitions in the Middle East and North Africa that began with the events in Tunisia in 2011 may have reversed this tendency. All of these uprisings have involved massive popular mobilizations. When the incumbent autocrats divested themselves of their leader with little violence from below (Tunisia, Egypt), their transitions would be classified as "reformist" (despite the revolutionary rhetoric); where the dictatorial ruler responded with armed violence from above and triggered a violent response from below (Libya, Syria), the transition would come closer to what we termed "revolutionary." So far, there have only been ambivalent efforts in this region at either transition by pacting (Tunisia) or by imposition (Morocco, Jordan).

11. For a substantiation of this argument with regard to Europe, see my *Parties Are Not What They Once Were* (Schmitter 2001).

12. Actually, there is one case: Portugal. The *golpe* by junior military officers on 25 April 1974 occurred in the complete absence of any prior popular manifestation and, ironically, it immediately triggered the most extensive and consequential mobilization of all recent cases of democratization (Schmitter 1975).

13. Unless, of course, they engage in unsuccessful military adventures. The transitions in Portugal, Greece, and Argentina were all triggered by such miscalculations and led to an immediate decline in popular support and a dramatic increase in internal factionalism, both of which subsequently contributed to bringing down their respective regimes. One could even stretch this observation to cover the former Soviet Union and the more delayed reaction to defeat in Afghanistan.

14. The important exception to this was the three semipublic German party foundations: Konrad Adenauer, Friedrich Ebert, and Hanns Seidel. Their role in Portugal and Spain was largely clandestine and much more significant than I was aware of at the time. Needless to say, throughout the post–World War II period there have been direct interventions in the process of regime change by the secret services of "real-existing" democracies—the balance of which seems to have favored autocratic outcomes. Hence, there existed and still exists a justified suspicion in Latin America, Africa, Asia, and (especially) the Middle East of the motives behind such actions.

15. For a theoretical analysis of this question for the period based on a highly skeptical set of

hypotheses about the likely impact of democracy promotion and protection, see Philippe Schmitter and Imco Brouwer (1999).

16. The importance of the EU in relation to democracy in Southern Europe was first explored in Pridham (1991). For a more comprehensive treatment of these changes in the international environment, see Whitehead (1996). For the emphasis on conditionality, see my *The Influence of the International Context upon the Choice of National Institutions and Policies in Neo-democracies* (Schmitter 1996).

17. This argument concerning the necessity of "stateness" is most prominently associated with Juan Linz and Alfred Stepan (1996: 16–37).

18. The notion that agreement upon the identity and boundary of the political unit is a "requisite" for a transition to democracy stems from Rustow (1970).

19. Hence, the famous *boutade* that, while the EU was an important promoter of democracy in its prospective member states, if it dared to apply for membership in itself it would have to be rejected since it did not satisfy the democratic criteria that it was imposing on applicants. Indeed, several of its already-member states would have failed the same test.

20. For a more extensive discussion and documentation of the recent evolution of these socio-economic inequalities in relation to globalization, depolarization, and democratization, see Terry Karl and Philippe Schmitter (forthcoming).

21. Machiavelli would most certainly not have approved of such an outcome. He was notoriously wary of the danger posed by survivors from the previous regime—and went so far as to advocate eliminating them physically.

PART II

THE POLITICAL ECONOMY
OF DEMOCRACY
AND AUTHORITARIANISM

CHAPTER 4

Rentier Populism and the Rise of Super-presidents in South America

SEBASTIÁN L. MAZZUCA

The "Left Turn" that swept across most South American countries during the early years of the twenty-first century has been the first continent-wide wave of political change about which Guillermo O'Donnell remained silent. His vast arsenal of concepts is nowhere to be found in the copious literature that deals with the Left Turn and its bifurcation into a radical and a moderate variant. O'Donnell decisively shaped the intellectual agenda for the study of the rise of repressive military dictatorships in the Southern Cone in the early 1970s; pioneered the analysis of authoritarian breakdowns and transitions to democracy throughout the 1980s; and broke new conceptual ground for understanding the issues of post-transition institutional quality during the 1990s. Yet research on the Left Turn has dispensed with the ideas that O'Donnell developed over four decades of a singularly distinguished scholarly career.

Two reasons explain the absence of O'Donnell's insights in the study of the Left Turn. First, the Left Turn has been seen mostly as an innovation at the level of policy outputs, whereas O'Donnell's concepts have almost obsessively focused on deeper variations located at the level of regime outcomes or at the even deeper level of state capacities. The two varieties of the Left Turn have in general been differentiated in terms of opposite policy responses to a prior period of neoliberal reform. These polar responses include, on the one hand, reversal of trade liberalization and privatization in the radical cases of Argentina, Bolivia, Ecuador, and especially Venezuela, and, on the other, center-left reform under free-market parameters in the moderate cases of Brazil, Chile, and Uruguay.[1] O'Donnell's analytical framework, designed for capturing large-scale institutional transformations, is not sensitive to variations along the spectrum of socioeconomic measures.

Second, even when the varieties of the Left Turn were characterized in terms of the government style under which the new policies were implemented, the key distinction observers make is one between populist versus institutional forms of rule, a contrast that resembles but cannot be equated to O'Donnell's celebrated distinction between low-quality "delegative" democracy versus high-quality representative democracy (O'Donnell 1994). Delegative democracy is simply not a proper characterization of, for instance, the case of Venezuela under President Hugo Chávez. The reason is certainly not the lack of delegative features but actually the weakening of the democratic ones.[2] The most pressing regime concern about Venezuela and, to a lesser extent, Ecuador and Bolivia under the Left Turn is that they are morphing into an "electoral" form of authoritarianism. Electoral authoritarianism is a regime type in which competition for power exists but is systematically biased against the opposition because of, for instance, excessive official control over the media (Levitsky and Way 2010). O'Donnell's latest work was an effort to craft a conceptual framework for the study of the quality of *democracies*, which by definition cannot be applied to cases that have gradually lost the attributes that form the basic package of a democratic regime.

The lack of an O'Donnellian perspective on the Left Turn and its varieties is, however, a serious loss. Adapting ideas from O'Donnell's theoretical legacy, old and recent, can yield substantial analytical gains for the understanding of the most significant ongoing political process in South America. Concomitant with the policy-level contrasts, a fundamental set of deeper but still underanalyzed differences at the level of macropolitical structures separates the radical from the moderate version of the Left Turn. O'Donnell's latest work on institutional quality and political accountability can help improve the *description* of such deeper variations.[3] Moreover, O'Donnell's early political economy work on the coalitional sources of different regime types can provide an *explanation* of the origins of the divide within the Left Turn, both as a contrast in policy contents and policy-making style but more crucially as a divergence in regime type.[4]

The first section of this chapter reconceptualizes the division between the moderate and radical versions of the Left Turn as a divergence at the level of the political regime, in addition to a contrasting cluster of social and economic policies, which so far has been the dominant account in the literature. The radical cases of the Left Turn all share, to different degrees, two regime attributes: plebiscitarianism and super-presidentialism. Such combination of regime features is, in turn, the outcome of the rise of "rentier populism," a new dominant sociopolitical coalition, which was made possible, but not unavoidable, by the price boom of natural resources. Section two provides a deeper analysis of the plebiscitarian form of super-presidential regimes that consolidated in the radical cases of the Left Turn, emphasizing innovations in relation to other experiences of concentration of political power in the history of Latin America. Section three introduces the theory of rentier populism, and section four traces its empirical origins in the cases of Argentina, Bolivia, Ecuador, and Venezuela. Section five specifies the mechanisms by which the dominance of rentier populism fosters the transition to, and consolidation of, a particularly intense and plebiscitarian version of the super-presidential regime.

The Varieties of the Left as Contrasting Regime Types and Coalitional Outcomes

The regime features that the radical cases of the Left Turn have in common are elements related to the form of *exercise* of state power. Argentina, Bolivia, Ecuador, and especially Venezuela consolidated a new, particularly intense and plebiscitarian version of "super-presidentialism," a form of exercise of power in which the president dominates the entire decision-making process at the expense of Congress and rules under only nominal scrutiny from other branches of government and nonpartisan agencies of oversight. Differences in the form of *access* to state power across the same set of cases, which can be more or less competitive, have unfortunately eclipsed the fundamental set of macroinstitutional commonalities at the level of exercise of power. However, the plebiscitarian form of super-presidential exercise of power is too systematic a feature across the radical cases of the Left Turn—and provides too stark a contrast with the moderate cases—to belong anywhere but in the forefront of analysis. Plebiscitarian super-presidentialism is an overarching constellation of attributes that covers both cases of illiberal democracy (e.g., Argentina) and electoral authoritarianism (e.g., Venezuela). The distinction between access to power and exercise of power provides a framework to characterize political regimes that adapts from—and makes more general—O'Donnell's distinction between issues of vertical versus horizontal accountability as well as the contrast later analyses have drawn between the democratic versus the liberal aspects of regimes.[5]

The similarities in the way power is exercised across the radical cases of the Left Turn have a common proximate cause: the rise of a new dominant sociopolitical coalition, which for lack of better terminology, could be called "rentier populism."[6] In its extreme form, rentier populism is a coalition crafted from the peak of the state, based on the economic incorporation of informal and unemployed workers, and funded by windfall gains from exports of natural resources. The coalition is made of two winning partners: the government, which redistributes income derived from mineral or agricultural sources to the informal sectors, and the informal sectors, which reward the government with political support. Redistribution of income occurs via extraction or expropriation from private owners of natural resources, the main losers from the emergence of rentier populism. O'Donnell was a central figure in the first generation of Latin America specialists who, adapting from Marx and Weber, viewed regime variations as reflecting, at least in part, transformations in coalitional dynamics caused by large changes in the underlying economic structures of nations. The rise of rentier populism as a dominant coalition is, to use Barrington Moore's (1966) terms, the "social basis" of the plebiscitarian form of super-presidentialism prevalent in the radical cases of the Left Turn.

The large economic change causing a new coalitional dynamics in South America was the boom in commodity prices that began in the second half of 2002, which in turn was a consequence of the rise of China and India as industrial superpowers and voracious consumers of raw materials and foodstuffs. The price boom of natural resources not only reversed a multidecade trend of "deteriorating terms of trade" for South American countries but also prompted an extraordinary period of economic growth, the consistency and speed of which has few antecedents in the economic history of the region. In 2000, buying the most basic model of cellular phone required fifteen barrels of oil. In 2013, a barrel and a half buys a last generation iPhone. In 2002, one hundred metric tons of soybeans had the same value as a small Honda car. Ten years later, they are worth a convertible BMW. The availability of a new source of national wealth made possible by the commodity boom was the key input in the construction of the rentier populist coalition.[7] However, as the case of Chile definitely shows, not all South American countries benefitting from the commodity boom experienced the rise of rentier populism and its political regime concomitant, plebiscitarian super-presidents. The commodity boom is a necessary but far from sufficient condition for the coalitional and regime underpinnings of the radical left.

The construction of the rentier populist coalition, like the formation of a plebiscitarian super-presidential regime, has been the result of political choices. Those choices were not blank-slate affairs, of course, but rather they have been shaped by a constellation of contextual conditions rooted in the structure of the national party system and the capital markets.[8] It can be safely assumed that all politicians, especially those who have what it takes to climb up the greasy pole, desire to accumulate as much power as possible and to preserve it for as long as possible. All politicians would like to become "super-presidents" and be reelected indefinitely, unless they face serious constraints.

The commodity boom threw a trinity of "temptations" in the path of South American presidents. The first temptation was to maximize the government's cut of the torrential income derived from natural resources. A larger government budget is simply the master key for power accumulation and preservation. This new opportunity faced by rulers in resource-rich countries under the commodity boom can be called the "expropriation temptation." The second opportunity, or "populist temptation," was to use the new income derived from natural resources to foster short-term consumption at the expense of long-term investment. This temptation, reflecting the general misalignment of the political and economic cycles, is hard to resist for presidents seeking to achieve peak levels of popularity, especially during election years. Finally, the "absolutist temptation," which is faced only by presidents who already fell into the first two ones, was to mobilize popular support, if necessary in a plebiscitarian fashion, to dismantle checks and balances that reduce the executive's freedom of action and remove constitutional brakes that ban presidential reelection. Presidents falling into the first two temptations give birth to rentier populism; and presidents who built the rentier populist coalition can hardly avoid the third temptation, which provides them with all the advantages that come with a plebiscitarian form of super-presidential regime.

Since the commodity boom laid the three temptations before all presidents in South America's resource-rich countries, and assuming that as power maximizers they would have given in to the temptations had they been unconstrained, the natural question is: Why and how barriers to the domination of rentier populism, which remained effective in the moderate cases, were lifted in the radical cases of Argentina, Bolivia, Ecuador, and Venezuela? Faced with the three opportunities presented by the commodity boom, presidents are dissuaded to capture them if they fear the reaction from direct rivals for power, that is, competing political parties, and from indirect sources of economic governability, essentially, large private firms and creditors. The vitality of the party system and the capital markets is then a key strategic element for presidents pondering a foray into rentier populism. The commodity boom hit all South American countries at the same time in the chronologic calendar, but at different junctures in their national political and economic trajectories. In the cases that would later become dominated by rentier populism, the beginning of the commodity boom intersected protracted national crises in the party system and the financial markets. The twin crises almost completely evaporated the citizens' trust on traditional politicians and the investors' confidence on macroeconomic conditions. As I will argue below, those crises bulldozed barriers against expropriation, economic populism, and super-presidentialism.

Super-presidential Regimes and Plebiscitarian Mobilization

For prevailing analyses of variations within the Left Turn in South America, the four radical cases of Argentina, Bolivia, Ecuador, and Venezuela share attributes at the level of policy contents (rejection of neoliberalism) but not at the level of macroinstitutional structures. Crucially, Argentina has kept a democratic regime but the three radical Andean countries, especially Venezuela, are increasingly authoritarian. However, despite the Argentine versus Andean contrast in terms of the competitiveness of access to power, Argentina is strikingly similar to the Bolivarian cases in terms of the form of exercise of power. The radical cases of the Left Turn may be more or less democratic, but all four of them have successfully sponsored the maximization of presidential control over the decision-making process, a concentration of political power that has occurred at the expense of liberal institutions of oversight and on the basis of plebiscitarian mobilization of political support.[9] By contrast, in the moderate cases of the

Left Turn, Congress, the judiciary, independent bureaucracies, comptrollers, or some combination of them, provide effective checks on presidential performance.

The rise of a plebiscitarian form of super-presidential regimes in the radical cases of the Left Turn may seem old news from the perspective of the "centralist tradition" that for some historians is the birthmark of Latin America's political trajectories. However, the plebiscitarian super-presidential regimes of South America involve a true break with the past. In fact, plebiscitarian super-presidentialism displays a constellation of features that set them apart from its two closest cousins: the classical forms of populist leadership of the mid-twentieth century and the delegative presidencies that led the introduction of market reforms in the 1990s. In contrast to delegative democracies, which were marked by the demobilization of the popular sectors and presidential delegation of economic decision making into the hands of technical experts, the new super-presidential regimes tend to intensify political mobilization of the public, especially the lower classes, and repudiate the role of economic technocrats (with the partial exception of President Rafael Correa). In contrast to classical populism, active popular support for the president is recruited mainly from the informal sectors of the economy rather than from the files of industrial workers.

Additionally, presidential superpowers in the new plebiscitarian cases became formally institutionalized, whereas prior experiences of presidential concentration of power, including delegative democracies, relied on informal agreements made in emergency situations, as well as on evolving balances of underlying political power. Formal institutionalization of presidential superpowers occurred either through constitutional reform in the Bolivarian cases or through a set of regular laws that in the case of Argentina transformed the emergency powers of the president over the economy into ordinary capabilities subject to only minimal scrutiny by Congress.[10]

Institutional similarities between Argentina and the Andean region's three radical cases run deeper and make the contrast with the moderate Left Turn cases even starker. In all four radical cases, the size of the state, measured by central-government expenditure as a proportion of annual GDP, grew from a "neoliberal" average of 27% by the end of the century to an average of nearly 40% a decade later—enough to land all these countries squarely in the "statist" category. In the moderate Left Turn cases, average state size was 32% before the Left Turn and actually shrank to 31% by 2010 (IMF 2012). Figure 4.1 illustrates the trajectory of state size in each of the radical cases versus the average of the moderate cases.

Thus, in all four radical cases, not only have presidents reached an historical peak in terms of control over government, but also the government itself is nearing an unprecedented level of control over the economy. The presidents of Argentina, Bolivia, Ecuador, and Venezuela dominate their societies to a degree that has few, if any, antecedents in their national modern histories. Concentration of political power in

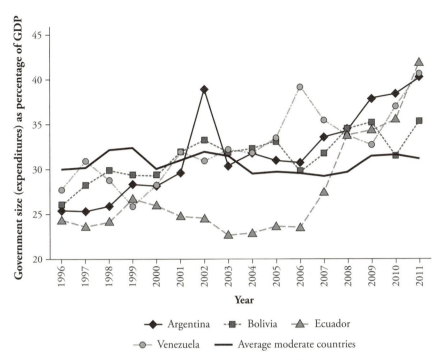

Figure 4.1. Government size (expenditures) as percentage of GDP. World Bank (2012).

the radical cases of the Left Turn, then, has proceeded in two steps (not necessarily sequential): the state expanded its control over the economy, and the presidents maximized their control over the government. The dual concentration of power introduces a contrast with the moderate cases of the Left Turn that is more fundamental than any other source of divergence, be it the magnetic personality traits or the militant neopopulist rhetoric of the radical presidents. These are either accidents or effects, not causes, of the dual concentration of power that underlies the radical cases.

Finally, cases of plebiscitarian super-presidentialism form an empirically distinct group, which, despite huge differences in other dimensions, cluster around a key selection of regime features for the first time in history. Plebiscitarian super-presidentialism emerged in countries with small economies and deep ethnic cleavages (Bolivia and Ecuador), a country with a large petroeconomy that used to have one of the most durable democratic regimes in Latin America's modern history (Venezuela), and a country with a large, diversified economy and one of the most unstable regime trajectories (Argentina). Besides, plebiscitarian super-presidential regimes consolidated in the radical cases of the Left Turn at the same time that countries of the moderate variant have shown undisputed signs of deepening the quality of their democracies. Such an array of cases provides the first set of hints for explaining the emergence of the new super-presidential regimes, for it helps to eliminate a number of good candidates for causes. Plebiscitarian super-presidentialism cannot be caused by the existence or deepening of ethnic cleavages (which are conspicuously absent in Argentina and Venezuela), by the presence of mineral wealth (which is negligible in the Argentine case), by the lack of democratic traditions of power sharing (which both Venezuela and to a lesser degree Bolivia used to have), by some Andean idiosyncratic feature (which Argentina of course does not share), or by cultural predispositions to paternalistic forms of rule (which should also be present in the moderate cases). Explaining the emergence of plebiscitarian super-presidentialism is a true challenge, but the very heterogeneity of the cases sharing the relevant regime attributes facilitates the process of searching for common background conditions—they are not that many. The main proximate cause behind the origins of plebiscitarian super-presidential regimes is the rise of rentier populism as a dominant coalition.

Rentier Populism I: The Theory

In the extreme case of rentier populism, an analytical caricature with no empirical instances in any place of the world or moment in history, only two actors form the ruling alliance: the government and the informal sectors. The government is the only owner of a natural resource that commands a high price on international markets. The government distributes the revenue from the natural resource to the informal sectors, which comprise a majority of the population. Exploiting the resource requires no substantial investments within the politically relevant time horizon. Either the necessary technology and physical capital are not expensive or they had been expropriated from private investors. In exchange for redistribution (economic incorporation), the informal sector provides votes to secure political victories and street mobilization to intimidate economic and political losers (political incorporation). The rentier populist coalition fully integrates itself into the international market for goods but it refrains from participating in financial markets. It needs the former as much as it can dispense with the latter. Foreign trade is the fundamental source of rent, whereas international capital is an unnecessary source of conditionalities.

The economic and political bases of rentier populism define its structure of accountability. Popular electoral ratification is the most affordable way of staying in power, because the vote of the informal sector is the least expensive to buy. The alternative of ignoring the majority and ruling through repression involves higher costs and more uncertain political benefits. Like any other dominant coalition, rentier populism has no spontaneous reasons to set checks and balances on presidential authority. The groups most interested in horizontal controls over the executive branch are those sectors in society that are least likely to become partners in the dominant coalition and are most worried about the discretionary use of political power. These include individuals or firms who have made heavy investments in physical and human capital, require long maturation periods, and present the most appealing targets for expropriation. The effectiveness of groups demanding checks and balances is a function of their relevance within the political economy of the dominant coalition. When rentier populism rules, the effectiveness of demands for horizontal accountability is negligible. Rentier populist rulers do not need the minorities in the formal economy for their reelection agenda, and the informal majority only requires the plebiscitarian mechanism to secure the uninterrupted flow of transfers. Plebiscitarian concentration of presidential power is a regime structure that is tailor-made for rentier populism: complete deactivation of horizontal controls (the super-presidential component) and high frequency of vertical ratifications (the plebiscitarian component). The rentier populist coalition "causes" plebiscitarian super-presidentialism.

Rentier populism and plebiscitarian super-presidents seem undefeatable. They are, so long as the three initial conditions hold at the same time: the price of the natural resource has to stay high, exploitation costs have to stay low, and the size of the informal sectors has to remain large. A small change in any of these conditions places a lot of pressure on the viability of the coalition and can provoke the collapse of the regime. If the international prices of the commodity fall below the threshold required for revenues to match the costs of the coalition or the size of the informal sectors shrinks so that they can no longer secure electoral success, it will be the end of the political regime. A new coalition replaces the old one, or the plebiscitarian super-president expands the coalition to sectors in the formal economy that demand institutional insurance against predation, for instance, effectiveness of legislatures in the economic policy process. Finally, if the costs of the technology for exploiting the natural resource become higher than the savings rate of the economy, rentier populism will be forced to end its isolation from international financial markets and, in exchange for fresh capital inflows, accept conditionalities that will curb the hegemonic features of the regime. Plebiscitarian super-presidents are strong while the conditions for rentier populism last, but they are extremely fragile in the face of small variations in the parameters of the underlying political economy.

Rentier Populism II: Comparative Political Origins

At the end of the twentieth century, rentier populism was an unimaginable phenomenon in Latin America. One of its components, the informal sectors, was available, but the other, the rent from natural resources, was politically irrelevant. The commodity boom of the early twenty-first century contributed the remaining piece of the rentier populist alliance. According to measures of the World Bank, total rents from natural

TABLE 4.1.
Rents from natural resources as percentage of GDP

Country	1990–2000	2002–2011
Argentina	2.45	9.83
Bolivia	6.78	29.61
Brazil	2.27	5.69
Chile	7.95	18.49
Colombia	5.28	8.13
Ecuador	14.02	24.35
Peru	2.85	9.78
Uruguay	0.51	0.98
Venezuela	26.86	34.81

Source: World Bank 2012.

resources during the commodity boom grew by at least 5% of GDP in six countries of South America: Argentina, Bolivia, Chile, Ecuador, Peru, and Venezuela (table 4.1). Since the data of the World Bank focus only on nonrenewable resources, the measure includes rents from minerals, oil, and gas but excludes rents from arable land. If the agricultural rents are included, Argentina becomes a major winner of the commodity lottery. There is no theoretical reason not to treat extraordinary gains in the prices of agricultural commodities as rent, which the government can appropriate without making a special effort to improve the business environment.[11]

The rent to fund a new type of populist coalition became available in most countries of South America, but rentier populism became dominant only in Venezuela, Bolivia, Ecuador, and Argentina. The reason for the divergence is that between the availability of the basic economic and demographic inputs and the effective construction of a new dominant alliance, a constellation of local economic and political conditions refracted the coalition-building process, preventing populism in some cases and encouraging it in others.

The original political decision in the process of building a rentier-populist coalition is whether to expropriate the booming natural resource, that is, whether to give in to the "expropriation temptation." In the ruler's cost-benefit analysis, the international price of the commodity, the scale of the national endowment, and the size of the informal sector define the potential reward. The costs, in contrast, are determined by the damage to the country's reputation in international capital markets and the resistance of national political forces that fear the risks that rentier populism create for their survival. The costs are shaped by financial markets and party systems, which are also structural constraints. These structures, however, are substantially more malleable and unstable than the ones that define the incentives, the rather fixed physical structure of the economy and the slow-moving social structure of the underlying population. Party system volatility in fact became endemic in Argentina, Bolivia, Ecuador, and Venezuela by the turn of the twenty-first century.

Financial reputation costs are especially high in countries with a long track record of receptiveness to foreign investment and debt repayment. All Andean countries are endowed with enough reserves of mineral wealth for expropriation to be a tempting political option in boom times. In three of them, Colombia, Peru, and especially Chile, the financial reputation costs have provided immunization against expropriation: flows of foreign investment are considerably higher than the expected gains of capture. This condition has been crucial in the Peruvian case, for in contrast to Colombia and Chile it meets all the other requirements for the rise and consolidation of a plebiscitarian super-presidential regime. President Ollanta Humala, who would otherwise be a natural architect of a rentier populist coalition, probably concluded that he had received too precious a legacy of financial reputation from the orthodox governments of Alejandro Toledo (2001–6) and Alan García (2006–11), which managed to achieve and keep investment grade status for the country. On the opposite extreme, the physical structure of the Argentine economy is considerably less attractive for rentier political ventures. Nevertheless, by the time commodities started to boom, the financial reputation costs of expropriation or confiscatory taxation had become negligible. In 2001 the Argentine government defaulted on a gigantic volume of foreign debt and doomed the country to years of abysmal credit ratings. For Néstor Kirchner, refraining from the rentier populist temptation would have only meant taking the first step in a necessarily long process for rebuilding reputation, the dividends of which would have started to flow well beyond the politically relevant horizon. When Evo Morales and Rafael Correa became presidents, credit ratings in Bolivia and Ecuador fell to all-time lows. For the fiscal needs of their coalitional projects, expropriation was much more effective than patient reconstruction.

Party systems, the other source of costs for the leader considering the construction of rentier populism, prevent expropriation if the incumbent party has a solid constituency in the formal economy or the opposition parties have enough organizational strength.[12] The economic recession of 1998–2002 was a watershed moment for party systems in South America. The political parties that had implemented neoliberal reforms lost vital reserves of political capital. Only two established left-wing parties had remained in the opposition during the era of market reforms: the Brazilian Partido dos Trabalhadores (PT) and the Uruguayan Frente Amplio. Free from the blame for economic pains, they supplied a fresh but institutionalized post-neoliberal option to the public. In Chile the economic crisis was very mild (the recession was over by 2000), neoliberal reform did not cause disappointment and, although they were partners in the ruling coalition, Socialistas also became a credible post-neoliberal choice. Once the PT, the Frente Amplio, and the Chilean Socialists gained power, the price for the creation of a rentier populist alliance would have been the destruction of their historic ties with formal labor. A more profitable course of action was the gradual incorporation of the informal sectors as an extra layer to their established constituencies. In Venezuela, Bolivia, and Ecuador, when the economic slowdown began, party systems were already experiencing a deep and protracted crisis caused by cartelization and corruption. In Argentina, the representation crisis actually followed economic recession. In all four cases, however, party system volatility peaked and, with the exception of the Argentine Peronistas, stable political parties virtually disappeared.[13] From that moment on, whoever became president would be able to rule without organized opposition. Political barriers to the emergence of rentier populism vanished as parties lost the strength to resist expropriation. In Argentina, Bolivia, Ecuador, and Venezuela, the flip side of party deinstitutionalization under economic collapse (Argentina and Venezuela) or stagnation (Bolivia and Ecuador) was mass praetorianism, especially informal sector mobilization. Massive street protests presented Chávez, Kirchner, Morales, and Correa with a unique opportunity for moving beyond the strictly economic incorporation adopted in Brazil, Chile, and Uruguay, to try the *political* incorporation of the informal sectors. Informal sectors became key allies in the electoral coalition, providing the base for plebiscitarian ratifications, as well as in the government coalition, supplying control of the streets and intimidation of the opposition.

Cases and Mechanisms of Rentier Populism

In 2001 the Chávez government decided that the state-owned Petróleos de Venezuela (PDVSA) should be the majority shareholder in all Venezuelan oilfields, which affected thirty-three multinational companies with operations in the Orinoco Basin. Two of them, Total and Eni, left the country. A year later, Chávez raised royalties on private oil companies from 1% to 30% and taxes from 34% to 50%. A presidential decree of 2007 raised the floor of PDVSA's share in exploitation joint ventures from 51% to 78%. Increased control over the flow of oil rents allowed for the creation of the Misiones Bolivarianas, Chávez's strategy of informal sector incorporation. In fact, PDVSA, rather than other state ministries, has administered the missions. The programs created between 2003 and 2004 included Misión Robinson and Misión Ribas to target literacy and basic education, Misión Barrio Adentro to provide health services, and Misión Mercal to provide subsidized food.

In Bolivia, Morales nationalized the country's hydrocarbon resources four months after assuming the presidency. In a primarily symbolic action, he sent troops to occupy the Tarija gasfields, the second largest reserves in Latin America. Petrobras, the

Brazilian oil giant, was the most affected firm, as its facilities came under the control of the Bolivian state company Yacimientos Petrolíferos Bolivianos (YPFB). At the same time, Morales repurchased the remaining privately held shares of YPFB and transformed the various drilling projects from joint ventures, in which private firms received a proportion of profits, to service contracts based on flat fees. Taxes also rose from 18% to 82%, reversing the division of earnings between the state and private firms. In relative terms, no government benefited from nationalization and the commodity boom more than Bolivia did. Revenues from mineral royalties grew 929% from 1997 to 2007, and hydrocarbon taxes 626%. The key political consideration behind hydrocarbon nationalization was the incorporation of the informal sector. Revenue from gas rents has financed the creation of the Bono Juancito Pinto, a family allowance of $29 for each child enrolled in primary school (October 2006), the Renta Dignidad, a payment of $340 to all seniors (April 2007), and the Bono Juana Azurduy, which gives $257 to pregnant women and mothers who undergo periodic medical checkups (May 2009). Despite the country's large oil deposits, the government of Ecuador was not dependent on mineral rents in the 1990s. Oil companies paid an average 20% of their revenues in taxes, which was far from enough to sustain a populist coalition. Yet, first as finance minister of Alfredo Palacio's transitional government (2005–6) and later as president, Correa raised hydrocarbon taxes, which reached 50% in 2006 and 80% in 2007. As a result, Petrobras decided to gradually leave the country and almost every other multinational firm stopped new investment. The new taxes strengthened Correa government's fiscal position and allowed it to launch the Bono de Desarrollo Humano, a redistribution program that covers 1.5 million households, or 45% of the population.

With much smaller reserves, Bolivia and Ecuador cannot reach the degree of rentierism of Venezuela. With an economy that is more diversified than Venezuela's and larger than those of Bolivia and Ecuador, Argentina remains the least dependent on rents. Further, its resource, land, has natural barriers against state expropriation and exploitation. Yet the state can still extract massive rents by setting up a monopsony for agricultural products, as it did under Perón in the late 1940s, or by taxing exports. Although President Carlos Menem eliminated export taxes in the 1990s, transitional president Eduardo Duhalde reinstated them in March 2002 under the name *retenciones*. Originally set at 5% for processed soybeans and 10% for unprocessed, the *retenciones* quickly rose to 20% in order to fund unemployment benefits for almost two million people. President Néstor Kirchner maintained the tariff levels and the allocation of revenues almost until the end of his term. Ahead of the 2007 presidential elections, Kirchner raised duties to 24% for processed soybeans and 27% for unprocessed to subsidize consumption in low-income sectors. After his wife, Cristina, won the presidential race in October, tariffs rose again to 32% and 34% to cover the debts incurred during the campaign. Soybean rents, which the central government has refused to share with the provinces, have brought Argentina closer to a rentier state than ever before.

No case perfectly fits the ideal type of rentier populism. During the commodity boom, however, Argentina, Bolivia, Ecuador, and Venezuela have moved closer to the ideal type, while Chile, Brazil, and Uruguay have moved away. Argentina, Bolivia, Ecuador, and Venezuela also differ among themselves in terms of proximity to the extreme case. The key point from the perspective of causal inference is that the degree of rentier populism in each case is concomitant with the extent of plebiscitarianism and presidential concentration. Venezuela, the case that best approximates rentier populism, is also the closest to plebiscitarian super-presidentialism. Argentina is the case with the most tenuous attributes of both types, while Bolivia and Ecuador are intermediate cases. But correlation is not causation. Since the number of cases is too small for statistical analysis, it is crucial to find causal mechanisms, that is, processes that connect rentier populist coalitions to the generation of the institutional features of plebiscitarian super-presidential regimes.

Once rentier populism has consolidated as the dominant coalition, two mechanisms foster concentration of power in the executive. The rising living standards of the informal sectors made possible by the boom and redistribution encourage presidents to intensify the use of plebiscites. In turn, popular ratification emboldens presidents to wrest remaining powers away from the other branches of government and portray resistances to hegemony as antidemocratic conspiracies. The string of ratifications dispels any doubt about the validity of the majority's verdict. Frequent plebiscitarian consultations extend a blank check for the unconstrained use of presidential superpowers. The other mechanism is fiscal. When prices are sufficiently high, rents from natural resources cover all the coalition's expenses. State control means the government doesn't have to negotiate with anyone to secure the flow of revenue and grants rulers independence from any group, national or international, that might otherwise make demands of institutional quality in exchange for taxation or investments.

Conclusions

The radical left differs from the moderate left in South America not only in terms of policy orientation but also, and more fundamentally, in terms of regime type and dominant coalition. The radical cases of the Left Turn share attributes of the regime of *exercise* of power—plebiscitarianism and super-presidentialism—that should not be eclipsed by differences in the regime of *access* to state power. The radical left may include cases of democracy (Argentina) and autocracy (Venezuela and to a lesser extent Bolivia and Ecuador). However, all of them exhibit virtually unconstrained domination of the government by the president, which was largely achieved through plebiscitarian methods of political mobilization. In terms of degree of power concentration and methods of consolidation, plebiscitarian super-presidential regimes form a distinct historical phenomenon.

The institutional innovations at the level of the regime type in the radical cases reflect a transformation in the underlying coalitional dynamics. The institutional concentration of power in Argentina, Bolivia, Ecuador, and Venezuela has been the result of the rise of rentier populism, a new political alliance between a government that has managed to gain control over the income from natural assets, and the informal sectors of the economy, which receive economic transfers in exchange for political support. The new coalition was in turn made possible by the commodity boom of the 2000s, a change in international prices that involved a global redistribution of economic wealth with substantial repercussions for national economies.

Ultimately, what differentiates the radical cases of the Left Turn from the moderate ones is that in the former it was the government, not a specific economic class or a particular production sector, the actor who became the main beneficiary from the price boom of natural resources. In order to be able to control the lion's share of the rent derived from the new international prices, the radical governments captured it. The moderate cases had one or more levels of institutional immunization against the expropriation, populist, and absolutist temptations faced by most South American presidents in the new century. In Argentina, Bolivia, Ecuador, and Venezuela, barriers in the party system and the capital market were ravaged by a combination of a protracted representation crisis and a deep financial crash. When they won the commodity lottery, radical presidents preferred rapid accumulation of power to patient reconstruction of multiparty institutions and ties to international investors.

Mainstream accounts depict variants of the Left Turn as variations in the spectrum of socioeconomic policies in which the choices by political leaders play a decisive role. In the spirit of the young O'Donnell, this chapter argues that policy differences within the Left Turn have been mere instruments for the construction and domination of alternative sociopolitical coalitions. As the young O'Donnell would have also done, this chapter portrayed leaders' choices under the Left Turn as strongly conditioned by underlying distributions of wealth and power, in particular, distinct combinations of international prices for natural resources, on the one hand, and national party systems and financial markets, on the other. The old O'Donnell showed little interest in the debate on the Left Turn in part, because it was never discussed as a regime question. This chapter reframed the divide within the South American left in terms of regime variations. However, in partial disagreement with the old O'Donnell, the different degrees of democracy observed across the radical cases were given less importance than the similar path that all four cases have followed toward the plebiscitarian accumulation of presidential superpowers. Will plebiscitarian super-presidents last? They will last as long as the price boom of natural resources. And no commodity boom lasts forever.

NOTES

1. For detailed and nuanced accounts of the Left Turn and its variants, see Levitsky and Roberts (2011a) and Weyland et al. (2010).

2. I acknowledge that classifying Venezuela under Chávez as not fully democratic is controversial. In this volume, for instance, Lucas González (chapter 11) codes the case as a democracy, whereas Enrique Peruzzotti (chapter 12) claims that Venezuela is no longer a polyarchy. Irrespective of the controversy regarding the form of *access* to power, as will be clear below, my own characterization of Venezuela, as well as Argentina, Bolivia, and Ecuador, centers on common features regarding the form of *exercise* of power, about which explicit research is scarce.

3. For O'Donnell's distinction between vertical and horizontal accountability, see O'Donnell 1998a.

4. For O'Donnell's "coalitional" analysis of regime change, see O'Donnell 1973 and especially O'Donnell 1977. For a critical review of O'Donnell's early perspective, see D. Collier 1978. Collier distinguishes regimes from policies and coalitions in order to clarify O'Donnell's contribution. Both O'Donnell's early coalitional perspective and Collier's triple distinction shape the explanation of the new super-presidential regimes advanced in this article.

5. For O'Donnell's distinction between vertical and horizontal accountability, see O'Donnell 1998a, and for the distinction between liberal and illiberal democracies, see Zakaria 1997. For a detailed discussion about how the distinction between access to power and exercise of power generalizes and clarifies distinctions made for the study of institutional quality, see Mazzuca 2010.

6. Both the term "rentier" and the term "populism" can create unnecessary controversy. To avoid it, I would happily replace them with more neutral terms, like "alpha" and "delta." I only keep them because they provide useful political evocation, and their use can be justified if properly differentiated from other meanings. In political science, "rentier states" are usually associated with mineral wealth, but in this article they also cover cases with extraordinary profits from agricultural assets, which is what allows for the inclusion of Argentina in the same group as Bolivia, Chile, Ecuador, and especially Venezuela. Standard definitions of "rent" in economics justify this usage. Also, populism in this article is defined as classical or "economic" populism: a social coalition based on redistribution policies that tend to incorporate formerly excluded sectors of the economy, sometimes hurting prospects for long-term investment (see D. Collier 1978). The economic definition of populism still dominates political discourse in many Latin American countries. For instance, Roberto Feletti, finance vice-minister during Cristina Kirchner's first term, defended the government's economic policy by claiming that "we must deepen populism" (Feletti 2011). Economic populism in this sense differs from the use of "neopopulism" that is increasingly dominant in American political science, which is a strictly political concept, centered on a type of leadership that resorts to intense antiestablishment rhetoric to mobilize popular support. For a recent review of the concept, see Barr 2009.

7. From a methodological point of view, the fact that the explanation of the new super-presidential regimes is ultimately based on an economic shock in international prices means that

the theory of rentier populism avoids the "endogeneity" problems that had plagued prior coalitional analyses of regime change, in which it was not clear whether coalitions caused regimes or vice-versa. Causality in my argument runs from a change in international prices (exogenous shock) to regime dynamics through the rise of the rentier populist coalition.

8. This structural explanation of regime features in the radical cases obviously differs from accounts based on the qualities of individual leaders, which usually focus on single countries (e.g., accounts of Venezuela's *Chavismo*). I see both approaches as perfectly complementary, each explaining different levels of political change, from more general regime attributes to more specific government features. For a subtle criticism of structural arguments for the Venezuelan case, with a compelling emphasis on Caldera's and Chávez's agency, see Mainwaring 2012.

9. Plebiscites in the technical sense were reactivated by the constitutional reforms in Venezuela, Bolivia, and Ecuador, and Presidents Hugo Chávez, Evo Morales, and Rafael Correa made frequent use of them in order to push their agendas and silence dissident movements. In Argentina, strong electoral majorities in presidential elections—based on a mix of vote shares over 50% and a wide margin of victory—have been repeatedly interpreted by government officials as an authorization to dismantle controls over the president and ignore the minority's claims. In the interview cited in note 6, Finance Vice-minister Roberto Feletti argued that "plebiscitarian" ratification in the 2011 presidential election would allow Cristina Kirchner to liquidate all checks (*frenos*) on presidential power. The main promoter of the plebiscitarian thesis in Argentina has been Cabinet Chief Aníbal Fernández. See, for instance, Fernández 2012.

10. For the key regime transition in Argentina in 2006, see Gelli (2006).

11. The rent is the difference between the total return to a factor of production (land, labor, capital, mines, gas/oilfields) and its supply price, that is, the minimum amount necessary to put it into work. Argentine farmers have continued to produce agricultural staples, especially soybeans, despite extraordinarily high taxes on exports of primary products, which have allowed the government to capture the lion's share of the return to land since 2003. The farmers' continued participation in the economy reveals the existence of a large agricultural rent in Argentina.

12. At least two works have also traced variations within the Left Turn to differences across parties and party systems. Nevertheless, they explain policy variations, not coalitional or regime outcomes. See Levitsky and Roberts (2011b) and Flores-Macías (2010).

13. For measures of party system volatility in the 1990s and 2000s, see Flores-Macías (2010: 423). For an in-depth analysis of party system volatility in Argentina, see Calvo and Murillo (2013).

CHAPTER 5

Democracy and Markets

Notes on a Twenty-First-Century Paradox

ROBERT M. FISHMAN

The more or less dominant meta-narrative of global transformation over roughly the past three and half decades presents the winds of change as favoring the simultaneous advance of both democracy and markets. Indeed, much of the scholarship written after Guillermo O'Donnell, Philippe Schmitter, and Laurence Whitehead's (1986) pioneering work on the political challenges of democratic transition has attempted to tie together logics of transformation in the political and economic arenas, assuming that the dynamics of liberal change in these two spheres tend to reinforce one another (Diamond and Plattner 1995; Fukuyama 1989, 1992; Simmons, Dobbin, and Garrett 2008). Granted, some scholarship has identified significant cross-national differences in the connection between economic and political liberalization (Haggard and Kaufman 1992, 1995), whereas others, somewhat outside this stream of work, have provided arguments on the potential contributions of mixed economies to democratic outcomes (Dahl 1998; Linz and Stepan 1996) or on tensions between markets and democracy (Przeworski 1991), but the predominant perspective has linked the resurgence of democracy to the advance of market logics. In this storyline, the progressive retreat of the state from meaningful economic ventures and the democratization of public authority are highly interrelated phenomena. This understanding of the contemporary epoch builds on a long and quite diverse theoretical tradition that—to one degree or another—has conceptualized markets and democracy as highly complementary, and in the extreme as actually mutually constitutive, approaches to the handling of complex challenges in modern society. In this chapter, I offer an alternative view, rooted in an analysis of contemporary developments and drawing intellectual inspiration from the work of O'Donnell. My analysis takes the form of what scholars often call a "think piece," in that it proposes a way to think about quite recent developments rather than attempting to offer definitive findings rooted in systematic empirical analysis.

The assumption that markets and democracy necessarily march together—and in its most extreme Hayekian version[1] the related claim that state involvement in the economy gravely endangers political liberty (Hayek 1946)—has long been subject to debate, in some instances from scholars strongly influenced by O'Donnell (Luebbert 1991; Rueschemeyer, Stephens, and Stephens 1992), but it has nonetheless exerted enormous force in the scholarly and political life of the West, especially in the post-1980 neoliberal era (on the neoliberal era, see Hall and Lamont 2013). Despite the overwhelming evidence undercutting the argument that Hayek presents in *The Road to Serfdom* (1946)—for example, the facts that dictatorship preceded economic centralization rather than following it in the Soviet case and that the social democratic societies of Nordic Europe have lively public spheres, relatively low levels of corruption and frequent party alternation in power, even such extreme forms of what Margaret Somers (2008) calls "market fundamentalism" have retained support, and more tempered assertions on the allegedly symbiotic linkage of democracy to markets remain highly influential. The more tempered claims, with their mix of historical and functional assumptions, tend to see the advance of market institutions and the eclipse of other allocation mechanisms as a development that strengthens the requisites for democracy. Even the great democratic theorist Robert Dahl, in his ambivalent treatment of this theme (1998), argues that markets are a precondition for democracy on two grounds—their alleged contribution to economic welfare and their presumed tendency to allocate social power and resources to nonstate actors—thus facilitating an undeniable requisite for democracy: the flourishing of autonomous social bases for politically meaningful opposition to power holders. Dahl also argues for negative consequences of unrestrained markets and offers a reasoned plea for a mixed approach to the handling of economic challenges but his learned effort to strike a balance on this question may yield too much ground to the market fundamentalists —perhaps because of a crucial methodological difference between his own approach to the fusion of theoretical and empirical analysis and that of neo-Weberians such as O'Donnell. For the neo-Weberians, the theoretical enterprise is thoroughly embedded in the analysis of historical and case-specific complexity rather than in a search for global commonalities. This case-sensitive methodology provides scholars such as O'Donnell with the ability to identify—and theorize—crucial departures from the outcomes expected by dominant theoretical narratives. This approach is especially useful for locating and making sense out of infelicitous outcomes, whether those classically theorized by O'Donnell, the recent developments highlighted in this chapter, or others.

It was precisely through his masterful use of the Weberian approach to social science that O'Donnell achieved his paradigmatic insights into the potentially deep tensions between economic development and democracy—in certain historical settings. Along with several other pioneering scholars of conditions for democracy—most notably Juan Linz, Alfred Stepan, and Philippe Schmitter—O'Donnell's work has been characterized by the classically Weberian dual embrace of two seemingly oppo-

specific interests (including political commitments) and, for the most part, intended also to promote broader developmental objectives. Yet both the developmental process writ large, and emergent strategies rooted in specific constellations of interests, constitute problematic and discontinuous endeavors characterized by ideational conflict and constant efforts of powerful actors to protect entrenched sources of privilege. Development, in this construction, is an often messy and discontinuous process rather than a functionally ideal model of reinforcing positive feedbacks. O'Donnell's ontological assumptions about the developmental process made it possible to theorize what he observed empirically: developmental advances associated with setbacks for democracy.

Thus O'Donnell makes theoretical sense of observed empirical reality by conceptualizing development—and its relationship to democracy—as embedded in an actor-centered world of complexity that is populated by more or less self-interested forces. Development in this rendering is a conflictual and problematic process that can easily empower actors driven by agendas that undermine the public good—both in the economy and the political system. O'Donnell offers us a compelling alternative to the rosy assumption that the nexus between development and democracy is guided by an abstract and simple functionality of positive feedbacks. In the place of that conventional view, he proposes an understanding rooted in the analysis of historical contingencies. This is precisely the perspective that I seek to apply to the relation between markets and democracy. I argue that the tension between the unrestrained pursuit of material advantage in economic exchange—in other words, the operation of more or less laissez-faire markets—and the robust practice of democracy is currently growing for reasons that are at least in part historically contingent but which, nonetheless, should be theorized. For reasons suggested above it is natural to turn to the work of O'Donnell for inspiration and guidance in this venture. Before turning to O'Donnell's work I offer a few observations on the contemporary paradox located in the nexus between markets and the fate of democratic polities.

Contemporary developments, especially in Europe, highlight the need to rethink the connection between markets and democracy, to theorize ways in which certain market dynamics currently threaten to erode the substance of democracy, and to identify political and regulatory arrangements capable of mitigating that danger. I am far from alone in holding this concern. A long list of observers, actors, and scholars have articulated concerns of one sort or another about erosion in the content of modern democracy (e.g., Crouch 2004). More specifically, scholars have noted ways in which market dynamics in contemporary Europe—and their complex linkage to not particularly democratic supranational European institutions (on these institutions, see Schmitter 2000, 2006)—have sharply reduced the space for democratic decision making within the theoretically sovereign states that share the Euro as their common currency. Paradoxically, it is the continent on which the marriage of markets to democracy seemed most firmly embedded in historical experience (admittedly, after some difficulties along the way) that now renders increasingly questionable the felicitous presumption of a natural symbiosis between liberal practice in the economic and political spheres. Wolfgang Streeck[3] (2011) and other social scientists have identified the danger of an epochal eclipse of democratic capitalism and the dawning of an era of uncertainty for democracy precisely because of dynamics endogenous to contemporary capitalism. This blunt warning—or preoccupation—has not been limited to scholarly voices; social movements and voices of protest in the streets, such as the 15-M movement of *indignados* in Spain,[4] have increasingly raised the specter of a threat to democracy from markets. The assumption of a positive symbiosis between market and political liberties is no longer a matter of easy consensus. What has motivated this broad-based rejection of a previously dominant meta-narrative?

The most dramatic developments promoting this growing skepticism over the alleged democratic beneficence of markets are related in one fashion or another to the crisis of the Eurozone[5] and of its sovereign debt, even though the problem is not limited to the polities sharing in Europe's common currency. The external imposition of a broad array of budgetary, regulatory and other policies on countries shunned by the international credit markets and then "rescued" by what has come to be known as the *troika* of the European Central Bank (ECB), the European Commission, and the International Monetary Fund (IMF) is perhaps the most persistent evidence of the broader problem but by no means its only manifestation.

When then Prime Minister Georgios Papandreou of Greece announced plans in late October 2011 to hold a national referendum to determine whether his country's citizens supported the austerity measures called for by the troika, that effort to incorporate the broad citizenry into the making of a watershed decision was widely denounced by political and economic elites in Europe as unthinkable and irresponsible. The skepticism of European elites—and their reluctance to allow Greek citizens to vote on the difficult decision about whether to embrace a devastating austerity program—was matched by the firm opposition to the referendum by many within the Greek political elite, including some within the governing party. Such pressures from actors opposed to the holding of a referendum thoroughly undermined a prime minister who had decided to subject his economic strategy to the will of the voters. Papandreou's referendum was never held and he lost his position as prime minister largely as a result of the promise to consult the electorate. Papandreou's replacement by an able and honest technocrat acceptable to both major parties was not as exceptional as the depth of the Greek crisis and instead proved emblematic of broader tendencies reflected elsewhere in the Eurozone, for example in the nonparty prime ministership of economist Mario Monti in Italy beginning in November 2011. The

to failure? Surely in the Greek case that verdict would hold some justification. In the years immediately following the collapse of interest rates charged for the country's issuance of sovereign debt—a seemingly benign development induced by Greece's incorporation into European monetary union—the country's political elites substantially increased public debt in a context of economic prosperity and (for that reason) improving living standards without directing most public expenditures toward useful investments holding the promise of sustaining the increased living standards paid for by the issuance of new debt. Granted, the tools through which Greek governments increased public debt included ones made available by major market actors now accused of masking the country's degree of indebtedness. Hence, the responsibility for unwise fiscal behavior is a shared one implicating both political and market actors. But if one wishes to argue that bad policies bring bad consequences—and as a result a substantial loss of room for maneuver by the governments that ultimately inherit the mess—Greece would seem to fit the story. That, however, is not the case for the other countries whose space for democratic decision making has been deeply eroded: Spanish and Irish governments were guilty of allowing real estate and construction bubbles to grow dangerously but not in any sense of "overspending" prior to the onset of economic crisis in 2007–8. Italian governments had their failures and embarrassments, but their public debt was a stable inheritance of decades past and seemed not to pose a problem, partly because of the country's large domestic savings rate.

The Portuguese case offers especially telling evidence of ways in which democratic erosion can be imposed by market actors and dynamics rather than as an inheritance of bad policy. I argue that the private credit rating agencies—the institutions that issue assessments of countries' creditworthiness for use by market participants—played a crucial role in this process. In April of 2011, Portugal was forced to seek an external "rescue" package when successive waves of credit downgrading by the rating agencies precipitated an increase in the country's borrowing costs across the threshold of 7% that was judged to mark the upper limit of sustainability. Despite solid evidence in Eurostat data and other sources that ongoing reforms were leading to an increase in exports, innovation within firms, and an improvement in student educational performance—and to reductions in government spending plans—the private rating agencies and other market participants came to see the country's finances as unsustainable. Voices within those circles called for fundamental policy transformations; their neoliberal framing of the country's challenges, coupled with the (strongly related) deterioration in the risk premium assigned to the country's sovereign debt in international bond markets, caused the Socialist government of José Sócrates to call early elections and led to a financial "rescue" that imposed harsh conditions on successor governments (Fishman 2011a). In an election held on June 5, voters decided to change governments, awarding a narrow majority to a center-right coalition, but that residual exercise in popular sovereignty exerted less of an impact on public policy than the outgoing government's negotiations with the troika over the external rescue ultimately agreed upon. Unelected actors such as the credit rating agencies, officials of the ECB and the IMF—along with their allies in the European Commission—ended up playing a decisive role both in analyzing Portugal's challenges and in opting for policy responses. Surely, some voters and elected politicians agreed with their analysis, but others did not, and the prebailout balance between the perspectives of domestic democratic actors was, in the end, of quite limited policy relevance.

Crucially, in the Portuguese case, market actors external to the country—including the private rating agencies—assumed that the country's institutions and ongoing policies required a fundamental remaking imposed from outside. That assumption—and the accompanying pressure intended to force domestic policy makers to act accordingly—marks a recurrent feature of the contemporary market-based challenge to democracy's substance. The rating agencies and other major market players have not shied away from making quite explicit pronouncements about the policies "required" to save one or another country from economic duress. These judgments, when they emanate from the market arena, are almost invariably rooted in an orthodox neoliberal perspective associated with policies likely to generate an increase in inequality and a loss of the state's ability to shape or somehow influence economic outcomes—whether through regulation, reallocation, public investment, state-sponsored credits to small and medium enterprises, or industrial policy of some other sort. The policies excluded or rendered unlikely by the emergent primacy of markets have their fully legitimate opponents in the democratic public sphere, but they also have their political proponents who point to many settings in which such policies have in fact contributed to favorable outcomes. Indeed, there is ample basis for arguing that the policy prescriptions being pushed by powerful market players reflect a misdiagnosis of the underlying structural problems besetting economies in the Eurozone's southern periphery and that, as a result, those prescriptions are likely to lead to structural damage—increasing the magnitude of long-term problems (Fishman 2012a). There is, of course, room for disagreement on this point as on so much else in the realm of policy analysis, but that is precisely the point: in the current European context market dynamics are tending to impose changes reflecting one side of ongoing policy debates, foreclosing alternative approaches and reducing the space for electorates to reach their own conclusions.

The Portuguese case itself, despite its moderately high debt load[7] and substantial external deficit at the time of the bailout, offers some evidence of the positive effects of policies and institutions (mis)judged by the markets to be failures. One can point to the country's vast increase in living standards during the two and half decades after Portugal's "liberation by *golpe*" (Schmitter 1975) and before the loss of monetary policy autonomy imposed by the inauguration of European monetary union in 1999. That improvement was accompanied by a number of other successes:

- a significant increase in labor productivity;
- an unemployment rate consistently lower than that of neighboring Spain—except for a very brief reversal of positions in late 2006 and early 2007 at the end of Spain's bubble economy (Fishman 2010);
- rapid (if still incomplete) catch-up with more developed countries in educational attainment; a level of poverty that, just prior to the financial "rescue," was the lowest in Southern Europe according to Eurostat data;
- high school educational performance, as measured by the PISA 2009 study, that was the highest in Southern Europe;
- a degree of innovation in private enterprise that Eurostat data showed to be above the EU average;
- and immediately prior to the "rescue," rapidly rising exports.

An analysis of cultural consumption patterns and their social determinants in the neighboring countries of the Iberian Peninsula has shown that, although the Spaniards and Portuguese born and socialized under authoritarian rule are relatively indistinguishable from one another, Portuguese young people born and educated under democracy have substantially more diverse and broad musical tastes than their Spanish counterparts and rank along with Danish and Finnish youth as the most "omnivorous" music consumers of Europe (Fishman and Lizardo 2013). In labor market participation by women, an element of economic life that has been theorized to represent a crucial underpinning of successful postindustrial economies (Esping-Andersen 1999), Portugal is the one southern European country to have attained levels of workforce participation similar to those of northern Europe. On various measures, prebailout Portugal appeared surprisingly successful; public expenditures as a proportion of GDP were higher than in neighboring Spain but lower than in the most successful societies of northern Europe. More important, given the social indicators mentioned above, they appeared to constitute a reasonable investment in the country's future.

I argue that such relatively felicitous outcomes rest on a form of (historically and culturally conditioned) democratic practice that has been more thoroughly egalitarian and inclusionary in certain respects than that found in otherwise similar polities such as Spain (Fishman 2011b). Yet, once the markets—under the influence of rating-agency downgrades—judged the country's sovereign debt to be an unwise investment, it became impossible for political leaders of the two largest parties to resist external pressures for budgetary and policy changes tied to the large troika-administered loan package.

The great weight of relatively few—but crucially placed and endowed—market players had shifted the ground on which the country's electoral competition and policy making was previously waged, thus highlighting major theoretical issues of wide significance: the principles defining free behavior and the determinants of collective outcomes are fundamentally different in markets from those understood to obtain in democratic polities. At least two defining features of democracy—the fundamental political equality of citizens and the effective location of executive authority in elective positions freely filled by the voters—are substantially emptied of meaning when market institutions characterized by the highly unequal weight of their participants and the absence of a full range of *political* debate acquire preeminence in the setting of policies. If that shifting of the locus of policy-making power also sharply alters the conditions shaping electoral competition and the debate among politically relevant ideas, the damage to democracy is even greater. To one degree or another, this is the fate shared by several countries at the periphery of the Eurozone. The Eurocrisis has evolved into a substantial disruption not only to national economies but also to democracy, and it has done so in ways that highlight the capacity of largely unregulated markets to diminish the space for democracy. The range of policy choices available to voters at election time has been reduced in ways that seem to privilege neoliberal outcomes and that undervalue policy alternatives that had generated substantially positive results—as the case of Portugal clearly shows.

Is the disturbing emergence of democratic erosion in Europe an isolated or unusual development? A great deal of evidence suggests that the problem is not unique to Europe or the contemporary era even though its current magnitude may well be so. Ongoing work by historians on a constellation of interrelated themes including colonialism, slavery, markets, and political freedom establishes the highly contingent and fluctuating nature of the relationship between the last two. The advance of markets and market-based economic liberties has been associated with the growth of political despotism in some historic settings and with the expansion of human freedoms in others.[8] Much of the contemporary European story will sound at least somewhat familiar to Latin Americans who suffered the political and economic effects of ratings downgrades and the self-fulfilling prophecies of bond markets driven by concerns over the creditworthiness of countries' sovereign debt in the closing decades of the twentieth century. And even the United States of America has recently been subject to a ratings downgrade and accompanying policy pronouncements by private rating agencies eager to delineate the future course of fiscal policy and budgetary outlays. Yet the current European crisis of democratic erosion is an especially severe and wide one. And—just as O'Donnell's perspective would lead us to expect—the reasons for that special severity are essentially historically contingent. Before turning to a consideration of the historical distinctiveness of this crisis, let us take up several themes in the work of O'Donnell that offer important guidance for analyzing Europe's current experience of democratic erosion.

I identify one overarching insight and several more specific points in O'Donnell's work that shed important light on the current market-based erosion of democracy. Most fundamentally and obviously, O'Donnell (1973) builds a powerful theoretical and empirical case for the proposition that the relationship between development and democracy is highly historically contingent. Even though development on average tends to favor democracy, in certain settings it may strengthen actors that behave in a fashion carrying antidemocratic consequences. Development, in O'Donnell's analysis, is a process fraught with struggle and with profound consequences for the changing balance of power among actors contending over an array of interests and objectives. In his historically embedded conception, the frustrations induced by developmental bottlenecks or failures may lead to doubly irresponsible conduct by dissatisfied actors whose behavior induces both economic and political difficulties.

The emergence of such obstacles to unilinear developmental success provides part of the basis for the emphasis that O'Donnell places on the growth of technocratic roles and policy orientations. But in a broader way, and following his friend David Apter (1965), he views the growth of such roles as an emergent component of the developmental process itself. O'Donnell's work on this theme contributed to scholarly appreciation of the increasing role of economists in politics (Markoff and Montecinos 1993) and identified the negative theoretical implications of this phenomenon for democracy. In O'Donnell's account, when problems induced by self-interested, and more or less irresponsible, actors give way to developmental disappointments, the temptation to trust all to the forceful imposition of technocratic policy outcomes contributes powerfully to the dynamic leading to bureaucratic authoritarianism. Much in that analysis holds carryover relevance for this chapter, but two other points also seem quite significant: O'Donnell's (1999a) concern over the authoritarianism of societal microtexts shaped by bureaucratic-authoritarianism (which I will refer to from here on as BA) highlights the complex interaction between social and political dynamics and between the macro and micro levels. And, perhaps most important, O'Donnell's major theoretical statement (2010a) on agency as a crucial foundation for democracy and on the state as a pillar underpinning the capacity of citizens to manifest that crucial property identifies important reasons why unrestrained markets may place democratic practice in danger. All of these contributions by O'Donnell offer insight into the issues raised here: if unregulated markets undercut citizens' capacity for agency and if the massive austerity imposed by the Eurocrisis leads to destructive outcomes within microcontexts (such as families or workplaces), the consequences for democracy's substance are quite serious.

Fundamental to O'Donnell's contributions was a general methodological and theoretical perspective underpinning his work, namely the assumption that the political and economic trajectories followed by national cases are in large measure historically contingent—a view that he shared with other great neo-Weberian students of democracy such as Linz and Stepan (1978, 1996). This perspective proves highly relevant for understanding the current tension between inadequately regulated financial markets and democracy in the Eurozone. The magnitude of the current market-based challenge to democracy's substance in Europe seems to rest on a distinctive constellation of unfavorable factors that have coincided in historical time. In that sense, the episodes of democratic erosion highlighted here and their (at least partial) rootedness in market dynamics is historically contingent. The unfavorable meta-context provided by the global neoliberal era has been negatively reinforced by a fundamental feature of European Monetary Union, namely the preeminence of German economic orthodoxy in the treaty and statutes guiding—or constraining—the actions of the ECB (Crouch 2000; Fishman and Messina 2006; McNamara 1998). The fact that by design the ECB lacks legal license to serve as lender of last resort, and thus to undertake substantial purchases of sovereign debt in the primary market (as opposed to "sanitized" purchases in the secondary market), has prevented the Eurozone's central bank from behaving in ways similar to the Federal Reserve and many other national central banks. Similarly, the ECB's asymmetric statutory charge to defend price stability (but not to guarantee economic growth and employment) limits its ability to respond aggressively to the severe and prolonged economic contraction of the Eurozone's southern periphery. The founding design of the Eurozone's central bank created an entity that left Eurozone states more vulnerable to the pressures of financial markets than were sovereign states with more activist central banks. This crucial feature of EMU has allowed private bond market actors a far greater ability to undercut the policy and political autonomy of Eurozone "sovereign" states than would have been the case if the ECB were willing to aggressively block speculative runs on the debt of countries subject to ratings downgrades. Given the low-inflation environment brought on by the financial crisis of 2008, the costs of aggressive ECB action would have been quite limited but nonetheless that path was not followed. The bank's hands had been legally and politically tied by the process leading to monetary union. Thus the Eurozone is more subject to the dictates of the bond market than other currency areas—with deep consequences for its democracies.

In the second half of 2012, the risk premium assigned by the bond market to the sovereign debt of states in the Eurozone's southern periphery declined significantly following a clear public commitment by ECB President Mario Draghi to aggressively purchase bonds in the secondary market in order to avoid a systemic crisis. Simply the threat to act—and that in a relatively limited way consistent with the bank's founding statutes—served to change the dynamic in the bond markets, thus reducing the danger that states would require massive new bailouts. But crucially, this relative flexibility and activism of the ECB was not only statutorily constrained in ways that differentiate ECB capacities from those of other major central banks but was also premised on the firm commitment of the periphery states to carry out policies shaped by the same neoliberal analysis as the prescriptions for change imposed by the troika in exchange for bailout assistance. Even when it acted to diminish the pressure applied by market forces on Eurozone states, the ECB did so in a way that required those states to embrace quite debatable neoliberal policy changes. The policy perspective driving the actions of powerful market participants also underpinned the ECB's initiatives and the expectations it communicated to member states. Instead of freeing Eurozone democracies from the policy-making constraints imposed by market dynamics, the ECB has in effect reinforced those constraints. Thus the historically quite concrete and unusual process that defined the charge and the powers of the Eurozone's new central bank proved to hold decisive importance not only for the currency area's economies but also for the democratic substance of participating states.

The economic downturn itself, beginning in 2007, and the related erosion of opportunities for market actors to attain the quick profits to which they had become accustomed may also be in certain respects related to the phenomena outlined here. Disappointing market outcomes should be expected to induce a change in strategies and a search for new avenues to profit, including perhaps the shorting of sovereign debt. The larger constellation has been quite unfavorable for European democracy.

In this context, the growth of technocratic roles and of a broader ethos underpinning them offers an unmistakable if distant echo of developmental tendencies highlighted by O'Donnell in his analysis of the making of BA. Indeed the recurring efforts of numerous European elites to turn the political game into a technocratic equation—conditioned of course by an anti-Keynesian epistemic community predominant both in the markets and within the ECB—is one of the defining features of Europe's contemporary crisis. The parallels with O'Donnell's 1973 formulation on the dynamics leading to BA are far from perfect but they are nonetheless quite real.

Perhaps most troubling are the potential spillover effects of market-induced democratic erosion on the capacities for citizen agency and on dynamics to be found in microcontexts where resignation and petty forms of discipline may undercut opportunities for political resilience in the face of crisis. But O'Donnell's (2010a) theoretical emphasis on law, social policy, and the state offers a key avenue in the search for democratic remedies to the challenges highlighted here.

Democracies should not and cannot eliminate the market but they can and should generate new forms of law, regulation, and social policy designed to prevent market actors from eroding the substance of democracy and to insure that the crucial principle of democratic equality among citizens is not sacrificed to the instincts and forces unleashed by "market fundamentalism" (Somers 2008). Markets are not in principle dangerous for democracy, as long as they are understood—and treated politically—as being sociologically "embedded" in the double sense highlighted by Swedberg (2003: 36–37), namely their rootedness in political and legal arrangements identified by Polanyi (1944) and in social networks specified by Granovetter (1985). The political and cultural frameworks within which markets operate are historically conditioned and subject to change. When markets are "disembedded" from regulations and monetary policy instruments capable of providing elected authorities with sovereign capacities for decision making, they raise the specter of dangerously deep democratic erosion. A re-embedding of markets in a regulatory, legal and monetary framework that permits central banks to freely purchase sovereign debt when appropriate, that regulates the decisively important rating agencies, and that reinforces social policies promoting the democratic agency of citizens would serve to end the danger of democratic erosion in Europe, thus closing off the unfortunate (but incomplete) parallels with elements of the road that O'Donnell discovered would lead to bureaucratic authoritarianism on another continent. Such a re-embedding of markets would represent an enormously positive legacy of O'Donnell's work—and of his hopes. If they are embedded in adequate state policies and legal regulations, markets can help to sustain democratic agency, instead of undermining it, but the political conditions required for that outcome are themselves subject to the danger of erosion. The connection between markets and democracy remains historically contingent.

Thus I argue that under contemporary conditions, strongly shaped by the nature of global financial flows, unregulated or weakly regulated markets lead to a "Schumpeter minus" form of democracy. Elections are still held and voters make choices among candidates but the assumed connections between the institutional core of modern democracy in the electoral arena and its substance in presumed popular control over policy making and government formation is badly eroded. O'Donnell's classic insights should, in this light, not be taken primarily as a set of fixed claims and predictions but instead as a set of general perspectives and instruments that can prove extraordinarily helpful for making sense out of the ever-changing challenges faced by modern democracy—many of them located precisely where O'Donnell concentrated so much of his pathbreaking work: in the nexus between the economy and the political system.

NOTES

I wish to thank Evelyne Huber, Tiago Fernandes, Julia Lopez, João Rodrigues, Casiano Hacker Cordon, and the volume editors for extremely helpful comments on an earlier draft. The errors and shortcomings are my own.

1. For a recent analysis of Hayek's work arguing for his recognition of the state's necessary role in building conditions for modern economic life, see Rodrigues (2012).

2. See the important work of Charles C. Ragin (1987) on configurational analysis.

3. Streeck's recent essay is full of insights but from my perspective undervalues the capacity of countercyclical deficit spending to sustain the viability of what he formulates as *democratic capitalism*—provided that other supporting conditions such as cooperative central banks also obtain.

4. For an analysis contextualizing the 15-M movement within the broader experience of Spanish public protest, see Fishman (2012b).

5. As a part-time resident of Spain and a scholar of southern Europe I have followed—and experienced—the crisis of the Eurozone's southern periphery since it began.

6. Spain did apply in 2012 for a partial rescue package aimed at the country's banking system, but both the dimensions of the request and its implications for national budgetary sovereignty were somewhat lesser in scope than had been the case for the Greek, Irish, and Portuguese loan requests.

7. Eurostat data for 2009 showed the Portuguese ratio of public debt to GDP to be the sixth largest at the time in the European Union. Since that time, and in part as a result of the economic contraction induced by the rescue package, Portugal's position on this measure has deteriorated, and the country now ranks third in the EU in the size of public debt relative to GDP.

8. I am indebted to historian Stephen Jacobson for discussions on this point.

CHAPTER 6

Inequality and Democracy
Latin American Lessons for the United States

TERRY LYNN KARL

A further word on the subject of issuing instructions on how the world ought to be . . . the owl of Minerva begins its flight only with the onset of dusk.
—Georg Wilhelm Friedrich Hegel, *Elements of the Philosophy of Right*

Guillermo O'Donnell's preoccupation with inequality could teach American exceptionalists a thing or two. Imbued with the moral imperative to overcome poverty and the exceptionally high levels of inequality characteristic of Latin America, O'Donnell showed that the outcome of exceptionally concentrated wealth was neither accidental nor beneficial. Beginning with his earliest scholarship on Argentina, O'Donnell illustrated how certain structural conditions influence and, in turn, are influenced by the intentions, ideologies, and policies of political and economic actors. Concerned with illuminating how dominance is exercised through choices encouraged or constrained by the structures and institutions within which they occurred, he foresaw how major corporate actors, facing crisis and pushed by fear of the future, shifted their attention from productive activities to what he called *la economía de saqueo*—the economy of looting (1982: 444). Influential actors increasingly captured portions of the state in their attempts to maximize short-term gains through rent seeking, making ministries (and ministers) their own, and thus eventually undermining the state's potential role as a guarantor of the capitalist order. The net result, as O'Donnell (1996b) showed, was the exacerbation of Latin America's notable concentration of wealth, the rise of poverty and the reshaping of institutions—all of which produced economic volatility and political instability.

O'Donnell could have been talking about the United States today. Where a keen observer like de Tocqueville once looked to the U.S. as a model—pointing out how its relative material equality produced egalitarian sentiments, exceptional opportunities for advancement, and a firm basis for democratic citizenship—this is no longer the case. Today, the United States is the most unequal longstanding democracy among developed countries in the world, and it has the highest concentration of wealth at the top.[1] Inequality, measured by the concentration of wealth at the very top, sets the United States apart from other rich countries and places it in a category more typical of Latin America. Notwithstanding real progress in combating race, gender, and other forms of discrimination, the country today faces its greatest challenge of social exclusion since the Great Depression. Not coincidentally, it also has the least effective government policies and social spending for alleviating poverty and inequality and the lowest level of income tax rates among all developed nations in the world.

This dramatic drop in the comparative standing of the United States is a remarkable change from the past, and one that has received insufficient scholarly or political attention.[2] This is a failure not only of politicians and public policy but also of American political science. Discussing the discipline, Jacobs and Soss (2010) place responsibility for ignoring the change in US inequality on the neglect of political economy in general, the inattentiveness to theories of power relations and social stratification writ large, and the pluralist tendency to overlook organized interests[3]—the very approaches that characterizes the work of O'Donnell and many comparativists. In this respect, the study of the United States has suffered from being a separate branch of the discipline of political science; it is implicitly considered exceptional and not subject to explicit comparison with other countries. But the United States is not exceptional when examined in comparative perspective.[4] Especially relevant to understanding its change in inequality status are the political economy and power-based approaches used to understand Latin America, most of which have been based precisely on the interaction between politics and economics as well as the study of organized interests that has been so strikingly absent in much of the study of American politics.[5]

Because Latin America has long been the most unequal region in the world, also marked by the concentration of wealth at the very top, this "lopsided continent"[6] is especially apt for lending insights into the reasons for and consequences of the huge increase in inequality in the United States. When examined through comparative lenses, the explanation presented here for the country's relatively abrupt change in levels of inequality will seem remarkably familiar to Latin Americanists: In the United States, as we shall see, dominant economic actors facing economic crisis embraced neoliberal formulas, then shifted their attention to the accumulation of what Adam Smith (1776) called rents,[7] especially in the financial sector. They accomplished this in part through a familiar pattern of state capture, reshaping key political institutions, and successfully redefining the policy agenda—just as in Latin America in the 1980s. As the US polity became more overtly and severely colonized by rent-seeking interests, inequality has soared, undermining the capacity of government to respond to policy preferences that might limit the rich and benefit the poor. This, then, threatens to solidify longstanding disparities in political voice, with grave implications for what democracy can and cannot do.

What is on the table in the United States—just has it has been in Latin America for so long—is whether it has entered a long-term "vicious cycle of inequality" that will continue to damage the quality of its democracy or whether this pattern will be reversed, as Brazil and other Latin American countries seek to do. This chapter first examines several key theoretical findings about point of departure, duration, crisis, and change in the interactive relationship between inequality and political institutions derived primarily from the Latin American experience; it then examines the US case through this rubric. The perverse impacts of huge wealth disparities are not well understood in the United States. But, as Latin Americans know, exceptionally high levels of inequality have serious consequences for the way people are forced to live and for democracy. They should not be considered the "natural ordering of things." Very high levels of inequality create dualism, that is, the coexistence of two separate worlds within the same national boundaries; this increases the social distance between people, erodes trust, and undermines the most basic notions of human solidarity essential for democracy. Ranking poorly in income inequality, as Wilkinson and Pickett's (2009) study of twenty-three countries demonstrates, carries a number of other worrisome indicators in its wake, and the United States is at the top of the list for all of these: high rates of poverty, imprisonment, homicides, teenage births, infant mortality, overweight children, poor health, drug use, and the decline of education.[8] High levels of inequality are a "drag on prosperity" (Goñi, López, and Servén 2011): they retard growth, imperil social mobility, democracy. and the rule of law.

When examining Latin America and the United States in comparative perspective, caution regarding the predictive capacity of the social sciences should be exercised. Neither the startling movement of the United States in a perverse inequality direction nor Latin America's very recent and surprisingly positive change could have been anticipated in 1980. In Latin America today, inequality has declined in thirteen of seventeen Latin American countries, which may represent a breakthrough in its history. As Lustig, López Calva, and Ortiz Juárez (2011) show, this decline in inequality since the early 2000s is substantial in at least ten countries, including those that benefited from high growth (Argentina, Chile, and Peru) and those that did not (Brazil and Mexico). This is a stunning reversal. Not too long ago, it would have been almost inconceivable that talk of soaring debt, threatened economic depression, pervasive uncertainty, exceptionally concentrated wealth, a "lost decade" for the poor, intense partisanship, deep polarization, and a paralyzed political system would describe the United States in the beginning of the twenty-first century—and not Brazil. Merely fifteen years ago, at the very time some were touting the success of "Reaganomics" in the United States[9] and others were claiming a "pathology of inequality" that threatened to become a permanent feature of Latin America's landscape,[10] Hegel's Owl of Minerva had already spread her wings; that is to say, just as these understandings were proffered, historic conditions were already changing in a new and largely unanticipated direction.

Inequality, Institutions, and the Quality of Democracy: The View from Latin America

A complete discussion of the interaction between inequality[11] and democracy[12] is not possible here, but extensive scholarship on Latin America (and other regions) illustrates a basic tenet: high levels of economic inequality shape and are shaped by political institutions, both directly and indirectly, thereby affecting the quality of democracy (Karl 1997). This is not the only explanation for different degrees of inequality by any means.[13] But even though the precise connection between poverty, inequality, stateness, growth, crisis, and democracy is still in debate,[14] there can be little doubt that high levels of inequality subsequently affect how political institutions are constructed and function, which, in turn, affects the quality of these institutions and their ability to adopt fair policies. Inequalities in wealth and income are created; they are not the product of some inescapable process of economic development or the inexorable working of the market but rather the outcome of specific laws and institutions regulating property rights, taxes, and public expenditures. In other words, the impact of gross inequalities is mediated through politics, and this causality is also reversed.[15]

What stands out in this mediation from the study of Latin America are certain understandings regarding how divergent patterns of inequality are constructed and changed. First is the *critical importance of how the point of departure* shapes the structure of property and role of the state. This, then rests to some extent on geographic conditions and initial factor endowments, especially natural resources and labor (Engerman and Sokoloff 2005a). But goals, laws, and institutions are important in themselves and not just through the way they are impacted by factor endowments. The identity and aims of different colonial powers (the Spanish or Portuguese versus the British);[16] their attitudes toward race, ethnicity, and gender; the relative centrality of a particular territory to a particular colonizer; and the degree of stateness established (or not) by different colonizers matter for laying the foundations for a highly inequitable development trajectory (Lange, Mahoney, and vom Hau 2006). Together, the interaction of factor endowments and colonial institutions sets a potentially durable path for inequality patterns—though seldom in the manner put forward by "new institutionalists."[17]

In Latin America, for example, comparative historical analysis shows how Spain granted Latin America's mineral and agricultural wealth to a fortunate few, centralizing economic and political power while relegating indigenous people to marginality as a means of extracting wealth. The Spanish operated most extensively in those areas that were already most densely settled by indigenous civilizations and/or where important deposits of gold or silver were located (e.g., Mexico, Guatemala, and the Andean countries), which meant that these areas also had the most significant impact of its colonial institutions and the greatest inequality[18] when contrasted to more peripheral areas marked by fewer sources of labor and minerals (e.g., Argentina, Chile, Uruguay, and Costa Rica).[19] While both groups were unequal, the difference in the Spanish legacy in these two groups, especially with regard to the treatment of indigenous people, affected the degree to which states became committed to the provision of public goods and the promotion of human welfare—with the latter countries faring far better. Nonetheless, neither group inherited state institutions that could promote any type of broad-based development.[20] Instead, in Latin America Spanish colonialism produced highly stratified societies, predatory states, and dysfunctional and inequitable markets (Evans 1995; Lockhart and Schwartz 1983).

A second lesson from Latin America is that *when significant changes toward greater equality or inequality do occur, they are generally the result of abnormal upheaval,* such as revolution, war, or economic crisis. Crisis represents the opportunity for change or the protection and persistence of a previous pattern. Whether inequality patterns improve, worsen, or persist depends on how political and economic actors and institutions respond to crisis. Crisis can be a great leveler, as it proved to be in the postcolonial period in parts of Asia—or not.

Neither the crisis of the nineteenth century nor the response was salutary in Latin America. The manner of collapse of Spanish imperial rule (not to mention Spain) and the internecine wars that characterized the nineteenth century resulted in (at minimum) a "lost half-century" for the countries of the region.[21] The tremendous cost of these wars had a perverse impact on the construction of state institutions that might have addressed existing inequalities, differing markedly from Tilly's (1975) observation about the favorable impact of war on state building in Europe (Centeno 2002; Karl 1997). Instead, because there was little institutional transfer from Spain, no stable mechanisms existed to encourage growth or equity or process conflict. In this context, asset inequality based on control of land and mineral resources reasserted itself, eventually making Latin America significantly more lopsided than other world regions.[22] Its natural resource bias in the context of weak institutions encouraged rampant rent seeking, manifested by how foreign borrowing and resource rents substituted for taxation. By the end of the nineteenth century, Latin America had settled into what became longstanding patterns of weak, overcentralized, and "captured" states, highly exclusionary political institutions, rentier private sectors, and dualism that have carried through, in some countries, to the present (Brockett 1988; Bulmer-Thomas 1995; Gootenberg 1991; Véliz 1980).

Third, *inequality patterns, once established, are strikingly resistant to significant change* (Alesina and Rodrik 1994; Karl 2000, 2003; Li, Squire, and Zou 1998; Lustig, López-Calva, and Ortiz Juárez 2011; Tokman and O'Donnell 1998). Relatively stable patterns of "virtuous" or "vicious" inequality cycles—that is, gradual, slow, and often almost imperceptible improvements or stagnation or deterioration—are most common. When change does occur, movements in a perverse direction appear to be the norm, with relatively few instances of dramatic and significant policy-induced changes in income distribution moving in a more equal direction.

Fourth, *economic inequality becomes political inequality (and vice versa), and over time this results in economic and political instability.* To the degree that highly exploitative economic relations are in place, they permit the construction of unfair, exclusionary, and biased institutions that grant unequal political influence to those of greater material means. High inequalities of wealth and income tilt the rules of the game, distort institutions of law and representation, and mold public policies in favor of the wealthy and privileged to differing degrees. Samuels and Snyder (2001), for example, show that Latin America has the most malapportioned legislatures in the world, which were initially drawn to over represent rural interests and produce a distinctive conservative bias in the polity, while Oxhorn (2003) and Bill Chávez (2004) demonstrate how the law becomes "marketized." Add influence trafficking, corruption, and vote buying or voter suppression—common mechanisms by which the wealthy convert assets into political power—and these institutional biases are compounded. But, if high inequalities encourage the wealthy to become politically active, they disempower weaker social groups by depressing political interest, discouraging action, and impeding the organization of the poor (Brinks and Botero 2010).[23] The short-term result is to create new opportunities for rent seeking while lowering the pressure for a more fair distribution of resources through taxes or transfers. In sum, high levels of inequality eventually express themselves through institutional harm.

Finally, *creating a fairer distribution of resources in today's globalized environment depends not only on growth and/or technological change but also on the capacity of political actors and institutions to form a "fairness coalition."* This requires, first and foremost, democratic institutions, yet they are a necessary but not sufficient condition.[24] Rent seeking and institutional harm over time lay the foundation for intense partisanship over the distribution of resources, political polarization, and dysfunctional politics, which themselves are economically very costly (Figueroa 1996). In this context, only the creation of a broad-based alliance of political parties, activists and government reformers, and unions and social movements can force the adoption of pro–middle class and propoor policies. A coalition of this sort is essential, not only to build majorities that will support a particular platform but also to impel democratic institutions (e.g., elections, various separate powers and their bureaucracies, etc.) to fulfill their accountability functions by limiting predatory behavior and encouraging participation.

Once again, the experience of Latin America is telling. After two decades of neoliberal market-oriented reforms and austerity programs that had a regressive impact on inequality, recession created the conditions for what K. Roberts (2012) calls "the logic of democratic competition" to politicize the region's terrible social deficits. Outbreaks of mass protest of unemployed workers, women, and indigenous groups rejected neoliberalism (Madrid 2012) and eventually contributed to unprecedented electoral victories by left-of-center candidates in eleven different Latin American countries.[25] Pushed by their constituencies, who overwhelmingly believed the distribution of income was unjust and that the state should take responsibility for reducing the gap between the rich and the poor,[26] all left-of-center presidents introduced new or expanded redistributive policies.[27] Cornia (2010) shows that a wide range of policies, ranging from social spending to raising the minimum wage, are primarily responsible for the recent reduction of inequalities in the region. This reduction came about largely through transfers, which were financed by favorable terms of trade, not taxes. The difference is important.[28] Tax collection in Latin America is still well below the international norm, reflecting the intense and longstanding opposition of the wealthy (Boylan 1996; Fairfield 2010). This restricts the scope for the further reduction of inequalities; thus whether reductions will continue still remains to be seen.

The Changing Face of Inequality in the United States

What do these observations mean for understanding the United States pattern of increasing inequalities since 1980? Before addressing this question, the extent of its rather astonishing transformation must be made clear. The country is now the most unequal of all democracies in the developed world. Not only does it have the greatest inequalities among the rich countries,[29] but the United States also stands out among this subset of countries for the size, extent, and uninterrupted nature of its change, as figure 6.1 demonstrates.

Concentration of income at the very top has driven this change. Figure 6.1 shows that the US today has returned to the inequality levels of the Great Depression, with the total market income accruing to the top decile close to 50%. This is a marked change from the postwar period, when it tended to stabilize around 33%. Piketty and Saez (2012: 3) observe that the magnitude of national income moving from the bottom 90% to the top is "truly enormous": In effect, it represents more than 15% of all national income over the past thirty years!

Much of this transformation was driven by the share of total income accrued by

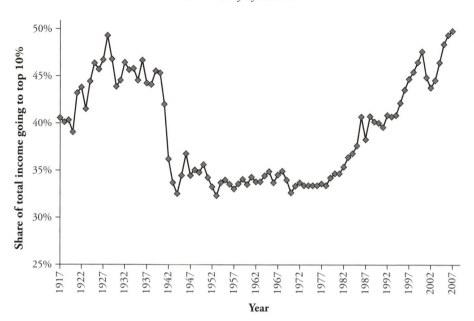

Figure 6.1. Income distribution in the United States by top decile: 1917–2007. Piketty and Saez (2012).

the richest 1% of households. Collectively, this group earned more than four fifths of the total increase in American incomes from 1980–2005 (Kristof 2010)—an average of $1.3 million a year. The top 1% is 288 times wealthier than the median US household. The shift in its status is startling: in 1979, the top 1% claimed about 40% of all capital income, while in 2007, it captured a whopping 65% of the total. Conversely, the bottom 90%, which claimed nearly a third of capital income in 1979, dropped to only about 15% in 2007.[30]

Moreover, as figure 6.2 illustrates, the super-rich (the top 0.1%) have benefitted the most from this pattern of upward redistribution. The richest thousandth of Americans have seen their incomes rise more than 400% since 1980 (Krugman 2011).[31] This group has an average annual family income of $27,342,212—compared with $31,244 of the bottom 90%. Even more remarkable, the richest of the super-rich, that is the top 0.01%, now share some 6% of national income, the highest share of income ever accruing to a mere 15,000 families (Piketty and Saez 2003). The gap between rich and poor based on accumulated wealth rather than income is even more extreme: the richest 400 individuals have as much wealth as the entire bottom 50%.[32] In what only can be called a Latin American pattern, one family alone (the Waltons) has as much wealth as the bottom 30% of the population of the entire United States. As the income shares of the top quintile soar, figure 6.3 shows how the income shares of the poor (bottom two quintiles) have stagnated and the middle have barely grown.

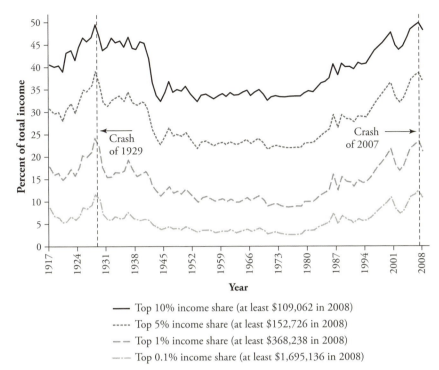

Figure 6.2. Wealthiest Americans' share of total income, 1917–2008. Based on U.S. Congress Joint Economic Committee (2010: 3).

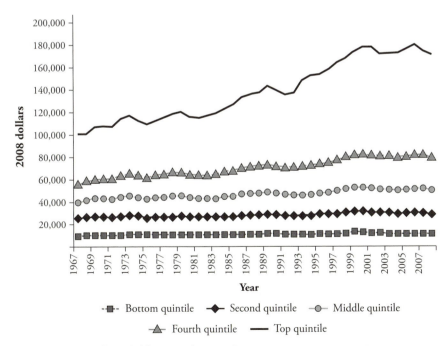

Figure 6.3. Average household incomes by quintile, 1967–2008. U.S. Congress Joint Economic Committee (2010: 4).

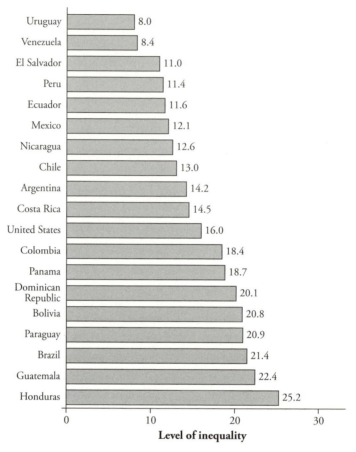

Figure 6.4. Inequality compared: Latin America and the United States. UN Economic Commission for Latin America and the Caribbean (2012).

These extremes augur poorly for social mobility (Ferrie 2005). The United States today has less relative mobility than Canada, Germany, France, and the Scandinavian countries (Corak 2006) and is only on a par with the notoriously class-based society in the United Kingdom.[33] As the middle class is hollowed out, the United States is now among the least mobile of the advanced economies (L. Levine 2012). Race and gender feature prominently in this lack of opportunity,[34] and the poorest of the poor are female single parent households (Hays 2004).

The US pattern of inequality is exceptional among the rich countries for its hyper-concentration of income at the very top,[35] but it is not unique when compared with Latin America. Even though Americans in general are very wealthy by world standards,[36] they do not compare well with Latin Americans in relative inequalities, as figure 6.4 shows. The United States falls in the middle—behind ten Latin American countries, according to statistics of the Economic Commission for Latin America and the Caribbean.

Reexamining US Inequality Patterns

This was not supposed to happen. If point-of-departure arguments (and the path dependence they often presume) are taken seriously, this extreme inequality is not an expected result. The colonial experience of the United States is widely understood to have been much more favorable than that of Latin America for both growth and equity. Because British colonialism in the New World concentrated on capital rather than terrain, this prevented the formation of powerful landed elites, except in the South.[37] Thus inequality was relatively low, if measured among the free whites who were permitted to earn an income. Indeed, measured in this way, incomes were supposedly much more equally distributed in colonial America than elsewhere.

In the nineteenth century, US and Latin American inequality are considered to have diverged even more. While the war of independence from Britain retarded economic development until the early nineteenth century, especially in the South, this was not comparable to Latin America's severe decline; the US independence war was far less costly. Once the country overcame the dual shocks of war and depression, this positively affected the capacity of political institutions to help direct development and provide public goods, such as in education and health care. The combination of America's enormous resource wealth and its fragmented, though effective, political institutions based on "self-government" produced one of the fastest growing economies in the world (at the very time Latin America was slumping, thus creating even greater divergence), with resources still distributed more equitably than in Latin America. Vanhanen (1997) estimates that by 1850 a full 60% of farms were owned by families in the United States, while in Latin America the figure was a mere 7.2%. This material equality, de Tocqueville noted, produced more egalitarian sentiments, which, in turn, formed the basis for the principle of equal citizenship. Thus politics became the province of the "common" white man, and not just a privileged few. "The soil of America," he wrote, "was opposed to a territorial aristocracy" (Tocqueville 1835: 21).

Well, not anymore. This suggests that either point of departure is less important than previously thought or that this "equality narrative" is overstated, and US inequality patterns have not changed so drastically. There is significant support for the latter position. In 1774, enslaved men and women, indentured servants, and free married women lived within households but had virtually no claim to the property held by the head of household head. Shammas (1993) shows that, when they are included (and when inequality is measured by the entire adult population rather than only white men), the result is a much more concentrated distribution of wealth. Even during the "Age of the Common Man" in the middle and late nineteenth century—when slavery ended, married women's property acts were passed, labor organizing began, and suffrage for white men improved—wealth remained highly concentrated in virtually the same pattern as before—with the majority of the population never managing to gain title to more than about 10% of the nation's wealth. Thus, from colonial times through the early 1980s, "the most salient characteristics of the wealth distribution [is] . . . the consistently large chunk of wealth held by the top 1%" (Shammas 1993: 428).

Nonetheless, inequality patterns in the United States did change substantially. Figures 6.1 and 6.2 above demonstrate the enormous shift toward reducing inequalities following the crisis of the Great Depression and the huge shift back beginning in the Reagan administration. What matters in both cases are government actions,[38] especially those related to the tax structure, regulation, labor relations, and social insurance. In the Great Depression, Roosevelt's Democratic majority instituted the "New Deal" by dramatically expanding social welfare programs, public infrastructure investment, financial regulation, and industrial cooperation while also changing the structure of government. Given the commitment to protecting incomes, alleviating poverty, and reducing inequality in order to avoid social collapse,[39] economic policies were based on creating new institutional arrangements, progressive taxation, and a high minimum wage in order to broadly distribute resources. Just as in Latin America after 2000, this road was not inevitable; instead, the very intensity of the crisis and the fear of mass protest pushed the construction of a political coalition based on greater fairness.

Crisis, Business Mobilization, and the Reshaping of the Polity

How is the present story different? From the perspective of a Latin Americanist, what happened in the United States sounds remarkably familiar: it is a tale of state capture and the subsequent reshaping of political institutions and economic policy. In the United States, 1980 was a watershed year for this process and for explaining the rise in inequality; just as in Latin America, it set the stage for neoliberal economic policies and the country's own version of "lost decades." Once again, crisis provides the backdrop. Record levels of inflation and high unemployment not seen since the Great Depression—provoked largely by the hidden costs of the Vietnam War, two huge OPEC oil price hikes, and the Federal Reserve's response of an exceptionally tight monetary policy[40]—plunged the country into recession. As a result, investors left the stock market in droves, causing the market to plunge, and reducing the book value of corporations. In response to these events, Vogel writes: "Virtually the entire American business community experienced a series of political setbacks without parallel in the post-war period" (1989: 59).

With hindsight, this crisis was the nail in the coffin of the more equitable social pact of "New Deal," setting the stage for an entirely new orientation of the federal government toward the economy. Based ideologically on neoliberalism and supply side economics, this was characterized by a package of policies: the deregulation of business and finance, sharp and "painful" cutbacks in social spending, a reduction of taxes on business and the wealthy, and a new normative framework in which market solutions to any and all problems became the order of the day (S. Fraser and Gerstle 1989; Prasad 2006). Ironically, in 1980 the United States submitted itself to the same economic recipe it had been pressing so relentlessly on Latin America.

This embrace of neoliberalism was no accident but instead the product of an unprecedented political mobilization by the corporate sector. Prompted by the crisis as well as by fears of a perceived rise in union and consumer power throughout the 1960s and 1970s, economic conservatives overtook the moderate wing of the Republican Party for the first time since 1964 and defined the policy agenda of the Reagan administration (Stockman 1987). Ramping up the frightful prospect of an "economic Dunkirk" and a "ticking regulatory time bomb" was an essential element of this policy takeover.[41] Rather than adopt the more modest mechanisms to deal with crisis that had been the previous norm, Wall Street and giant firms convinced the new Reagan administration to adopt a radical neoliberal package to fix the economy.

This intensive mobilization of business interests successfully altered the political system. Motivated by the goal of winning the 1980 elections, organized business interests gave shape to a new order in which a small network of campaign specialists, fundraisers, and lobbyists placed political power in the hands of the wealthy to a previously unimaginable degree. Inequality inducing institutions were nothing new: the United States has always had an unusually high number of electorally based veto players with the capacity to block social change as well as the most malapportioned upper house (the Senate) among longstanding democracies. From the beginning of its democracy, this built a strong conservative bias into the polity that had a major effect on policy choices.[42] But since 1980, politics in America became "a game increasingly played by and for the wealthy" in a qualitatively new way (Edsall 1989). In effect, oversized economic power translated into disproportionate political influence to create corporate-driven government.

The change in the early 1980s is extraordinary by any measure. The rise in lobbying was exceptionally rapid; in 1971, only 175 firms had registered in Washington as lobbyists, but, by 1982, this figure had risen to a whopping 2,445 (Hacker and Pierson 2010: 176; Kaiser 2009). Political action committees (PACs) soared from a mere eighty-nine corporate PACs registered with the Federal Election Commission (FEC) in 1974 to 1,206 by 1980; by 1984 there were 1,682. Individual political donations also climbed and skewed very noticeably toward Republicans.[43] This corporate political mobilization had a considerable impact on election outcomes[44] as well as public policy. Most important, it led to an ideological framework that strongly favored market rather than administrative or regulatory solutions to economic problems—an orientation that has endured in the polity even though it has led to repeated economic crises (Crouch 2011).

The cumulative impact of this organizational and financial mobilization remains undeniable (and this was true well before the Supreme Court *Citizens United* ruling). To this day, US politics is completely monetized. Elections cannot be won without money: the average cost of a Senate seat in 2008 was $8.5 million, while House seats were a bargain at $1.4 million (Gilson 2010). This cost has constrained the range of people and viewpoints that politicians encounter, because large donors represent an extremely narrow and unrepresentative cross section of the public,[45] and this shapes outcomes. Furthermore, in situations of high inequality, richer Americans, just like upper classes elsewhere, are more likely to engage in campaign work, affiliate with political organizations, give campaign contributions, and vote when compared with the poor (APSA 2004). As a result congressional representatives allocate funds to especially narrow segments of their districts. The net result is that the votes of US senators correspond far more closely with the policy preferences of rich constituents than with the poor: the top of the income distribution pyramid has almost three times as much influence on a senator's vote than those at or near the bottom; and the very poorest have little or no effect on senators' votes (Jacobs and Shapiro 2000). The same is true in national government more general (Bartels 2008).

Countervailing forces have great difficulty competing. In the 1980s, just as business interests and public officials mobilized to saturate the political process, forces that objected to their agenda grew more vulnerable. This is evident in the decline of the unions after 1981[46] and the shift in focus of middle-class nongovernmental organizations away from economic issues (Skocpol 2003a). The most effective grassroots organizing that took place between 1980–2008 in the religious right and eventually the Tea Party was financed by members of the superrich. These groups fought redistributive efforts as a form of socialism (Rich 2010).[47] As a result, there has been "a fundamental 'policy realignment' in which government policy, regardless of whether Republicans or Democrats control Washington, favors the well-to-do and penalizes the poor" (Fraser and Gerstle 1989: xxiii).

The Road to Crisis: Public Policy by and for the Rich

The well-organized pressure of business interests resulted in the implementation of qualitatively new institutional rules that were an important departure from the past (Useem 1984). The new consensus that restoring economic growth without government interference should be the core of public policy permeated almost every aspect of policy. From the start, the Reagan administration sent clear signals that it embraced this overarching concept of public policy. President Reagan's first legislative act was a huge tax cut for business and individuals, followed by opposition to raising the minimum wage,[48] the suspension of antitrust laws, and breaking the air traffic control union. Although the Reagan administration rolled back its own tax cuts to try to control the soaring deficit, supply siders eventually "hooked Republicans for good on the delusion that the economy will outgrow the deficit if plied with enough tax cuts" (Stockman 2010). Thus, when the Bush administration reaped the benefits of the Clinton's deficit reduction, it was free to return to the neoliberal package of policies while engaging in two unfinanced foreign wars and raising domestic spending to previously unheard of levels.

These new rules and practices granted business a thirty-year run to dominate the political process. This occurred not only through policies favorable to the rich that rigged the system (Kuttner 2007) but also through what Hacker and Pierson (2010) call policy "drift," meaning the protection of the interests of the rich through nondecisions. This is evident in a variety of areas, but deregulation is among the most crucial. The general retreat from regulation between 1980 and the 2008 "Great Recession" was premised on the assumption that the market was always right; where agencies could not be abolished, wealthy interests used their political influence to get sympathetic directors appointed in a form of "regulatory capture" (Stiglitz 2012: 47). The 1980 Depository Institutions Deregulation and Monetary Control Act, perhaps the most important deregulation permitting bank mergers that were "too big to fail," repealed important banking regulations that had been implemented in 1933 in order to oversee financial institutions, avoid speculation, and inhibit market crashes in the wake of the Great Depression. Other deregulation permitted CEO pay to be tied directly to stock performance, thus creating perverse incentives for their decisions.[49] Moreover, the Federal Reserve and the Securities and Exchange Commission, directed by market fundamentalists who embraced deregulation, withdrew from their previous oversight role. This meant that they became increasingly unable to recognize a bubble until it broke, doing "untold damage" to the economy.[50]

This systematic removal of oversight then led to the profound "financialization" of the economy as a way of restructuring US capitalism.[51] Stockman (2010) notes that the combined assets of conventional banks, investment banks, and finance companies soared from a mere $500 billion in 1970 to $30 trillion by 2008. Key changes in laws and practices increased the concentration of finance capital and the centrality of these large financial institutions to the economy. A huge merger movement, fed by "corporate raiders" that bought and sold assets at huge profits, gave the financial sector increased power to structure the market as it wished. As new practices linking the pay of managers to the performance of firms began to encourage the inflating of profits and manipulation of books, this became one of the key engines for concentrating income at the very top (Fligstein 2010). It also created powerful incentives to engage in short-term speculation and excessive risk taking over long-term growth. In the context of lack of regulation, the drive for immediate profits and fees resulted in bad lending practices that increasingly gave funds to people on terms they would be unable to pay.

Tax policy was a second important mechanism of distribution to the rich and superrich. Even though taxes in the United States were already low relative to those in other developed countries, tax relief to "grow the economy" became the rallying cry of the business community. In 1981, Congress passed the Economic Recovery Tax Act, which gave a 25%, across-the-board tax cut to individuals in all tax brackets, then passed the Tax Reform Act of 1986, which, among other changes, lowered the highest marginal tax rate from 50 to 28% and reduced the corporate tax rate even though spending and especially military spending rose. Faced with a climbing deficit, the Clinton administration repealed some of the Reagan tax cuts in 1993 and accepted tough budget controls, leading to budget surplus of $230 billion in 2000 that was projected to grow if policy remained the same.[52] But tax rates on capital gains were lowered, and the Bush administration returned to tax cuts of $1.7 trillion in 2001. This was followed by additional cuts in 2002, 2003, 2004, 2006, and 2008 that included the estate tax, thus making the role of inherited wealth more important. The Bush administration also removed budget controls, dropped the top marginal rate, provided major tax incentives for businesses, and permitted a significant rise in tax shelters.[53] This cut revenues to the lowest rate since the 1940s when the administration was also dramatically increased spending. The results were a budget deficit in 2008 of almost half a trillion dollars and a $1.6 trillion increase in the national debt. In effect, just like many Latin American governments in the past, tax cutters substituted debt for taxation.

The results of deregulation of the financial sector and tax policy, along with other factors, laid the basis for a remarkable series of financial bubbles that left the economy in full-blown crisis.[54] On the one hand, regressive tax policy did not advance the economy and, contrary to its justification, was associated with slow growth, declining investment, and huge borrowing (Hungerford 2012). While the United States paid the lowest taxes of the rich OECD countries (with only Mexico, Chile, and Turkey having lower taxes),[55] it grew more slowly than its more highly taxes counterparts in Europe. On the other hand, deregulation hid the fact that borrowing was helping to finance not only a tax cut for the rich but also a housing boom and an unsustainable financial bubble. In effect, in Crouch and Keune's (2012) words, financial irresponsibility became a "collective good." The cost of these policies has been enormous: one estimate of a whopping $12.8 trillion is only a start at measurement; it includes neither

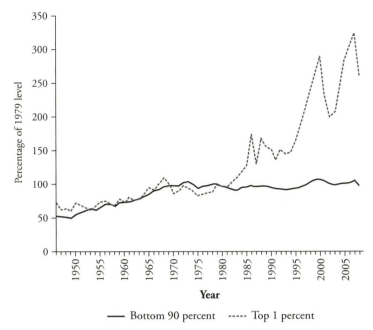

Figure 6.5. Average income between 1946 and 2008, as a percentage of 1979 level. Shaw and Stone (2010).

the loss in home equity by millions of Americans nor the price of government bailouts (Better Markets 2012).

Nonetheless, the wealthy gained hugely, as the top income brackets cleaned up from the economic policy they had designed. In the United States and the United Kingdom, the two countries where top marginal income tax rates were cut the most, top income shares also increased the most (Piketty and Saez 2012). Tax rates affecting the top of the income distribution fell to their lowest levels since the end of the Second World War, but income distributions was more skewed than ever due to policy changes in taxation.[56] Deregulation also drove inequality from the top. Executive salaries skyrocketed, rising from forty-two times the pay of an average worker in 1982 to 325 times in 2010, with a number of sources putting this figure far higher. Tomaskovic-Devy and Ken-Hou Lin (2011) calculate that rule changes associated with deregulation transferred somewhere between $4.5 and $5.1 trillion to the financial sector between 1980 and 2008, with about half of this occurring after 2000. These benefits are reflected in changes in inequality apparent in the results depicted in figure 6.5.

Both political parties protect these corporate gains to differing extents. Because the shift in economic policy is directly related to the changes in lobbying and political donations, as S. Anderson et al. (2011) demonstrate, Republicans and Democrats alike are influenced to protect the top, especially by single donors and corporations.[57]

Bartels (2008) and Piketty and Saez (2012) show, however, that Republican administrations produce the most disequalizing effects, particularly at the upper end of the earning scale, which is due to their complete embrace of market fundamentalism and the nature of their party's constituency.

The "logic of democratic competition" that K. Roberts (2012) holds responsible for the reduction of inequalities in Latin America has instead resulted in gridlock in the U.S. Democrats, pushed by party constituencies and electoral logic, have sought increasingly to build a new progressive coalition aimed at much of the 90% pictured in figure 6.5, and this, as a result, has produced a widening schism between the parties. By almost all measures of partisan polarization, the divide manifested in Congress has widened deeply over the past twenty-five years, thus making it harder to build workable coalitions. The resulting stalemate creates difficulty for designing any economic policy at all (witness the budget debacle), lowers confidence in the economy, and creates new difficulties for responding to future economic shocks. High inequalities are a significant underlying cause of the increase of political polarization.[58]

The net effect of intense polarization is conservative; thus, despite campaigning on slogans of "Hope" and "Change" in 2008, the Obama administration in its first term was able to pass bailouts and recapitalize the banks, but it could not restructure mortgages to force financial institutions to recognize their risky behavior and significantly help homeowners. The outcome has not been pretty: the response to the Great Recession of 2008 appears unlikely to reverse the dramatic inequality trend (Piketty and Saez 2012), which, in turn, suggests that the United States may be entering its own "vicious cycle of inequality."

Conclusion

This exercise in inequality comparison between Latin America and the United States points to some interesting findings. First, exceptionally high levels of inequality are relatively easy to create but are extremely hard to undo. Because huge economic and social disparities shape (and are shaped by) political institutions, they have a direct (and indirect) impact on the distribution of political power. This makes it especially difficult to reverse directions. In both regions, in every case that a reversal occurs (either through an increase or reduction of inequality), crisis is the catalyst. And in both regions, these crises were precipitated by economic disasters brought about by policy packages that not only showed a striking disregard for equity considerations but also reflected unequal power relations when they were adopted. It may prove to be that the deeper the crisis, the greater the subsequent reversal.

Second, crisis is a necessary but not sufficient condition for reversal. In both countries, social and political mobilization has been crucial for changing public policy, though it is mobilization of a very different sort. In Latin America, beginning in 2000, a revival of social mobilization from below politicized the problem of inequality and made redistributive policies a central focus of the economic policy agenda. In the United States, beginning in 1980, mobilization was from the top as business interests worked to change the polity, especially through its monetization. They succeeded in justifying gross inequalities as necessary for growth and investment (which has proved not to be true) while labeling equity concerns as "socialist." This has meant that the inequality patterns of two regions appear to be converging—which is good news for Latin America but not for the United States. It is interesting to note that these patterns may not have been as different in their colonial points of departure as generally argued, when measurements are altered to reflect the entire adult population, not just white men. It appears that the largest inequality divergence occurred in the nineteenth century due especially to Latin America's almost perpetual conflict, but it would be important to contrast this pattern to those following the Great Depression to be certain.

Finally, although the United States appears to be in a "vicious cycle" in which huge inequalities now express themselves through political gridlock and hence the threat of repeated crises, this may be an "Owl of Minerva" moment; that is, just as this phenomenon of gross inequalities seems institutionalized, it is turning into something else. A growing sense of "haves" and "have-nots" indicates that astonishing levels of inequality do not sit well with most citizens, and it was not an accident that "fairness" was the theme of the 2012 Obama campaign. Teixeira and Halpin (2012) argue that a progressive coalition of African Americans, Latinos, Asian Americans, young adults, women, and highly educated professionals is in the works. Within this group, the young especially favor more government services and (by a very large margin) want the government to become more active in solving problems. Since the 2012 elections, 60% of Americans favor tax increases on the wealthy and large corporations, and a majority believe that government should do more to close the gap between the rich and the poor (Pew Research Center 2012). Nonetheless, the polity is deeply split about how this should occur, with one party arguing for the failed policies of growth through tax and spending cuts and deregulation that brought about crisis, while the other calls, rather timidly, for the opposite. This polarization makes change significantly more difficult[59] and is likely to cause new economic crises. Should crisis deepen, a "fairness" coalition could begin to alter outcomes, just as it has in Latin America.

Trickle down, it turns out, is trickle up. As Nel puts it: "A rising tide can lift all boats, but not if some are moored to the bottom by inflexible shackles" (2005: 17). Very high levels of inequality are a hazard, not only to economic growth but also to the fundamental sense of solidarity that necessarily undergirds democracy. Guillermo

O'Donnell knew that ultimately the fates of the rich and the poor are intertwined and that a "quality" democracy had to be based on perceived fairness. As the quintessential engaged scholar, O'Donnell would have labeled this regressive change "a scandal," as he did in Latin America, and urge his North American colleagues to make the reduction of gross inequalities an intellectual and moral commitment.

NOTES

Epigraph. Hegel (1820) 2002.

1. Of the thirty-four nations that make of the Organization for Economic Co-operation and Development (OECD), only Chile, Mexico, and Turkey have higher income disparities than the United States, as measured by the Gini index. See OECD 2013a, 2013b, and 2013c.

2. A plethora of studies with telling titles have emerged in the past few years, including Larry M. Bartels, *Unequal Democracy: The Political Economy of the New Gilded Age* (2008); Jacob Hacker and Paul Pierson, "Winner-Take-All Politics: Public Policy, Political Organization, and the Precipitous Rise of Top Incomes in the United States" (2010); Joseph Stiglitz, *The Price of Inequality: How Today's Divided Society Endangers Our Future* (2012); Crystia Freeland, *Plutocrats: The Rise of the New Global Super-rich and Fall of Everyone Else* (2012); and Sophia Parker, *The Squeezed Middle: The Pressure on Ordinary Workers in America and Britain* (2013).

3. Along with others, they also attribute this failure on the rise of methodological individualism and the overattention to the "median voter" theory as well as the hyperfragmentation of the field of American politics.

4. This is not to say it is not unique or does not have qualities that make it exceptional. But every country has unique features that make it exceptional in some respects based on the principle and nature of comparison.

5. This is a longstanding tradition in the study of Latin America, dating back to the early work of the Economic Commission on Latin America and the very strong influence of Albert Hirschman's (1968, 1971, 1979, 1981) political economy contributions, Cardoso and Faletto's (1969) dependency approaches, O'Donnell's (1982) emphasis on the state, and Schmitter's (1971) work on corporatism and organized interests—all of which was initially developed in the late 1960s and early 1970s. For important case studies that also illustrate how inequality affects the construction of different types of political institutions, see Weyland (1996), K. Roberts (1998), Friedman (2000), Wise (2003), and Bill Chávez (2004), but there are many others.

6. The phrase is from Hoffman and Centeno (2003). On the concentration of wealth at the top in Latin America, see the Inter-American Development Bank (1999) and Birdsall and Jaspersen (1997).

7. Adam Smith (1776, 1: 59) defined "rents" as reaping what one does not sow, and Stiglitz (2012: 32) calls them "large gifts" extracted from the public. Rent is different than profit. It is not about creating wealth but rather using the political process to seek hidden and open excess profits and transfers by manipulating the political, economic, and legal rules of the game.

8. The US ranks worst in most of these indicators but ranks at the top in three other areas: military spending per capita, the cost of medical care, and income per capita.

9. This refers to a package of widespread tax cuts, decreased social spending, increased military spending, and the deregulation of markets implemented first by President Reagan in the US. Using

the principles of supply-side economics and trickle-down theories, this is based on the notion that freeing corporations from taxes and deregulation is the best way to stimulate economic growth.

10. This was the argument of Tokman and O'Donnell (1998), the Inter-American Development Bank (1999), and Karl (2000, 2003).

11. By inequality, I mean the disparity or dispersion in condition, distribution, and/or opportunities that results over time in social disparities. What matters here is not perfect equality, which carries its own dangers, but exceptionally high levels of inequality. For purposes of this essay, specific types of inequality based on class, gender, race, and ethnicity are not addressed even though they are critically important for understanding power and marginalization in both Latin America and the US. Finally, there are numerous ways of measuring inequality, including the Gini coefficient, the Theill index, the decile dispersion ratio, and the share of income/consumption of the poorest percentage of the population. For a discussion of these various methods and more thorough definitions, see the World Bank website on Inequality, Poverty, and Socioeconomic Performance, available at http://www.worldbank.org/poverty/inequal/index.htm.

12. Definitions of democracy (see Schmitter and Karl 1991) and measurements (see Munck 2009) are not addressed here, including the notoriously fuzzy concept of "the quality of democracy" (see Diamond and Morlino 2005; O'Donnell et al. 2004).

13. For a discussion of the economic causes of inequality and increased equality, see the essays in López-Calva and Lustig (2010) and Cornia (2010). They include whether or not external conditions are favorable, cyclical factors, improvements in education, and relative skill premiums. The claim here is *not* that inequality solely affects political institutions or vice versa. There are other important determinants of inequality as well as the nature of political institutions, but this relationship is the focus here.

14. The relationship between different forms of inequality and transitions to democracy is not discussed here. There is an extensive literature on this question, but it is not especially relevant to a huge shift in levels of inequality that takes place in a longstanding democracy.

15. Birdsall, Lustig, and McLeod put it this way: "Economics explains the politics which explains the economics" (2011: 1). But the causal relationship could run a different way. That they are interactive is demonstrated by a large body of work based on historical political economy. On Latin America, see, for example, Schmitter (1972), O'Donnell (1982), Evans (1995), Karl (1997), the essays in Eckstein and Wickham-Crowley (2003), and Hagopian and Mainwaring (2005).

16. In the neoinstitutionalist (and other) approaches, Spain is the "bad" colonizer and England is "good" based on its institutional legacies. To the extent this is accurate, this description is confined to England's settler colonies, that is, those in the United States and Canada but not its Asian, sub-Saharan Africa, or other colonies. Both Spanish and English colonialism had tremendously negative consequences for indigenous people in Latin America. But Spanish colonies in the New World granted a wider franchise to men, abolished key legal distinctions between whites and indigenous people over time, and emancipated slaves more quickly (Guerra 1994).

17. There are several problems with their narrative. North (1989), for example, credits the "centralized monarchy in Castile" with defining the institutional evolution of Latin America and claims that it imposed a type of uniformity that contrasted unfavorably with the diversity permitted by the English. But Spanish historians dispute this view and demonstrate the ineffectiveness of Spanish absolutist rule (Halperín Donghi 1992; Lynch 2001). Karl's (1997) chapter on Spain illustrates that the state had neither the fiscal discipline nor organizational control to operationalize the type of absolutism attributed to it. For example, there was no single Spanish authority

responsible for the collection of taxes from the New World. Spain's behavior, as Grafe and Irigoin (2006: 14) show, "contrasts sharply with the notion of a relatively modern fiscal administration at the service of a predatory, absolutist, all-powerful Spanish state that the institutionalist approach has painted."

18. The Caribbean did not have these highly developed indigenous civilizations, but the introduction of slavery also made it central (Lockhart and Schwartz 1983).

19. Since these countries had virtually no minerals or large indigenous populations that could work plantations, their patterns were different; even today, Costa Rica and Uruguay remain among the cases with the least inequality and measure well on quality of democracy indicators.

20. The Spanish state, though seeming absolutist, was strikingly unable to create these institutions for itself.

21. The independence wars were compounded by at least sixteen other wars in the region in the postindependence period. These wars occurred later than the US independence struggle, lasted longer, and were immensely destructive (Archer 2000). Their long-term perverse impact on the construction of stateness cannot be overemphasized. In Venezuela, for example, which was the center of a continental civil war, close to 40% of the population was killed and virtually all vestiges of its previous bureaucratic system were destroyed. A centralized state did not exist until the beginning of the twentieth century (Karl 1997: 74–7). Coatsworth (2005) calls the postindependence period "catastrophic," leading to a marked decline throughout the latter half of the nineteenth century.

22. For example, Deininger and Olinto (2000) show that the Gini coefficient of the distribution of holdings of agricultural land is about 0.81 for Latin America, while in other world regions it hovers around 0.60. High-income inequality usually reflects an unequal distribution of assets, such as land and human capital. Across countries, asset inequality and income inequality are closely associated, and this is certainly the case in Latin America.

23. Latin America vividly demonstrates that where income inequality is greatest, people are more likely to accept forms of authoritarian rule, more willing to violate human rights, and less likely to be satisfied with the way democratic institutions work. Contrast, for example, the opinion polls in the 1990s of the two most historically equitable countries in Latin America (Cuba is not in this sample)—Costa Rica and Uruguay—with their highly inequitable counterparts: Brazil, Paraguay, Venezuela, and Colombia. By the turn of the century, this latter group exhibited a crisis in their attitudes toward democracy.

24. To be clear, democracies do not automatically ease inequalities. The median voter argument, upon which this belief is based, does not hold in the context of great inequalities. As we have seen repeatedly, fair elections do not mean that the poor will always favor distribution, especially when the rich both have greater control of these elections and are more apt to participate.

25. For the first time in its history, this placed two-thirds of the region's population under left national governments. On the rise of this left, see Weyland, Madrid, and Hunter (2010) and Levitsky and Roberts (2011a).

26. When asked: "Do you believe the distribution of income is just?" a whopping 75–85% of respondents in Latin America answer "unjust," with almost half saying "very unjust." (K. Roberts 2012: 10). Earlier, an overwhelming majority agreed that the state should reduce inequalities.

27. This is the case for left regimes whether their orientation is populist (e.g., Venezuela, Ecuador, Bolivia, Argentina) or social democratic (e.g., Chile, Brazil, Uruguay). Lustig and McLeod (2009) show that there is evidence that both types of left regimes have reduced inequality in Latin

America more than nonleft regimes. Within the different types of left regimes, that it is the social democratic and populist, social democratic regimes appear to have done better. Also see Birdsall, Lustig, and McLeod (2011). Where more conservative candidates won elections, they too had to respond to demands for social inclusion.

28. Goñi, López, and Servén (2011) show the difference in distribution by comparing Latin America and Europe with regard to their tax and transfer systems. Latin America's fiscal system has proved to be of little use in reducing inequality over the long term, because they rely on transfers (that do help redistribution but not as much as taxes). In recent years, these transfers have been largely paid for through commodity booms and not through taxes. Note that populist left regimes (Venezuela, Ecuador, Bolivia, and Argentina) have enjoyed better terms of trade and have higher fuel exports as a percentage of merchandise trade, thus in the long run they are more vulnerable to "the paradox of plenty" (Karl 1997).

29. The United Kingdom is another outlier, but most rich countries show either a modest growth in inequality or like the Scandinavian countries have held relatively steady.

30. See "The State of Working America" for its sobering report. Available at http://stateof workingamerica.org/fact-sheets.

31. Had their share remained constant, R. Freeman (2011) estimates that the incomes of all others in the United States could have increased 10%!

32. This information is available through the Board of Governors of the Federal Reserve's Survey of Consumer Finances. See http://www.federalreserve.gov/econresdata/scf/scf_2009p.htm.

33. Germany has 1.5 times more mobility than the United States, Canada is 2.5 times greater, and Denmark is 3 times more mobile. See Isabel Sawhill and John Morton (2007).

34. The gap between men's and women's wages has remained stagnant in the twenty-first century. Women's earnings were 77% of men's in 2011, according to Census statistics released September 12, 2012. This means that a typical woman who worked full-time, year round would lose $443,360 in a forty-year period due to the wage gap. A woman would have to work almost twelve years longer to make up this gap. The median white household still earns at least 62% more income and possesses *twelvefold* more wealth than the median black household, and nearly two-thirds of black households and half of Hispanic households lack any financial assets whatsoever (APSA 2004: 3). The wage gap persists between women and men, inhibiting the advance of especially low paid female workers.

35. The United Kingdom, though not as regressive as the US, is the other outlier when compared with the rich countries.

36. With an average per capita income of $47,500, the United States ranks fifth in the Top 10 in the world.

37. The South proved to be a different story, with plantation systems similar to Latin America and institutions dominated by landowners (Beckford 1983), but economists argue that this did not abrogate the relative egalitarianism and institutional transfer that characterized the country as a whole. This is reflected in the very different patterns of land ownership between the United States and Latin America.

38. While there is still no agreement regarding the impact of various policies for economic recovery or the cost efficiency of the financial regulations adopted, agreement does exist over the types of actions taken and their impact on inequality. See, for example, Shammas (1993), Levy and Temin (2007), and Wallis (2010).

39. When Roosevelt took office in 1933, unemployment was at 25%. Over the previous three

years, real income dropped 25% and nominal income by almost 50%. The banking and financial system were near complete collapse. This was decisive in creating change. As Roosevelt said in his speech at the 1936 Democratic Party Convention in Philadelphia: "For too many of us the political equality we once had won was meaningless in the face of economic inequality. A small group had concentrated into their own hands an almost complete control over other people's property, other people's money, other people's labor—other people's lives." Available at http://www.austincc.edu/lpatrick/his2341/fdr36acceptancespeech.htm.

40. The Federal Reserve, determined to drive double digit inflation out of the economy, raised interest rates to exceptionally high levels. The prime interest rate eventually reached a whopping 21.5% in June 1982.

41. Dire predictions by supply side economists of double dip recession, and budget and credit disasters threatened that the limits of US economic growth soon would be reached. See, for example, "Two Advisers Warn of Economic Dunkirk," *New York Times*, December 11, 1980.

42. Stepan and Linz (2011: 844) note that the principle that every state has an equal vote in the Senate generates "the greatest violation of the classic majority principal of 'one person, one vote' of any of the eight federal democracies" they studied. On malapportionment, see M. Thies (1998) and Samuels and Snyder (2001).

43. Burris (2001) compared the PAC contributions of 394 large corporations in 1980 with the individual contributions of 592 top officers of those same corporations, finding that corporate PACs contributed mainly to congressional races and individual capitalists directed a larger share of their contributions to presidential candidates. While both heavily favored the Republican presidential candidate in the 1980 elections, on average individual capitalists' contributions were more strongly skewed toward Republicans.

44. This is evidenced by the unusually high number of Democratic incumbents who were defeated in the congressional election of 1980, giving Republicans control of the Senate (Ashford 1986).

45. Only 12% of American households had incomes over $100,000 in 2000, for example, but these households account for 95% of the donors who made substantial contributions to the elections (APSA 2004: 7).

46. The breaking of the Air Traffic Controllers strike sent the message that public sector unionization would no longer be tolerated. By 2010, the percentage of workers belonging to a union in the United States was 11.4%, compared with 18.6% in Germany, 27.5% in Canada, and 70% in Finland (OECD 2013c). Union membership in the private sector fell to under 7%—levels not seen since 1932 (Bureau of Labor Statistics, Union Members Summary 2012, see http://www.bls.gov/news.release/union2.nro.htm).

47. In a study of the 2008 elections, Project Vote's survey demonstrates that, despite their anger over government spending on social programs, the vast majority of tea party sympathizers were white and affluent. Increased government spending on infrastructure, education, and welfare programs like food stamps and Social Security were favored by large majorities of the electorate, especially blacks, youths, and low-income voters but rejected by the tea parties. The poll also found that most respondents felt the government should do more to bolster the economy and secure Americans' well-being, including raising the minimum wage and protecting consumer from fraudulent business practices, whereas tea party conservatives wanted less spending and smaller taxes (see http://projectvote.org/voter-poll-results.html). The survey accounts for views expressed by 1,947 Americans who voted in 2008 and carries a margin of error of plus or minus 3%.

48. The minimum wage, which had reached $9.20 during Lyndon Johnson's Great Society, fell to $5.40 during the Reagan presidency, rose slightly under Clinton, then declined to $5.30 during the George W. Bush presidency—the lowest since the antiunion Taft Hartley Act was passed in 1949.

49. In the wake of the Crash of 1929, the Glass-Steagall Act of 1933 was passed regulating risk in the financial sector, preventing speculation and the concentration of capital in finance. This new law, to the contrary, permitted banks to merge and removed regulatory controls, which in turn encouraged banks to rely upon fees for financial services for financial investment instead of their traditional deposits (G. Davis 2009). Other deregulation removed oversight from the financial sector and permitted extensive and intensive capital concentration. The 1994 Riegle-Neal Interstate Banking Act repealed the prohibition on interstate banking and thus permitted greater concentration. This was followed by other legislation that made it legal, for the first time, for investment and commercial banks to combine operations with insurance companies. Finally, CEO pay was directly tied to stock performance (Tomaskovic-Devy and Lin 2011).

50. Stiglitz's (2009) critique is devastating in this respect.

51. This means both the growing importance of firms specializing in financial services as well as the increased involvement of nonfinancial firms in financial activities.

52. The Clinton administration passed the Omnibus Budget Reconciliation Act of 1993, which raised individual rates from 28% to 36–39% at the top, with a 35% rate for corporations. Just as George W. Bush took office, the Congressional Budget Office projected in January 2001 that the federal government would run a total budget surplus of $3.5 trillion through 2008 if tax policy remained unchanged (Bartlett 2012).

53. One Senate Committee estimated that these tax havens cost the federal treasury $100 billion per year, enough to pay the budget deficit of Great Britain, buy an iPad for every student in the United States, or bail out most of Greece. See United States Senate 2008.

54. These bubbles include the early 1980s international debt crisis; the real estate bubble and savings and loan crises of the 1980s; the stock market collapse of the late 1980s; the dot-com and hedge fund bubbles of the late 1990s; and the real estate, consumer lending, and stock market bubbles of the first decade of the new century.

55. In 2008, US taxes at all levels of government were 27.3% of GDP, compared with an average of 36.3% of GDP for the 33 member countries of the Organization for Economic Co-operation and Development. Only Mexico, Chile and Turkey had lower taxes than the United States when measured as a percentage of GDP. See OECD 2010.

56. Estimates by the Urban Institute/Brookings Institution Tax Policy Center that consider *only* the impact of the tax policy changes demonstrate that 2001 tax cuts alone have widened income inequality. It found that the 2001 cuts alone had these results: in 2007 households in the bottom fifth of income distribution received tax cuts averaging $29, while the top 1% received cuts averaging a $41,077, and those with annual incomes exceeding $1 million received cuts averaging $114,000. On a percentage basis, this meant that the poorest households raised their after-tax incomes by 0.4% while the richest raised theirs by 5.7%. See Tax Policy Center tables T06-0035 and T06-0036 at http://www.taxpolicycenter.org.

57. Their data are startling: For example, in 2010, twenty-five of the hundred highest paid corporate executives captured more in CEO pay than their entire company paid in federal tax income. Most of their companies actually collected an average of $304 million in tax refunds despite the fact that these same 25 firms reported average profits of $1.9 billion! These benefits are direct

political rents: these companies spent more on lobbying and political donations than they paid in corporate taxes in general.

58. Many scholars have shown this. See, for example, McCarty, Poole, and Rosenthal (1997) and Hicks (2003). Note, however, that this is not the only reason for the increase polarization, which is also due to redistricting and other factors.

59. In the Senate, for example, the filibuster and other procedural tactics permit a minority to block the majority, and this is now becoming a routine legislative tactic. In the House, because of redistricting and the distribution of Republican voters, the Republican Party has an estimated 5% advantage. Thus, even though Democrats received 1.3 million more votes for House candidates than Republicans in 2012, they won only 201 seats compared with 234 for Republicans (Galston 2013).

CHAPTER 7

Economic Performance, Political Competition, and Regime Stability in Postwar Latin America

MARCELO LEIRAS

Guillermo O'Donnell's work examined many practically pressing and intellectually challenging problems. This chapter returns to one of them: the influence of economic performance on the stability of political regimes in Latin America. Like *Modernization and Bureaucratic-Authoritarianism* (1973), the chapter presents an empirical fact to motivate an evaluation of influential theories in contemporary studies of democracy and then advances an alternative interpretation. The empirical fact is that, in postwar Latin America, economic performance seems to have had less of an impact on the survival of competitive regimes than on the stability of authoritarian governments. Most theories of the effect of economic performance on the stability of political regimes, including O'Donnell's, predict, on the contrary, that democracies should not be less vulnerable to economic outcomes than dictatorships are. My main contention is that these theories place excessive emphasis on the impact of economic performance on income and downplay the relevance of political ambition as a motivation and political competition as a stabilizing mechanism. The alternative interpretation that this chapter advances is that economic performance affects the stability of regimes more because it sets in motion those aspiring to compete for political power than because it ignites the resistance of those hurt by economic outcomes. When political competition is not institutionalized or when it is blocked, poor economic results may encourage and provide aspiring elites with an excuse to irregularly replace incumbents. Thus, signs of government weakness or incompetence, such as bad economic results, should make dictatorships more vulnerable than democracies to coups and other forms of elite activity that compromise the stability of political regimes.

The literature offers five alternative accounts of the effect of economic performance on the stability of political regimes. Four of them predict that democracies should not be less vulnerable than authoritarian regimes to economic performance. This does not fit the experience of Latin America in the post war, as the evidence presented in this chapter suggests. The fifth argument posits that democracies should be less vulnerable to economic performance than dictatorships, which is consistent with my empirical findings.

This chapter develops an argument inspired in this fifth prediction. Bad economic performance creates problems and hurts governments. Good economic performance generates benefits and helps governments. Those problems and benefits affect the stability of regimes depending on the credibility of the promise of leadership turnover that the rules of political competition under each regime entail. Governments tend to be stable when economic times are good (Gil-Serrate et al. 2011; Kennedy 2010). Bad economic times encourage challenges to incumbents.

Challenges to governments may or may not succeed; successful challenges lead to the irregular replacement of governments but may not lead to regime change. This chapter focuses on the effect of economic performance on the odds that a challenge takes place. The probability that a challenge succeeds depends on the resistance capabilities of incumbents. As recent contributions find, those capabilities include the costs of making political transactions and forming coalitions, the normative attachments to regimes prevailing among political elites, the degree of radicalization of political actors, and the support in neighbor countries or in regional hegemonic powers to incumbent authorities and to the established regime (Ahlquist and Wibbels 2012; Boix 2011; Pérez-Liñán and Mainwaring, chapter 1 of this volume; Torfason and Ingram 2010; Wejnert 2005). By focusing on the incentives of potential challengers, this chapter accounts for a necessary condition of successful challenges, which are themselves a facilitating condition (neither necessary nor sufficient) of regime change.[1] In this sense, the chapter is intended as an analysis of one significant link in the causal chain that goes from economic outcomes to the survival of political regimes. This chain also interested O'Donnell. In *Modernization and Bureaucratic-Authoritarianism*, he presented economic performance as a sign of the possibilities and limits of different political regimes. He recognized that economic crises destabilized authoritarian governments but stressed the debilitating effect of crises on competitive regimes. This chapter, in contrast, views economic performance as a sign of the competence of governments and stresses the robustness of competitive regimes. Bad performance does not compromise the stability of regimes when institutionalized political competition facilitates the replacement of governments that are perceived as incompetent.

The argument is based upon the conviction that credible leadership replacement, typically a result of unrestricted political competition, plays a key role in the survival of regimes, as has been forcefully expressed in an early evaluation of the experience of new democracies in South America (Remmer 1996) and persuasively presented in a more recent contribution (Lehoucq and Pérez-Liñán forthcoming). It is intended as an invitation to develop theories of regime stability that are more sensitive to the specifically political incentives of actors. Chapters by Pérez-Liñán and Mainwaring (chapter 1) and by Gervasoni (chapter 2) in this volume point in the same direction.

Previous empirical studies have found democracies to be less vulnerable to economic results than dictatorships (Burke and Leigh 2010; Przeworski et al. 2000: 123) and evaluated this independence as the source of a democratic advantage (Remmer 1996). My finding then, is not new, though it partially deviates from the conclusions of several studies (Ahlquist and Wibbels 2012; Epstein et al. 2006; Feng 1997; Gasiorowski 1998; Gasiorowski and Power 1998; Gil-Serrate et al. 2011; Hegre et al. 2012; Kennedy 2010; Londregan and Poole 1990; Svolik 2008). These studies find that economic performance affects the stability of all regimes, though they do not always examine specifically the contrast between authoritarianism and competitive regimes as I do here.

This chapter makes theoretical and empirical contributions. It presents a comprehensive critical review of theories about the effect of economic performance on the stability of political regimes. On this basis, it discusses in detail the relevance of elite aspirations to the understanding of regime stability and examines the validity of these theoretical insights by testing the effect of economic performance on different measures of regime stability in postwar Latin America. First, it highlights a negative finding: economic performance did not affect the stability of competitive regimes in this region over this period. The negative finding is important, for it belies the most common prediction of the literature, which is that democracies should be vulnerable to bad economic results. Second, it compares the effect of economic performance on the stability of competitive and noncompetitive regimes. To do so, it focuses on a usually overlooked phenomenon: coup attempts.

Conclusions from these theoretical and empirical exercises speak to two important questions in contemporary theoretical discussions on regime stability. One is the correspondence between regimes and policies. In contemporary political economy, the distinction between democratic and nondemocratic regimes is modeled as a difference in tax rates. Insights from this chapter suggest, in contrast, that competitive regimes are more flexible in terms of policy than these models allow. This does not necessarily deny the existence of a systematic difference between the policies that democracies and dictatorships are likely to implement, but it casts doubt on the relevance of this difference, should it exist, for the understanding of regime stability. The second question relates to the significance of policy safeguards for the survival of competitive regimes. Approaches to democratic stability that focus on distributive disputes, posit that constraining the range of policy variation dissipates redistributive threats and thus helps democracies survive. Conclusions from this chapter suggest that policy warranties may not be indispensable when the expectation of leadership replacement is sufficiently firm. Policy restrictions may also be counterproductive when they lead to excessive rigidity.

The exposition is organized as follows. The first section reviews hypotheses about the effect of economic performance on the survival of political regimes and derives their observable implications. The second section estimates the effect of different economic outcomes on the survival of competitive regimes using the same data and modeling strategy as the study of Pérez-Liñán and Mainwaring in this volume. Later, it tests the effect of economic performance on the probability that coups d'état take place and succeed. The third section underlines some of the theoretical lessons that may be derived from the empirical exercise for the understanding of the stability of democratic regimes. It argues in favor of a conception of democratic stability that acknowledges the central role of political competition and its two main components: leadership replacement and policy change. A fourth section summarizes the insights and findings of the previous three and explains their relevance for the study of contemporary challenges to the stability of democracies in Latin America.

Theories about the Impact of Economic Performance on Regime Survival

This section presents explanations about the effect of economic performance on the survival of political regimes and indicates the outcomes we expect to observe if these explanations were correct. *Economic performance* designates short- to medium-term economic outcomes that are publicly relevant and that in most modern polities are usually taken to be influenced, at least in part, by government policies. Typical measures of economic performance are yearly per capita GDP growth, inflation, and unemployment. *Political regimes* refers to the combination of formal rules, informal rules, and established practices that regulate access to government positions. The literature offers a series of classifications of political regimes.[2] The chapter focuses on the contrast between competitive regimes (democracies and semi-democracies) and authoritarian ones.

Numerous empirical explorations either directly test the effect of economic performance on regime stability or control for this effect in analyses of other factors (Ahlquist and Wibbels 2012; Epstein et al. 2006; Gasiorowski 1995, 1998; Gasiorowski and Power 1998; Gil-Serrate et al. 2011; Hegre et al. 2012; Kennedy 2010; Londregan and Poole 1990; Przeworski et al. 1996, 2000; Remmer 1996; Reuter and Gandhi 2011; Svolik 2008). Though empirical studies abound and economic performance is widely assumed to determine the fate of governments under any political regime, specific theoretical analyses of this effect are relatively scarce. Still, five alternative accounts may be found among available explanations.

According to the most common accounts, the effect of economic performance on regime survival is either positive or neutral.[3] Arguments that good economic performance destabilizes political regimes are rare,[4] as are arguments that bad economic performance could stabilize some regimes.[5] The accounts summarized here propose different mechanisms and different conceptions about the effect that performance may have on stability under different political regimes.

The first thesis is unconditional: bad economic performance decreases and good performance increases the probability that any kind of regime survives. Acemoglu and Robinson (2001, 2006) developed the most influential version of this kind of explanation. In their account, economic crises may lower the costs of collective action for those opposed to established regimes. Thus, crises may help the poor rebel against dictatorships dominated by elites and they may also help elites mount challenges to democratic authorities when the costs of redistribution are larger than the costs of confrontation. The probability that any kind of rebellion takes place falls when economic performance is good. Therefore, we should observe that growth makes both competitive and authoritarian regimes more stable.

Three explanations in a second group hold that good economic performance prevents democracies from breaking down. In this view, the effect on authoritarian regimes is weaker or nonexistent.

The first kind of explanation in this group relates to the intensity of distributive conflicts and may be found in the seminal piece by Lipset (1959: 83). According to this portrayal, as income grows, workers become less impatient, diversify their social connections, and loosen their ties to narrow class-based groups; the middle class grows in size; and the upper classes become more inclined to extend rights to the lower classes. The outcome of all these developments is a reduction of the intensity of distributive conflicts among social classes. Intense distributive conflicts make social actors more reluctant to accept the results of democratic mechanisms of political competition. Good economic performance protects democracies from this danger. Arguably, intense distributive conflicts may also compromise government stability under authoritarian regimes. However, autocratic rulers may rely on repression at a lower cost than democratic governments. Moreover, reasoning along these lines, the fall of an authoritarian government in a context of distributive conflict is unlikely to bring about a change of regime. Therefore, if bad economic results make distributive conflicts prevail, all else being equal, we should see democracies falling at a higher rate than dictatorships.[6]

Another kind of conditional explanation may be elaborated considering the direct impact of economic performance on income levels, in line with analyses by Przeworski (2003, 2005).[7] To the extent that the effect operates through the intensity of distributive conflicts, it could be considered as a version of the explanation in the preceding paragraph. However, this account is quite specific and merits a separate consideration. According to Przeworski, democracies survive when all representatives of social sectors choose to obey the results of elections. Actors maximize utility. Obedience depends on average income levels and on the results of elections. Both winners and losers of elections rebel in poor countries. Only those who lose elections rebel in countries with intermediate income levels. In richer countries no one rebels, not even those who never win elections. Improvements in economic performance increase the size of the set of distributive schemes that would be acceptable to all social sectors. It makes irrelevant the losses that actors may incur when they lose elections. Dictators impose their most preferred distributive schemes. They fight distributive conflicts before becoming dictators and are therefore less dependent on the distributive preferences of other sectors. For this reason, they are less vulnerable to economic performance. Growth deprives distributive conflicts from their corrosive effects on the stability of democratic institutions. Therefore, good economic performance protects democracies more than it protects dictatorships. Interesting from the point of view of this chapter, it also makes political competition inconsequential for the survival of competitive regimes in rich countries.

A third explanation in which democracies appear as more sensitive to economic performance than dictatorships may be found in Gasiorowski's work on economic crises (1995). One of the arguments the author evaluates is, unlike the previous ones, centered on elites.[8] According to it, democracies are more vulnerable to bad economic performance, for example, to economic crises, when "certain political actors who are capable of bringing about regime change believe that democratic and semi-democratic regimes hinder the resolution of these crises because governments under such regimes are more responsive to popular pressure and therefore less capable of carrying out the painful measures needed to resolve these crises" (Gasiorowski 1995: 884). The diffusion of the belief that economic crises may not be overcome under democratic rules is central to the interpretation of the fall of Southern Cone democracies that O'Donnell presented in *Modernization and Bureaucratic-Authoritarianism*. For the same reason, because robust growth demands the adoption of socially costly measures and dictatorships are deemed to be less vulnerable to the imposition of social costs, authoritarian regimes should become more robust when economic results are negative. Gasiorowski labels this effect of economic performance on the probability of regime change in each direction "complementary."[9]

A fifth approach to the effect of economic performance on regime stability is also elite based and conditional on the type of regime, but, unlike the previous ones, predicts economic performance to be more consequential to the survival of autocracies than to the stability of competitive regimes. Remmer (1996) advances a clear and persuasive interpretation of the problem. According to Remmer: "Regime durability may be expected to vary indirectly with the incentives and opportunities of political actors to achieve their goals by changing the existing regime framework. Democracy dampens those incentives by institutionalizing opportunities for leadership and policy change" (1996: 617).

Remmer's insight could be interpreted as an elaboration of the conviction that democratic legitimacy offers more reliable support to face the problem of succession than the various legitimacy formulae to which authoritarian regimes resorted. This conviction was widely influential among classic studies on political regimes (Linz 1975), including O'Donnell's (1979b), and also inspires contemporary work on the efficacy of alternative power sharing arrangements under different types of authoritarianism (Gandhi 2008; Gandhi and Przeworski 2007; Magaloni 2008; Reuter and Gandhi 2011; Svolik 2009). According to this rich tradition, the stability of political regimes depends crucially on the credibility of the paths to power they offer to organized political elites. Remmer's contention is that, in general, the promise that paths to power will not be permanently blocked is more credible under competitive than under noncompetitive regimes.

This explanation shares with the previous one the advantage of focusing on elite incentives but it is less dependent than accounts by Gasiorowski and O'Donnell (in *Modernization and Bureaucratic-Authoritarianism*) on the general prevalence among political actors of a particular interpretation of the possibilities of alternative regimes. The emphasis on elite incentives is important for two reasons. First, it places attention on a factor—elite behavior—that immediately precedes the outcome of interest: regime survival.[10] Second, it emphasizes political ambition as a trigger of potentially destabilizing behavior. In my view, political ambition offers a more persuasive reason than dislike for policies to account for the risky and unusual decision to challenge governments. An account based on elite incentives cannot completely dispense of relative support for policies. Challengers feel encouraged to act only when someone blames incumbents for prevailing outcomes. But the trigger is elite intervention not policy evaluation by some social sector.

From this review, three different sets of predictions about the relative vulnerability to economic outcomes of competitive regimes and dictatorships may be derived. If the effect of economic conditions runs through the costs of collective action that social sectors face, as in Acemoglu and Robinson, good performance should increase the stability of both kinds of regimes. Democracies should be more dependent on economic outcomes if the main impact of performance runs through class-based distributive conflicts or if, as O'Donnell's early study posited, elites distrust the ability of democratic regimes to effectively administer them. A finding that autocracies are more dependent on economic performance than competitive regimes would speak in favor of the argument about the power concerns of political elites. As the next section shows, the experience of Latin American countries in the postwar period comes closest to this third possibility.

Economic Performance and Regime Stability in Latin America: 1945–2010

This section examines the relationship between economic performance and the stability of political regimes in Latin America after 1945. It presents evidence suggestive that economic outcomes have been more relevant for the survival of governments under authoritarian rules than for the stability of competitive regimes.

The exposition is divided in two parts. The first one replicates the analysis of the survival of competitive regimes that Pérez-Liñán and Mainwaring perform in their chapter, adding new measures of economic performance to test the prediction, quite frequent in the literature, that the stability of competitive regimes should be sensitive to economic outcomes. The second part of the section, turning more directly to the theoretical argument that this chapter advances, tests the effect of economic performance on the probability that challenges to incumbent authorities, in the form of coups d'état, are mounted and on the probability that they succeed. In both of these exercises, the variables of interest are those that represent the effect of economic conditions on the probability that attempts are made to irregularly replace governments.

Effects of Economic Performance on the Survival of Democracies and Semi-democracies

I test the effect of three different measures of economic performance on the survival of competitive regimes. The test follows the modeling strategy that Pérez-Liñán and Mainwaring propose in their chapter. As in that piece, I work with a panel of twenty Latin American countries observed between 1945 and 2010.[11] The analysis in this chapter includes different measures of economic performance to check the possibility that a significant economic result was overlooked.

The outcome of interest is a dummy variable coded as 1 in the country-year in which a democratic or semi-democratic regime breaks down.[12] A second measure of the dependent variable is presented. In this case, observations are coded as 1 when they transit from democracies to dictatorships as defined by Cheibub, Gandhi, and Vreeland (2010).[13]

Alternative measures for both the dependent and the independent variables are included to establish on firmer ground estimations about the vulnerability of competitive regimes to economic outcomes.

The analysis includes four measures of economic performance. The first one is the rate of per capita GDP growth one year before the observation (GDP growth, $t - 1$), the measure that Pérez-Liñán and Mainwaring report. Economic growth is expected to protect governments from threats. In line with the theoretical argument previously exposed, this protective effect should be felt more strongly under authoritarian regimes than under competitive regimes; this includes the possibility that growth does not affect the survival of competitive regimes at all.

The second measure is a logarithmic transformation of the inflation rate, also registered in the year previous to the observation. Inflation has been posited to negatively affect economic growth and therefore welfare (Dotsey and Ireland 1996; Feldstein 1979). Determining the exact size of this effect in developed economies has led to controversies (Lucas 2000), but in developing economies typically larger inflation rates have been widely regarded as signs of macroeconomic inconsistency and policy mismanagement (Dornbusch 1992). Large inflation rates have a direct impact on personal income, and increasing uncertainty about the near future reduces the utility that may be derived from that income, sometimes very significantly. Feelings of social disorder that go together with high inflation rates should then encourage challenges to incumbent authorities. Again, the encouraging effect should be felt more strongly when political competition is not institutionalized. Therefore, inflation should affect the survival of authoritarian regimes more than the survival of competitive ones, including the possibility that it does not affect at all the survival of democracies and semi-democracies.

Two additional measures intend to capture the effect of recessions. Recessions may be important for perceptual or symbolic reasons. The relevance and potential political damage associated with recessions depend on their magnitude, yet the mere fact that an economy does not grow is usually portrayed in public discourse as a worrisome sign and, in political debate, as a sign of policy failure. For these reasons, the test includes two dummy measures of negative growth: the first one, codes country-years with negative growth in the year immediately preceding as 1; the second one coded country-years preceded by two consecutive years of negative growth as 1. Multiyear recessions are included in the analysis to capture effects that may not be perceptible with shorter episodes, for example, because shorter recessions are interpreted as cyclical variations not reflective of the competence of governments. Long recessions should make clear that governments fail to put the economy back on track, whatever the reason of the previous disruption.

Like in Pérez-Liñán and Mainwaring, the model is a logistic regression with random effects. Covariates are those the authors propose. Table 7.1 reports the results of three different models. The table includes two versions for each model: one, with the Mainwaring, Brinks, and Pérez-Liñán (2001) indicator of breakdowns (MBP), the other one with the measure by Cheibub, Gandhi, and Vreeland (2009; CGV).

TABLE 7.1.
*Survival of competitive regimes (logistic regression of random effects
with breakdown as the dependent variable)*

Regime indicator	Models					
	1.1 MBP	1.2 CGV	2.1 MBP	2.2 CGV	3.1 MBP	3.2 CGV
GDP growth, $t-1$	3.81 (6.31)	−7.91 (6.63)				
Inflation (ln), $t-1$	0.11 (0.19)	0.09 (0.18)				
Negative growth, $t-1$			−0.40 (0.52)	0.59 (0.48)		
Negative growth, $t-1$ & $t-2$					−0.87 (0.73)	−0.55 (0.80)
Age	0.02 (0.18)	−0.03 (0.15)	0.05 (0.16)	−0.09 (0.13)	0.07 (0.16)	−0.07 (0.13)
Age^2	0.00 (0.01)	0.00 (0.01)	0.00 (0.01)	0.00 (0.01)	0.00 (0.01)	0.00 (0.01)
Age^3	0.00 (0.00)	0.00 (0.00)	0.00 (0.00)	0.00 (0.00)	0.00 (0.00)	0.00 (0.00)
Prefers democracy	−3.08* (1.67)	−1.83 (1.61)	−2.79* (1.55)	−2.03 (1.48)	−2.83* (1.57)	−1.72* (1.48)
Radicalization	2.32* (1.19)	2.89** (1.45)	2.55** (1.14)	2.40* (1.26)	2.70** (1.14)	2.77** (1.28)
Democracies region	6.18** (2.37)	−3.02 (2.00)	−4.44** (1.90)	−3.15* (1.65)	−4.30** (1.91)	−2.79** (1.62)
Presidential powers	−0.25** (0.10)	−0.13 (0.10)	−0.19** (0.09)	−0.08 (0.09)	−0.19** (0.09)	−0.08** (0.09)
Pc GDP (ln)	−7.35 (7.31)	−10.72 (9.51)	−5.71 (7.04)	−2.19 (8.98)	−6.37 (7.04)	−5.27 (9.05)
Pc GDP ^ 2 (ln)	0.50 (0.48)	0.69 (0.62)	0.39 (0.46)	0.14 (0.59)	0.43 (0.46)	0.34 (0.59)
Multipartism	0.14 (0.59)	0.51 (0.54)	−0.12 (0.52)	0.39 (0.50)	−0.19 (0.53)	0.36 (0.51)
US policy	−0.10 (1.00)	−0.33 (0.97)	−0.65 (0.81)	−0.17 (0.80)	−0.72 (0.83)	−0.34 (0.81)
Share industrial labor	0.00 (0.04)	0.07 (0.05)	0.03 (0.04)	0.08* (0.04)	0.03 (0.04)	0.08* (0.04)
Mineral exports	−1.22 (0.81)	−0.82 (0.79)	−0.47 (0.66)	−0.64 (0.75)	−0.41 (0.67)	−0.50 (0.76)
Constant	29.55 (27.04)	39.04 (36.23)	21.71 (26.18)	5.56 (34.26)	24.13 (26.19)	16.96 (34.51)
Observations	522	517	652	645	652	645
No. of countries	19	17	20	18	20	18

Note: Standard errors in parentheses. Pc = per capita; MBP = Mainwaring, Brinks, and Pérez-Liñán; CGV = Cheibub, Gandhi, and Vreeland.
*$p < 0.1$; ** $p < 0.05$

The analysis aims to determine to what extent measures of economic performance affect the odds that a competitive regime breaks down in a given country on a particular year, considering that it survived until that point and a set of attributes including the following: the average normative commitment to democracy of relevant political actors (prefer democracy in table 7.1); the level of radicalization prevailing among them; the proportion of democratic countries observed in Latin America; the extension of the legal authority that the constitution grants to the president; the level of economic development (Pc GDP, ln) and, to test for nonlinear effects, its quadratic transformation; whether the national legislature seats more than three effective parties (multipartism); US policy toward the region; the incidence of industrial labor in the working force (share industrial labor); and whether the incidence of mineral exports exceeds 10% of total exports (mineral exports). A measure of the age of the regime, its square, and its cubic transformations are included to verify whether the underlying unconditional probability that a competitive regime breaks down in a particular year changes over time. Coefficients represent variations in the log of the odds that a breakdown takes place associated with changes in the independent variables. Positive signs represent variables that increase the odds that a competitive regime breaks down. Negative signs admit the opposite interpretation.

It is not surprising that table 7.1 reports results very similar to those obtained by Pérez-Liñán and Mainwaring, for the specification is the same and the sample almost identical.[14] The first set of models (1.1 and 1.2) adds lagged inflation to the base model. The second set tests the effect of a recession in the year preceding the observation, and the third analyzes recessions that lasted two years before the country-year of interest. Conditional on this set of controls, economic performance seems to have had no impact whatsoever on the probability that a democracy or a semi-democracy died in a Latin American country in any year since 1945. It is significant that results are robust to different measures of the dependent variable. Models testing for nonlinear effects of previous growth and inflation (not shown) yielded similar results.

The negative finding is theoretically relevant, for most interpretations of the effect of economic performance predict democratic stability to benefit from good economic times and to suffer in bad times. This is not what happened in Latin America in the second half of the twentieth century. Though the sample is limited, economic performance varied widely, both across countries and over time. Had it had any bearing on the odds that a competitive regime survived, the statistical analysis should have captured it. Yet competitive regimes in this region and period seem to have perished or survived for reasons unrelated to economic outcomes.

The finding is also consistent with the argument made in other chapters and in the introduction to this volume: normative commitments and dispositions of political actors, as well as features of the international environment, are much more reliable guides than economic factors in the search for the roots of democratic stability in Latin America.

These results do not undermine the idea that where political competition is institutionalized, bad economic performance presents no special challenge to established authorities and good economic performance grants no additional protection against other threats to regime stability. Does this happen because the possibility of replacing leaders and policies in bad times discourages extra constitutional threats?

Effects of Economic Performance on Challenges to Incumbent Authorities

To answer this question a second test is performed. In this case I estimate the odds that a coup attempt takes place. Data on coup attempts have been drawn from Powell and Thyne (2011), who define these events as "overt attempts by the military or other elites within the state apparatus to unseat the sitting head of state using unconstitutional means" (252). The list includes both successful coups[15] and unsuccessful ones. Though vulnerable to different sources of measurement error,[16] coup attempts approximate the phenomenon on which this chapter focuses; that is, the fact that economic outcomes encourage or discourage those aspiring to unseat incumbents to present a challenge.

Coup attempts may take place in competitive regimes as well as in authoritarian ones and represent, as previously explained, a necessary condition of irregular government replacement, which is a facilitating condition of regime change. In order to explore the effect of economic performance on irregular government replacement—an outcome that is one conceptual step closer to regime change—a second dependent variable is introduced. It is the measure of coups that Lehoucq and Pérez-Liñán (forthcoming) propose. The authors define a coup as "a successful attempt to overthrow the president by a group of state officials, typically executed by a part or the entire armed forces. A coup is an extraconstitutional and illegal replacement of the chief executive" (2009: 4).

The correlation between the measures of coup attempts and successful coups in this sample is 0.69, but the indicators capture different phenomena. This chapter is centrally concerned with one particular source of regime instability: the reaction of challengers to economic performance. Excluding unsuccessful attempts runs the risk of underreporting these reactions. The comparison between the determinants of coup attempts and successful coups sheds light not only on the incentives of challengers but also on the defensive capabilities of incumbents.

Table 7.2 presents the results of three sets of models. Models in each set regress the dependent variables against the same group of independent variables and con-

TABLE 7.2.
Determinants of political instability (logistic regression of random effects with coup attempts and coups as the dependent variable)

	Model					
Measure of instability	4.1 Coup attempts PT	4.2 Coups LP	5.1 Coup attempts PT	5.2 Coups LP	6.1 Coup attempts PT	6.2 Coups LP
GDP growth, $t-1$	−5.8* (3.35)	−3.72* (4.09)				
Negative growth (t − 1 & t − 2)			0.74** (0.33)	0.44** (0.42)	1.10** (0.56)	0.80 (0.60)
Inflation (ln), t − 1	−0.13 (0.09)	−0.08 (0.11)	−0.14 (0.09)	−0.09 (0.11)	−0.32* (0.18)	−0.24 (0.19)
Age of the regime	−0.07 (0.07)	0.08 (0.09)	−0.07 (0.07)	0.08 (0.09)	−0.11 (0.13)	0.16 (0.14)
Age^2	0.00 (0.00)	−0.01 (0.00)	0.00 (0.00)	0.01 (0.00)	0.00 (0.00)	0.00 (0.01)
Age^3	0.00 (0.00)	0.00 (0.00)	0.00 (0.00)	0.00 (0.00)	0.00 (0.00)	0.00 (0.00)
Prefer democracy	−2.61** (0.76)	−1.84** (0.95)	−2.64* (0.77)	−1.89** (0.95)	−0.62 (1.46)	1.49 (1.6)
Radicalization	0.45 (0.56)	0.78 (0.68)	0.40 (0.57)	0.75 (0.69)	−0.23 (1.05)	0.67 (1.22)
Democracies region	−0.31 (1.02)	−1.94 (1.25)	−0.29 (1.02)	−1.91 (1.25)	0.05 (1.95)	1.89 (2.13)
Pc GDP (ln)	−5.08 (3.85)	−6.04 (4.87)	−4.94 (3.87)	−6.01 (4.89)	0.18 (8.09)	4.03 (9.54)
Pc GDP^2 (ln)	0.35 (0.25)	0.40 (0.32)	0.34 (0.25)	0.40 (0.32)	−0.05 (0.56)	−0.33 (0.66)
Multipartism	0.37 (0.29)	**0.86**** (0.36)	0.41 (0.29)	**0.89**** (0.36)	0.56 (0.57)	0.40 (0.63)
US policy	−0.50 (0.52)	−0.30 (0.57)	−0.46 (0.52)	−0.30 (0.57)	0.32 (0.76)	0.52 (0.85)
Share industrial labor	0.01 (0.02)	−0.01 (0.03)	0.01 (0.02)	−0.02 (0.03)	0.01 (0.04)	0.00 (0.04)
Mineral exports	0.29 (0.34)	0.05 (0.44)	0.23 (0.34)	0.04 (0.44)	0.24 (0.75)	1.12 (0.67)
Competitive regime	−0.06 (0.33)	−0.52 (0.40)	−0.11 (0.33)	−0.55 (0.40)		
Constant	17.62 (14.48)	21.27 (18.27)	15.05 (14.71)	17.43 (18.72)	0.46 (29.83)	−15.36 (34.98)
Observations	793	793	793	793	271	271
No. of countries	19	20	19	19	19	19

Note: Standard errors are in parentheses. Models 6.1 and 6.2 look only at authoritarian regimes. LP = Lehoucq and Pérez Liñán; PT = Powell and Thyne; Pc = per capita.
*$p < 0.1$; ** $p < 0.05$

trols. Models 4.1, 5.1 and 6.1 use coup attempts as dependent variables. Models 4.2, 5.2, and 6.2 use successful coups. Model 4 tests the effect of per capita GDP growth lagged one year and inflation, also lagged. Model 5 looks into the effects of multiyear recessions and inflation. Model 6 replicates model 5 but on a subsample of only authoritarian regimes (as coded by MBP). This is one of two strategies to explore whether different regimes have run different risks of experiencing instability. To the same purpose, models 4 and 5 include a dummy variable coded 1 for country-years under a competitive regime.[17] According to the theoretical discussion, coefficients of economic performance indicators should be higher in the subsample of authoritarian country-years than in the whole sample, and the coefficient for the dummy representing competitive regimes should be negative.

Results of models 4.1 and 5.1 are consistent with the hypothesis that economic growth affects the incentives of those who aspire to unseat governments. A 1% increase in per capita GDP significantly reduces the odds that a coup is attempted the following year. In line with this result, two consecutive years of negative growth increase by 20% the odds that a coup takes place on the third year. Growth seems to be a powerful deterrent and multiyear recessions an encouraging sign for challengers.

The contrast between the effects of growth under alternative political regimes also lends support to the expectations derived from the theoretical discussion. The dummy variable for competitive regimes presents the expected negative sign in all models, although the estimation is imprecise and coefficients fail to reach significance at standard levels. Coefficients for multiyear recessions under authoritarianism (model 6.1) are higher than for the whole sample (5.1).[18] Challengers in an authoritarian regime are 10 percentage points more likely to find encouragement to mount a coup in a multiyear recession than are challengers in the whole sample of country-years. This finding is consistent with the interpretation this chapter proposes: when the promise of leadership turnover is credible, as it typically is in competitive regimes, challengers should be less inclined to conspire against incumbents; therefore, the deterrence effect of growth and the encouraging effect of recession should be weaker when political competition is institutionalized.

Inflation, in contrast, does not seem to have played an important role. Coefficients for this indicator are statistically significant at the 0.1 level in only one of six models. The sign of these coefficients is always negative, in contrast to the hypothesis that inflation should make governments more vulnerable to conspiracies.[19] The evidence suggests that inflation has neither inspired nor has it deterred conspiracies against governments in postwar Latin America.[20]

Estimates of the effects of growth and multiyear recessions do not correlate with successful coups as strongly or precisely as they do with coup attempts. Coefficients in models 4.2, 5.2, and 6.2 show the same signs as their pairs in the previous models, but their magnitude is smaller and standard errors are larger. Coup attempts are, of course, a necessary condition of successful coups. It is therefore not surprising that analyses of their determinants yield some similar results. But the observed differences are, I believe, theoretically relevant. The success of conspiracies depends not only on the motivations of challengers but also on the resolve and ability of defenders. It is possible the reason that economic performance shows no clearly discernible effect on successful coups is that signals encouraging challengers also prompt incumbents to raise their guard and prepare for battle. This observation suggests that a more comprehensive analysis of elite behavior as a determinant of regime stability should look at the incentives and capabilities of both incumbents and potential challengers.

Estimates for one of the control variables are consistent with the preceding interpretation. Multipartism in legislatures[21] seems to be a strong predictor of the success of coups but not of coup attempts. This fact suggests that legislative fragmentation is related to the ability to defend established regimes from challengers. The positive coefficient may represent the higher transaction costs that a more fragmented incumbent coalition must pay in the face of a serious political threat. Further studies on this topic should delve more deeply into the factors that affect the size, resilience, and effectiveness of both challenging and incumbent coalitions.

Some of the results for the covariates are consistent with previous studies but nevertheless, I think, interesting. A normative commitment to democracy is strongly and negatively associated with the odds that a coup takes place or succeeds. However, it seems to have had no bearing on those intent on forcefully deposing dictators (as models 6.1 and 6.2 show), perhaps because in postwar Latin America most conspirators against dictatorial governments were not intransigent defenders of democracy but aspiring dictators themselves.

Estimates of the impact of the degree of radicalization of the main political actors show the expected positive sign, though they are imprecise. One possible interpretation for this fact is that policy radicalization affects the survival only of competitive regimes but not of dictatorships. Though the matter requires further exploration, it seems likely that authoritarian governments are neither sensitive nor vulnerable to actors with radical preferences.

Estimates for the number of democracies in the region are also imprecise. This occurs, perhaps, because international factors and diffusion effects kick in only when the irregular replacement of authorities derives in a change of regime. As the events unfold, irregular replacements may be difficult to tell from regime changes. Indeed, they often lead to regime change, but they don't always. This seems to be the reason that estimates for the number of democracies in the region show the expected sign but predict the odds that a coup is attempted or succeeds imprecisely.

Significantly, levels of wealth, as represented by per capita GDP, seem to be unrelated to the stability of any kind of regime. In Latin America, unconstitutional succession has been perversely egalitarian: open to all, both poor and rich.[22]

In sum, in postwar Latin America some economic outcomes have affected the odds that governments are challenged. The analysis of the determinants of coup attempts shows that growth deterred and recessions encouraged challenges to incumbents. Inflation seems to have been less relevant. As expected, the encouraging and deterrent effects of growth were felt more strongly under authoritarian regimes than under competitive ones. Economic performance does not appear to have had as strong an impact on the odds that an attempt to irregularly replace incumbents succeeds, possibly because the signals that affect challengers also alert incumbents and thus increase the odds that they present an effective resistance. These findings are consistent with the most recent empirical studies on regime stability, which control for potential sources of endogeneity of economic performance (Burke and Leigh 2010) and lend support to the theoretical argument advanced in the previous section.

In postwar Latin America, governments have been more vulnerable to conspiracies under authoritarian regimes than under democracies or semi-democracies. This happens, I argue, because a credible promise of leadership replacement makes challengers less prone to adopting irregular tactics and weakens their public justifications for resorting to those tactics. If this is correct, more sensitive measures of political competitiveness—measures that allow for finer distinctions among both democracies and autocracies—could lead to different results. In that case, according to the reasoning proposed in this chapter, democracies with restrictions on political competition should be more vulnerable to attacks and autocracies with credible succession rules should be less vulnerable.[23] However, on average, leadership replacement should be more credible under competitive regimes, so the effect of institutionalized political competition should be discernible in every contrast of political regimes. This hypothesis merits systematic examination in further studies.

Studies of political regimes have long recognized electoral competition as a more legitimate mechanism for the replacement of leaders than many of the various formulae that authoritarian regimes have proposed in modern times. The argument I present here is consistent with this thesis. Institutionalized political competition may be interpreted as one of the components of the legitimacy of democratic rule. It is surprising that theoretical discussions of the effect of economic performance on regime stability have so often overlooked this thesis. Instead, attention has focused on economic motivations and the distributive confrontations they could unleash. The institutionalization of distributive conflicts is, no doubt, part of the puzzle that erecting stable democracies entails. But a focus on economic motivations and distributive confrontations is, as several contributions to this volume make abundantly clear, particularly ill-suited to account for the experience of Latin American countries. Conversely, a systematic exploration of the link between economic performance and regime stability in Latin America sheds light on the shortcomings of some of the conceptions that infuse contemporary discussions of regime stability. Drawing on the insights from the previous study, the next section turns to identifying those shortcomings, discussing the problems they entail, and suggesting some remedies.

Policy Restriction, Political Competition, and the Stability of Democracy

This section presents some theoretical lessons that may be drawn from the study of regime stability and coups in Latin America since 1945. I believe these lessons shed light on contemporary discussions of the sources of stability of political regimes; especially on those referred to the stability of democracies. I make two points. First, that a focus on the potential effect of policies on the income of social sectors yields no definite prediction on the stability of governments or regimes if it does not take into account the crucial mediating effect of political competition. Political competition is important because it allows for both leadership replacement and policy change. My second point is that the institutionalization of both leadership replacement and policy change helps democracies survive. The stress on policy change is important because several contemporary approaches to democratic stability posit, on the contrary, that democracies survive by restricting policy variation.

Let us begin by exploring one corollary of the main finding in the empirical section. Why would economically ineffective dictators run a higher risk of being challenged and overthrown than ineffective constitutional presidents? Focusing only on the effect of policies under each regime on the income of social sectors does not lead to a plausible answer to this question. Suppose that an increase in income raises personal utility and a reduction in income lowers personal utility more under an authoritarian government than under a competitive government. This is conceivable but odd. It is far easier to accept the idea that the relationship between income and utility is the same under both regimes but that changes in the income of social sectors unleash different political dynamics depending on the prevailing fundamental rules. According to the argument advanced here, bad economic performance, construed as a sign of incumbent incompetence, may encourage those aspiring to unseat incumbents. Signs of government incompetence may motivate public acquiescence in and elite support for coups. But economic shocks of similar size should lead to wider challenging coalitions when the regime makes the prospect of leadership replacement less certain. Otherwise, political insiders have little incentives to join conspiracies. An explanation of democratic stability that pays attention only to the impact of economic outcomes on income levels or distributions is likely to miss the key mediating factor: political competition, which is more vigorous under democratic rules.

Recognition of the relevance of leadership turnover for regime stability leads to a consideration of a closely associated problem: policy change. Insensitivity to leadership turnover leads us to underestimate the potential for policy change of competitive regimes.[24] This has consequences for the way we think about democratic rule and its chances of survival.

Influential recent studies (Acemoglu and Robinson 2006; Boix 2003) have narrowed the inquiry about the sources of democratic survival to a search for the conditions that make distributive conflicts manageable. This narrower question admits two general answers. One possible answer is that democracies endure to the extent that they restrict the range of policy change. The other one is that democracies endure because they make policy change reversible.

Contemporary political economy studies of democratic stability devote themselves almost exclusively to advancing different versions of the first kind of answer. From this perspective, conflicts over political regimes are reducible to conflicts over levels of taxation. Thus, structural circumstances such as a more equal distribution of assets and income, weaken the demand for higher taxes (Acemoglu and Robinson 2006; Ardanaz and Mares 2012; Boix 2003; Boix and Stokes 2003). Other structural features such as assets that can move between economic sectors (Boix 2003) or countries (Freeman and Quinn 2012) make high tax rates unfeasible. Structural restrictions to high taxation are posited to strengthen democracies.

These studies are illuminating and do more than discuss safeguards to the interests of powerful social actors. However important, recent contributions cast doubt on the empirical validity of factor-based accounts (Ahlquist and Wibbels 2012; Haggard and Kaufman 2012). Part of the empirical inaccuracy of this general approach may stem from the privileged focus on domestic factors. Several contributions have convincingly demonstrated that international systemic and regional diffusion effects play a crucial role in democratization, particularly in the third wave and in Latin America (Brinks and Coppedge 2006; Gleditsch and Ward 2006; Mainwaring and Pérez-Liñán 2007; Torfason and Ingram 2010; Wejnert 2005). Recent efforts in the structurally inspired tradition include a systematic exploration of international factors (Boix 2011). Yet the empirical inaccuracy may reflect a more fundamental theoretical oversight: democracies may handle intense distributive conflicts when electoral competition offers credible opportunities for both leadership replacement and policy reversal.

To illustrate the previous point, I refer to the fall of the party system and consequent erosion of democracy in Venezuela before 1998, an example of frequent leadership replacement without policy change. Studies performed before (Coppedge 1994) and after the ascent of Hugo Chávez (Mainwaring 2012; Seawright 2012) portray the ideological and policy similarities between the Acción Democrática (AD) and Copei administrations as a corrosive factor for democracy. Ideological similarities did not prevent first AD's Carlos Andrés Pérez and later former Copei's leader Rafael Caldera to attempt different changes in economic policies during their last presidencies. However, these attempts failed to significantly alter the policy status quo.

The frequent rotation in power of the two traditional Venezuelan parties does not seem to have protected Venezuelan democracy from erosion in the face of the very bad economic results of the 1980s and 1990s. Evidence of government inefficacy undermined a competitive regime even when the promise of leadership replacement was credible.

The question challenges us to think more clearly about the stabilizing role of political competition. Institutionalized access to power is relevant for government and regime stability per se. The survival of political regimes requires that political insiders trust them, regardless of what they do once they reach power. But credible leadership replacement is not sufficient to stabilize democracies. Policy flexibility is also necessary. Without policy flexibility, established elites are vulnerable to the mobilization of those who do not see themselves represented by established players. Universal franchise increases the size of the set of potentially mobilizable sectors and therefore makes the requirement for policy flexibility a more central component of political competition under democratic rules.

Chávez rose to power mobilizing sectors that, he claimed, policies adopted during the previous party system left out. So did Evo Morales in Bolivia and Rafael Correa in Ecuador. Arguably, the consolidation of these populist leaderships contributed to the erosion of democracy in those countries. The erosion often consisted in imposing restrictions on political competition. They were usually justified as a means to anchor the changes of policy that these presidents brought about. This illustrative story suggests that it is the combination between leadership replacement and policy change that helps democracies survive.

The complementary theoretical risk is to think that policy flexibility is all that matters for regime stability. If actors associate their welfare with particular policies, they would not conspire against a particular regime as long as they believe that the regime makes the policy they prefer sufficiently likely (and the policies they oppose sufficiently unlikely). In this view, leadership turnover matters only because it is a vehicle for policy change and policy change matters because it mitigates distributive conflicts. This view is incorrect.

Recent studies find that the proportion of democracies that fall in the context of intense class-based distributive conflicts is far from overwhelming (Haggard and

Kaufman 2012), and other studies find that even when class-based conflict is intense, such as in Bismarck Germany, exclusively political motivations may lead representatives to support regime changes that could threaten the economic interests of their constituencies (Ziblatt 2008). Political aspirations of elites may contribute, independently from the economic interests of constituencies, to the stability or change of political regimes. In other words, policy changes in which social sectors may be interested need to be brought about by individuals and organizations with specifically political motivations.[25]

Contemporary political economy discussions of the survival of political regimes focus on the direct impact that policies adopted under alternative regimes are likely to have on the income of social sectors. This is, I believe, the main reason they conceive of the survival of democracy as a matter of restricting the range of policy change. The finding that in postwar Latin America autocratic governments were more vulnerable to irregular challenges than governments under competitive regimes suggests, instead, that income variations are relevant only as long as they prompt political elites to act. However, elites intent on exercising power may bring about the policy changes that could make social actors acquiescent, if not loyal, to democratic rules.

Conclusions

Numerous empirical studies identify an effect of economic performance on the survival of political regimes. The evidence in this chapter suggests that this effect is stronger for authoritarian than for competitive regimes. The most convincing theoretical argument points in the same direction.

The effect of economic performance on regime survival does not seem to run through its direct impact on personal income but, more indirectly, through its effect on the perceptions and incentives of political elites. Bad economic outcomes under both authoritarianism and competitive regimes encourage elites intent on unseating incumbents to mount coup attempts. Good economic outcomes deter potential challengers from attempting coups. The incentive to challenge in bad times and the protective effect of good performance should be more powerful when the rules of the political game do not offer a credible promise of leadership replacement. The credibility of this promise is then closely related to all factors that shape political competition and should, on average, be higher under democratic rules than under authoritarianism and higher in authoritarian regimes that have some rule to handle the problem of succession.

Results from an empirical exploration of the sensitivity of democratic survival and government stability to economic performance in postwar Latin America support this interpretation. Since 1945, the survival of competitive regimes has not been affected by growth or inflation. This negative result is robust to alternative specifications and codings of the dependent variable. Economic growth seems to prevent coup attempts from taking place under either authoritarian or democratic rule. The effect appears to be stronger in authoritarian regimes. The fact that economic performance encourages conspiracies and that this happens more often when political competition is restricted are consistent with the previous theoretical examination.

From the point of view of interpreting democratization trends in Latin America, these results and findings should be put in the wider context of the arguments that the literature and other contributions to this volume offer. Two stand out among those proposed more recently.

First, regional diffusion effects, international systemic effects, and the foreign policy of international hegemons crucially determine the chances of democratization and democratic survival. In the context of the discussion in this chapter, international factors could be interpreted as determinants of the credibility that leadership turnover may take place or, alternatively, as components of the cost of trying an extraconstitutional strategy. The interaction between international factors and the credibility of political competition appears as an area for potentially fertile further exploration.

Second, normative commitments are important. An unconditional disposition to play by the rules appears to have had a highly significant effect both on the survival of democracy and on the probability that a coup takes place. In the context of the argument developed in this chapter, normative commitments to democracy may be interpreted as signals that actors receive about the disposition of other actors to keep the regime competitive. Reciprocally, the experience of effective and institutionalized political competition may help forge and galvanize these commitments. This problem also seems to merit further consideration.

Acknowledging the relevance of specifically political incentives and the stabilizing role of political competition offers a portrait of democracy that seems to be theoretically more convincing and empirically more accurate than other portraits that may be composed relying on some conceptions that are common in political economy studies of democratization. In particular, the stability of democracy does not seem to hinge on restrictions to policy change but rather on the credibility of leadership turnover and policy reversal. Significantly for the purposes of this discussion, leadership turnover may not suffice to make democracy stable when it goes together with policy rigidity.

It is interesting to note that some of the most significant threats to democratic stability in contemporary Latin America seem to derive from governments that in the name of drastic policy change attempt to impose restrictions to political competition. If the arguments in this chapter are correct and in line with Mazzuca's argument in chapter 4 of this volume, by restricting political competition, these governments are making their stability more dependent on the quality of economic outcomes. Paradoxically, by imposing restrictions on competition these governments may be undermining one of the most powerful pillars of democratic survival and of the independence of democratic rules from economic outcomes in the third wave: the conviction that no economic result merits a rebellion, for whatever happens with inflation or growth, incumbents may be replaced in the next election.

NOTES

I thank Antonella Bandiera for her superb research assistance. I am grateful to Scott Mainwaring and Aníbal Pérez-Liñán who generously shared their data set on political regimes in Latin America. Victoria Murillo, Patricio Navia, Pablo Pinto, Nicolás Zaharya, and Rodrigo Zarazaga made provocative and insightful comments on a previous version of this chapter. Extensive comments and editorial suggestions by Scott Mainwaring and Daniel Brinks helped me understand and formulate, I hope, more clearly my argument.

1. Regimes may break down, erode, or be replaced through negotiations; this is why successful challenges are not a necessary condition. These challenges do not always lead to new rules of the game. This is why they are not a sufficient condition for regime change either. However, successful challenges to established authorities, especially when they are repeated, undermine and thus contribute to the replacement of regimes.

2. McGuire's chapter 13 in this volume discusses the strengths and weaknesses of more complex or more simple classifications.

3. Of course, part of the literature accepts the possibility that performance affects governments but has no impact over any regime. Regimes are sets of broad and general rules that allow for a wide array of outcomes. In this sense, it may sound reasonable that the fate of all regimes has very little to do with economic performance, particularly in the sense of "short to medium term outcomes" proposed here. This is a sound observation, but, if governments may be affected, it seems more plausible that regimes could be affected as well, though under some specific condition (for instance, when recessions are deep or long). Indeed, this chapter may be interpreted as an effort to identify some of those conditions.

4. Only in some interpretations of Samuel Huntington's (1968) argument, economic performance is posited to compromise the stability of political regimes. I am not sure that this is the most faithful interpretation of his argument. I believe that the effect of performance Huntington proposes is conditional on the level of institutional development. This thesis is certainly not an accurate portrayal of O'Donnell's analysis in *Modernization and Bureaucratic-Authoritarianism*. In that case, the argument is clearly that uneven and disappointing economic performance helped destabilize democracy in Argentina in 1966. The extent to which that was an accurate assessment of the evolution of the Argentine economy at that point—a contemporary review argued it was not (Brodersohn 1973)—is a different matter.

5. However, Gasiorowski (1995) considers one such argument. It will be analyzed below.

6. Lipset's (1959) account included also the possibility that democracies survive because they are perceived as legitimate and regardless of economic outcomes. The effect of economic performance is not the only one he discussed.

7. Notice, however that these arguments differ from the one Przeworski presented in *Democracy and the Market* (1991) in which he argued that the expectation of party turnover mitigated distributive conflicts and contributed to the stability of democracies.

8. Which is not necessarily the one the author espouses.

9. Gasiorowski's piece discusses other possible effects, but they are similar to the ones discussed previously.

10. Regimes may survive or perish for reasons independent from what elites intend to do. However, some kind of elite behavior is necessary if a government replacement turns into regime change. Though elite intervention is not always the efficient cause, it is rarely irrelevant for regime survival.

11. The number of country-years effectively observed is, in some cases, reduced, due to data restrictions.

12. Breakdowns are switches to the category "authoritarian" in the coding system proposed by Mainwaring, Brinks, and Pérez-Liñán (2001). The switch may happen through a coup d'état, a self-coup, or erosions of rules of competition, civil liberties, or constitutional checks that are not traceable to any particular event.

13. These two data sets use different coding criteria and therefore classify some cases differently. Yet the correlation between these two dichotomous measures is 0.86.

14. In some cases I recoded the age of the regime to make it consistent with the coding of the breakdown indicator.

15. Successful coups are those in which "perpetrators seize and hold power for at least seven days" (Powell and Thyne 2011: 252).

16. Coups are usually plotted in secrecy. In several instances it might be very difficult to distinguish a coup attempt from a minor conspiracy that never got off the ground. Though subject to this source of measurement error, the indicator may be interpreted as an approximation to the sort of intra elite tension we are exploring.

17. The simultaneous inclusion of this variable with the measure of executive powers created problems of multicollinearity. For this reason, the variable *executive powers* has not been included as a control in this analysis.

18. A model with the indicator of growth as independent variable, not shown to save space, also yields higher coefficients.

19. Gasiorowski (1995, 1998) also finds that inflation *decreases* the odds that incumbents are replaced, particularly incumbents under authoritarian regimes.

20. Someone that finds the result in model 6.1 and the consistently negative signs of the coefficients more persuasive could argue that inflation has protected governments against conspiracies. I do not find this interpretation convincing, yet I do not believe the results suffice to rule it out completely.

21. Multipartism is coded as 1 when the regime, competitive or not, has a legislature with more than three effective parties. Otherwise (if fragmentation is lower or if there is no legislature) the code is 0.

22. In light of previous studies on coups (for example, Londregan and Poole 1990), I expected to find a positive effect for the relative incidence of previous coups in each country. I did not. This is intriguing and may be related to the fact that most previous studies use dynamic probit models, which estimate determinants of switches between alternative states instead of correlates of the odds that one particular event takes place.

23. The exploration of political instability that Lehoucq and Pérez-Liñán (forthcoming) are carrying out is headed in this direction. Credibility of succession rules may be part of the consistency of political regimes that Gates and coauthors (2006) posit to be a strong predictor of regime stability.

24. Of course, policy may change even if leaders do not, but policy variation is more probable when leaders are replaced.

25. This is consistent with one of the arguments of the introduction to this volume and Pérez-Liñán and Mainwaring's chapter: preferences over political regimes may not be derived from preferences over distributive schemes. This is because normative commitments that are independent from economic interests often drive political behavior. Economic concerns may be an imprecise guide in the selection of regimes even when they prevail, for the correlation between basic political institutions and public policy has been, as the experience of Latin America in the postwar attests, weaker than some contemporary theories would allow.

PART III

WEAK FORMAL INSTITUTIONS, RULE OF LAW, AND DELEGATIVE DEMOCRACY

CHAPTER 8

Theorizing a Moving Target

O'Donnell's Changing Views of Postauthoritarian Regimes

TIMOTHY J. POWER

The central problem of democratic consolidation is to prevent a successful military coup.

>—Guillermo O'Donnell, "Notes for the Study of Democratic
> Consolidation in Contemporary Latin America," 1985

Delegative democracies, weak horizontal accountability, schizophrenic states, brown areas, and low-intensity citizenship are part of the foreseeable future of many new democracies.

>—Guillermo O'Donnell, "On the State, Democratization,
> and Some Conceptual Problems," 1993

"Democracy" and "consolidation" are terms too polysemic to make a good pair.

>—Guillermo O'Donnell, "Illusions about Consolidation," 1996a

Guillermo O'Donnell's life and scholarship were centrally concerned with the prospects for democracy in Latin America. As this volume makes clear, his influence in this area is nothing short of colossal. If we look back over the past forty years of research on democratization and adopt a simple sequential, tripartite classification of the scholarly literature—breakdown of democracy, transitions to democracy, consolidation of democracy—we can easily observe that O'Donnell is among the few voices that dominated all three debates. His theory of bureaucratic-authoritarianism addressed the collapse of democracy in the Southern Cone; he was among the first to identify contradictions in authoritarian coalitions that would lead to pressures for liberalization; his innumerable insights into the dynamics of regime change pervade the modern literature on transitions to democracy.

In all of this O'Donnell was the very definition of a pioneer: he was consistently in the theoretical vanguard. By the mid-1980s, even before the third wave of democratization was complete in South America, O'Donnell was already exhorting his colleagues to begin theorizing postauthoritarian politics. As a natural extension of his earlier work on transitions with Philippe Schmitter (O'Donnell and Schmitter 1986)—an enterprise characterized by Abraham Lowenthal as "thoughtful wishing" (1986: viii)—the proposed new research program would examine the prospects for sustainability of Latin America's nascent polyarchies. In seeking an umbrella term for this avenue of inquiry, O'Donnell and collaborators began using the shorthand term "democratic consolidation." For better or worse, the term stuck. Seemingly overnight, a phrase that had barely appeared in the comparative politics literature prior to the mid-1980s suddenly became the buzzword for countless conferences, papers, articles, and books over the next decade.[1] This was essentially the third time that O'Donnell had helped launch a scholarly industry, but on this occasion his role in the vanguard would prove to be very different. Although he and his collaborators quickly expended significant energy on conceptual and definitional questions pertaining to democratic consolidation, by the early 1990s O'Donnell was already signaling a change of theoretical course, and in 1996 his vivid essay "Illusions about Consolidation" advocated a complete rethinking of the dynamics of postauthoritarian regimes. Why did this shift occur? What led Latin America's premier scholar of democratization to disinvest from a research program that he himself pioneered?

This chapter attempts to answer these questions by retracing O'Donnell's thinking per se as well as the "moving targets" he was tracking: the new democracies in Latin America born between 1978 and 1990. I argue here that O'Donnell's changing views on consolidation were driven not only by new regional dynamics in Latin America— that is, by constant "status updates" in new democracies, to which O'Donnell was acutely attentive—but also by the inadequacy of certain theoretical assumptions that he carried over from his celebrated work on transitions and that constrained his early thinking about consolidation. To a lesser extent, O'Donnell's views were also subject to a professional feedback loop: they were shaped by his own negative evaluations of the ways in which the consolidation debate was being processed by fellow political scientists.

I document how from the mid-1980s to the mid-1990s, O'Donnell's concern moved from the abstract possibility of democratic breakdown to visible shortcomings in democratic quality. O'Donnell's theoretical focus mirrored the evolution of these two factors in Latin America, a region where the receding likelihood of the former variable was eclipsed by the painful certainty of the latter. Thus, O'Donnell's gradual disinvestment in the consolidation literature is directly linked to his subsequent major contributions on the rule of law and the quality of democracy (e.g., 1999c, 2001, 2004a, 2010a). Although I do not address those later contributions here, the content of this final phase of his work (completed between the mid-1990s and 2010) can be seen as inspired by "omitted variables" that were absent from the first wave of studies on democratic consolidation. O'Donnell's shift in empirical focus over time—from coup avoidance to a new emphasis on effective citizenship—was mirrored by a similar shift in theoretical perspective, in which bold assumptions of fluidity and actor-centrism were gradually supplanted by greater attention to the state, social structure, and longstanding political practices in Latin America.

The discussion below documents some inconsistencies in O'Donnell's work, including at least one dramatic recantation (O'Donnell 1996a) that was accompanied by public self-criticism. None of this is news to readers who followed O'Donnell's career closely. In revisiting these issues, my intent is not to criticize O'Donnell: in fact, my goal is quite the opposite. O'Donnell would be the first to admit that his analysis of postauthoritarian regimes was built (like all good science) on trial and error. However, his willingness to externalize his own doubts in a long paper trail of brilliant essays— and his willingness to add and subtract explanatory variables as necessary—led to significant theoretical advances in comparative politics. His decade-long engagement with democratic consolidation as a dependent variable, though ultimately unsatisfying to him, launched countless beneficial by-products; O'Donnell's interrogation of postauthoritarian politics spun off exciting new literatures on delegative democracy, accountability, stateness, the rule of law, and informal institutions.

O'Donnell's Early Approaches to Democratic Consolidation

On the heels of the successful *Transitions from Authoritarian Rule* project (by then completed and on its way to the publisher), O'Donnell partnered with José Nun to create a working group on "Opportunities and Dilemmas in the Consolidation of Democracy in Latin America." This group met for the first time in São Paulo in December 1985.[2] O'Donnell's unpublished think piece for the meeting (henceforth "Notes") is the best extant record of how he first approached the problem of democratic consolidation in post-transitional settings.[3]

"Notes" begins with the bald statement that "the central problem of democratic consolidation is to prevent a successful military coup."[4] The paper then goes on to depict democratic consolidation as a series of strategic interactions among actors defined solely by their regime preferences. In his stylized model, O'Donnell drew distinctions among what he called C actors (those seeking democratic consolidation), B actors (those actively seeking democratic breakdown), and N actors (those adopting a position of neutrality or indifference). The N camp is presumed to be large, and both C and B actors seek to convert N actors to their respective causes. C and B actors compete for N actors at two levels: at the level of public opinion and at the level of organized actors. With regard to organized actors, O'Donnell gives particular weight to the armed forces and to the bourgeoisie. His approach is clearly influenced by threshold models drawn from game theory: the goal is to prevent the coalition favoring breakdown from becoming a Schelling-like k-group (Schelling 1978; see also Przeworski 1986). The assumption is that if C actors can successfully block the formation of a breakdown coalition, they can use time to their advantage: "the longer a democratic 'situation' endures, the better the chances are that political democracy will be consolidated" (O'Donnell 1985: 5). With these theoretical building blocks in hand, O'Donnell then goes on to analyze how the C–B game may play out abstractly in a large number of domains, including economic management, public opinion, and civil-military relations. At more than seventy-five pages, this still-unpublished text is noteworthy for its topical diversity.

Rereading "Notes" over a quarter century later, two aspects of this early work immediately stand out. First is the pervasive attention to coup avoidance. O'Donnell reviewed the previous two decades of Latin American history and noted that, while democracies had died both "sudden deaths" and "slow deaths," in the end the final blow was always dealt by the armed forces. Memories of military coups were fresh in his mind (it is incredible now to think that he wrote this paper about democratic consolidation a mere nine years after the 1976 coup in Argentina), and so he naturally placed immense importance on traditional and potential allies of the military, such as the bourgeoisie. Second, it is notable that O'Donnell argued explicitly for an "actor-centered," choice-theoretic approach to democratic consolidation. In 1985 he advocated actor-centrism over what he saw as three plausible but inferior alternatives: a "procedural approach" that would highlight milestones like elections and alternations in power, a "public opinion" approach that would use survey research to trace regime support, and a "substantive approach" that would highlight the role of discrete political institutions (e.g., parliamentary strengthening).[5] Yet, although he opted for actors, O'Donnell was reluctant to use a "concrete-actor centered approach" (i.e., one with proper names) and preferred what he termed an "abstract-actor, preference-centered approach." Only with a stylized model, he insisted, could he highlight the strategic interactions that would shape the trajectory of a postauthoritarian regime (1985: 13–18).[6]

What came of these provocative ideas? O'Donnell would subsequently abandon both (1) his overriding concern with coup avoidance and (2) his abstract actor-centered approach to democratic consolidation, which assumed a high degree of autonomy of politics. The first was presumably discarded for empirical reasons—by and large, military putschism did not turn out to be a central issue in postauthoritarian Latin America—yet O'Donnell's move away from the strategic interaction model needs a bit more explanation. Perhaps O'Donnell viewed these two aspects of his work as mutually interdependent, though logically it would have been possible to drop the concern with *golpismo* while continuing to apply strategic choice models to other aspects of macropolitics (e.g., economic reform, coalition formation, or state-society relations). One possibility is that "Notes" is simply the one-off product of a brief dalliance with game-theoretic approaches,[7] but another (more persuasive) explanation is that that strategic choice analysis simply did not lend itself well to the variables that O'Donnell came later to identify as more important than coup avoidance: horizontal accountability, state responsiveness, social authoritarianism, and delegative forms of rule.

"Notes" illustrates O'Donnell's characteristic care and caution when entering unfamiliar terrain. The essay is replete with warnings and disclaimers about the slippery nature of democratic consolidation, and every possible theoretical entry point to consolidation (including the ones that O'Donnell favored) is preemptively criticized. Influenced by Schmitter's early thoughts on "partial regimes" (later published as Schmitter 1992), O'Donnell wrote that "we may agree that, first, consolidation is a complex and multidimensional process, and second, that whichever the relevant dimensions are, it is very unlikely that they will move at an equal pace" (1985: 73). O'Donnell cautioned against using discrete events (e.g., an alternation in power or a certain number of parliamentary sessions) as unambiguous empirical indicators of consolidation, yet at the same time he was unwilling to discard these milestones entirely—such indicators could be taken as proxies for "eventual processes of routinization/institutionalization" (74). As a working definition of democratic consolidation, O'Donnell preferred instead to emphasize the termination of decisional constraints on the democratizing coalition:

> [I advance] a criterion that I find more indicative than the ones provided by discrete events, more easily graspable than the mapping of continuous process, and that can be jointly used with these two: *consolidation of democracy is achieved when C actors playing high politics eliminate from their decision function the constraint of playing into the hands of B actors.* (1985: 75, italics added)

Thus O'Donnell's original model of democratic consolidation described a political world in which actors defined by their regime preferences either "played consolidation" or "played breakdown" and in which the sudden death of democracy was a distinct possibility.

The fluidity and indeterminacy of this model seems a natural extension of O'Donnell's then-recently completed work with Schmitter, *Tentative Conclusions* (O'Donnell and Schmitter 1986). In that monograph, the authors claimed that the hallmark of democratic transitions was uncertainty and that, as a consequence of this, "normal science" models of political analysis would not be of much help (O'Donnell and Schmitter 1986: 19). The central contention is that in periods of extreme uncertainty, politics becomes less constrained by structural factors than is normally the case, and actors and their choices matter much more. The autonomy of politics is greatly enhanced, albeit temporarily. In an interview with Gerardo Munck, O'Donnell freely conceded that *Tentative Conclusions* was a "politicist text" (Munck and Snyder 2007: 292).

Why was this strong assumption of fluidity carried forward by O'Donnell from transition theory into consolidation theory? First, there is little doubt that this methodological choice was a reasonable one at the time, especially given the "moving target" problem of mid-1980s Latin America: it is difficult to see why the first year of a democratic regime would be any less fluid than the final year of a military dictatorship.[8] Second, the fluidity assumption was useful for comparative purposes, because it helped to distinguish Latin America from the other democratizing region of the time, Southern Europe. At various points in "Notes," O'Donnell signals his skepticism that the parliamentary arena would ever prove as important to democratic consolidation in Latin America as it clearly was in Greece, Portugal, and Spain; additionally, Southern Europe enjoyed a far more favorable international context, which reduced uncertainty by raising the cost of democratic backsliding (Whitehead 1986). The clear implication here is that "normal science" models might recover their relevance much sooner in the European cases but that Latin American analyses would be better served by retaining the indeterminacy assumption—so prominent in *Tentative Conclusions*—for a while longer.

Yet, as we shall see below, O'Donnell soon distanced himself from the fluidity assumption. He progressively reduced the space given to the autonomy of politics and began to give more attention to "structural" problems long engrained in the sociopolitical fabric of Latin America: particularism, personalism, unresponsive states, and the weak rule of law. In retrospect, "Notes" is a clear outlier in O'Donnell's work on consolidation: none of his other essays comes even close to assuming the level of uncertainty and fluidity that we see in this 1985 work.

The "Two Transitions" Approach

O'Donnell's next treatments of consolidation turned to the topic of authoritarian legacies while experimenting with a different framework for understanding democratic consolidation. In "Notes," O'Donnell had already questioned the "modes of transition" approach, which assumed that new democracies would be strongly influenced by the specific path they took from dictatorship.[9] In essays written circa 1987–88, he began to deepen this critique, questioning whether even specific legacies of authoritarianism (as opposed to paths or routes to democracy) would shape new polyarchies, or if they did, whether we could account for political learning that might confound the expected effects of these legacies. Hence his brilliant comparison of late

1980s Brazil and Argentina in "Transitions, Continuities, and Paradoxes" (O'Donnell 1992).[10] Conventional wisdom had held that democratic consolidation would be easier in countries where the outgoing dictatorship had been more economically successful and less physically repressive (e.g., Brazil, not Argentina). O'Donnell made a persuasive case for the opposite hypothesis. In countries where the political class and bourgeoisie had been thoroughly scarred by prior experiences with military rule (e.g., Argentina, not Brazil), they would work harder to avoid an authoritarian involution. Conversely, Brazilian capitalists and party politicians had good historical reasons to believe that a military coup would not put them out of business, and this would explain their somewhat irresponsible *leviano* behavior during the Sarney years. Subsequent survey data on regime preference and on trust in the military lent credence to O'Donnell's comparative insights. Over the past twenty-five years public support for democracy has consistently been higher in Argentina than in Brazil, despite greater political instability and more severe socioeconomic crises in Argentina.[11]

More important for consolidation theory, it is at this point in his work that O'Donnell begins to conceive of democratic consolidation as a "second transition." The first transition would be from an authoritarian regime to the inauguration of a democratic government, while the second transition would be from a democratic government to the "effective functioning of a *democratic regime*" (O'Donnell 1992: 18, italics in original). Whereas in "Notes" O'Donnell had referred to postauthoritarian "situations"—a catch-all term that implies no direction of movement or no movement at all—the switch to "transitions" could be read as implying forward motion of some type. Because O'Donnell clearly recognizes (1992: 19) that this second transition may result in retrogression or breakdown, he is not guilty of premeditated teleology. Yet the use of the term "second transition" to describe postauthoritarian politics is a foretaste of what O'Donnell would later deride as the "teleological flavor" of the consolidation literature (1996a: 36).

In this phase of his work, O'Donnell was still concerned with coup avoidance, but he began to expand the research agenda for consolidation. In his jointly authored book introduction with Mainwaring and Valenzuela (Mainwaring, O'Donnell, and Valenzuela 1992: 4–5), the authors pose no fewer than eleven new questions that should be considered above and beyond the narrow issue of possible breakdown. These questions cover issues such as economic performance, civil-military relations, transitional justice, political learning, channels of representation, social policy, and the quality of political leadership. The temporal lens was widened somewhat but still not enough to engage with deep structural questions about Latin American states and societies: none of the items on the research agenda fully anticipated the broad issues of citizenship and the rule of law to which O'Donnell would later turn.

"On the State" and "Delegative Democracy"

A key turning point in O'Donnell's work was his essay "On the State, Democratization and Some Conceptual Problems: A Latin American View with Glances at Some Postcommunist Countries," written in 1992 and published in 1993. This paper (henceforth "On the State") is best remembered for its proposed mapping of state presence in Latin America (the memorable blue, green, and brown areas) that would illustrate unevenness in the territorial penetration of the state in its day-to-day functionality and in the presence of a democratically sanctioned rule of law. The topographical scheme is familiar and I will not revisit it here. Instead I wish to advance three reasons why we can consider "On the State" to be an inflection point in O'Donnell's thinking.

The first is obvious from the title: with this essay, O'Donnell marks a sharp return to *the state*. O'Donnell had been centrally concerned with the state in his mature work on bureaucratic-authoritarianism (1978b, 1978c, 1979b, 1982), but much less so in his process-driven and actor-centered approaches to transition and consolidation, respectively. His strong emphasis on the autonomy of politics tended to obscure the role of the state, so prior to 1992 and 1993 O'Donnell had not yet given the state any extensive analytical treatment under conditions of polyarchy. Yet, from this point forward, the relationship between the state and democracy would be the central theme of his work until the end of his life.

Second, this essay is the first in which O'Donnell opines on the burgeoning literature on democratic consolidation, which he himself had initiated. He was clearly unimpressed. He lamented that with relation to new democracies, "the existing literature does not go much beyond indicating what attributes (representativeness, institutionalization, and the like) they do not have, along with a descriptive narration of their various political and economic misadventures" (1993: 1356). Impatient with the mainstream tendency to define postauthoritarian regimes by what they lacked, O'Donnell acquired a new motive to theorize the new regimes as they really were—thus leading directly into his work on delegative democracy and informal institutionalization.

Third, "On the State" also carried a warning against universalistic, or "flat," theories of democratization. O'Donnell worried that triumphalism about capitalism and democracy would cause analysts to overlook the immense heterogeneity of democratic practices within existing polyarchies, that is, the brown patches. He cautioned that "we may be going back to some mistakes of the 1960s, when many theories and comparisons were flat, if not ethnocentric; they consisted of the application of supposedly universally valid paradigms which ignored the structured variation to be found outside of the developed world" (1993: 1360).

The warning against universalism in "On the State" leads logically into "Delegative Democracy" (henceforth DD), a far more widely cited essay that was published a year later (O'Donnell 1994).[12] Here O'Donnell makes a strong case to discard "Northwestern" models of democracy altogether and to engage with new democracies on their own terms. Hence the remarkable opening sentence: "Here I depict a 'new species,' a type of existing democracy that has yet to be theorized" (1994: 55). O'Donnell explains that DDs are certainly a form of polyarchy, in the sense that Dahl (1971) used the term, but that they are not *representative* democracies. DDs hold elections and these contests are institutionalized, yet they are not intended to generate accountable representation: elections are geared toward empowering strong executives to govern the nation as they see fit, usually with a view to "magically" resolving a pressing socioeconomic crisis. O'Donnell claims that delegative democracies, or DDs, result from an "interaction effect" (his term, 1994: 56), and the two constitutive variables are (1) social and economic crises inherited from outgoing authoritarian regimes and (2) cultural patterns pertaining to executive authority. Each of these variables reinforces the other, such that the winners of presidential elections see their mandate as a limitless delegation of power. Of course, delegation is part of representative democracy (RD) too—but RD differs from DD in that the former has channels of accountability. DD generally lacks these channels: it is a system of weak institutionalization. Instead, DD relies on technocratic and especially personalistic forms of rule: "it is more democratic, but less liberal, than representative democracy" (1994: 60).

"Delegative Democracy" is an essay devoted to constructing an ideal type. It does not invest heavily in causal explanation concerning democratic consolidation, but there are some interesting nuances that show a changing conception of what consolidation really entails. O'Donnell greatly downplays the term "consolidation" in this piece, preferring to speak of "institutionalization." The essay is memorable for its lengthy defense (57–59) of why institutions are important to new democracies: they reduce uncertainty, they induce patterns of representation, they lengthen the time horizons of key actors, and they serve to overcome one-shot prisoner's dilemmas. O'Donnell claims that DDs lack strong democratic institutions that would make representation possible and that these spaces are frequently filled by clientelism, patrimonialism, and corruption (59). Though DD is both a cause and a consequence of weak institutions, it is nonetheless a subtype of democracy.

Again, it is possible to identify in "Delegative Democracy" some subtle changes in O'Donnell's thinking about postauthoritarian regimes. First, consolidation is now *implicitly* defined as a kind of formal institutionalization that would provide representation and accountability. DD implies the absence or distortion of these desirable properties. Second, O'Donnell distances himself from the connotation of forward movement implied by a "second transition." He states clearly that "DDs are not consolidated (i.e., institutionalized) democracies, but they may be *enduring. . . .* In many cases, there is no sign either of any imminent threat of an authoritarian regression, or of advances toward representative democracy" (56, italics in original). But this apparent limbo is not a residual category—it is a new species that must be described and theorized. Third, there is an acceptance that historical, structural, and even cultural factors need to be brought back into the analysis of postauthoritarian regimes. It is striking to see O'Donnell employ "certain practices and conceptions about the proper exercise of political authority" (56) as an explanatory variable, or to wonder aloud whether the plebiscitarian impulse of DD is due to "culture, tradition, or historically-structured learning" (62). The postulation of culturally bound practices incompatible with formal institutionalization would foreshadow his last work on democratic consolidation.

Disowning and Atoning: "Illusions"

As is well known, O'Donnell's 1996 essay "Illusions about Consolidation" (henceforth "Illusions") represented a dramatic break with much of his earlier work. Published in the *Journal of Democracy*—an outlet that was itself a product of the consolidation literature, being created specifically to study the sustainability of third wave democracies—it became one of O'Donnell's most cited and debated papers. The article essentially does three things: (1) it directs withering criticism at the mounting scholarly literature on democratic consolidation, (2) it offers a recantation and mea culpa on the part of O'Donnell for his own role in this literature, and (3) it innovates a new research agenda on the "informal institutionalization" of new democracies. I now take each of these aspects in turn.

"Illusions" takes consolidologists to task for several reasons. O'Donnell argued that the institutionalist variant of the consolidation literature was too focused on how the parties, legislatures, courts, and other trappings of new democracies failed to live up to certain high standards set by the analysts themselves. The implicit yardstick was usually some idealized version of these same institutions as constituted in advanced democracies, but the lack of clarity about this yardstick was a recurrent problem. Most scholars seemed to be looking for forms of institutionalization that they would recognize and of which they would approve, thus preventing them from seeing any alternative forms of institutionalization that could in fact be under way.[13] The criticism and impatience that scholars displayed in their treatment of new democracies seemed to O'Donnell to reflect a teleological bias (1996a: 38).

In criticizing other scholars in "Illusions," O'Donnell also criticizes himself for making some of the same mistakes. He admits that by using terms such as "stunted democracies" that he reinforced the fallacy of seeing new democracies as necessarily incomplete. He notes that by developing the concept of the "second transition" that he dabbled in teleology himself (38, n14). Most radically, he essentially disowns the very concept of democratic consolidation: "the terms 'democracy' and 'consolidation' are terms too polysemic to make a good pair" (38). O'Donnell concludes that the term "consolidation of democracy" is best left to politicians rather than to political scientists:

> As an author who has committed most of the mistakes I criticize here, I suspect that we students of democratization are still swayed by the mood of the times that many countries have more or less recently passed through. . . . The Northwest was seen as the endpoint of a trajectory that would be largely traversed by getting rid of the authoritarian rulers. This illusion was extremely powerful during the hard and uncertain times of the transition. Its residue is still strong enough to make democracy and consolidation powerful, and consequently pragmatically valid, terms of political discourse. Their analytical cogency is another matter. (1996a: 47)

O'Donnell concludes that only by "freeing ourselves from some illusions" can political scientists make sense of postauthoritarian regimes. These regimes may institutionalize in "ways we dislike and often overlook" (46). The remainder of his essay consists of a strong argument in favor of a new research agenda on informal institutionalization, in particular by examining the ways in which pervasive particularism (by which O'Donnell means a diverse set of antirepublican practices including clientelism, patrimonalism, and personalism) ingrains certain contradictions in new democracies. The contradiction most interesting to O'Donnell—and one that he would explore over the next decade—was the strong presence of *democratic* freedoms combined with the weak presence of *liberal* freedoms in Latin America (45). The weakness of liberalism and republicanism justified his increasing attention to the central role of the state, and this new focus led into his major contributions on citizenship and the rule of law. But after "Illusions" O'Donnell no longer embedded his observations in the ongoing debate on "democratic consolidation." Having initiated this literature, watched it unfold, and catalogued its many errors (including some of his own), he essentially divested from the consolidation debate in the mid-1990s.

Explaining the Shift in O'Donnell's Views

Why did a key pioneer of the consolidation debate withdraw from it only a decade later, seemingly disillusioned? Part of the answer lies in a professional feedback loop, that is, in O'Donnell's great dissatisfaction with the way that so-called consolidology was taking shape in comparative political science. His critiques of the literature are well developed in "Illusions," and there is no need to revisit them here. But the more compelling reasons for O'Donnell's evolution are connected to the "moving target" problem he faced in analyzing the new Latin American democracies of the 1980s and early 1990s. This moving target problem can in turn be disaggregated into distinct empirical and theoretical dimensions.

Empirically, Latin America changed in important ways from the mid-1980s and the mid-1990s, and so did the zeitgeist in which it was inserted. When O'Donnell first began writing about democratic consolidation in the region, about 40% of its current polyarchies did not yet exist (Chile, Paraguay, Mexico, and most of Central America were still under authoritarian rule). There was no democratization—nor even liberalization—in Eastern Europe, and the idea of a global "Third Wave" (Huntington 1991) had not yet been conceived. O'Donnell could not yet fully appreciate the more favorable international environment for democracy that would emerge, nor had political scientists identified the strong "neighborhood" and diffusion effects that improve democratic sustainability and discourage authoritarian retrogressions.[14] In this environment, it seemed reasonable to assume that the main threat to democracy in Latin America lay in possible military intervention (as in the 1960s and 1970s) and that the main goal of democratic consolidation would be to thwart the formation of any breakdown coalition that would include the armed forces.

Yet from the mid-1980s on most South American militaries did not turn out to be major veto players, having been scarred by their own poor performance in power, underfunded in times of austerity, and gradually marginalized by ambitious civilian politicians (e.g., Hunter 1997). The regional and international environments discouraged coups. Social groups that had looked to military salvation twenty years earlier (e.g., capitalists, the urban middle classes, the civilian political right, the Catholic Church) had undergone internal changes that disposed them more favorably to polyarchy: the coup coalitions that O'Donnell had described so vividly in *Modernization and Bureaucratic-Authoritarianism* (1973) did not regroup. In part, this is because several of the military's former allies no longer feared polyarchy. The possibility of socialist revolution had sharply declined; some form of capitalism seemed secure almost everywhere; and parties of the left did not fare particularly well in founding elections in the region.

The decline of coup avoidance as an overriding goal was a permissive condition for O'Donnell to alter his thinking about consolidation, but the direct causal factor was the acquisition of new democratic experience in Latin America. His 1985 paper on consolidation ("Notes") contains virtually zero analysis of the actual policy performance of new democratic governments for a simple reason: O'Donnell had almost no record to go on. However, as the new regimes engaged with political and economic realities—inflation crises, stabilization packages, corruption scandals, second elections and the like—new data became available and nascent democracies acquired their initial reputations. O'Donnell formed mostly negative opinions of the early record of Latin American democracy; in the series of essays reviewed above, only Chile and Uruguay are singled out for praise of their performance. The reason given is that these two regimes (unlike their neighbors) were authentic cases of *re*-democratization, having dense formal institutions that were highly congruent with actual political practices. But, looking at the rest of South America, O'Donnell observed trends that worried him greatly. These included hyperpresidentialism, bait-and-switch populism, rampant particularism, and weak channels of accountability, all of which eventually found their way into his ideal type of delegative democracy (of which he considered Brazil, Ecuador, and Peru as the purest cases circa 1992).

Over time, however, O'Donnell focused on the increasingly evident illiberalism of Latin American democracy, drawing attention to major deficits in citizenship and the rule of law. "On the State" is the essay that best exhibits the turning point in his thinking, as it points to immense heterogeneity in the penetration and effectiveness of the Latin American state, conceived not only as a network of administrative structures but also as a set of social relations (or "mediations") that strongly shaped popular perceptions of the political regime. These themes dominated O'Donnell's work from the early 1990s until his death in 2011. Taking a longer view of his output, the shift in emphasis from coup avoidance in "Notes" to democratic quality in "On the State" is rather rapid, but it shows what a difference new data can make, even if based only on five to seven years of observation of democratic practice.

The "moving target" problem had an empirical as well as a theoretical dimension. As O'Donnell pondered the possibility of military coups in 1985, he needed a theoretical framework that would allow him to capture the formation and interaction of regime-oriented coalitions (the *B* and *C* actors in his model). Given the restricted temporal domain and the advent of untested regimes, it seemed logical to carry forward some of the assumptions that O'Donnell had used with Schmitter in *Tentative Conclusions*: widespread uncertainty, the enhanced autonomy of the political sphere, and the importance of individual actors. O'Donnell assumed that the *C* camp would be constantly engaged in trying to neutralize the formation of a *B* coalition. But for the most part, *C* actors did not have to do that and simply went on with the business of "governing." Within a few years the accumulated experiences of new governments had added a host of new items to the research agenda on democratic consolidation, many of which were big, structural, slow-moving factors. To come to grips with these factors, O'Donnell needed to distance himself from the choice-theoretic, process-oriented approach that had characterized his work on democratic transition in the first half of the 1980s. This approach constrained his thinking about new democracies, and he soon discarded it.

O'Donnell made the appropriate theoretical modifications rather quickly after

"Notes." The sphere of day-to-day politics became less autonomous in his work. His time horizon was lengthened from short to medium and then to long. The concept of "modes of transition" was thoroughly abandoned. The centrality of concrete political actors (the military, the bourgeoisie, political parties) was sharply reduced. Instead, O'Donnell brought new variables to the fore, most of which were stickier and more structural. These included the role of the state, the legal system and the rule of law, the citizenship deficit, and centuries-old political practices such as particularism, clientelism, and personalism. Historical, structural, and even some cultural variables made a rapid rebound in O'Donnell's work as he attempted to match his theoretical approach to the changing empirics of Latin American democracy. These adjustments, which he revealed incrementally in his series of provocative essays in the early 1990s, led O'Donnell to the strong conclusion that it was more profitable to analyze state-society relations and "real-existing" political practices than the abstract concept of "democratic consolidation." At every point along the way, O'Donnell's own doubts and his subsequent course corrections were externalized to the scholarly community, so that his work was always in very close pursuit of a moving target.

Conclusions

This chapter has retraced O'Donnell's engagement with democratic consolidation theory, but that is only one phase of his long career. It would be profitable to assess his consolidation work against the full forty years of his prodigious output. Although that task is beyond me, one brief point bears mention here. O'Donnell had a strong Weberian bent and found ideal types an essential tool of modern social science. Not only did he enjoy ideal types, but he was amazingly good at producing them himself: think of the memorable depictions of bureaucratic-authoritarianism found in "State and Alliances" (1978c) or "Tensions" (1979b) or reread the more recent "Delegative Democracy" (1994). These are jaw-droppingly vivid portraits, full of nuance and creativity at every turn, and they will be cited and used by comparative political scientists for decades to come. But it seems to me that either one "believes" in ideal types or one does not—if we believe in them, then we construct them and accept (as Weber did) that no empirical case will ever perfectly correspond to the stylized model.

O'Donnell employed ideal types successfully with bureaucratic-authoritarianism and delegative democracy, which makes his refusal to sign off on a model of "consolidated democracy" puzzling at first glance. His protestation that this would simply end up as a caricature of "Northwestern" democracy is not persuasive from a Weberian standpoint, because once again ideal types allow us precisely to focus on the differences between models and reality. Yet O'Donnell loathed the ethnocentrism that he feared would plague such a Northwestern approach. Thus, O'Donnell avoided a universalistic model of consolidated democracy and preferred to create regionally based ideal types suited to Latin America (and partially to postcommunist Europe), the best example of which is delegative democracy. This "new species" may be regionally bound, but that was precisely the point: O'Donnell believed it was more useful to theorize "up" from the properties of really existing polyarchies (delegation, weak accountability, particularism, and informal institutionalization) than "down" from the properties of Northwestern democracies. To do otherwise would be to partake of "illusions about consolidation." But the "illusions" in question plainly refer to third wave democracies: nowhere did O'Donnell really tell us whether the concept of consolidation would also be an illusion in advanced industrial democracies. His work is similarly silent with regard to longstanding polyarchies in South America: O'Donnell's passing characterization of Uruguay and Chile as successful cases of *re*-democratization skirts the fascinating question of whether these countries could have been considered consolidated democracies prior to 1973, during the second wave of democracy.

For a scholar so reliant on regime-related ideal types, O'Donnell's ultimate reluctance to include "consolidated democracy" in his taxonomy is rather striking. Yet, despite his abrupt disinvestment in the consolidation debate and the lingering of some unanswered questions, O'Donnell's careful engagement with the topic generated innumerable insights. Some of these insights are specific to certain scholarly outputs and could not be reviewed here, while others were "spun off" by O'Donnell and other scholars in ways that ignited new debates and spawned several allied literatures. Contemporary social science research on delegative democracy, accountability, stateness, the rule of law, and informal institutions owes much to Guillermo O'Donnell's decade-long research into the prospects for democratic consolidation in postauthoritarian regimes.

NOTES

I thank Cynthia Arnson, Gerardo Munck, and the editors of this volume for helpful comments on the first draft of this chapter.

Epigraphs. O'Donnell (1985:1); O'Donnell (1993: 1367); O'Donnell (1996a: 38).

1. Looking at the foundational texts of the modern democratization literature, Rustow (1970) uses the term "consolidation" only once in his classic article, compared with seven instances of his preferred behavioralist cognate, "habituation." Dahl (1971) does not use the term "consolidation" at all. The term seems to have first gained widespread usage in the literature on the new Southern European democracies of the 1970s, spreading shortly thereafter to Latin America.

2. The São Paulo meeting is well documented by Mainwaring (1986). The working group met again in Buenos Aires from March 21–23, 1986. In April 1987, an expanded group met at Notre Dame to consider comparisons between Latin America and Southern Europe (see Power and Powers 1988).

3. O'Donnell never returned to this unpublished draft, and the surviving mimeo version carries an explicit request not to cite or quote. But the central ideas of this text have been disseminated previously: Mainwaring (1986) synthesized the oral delivery of O'Donnell's arguments at the December 1985 consolidation workshop in São Paulo, and later O'Donnell gave permission to David Collier and Deborah Norden to summarize his game-theoretic model in their review article on strategic choice analysis (1992). Here I quote the original version of "Notes" with permission from his literary estate.

4. The very next sentence carries the disclaimer that this statement is an "abysmal platitude," yet a useful starting point for the model that follows.

5. These three alternatives were all developed in the broader literature on consolidation. An example of the first type would be Huntington's later "two-turnover test" (Huntington 1991: 77). An example of the second type would be the focus on legitimation used by Linz and Stepan (1996) or Diamond (1999a), both of which drew on early Latinobarómetro data. The third type shared common origins with the new institutionalism in the study of Latin American politics, although by the mid-1990s this literature had become more inward-looking and progressively less concerned with the theme of democratic consolidation (Weyland 2002).

6. This approach contrasts sharply with the one used in his classic essay "An Impossible 'Game': Party Competition in Argentina, 1955–66" (chapter 4 in O'Donnell 1973). In that essay, players in the game were identified as real actors, such as Peronists, Radicals, and the military. Of course O'Donnell was describing the Argentine game post hoc, differently from the future-oriented and case-blind approach of "Notes."

7. As noted, O'Donnell's interest in game theory was foreshadowed much earlier by "An Impossible 'Game.'" In the mid-1980s he briefly became very interested in N-person prisoners' dilemma and threshold models, rereading and discussing classic works by Olson, Granovetter, and Schelling, among others. In 1986 he even taught a one-off graduate seminar on collective action theory at Notre Dame.

8. To remind the reader of the context in which O'Donnell was writing "Notes," in December 1985 the democratic governments of Uruguay (Sanguinetti) and Brazil (Sarney) were nine months old. In Argentina, President Alfonsín had been in office for two years, but the country was under a state of emergency during the sentencing phase of the Trial of the Juntas.

9. For an excellent review of the first decade of the modes of transition debate, see Munck and Leff (1997).

10. The 1992 book chapter in English is in fact a merger and updating of two essays that first appeared in Reis and O'Donnell (1988). I served as translator and editor of the English-language version.

11. See, for example, the Latinobarómetro time series data presented in the statistical appendix to *Democracy in Latin America: Toward a Citizen's Democracy*, a comprehensive report of the United Nations Development Programme on which O'Donnell served as lead consultant (UNDP 2004).

12. O'Donnell began using this term in public presentations around the end of 1990. A first draft of this essay appeared as Kellogg working paper number 172 in March 1992.

13. O'Donnell noted the irony that many analysts did not appreciate that elections were also institutions and thus overlooked the one institutional characteristic that both old and new democracies reliably share (1996a: 38).

14. For empirical support of the democratic diffusion hypothesis, see Gasiorowski and Power (1998), Brinks and Coppedge (2006), and Gleditsch and Ward (2006).

CHAPTER 9

Building Institutions on Weak Foundations
Lessons from Latin America

STEVEN LEVITSKY AND MARÍA VICTORIA MURILLO

> The liberal and democratic ideology, far from expressing our concrete historical situation, obscured it. The political lie installed itself almost constitutionally among our countries. The moral damage has been incalculable and reaches into deep layers of our character. Lies are something we move in with ease. During more than a hundred years we have suffered regimes of brute force, which were at the service of feudal oligarchies, but utilized the language of liberty
>
> —Octavio Paz

Throughout his career, Guillermo O'Donnell used Latin American cases to challenge and refine dominant theories and concepts in comparative politics—often ones that were based, either explicitly or implicitly, on studies of advanced industrialized countries. Indeed, O'Donnell's writings on bureaucratic authoritarianism, democratic transitions, and the problems facing new democracies—delegative democracy, informal institutionalization, state weakness and the (un)rule of law—all used Latin American reality to challenge some basic assumptions underlying existing theories of democracy.

Much of O'Donnell's later work focused on how state and institutional weakness shaped the character of new democracies.[1] During the early 1990s, when the literature on (formal) institutional design was taking off, O'Donnell highlighted the importance of weak (1993, 1994) and informal (1996a) institutions. These writings pointed to a key problem in the new institutionalist literature in Latin America. Many studies of democratic institutions are based on an assumption of institutional strength: that is, they assume that the rules that are written into parchment are minimally stable and regularly enforced. Although such assumptions may be appropriate for analyses of advanced industrialized democracies, they travel less well to Latin America and other developing regions. Institutions in the developing world vary widely, both in terms of their enforcement and in terms of their durability (Levitsky and Murillo 2009). This variation has important implications for how institutions work, how (and why) they are created, and how they change. Although formal institutions are not uniformly weak in developing countries (nor uniformly strong in developed ones), the vast differences in the enforcement and stability of rules in Latin America suggests that institutional strength should be treated as a variable, rather than being taken for granted.

A central insight of O'Donnell's later work, then, is that democratic politics work very differently in a weak institutional environment. By weak institutional environment, we mean a context in which (1) enforcement of the rules is low or there exists broad de facto discretion with respect to their application and (2) institutional durability is low, in that formal rules change repeatedly, rarely surviving fluctuations in power and preference distributions.[2] Because actors in such a context are often uncertain about whether rule violations will trigger sanctions, and because they are less likely to view unstable rules as legitimate or "taken for granted" (Henisz and Zellner 2005), their incentives for compliance with formal rules are weaker.[3] The result is high uncertainty and short time horizons, as actors cannot reliably use formal rules to guide their expectations about others' behavior.

Latin America is a particularly useful place to study the causes and consequences of institutional weakness. Although institutional weakness is hardly confined to Latin America, it is more common—and more extreme—in the region than in the advanced industrialized countries upon which much of the institutionalist literature is based. Moreover, one finds considerable variation in institutional strength *within* Latin America, both across countries and within national territories (O'Donnell 1993).[4] This variation in institutional strength creates opportunities for scholars to refine existing theories of institutions while broadening their comparative scope.

This chapter examines issues of institutional change in a weak institutional environment. Taking as our point of departure the pioneering work by Kathleen Thelen and her collaborators (Mahoney and Thelen 2010; Streeck and Thelen 2005; Thelen 1999, 2004), we argue that institutional change in Latin America often approximates neither punctuated equilibrium models nor the modes of gradual change described by Thelen and colleagues. Rather, institutional change often takes the form of "serial replacement," in which institutions repeatedly undergo abrupt and wholesale transformation. The chapter then examines the conditions that give rise to patterns of serial replacement. The second part of the chapter turns to the relationship between enforcement and institutional change. It argues that systematic nonenforcement can be an important source of institutional stability and that increased or reduced enforcement can itself be an important mode of institutional change.

We limit our discussion to cases in which states possess a minimum of control over the national territory (that is, where it exercises a legitimate monopoly of force in a Weberian sense). Where the state does not exist in much of the national territory (e.g., guerrilla-controlled zones in Peru in the 1980s or Colombia in the 1990s) or where the state is so weak that it fails to enforce even when governments attempt to do so (e.g., Haiti in the 2000s), it is virtually meaningless to talk about formal institutional enforcement. Our focus, then, is on cases in which the reach of the state makes enforcement possible—and uneven enforcement is thus rooted in choices made by elites, rather than the state's absence or failure.

Rethinking Institutional Change in the Advanced Industrialized Countries: From Punctuated Equilibrium to Gradual Change

Institutionalism dominated the study of comparative politics in the 1990s and into the 2000s. Whereas an initial wave of literature focused on institutional effects,[5] subsequent scholarship turned to questions of institutional origins and change (Greif and Laitin 2004; Mahoney and Thelen 2010; Pierson 2004; Streeck and Thelen 2005; Thelen 1999, 2004; Weingast 2005). The impulse to study institutional change originated within the historical institutionalist tradition. Rational choice institutionalists did not view institutional change as particularly problematic. Because rational choice approaches to institutions generally treat them as in equilibrium, they expect institutional change whenever underlying power and preference distributions change.[6] Historical institutionalists, by contrast, highlighted the "stickiness" of institutions— or the fact that many institutional arrangements persisted long after their originating power and preference distributions had changed (Steinmo, Thelen, and Longstreth 1992). Still, as Thelen observed, historical institutionalists' focus on institutional continuities limited their capacity to explain change (1999; also Thelen and Steinmo 1992). Much of the early historical institutionalist literature employed a "punctuated equilibrium" model of change, in which long periods of continuity are punctuated by periods of abrupt and far-reaching change (Krasner 1984; Pempel 1998: 1–3). These studies thus distinguished between what Swidler calls "settled" times (1986: 278), in which the rules of the game are firmly established, and "unsettled times," when the rules are up for grabs and radical change becomes possible (1986: 283). Such "discontinuous" models of change underlie many path-dependent analyses, which tend to treat periods of institutional change as "critical junctures," after which institutional arrangements were expected to "lock in" (Mahoney and Thelen 2010: 7; Streeck and Thelen 2005: 6–7).[7]

Yet, as Thelen and her collaborators show, punctuated equilibrium models fail to capture many forms of institutional change. Institutional change is often *not* abrupt and discontinuous but rather slow and gradual (Mahoney and Thelen 2010; Streeck and Thelen 2005; Thelen 2004). Mahoney and Thelen (2010) identify four modes of gradual institutional change: (1) *displacement,* or the "removal of existing rules and the introduction of new ones" (Mahoney and Thelen 2010: 15–16); (2) *layering*, or the creation of new rules alongside old ones, thereby changing the way the original rules structure behavior; (3) *drift*, in which the original rules remain intact but their impact is altered by changes in the external environment (Mahoney and Thelen 2010: 17); and (4) *conversion*, in which "rules remain formally the same but are interpreted and enacted in new ways" (Mahoney and Thelen 2010: 17–18). Although these changes may occur rapidly, Thelen and her coauthors argue that institutional change is more often a "slow-moving process" (Mahoney and Thelen 2010: 15; Streeck and Thelen 2005: 19–22). Rather than abruptly dismantling the rules, then, actors slowly subvert, build around, or redirect them.

Thelen and her coauthors are correct in asserting that institutional change is often gradual and subtle, rather than abrupt and discontinuous. However, their emphasis on gradual change is most appropriate in a strong institutional environment (such as those in most advanced industrialized democracies), in which the core rules of the game (i.e., political regime, legal system) are entrenched and actors expect that existing rules will endure and be regularly enforced. In weak institutional environments, in which actors do *not* necessarily expect existing rules to endure (and may expect them to fail), processes such as layering, drift, and conversion—in which actors seek to change behavior and outcomes while leaving the old rules formally intact—are less common. Indeed, patterns of formal institutional change are likely to resemble neither the punctuated equilibrium model nor the modes of gradual change developed by Thelen and her collaborators. Rather, they often take the form of serial replacement, in which change is both *radical and recurrent*.

A Latin American View: Serial Replacement as a Distinct Pattern of Institutional Change

Latin American reality poses challenges to both "punctuated equilibrium" models of institutional change and the models of gradual change described in the previous section. On the one hand, punctuated equilibrium models are often of limited utility, for as Kurt Weyland observes, institutional change in Latin America is "surprisingly discontinuous" (2008: 283). For example, scholars of democratization developed path-dependent arguments linking the institutional arrangements created during transitions to longer-term regime outcomes (Agüero 2000; Karl and Schmitter 1991; Munck and Leff 1997; Schmitter and Karl 1992; J. S. Valenzuela 1992). Transitions were treated as critical junctures in which the rules of the game were up for grabs, and it was assumed that the new rules would "lock in" and then shape subsequent regime trajectories (Agüero 2000; Karl 1990; Karl and Schmitter 1991; Schmitter and Karl 1992; J. S. Valenzuela 1992). Thus, Schmitter and Karl argued that conditions during transitions "would determine the initial distribution of resources among actors, and that these temporary disparities would be converted—through rules, guarantees, and roles—into enduring structures" (1992: 59). Scholars paid particular attention to the institutional prerogatives of the military, arguing that military-led transitions would result in "perverse institutionalization" and the consolidation of "tutelary democracies" (J. S. Valenzuela 1992). Thus, in countries like Brazil, Chile, and Ecuador, where militaries retained considerable power during transitions, the institutionalization of military pre-rogatives was expected to be a "major obstacle to future democratic self-transformation" (Schmitter and Karl 1992: 62–63; also Hagopian 1990; J. S. Valenzuela 1992). These predictions were off the mark, however. In most cases, the institutions created during transitions did not "lock in" but were instead quickly modified or dismantled (Hunter 1997). In Ecuador and Peru, constitutions written during transitions were replaced in the 1990s; in Brazil, many military prerogatives were stripped away within a decade; even in Chile, where institutions have historically been stable, Pinochet's "protected democracy" was largely dismantled by 2005. Thus, punctuated equilibrium models led scholars to overstate institutional continuity in new Latin American democracies.

On the other hand, institutional change in Latin America often does not approximate the gradual modes of change described by Mahoney and Thelen (2010). Rather than being infrequent and radical (i.e., punctuated equilibrium models) or ongoing and gradual, institutional change in much of Latin America is *frequent and radical*. Indeed, in some cases, the rules are overhauled with such frequency that—to use Swidler's (1986) language—they appear to be permanently "unsettled." We call this pattern serial replacement.

Examples of serial replacement abound. Take Latin American constitutions. Bolivia's first postcolonial constitution, which was drafted in 1826, lasted only five years; its successor, the 1831 constitution, lasted only three years. Constitutions were replaced again in 1834, 1839, 1843, 1851, 1861, 1868, 1871, and 1878 (Loveman 1993: 237–55). The 1880 constitution was thus Bolivia's tenth in barely half a century. Bolivia was hardly unique. In the Dominican Republic, Ecuador, Peru, and Venezuela, constitutions were replaced at least ten times during the first century of independence—a stark contrast to the US constitution, on which most Latin American charters were originally modeled (Elkins, Ginsburg, and Melton 2009: Appendix, table A.1). In some countries, these patterns have persisted in the contemporary period. For example, Ecuador changed constitutions in 1978, 1998, and 2008, and it has now done so more than twenty times in fewer than 200 years of independence (Pachano 2010).

Serial replacement can also be seen in processes of economic liberalization in the 1980s and 1990s. In the advanced industrialized countries, economic liberalization took place "incrementally, without dramatic disruptions" (Streeck and Thelen 2005: 4). Indeed, according to Streeck and Thelen, "an essential and defining characteristic of the ongoing worldwide liberalization of advanced political economies is that it evolves in the form of gradual change" (2005: 4). Welfare state institutions also evolved in a gradual manner (Pierson 1994). Even in the most radical reform cases, such as Reagan and Thatcher, "the fundamental structure of social policy remain[ed] comparatively stable" (Pierson 1994: 182). Pension systems in particular were found to be particularly "sticky," as even the most ambitious reform-minded governments were "strongly conditioned by the structure of programs already in place" (Pierson 1994: 73).

In Latin America, by contrast, economic liberalization often entailed the rapid and wholesale dismantling of economic institutions. In Argentina, Bolivia, and Peru, among other countries, governments undertook sweeping institutional reforms—including large-scale privatization and deregulation and a dramatic restructuring of trade and foreign investment regimes—of a kind that had previously been associated only with Pinochet-style dictatorships. Welfare state institutions were also radically reconfigured. In Argentina, Bolivia, El Salvador, and Peru, for example, governments dramatically overhauled pension systems, replacing pay-as-you-go systems with privatized systems. Not only were Latin American reforms more rapid and far reaching than in the advanced industrialized countries, but in many countries, new market institutions proved short-lived. In Venezuela, Argentina, Bolivia, and elsewhere, a variety of market-oriented institutions that were created during the 1980s and 1990s—including new private pension systems in Argentina and Bolivia—were dismantled in the 2000s.

Serial replacement is also evident in the area of electoral reform. Scholars of electoral systems—particularly those in advanced industrialized countries—have highlighted their stability. Arend Lijphart writes that "[o]ne of the best-known generalizations about electoral rules is that they tend to be very stable" (1994: 6), while Dieter Nohlen argued that major changes in electoral systems "are rare and arise only in extraordinary historical circumstances (1984: 218). However, as Karen Remmer observes, electoral rules in Latin America "are notable less for their 'stickiness' than for their fluidity" (2008: 7).[8] For example, Venezuela employed thirteen different electoral laws between 1958 and 1998, which meant that electoral reforms were "more frequent than elections" (Remmer 2008: 7; also Crisp and Rey 2001: 176). Likewise, Ecuador's electoral system has undergone "incessant" change since 1978: "not a single election has been carried out under the same rules as the previous election" (Pachano 2010: 80). Finally, Argentina's twenty-four provinces undertook thirty-four electoral reforms between 1983 and 2003, adopting—and discarding—a wide range of electoral systems (Calvo and Micozzi 2005). For example, ten provinces adopted the double simultaneous vote (*ley de lemas*) system between 1987 and 1991; by 2003, however, six of these provinces had eliminated the system (Calvo and Escolar 2005: 106–7).

A fourth example of serial replacement is decentralization. Decentralizing reforms are widely viewed as sticky. Many analyses of the origins of federalism treat it as a path-dependent process, in which initial center-periphery bargains prove enduring (Gibson 2004; Gibson and Falleti 2004; Ziblatt 2006). In Peru, however, decentralization has been a fluid and reversible process. Whereas Peru was a centralized state in the 1960s and 1970s, broken down into twenty-five departments with limited autonomy and no elected government, the 1979 constitution "mandated a federal-like system of regional governments" (Mauceri 2006: 51). The change was implemented in the late 1980s, when Congress hurriedly passed a law that subsumed Peru's twenty-five departments into twelve regions to be governed by elected regional assemblies and indirectly elected presidents (Levitt 2012: 62–63; McNulty 2011: 28–29). The new arrangement proved short-lived, however. Following Alberto Fujimori's 1992 presidential coup, the regional governments were dissolved and replaced by appointed Transitional Regional Administration Councils (CTAR), based on the old departments. The CTARs, in turn, were dismantled after Fujimori's fall, and in 2002, a decentralization law established a new system of twenty-five regions, to be governed by directly elected regional presidents (McNulty 2011).

Explaining Serial Replacement

What explains serial replacement—and why is it so widespread in Latin America? To a significant extent, the causes of serial replacement lie in institutional origins. Much of the literature assumes that institutions are born strong (or in equilibrium), in the sense that they are designed more or less in line with domestic power and preference distributions and with existing social and political norms. In other words, all actors initially accept the rules or lack the power to overturn them. Although institutions may subsequently experience drift or conversion, at the time of their creation, they are assumed to represent the preferences of (or a settlement among) key power holders.[9] In most established democracies, where formal rule-making authorities (e.g., executives, parliaments, courts) are fully vested with power and either represent or are able to impose rules upon powerful state and societal actors, these assumptions generally hold.

Such conditions do not always hold in Latin America, however. Historically, formal institutions in Latin America have often been "born weak," or out of equilibrium. Such stillborn or transient institutions appear to be rooted in two conditions. One is extreme uncertainty. O'Donnell and Schmitter (1986) highlighted the role of uncertainty in transitions, arguing that it heightens the importance of contingency—and agency—in institutional design. Yet uncertainty—either about the underlying rules of the game or about power and preference distributions—also increases the likelihood of miscalculation. When uncertainty is high, those in control of the rule-writing process are more likely to misjudge the preferences and/or strength of powerful actors, leaving newly designed institutions vulnerable to displacement.

A second condition that gives rise to stillborn or transient institutions is incongruence between formal rule-making processes and de facto power holders. In established democracies, powerful veto players are generally incorporated into the formal rule-making process, through political parties, legislative representation, corporatist bargaining, and legalized interest group activity (or lobbying).[10] This has not always been the case in Latin America. Although elections, political parties, legislatures, and nominally independent judiciaries have existed throughout much of the region's history, the degree of correspondence between those formal institutions and actual power distributions and decision-making centers has varied widely. In extreme cases (e.g., Somoza, Trujillo), formal democratic institutions served as little more than window dressing. In other cases—including hybrid regimes and many new democracies —their power was ambiguous and contested. Elections produced governments and legislatures whose authority to make binding rules was often constrained by informal veto players such as military, the Catholic Church, and economic elites (Karl 1995). The role of informal veto players was especially manifest where conservative forces failed to translate their de facto power into electoral strength (e.g., post-1912 Argentina; Gibson 1996), where the proscription of major parties left powerful socioeconomic actors without formal representation (e.g., Argentina between 1955 and 1973; McGuire 1997), and in hybrid or "tutelary" regimes in which militaries retained de facto veto power despite formal transitions to civilian rule (e.g., El Salvador, Honduras, Guatemala, and Panama in the 1980s; Karl 1995).

The existence of powerful informal veto players may give rise to transient institutions in two ways. First, it increases the likelihood of miscalculation: where veto players are not formally incorporated into the rule-making process, rule writers are more likely to misjudge their power and/or preferences. Second, a disjuncture between rule writers and informal power holders may create incentives for the former to design institutions aimed at weakening the latter. Although such efforts are sometimes successful, they often fail, resulting in institutional displacement.[11]

Why have levels of uncertainty and/or incongruity between rule writers and power holders been higher, historically, in Latin America than in the established industrial democracies? Several factors appear to be important.

Regime Instability

Latin America has long been characterized by regime instability. Prior to the Third Wave of democratization, many countries in the region experienced regime transitions

—between civilian and military rule or from dictatorship to dictatorship—at a rate of more than one per decade.[12] Transitions are often characterized by uncertainty regarding power distribution and actors' preferences (O'Donnell and Schmitter 1986), as well as a disjuncture between rule writers and de facto power holders. In such a context, those in temporary control of the rule-writing process (constituent assemblies, transitional or weak civilian governments) may ignore the preferences of —or misjudge the strength of—powerful veto players, leaving new institutions vulnerable to displacement.

Frequent transitions thus increase the likelihood that institutions will be born weak. Indeed, as Elkins, Ginsburg, and Melton note, Latin American history is "littered with" transitional constitutions—often written by constituent assemblies that were insufficiently representative of powerful leaders—that met an early demise because they "stood in the way of executive ambition" (2009: 73). For example, Peruvian *caudillo* Ramón Castilla seized power in 1855 in alliance with radical liberals inspired by the 1848 European revolutions (Loveman 1993: 224). A constitutional convention, which was "dominated by liberals," then produced "the most radical constitution Peru had yet seen" (Sobrevilla Perea 2010: 34–35). The new charter weakened the executive and reduced the influence of the church and the armed forces (Loveman 1993: 224–25). However, the liberal constitutional framework was "compatible neither with President Castilla's own powerful personality and charismatic leadership nor with the political power of the new social groups rising with the economic expansion of the 1850s" (Loveman 1993: 224). Castilla, who "preferred a flexible, centralist, authoritarian constitution," pushed through a new constitution in 1860 (Loveman 1993: 227). Likewise, Brazil's 1934 constitution, which was written by an elected constituent assembly—influenced by Weimar Germany—in the wake of the 1930 transition, greatly strengthened the legislative and judicial branches vis-à-vis the executive. However, Brazil's powerful president, Getulio Vargas, "chafed under the charter's restrictions" (which, among other things, would have prevented his reelection in 1938) and dissolved it in 1937, replacing it with a far less liberal constitution (Elkins, Ginsburg, and Melton 2009: 73).

Electoral Volatility

Although regime instability declined in Latin America after the 1980s, levels of electoral volatility remained high—or increased—throughout much of the region (Roberts and Wibbels 1999), often producing dramatic shifts in political power configurations from election to election. In Ecuador, Guatemala, and Peru, for example, party collapse was so extreme in the 2000s that party systems were effectively created anew at each election (Sanchez 2009).[13] Thus, parties that controlled the presidency and/

or Congress in one period virtually disappeared in the next one.[14] Electoral volatility may have two possible effects. First, like regime transitions, electoral volatility generates uncertainty about power distributions, which increases the likelihood of miscalculation. Second, rapid and dramatic shifts in power distributions make it less likely that newly created institutions will take hold. Even when actors design rules in line with underlying power distributions at T-1, a radical reconfiguration of the party system from one election to the next may leave the actors who designed the rules too weak to defend them at T-2 (effectively creating an inter-temporal incongruence between rule writers and political power holders). In such cases, the new rules may simply lack the time to take root. Whether it is due to public legitimacy, the emergence of constituencies with a vested interest in their preservation, or simple "taken for grantedness," the passage of time tends to have a stabilizing effect on institutions (Pierson 2004).[15] Hence, institutions that emerge amid rapidly changing power constellations should—all else equal—be less likely to endure.

Electoral volatility may explain the repeated reconfiguration of electoral rules in much of Latin America (Remmer 2008). If parties in power often design electoral rules in their own self-interest, then extreme volatility—in which the dominant parties repeatedly lose power to new ones—should result in frequent electoral redesign. Electoral volatility may also help explain recent constitutional fluidity in Ecuador. Ecuador's 1998 constitution was designed by established parties in consultation with indigenous groups, which had emerged as powerful actors in the 1990s (De la Torre 2010). However, before the new constitution could gain a minimum of societal legitimacy, the indigenous movement divided and weakened, and established parties were displaced by outsiders. When newly elected outsider Rafael Correa called a constituent assembly in 2007, the political forces responsible for the 1998 constitution were marginal, and pro-Correa forces—nonexistent in 1998—won a majority. Likewise, Peru's decentralization in the 1980s was passed by a legislature dominated by APRA (Alianza Popular Revolucionaria Americana or American Popular Revolutionary Alliance; Levitt 2012: 62–63; McNulty 2011: 28–29). However, APRA and other established parties were displaced in the early 1990s by outsider Alberto Fujimori. A personalistic autocrat with little organized regional-level support, Fujimori dismantled the newly elected regional governments after his 1992 coup (O'Neill 2005: 200–201). Regional governments were "not yet anchored in the conscience of the population" (Thedieck and Buller 1995: 219); thus, when Fujimori moved to recentralize, "the public did not clamor to keep the regional governments intact" (McNulty 2011: 31). Fujimori's fall from power triggered another dramatic shift in the party system, and anti-Fujimori forces, which dominated the 2001–6 legislature, passed a new decentralization law in 2002 (McNulty 2011).

Social Inequality

Most Latin American states have for decades granted full political rights to all citizens, despite the persistence of extreme socioeconomic inequality (see Brinks and Botero, in the next chapter). Yet, the coexistence of political equality and extreme socioeconomic inequality often creates a disjuncture between formal rule writers elected by politically equal citizens and powerful socioeconomic actors who are not necessarily represented as such in the formal political system. Such a disjuncture increases the likelihood that elected governments will overestimate their capacity to sustain the rules they create—or to enforce the rules without triggering a fatal attack on them. An interesting example in this regard is Chile. Chile's institutional stability during the mid-twentieth century—despite extreme inequality—may have been facilitated by a 1914 reform that sharply restricted the electorate, thereby preserving congruence between rule writers and power holders. However, the establishment of universal suffrage in the 1960s undermined this congruence, particularly after the election of Socialist president Salvador Allende (A. Valenzuela 1978). Once the economic elite lost control of the rule-writing process, it first sought to change the rules to weaken the presidency and then backed a military coup.[16]

Institutional Borrowing

Like many former colonies, Latin American states are prone to import institutions from abroad.[17] As Weyland (2007, 2008) has shown, Latin American governments routinely emulate institutional models employed by successful neighbors, often without serious regard to how those institutions align with domestic power structures or preexisting norms.[18] Incentives to borrow from abroad are often reinforced by conditionality imposed by Western governments or international financial institutions. Whether the mechanism is diffusion or conditionality, a tendency to adopt foreign institutional models exacerbates problems of incongruence between rule writers and power holders, as governments necessarily pay less attention to how those institutions correspond to domestic norms and power structures (indeed, they may adopt institutions in an effort to alter those norms and power structures). Although borrowed institutions sometimes take root, they are more likely, *ceteris paribus*, to suffer displacement. Mismatches between domestic conditions and those in the institution's country of origin have been shown to undermine institutional performance (Mukand and Rodrik 2005). An example is the diffusion of regulatory institutions (Jordana and Levi-Faur 2005). During the 1990s, Latin American governments adopted regulatory institutions in telecommunications and electricity under pressure from international

finance institutions (Henisz, Zelner, and Guillén 2005). Yet many of these new arrangements failed to take root, as a disjuncture between the adopted institutions and
local perceptions of fairness left them vulnerable to attack by local opponents during
crises (Henisz and Zelner 2005).

Rapid Institutional Design

As Anna Grzymala-Busse (2011) has argued, the pace of institutional design affects
institutional durability. When institutions are created in a slow-paced manner, actors have
time to evaluate their (often unintended) consequences, calculate how the rules affect
their interests, and organize collectively in defense of (or opposition to) the rules.
Rules that survive a slow-paced process of formation are thus more likely to enjoy
organized support and other means of institutional reproduction. By contrast, when
rules are designed quickly, actors are more likely to miscalculate their potential consequences and/or how their interests are affected, and mechanisms of reproduction
have less time to emerge (Grzymala-Busse 2011). Elkins, Ginsburg, and Melton make
a similar argument in their study of constitutional endurance, arguing that constitutions born of an "inclusive" drafting process, in which a wide range of groups are
consulted, are more likely to endure (2009: 78–81).

In Latin America, formal institutions are often created quickly, for at least two reasons. First, as O'Donnell argued in his essay on delegative democracy, institutions of

> horizontal accountability—in particular, legislative and judicial bodies—are weak
> in much of the region, such that parchment "veto players" are, in effect, paper ti-
> gers. By using decree authority or plebiscitary appeals to circumvent parties, legisla-
> tures, and other agents of horizontal accountability, executives can often undertake
> sweeping institutional reforms in little time. However, because such reforms are
> undertaken in the absence of extensive consultation or public debate, they often
> are flawed or politically unsustainable. (O'Donnell 1994: 64)

Second, the de facto weakness of institutional veto players is exacerbated in much of
Latin America by the frequency and depth of crises (O'Donnell 1993, 1994). Severe
socioeconomic or political crises—and the perceived need for quick action to restore
governability—are often used to justify executive rule by decree and sweeping reform
initiatives (or "packages") undertaken without public consultation or debate, which
undermines their sustainability (O'Donnell 1994). Argentina provides an example
of this dynamic. After taking office in a context of hyperinflation in 1989, President
Carlos Menem initiated a rapid economic liberalization process in which many of the
country's public and economic institutions—including trade and investment laws,
the public bureaucracy, and the tax, financial, and regulatory systems—were radi-

cally redesigned. Many reforms were adopted by decree or pushed through Congress quickly and with limited public debate. Just over a decade later, however, another profound socioeconomic crisis paved the way for another round of sweeping reforms—many of which reversed the reforms of the 1990s—under President Néstor Kirchner.

In sum, serial replacement is most likely where power distributions are uncertain or rapidly shifting and where greater incongruence occurs between the formal rule-writing process and underlying power structures. Uncertainty and incongruence are exacerbated by regime instability, electoral volatility, social inequality, frequent borrowing from abroad, and rapid institutional design encouraged by crises and the de facto weakness of formal institutional veto players. When powerful actors are excluded from the rule-writing process, they are likely to attack fledgling institutions early on. Consequently, new institutions are unlikely to endure long enough to gain broad public legitimacy, stabilize actors' expectations, or generate the kinds of vested interest and institution-specific investments that increase the costs of replacement.

This process of institutional failure and replacement may be self-reinforcing. As scholars such as North (1990) and Pierson (2000) have argued, institutional stability is often self-reinforcing. An initial period of institutional persistence generates expectations of stability. When actors expect institutions to endure, they are more likely to invest in them; thus, initial durability allows actors to make institution specific investments. As institutions gain legitimacy and become taken for granted, actors adapt their strategies to them rather seeking to change them. As these investments accumulate, existing institutional arrangements grow increasingly attractive relative to their alternatives, raising the cost of replacement. Institutional instability may follow a similar path-dependent logic,[19] in which an initial period of institutional failure —rooted in historically contingent circumstances—effectively locks a polity into what Helmke (2007: 28) calls an "institutional instability trap." Where institutions are repeatedly overturned, actors may develop expectations of instability (Grzymala-Busse 2011; Przeworski 1991: 82). If actors believe that institutions are unlikely to endure, they will become less invested in those institutions; indeed, they may invest in skills and technologies appropriate to a weak institutional environment (and thus develop a stake in noninstitutional politics). Finally, repeated crises may undermine public support for particular institutions, thereby lowering the cost of future attacks on them (Helmke 2007: 28). Consequently, the cost of institutional replacement remains low, which increases the likelihood of change—and reinforces expectations of institutional weakness.

Argentina followed such a path of institutional instability after 1930 (Levitsky and Murillo 2005a). Decades of regime instability had a powerful effect on actor expectations (Spiller and Tommasi 2007). Due to the frequent collapse, suspension, or purge of core regime institutions, Argentines came to expect instability. Betting that institutions would be replaced or purged with each change of government or regime, political and economic actors did not investment in them. In fact, many actors—including Peronist unions, economic elites, and conservative politicians—invested in skills, organizations, and alliances that helped them survive in a context of regime instability (Cavarozzi 1987; McGuire 1997). As a result, the cost of institutional change remained persistently low.

Enforcement and Institutional Change

Variation in enforcement and compliance is central to understanding institutional change in weak institutional environments. As Mahoney and Thelen observe, gaps between formal rules and actual compliance—a product of factors such as ambiguity in the rules, cognitive limitations, the character of underlying norms, and problems of implementation—create opportunities for contestation and serve as sources of incremental change (2010: 10–14). They suggest that the level of discretion in interpreting or enforcing the rules shapes the character of institutional change. Where actors enjoy wide discretion, change is likely to occur within the institution itself—through drift or conversion—rather than through displacement and the creation of new rules (Mahoney and Thelen 2010: 18–22).

Mahoney and Thelen (2010) focus on de jure variation in discretion over enforcement or discretion that is prescribed (or at least permitted) by the rules. Such discretion is important to understanding patterns of institutional change. Take immigration regulation in the United States. Since 1986, US immigration laws on the books have remained largely unmodified. However, this stability obscured important policy shifts, as governments varied enforcement levels depending on political conditions and the demands of their core constituencies. Strict enforcement of immigration laws imposes heavy costs on many US businesses and well-to-do households. Hence, legal restrictions on immigration in the United States were weakly enforced in the 1990s, when, in the context of a booming economy, the interests of employers prevailed. Although the subsequent growth of the undocumented population generated demand for comprehensive immigration reform, such a reform proved politically impossible, particularly in the wake of the 2008 recession (which reduced employers' demand for labor and increased public hostility to liberal immigration policies). Unable to reform the immigration laws, the Obama administration responded to increased public opposition to illegal immigration by stepping up enforcement. In 2011, under pressure from core constituencies, the government again relaxed enforcement of deportation policies. These changes were done through formal directives issued by the executive.[20] In other words, discretion over enforcement was largely de jure, or built into the rules.

In weak institutional environments, discretion over enforcement is often much wider, for it is rooted not only in the inevitable ambiguities found in the letter of the law (de jure discretion) but also in actors' ability to avoid enforcement in direct violation of the rules (de facto discretion). In much of Latin America, a weak or uneven rule of law has long enabled powerful actors to violate or ignore certain rules with impunity (Acemoglu, Johnson, and Robinson 2001; Centeno 2002; O'Donnell 1993, 1999c). Thus, even where the formal rules are relatively unambiguous, de facto discretion over enforcement yields considerable variation in terms of actual compliance. Rulers thus enjoy a broader range of options: they may enforce the rules, use de jure discretion to limit enforcement, or use de facto discretion to permit—or engage in—the outright violation of the rules.

Two examples serve to highlight the role of de facto discretion over enforcement in Latin America: civil service laws and judicial independence. All Latin American countries have civil service laws on the books mandating merit-based appointments in the public sector and restricting the executive's capacity to make patronage appointments (Echebarría 2006; Grindle 2010, 2012: 265–66). As in all countries, these civil service laws contain a range of legal loopholes and ambiguities.[21] Yet, neither formal rules nor de jure discretion tells us much about actual hiring practices in Latin American bureaucracies, for one finds "significant differences between de jure and de facto practices in the region" (Grindle 2010: 6–7). Whereas merit-based hiring systems are respected in a few countries (e.g., Brazil, and to a lesser extent, Chile and Costa Rica), in many other countries (e.g., El Salvador, Guatemala, Nicaragua, Paraguay), government authorities enjoy near-total de facto discretion in making patronage appointments (Grindle 2010: 7).

Likewise, although rules protecting judicial tenure security are fairly clear in most of Latin America, countries vary widely in terms of how well Supreme Court justices are actually protected from executive intervention (Stein et al. 2006). According to Brinks and Blass (2011), many Latin American constitutions contain "engine room attributes," or formal procedural details,[22] which serve as (often little noticed) "poison pills" that transform what are nominally independent Supreme Courts into Potemkin courts. Although such engine room attributes are sources of de jure discretion, governments in much of the region also exercise considerable de facto discretion over court appointments. In Argentina, for example, despite the existence of a US-style constitutional clause granting lifetime tenure security to Supreme Court justices, nearly every incoming president purged or packed the court between the 1940s and the mid-2000s (Helmke 2004). Indeed, scholars have found no relationship between levels of de jure and de facto independence in Latin American judiciaries (Sousa 2007).[23]

Latin American reality thus suggests the need to broaden our understanding of discretion to include both the ambiguities found within the parchment rules and actors' de facto discretion in applying those rules. De facto discretion over enforcement grants authorities with a critical degree of agency. Where such discretion exists, authorities effectively have two options when rules come under pressure from powerful actors: they may change the rules or they may cease to enforce them. In the sections below, we explore some of the theoretical and practical implications of these two strategies, showing how low enforcement can be a source of institutional stability and how varying enforcement levels can be an important—and deliberate—source of institutional change.

Low Enforcement as a Source of Institutional Stability

Nonenforcement may be a source of formal institutional stability. Enforcement and stability are often viewed as complementary. In their work on constitutional endurance, for example, Elkins et al. write that "fealty to the dictates of the constitution . . . and [constitutional] endurance are inextricably linked" (2009: 77). Yet, in some cases, institutional endurance is rooted in the *systematic absence* of such fealty. Weak enforcement lowers the stakes surrounding formal institutional outcomes, which can dampen opposition to those institutions. By softening (or eliminating) an institution's effects on informal veto players and other potential losers, weak enforcement may induce powerful actors to accept rules they would otherwise seek to overturn.

The relationship between nonenforcement and stability can be seen in the case of Mexico under the PRI (Institutional Revolutionary Party or Partido Revolucionario Institucional). Constitutionally, Mexico's postrevolutionary order was remarkably stable. The 1917 constitution was among the most enduring in Latin American history, surviving into the twenty-first century. However, constitutional clauses that threatened the vital interests of the ruling party and its allies, including free and fair elections, limits on executive power, judicial tenure security, and a variety of progressive social rights, were routinely violated. Thus, formal institutional stability in twentieth-century Mexico was rooted less in veto possibilities (PRI governments could easily change the rules) than in PRI elites' preference for nonenforcement. Had the alternative of nonenforcement not been available, demands for institutional change would have likely been more intense.

By contrast, increased enforcement of Argentine electoral institutions during the twentieth century undermined their stability. Electoral fraud had been pervasive in the 1930s as Argentine elites, like their Mexican counterparts, developed alternative power arrangements (Cantu and Saiegh 2010). However, after the activation of the popular sector by Perón weakened older patronage networks and increased monitoring, electoral fraud grew costly. The enforcement of electoral results generated stronger incentives for military intervention and the dismantling and rewriting of electoral rules, thereby generating a pattern of serial replacement that contrasted sharply with the stable-but-weakly enforced institutions observed in Mexico.

Formal rules may thus remain on the books because de facto discretion over enforcement protects powerful actors from their undesirable effects. When do actors choose to maintain the formal rules and instead invest their energy into shaping (and in many cases, preventing) enforcement? Generally, they do so when the existence of the formal institutions is perceived to generate some positive value for a domestic or international audience. For example, elites in peripheral states may deem certain institutions to be essential to gaining or maintaining international standing. Elections are a clear example. Though often marred by fraud and abuse, elections have been widely retained by autocrats as a means of retaining international support (Herman and Brodhead 1984; Karl 1986). Likewise, many governments maintain on the books (but do not rigorously enforce) child labor statutes, laws protecting the rights of women, indigenous people, or ethnic minorities, and other laws deemed critical to maintaining their standing in the international community.[24]

The maintenance of weakly or unevenly enforced institutions may also have domestic value. In postrevolutionary Mexico, for example, regular elections were viewed for decades as essential to regime legitimacy and elite cohesion. In other cases, weakly enforced laws remain on the books because governing elites deem that their removal would generate politically costly societal opposition. For example, most Latin American states have maintained laws banning abortion—in many cases, despite very limited enforcement—because removing them would trigger public opposition from the Catholic Church.

"Window dressing" institutions are often accompanied by informal rules that help guide actors' expectations in a context of low or uneven enforcement. To the extent that such informal institutions stabilize actors' expectations and lower the stakes associated with formal institutional outcomes, informal institutions may serve to reinforce or enhance the stability of the formal rules. Informal rules were widespread, for example, in postrevolutionary Mexico. PRI elites faced the problem of presidential succession in a context of regular, but de facto noncompetitive, elections (and an enforced ban on reelection). Over time, they developed an informal institution, called the *dedazo*, in which sitting presidents unilaterally chose their successor from a select pool of candidates (cabinet members) who followed a set of clear rules (e.g., abstain from campaigning, mobilizing supporters, or attacking rivals, publicly support the eventual nominee). Outgoing presidents would then retire from political life (Langston 2006). The *dedazo* shaped leadership succession in Mexico for half a century, contributing in a central way to the stability of Mexico's formal electoral regime.[25] Another example is the informal norms governing police killing. As Daniel Brinks (2006, 2008) has shown, widespread police killing of suspected criminals in parts of Brazil is rooted not only in the weak enforcement of the law but also in a set of informal norms within the law enforcement community that permits—and in some cases, encourages—such killing.

Although informal institutions are often viewed as deeply entrenched and thus slow to change, in fact, many of them collapse or change quickly when levels of formal institutional enforcement change. For example, the *dedazo* and other informal institutions in Mexico (e.g., *concertacesiones*, the "metaconstitutional" powers of the presidency), which survived for years while electoral institutions were weakly enforced, collapsed quickly in the 1990s due to heightened enforcement of those institutions (Eisenstadt 2006; Langston 2006).

Variation in Enforcement as a Source of Institutional Change

Altering the de facto level of enforcement may be an important mode of more incremental institutional change. Indeed, it may be understood as a form of institutional "conversion" (Mahoney and Thelen 2010: 17–18), in that the parchment rules remain the same but their impact changes considerably. For example, relaxed enforcement may provide an under-the-radar means of abandoning the status quo without publicly recognizing a major policy reversal.

De facto institutional change by means of reduced enforcement can be seen in the area of labor regulation in Latin America. Latin American labor laws have proven surprisingly resilient, even during the heyday of the Washington Consensus (Murillo 2005). Yet enforcement levels have varied considerably across time. As scholars such as Graciela Bensusan (2006) and Maria Lorena Cook (2007) have shown, reduced enforcement was frequently employed as a means of achieving "*de facto* labor flexibility." Throughout Latin America, governments came under pressure to "flexibilize" labor laws during the 1990s (Murillo 2005). In a few cases, such as Fujimori's Peru, this was done by formally dismantling preexisting labor codes. However, other governments—particularly those with ties to organized labor—found the political costs of labor reform to be too high (Murillo 2005). Many of these governments pursued "*de facto* flexibility" by means of reduced enforcement. For example, Mexico's Federal Labor Law has remained unchanged since the 1930s, but during the neoliberal 1990s, enforcement agencies dramatically altered the way the law was applied (Bensusan 2006). Similarly, although the Menem government made only minor reforms to Argentina's labor law, it drastically reduced resources for monitoring and enforcement of the law.[26] In Mexico and Argentina, then, the stability of labor institutions was enhanced by weak enforcement in the 1990s. Although the formal rules were relatively unambiguous, governments used their discretion over enforcement to achieve de facto labor flexibility. Rather than pursuing the more politically costly path of changing the letter of the laws, governments simply weakened their enforcement.

Institutional change may also be achieved through the enforcement or "activation" of previously dormant formal institutions.[27] An example is democratization in Mexico. Unlike many third wave transitions in Latin America, Mexico's democratization was not accompanied by constitutional change. Rather, it entailed the activation of key elements of the formally democratic—but weakly enforced—1917 constitution. Stricter enforcement of electoral rules and increased electoral competition during the 1990s put an end to de facto presidential dominance and gradually empowered Congress, state governments, and other institutions.[28] The weakening of the presidency and the strengthening of federalism brought the regime much closer to the design of the 1917 constitution. To a significant extent, then, Mexico's democratization occurred by constitutional *activation* rather than constitutional change.

The activation of previously dormant institutions is often rooted in a combination of civic and judicial activism (see Gauri and Brinks 2008; Brinks and Botero, this volume). This process can be seen in the diffusion of new social or "third generation" rights (e.g., right to health care, shelter, ethnic recognition, communal lands, and a clean environment) in Latin America in the 1990s and 2000s. As the chapter by Brinks and Botero (this volume) argues, the enforcement of new constitutional rights requires that beneficiaries have a dense infrastructure of "lateral support," including civil society groups, international NGOs, and allies in the legal system, to ensure that those rights are enforced. In the absence of such support, particularly in highly unequal societies, new rights are likely to remain "token gestures" (Brinks and Botero, this volume). Indeed, when new social rights were initially incorporated into constitution-writing processes in Argentina, Brazil, Colombia, and elsewhere, few observers expected them to be enforced (Htun 2003: 126; H. Klug 2000). (Expectations of low enforcement may have been what permitted their inclusion in the first place.) Many of these new constitutional rights did, in fact, remain window dressing (Brinks and Botero, this volume). Yet in some cases, such as Colombia and Brazil, civil society groups mobilized effectively for enforcement, using the legal system to activate the social rights written into new constitutions. On several occasions, constitutional court rulings compelled governments to implement policies aimed at enforcing these rights (Cepeda-Espinosa 2004; Gauri and Brinks 2008). For example, the Colombia's 1991 constitution grants indigenous peoples property rights over ancestral territories and, consequently, the natural resources located therein (art. 329–31). Thus, indigenous groups were given the constitutional right to be consulted over all resource exploitation projects in these territories. Initially, this right was not respected, but in 1997, the Constitutional Court compelled enforcement by ordering the suspension of an oil exploration project in the U'wa territory because the consultation requirement had not been met (Cepeda-Espinosa 2004: 623).

Another example of institutional activation is the prohibition of vote buying in Brazil. Although vote buying has been formally prohibited in Brazil for decades, these bans were rarely enforced prior to the adoption of Law 9840 in 1999 (Nichter 2011: 4–7). Under Law 9840, enforcement increased markedly: nearly 700 politicians were removed from office for vote buying between 1999 and 2010 (Nichter 2011: 7). According to Simeon Nichter (2011), civil society contributed in an important way to the unprecedented (if still partial) enforcement of Law 9840. The church-based Brazilian Commission on Justice and Peace and other civil society groups formed more than 300 "9840 Committees" to monitor local politicians and report acts of vote buying, and preliminary evidence suggests that prosecution for vote buying is more frequent where such church-based organizations are present (Nichter 2011: 19–23).

Institutional activation may also be a product of international pressure, especially in smaller, peripheral states seeking access to international assistance or markets. For example, in countries where elections and other democratic institutions were on the books but not seriously enforced during the Cold War (e.g., Dominican Republic, El Salvador, Guyana), a combination of heightened international scrutiny and a credible threat of international punitive action raised the cost of nonenforcement—thereby creating incentives for institutional activation—in the post–Cold War era (Levitsky and Way 2010). Another example is the impact of US trade agreements on the enforcement of Latin American labor laws. All but one of the eleven regional and bilateral trade agreements (RBTAs) signed between the United States and Latin American governments in the 1990s and 2000s include labor law enforcement as an explicit condition for membership.[29] A study by Murillo, Schrank, and Ronconi (2011) found that states that negotiate a trade agreement with the United States invest twice as heavily in labor inspectors as do those which do not sign trade agreements.[30] In these cases, exogenous changes in US preferences—rooted in the end of the Cold War and the rise of a labor-backed Democratic administration—encouraged not only the adoption of new institutions but also the enforcement of existing ones by shifting the preferences of domestic power holders who sought to maintain the support of key external allies.

In sum, de facto discretion over enforcement in Latin America is qualitatively different from de jure discretion over enforcement of regulations in advanced democracies. Actors exploit ambiguities in the formal rules, and, in many cases, they choose not to enforce them. This dimension of de facto variation in enforcement is critical to understanding institutional stability and change in weak institutional environments. We have argued that weak enforcement can be an important source of formal institutional stability. In a context of incongruence between rule writers and informal power holders, uneven enforcement may contribute to institutional stability by shielding powerful actors from undesired effects of the rules. We also argued that the activation/deactivation of formal rules through changes in enforcement may be a substantively important form of institutional change. In some cases, pressure from civil society or external actors may activate dormant institutions without need for legal change. In fact, the focal point provided by existing rules should make mobilization for enforcement easier to achieve than agreement over a new institutional design.

We have thus identified two distinct patterns of institutional change—serial replacement and institutional activation/deactivation—that merit study alongside the patterns of models of gradual change identified by scholars of advanced democracies.

Conclusion

This chapter has examined patterns of institutional change in a context in which the rules are unstable and/or unevenly enforced. In such an environment, institutional change often approximates neither a punctuated equilibrium model of infrequent but dramatic change nor the modes of gradual change outlined by Thelen and her collaborators. Rather, it often follows a pattern of serial replacement, characterized by repeated episodes of wholesale change. In such cases, the cost of institutional replacement for powerful actors is low. Where the cost of replacement is low, institutional stability is often rooted in the preferences, rather than the strength, of key veto players. Under some conditions, powerful opponents of an institution prefer nonenforcement to displacement. The chapter also examines how gradual change may occur in a weak institutional environment. For example, where de facto discretion over enforcement is high, decreased enforcement may yield a process of conversion in which real institutions are converted into "window dressing" ones. Alternatively, increased enforcement may "activate" previously dormant institutions.

Future research should exploit the considerable within-country variation that exists along the different dimensions of institutional strength to better understand the sources of institutional strength and weakness. Even in countries with weak institutional environments, one can find striking variation in durability and enforcement, both across institutions and over time. For example, Argentine labor laws have proven far more durable than other Argentinian institutions. Whereas the financial system, the pension system, trade and investment rules, and other social and economic institutions were dramatically reformed—often more than once—in the 1990s and 2000s, collective labor law remained untouched, despite two major attempts to reform it (Murillo 2005, 2011). Similarly, in Peru, enforcement of civil service laws and other bureaucratic rules increased markedly within the Central Bank and Finance Ministry during the 1990s and 2000s, but enforcement within other areas of the state did not

(Dargent forthcoming). Future research might also explore sources of change in patterns of institutional durability and/or enforcement. One question might be how patterns of serial replacement may be overcome. In parts of Latin America, some of the conditions that we associated with serial replacement have changed in recent years. For example, regime instability has declined markedly since the 1980s (Mainwaring and Pérez-Liñán 2005). Has stable democracy resulted in more gradual and incremental processes of institutional change? Socioeconomic inequality has also declined (albeit less dramatically) over the past decade (López-Calva and Lustig 2010). Might this change bring greater congruence between rule writers and power holders?

In the spirit of O'Donnell's search for a more effective and progressive citizenship in Latin America, we conclude by highlighting two important sources of tension in our argument. First, there may be an inherent trade-off between institutional scope and stability in weak institutional environments.[31] Institutions that are not very ambitious in their design—those that seek to affect less change—are less likely to trigger opposition from informal veto players and thus more likely to take root. By contrast, institutions that are more ambitious in their design—those that seek to affect greater change—are more likely to threaten the interests of powerful actors. Two scenarios exist in such a context. If the rules are enforced, the probability of institutional instability is high. Alternatively, limited enforcement of ambitious rules may enhance their stability. Chile's 1980 constitution is an example of a limited-scope institution—for example, it includes few social rights—that proved both enforceable and durable. Argentina's 1949 (Peronist) constitution, which "set forth a series of new guarantees regarding the worker, the aged, the family, education, and property" (Ilsley 1952: 230), is an example of an ambitious constitution that proved short-lived, whereas Mexico's 1917 constitution is an example of an ambitious constitution that endured due to low enforcement. A potential path out of this dilemma may be the activation over time of ambitious but weakly enforced institutions. As noted above, Brazil's 1988 constitution and Colombia's 1991 constitution approximate this dynamic.

Second, it is easier to create durable and effective institutions when the informal power holders are included in the rule-writing process—so that such actors have no incentive to block the enforcement of fledgling institutions or dismantle them before they take root. Thus, more effective institutions should emerge where the formal incorporation of powerful actors into the rule-writing process gives them a legal veto over rules that affect their interests. In highly unequal societies, however, such institutions may suffer from a lack of legitimacy among the majority of citizens who, their political equality notwithstanding, are not endowed with such power. In a democracy, then, politicians will be tempted to use electoral majorities to create more broadly appealing institutions that, if enforced, will be vulnerable to attack by informal veto players—which could easily generate patterns of serial replacement. The way out, perhaps, is something akin to O'Donnell and Schmitter's (1986) democratization "on the installment plan": ambitious institutional reforms that, with the help of civil society, may be activated once they have taken root. As in O'Donnell and Schmitter's (1986) work on transitions, the role of agency thus remains vital.

NOTES

Epigraph. Paz 1959, 110–111.

1. See, for example, O'Donnell 1993, 1994, 1996a, 1999c and 2010a.

2. It should be noted that rational choice approaches to institutions do not expect institutions to survive changes in power and preference distributions, as such changes undermine the equilibrium upon which the rules are based. However, rational choice accounts cannot explain why, in some contexts, institutional equilibria tend to be so ephemeral.

3. On the distinction—and relationship—between enforcement and compliance, see Levi (1988) and Bergman (2009).

4. One also finds considerable within-country variation across institutions.

5. For an excellent review, see Carey (2000).

6. Some rational choice institutionalists have explored patterns of institutional change; see in particular, Greif and Laitin (2004) and Weingast (2005).

7. On critical junctures and their relationship to path-dependent arguments, see Collier and Collier (1991).

8. Excluding democratic transitions, rules governing presidential runoffs, and rules translating votes into seats, Remmer identifies 28 "distinct [electoral] reform episodes" in Latin America between 1978 and 2002 (2008: 13).

9. Indeed, for rational choice institutionalists, rules would not be created in the absence of such equilibrium.

10. Moe (1995) describes how power holders are represented in the US Congress and use their institutional power to shape the structure of new agencies. As a result, even when they cannot prevent the creation of new institutions, they influence their powers and functioning.

11. For example, Argentina's military government attempted to prevent a Peronist electoral victory in 1973 by imposing an electoral reform that replaced the Electoral College with a presidential runoff system and established a residency requirement to keep the exiled Perón off the ballot. However, Perón ally Héctor Cámpora won, called new elections (which Perón won), and the presidential runoff system was subsequently abandoned.

12. For example, Argentina experienced five transitions to democracy or semi-democracy and six military coups between 1912 and 1983, for an average of one transition every seven years. Bolivia experienced eight transitions between 1936 and 1982, for an average of one transition every six years. Peru experienced six transitions between 1948 and 2000, for an average of one transition every eight years.

13. In Ecuador, the 2002 and 2006 presidential elections were won by political forces that did not exist in the previous election. In Guatemala, none of the top four parties in the 2007 and 2011 elections existed in 2000.

14. In Peru, for example, Alejandro Toledo's Possible Peru, which controlled the presidency

and Congress in the 2001–6 period, won just two legislative seats (down from 45) in 2006, and APRA, which controlled the presidency and Congress in the 2006–11 period, won only four seats in Congress (down from 36) in 2011.

15. Although some institutional arrangements (for example, pay-as-you-go pension systems) may develop supportive constituencies quickly, many others do not. Moreover, shifts in overall policy performance, themselves a product of high levels of economic volatility, often shape the preferences of beneficiaries.

16. The Pinochet dictatorship's constitutional, legal, and electoral reforms aimed at creating a "protected" democracy (e.g., appointed senators, military autonomy, binomial electoral system, independent central bank) may be understood as an effort to restore congruence between rule makers and power holders; indeed, the success of these efforts likely contributed to Chile's relative institutional stability between 1990 and 2010.

17. For example, close ties between the creole elite and Western Europe (and later, the United States) encouraged postcolonial elites to adopt Western-style institutions—such as US-style constitutions and presidential systems—in an effort to emulate Western political systems. Other examples include the extension of male suffrage and the adoption of Southern European–style labor regulation during the twentieth century.

18. This pattern of institutional emulation can be traced back to the early independence period, during which creole elites self-consciously sought to model their countries on the United States and Western Europe. Albert Hirschman's description of the evolution of Latin American ideologies of development is telling. He traces the evolution from Bolivar's "self-laceration" to the late nineteenth-century Argentine elite's strategy of borrowing institutional designs from the United States (Hirschman 1961: 275). For an alternative view of the causes of institutional and policy diffusion, see Simmons and Elkins (2004).

19. See also Grzymala-Busse (2011).

20. The fact that the directives were formal allowed for a degree of internal and public debate. See "US to Review Cases Seeking Deportation" (http://www.nytimes.com/2011/11/17/us/deportation-cases-of-illegal-immigrants-to-be-reviewed.html?ref=opinion); "Deportations under New US Policy Are Inconsistent" (http://www.nytimes.com/2011/11/13/us/politics/president-obamas-policy-on-deportation-is-unevenly-applied.html?ref=us). Also, see the union webpage for their opposition to the new enforcement patterns: http://www.iceunion.org/.

21. According to Grindle, the percentage of public jobs that are legally available for patronage appointments ranges from less than 2% in Argentina, Colombia, Chile, Mexico, and Peru, to 9–10% in Bolivia and Brazil, to 18% in Guatemala (2010: 5–6).

22. These include rules and procedures that cover the number of actors involved in the appointment process, the process of judicial renewal, internal voting rules (e.g., requirements for supermajorities), and the ease with which governments are able to invoke the courts.

23. Likewise, Rosenbluth and Helmke (2009) argue that justices' de jure independence is not necessarily a good predictor of their de facto independence.

24. Of course, such laws may also be kept on the books for the purposes of maintaining domestic legitimacy.

25. Likewise, the Mexican constitution created a weak executive branch, but a set of informal or "metaconstitutional" powers greatly strengthened the presidency under PRI rule (Weldon 1997).

26. The number of federal labor inspectors declined from 212 in the 1980s to just 71 in 1994

(Murillo, Schrank, and Ronconi 2011). It is interesting to note that, after 2003, when tighter labor markets and the election of a left-of-center Peronist government strengthened union bargaining power, labor law enforcement increased dramatically. The number of federal labor inspectors increased nearly sevenfold, from 71 in the mid-1990s to 475 in 2007 (Murillo et al., 2011).

27. Awapara (2010) calls these "latent" institutions.

28. Stricter enforcement was rooted in the creation of an independent electoral authority (with members selected by legislative supermajorities (Magaloni 2005), which, in turn, was a product of the PRI government's efforts to maintain international legitimacy and ward off domestic opposition mobilization.

29. For example, the US-Chile Free Trade Agreement stipulated that member countries had to enforce their own labor laws (Martin 2005: 203). Similar language was inserted into subsequent agreements with Panama, Peru, Colombia, and the so-called CAFTA countries (Costa Rica, El Salvador, Guatemala, Honduras, Nicaragua, and the Dominican Republic) (Schrank and Piore 2007). The lone exception is the North American Free Trade Agreement (NAFTA), which relegates labor standards to a controversial "side agreement" between the United States, Canada, and Mexico.

30. The study compares the ratio of labor inspectors to economically active workers in countries that negotiate a trade agreement with the United States versus those that do not.

31. In their analysis of constitutional endurance, Elkins, Ginsburg, and Melton (2009) question the relationship between scope and durability, arguing that constitutions with broad scope may endure if the constitution-making process includes a broad range of actors.

CHAPTER 10

Inequality and the Rule of Law
Ineffective Rights in Latin American Democracies

DANIEL M. BRINKS AND SANDRA BOTERO

In public discourse and academic writing, the words "democracy and the rule of law" appear inextricably linked. Nowhere is this truer than in the literature on Latin American democracies. Guillermo O'Donnell was perhaps the most insistent on the role of the law and a democratic *Rechtsstaat* in supporting democracy. Among other things, he argued that an effective democratic legal order provides the necessary underpinning for elections to be truly free and fair, and thus for democracy to exist at all (O'Donnell 2001: 17, et seq.). Mainwaring et al. also argue that the rule of law is "intrinsic to democracy" (2009: 14). O'Donnell reemphasized the centrality of the rule of law to the quality of democracy: "What is needed . . . is a truly democratic rule of law that ensures political rights, civil liberties, and mechanisms of accountability which in turn affirm the political equality of all citizens and constrain potential abuses of state power" (2004a). His last project on the meaning and practice of democracy (2010a) again places law at the center of democratic theory.

And yet, in the nearly thirty years since the latest wave of democratization swept over Latin America, many of the emerging democracies across the developing world continue to struggle to install a truly democratic rule of law (Foweraker and Krznaric 2002; Mainwaring and Welna 2003; Méndez et al. 1999; Schedler et al. 1999). Indeed, some have argued not only that recent declines in levels of democracy are substantially attributable to deficiencies in the rule of law (Diamond 1996, 1999b) but also that democratic politics has actually played a role in undermining the rule of law, at least for certain underprivileged groups (Ahnen 2007). Central to the problem is the failure to extend the benefits of crucial democratic rights, and of the law more generally, to the underprivileged (Foweraker and Krznaric 2002; Méndez et al. 1999). The question addressed in this chapter strikes at the heart of this democratic dilemma: Why have so many of the formal legal improvements that are concomitants of twenty-first-century democracy—new constitutions, better laws, improved judiciaries, more accountable security forces—failed in so many respects to produce more "democratic rule of law," especially for the underprivileged?

The answer we propose rests on the gap, in highly unequal democracies, between the extension of voting rights—essentially one person/one vote—and the distribution of social and economic resources. The main point, developed in detail below, is that many formerly marginalized populations in Latin America secured greater political participation and greater international support since the 1970s. As a result, these groups gained greater influence over legislative outcomes, which, in turn, allowed them to secure greater formal rights. But the continued socioeconomic marginalization of some of these groups made it difficult for them to first create and then engage with the structures, also described below, required to make these formal rights effective. In effect, then, they gained sufficient influence to shape the creation of a basic set of substantive legal rights that favor their interests but have consistently failed to gain sufficient influence over the creation and operation of the infraconstitutional and infralegislative structures that are necessary to make these rights a reality.

Latin American democracies have always included a range of liberal protections (Gargarella 2010). In recent years, however, they have witnessed a proliferation of formal rights for traditionally marginalized populations—the indigenous, women, the poor—but without a corresponding growth of the infrastructure required to generate compliance for all of them. The development of this dense structure of lateral support within the state and in society (ancillary rules as well as support organizations) hinges on the sustained political clout of the groups in question. In this sense, effective law and rights are a reflection and an extension of politics, not a substitute for them. There are, of course, other failures of the rule of law—the high levels of violent crime that afflict the region, for instance—but the failure of new (and some old) rights regimes is a prominent characteristic of Latin American legality today and is what we address in this chapter.

In the following sections, we first offer and defend a relatively thin definition of rule of law, in an effort to avoid some of the conceptual confusion around the term. We then use insights from the economics, sociolegal, and political science literatures on the rule of law to offer an account of this failure. Among other things, we argue that the search for the indicators and causes of a single, national level, "rule of law" is at least partially misguided, as a country's legal texture is made up of a wide diversity of normative regimes, within each of which there may be more or less rule of law. We also, however, aggregate this more granular account into an explanation for the observed cross-national variation in the rule of law. In the empirical portion of this chapter, we examine how well the theory can account for the development and success of legal regimes surrounding particular issues, specifically, women's rights, indigenous and afro-descendant land rights, and environmental protection. The analysis, based mostly on secondary sources, demonstrates that the proposed explanation accounts for both cross-national and within-country variation in the effectiveness of rights and laws more generally.

The quite uniformly negative view presented in *The Underprivileged and the (Un) Rule of Law in Latin America*, the volume coedited by Juan Méndez, Paulo Sérgio Pinheiro, and Guillermo O'Donnell (1999), is no longer completely justified. Latin America has now become a place where, in some contexts and for some people, the law effectively guides social interactions and becomes a source of both rights and responsibilities. The problem, however, is that this new rule of law regime is poorly distributed, both across countries and across social groups within countries. This chapter explores the social and political roots of that maldistribution.

Defining the Rule of Law

In order to set the conceptual foundations for this discussion, we must first clarify what we mean by the rule of law and what we hope to achieve by it. Many have noted the conceptual confusion surrounding the subject and have proposed various definitions—some "thick," some "thin," some more institutional, and some more laden with substantive requirements (see Domingo and Sieder 2001; Kleinfeld 2006; O'Donnell 2004a; A. Santos 2006; Trebilcock and Daniels 2008). We propose a thin definition that includes more than the effective application of rules by the government —what might be called rule *by* law (Holmes 2003)—but that incorporates neither specified substantive requirements nor a catalogue of institutional elements that are believed to be necessary for the rule of law to exist.

A commonly used minimal and thin conception of the rule of law borrows from Rawls: "the impartial and regular administration of rules, whatever these are" (1971: 235, quoted in Trebilcock and Daniels 2008: 20). This definition is incomplete, however, as the rule *of* law implies that law structures not only interactions between citizens and the state but also those between citizens (Magaloni 2003: 269–71). We add this second dimension to a still thin definition: the rule of law is prevalent to the extent that regulated interactions among citizens or between them and the state are structured by (that is, predictable according to) preexisting rules that have the status of law within that political system. This definition requires compliance with the law by official instances as well as substantial compliance with the law in ordinary affairs. Its only substantive requirement is that these laws be preexisting—the alternative would allow a ruler to dress up arbitrary, ad hoc, rule in legal clothing. The lack of substantive requirements in the thin definition allows us to examine various interesting questions, including, for example, whether the rule of law, regardless of the law's substantive justice, eventually leads to more democracy, or more justice, or more regard for human rights. Although the ultimate goal might be to develop, as

O'Donnell suggests, a democratic rule of law, or a more just, or a more egalitarian, or a more progressive, rule of law, this definition suits our more empirical purposes well.[1]

Given this definition, the question is this: what contributes to a regime in which interactions are structured by the relevant substantive rules? Or, to state it differently, what has to happen for a rule of behavior to "take," to produce the desired substantive effects in actual behavior? The answer has much to do with power disparities and, in particular, with inequality of resources between the nominal beneficiaries of a legal right and those on whom that right imposes a burden—disparities that are more likely and more pronounced in the context of socioeconomic inequality. The argument presented here develops this connection between inequality and rule of law and accounts for examples from different normative regimes in Latin American democracies—some that have failed to "take," thus exhibiting low levels of rule of law, and some that have taken root and produce higher levels of compliance. Levitsky and Murillo, in chapter 9 of this volume, also focus on the disparity between the distribution of power at the rule-making stage and the implementation or compliance stage. They propose a number of reasons in addition to socioeconomic inequality for the ensuing disjuncture between formal rules and outcomes, focusing largely on various political institutions. Our concern in this chapter is for those normative regimes that purport to grant rights to particular social groups, where, we believe, the role of socioeconomic inequality is particularly important.

Existing Arguments Do Not Account for Subnational Variation

Many recent arguments assume that each political system, or at least its legal component, demonstrates sufficient internal homogeneity that it could be scored as a unit. The most commonly used rule of law indicators (e.g., Kaufmann et al. 2005) produce a single value for each country. Models of the establishment of the rule of law treat this as something that has a "founding moment" for the system as a whole (Levi and Epperly 2008). Weingast (2008) goes further, arguing that developing countries (or, more precisely, "natural states," a term that is applied to the vast majority of all regimes in the world today and historically, including all developing countries) are incapable of establishing or sustaining the rule of law. In this view, the rule of law is something that should respond primarily to regime level variables: the existence of "principled principals" at the national level, in Levi and Epperly's argument, or control over the production of violence and various "threshold conditions" in Weingast's model.

But O'Donnell noticed long ago, in his "brown areas" article (O'Donnell 1993), that a country's legal texture is much more variegated than what these authors describe. It varies, as O'Donnell noted, along both geographic and functional dimensions. It is clear that we need to look at the individual and group level to understand whose rights become effective, and that this varies in response to social, geographic, and economic variables. The individual-level complement to the rule of law is what we might label *legal agency*: a relatively low probability of being denied one's rights, a relatively high probability of securing redress when those rights are violated, and the capacity to make effective and proactive use of law and legal processes when and as desired in the pursuit of all legally sanctioned life objectives.[2] Legal agency is an individual-level variable and can vary significantly within a single political system, in response to other individual-level variables such as access to lawyers, to take a simple example, or according to group level variables such as race or ethnicity. This is self-evidently true even in countries in which there is otherwise a fairly high degree of rule of law.

It becomes perhaps more apparent, when we leave the advanced industrial democracies and enter the world of weaker states. Pistor, Haldar, and Amirapu (2008) show how social norms deny the bulk of Indian women legal agency, despite relatively high scores for "rule of law" at the national level. Helfer, Alter, and Guerzovich (2009) show how the Andean countries managed to construct a "rule of law island" for intellectual property protection under the aegis of the Andean Court, despite a generalized legal weakness in other areas. Levitsky and Murillo (in this volume) discuss how powerful actors in what they call weak institutional environments have great de facto discretion over the enforcement of formal rules, which results in important variation in terms of actual compliance. As we will see below, some of the new legal regimes put in place in Latin America since the 1970s have become effective rule of law regimes (in some places) while others have not. The national-level analyses and models detailed above may tell us something interesting about necessary or threshold conditions or about national-level variables that make it easier or more difficult for individuals and groups to acquire legal agency, but they say little about the sources of subnational and individual variation.

What we need, then, is an explanation that can account for the observed variation at the individual, group, and national levels. There are valuable contributions on particular institutional elements that contribute to the rule of law, such as strong courts (Ríos-Figueroa and Taylor 2006) but rarely a consideration of the more sociopolitical bases of the rule of law. The argument we make below suggests that much of the discontinuity in the rule of law has its immediate causes further down the legal system—at the level of claimants, police, support organizations, prosecutors, and trial courts—where society meets the state. Yet studies that focus on that level often explore inequality without considering the political component. Adorno (1994, 1995), for example, reports on the extent of legal inequality in São Paulo without addressing its political construction.

Institutional economists have long been interested in the relationship between the rule of law (or some aspect of it) and economic development and carry out large-N empirical analyses to test that relationship (see, e.g., Acemoglu et al. 2001; Barro 2000; Berkowitz et al. 2003). Some argue that economic development, channeled primarily through institutional mechanisms, produces more rule of law by allowing wealthier countries to build better legal institutions, while others argue that better institutions (and the rule of law they produce) lead to wealthier countries (Kaufmann et al. 2005: 36). The causal direction of the relationship between wealth and the rule of law is difficult to disentangle. Barro (2000), like us, argues for the importance of inequality, finding higher inequality consistently and robustly associated with lower levels of the rule of law, but he does not hazard a theoretical explanation for the relationship (his primary concern is explaining economic development, not the rule of law). Others have argued that governments are more likely to respect and promote the rule of law when they are more exposed to democratic pressures (Ahnen 2007; Moreno et al. 2003; Poe and Tate 1994). The failure of the rule of law in new democracies, in this view, might be traced to the shortcomings in electoral competition characteristic of imperfect democratic governments.

The theory we have presented here accounts for the association between inequality and lower levels of rule of law that Barro (2000) notices. It also complements the argument that it is the failure of political representation that contributes to the lack of rule of law (cf. Moreno et al. 2003), but it offers an explanation for the failure that goes beyond institutional design, to its roots in socioeconomic inequality. Finally, it complements Levitsky and Murillo's argument (in chapter 9 of this volume) that a disjuncture between a group's power at the time of lawmaking and its power at the time of implementation is at the root of the problem. In our view, economic development, and the consequent state capacity to create effective lateral institutional support, is a constraining factor: development provides the resources to spend on those institutions the polity decides are important. But it is the social and economic power of the rights-bearing group that generates the incentives to devote whatever state resources there are to a particular normative regime. The incentives must come from concerted and prolonged political and legal activity on the part of those who would attain the rights promised in laws and constitutions. Our theory thus pulls all three of these insights—the role of wealth, inequality, and more democracy—into one comprehensive account.

To develop our explanation, we examine the construction of individual normative regimes within the national legal context. We define a normative regime as the complex of actors, institutions (formal and informal, including laws, social norms and other rules), and organizations that structure human activity around a particular social end. This definition is similar to the definition of regimes used in international relations theory (see, e.g., Keohane 1984; Krasner 1983). We include informal institutions and social forces, for the simple reason that the rule of law cannot rest on state action alone.

The Institutional Underpinnings of the Rule of Law

So what are the elements of a typical normative regime and how do they add up to more rule observance? A comprehensive regime will have *rules of recognition*—what Ellickson (1991) calls "constitutive rules"—that define who can make the rules and under what conditions an aspirational statement is a valid rule, *substantive rules* of behavior that specify favored or disfavored behavior, *rules defining sanctions and rewards*—what Ellickson calls "remedial rules"—and *controller selecting rules* that determine which set of controls and controllers will apply to particular behavior (we take these elements mostly from H. L. A. Hart [1961] and Ellickson [1991]). In addition to rules, of course, a regime is defined by its individual and collective actors. The actors fall into three categories: first parties (the actors on whom falls the burden of a duty), second parties (those who are meant to enjoy the benefits of that duty, sometimes referred to as rights bearers), and third parties (explained in more detail below). Many regimes will have national-level structures in common—a national police and judiciary, for example—but will have many more discrete, geographically and substantively specific, sometimes hierarchically arranged subsystems that may or may not feed into these national structures.

Critically, in addition to first- and second-party controls,[3] regimes may include three kinds of third-party controllers: governmental agencies, nongovernmental organizations, and unorganized social forces (Ellickson 1991: 130–32). The same rule, say "thou shalt not steal," may find reflection in laws, social norms, corporate rules, family rules, and religious edicts. Within each system of social control, the regime may define a separate controller—the criminal justice system might prosecute the thief, neighbors and coworkers may shun him, his boss may fire him, parents may discipline their child, and a religious leader may expel her congregant. It may be the case that each system's controller-selecting rules prescribe that an offender be turned over to another controller (the boss should call the police in addition to firing an employee) or not (parents should punish a child who takes their money, but should not call the police on her).

The normative regime surrounding the protection of property from theft thus includes a host of interrelated and mutually supportive rules, sanctions, and controllers. It might also include third-party facilitators, who provide support for first- and second-party actors in their interactions with controllers (for example, lawyers, NGOs, victim support groups, even neighbors). When the second parties are disadvantaged relative to the first parties, as we argue below, third-party facilitators may be as or more important than controllers. The crucial point here is that new legal regimes, especially if they benefit socially and economically marginalized groups, are unlikely to have this sort of layered social support and thus will rely more on self-help (second-party controls) or state structures (state-based third-party controllers) to become effective. Our example, below, of the legal regime meant to protect women from violence in Guatemala, is an example of this. A constant cycling of new institutional arrangements, as described by Levitsky and Murillo in chapter 9, may lead to institutional weakness in no small part because they have not yet been able to develop this layered underpinning of social and institutional support.

Inequality within Normative Regimes

The construction and operation of a normative regime is affected by inequality in two ways: inequality structures the interaction between first and second parties, and it also affects the capacity of second parties to build, influence, and engage with third-party (especially state-based) controllers and facilitators over the resistance of the first parties. At the level of individual normative regimes, the greater the disparity in resources between the first and second party, the less likely it is that first- and second-party controls will be effective. Neither self-restraint by the first party nor self-help by the second party is likely to operate well when the first party has a great social and economic advantage. As a result, disadvantaged second parties will have a greater need for third-party controllers and facilitators. Moreover, the greater the socioeconomic disadvantage of the second parties in a regime, the less likely they will prevail in the political struggle to build an effective infrastructure of state-based controllers and facilitators. Finally, the more marginalized the second parties, as a class, the less likely they will be to effectively build and support a non-state-based system of controllers and facilitators (such as voluntary associations, NGOs, private lobbyists and consultants, or privately hired enforcers). Under these conditions, substantive rules will remain symbolic gestures, devoid of a well-developed system of lateral support, the distance between formal rules and actual behavior will remain great, and the rule of law will remain tenuous.

Note that what is important is the difference between the capacity of the first and second parties in a normative regime to engage with the state and build what we have called lateral support. This means that, unsurprisingly, the poor are most likely to lose in many of the key normative regimes, but also that the middle class is likely to lose when confronting interests with greater access to the state, and that even the wealthy might lose in the legal arena when political power does not track economic resources. Indeed, there may be legal arenas, say the regime for regulating street vendors or property rights in informal settlements, where the relevant resources—local knowledge and information, for example—may be in the hands of the poor. This is not, then, simply a story about why the poor do poorly.

Both increased political participation and new normative ideals can contribute to bringing about changes in formal laws. Transitions to a new regime type, like (re)democratization, often come with reforms to the formal legal framework. Furthermore, even a modest increase in political power—say, the voting power of a previously marginalized group, coupled with international pressures—can also produce significant changes in formal rules of behavior in favor of that group (e.g., the adoption of an international treaty, the passage of indigenous rights legislation). However, reforms do not all go on to effectively structure interactions. Substantive rules are (relatively) cheap and can be enacted for symbolic reasons, whether to temporarily appease a domestic group or to satisfy international demands. The effectiveness of these rules rests on the subsequent development of a dense structure of lateral support composed of ancillary rules and of third-party facilitators and controllers, often but not only within the state. Substantive innovations fail to "take" when no lateral support develops for the new rule.[4]

Developing the necessary lateral support for those new rules requires much more costly and sustained political engagement than merely passing new substantive rules, especially if these rules purport to bind powerful interests, and thus meet considerable resistance. The development of and effective engagement with lateral support will largely depend on the balance of individual capabilities between the second and first parties. The outcome is not so much a function of the absolute level of capability of one or the other group but of their relative levels. When the second parties are at a social, political, and economic disadvantage relative to the first parties, we are likely to find that the legal regime is ineffective—that within this regime, at least, the rule of law is lacking.

The Effect of Inequality in a Democracy

So far, we have explained uneven institutional development and highlighted the importance of relative inequality across parties within a given regime—this, however, does not account for the proliferation of ineffective substantive norms in the first place. To understand that, we must look to further causes: socioeconomic inequality and democratization. This is because numerous but economically disadvantaged actors in a democracy have sufficient political power to produce the (relatively cheap) formal rules that favor them, through social or electoral mobilization. Crucially, however, they lack the social, economic, and political resources to develop and use a (costly) dense structure of lateral support for their rights. Their rights are thus more likely to remain token gestures that cannot overcome the resistance of traditionally dominant actors. The result is the particular failure of the rule of law that is visible in Latin American democracies today: a marked improvement in formal rights, with uneven changes in actual practices, that is, many failing (new) normative regimes.

In general, then, newly minted rights are effective when they benefit those who have the capacity to generate and make use of lateral support. Environmental rights, for example, which are largely promoted by and benefit the middle class and enjoy both international and domestic support, are noticeably successful in places like Brazil and Argentina. The poor benefit when their interests align with those of this environmentally conscious middle class; they lose when those interests are misaligned, as when informal settlements infringe on environmentally protected areas. For the less advantaged, effectively exercising some of their newly acquired rights is often a lost battle. A striking example is police violence—in spite of concerted efforts at legal reform, most police forces in the region no longer target political opponents but continue to torture and kill on a large scale in the interest of social order.[5] The key to the failure is that these violations target one of the most economically, socially, and politically disadvantaged populations in the region: young urban males, often unemployed, often black, often suspected (or guilty) of petty crimes (Brinks 2008, 2010). Almost completely lacking in political power, and thus, in state assistance, devoid of personal resources to support their rights claims, and facing police with no first-party constraints, they experience high rates of violations, committed with almost complete impunity. The exception to this rule comes not in the location that has the strongest or most modern state structures but in the locations that have the lowest levels of socioeconomic and political marginalization, where third-party controllers and facilitators are placed at the service of their claims (Brinks 2008: chap. 9).

We now have a proposed answer to the question of why so many Latin American countries are characterized by the presence of many failing legal regimes. Countries in which political, social, and economic power is more aligned are more likely to exhibit the rule of law, whether this rule of law is democratic or not. Democracies marked by high levels of economic and social inequality are less likely to exhibit the rule of law, as law-making power for the poor runs ahead of the social and economic power required to make their formal rights effective.

This fairly abstract account of the preconditions for effective rights generates four concrete predictions for the enforcement of particular rights and rights regimes:

1. Ordinarily, higher socioeconomic inequality should be associated with less lateral institutional development in support of the rights of subordinate groups.
2. As a result, at the aggregate, system-wide level, there should be lower levels of rights-effectiveness in democracies in which inequality creates a large pool of

disadvantaged potential claimants, especially in normative regimes that narrowly target this population (i.e., when they define special rights for the disadvantaged).

3. On the more positive side, when the formerly disadvantaged gain substantial political power, over time we should see the development of state-based controller and facilitator institutions helping the second parties to overcome their disadvantage and ultimately leading to more legal effectiveness.

4. A successful legal regime should develop relatively quickly, however, when a right favors groups that are either privileged or largely representative of the (politically relevant) population.

Under these conditions, we should see lateral support—either from the state or from society—mobilized on behalf of the right in question.

Evidence in Support of the Theory

In what follows we use the theory outlined above to explain variation in rights effectiveness across countries and selected legal regimes in Latin America. First, we offer a broad overview of the evolution of formal rights in the region in the wake of democratization and then apply our theoretical framework to empirical accounts of the success or failure of various normative regimes within six Latin American countries. In doing so, we shed new light on cross-national and within-country variation in the development of three legal regimes in particular: collective land rights, women's rights, and environmental law.

The cases maximize variation in the independent and outcome variables across regimes and countries. The experiences of Nicaraguan, Colombian, and Brazilian afro-descendant minorities in effectively titling their collective lands show how marginalization across the board affects groups' ability to engage the legal system and how variations in levels of political and economic power across groups in different countries impact their ability to generate a lateral support structure, thus explaining moderately successful titling rates in the Colombian case. A comparison of the Guatemalan and Argentine legal regimes protecting women from gender-based violence illustrates how stark differences in levels of socioeconomic marginalization between otherwise comparably vulnerable groups (a majority indigenous female population in Guatemala, and a politically and economically active largely middle-class female population in Argentina) result in disparately dense support structures, particularly in terms of third-party facilitators and controllers and therefore a dismal, possibly worsening, situation for women in Guatemala. Finally, we discuss evidence from a case study of Brazilian environmental law to analyze the process of development of the lateral support structure in a successful normative regime. This case study provides a longitudinal comparison of the different stages of effectiveness of this particular right, to illustrate the effects of the variation (i.e., densification) of environmentalists' lateral support structure as a result of continued political engagement.

As noted above, the argument, in its simplest form, is that a naked legal right is unlikely to be effective if not supported by a network of ancillary institutions that support claimants and impose costs on potential violators. Moreover, unequal democracies typically grant just enough power to the economically marginalized to create new substantive rules but not enough to develop more costly and complex lateral support. Specifically, the prediction is that "thin" democratization, particularly in unequal societies, should produce *less*, not more, rule of law, not because behavior deteriorates (although in some instances it might) but because legal standards improve ahead of behavior.

An Overview of the Region

A survey of legal developments in Latin America shows the disjuncture between evolving formal rights and lagging realization of those rights. Since the early 1980s, the movement toward greater democracy and political participation in the region brought greater formal recognition to the set of substantive rights typically associated with liberal democracy, as well as rights for various disadvantaged groups like the indigenous, or women. But democratizers have so far failed to carry out the much more arduous work of creating and populating the ancillary institutions that would be required to make these rights effective. The lack of rule of law in Latin America, then, is not primarily a matter of inadequate substantive legislation, but is instead characterized by the failure to comply with an increasingly well-developed legal framework. Much of the gap is attributable to raising the bar, not to lowering performance.

In the late 1970s and early 1980s, most of the region underwent a dramatic period of (re)democratization, including not only regime change but also the political inclusion of previously marginalized social groups. Notably, the wave of democratization triggered the adoption of human rights language and international human rights instruments into domestic legislation and constitutions (Elkins and Ginsburg 2010). Thus, we have the 1988 constitution of Brazil, which incorporates a great variety of rights into the formal laws of Brazil; the 1994 reform to Argentina's constitution, which gives human rights treaties quasi-constitutional status; Colombia's 1991 constitution, which highlighted social and economic rights and added a new mechanism for enforcing them and many others.

This process of formal legal democratization goes far beyond new constitutions. Many Latin American countries have enacted laws addressing torture, racial discrimination, indigenous rights, children's rights, prison conditions, and more. All the countries of the region have now ratified the Convention on the Elimination of All Forms of Discrimination against Women (CEDAW)[6] and have made various other legal changes to benefit women in politics, the workplace, and the home. Across Latin America, indigenous movements using the tools of democracy have pushed countries to add cultural and land rights to their constitution (Van Cott 2005; Yashar 1999, 2005).[7] Criminal procedure reforms have consistently increased due process protections for criminal defendants (Langer 2007), and judicial reform has paid considerable attention to access to justice issues (Domingo and Sieder 2001). Twenty years of democracy have had a noticeably democratizing, progressive impact on the written laws and constitutions of Latin America, yet the de facto world of discrimination and rights violations continues to challenge the de jure world of equal rights for all.

Developing a Legal Regime around Indigenous and Afro-Descendant Land Rights

The extension of land rights, especially collective land rights, offers just one example. Indigenous and afro-descendant groups have made great strides in transforming formal legal regimes to incorporate their demands, only to find their constitutionally and legally recognized rights unrealized in practice. Over the previous two or three decades, many Latin American countries have granted these rights, including Argentina, Brazil, Colombia, Ecuador, Nicaragua, and Mexico. They have formally recognized the rights of the indigenous and afro-descendant groups in constitutions and laws, through adoption of ILO Convention No. 169, through modification of land tenure regimes and other means (Sieder 2002). Nevertheless, these groups continue to experience the de facto denial of rights, even longstanding ones like the right to land (D. Davis 1999; Rapoport Center for Human Rights and Justice 2007, 2008). Where they butt up against other, more powerful interests, they lose, sometimes through violence (Rapoport Center for Human Rights and Justice 2007). In short, these socioeconomically marginalized groups have won formal rights but are struggling to make them work, especially where there is considerable resistance. The one exception, again, supports the argument made above: indigenous rights are more effective in Bolivia, where the indigenous have gained access to considerably more political power and state backing.

Even degrees of marginalization matter, as in most cases indigenous groups have fared better than afro-descendants in realizing land rights (Rapoport Center for Human Rights and Justice 2007). Afro-descendants struggle with smaller population sizes and less political organization and mobilization around collective rights (Hooker 2005). The afro-descendant populations making collective land claims in these countries are among the poorest and most marginalized social groups in an already unequal region. They often live in remote rural areas, as in Nicaragua, Colombia, or Brazil, or are overrepresented among the urban poor and unemployed, as in Brazil. They lack the international networks of support that have sprung up around indigenous rights. When they secure formal collective rights, it is often as an appendage to the more visible indigenous collective claims. Their rights are often defined in terms that match more closely the traditional claims of indigenous groups, requiring evidence of a separate culture, traditional occupation of land, and the like. Afro-descendant land rights are the poor cousins of collective land rights more generally.

Moreover, exercising their right to the communal ownership of lands not only pits afro-descendants against a recalcitrant state, it often confronts them with powerful economic interests. In Brazil, where the titling process is open to contestation by third parties, *quilombolas* (the afro-descendant occupants of communal settlements known as *quilombos*), often enter into unequal disputes with landowners, who have greater capacities to furnish the materials required to prove previous use or ownership of the lands or who can, at the very least, easily influence the processing of the original claim and protract it (Rapoport Center for Human Rights and Justice 2008). In Nicaragua, the Atlantic coast is the object of bitter disputes over ambitious tourist and agricultural development projects. The contested nature of the area has mobilized strong opposing interests and played a large role in the government's reticence to relinquish full tenure and control of their lands to afro-descendant communities (Goett 2004). Although the indigenous have long been accepted as "original inhabitants"—and thus associated to a degree with a normative entitlement to the land they occupy— afro-descendants have largely not been accorded such recognition, which generates even greater political resistance to crafting state-based third-party facilitators and enforcers. As a result, the latter communities have nowhere managed to secure even the limited measure of legal agency regarding their land claims that indigenous groups have.

In spite of afro-descendant marginalization, however, in the early 1990s Latin American constitutions began incorporating provisions that guaranteed these minorities the right to inhabit and title their communal lands. The Brazilian (1988), Colombian (1991), and Nicaraguan (1995) constitutions, for example, recognize the collective land property of afro-descendant communities as well as their right to a distinctive culture. To varying degrees, none of these promises have been realized. Colombia presents the moderately optimistic case, where 159 collective titles have been issued to afro-descendant communities in the Pacific Basin between 1996 and 2010 (Comisión Colombiana de Juristas 2011). In Brazil, afro-descendant groups (known as *quilombos*) must first be formally recognized by a state agency to be eligible for a communal land title. As of 2003, thirty-one communities were officially recognized and only five titles had been granted (UN Committee on the Elimination of Racial Discrimination 2003). More recent reports indicate that of the 3,550 *quilombos* currently recognized by the Brazilian government, only eighty-seven have title to their lands. Afro-descendant communities in Nicaragua (creoles and *garifunas*) have faced increasing difficulties to make good on the constitutional text, which recognizes communal forms of ownership of land in the Atlantic Coast. Since the mid-1990s, the Nicaraguan state has held on to the administrative control of the land, and only in 2002, almost a decade later, was Law 445 approved, providing a framework for the demarcation and collective titling of indigenous and afro-descendant territories.

A closer look at the legal regime surrounding the protection of collective land rights for afro-descendant populations in Latin America shows how their socioeconomic and political marginalization hampered the development and harnessing of a comprehensive normative regime and thus the effectiveness of the laws. Across the board, we find evidence of resistance by the first parties and the inability of afro-descendant groups to overcome it. The limited success of afro-descendant communities in the Colombian Pacific Coast when compared with their Brazilian and Nicaraguan counterparts underscores the point that political backing is important to develop effective state-based third-party controllers and facilitators and for the successful mobilization of the support network in displacing the preexisting normative regime, in which powerful interests could use this land at will. It is true that Colombian afro-descendants are partly the unintended beneficiaries of the development of a strong enforcement regime for all constitutional rights, which responds to a broader politics than the politics of communal land tenure (see, e.g., Bonilla Maldonado 2013; Cepeda-Espinosa 2009). But it is also true that without developing their own, more specific support structure, they might have been left out of that regime, as many others have.

After the enactment of new constitutions in Brazil and Colombia, afro-descendant NGOs and grassroots organizations participated in a long process to garner support and develop the necessary legislation that would provide a legal framework for the rights consigned in these charters (Agudelo 1999; Linhares 2004). In Colombia, the political momentum surrounding the drafting of the 1991 constitution in a popularly elected assembly brought some level of attention and political support to the claims of afro-descendants and strengthened their organizations. Law 70 of 1993 and Decree 1445 created state-coordinated mechanisms of participation (Dirección de Asuntos de Comunidades Negras, Comisión Consultiva de Alto Nivel), defined third-party controllers (mainly the Instituto Colombiano de la Reforma Agraria, and later on, INCODER), and laid out a specific titling procedure. The titling process is not without obstacles and is limited in its geographic scope, yet according to official figures, 3,475 families were issued collective titles to 127,467.40 hectares between 2006 and

2010 (Instituto Colombiano de Desarrollo Rural 2010). Beyond large-scale national third-party enforcement institutions like the Constitutional Court and so on, it is these third-party facilitators that appear to play the greatest role in making land rights effective in Colombia.

This contrasts sharply with the situation in Brazil and Nicaragua, where the domestic legislation that defines controllers, facilitators, and ancillary rules has failed to crystallize. In Brazil in particular, sharper inequality and the control of local state structures by first-party landowners facilitate the use of violence to squelch demands. Nonstate facilitators are scarce in the remote areas where the struggle is taking place, and overly bold individuals, such as Dorothy Stang, are simply murdered. The *quilombolas* in Brazil and the creoles and *garifunas* in Nicaragua did not enjoy the political backing their colleagues in Colombia had. In Brazil, efforts by *quilombola* organizers and NGOs to see the creation of regulatory policies for transitory Article 68 (which defined the constitutional right to culture and collective lands) were mostly futile for over a decade. Shifting definitions of the requirements for official recognition as a *quilombo*, repeated changes in the controller institutions, and, principally, the lack of a clear titling procedure stalled any advance toward its effective implementation (Rapoport Center for Human Rights and Justice 2008). Afro-Brazilian groups have historically faced notorious difficulties in organizing for identity-based mobilization (Fry 1999; Htun 2004).

In 2001, the World Conference on Racial Discrimination held in Durban, South Africa, marked a breaking point in the politics of racial discrimination issues in Brazil (Htun 2004). Afro-descendant groups began to organize more consciously around identity issues, gaining significant political strength and social visibility. As the government committed to specific policies to redress racial inequality, the issue of *quilombo* land titling slowly gained some relevance and political space (Linhares 2004). Only in 2003, fifteen years after the new constitution, did presidential Decree 4887 specify a titling mechanism (albeit only at the federal level) and reinstate the Instituto Nacional de Colonização e Reforma Agraria (National Institute of Colonization and Agrarian Reform, INCRA) as the principal agency in charge. These institutional developments still lack coherence and substance, however, leaving the communities without sufficient protection and assistance in their titling efforts. The lack of political backing is also notorious in Nicaragua, where the government openly opposed diagnostic studies of communal land titling disputes in the Atlantic Coast (Gordon et al. 2003) and where we find evidence of a similar lengthy lag in the development of ancillary rules, third-party controllers and facilitators, which did not come into existence until 2002 with the approval of Law 1445.

As expected, nonlaw, nonstate elements that support rights play an important role in the struggle to develop an effective normative regime. In the face of first-party resistance, which is abundant throughout the cases studied here, and given prevalent social norms marginalizing afro-descendants, the role of third-party facilitators in overcoming these hurdles and aiding in the navigation of legal labyrinths is crucial. In Colombia, the Proceso de Comunidades Negras (PCN), an NGO that spearheaded afro-Colombian mobilization efforts during the constitutional assembly, actively informed, organized, and provided aid to rural communities in the Pacific Coast with regard to the rights and procedures in Law 70 and Decree 1745. The PCN was instrumental in the titling wave under way in the first decade after 1991, providing assistance but also raising political support for the initiative. This initial burst of activity fueled local political organization processes (in the form of Juntas de Acción Comunal and, more recently, Consejos Comunitarios Locales) that have continued to struggle for land titling, even in the wake of forced displacement and violence in more recent years (Martínez Basallo 2010; Romaña Palacios et al. 2010). In Brazil and Nicaragua, meanwhile, neither clear titling procedures nor third-party facilitators emerged to assist in the compliance and enforcement process. The Brazilian experience suggests that this is exactly what hampered realization of formal rights, as *quilombo* members report that the lengthy, cumbersome, and resource-intensive seventeen-step titling procedure currently in place cannot possibly be attempted without third-party aid (Rapoport Center for Human Rights and Justice 2008).

In sum, the failed afro-descendant land-titling efforts confirm the connection between democracy and an initial burst of formal right granting, on the one hand, and socioeconomic and political marginalization and the ineffectiveness of these formal rights, on the other. The more successful regimes are marked by a gradual increase in political and economic power, slowly increasing access to state and governmental structures, leading to the gradual densification of the normative regime and the gradual realization of the right in question.

Developing a Legal Regime around Gender-Based Violence

Despite the region-wide ratification of the CEDAW throughout the eighties and the subsequent expansion of formal rights, there are wide differences in the extent to which support structures have developed nationally to help make women's rights effective. In this section we offer an overview of the development of the legal regime surrounding gender-based violence, focusing on two cases at opposite ends of the spectrum: Argentina and Guatemala. Both countries, like most other nations in Latin America, began incorporating a catalog of women's rights into their national frameworks starting in the 1980s. Today, Argentina ranks forty-ninth in the UNDP's worldwide Gender Empowerment Index (GEM), second in Latin America only to Chile (forty-fourth). This contrasts sharply to Guatemala, ranked 103rd in the GEM, where women are just as vulnerable to violence and discrimination as before ratification, if not more so. The evidence confirms that a crucial difference lies in the relatively lower levels of social and political marginalization of Argentine women when compared with their Guatemalan counterparts. Argentine women, particularly those in the middle class, have continually and increasingly organized and gained political relevance since the 1980s, developing a textured network of organizations that has made incremental but important progress toward pushing for formal rights as well as for generating and populating the institutions that raise awareness and buttress the ability of women to seek help against gender-based violence.

Since the mid-1990s, Guatemala has enacted laws meant to protect women from domestic and other forms of violence, culminating most recently with the 2008 law against "femicide," a term coined to describe the epidemic of murders of women in the country. In spite of these laws, "Guatemala remains a 'killer's paradise,' with one of the highest levels of homicide of women and one of the highest levels of impunity for violence against women in the world" (Walsh 2008: 49). In addition to the femicides, the country is experiencing extremely high levels of sexual and domestic violence, with equal or higher levels of impunity. One of the key elements in crafting this level of impunity is the failure to develop an effective normative regime, especially in the form of third-party controller and facilitator organizations that might either prevent or investigate and punish violence against women.

Walsh (2008: 51, table 1) lists many of the organizations that have been developed since the 1990s to support the normative regime. These organizations—both facilitators, such as a free legal assistance to victims of domestic violence, and controllers, like the Special Prosecutor for Women—were proposed by women fighting the violence and are the clear result of periodic mobilization by newly empowered women's groups, acting in the aftermath of the civil war and repression that had marked the 1980s. At the same time, given the ever-rising level of violence in the country, it is clear that these organizations have been largely ineffective. A much more robust system of controllers and facilitators would need to emerge to provide a truly effective response.

The weakness of the normative regime can be traced back to the disparity between a male-dominated, patriarchal culture of *machismo* and subordination of women, on the one hand, and the resources women can bring to bear on the struggle to change those norms, on the other. Indigenous women in particular (who are overrepresented among the victims of violence) are socially and economically marginalized. Fifty-one percent of indigenous women are illiterate (compared with an overall illiteracy rate of 36%), "only 17 of every 100 girls complete primary school, and in rural areas 66 per cent of them drop out of school before completing the third grade" (Montenegro 2002: 1). Women are largely excluded from holding title to land, appearing on only 27% of real property titles, despite constituting 52% of the population (ibid.). Their socioeconomic marginalization translates into limited political participation. Only ten of 113 representatives in the lower chamber of the national legislature are women; only three of 331 mayors in 2002 were women (Montenegro 2002: 2–3). They are excluded from leadership roles in mainstream political parties.

The inequality is rooted in longstanding patterns of "patriarchy and exclusion [that] persist as the bases of societal arrangements, in which values are gauged through macho and racist socio-cultural standards" (ibid: 3). Not surprisingly, women have, to some extent, internalized these social norms, further disempowering them: "The group of women organized around gender issues is very small. . . . The typical woman has accepted her circumstances" (ibid.). What there is of a women's movement in Guatemala is fragmented and divided over both strategies and goals (Walsh 2008: 52–53). One result of this is that even the third-party controller organizations that are supposed to enforce the law are populated by individuals who do not accept the normative premises of the new regime: "Guatemalan police are in the habit of not only not applying, but consistently undermining, the laws that protect women from violence" (Walsh 2008: 54). In short, existing social norms construct a powerful normatively based opposition to women's exercise of their formal rights, and women do not have the political power needed to develop the set of structures and institutions that could overcome that resistance.

Like Guatemala, Argentina has developed an increasingly rich national legal framework to protect women from gender-based violence. Aside from the CEDAW, Argentina also grants constitutional status to the Interamerican Convention to Prevent and Eradicate Violence against Women. Further, throughout the nineties, all the provinces reformed their penal law codes to include domestic violence as a felony and, since 1999, a framework for the judicialization of sexual crimes is also in place. Although the figures for gender-based violence have risen nationally in recent years, there is agreement that this rise reflects increased awareness of the topic as well as improved access of women to the legal mechanisms and the (third-party) governmental and nongovernmental instances put into place to address gender-based violence. Thus, although there is clearly still room for improvement, comparatively speaking, the mere availability of some data regarding gender-based violence sets Argentina apart from most Latin American countries, including Guatemala, where even the most basic indicators are missing.[8]

When compared with their Guatemalan counterparts, the overall greater ability of Argentine women to gain ground in making effective the laws addressing gender-based violence is directly related to their comparatively higher degree of socioeconomic and political integration and, thus, their greater ability to develop a third-party support structure. Female adult literacy rates in Argentina have risen over the years until their present 97.7%, equivalent to those of Argentine men. Although still earning less than their male counterparts, the majority of women in Argentina are comparatively well integrated into the labor market. This facilitates greater levels of political mobilization; women's collective organization, for example, has a strong history in Argentina starting with the founding of the Madres de Plaza de Mayo in 1977. This trend continued throughout the 1990s; according to Di Marco (2010), a multiplicity of women's urban and rural collective organizations emerged during this decade, which resulted in the growing visibility of working class women in the public sphere.

Coupled with the gradual increase in the number of women in legislative and management positions (according to UNDP's Human Development indicators, 23% of legislators and senior managers are female), the mobilization of middle-class women not only put the gender-equity agenda on the table but also has been able to furnish the resources necessary to create organizations that continue to demand and facilitate compliance with it. National and federal level governmental controllers (Defensoría del Pueblo and Secretaría de Derechos Humanos) as well as facilitators like the Consejo Nacional de la Mujer and Municipal Women Councils (for a list, see Birgin and Pastorino 2005: tables 1.7 and 8.11) are surrounded by a network of women's rights NGOs that provide services from legal aid and psychological counseling to awareness campaigns (for a detailed list, see Equipo Latinoamericano de Justicia y Género 2009). Women's organizations in the country have worked tirelessly to keep the topic relevant—their latest victories are the approval of a national law against gender violence in 2009 and the creation in 2008 of a state-based controller in the Office for Domestic Violence (Oficina de Violencia Doméstica) within Argentina's Supreme Court. All of these elements illustrate the gradual densification of the normative regime surrounding women's rights in Argentina.

Rights for the Middle Class: Developing a Legal Regime around Environmental Law

Similarly, some regimes have proven to be remarkably effective even in countries that are traditionally considered to have very low levels of rule of law. The example cited earlier, of an "island of rule of law" surrounding intellectual property rights in the Andean countries is indicative (Helfer et al. 2009). These authors attribute the success of this "island" not to institutional design but rather to the presence of an active and effective constituency in support of the normative regime. In Brazil—which fails abysmally to protect the basic rights of poor, urban men who fall afoul of the police (Brinks 2008)—litigation for access to medications under the right to health is surprisingly effective and widespread. As Hoffmann and Bentes (2008) argue, this is in no small part because it is promoted by middle-class concerns and possibly even the economic interests of pharmaceutical companies. The quintessentially middle-class legal regimes supporting consumer rights in places like Argentina are significantly stronger now than at any previous time in history, aided and abetted by changes in the law and also by the creation of nongovernmental consumer organizations, state-based ombudsman and prosecutorial organizations, small claims courts, and more. All these more successful regimes have the support of more affluent groups and therefore have developed a denser support structure, in line with the predictions of the model. A closer look at one of these normative regimes—the relatively successful Brazilian environmental law system—buttresses these observations.

Over the course of about forty years, environmental rights in Brazil struggled to rise above the resistance of prodevelopment forces in society and the government. In recent years, environmental laws are finally finding enforcement, under the zealous eye of federal and state prosecutors. As the political prominence of the issue rises, these laws gain ever more social acceptability. In addition, as the economy strengthens, the clout of the developmentalist forces that opposed them is reduced (Hochstetler and Keck 2007). The process has been noticeably marked by institutional developments. As environmental activists gain political power, both through organizational changes and large-scale political changes, state-based controller and facilitator organizations grow in strength. As the latter become more active, purely formal rights become more and more effective. "Making law real," say Hochstetler and Keck (2007: 226), "required a much longer—and protracted—struggle [than simply enacting formal laws], and it required state building." The following paragraph sums up much of the story, in terms strikingly consistent with the theoretical account offered above:

> Since the Brazilian military government created a tiny, three-person national secretariat to deal with environmental issues in 1973 [in response to international pressures], Brazil's formal environmental capacity has been radically transformed. The national environmental agencies themselves were reconfigured many times, gradually gaining personnel and responsibilities until they took the form of the full-fledged institutional structure that we see today. Environmental legislation was written throughout the period, by the military regime and then by its civilian successor governments. The 1988 constitution devoted a chapter to the environment; other innovations not specifically about the environment gave Brazil a powerful "fourth branch" of government in the form of the Ministério Público, empowered to defend collective rights like the right to a healthy environment in the courts and through extrajudicial agreements—even against the state. All these changes were the result of political struggles by a variety of primarily domestic actors, both state and nonstate (and sometimes both at once). . . . Environmental proponents confronted the undertow of Brazilian politics, with the powerful often above the law

and the drive to develop trumping most other aims. . . . The Ministério Público has shown surprising ability to cut through the cacophony, and it will be interesting to see whether its success in taking on the powerful eventually generates some kind of backlash. (Hochstetler and Keck 2007: 61–62)

The story begins in 1985 with largely symbolic legislation that has little effect (prompted mostly by international pressures). This legislation is followed by a gradually developing lateral support structure (promoted primarily by domestic actors) that grows to address the gap between law on the books and law in action. From 1985 to 1989, we see the gradual strengthening of the national environmental agency, a crucial third-party enforcer and facilitator, though still with very limited budgets, given the resistance of prodevelopment forces. In the 1990s, this gives way to an explosion of third-party enforcement agencies in the form of specialized prosecutorial offices, resting on the 1988 constitution. These efforts show considerable results in the case of both urban pollution and the protection of the Amazon, through increasing judicial interventions. Finally, in the 2000s, environmentalism becomes fashionable, social norms and prosecutorial action coincide, and cities sign up to boycott forbidden lumber. Whereas before the government was only spending about 34% of the funds budgeted for the environment, that figure now grows to 93%. Tellingly, the greatest weakness of the environmental rights regime continues to be in the Northeast, where large landowners still control local state third-party enforcement structures. Overall, however, this process of lateral support development culminates in a regime that actually has some constraining effect on the behavior of even the most powerful corporations and landowners.

The process was, as Hochstetler and Keck emphasize, nonlinear and subject to reversals and setbacks as well as to jumps forward. But the key to progress, when it occurred, was the continued engagement of environmental proponents with the state, the gradual building up of a network of support for the underlying substantive rules, and even the creation of social norms that support these substantive rules, thus easing the burden on state actors of monitoring compliance. The role of prosecutors and courts as third-party controllers was essential, but so was the fact that "air pollution was perceived as the neighborhood-level environmental problem" and that "people who took their cars out on forbidden days got 'gestures, words, little arguments, expressions of disdain, insistent honking'" (Hochstetler and Keck 2007: 214, quoting a 1998 survey). The growing "mainstreaming" of the movement and its supporters brought into existence a dense network of third-party enforcers and facilitators, both governmental and not, that led to a fairly successful normative regime embedded in one of the countries that has traditionally been associated with a weak rule of law.

Conclusion

Existing accounts of the establishment of the rule of law obscure the empirical variety evident in the preceding discussion. The literature has made headway in understanding how certain institutions and their increased ability to function as mechanisms of horizontal accountability can contribute to effective checks and balances, as well as how greater political participation and increased access to legal services may promote processes of societal accountability vis-à-vis the state. These accounts, however, cannot explain the pattern of failures and successes of substantive rules to effectively structure interactions among individual citizens, between different groups, and between citizens and the state. Moreover, single variable explanations that focus on, for example, the state's ability to control violence remain incomplete, as even countries like Brazil with high levels of crime (and the impunity often associated with it) protect and effectively promote certain other rights.

The cases also show that, across normative regimes and countries, understanding an individual's legal agency involves looking at the political, institutional, and structural factors that together hinder or facilitate his or her ability to engage the legal system. Political power matters to bring about changes in the formal framework, but increased electoral participation alone cannot explain subsequent compliance with and the effectiveness or failure of a particular reform. As for structural factors, our explanation confirms that socioeconomic inequality matters, as other studies have suggested. However, our model indicates, and the cases confirm, that to fully understand how and why inequality plays in we need to look at the institutions involved in a particular normative regime. The existence of nonstate controllers and facilitators (what we have called a lateral support structure) can prove essential for individuals to successfully engage the legal system, particularly so if they are socioeconomically marginalized.

In short, the greatest shortcomings in the rule of law are found in normative regimes that favor marginalized groups. These groups have managed to secure formal rights, but their social circumstances have not changed since redemocratization, impeding their ability to make their rights effective. The police target poor, unemployed shantytown residents. Women in Guatemala continue to suffer violence and discrimination—but those in Argentina, less socially and economically marginalized, have managed to make important strides in making their rights effective. Indigenous groups in Mexico, Guatemala, and elsewhere have failed to solidify their cultural and property rights—but this is less true in Bolivia, where they now have continued access to the state, through the election of a president that emerged from the indigenous movement. Afro-descendant land rights, which benefit groups with even less socioeconomic and political clout than the indigenous, lag even further behind—but afro-descendants do better in Colombia where they have slightly more influence.

In contrast, other legal regimes, including those protecting health, consumer, and environmental rights, are much more effective, at least in some countries. These regimes prosper when their proponents can support their substantive rights with substantial political capacity and socioeconomic participation. In this sense, our review of the cases also tells us something interesting about when these structures might come about. The experiences of environmental activists in Brazil, of indigenous organizers in Bolivia, of afro-Colombians, and of women's rights activists in Argentina suggest that a key condition to successfully building lateral support structures for a given group is to gain access to the state and its decision-making instances. Fleshing out these processes is a fruitful avenue for future research.

As is evident across Latin America, a shift to democracy from an oligarchic or authoritarian regime—or even a move toward broader political participation within an existing democracy—implies a reallocation of influence on the law-making process. This, in theory, severs the link between social and economic advantage and the content of laws and could, again in theory, lead to a more redistributive legal order and maybe a more democratic rule of law. This is precisely the presupposition upon which T. H. Marshall (1950a) built his argument about the progression from civil to political to social rights. To some extent, the Latin American experience turns Marshall's account on its head—not with respect to the historical sequence as others have suggested, but rather in terms of the logical progression. It is a certain basic measure of social and economic participation that is the prerequisite for the creation of truly effective regimes that can protect even civil and political rights.

It seems to be true that the expansion of political participation and the growth of civil rights over the past thirty-five years in Latin America have led to a proliferation of formal rights, many of which seek to address longstanding economic and cultural demands as well as more basic civil and political rights. But this extension of formal rights in a context marked by sharp socioeconomic inequality and marginalization has often failed to secure effective rights. On the contrary, where new formal rights seek to benefit perennially marginalized groups, traditional power holders easily resist their implementation. The result has been a region whose legality is characterized by wonderfully developed, progressive formal rights regimes that have little purchase on the everyday experience of ordinary citizens.

The effectiveness of these rights regimes depends on the development and activation of a dense system of lateral support, which includes both state and nonstate components, requires third-party controllers and facilitators, and might even demand reshaping social norms. The persistently high levels of inequality in Latin America, and the consequently "thin" political citizenship of traditionally excluded groups, has hampered the development of truly strong lateral support. And when it comes time for the poor and marginalized to exercise their rights in this weak institutional context, they face ineffectiveness at best and violence and intimidation at worst. Perfect equality between claimants and those who oppose them is not, of course, a prerequisite, or there would be no effective rights regime anywhere. But it is clear that both the development and the operation of the institutions meant to buttress a rights regime respond to the core inequalities present in society. Until those inequalities are addressed, it is unlikely that the rule of law will prevail in those normative regimes that surround the rights of the underprivileged.

NOTES

We are grateful for helpful and insightful comments by Scott Mainwaring and Marcelo Leiras, by Paola Bergallo, and by Vicky Murillo. All errors remain ours.

1. "Institutional" definitions of the rule of law retain this substantive agnosticism but typically specify a set of institutions that must be present for a state to have the rule of law (Trebilcock and Daniels 2008, citing Raz 1979: 211–14). It is immediately clear that this is not so much a definition as a prescription for what must be done if law is to fulfill its intended social coordination function. A truly "thick" definition of the rule of law, meanwhile, specifies at least some of the values that must be protected by the laws. Typically these might include human rights or broader notions of substantive justice—thus not only requiring that everyone be granted the same rights but also specifying some minimal list of rights that must be included in the system of laws (Kleinfeld 2006).

2. See O'Donnell (2001) for a parallel discussion of the connection between agency tout court (of which what we have called "legal agency" is but one component) as the individual-level complement to democracy.

3. First-party controls are those completely internal to the first party—those that manifest in self-restraint, for whatever reason, whether conscience or economic calculus. Second-party controls are self-help mechanisms exercised by the person who has suffered a violation, including, of course, force and coercion, but also moral suasion, economic incentives, withholding promised services or pay, and the like. Neither of these involves third parties.

4. Note that this goes beyond Epp's (1998) argument about the support structure required for a "rights revolution" in at least two ways. First, his "support structure" focuses exclusively on the role that rights advocacy lawyers, legal organizations and resources play in generating changes through litigation. In contrast, our notion of lateral support encompasses organizations and institutions in and outside of the state. Moreover, his theory is based on the resources needed to effectively mount a litigation campaign, while we focus on the key role of what we have called lateral support in the actual effectiveness of legal rights (including voluntary compliance by government and private actors), not just the success of litigation.

5. From 1990 to the end of 2000, for example, the police in the state of São Paulo killed more than 7,500 people in the name of public safety. While São Paulo's vast population produces truly striking numbers of victims, this city is not alone in relying on deadly violence as a means of crime

control. The per capita rate in Salvador de Bahia in the mid-nineties, more than six per hundred thousand, was nearly three times higher than the three worst years of that decade in São Paulo. Buenos Aires, in the second half of the decade, averaged a per capita rate of police homicides (almost two per hundred thousand) that was just as high as São Paulo's for that same period (Brinks 2008). The level of impunity for these violations is as striking as their number (Brinks 2010).

6. See the list of states parties to the Convention, at http://treaties.un.org/Pages/ViewDetails .aspx?src=TREATY&mtdsg_no=IV-8&chapter=4&lang=en.

7. See also Assies et al. (2000) for a discussion of the multiplicity of pressures that led to these constitutional transformations.

8. For data and a discussion of the federal legislation, see Birgin and Pastorino (2005).

CHAPTER 11

Unpacking Delegative Democracy

Digging into the Empirical Content
of a Rich Theoretical Concept

LUCAS GONZÁLEZ

In his work on delegative democracies, Guillermo O'Donnell appealed for more "empirical research, as well as more refined analytical work" on the "new species" he depicted (O'Donnell 1994: 55). This is what I intend to do in this chapter: first, I provide an empirical classification of some Latin American cases based on the different dimensions in O'Donnell's definition of delegative democracies.[1] In this descriptive section, I observe cross-case variation between delegative and representative democracies (something O'Donnell obviously recognized) but also variation inside each of the two groups. Even more important, there is also within-case variation over time: in some countries, there has been a continuous erosion of their representative democracies. Others have been going through a gradual but steady "second transition" to a more representative democracy. In a third group of cases, there has been an oscillating trend, or "recurring delegativeness." Second, I explore some possible causes of this variation by identifying the main conditions under which delegative democracies are more likely to occur and why delegative democracies are enduring and recurrent in some countries, while not in others.

The chapter is structured as follows: In the first section, and after reviewing the research and justifying the main contribution of this work to the empirical literature on the topic, I present O'Donnell's definition of delegative democracy and the discussions over the concept. Based on the main dimensions in the definition, I classify cases and analyze the empirical data. In the second part, I review the theoretical argument on the origins of delegative democracies and the conditions that could explain variation among them and representative democracies. I empirically assess some of these propositions, relying on a quantitative analysis (descriptive statistics and linear and ordinal logistic regression analysis) and explore whether some specific structural, cultural, and politico-institutional factors in the theoretical argument may account for some of the variation across and within cases. O'Donnell contended that tools in political science cannot be an end in itself. As such, they shall be used to help developing or complementing a theory. He developed the theory; here, I use some simple tools to analyze the empirical content of his work and (hopefully) contribute to more debate on the topic.

In this chapter I show that, under conditions of economic growth, low inflation, and large public support for democracy, Latin American countries are more likely to be representative than delegative democracies. When structural conditions deteriorate and public confidence diminishes, the probability of having a delegative democracy increases dramatically. Empirical results also demonstrate that there is a quadratic relationship between partisan polarization and volatility and the odds of a country being a delegative democracy. I review the main findings and their limitations and highlight some questions that could be addressed in a future research agenda in the conclusion.

State of Research

O'Donnell's concept of delegative democracy generated stimulating debates, both theoretical and empirical (something the author himself demanded). In the theoretical realm, some of the discussions explored the connections between delegative democracies and the literature on transition from authoritarian rule and democratic consolidation or quality of democracy (Diamond 1997: 16; O'Donnell 1996a). Other studies delved into the similarities and differences with other concepts, such as populism,[2] *"decisionismo"* (Quiroga 2011), and presidential leadership (Ollier 2011), or elaborated on the theoretical consequences of delegation on accountability and representation (Quiroga 2011; Stokes 1999). Despite the important contributions at the theoretical level, part of this literature developed weak connections and exchanges with empirical studies on the abovementioned concepts. This chapter works on the links between these fields.

The empirical research agenda on delegative democracy can be divided into several areas, broadly defined out of the different features of the concept being studied. One of them concentrated on the role of presidential power and executive-legislative relations in weakly institutionalized democracies, particularly in Latin America.[3] Another large body of research focused its efforts on a different attribute of delegative democracies: the weaknesses of control institutions and accountability in its horizontal and societal versions.[4] A third group studied informal institutions (Helmke and Levitsky 2006a; Levitsky and Murillo 2009) and a fourth, the specific characteristics of their policy-making process, especially policy switches, and their implications over broader discussions on accountability and representation (Stokes 1999).

Some empirical work has been conducted in the format of case studies, but most of these works have studied specific dimensions of the concept in a particular case,[5] without considering all of them together or in a broad comparative way. International organizations, such as the United Nations Development Programme (UNDP), or think tanks, such as Freedom House, Polity, or Estado de la Nación, developed comparative analysis by regularly presenting descriptive diagnoses on the functioning of democracies either globally (Freedom House, Polity) or in Latin America (UNDP 2004).[6] These studies take different definitions of democracy (see Collier and Levitsky [1997] and Munck and Verkuilen [2002] for excellent reviews and critiques on these measures), but none of them specifically focuses on delegative democracy.[7]

These research agendas have significantly advanced our theoretical and empirical knowledge on democracy in Latin America and beyond. Despite the large and productive discussions generated, there is no systematic empirical comparative work, at least to the best of my knowledge, focused specifically on the concept of delegative democracy or large-*N* empirical study to account for some of the observed features across cases.

Unpacking Delegative Democracy (Its Definition and a Preliminary Classification)

In his well-known work on delegative democracies, O'Donnell introduces a conceptual framework to analyze a "new species," a new type of democracy (O'Donnell 1994: 55). Delegative democracies meet Dahl's (1971) criteria for the definition of polyarchy, yet they are neither representative nor consolidated (i.e., institutionalized) democracies, because they maintain serious deficits in the mechanisms of horizontal accountability (O'Donnell et al. 2011: 10). Besides, these democracies are also characterized by informal institutional practices related to the exercise of power: "Delegative democracies rest on the premise that whoever wins the election to the presidency is thereby entitled to govern as he or she sees fit, constrained only by the hard facts of existing power relations and by a constitutionally limited term of office" (O'Donnell 1994: 59). As a result of these practices, delegative democracies have not yet transitioned "from a democratically elected *government* to an institutionalized, consolidated democratic *regime*" (O'Donnell 1994: 56).

O'Donnell presents a definition that is a full instance of the root definition of polyarchy, but at the same time he provides useful conceptual differentiation and fine-grained distinction by identifying the key attributes of the subtype (Collier and Levitsky 1997: 435). Based on O'Donnell's (1994: 60–62 and 2011: 21–23) characterization, I specify the main features or attributes that define the subtype delegative democracy (and use these features to classify cases across the region in the next section). These attributes are:

- The president is taken to be the embodiment of the nation, custodian, and definer of its interests;

- The policies of his government need bear no resemblance to the promises of his campaign;
- The president's political base is a political movement; the president presents herself as above both political parties and organized interests;
- Other institutions, such as courts and legislatures, are considered impediments to the exercise of power;
- The exercise of power is noninstitutionalized;
- The president nominates isolated and shielded *técnicos* to office;
- There is extremely weak or nonexistent horizontal accountability; and
- There is swift policy making (and a higher likelihood of gross mistakes, hazardous implementation, and the president taking responsibility for the outcome).

In contrast, the main features that characterize representative democracies are a series of constitutional restrictions and historically embedded practices to institutionalize the exercise of power, strong horizontal accountability, an institutionalized legislature, slow and incremental decision making, a decisive coalition of broadly supported political leaders who take great care in creating and strengthening democratic political institutions, and a clear distinction between the public and private interests of office holders (O'Donnell 1994: 56, 61–64).

Based on the previous definition, I categorize countries in the region as delegative or representative democracies. I classify each country from 1980 or from its transition to democracy if that occurred later, until the last year for which we have access to data (2010). First, I follow O'Donnell's own classification in his 1994 piece: Argentina, Brazil, Bolivia, Ecuador, and Peru are delegative democracies (56); Chile and Uruguay are classified as representative democracies (56, 63–64).

O'Donnell's work on delegative democracy is, above all, theoretical. Its immense strength in this realm (that can be measured by the amount of discussion it generated in the literature) rivals with the enormous empirical challenges it left. I find some of these challenges in this initial classification. One of them is that it does not explicitly incorporate a dynamic component into it: democratic regimes are either delegative or representative, and it is not clear whether this situation can change over time.[8] However, we *can* see some changes during the period of analysis in the main defining features of delegative democracies. Brazil is a case in point. O'Donnell classified Brazil into the first group. At the time he wrote the article, this country was under the presidency of Fernando Collor de Mello, the epitome of this new species (we can roughly say the same about the previous presidency of José Sarney). However, some features of this delegative democracy began to change during Itamar Franco (for instance, the interim president worked along with congress instead of bypassing it as Collor did).[9] Arguably, some of these trends continued during Fernando Henrique

TABLE II.I.
Attributes of delegative democracies (averages of country experts' codings, 1980–2010)

Year	Argentina	Bolivia	Brazil	Chile	Colombia	Ecuador	Mexico	Paraguay	Peru	Uruguay	Venezuela
1980					5	4	3				1
1981					5	4	3		3		1
1982					2	4	3		3		1
1983	1	1			0	4	2		3		1
1984	1	1			0	4	2		3		3
1985	2	1	6		2	5	2		3	0	3
1986	2	4	6		5	5	2		5	0	3
1987	1	4	6		0	5	2		5	0	3
1988	1	4	6		0	5	2		5	0	3
1989	1	4	6		1	1	3		5	0	5
1990	8	2	8	1	4	1	3		5	0	5
1991	8	2	8	1	1	1	3		8	0	5
1992	8	2	8	1	0	1	3		8	0	5
1993	8	2	2	1	0	3	3		8	0	1
1994	8	2	2	1	1	3	3	4	8	0	2
1995	8	2	4	1	5	3	3	4	8	0	2
1996	7	2	4	1	4	7	3	4	7	0	5
1997	7	2	3	1	5	2	3	4	7	0	5
1998	6	2	3	1	5	2	3	4	6	0	5
1999	6	2	2	1	2	4	3	3	6	0	8
2000	1	2	2	0	1	2	3	3	6	0	8
2001	3	2	2	0	3	2	1	3	2	0	8
2002	5	0	2	0	4	2	1	3	3	0	8
2003	7	2	1	0	1	8	1	3	3	0	8
2004	7	0	1	0	1	8	1	7	3	0	8
2005	7	0	1	0	3	3	1	7	3	0	8
2006	7	6	1	1	4	3	1	6	3	0	8
2007	7	6	1	1	5	7	2	6	3	0	8
2008	7	6	1	1	4	7	2	6	3	0	8
2009	6	6	1	1	6	7	2	6	3	0	8
2010	8	6	1	1	6	7	2	6	3	0	8

Cardoso, and many of them were reinforced during Luiz Inácio Lula da Silva and more recently with Dilma Rousseff.[10] Venezuela is another case in which there has also been variation over time. One could probably classify it as a relatively institutionalized democracy from 1959 until 1999 (despite all the problems this democracy had at the time), but it looks more like a delegative democracy after that.[11]

Another problem is how to classify cases that do not clearly belong to one group or the other. In other words, it is not clear where the cut point between the two categories, delegative and representative democracy, should be. Nor is it clear what the boundary is between a delegative democracy and an authoritarian regime. This may be a problem as we intend to classify other cases in the region or outside it (such as postcommunist countries, an option O'Donnell considered possible). Mexico, for instance, is a case in point. To begin with, some of the basic elements in Dahl's definition of polyarchy were seriously questioned during most years of PRI rule, especially until 1994.[12] Therefore, I decided to code it since this year and not before it. Moreover, in the post-1994 classification, several of the features in the definition of delegative democracy are present (e.g., noninstitutionalized exercise of power or isolated and shielded *técnicos* during some periods), but others are not (such as a political movement being the presidents' political base or the weakness of congress in some periods).

Based on these impressions, I try to incorporate a dynamic component into the initial classification: with the help of several country specialists,[13] I classify each president-year in eleven cases (Argentina, Brazil, Bolivia, Chile, Colombia, Ecuador, Mexico, Paraguay, Peru, Uruguay, and Venezuela) in all of the main dimensions that define delegative democracies according to O'Donnell. With this classification, one country can be either a delegative or representative democracy depending on the category it fits at a moment in time, but then change in some of its dimensions in another (as happened in Brazil or Venezuela). Table 11.1 reports averages of the final country experts' codings.[14]

As the values taken in each dimension add up to each of the two categories (delegative or representative), we can also incorporate a cut point for each of the two. Each of the dimensions of delegative democracies is coded 1 if it is present in the country in a given year, 0 otherwise; all the values add up to an index of "delegativeness," divided in eight categories[15] that range from 0 (full representative democracy) to 8 (full delegative democracy; i.e., all the dimensions in the definition of delegative democracy are present in the country in a year; table 11.1). I run a test of internal consistency to estimate the reliability of the index. The value of Cronbach's alpha is 0.87, indicating high internal consistency across the eight items in the index and that this set of items measures a single unidimensional latent construct.

Results indicate some variation over time, particularly in the group O'Donnell

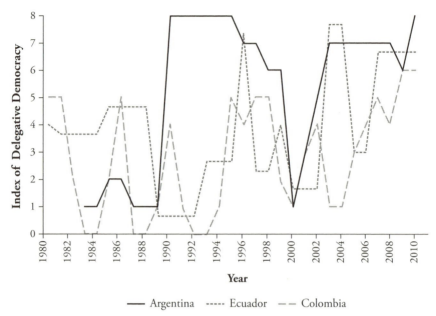

Figure 11.1. Recurring delegative democracies (1980–2010)

classified as delegative democracies. I distinguish different tendencies that I cluster into four different categories: recurrent (or cyclical) delegative democracies, eroding delegative democracies, intensifying delegative democracies, and stable representative democracies.[16] Using this classification, I analyze their final or average scores as well as the tendencies the cases show over time. The first three categories reveal significant variation inside the delegative group.

I examine recurrent delegative democracies first. I include Argentina, Ecuador, and Colombia in this group. The average index for Argentina is the highest for the cases and years covered in the study (5.5 out of a maximum of 8) with a high standard deviation (2.8), indicating substantial variation across time as a result of a cyclical trend.[17] The classification for Ecuador reveals a similar trend, although with lower average results (the average of the overall index is 3.8; the standard deviation is 2.2). Colombia, despite not being classified as a delegative democracy in the initial coding, alternates periods in the delegative and the representative camps (and that is the reason why I classified it as "recurrent"). The average value is relatively low and in the representative camp (2.7), but with a relatively high standard deviation (2.1) that reflects the cycles across time (figure 11.1).[18]

I include Brazil and Peru in the group of eroding delegative democracies. The average index for Peru is 4.6 with a standard deviation of 2.1, indicating also varia-

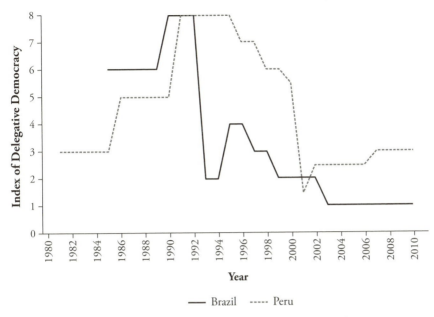

Figure 11.2. Eroding delegative democracies (1980–2010).

tion over time but with a different trend than in the previous group: during the early years of Alberto Fujimori, the index was at its highest (8).[19] But scores decreased since then[20] to enter a period with low average values in the index. Brazil, despite being categorized as a delegative democracy in O'Donnell's first classification, reveals a smaller average value than all the previous cases (except Colombia) and a similar trend than Peru. The average index is relatively low (3.4), but with a large standard deviation (2.5). From the 1985 transition to Collor's impeachment, this case was clearly a delegative democracy: the values for the index range from 5 during Sarney's presidency to 8 during Collor's. But these values decreased dramatically after that (figure 11.2).[21]

Venezuela, Bolivia, and Paraguay are intensifying delegative democracies. Venezuela was classified as a representative democracy at the beginning of the period under study, during Luis Herrera Campins's term in office (who scored 1) or during Jaime Lusinchi's (3), but moved progressively into the delegative camp.[22] It finally entered into a clear delegative phase with Hugo Chávez, who scores the highest value in the index. It is interesting to note that Venezuela has a relatively high average value for the index over the period (5), with a high standard deviation (2.7).[23] Paraguay has a midrange average value (4.4) and a relatively low standard deviation (1.4), with the highest values at the end of the period under analysis, during the presidencies of Du-

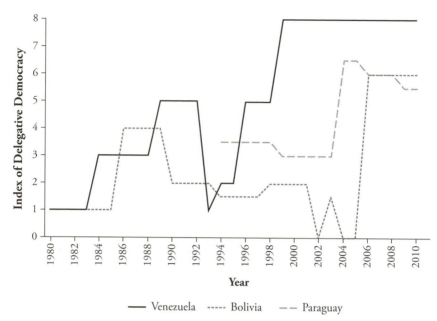

Figure 11.3. Intensifying delegative democracies (1980–2010).

arte Frutos (7 during the first two years in office) and Fernando Lugo (6). Bolivia has even lower average values: the index for the entire period is 2.6, in the representative camp rather than in the delegative, with a relatively high standard deviation (of almost 2). But the trend is similar to the one in the previous two cases: values are at their highest at the end of the period under study (6 during Evo Morales's government; figure 11.3).

Chile and Uruguay are stable representative democracies. There is very little variation inside this more institutionalized group. Chile scored 1 during the terms of Aylwin, Frei, and Bachelet because shielded *técnicos* were present during these governments. The average index and the standard deviation are very low (0.6 and 0.4). In Uruguay, there are no changes over time: all the country specialists coding this country agreed that none of the dimensions of delegative democracy have been present in this case since 1985 (figure 11.4).

Some cases do not clearly fit into any of the categories or tendencies and are difficult to classify; Mexico is clearly one of them. Its overall index is much larger than the previous two cases but relatively low compared with the rest (2.1), with a low standard deviation (0.9) indicating a steadier trend than in the other categories (figure 11.4).

Remarkably, the average index for the eleven cases in the region for the 30 years under study (1980–2010, without considering the years of authoritarian rule) is relatively low (3.1), or in the "very weakly representative" category.[24] The average standard

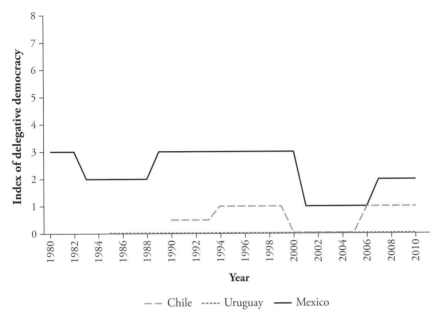

Figure 11.4. Stable representative democracies and Mexico (1980–2010).

deviation, though, is relatively high (2.6), revealing substantial variation among cases and across time, particularly in the delegative group, that we see in the previous analysis of each case.

The results of this classification effort may contribute to the empirical study and better understanding of delegative democracies in the region and even beyond it. In this sense, we can use the index and the classification to measure delegativeness in postcommunist countries (something O'Donnell himself encouraged) and even other institutionalized democracies in which some of these dimensions may be present (such as the United States, especially during the George W. Bush era, or nowadays in some European countries where shielded *técnicos* are in office, swift policy making seems to be widespread, and horizontal accountability may be imperiled). We could probably see that the concept of delegative democracy (or some of its specific dimensions) does not necessarily relate only to a circumscribed geographical area. Furthermore, this short (and somewhat sketchy) analysis can be useful to examine together all the dimensions that the literature tended to study separately.[25] This is precisely one of the main strengths in the concept of delegative democracy: the capacity to integrate all these dimensions into a unique theoretical framework.

The previous classification effort also serves one of the main purposes of this chapter: to highlight that delegative democracies vary and to have more precision about this fact. There is cross-case variation between delegative and representative democracies and inside each of these two groups. For instance, there are clear differences among delegative democracies, between the most delegative cases (such as Argentina and Venezuela) and others less delegative (such as Peru, Bolivia, and Brazil). But even more important, there is also variation over time within cases: the index increased over time in some countries (Venezuela and Bolivia), declined in others (Brazil and Peru), and revealed an oscillating trend and "recurring delegativeness" in a third set of cases (Argentina and Ecuador).

What explains these variations among cases? Why are delegative democracies enduring and recurrent in some countries, while not in others? What accounts for the progressive decline in delegativeness in some cases? In the next section, I put forward O'Donnell's argument to explain the emergence of delegative democracies and the recurring trends in some of these cases. In doing so, I try to identify some of the main factors in the theoretical argument that may account for some variation across cases.

The Emergence of Delegative Democracies

In this section, I analyze the main conditions under which delegative democracies emerged.[26] To begin with, O'Donnell claims this is not a recent process. He stresses that the plebiscitary tendencies of delegative democracies were detectable in most Latin American countries long before the present and that they have been studied under the guise of authoritarianism, caesarism, bonapartism, caudillismo, or populism. It is not the aim of this chapter to enter into the theoretical discussion or the historical details to differentiate these concepts (for a theoretical discussion on the topic, see Collier and Levitsky [1997] and Diamond [1997]) but rather to assess the main factors that contribute to the emergence of delegative democracies.

O'Donnell also underscores the relevance of previous democratic experiences. "Delegative democracy is not alien to the democratic tradition" (O'Donnell 1994: 60).[27] These legacies and their long-lasting influence can be studied using a historical comparative analysis or in-depth within-case studies (relying, for instance, on some tools such as process tracing or path-dependency analysis). I rely on a different methodological approach to empirically assess whether some of the factors leading to the outcome in the theoretical argument are relevant across cases and years and, if so, how much.

When talking about the emergence of delegative democracy, O'Donnell mainly refers to the experience of some specific countries after their transitions to democracy. Being loyal to his epistemological tradition, he presented a theoretically bounded argument. Bearing this in mind, a crucial feature that recurrently appears in his theoretical account is the economic crisis. The emergence of delegative democracies is very much linked to "the depth of the crisis that these countries inherited from their respective authoritarian regimes" (O'Donnell 1994: 65).[28] By economic crisis, the author means high inflation, economic stagnation, financial crisis of the state, huge foreign and domestic public debt, increased inequality, and deterioration in welfare provisions (O'Donnell 1994: 63).[29]

Other elements in the theoretical claim that explain the emergence of delegative democracies are linked to the abovementioned crises: a strong sense of urgency in the population (O'Donnell 1994: 65), low confidence in government, and low prestige of all parties and politicians that translate into demands for urgent action and delegation in the person of the president (O'Donnell 1994: 65).

I cluster these claims into a structural and cultural component and, based on them, I formulate the first set of hypotheses: delegative democracies are more likely to *emerge* when economic crises are deeper (structural component) and confidence in government, parties, and politicians is lower (cultural component). I further specify these hypotheses below.

Explaining "Delegativeness"? Stability and Change in Delegative Democracies

Can we explain why there is a recurring cycle of delegation in some democracies? And more generally, can we account for changes in the delegative democracy index? O'Donnell had a clear theoretical argument on the conditions for the emergence of delegative democracies after transitions to democracy. What he called the "cycle of crisis" can explain recurring trends in some delegative cases: for him, the logic of delegation means that the executive does nothing to strengthen other institutions, placing enormous responsibility on the president. In a context of crisis, the fate of his government depends on policies that entail substantial costs for many parts of the population. Policy making under conditions of despair can result in this shift from governmental omnipotence (during the enactment of stabilization packages) to impotence, when failures accumulate. Under those conditions, a new cycle of crisis, delegation, and concentration of power will take place (O'Donnell 1994: 66–67). This part of the argument does not appear to be historically bounded to transitions from authoritarian rule (although it describes some trends after the implementation of stabilization packages in the cases he selected) and seems to have more extension (in Sartori's [1970] terms): weakly institutionalized democracies may suffer from "recurrent cycles" of crises and delegation.

It is very difficult, if not impossible, to evaluate the relevance of some other factors in the argument using the methodological approach I chose.[30] The role of economic crisis or individual perceptions about political institutions and politicians can be empirically assessed using quantitative tools and the data we have available. I focus on these variables, recognizing the limitations in the approach and the relevance of the missing conditions in the argument. Hence, we could expect a cycle of delegation to begin when economic crises are deep (or recurrent; this is the economic component) and confidence in government, parties, and politicians (or confidence in democracy as a whole) is low (or drops drastically; this is the cultural component).

I am not trying to empirically evaluate O'Donnell's argument since he did not attempt to explain variation across cases; rather, I am pushing it forward to test some of its possible implications and its reach. I explore whether the structural and cultural components in the abovementioned hypothesis account for changes in the index of delegative democracies: that is, whether delegative democracies are more likely to *intensify* (values in the index will be higher) when economic crises are deeper and confidence in democracy, government, parties, and politicians is lower. Following the logic in the model, we could expect delegative democracies to *weaken* (values in the index will be lower) when the economic context is more favorable and confidence in government, parties, and politicians is higher (second hypothesis). I test these propositions and see whether there is empirical support for them in the next sections.

Variables and Data

To explain changes across and within cases over time, I use the values of the delegative democracy index. Each of the eight main features that define delegative democracies according to O'Donnell (1994: 60–62) are coded 1 in case the dimension is present in a country in a given year, 0 otherwise.[31] The index is composed by the simple (unweighted) sum of all values present in a country in a given year.

I grouped the main independent variables into structural and cultural components or dimensions (see description of variables and data sources in table 11.2). In relation to the structural factors, I use economic and fiscal variables to account for economic crisis: inflation (natural logarithm of the annual percentage change in consumer prices, to normalize the data), economic growth (annual percentage change in GDP), public debt (total debt stock as a percentage of gross national income), and inequality (measured using the Gini index). I also include (the natural logarithm of) GDP per capita to control for differences in income across cases. I accessed data on these variables from the World Bank's World Development Indicators (WDI) and Global Development Finance (GDF; see tables 11.2 and 11.3).

I include data on individual confidence in government, parties, and congress as well as variables to measure support for democracy and satisfaction with democracy and test the relevance of the cultural component. Pairwise correlations among these variables for the selected cases are high, so I report basic descriptive statistics for all of them (table 11.4) and use only one of them, support for democracy, in the regression analysis.[32]

These data are available from Latinobarómetro for all the cases in this study. As indicated above, the main problem with these series is that data are only available for recent years (after 1995 and, for some variables, 1997), so we cannot analyze the legacies from authoritarian rule in terms of individual perceptions. However, we can explore whether changes in these variables have an impact on the outcome. In other words, we can investigate whether diminishing levels of individuals' confidence in politicians or political institutions affect the delegativeness of the democratic regime.

O'Donnell also stressed the role of party system fragmentation, institutionalization, and polarization in delegative democracies in a later piece (2011: 24–27; see also Ollier 2011). This is a third component or an alternative argument, which I call politico-institutional. I use some proxies that could measure how hard (or easy) it is for the president to construct political power in her party or coalition and in congress (and not only in public opinion). I use data on party systems' fragmentation and polarization (Coppedge 2007), assuming (in line with several other works in the literature) that presidents will have more difficulties governing in a more fragmented and polarized party system, especially in presidential systems (Diamond 1997; Linz 1978b; Mainwaring and Scully 1995; Sartori 1976). Under conditions of high fragmentation and polarization, we would expect larger chances of a cycle of crisis and delegation. These data are available for longer time series (1973–2009). I also included two variables measuring the institutional power of the president. To that effect, I use Shugart and Carey's (1992: 155) index of presidential institutional powers and Negretto's (2009: 139) index of legislative presidential powers[33] (see description of variables and data sources in table 11.2).

Model

In the first part of the analysis, I provide a basic description of the values the main variables take before and after the transition from authoritarian rule to delegative and representative democracies. Here I explore the legacies of authoritarian regimes after their transitions to democracy. In the second part of this section, I analyze whether there is empirical support for the hypotheses presented above relying on regression analysis.

When trying to account for changes in the Index of Delegative Democracy, I ran an ordered logistic regression, which is specifically designed for ordinal outcomes. The dependent variable in this study is ordinal, since it has several categories, ranging from a full representative to a full delegative democracy, with no precise distinctions among them. Long and Freese (2001: 137) claim that ordinal variables are often coded as consecutive integers from 1 to the number of categories. They argue that perhaps as a consequence of this coding, it is tempting to analyze ordinal outcomes with the linear

TABLE 11.2
Description of variables and data sources

Variables	Description	Source	Years
Index of Delegative Democracy	See the chapter text for a description of the index. The index has the following categories: fully representative (value of 0 in the index), almost fully representative (1), weakly representative (2), very weakly representative (3), representative-delegative (4), very weakly delegative (5), weakly delegative (6), almost fully delegative (7), and fully delegative democracy (8).	Countries were categorized by the chapter author and country specialists.	1980–2011
Inflation	Natural logarithm of the annual percentage change in consumer prices; GDP deflator.	World Development Indicators (WDI) & Global Development Finance (GDF)	1972–2010
Economic growth	Annual percentage change in GDP	WDI-GDF	1972–2010
GDP per capita	Natural logarithm of GDP per capita (constant values)	WDI-GDF	1972–2010
Public debt	External debt stocks as a percentage of gross national income (GNI).	WDI-GDF	1980–2010
Inequality	GINI index	WDI-GDF	1981–2009
Unemployment	Total unemployment as a share of the total labor force.	WDI-GDF	1981–2009
Confidence in government	Percentage of respondents having "no confidence at all" in government.	Latinobarómetro	1995–2010
Confidence in the president	Percentage of respondents having "no confidence at all" in the president.	Latinobarómetro	1997–2007
Confidence in parties and congress	Percentage of respondents having "no confidence at all" in parties and congress.	Latinobarómetro	1995–2010
Support for democracy	Percentage of respondents agreeing with the statement: "Democracy is preferable to any other form of government."	Latinobarómetro	1995–2010
Satisfaction with democracy	Percentage of respondents "Not being satisfied at all with democracy."	Latinobarómetro	1995–2010
President can bypass Congress and Parties	Share of respondents who agreed with the statement: "In case of difficulties, the president can bypass congress and parties."	Latinobarómetro	2002, 2008
Desire to eliminate Congress	Share of respondents who agreed with the statement: "Democracy can work without Congress."	Latinobarómetro	1997–2010
Fragmentation	Effective Number of Parties, in terms of seats.	Coppedge (2007)	1973–2009
Polarization	Coppedge's Index of Polarization (IP), which measures the dispersion of the vote away from the relative center of the party system.	Coppedge (2007)	1973–2009
Volatility	Pedersen's Index of Volatility: sum of the absolute value of the changes in all parties' vote shares from one election to the next, divided by two.	Coppedge (2007)	1973–2009

TABLE II.3.
Main structural variables for delegative and representative democracies

Country	Previous economic growth (2 yrs.)	Previous economic growth (4 yrs.)	Previous inflation (2 yrs.)	Previous inflation (4 yrs.)
Delegative democracies				
Argentina	−5.3	0.9	157.0	138.1
Bolivia	−0.5	0.3	27.3	22.1
Brazil	0.9	−0.5	176.5	141.3
Ecuador	4.6	6.3	12.1	11.8
Paraguay	5.3	3.7	18.9	26.3
Peru	3.0	2.1	3.0	2.0
Representative democracies				
Chile	8.9	7.5	18.0	21.0
Uruguay	−5.7	−4.9	55.0	38.9

Source: World Bank's World Development Indicators (WDI) and Global Development Finance (GDF).
Note: Columns represent average values of the variables for the two and four years before the transition to democracy in each of the cases studied. Economic growth = GDP growth (annual %); inflation = consumer prices (annual %).

regression model. However, they alert that an ordinal dependent variable violates the assumptions of the linear regression model and this can lead to incorrect conclusions (see also McKelvey and Zavoina 1975: 117 and Winship and Mare 1984: 521–23). I follow the authors' recommendation that with ordinal outcomes it is much better to use models that avoid the assumption that the distances between categories are equal. In order to test for robustness in the results, I also run a simple linear (OLS) regression and a linear regression with panel corrected standard errors (PCSEs) to account for the panel structure in the data.

Descriptive Statistics

First, I analyze the values in the different variables of the economic dimension in each of the countries that transitioned to democracy during the 1980s (table 11.3). Here, I take O'Donnell's classification to divide delegative and representative democracies.

I evaluate economic growth first. Some delegative democracies received a heavy burden in terms of economic growth from previous authoritarian regimes.[34] Argentina experienced the largest fall in GDP before the transition to democracy, followed by Bolivia and Brazil. In contrast, Chile, a case in the representative camp, inherited a much more healthy economy. These cases support the argument on the role of economic crisis played during the transition from authoritarian rule to delegative or representative democracies. However, other cases do not fit the theoretical expectations very well. Some representative democracies did not receive a comfortable economic situation from their authoritarian governments (e.g., Uruguay), and other delegative democracies did not inherit economic turmoil (e.g., Paraguay, Peru, and Ecuador).[35]

In terms of inflation, Brazil and Argentina inherited the highest values from their transitions to democracy. These values were relatively high in the case of Bolivia but relatively low in the case of Ecuador and Peru. The two cases of representative democracies, Chile and Uruguay, received moderate to relatively high levels of inflation after their transitions. These averages, though, were much lower than in the Argentine and Brazilian cases (especially for Chile).

Other variables do not seem to support the theoretical expectations. The legacy in external debt stocks (as a percentage of gross national income) is very diverse.[36] In terms of inequality, results are even less conclusive: most of the cases have high Gini indexes for income distribution. Delegative and representative democracies are among the most and least unequal countries.[37] Finally, and contrary to what we could have expected, delegative democracies had lighter legacies in terms of unemployment rates than representative ones did.[38]

Summing up, delegative democracies received a somewhat heavier burden from their authoritarian regimes in terms of economic growth and inflation, especially in Argentina and Brazil compared with Chile. But the same conclusion cannot be reached for other variables, such as unemployment rates and debt burden. The economic legacy in Uruguay seems to be as heavy as in the delegative cases for some variables, despite being a representative democracy after 1985. There are also some cases in the delegative group that performed better than representative democracies in some variables.

Some questions can be raised regarding Mexico, Colombia, and Venezuela. O'Donnell's argument was very likely restricted in scope and reach and perhaps very much based in the Southern Cone cases (Argentina, Brazil, Chile, and Uruguay) and Peru, so this may limit the capacity of the theory to travel beyond the cases he explicitly referred to (although he recognized some postcommunist countries can be included in the delegative group). In any case, and despite the theoretical and empirical prudence of the author, I explore the empirical incidence of economic crisis on the likelihood of a country being a delegative or representative democracy in the following sections.

Before that, I examine whether individual perceptions (confidence in political institutions, support for democracy, and satisfaction with democracy) vary across the two categories (table 11.4).

Some interesting results emerge out of basic descriptive statistics: about 60% of citizens in delegative democracies (e.g., Argentina, Brazil, Bolivia, Ecuador, and Peru) support democracy as preferable to any other form of government;[39] this average is 9.1

TABLE II.4.

Main cultural variables for delegative and representative democracies,
national averages, 1995–2010

Variable	Number of observations	Mean delegative democracies	Standard deviation	Minimum	Maximum
Delegative democracies					
Support for democracy	73	60.1	10.2	38.2	81.8
Respondent not satisfied with democracy	73	21.1	8.9	2.4	47.9
Respondent has no confidence in parties	73	51.6	10.3	31.2	80.6
Respondent has no confidence in Congress	73	39.8	13.1	18.7	72.6
Respondent has confidence in president	45	35.2	16.8	7.2	72.0
Respondent has no confidence in president	45	64.8	16.8	28.0	92.8
Respondent has no confidence in government	53	67.3	15.8	29.3	93.4
President can bypass Congress and parties[a]	10	40.8	10.9	24.9	60.4
Desire to eliminate Congress[b]	45	40.3	13.3	18.3	72.3
Representative democracies					
Support for democracy	30	69.2	13.7	47.8	87.6
Respondent not satisfied with democracy	30	11.0	5.9	2.3	25.3
Respondent has no confidence in parties	30	33.3	10.8	·16.7	61.0
Respondent has no confidence in Congress	30	20.9	7.9	9.9	41.0
Respondent has confidence in president	18	53.9	15.4	14.9	77.6
Respondent has no confidence in president	18	46.1	15.4	22.4	85.1
Respondent has no confidence in government	22	48.0	14.9	28.1	83.8
President can bypass Congress and parties[a]	4	26.4	9.9	17.8	36.2
Desire to eliminate Congress[b]	18	22.2	7.5	11.3	38.2

Source: Latinobarómetro.
Note: 1995–2010 for most variables; see also table 11.2
[a] Share of respondents who agreed with the statement: "In case of difficulties, the president can bypass congress and parties."
[b] Share of respondents who agreed with the statement: "Democracy can work without Congress."

points higher in representative democracies (e.g., Uruguay and Chile). The average of those who report not being satisfied at all with democracy is 21% in the delegative camp, while it is 11% in the representative one.[40] Those not having confidence in parties are almost 52% in the first group and 33% in the second. These sharp differences are similar for those not having confidence in congress (40% versus 21%), not having confidence in the government (67% versus 48%), and not having confidence in the president (65% versus 46%).[41] The average of respondents who agreed with the statement: "democracy can work without the national congress" was 40% in the delegative group, 22% in the representative one. The average of those who agreed with the statement "in case of difficulties, the president can bypass congress and parties" was 41% against 26%.[42]

These figures indicate that individual political perceptions vary between delegative and representative democracies. In line with O'Donnell's theoretical expectations, citizens report more support and satisfaction with democracy as well as less distrust in parties, congress, government, and the president in more institutionalized democracies.[43]

It is difficult to assess presidential popularity in delegative democracies and its variation from wide public support to general vilification with the partial data we have. Ideally, we would need measures of presidential support for each year in each country.[44] We only have responses on confidence in the president for eight years in each country between 1997 and 2007 (there are no data for years 1999 and 2002). Taking into account these limitations, the average confidence in the president for these years in delegative democracies is 35%; compared with 54% in representative democracies.[45]

These basic descriptive statistics show some variation in the values the main variables take in delegative and representative democracies. These results offer some preliminary support for O'Donnell's expectations. The next step is to analyze whether changes in these independent variables produce changes in the outcome. To do this, I turn to another tool, regression analysis.

Regression Results

Regression results support some of the main theoretical expectations in the model to account for variations in the delegative democracy index. I ran an ordered logistic regression model and controlled for the robustness of results with an OLS and a linear regression with PCSE. The outcomes across models show little variation, with substantive conclusions holding in all of them, so I only report results from the first (table 11.5).

According to the results, more inflation positively affects the odds of a country being a delegative democracy. The coefficient for this variable is robust and statistically significant. More economic growth, in contrast, has a negative effect on those

TABLE 11.5.
Ordered logistic regression results with a dependent variable of Index of Delegative Democracy

Variable	Index of Delegative Democracy
Inflation (ln)	0.2670*
	(0.1757)
GDP growth	−0.0004
	(0.0436)
GDP per capita (ln)	−0.2560***
	(0.0661)
Support for democracy	−0.0480***
	(0.0194)
Partisan fragmentation	−0.1574
	(0.1107)
Volatility	0.0564***
	(0.0142)
Polarization	−0.0396***
	(0.0137)
Pseudo R^2	0.16
Observations	123

Note: Standard errors in parentheses. The Index of Delegative Democracy is the dependent variable and figures in the second column are the coefficients (and standard errors) of the model that account for variation in this index.
*significant at 10%; **significant at 5%; ***significant at 1%

odds but the coefficient is very small and the statistical significance is below the accepted standards.

The cultural variable has a coefficient with the expected sign and is robust and statistically significant in the ordered logistic model (and moves in the expected direction in the PCSE regression). As our theory predicted, larger support for democracy reduces the probability of having a delegative democracy.

There is some empirical support for alternative arguments also. Volatility positively affects the odds of a country being a delegative democracy, as we anticipated. However, more party system fragmentation and polarization are negatively associated to the probability of having a delegative democracy in a given year. Results for fragmentation are not statistically significant (p = 0.155; table 11.5). These results suggest the opposite of what we theoretically expected: some level of party system fragmentation and polarization might be good for having a representative democracy in the sense that under low levels of both variables more negotiation might be needed to take decisions or pass bills in congress (and hence, less unilateral imposition is possible). We could argue that party system fragmentation and polarization have a U-shaped relationship with the index of delegative democracy.[46] To test this, I decided to include the squared term of both independent variables, generating a quadratic

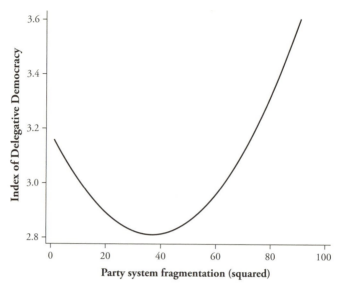

Figure 11.5. The quadratic relationship between the Index of Delegative Democracy and Party System Fragmentation.

curve. Regression results with these new variables and figures 11.5 and 11.6 effectively indicate that there is a quadratic relationship between party system fragmentation and polarization:[47] holding all other variables constant, the probability of having a delegative democracy diminishes as the values for both independent variables augment, to increase again in a U-shaped relationship. I also ran an additional model, including Shugart and Carey's (1992: 155) Index of Presidential Institutional Powers and Negretto's (2009: 139) Index of Legislative Presidential Powers. The coefficients for both variables move in the expected direction, but only the first one is robust and statistically significant, indicating that institutionally powerful presidents and delegative democracies tend to be empirically associated.[48]

The advantage in the ordered logistic regression (besides the ones mentioned in the models' section) is that I can calculate predicted probabilities for each of the categories in the dependent variable. Out of the results, when all variables in the model are at their means, the countries in the sample have 76% probability of being in one of the four categories in the representative camp. The larger probabilities are in the two categories next to the full representative democracy (almost fully representative, with 24%, and weakly representative, with 29%). The predicted probabilities of being in the delegative democracy camp are only 21%, with the different categories ranging from 5% to 6% each. Under more negative economic conditions (no growth and average inflation),[49] the probabilities of being a representative democracy diminish to 65% (or 11% less than in an average scenario). Under very critical economic conditions (the lowest values in

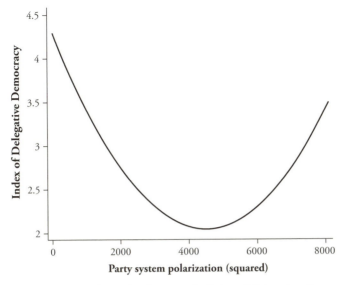

Figure 11.6. The quadratic relationship between the Index of Delegative Democracy and Party System Polarization.

GDP growth, the highest inflation),[50] and all the other variables at their means, a country has a 63% probability of being in any of the delegative democracy categories. The largest predicted probability, 24%, is that of being a fully delegative democracy.

At this stage, I included individual perceptions supporting democracy in the analysis. When all the variables are at their means and support for democracy at its highest, the largest probability (38%) is that of being an almost fully representative democracy. All the categories in the representative camp add up to 92%. When support for democracy diminishes to the minimum (34%), economic growth is at the lowest, and inflation at the highest values, the predicted probability of being in any of the categories in the delegative camp is 86%. The largest probability (55%) is that of being a fully delegative democracy.

Discussion

These results indicate that under very critical economic conditions and dramatic drops in public opinion's confidence in democracy, there is 86% probability for a given country to be a delegative democracy. Argentina was under conditions similar to these twice in recent history (in 1988–90 and 2001–2) and both times ended up in the delegative camp. Crises in this country were regularly larger and more recurrent than in Brazil, for instance, a case that moved gradually into the representative camp.[51]

When conditions of crisis urge presidents to concentrate political power and take

swift policy decisions and when individual perceptions are more prone to delegation, the key is whether presidents can concentrate political power or are forced to
negotiate. This brings the political (or partisan) dimension into the analysis, vis-à-vis
structural and cultural variables.

Argentine presidents, for instance, although forced to negotiate permanently, were
able to concentrate more political power in Congress and inside their parties than
any of their Brazilian counterparts ever did.[52] Under conditions of recurrent crises,
more concentration, delegation, and rushed policy making have been more likely in
Argentina than in Brazil. There, and especially after Collor's term in office, policy
making has been more protracted and slow but also more negotiated and, in the end,
more institutionalized (as the classification shows).

Conclusion

This work intends to contribute to the literature on delegative democracies that Guillermo O'Donnell inaugurated by providing a classification of the cases and presenting
some evidence to account for variation among them and within the two groups, delegative and representative democracies. This classification and descriptive effort can
be useful for exploring and analyzing delegative democracies in more detail as well as
for explaining causes and consequences of specific changes in some dimensions. As
Collier and Levitsky (1997: 432) stressed, "improved description . . . is essential for
assessing the *causes* and *consequences* of democracy" (emphasis in the original text).

This classification also intends to contribute to empirical analysis of democracies
in Latin America and to allow for comparison among them with other cases and regions. Some of the dimensions in the concept may be present even in institutionalized
democracies, particularly under conditions of crisis. If that is the case, we could argue
that delegative democracy is not a phenomenon circumscribed to a geographical area
(or cultural community) but rather a more general phenomenon. Once again, if that
is the case, a more detailed empirical analysis can contribute to the broader theoretical discussion.

This chapter also shows that Latin American countries have larger probabilities
of being (weakly) representative rather than (fully) delegative democracies. It is only
when economic conditions deteriorate dramatically or when support for democracy
in the population erodes significantly or when partisan volatility and polarization
increase substantially that the probabilities of ending in the delegative camp increase.
The theoretical argument and the empirical results reveal a paradox: a key way to end
the cycle of delegation requires weakening the factors that explained its emergence,
strength, and the very sources of power of the delegative president: the context of

urgency under economic crisis and the lack of public confidence in democratic institutions.

This chapter shows that O'Donnell's conceptual framework is a powerful device to analyze and understand institutionalizing, deinstitutionalizing, and institutionalized democracies. Unpacking delegative democracy, I demonstrated that instances of this concept vary and I argue that this variation may not only be circumscribed to Latin America. Although clearly more research is needed, the findings in this work may be empirically and theoretically meaningful for discussions on delegative democracies in particular and democratic regimes in general.

NOTES

This chapter is dedicated to the memory of my great professor, advisor, and friend, Guillermo O'Donnell.

I would like to thank Scott Mainwaring, Daniel Brinks, and Marcelo Leiras for their crucial comments and advice. Gabriela Ippolito-O'Donnell, James McGuire, and Gerardo Munck read the manuscript and gave me generous suggestions on it. I also thank the observations Johns Hopkins University Press's reviewer provided. This work has also been possible due to the generous advice and time offered by several country experts. My enormous gratitude to Diego Abente Brun, David Altman, Angel Alvarez, George Avelino, Santiago Basabe, John Crabtree, Guillermo Cejudo, José Cepeda, Claudia Dangond Gibsone, Eduardo Dargent Bocanegra, Marcelo Escolar, Alfredo Roberto Joignant Rondon, Carlos Huneeus, Juan Fernando Ibarra, Ignacio Labaqui, Marcelo Leiras, Arturo Maldonado, Claudia Maldonado Trujillo, Ignacio Mamone, René Mayorga, Andrés Mejía Acosta, Carlos Meléndez, Marcus Melo, José Enrique Molina Vega, Juan Andrés Moraes, Andrew Nickson, Rafael Piñeiro, John Polga Hacimovich, Maria Isabel Puerta Riera, Ximena Simpson, and Dominica Zabala. Any mistake is my sole responsibility.

1. The original piece on delegative democracy first appeared published in Portuguese (in CEBRAP's *Revista Novos Estudos*) in 1991, then in Spanish (*Cuadernos del CLAEH*) and in English (*Kellogg Institute's Working Papers*), both in 1992 and later on in 1994 (*Journal of Democracy*). It was reproduced in several other places (including O'Donnell's *Contrapuntos*, 1997; and *Counterpoints*, 1999a). O'Donnell presented new thoughts on delegative democracy in O'Donnell 2011.

2. Some authors argued that the two concepts, delegative democracy and populism, are very similar, particularly in their cultural components (Peruzzotti 2001: 136–137). Nevertheless, O'Donnell (1993: 1355–56) clearly differentiated between the two (see also O'Donnell et al. [2011: 14–15], O'Donnell [2011: 30–31], and Weffort [1993:171] for further differentiation between the two concepts). He claimed that although the two concepts share some common characteristics, populism (at least in Latin America) led to larger political mobilization and organization, although vertically controlled, and coincided with periods of expansion of the national economy. On the contrary, delegative democracies tended to demobilize their populations, with the exception of periods in which they needed their plebiscitary support, and coincided with periods of profound economic crisis. In the definition I use, delegative democracy is not the same as populism.

3. A part of this debate focused on whether the president effectively "governs alone" (Ferreira

Rubio and Goretti 1996; Negretto 2002) or negotiates with congress when producing legislation, and, if it does, under what conditions (Cox et al. 2001; Cox and Morgenstern 2001; Llanos 1998, 2001; Mustapic 2000; Negretto 2001, 2006; Panizza 2000; Peruzzotti 2001).

4. See, for instance: L. Anderson 2006; Canache and Allison 2005; Dodson and Jackson 2004; Larkins 1998; O'Donnell 2006; Peruzzotti and Smulovitz 2006; Przeworski 2006; Smulovitz and Peruzzotti 2000; and Stanley 2005. Some of these scholars paid particular attention to these aspects of delegative democracies during the neoliberal economic reforms of the 1990s (Conaghan et al. 1997; K. Roberts 1995; Samuels 2004; Weyland 2004), but other authors underlined that this was "something more than a simple momentary authoritarian deviation" (O'Donnell et al. 2011: 13).

5. See, for instance: Álvarez 2000; Anderson 2006; Avritzer 2000; Croissant 2003; Kubiček 1994; Larkins 1998; Morgan Kelly 2003; Schmidt 2000. Ippolito-O'Donnell (2011: 54) presents a list of case studies that applied the concept of delegative democracy in the analysis of different countries, including Colombia, Dominican Republic, Ecuador, Kazakhstan, Mexico, Nicaragua, Panama, the Philippines, Russia, South Korea, Ukraine, and Venezuela.

6. Some studies concentrated on a particular subregion, such as Central America (Programa Estado de la Nación 2011a), or particular cases, such as Costa Rica (Programa Estado de la Nación 2010). Ippolito-O'Donnell (2011) conducted public opinion polls in Buenos Aires and São Paulo to study citizens' representations on delegation.

7. Ippolito-O'Donnell (2011) is an exception to this, but she conducted the polls only in one year, 1992. Latinobarómetro asked questions directly related to perceptions on delegation in their polls, but only in one year also, in 2003.

8. O'Donnell recognized changes over time in delegative democracies in his 2011 piece.

9. I further analyze several other changes below.

10. O'Donnell et al. (2011: 13) acknowledged these changes that led the Brazilian case into a more institutionalized direction, although Weffort questioned this in a comment in this paper.

11. Other authors classify Venezuela during Chávez as a competitive authoritarianism (Levitsky and Way 2010: 4, 16, 32, 82, 178) or as semi-democratic (Mainwaring and Pérez-Liñán 2013). Mazzuca (chapter 4 in this volume) claims that "[d]elegative democracy is simply not a proper characterization of . . . Venezuela under President Hugo Chávez." For him, Venezuela is "morphing into an 'electoral' form of authoritarianism." This is also the case of Ecuador under Correa and Bolivia under Morales. For the author, these cases fall short of the procedural minimum of democracy and thus should not be characterized as delegative democracies. Peruzzotti (chapter 12 in this volume) tends to side with Mazzuca, claiming that Venezuela under Chavez and Ecuador under Correa have undermined key aspects of the notion of polyarchy. The country coders (see note 13 below), though, agreed on classifying these cases as delegative democracies (despite some disagreement among the coders on which dimensions of delegative democracy were present during the abovementioned presidencies). Due to these disagreements, I simply acknowledge that I am including cases that, according to some scholars, have competitive elections and are classified as delegative democracies, but other authors questioned their democratic credentials and consider them as authoritarian or semi-democratic regimes.

12. Peru from the April 5, 1992, coup until 1995 could also be considered an authoritarian regime and not a delegative democracy. I owe this comment to Scott Mainwaring. I make explicit the disagreements among analysts on some specific cases and during some periods rather than taking a definite position on them (see previous footnote).

13. Marcelo Escolar (Universidad Nacional de San Martín), Marcelo Leiras (Universidad de

San Andrés), and Ignacio Labaqui and Ignacio Mamone (Universidad Católica Argentina) helped me classify and code Argentina; George Avelino (Fundação Getulio Vargas-São Paulo), Marcus Melo (Universidade Federal de Pernambuco), and Ximena Simpson (Universidad Nacional de San Martín) with Brazil; René Mayorga (Centro Boliviano de Estudios Multidisciplinarios and Flacso) and John Crabtree (University of Oxford) with Bolivia; Carlos Huneeus (Universidad de Chile) and Alfredo Roberto Joignant Rondon (Universidad Diego Portales) with Chile; Claudia Dangond Gibsone and José Cepeda (Pontificia Universidad Javeriana) with Colombia; Andrés Mejía Acosta (University of Sussex), Santiago Basabe (FLACSO Ecuador), and John Polga Hacimovich (University of Pittsburgh) with Ecuador; Claudia Maldonado Trujillo, Guillermo Cejudo, and Juan Fernando Ibarra (Centro de Investigación y Docencia Económicas, CIDE) with the Mexican case; Diego Abente Brun (National Endowment for Democracy and Centro de Análisis y Difusión de la Economía Paraguaya, CADEP), Andrew Nickson (University of Birmingham), and Dominica Zabala (London School of Economics) with Paraguay; Carlos Meléndez (University of Notre Dame), Eduardo Dargent Bocanegra (University of Texas, Austin), and Arturo Maldonado (Vanderbilt University) with Peru; David Altman (Universidad Católica de Chile), Juan Andrés Moraes, and Rafael Piñeiro (Universidad de la República) assisted me with Uruguay; Ángel Álvarez (Universidad Central de Venezuela), María Isabel Puerta Riera (Universidad de Carabobo) and José Enrique Molina Vega (Universidad del Zulia) helped me with Venezuela.

14. Intercoder reliability is relatively high. The average pairwise percent agreement is 86.27%, ranging from Uruguay, with complete agreement among the coders, to Colombia, with the lowest value (53.34). The average Fleiss' kappa for all the cases is 0.66, the average pairwise Cohen's kappa is 0.72, and the Krippendorff's alpha is 0.67. The coding for each country and the intercoder reliability tests are available upon request. I recognize the limitations in the strategy of country experts' coding and the need to move toward more reliable indicators. Both Daniel Brinks and Gerardo Munck recommended this to me. An alternative measure could rely on observable and easier to operationalize institutional dimensions. The dimensions that can be included are accountability, regulatory quality, rule of law, government effectiveness, and control of corruption (from the World Bank's Worldwide Governance Indicators). These are useful measures for the institutional dimensions in the index of delegative democracies. But there is a high cost in relying solely on them: they mostly measure institutional variables (related to accountability), leaving aside other important "informal" dimensions of delegative democracies (mostly linked to the exercise of power). O'Donnell considered these dimensions crucial. Hence, in this work, I use the experts' coding, recognizing the limitations in this strategy, and leave for future research more sophisticated, observable measures of delegativeness both in its formal (institutional) and informal dimensions.

15. These categories are: fully representative (value of 0 in the index), almost fully representative (1), weakly representative (2), very weakly representative (3), representative-delegative (4), very weakly delegative (5), weakly delegative (6), almost fully delegative (7), and fully delegative democracy (8).

16. In a later piece, O'Donnell (2011: 28) argued that delegative democracies can take different paths: to a representative democracy, through another crisis to a new delegative democracy, and by a gradual descent (*deslizamiento*) into authoritarianism.

17. In fact, Argentina's index oscillated from 1 during most of Alfonsín's term in office, to a maximum of 8 during the early years of Menem (the period O'Donnell refers to in his article). Peruzzotti (2001: 148–49), in his critique to O'Donnell's argument (1994), claimed that "Both in its rhetoric and political practices, the [Alfonsín] government disconfirmed the delegativeness ar-

gument. Under Alfonsín's administration, the executive power made a conscious effort at political self-limitation, particularly in relation to the judicial power." This cycle repeats itself again during De la Rúa's administration (it had a 1 during the first year in office and 3 in the second), Duhalde's (5) and the Kirchners' (7 during Néstor Kirchner's and between 6 and 8 during Cristina Fernández de Kirchner's term).

18. It scores relatively high values at the beginning of the period under consideration, during the presidency of Julio César Turbay (5); followed by low values in the following presidency, during the first two years of Belisario Betancourt (0), who then entered into a more delegative phase (5 in the last year of his term). These ups and downs continued: low values during César Gaviria's presidency contrasted with higher values during Ernesto Samper's and Álvaro Uribe's at the end of his second term. O'Donnell (2011: 24) also classified Uribe's presidency as delegative.

19. Scott Mainwaring argues that Peru met no reasonable threshold of being a democracy between 1992 and 1995. For him this is not a case of a delegative democracy but rather an authoritarian regime. If we agree on this classification, we should exclude Peru during those years from the analysis. I decided to keep the original classification made by the country experts in the paper, mentioning this disagreement in the classification. Substantive results do not change if we exclude these four country-years from the regression analysis.

20. The values in the index decreased to 7 after 1996 and 6 later on: the president did not oppose his campaign policies once in office during his second term (1995–2000) and the courts and congress were not impediments to him. The president did not clash with them but not because they were independent powers and separation among them was guaranteed but rather because they were loyal (and subordinated) to the president (mechanisms of horizontal accountability remained very weak). We could probably revise this dimension to express more precisely the type of relations between the executive and the legislative and judiciary that we refer to when we examine a delegative democracy.

21. Cardoso's government scored 4 during the first two years in office, 3 in the following two years, and 2 during his second term in office. Lula's presidency has even lower values (1).

22. Carlos Andrés Pérez's second presidency scored 5 and Rafael Caldera began his government with a 2 during the first two years in office, but moved to 5 in the last three.

23. The persistently high values during Chávez's terms in office contribute to this overall high average value. The average for the presidencies before Chávez was 3.1 and the standard deviation, 1.7.

24. It would be interesting to compare this average with the values for other regions, such as postcommunist or southern countries in Europe.

25. Such as executive-legislative or executive-judiciary relations, horizontal accountability, informal institutions, campaign promises and policy switches, types of policy making, political parties and political movements, presidential discourses, among others.

26. It has not been an easy task to differentiate the main features defining the concept from the factors that may contribute to their emergence (see, for instance, II.10 in O'Donnell 2011, p.23). Diamond (1997: 18), when studying the causes of democratic consolidation, also noted "it is hard to separate the concept from some of its causes."

27. Redemocratization was crucial in Uruguay and Chile. These two countries had a "strongly institutionalized legislature, and a series of constitutional restrictions and historically embedded practices," long before their authoritarian governments. These institutions and practices reemerged after democratization and contributed to put limits to the way presidents have exercised power (O'Donnell 1994: 64).

28. See also O'Donnell (1993: 1362–65) for a detailed link between the two variables; and O'Donnell (2011: 23–24) for further precision. In this latter piece, O'Donnell argues that some delegative democracies also emerged as a consequence of "serious socio-economic crises and/or in some cases, prolonged and violent situations of internal war" (O'Donnell 2011: 24).

29. Several authors developed the link between times of economic crises and the need of a president with temporarily heightened powers (see L. Anderson 2006: 162).

30. That is the case, as indicated above, of the existence of historically embedded practices previous to the democratic transition. Others—such as a "decisive segment of the political leadership recognizing the self-destructive quality of those cycles, and agreeing to change the terms on which they compete and govern" (O'Donnell 1994: 68)—are very difficult to assess.

31. At least three different country specialists classified each case: two persons helped me code all the cases and each of the cases had two, three, and up to four coders each (depending on the replies I received). The final coding is available upon request.

32. Pairwise correlation between support for democracy (percentage of respondents who agree with the statement "democracy is preferable to any other form of government") and satisfaction with democracy (here I include the percentage of respondents in the three categories that include "very satisfied," "fairly satisfied," and "not very satisfied," excluding "not at all satisfied") is 0.7. Pairwise correlations among confidence in parties, congress, and government oscillate between 0.7 and 0.9. All correlations are statistically significant (at less than 1%).

33. Scott Mainwaring advised me to include these variables.

34. I take the period of two or four years before the transition to democracy because, first, I assume the effect of these periods is stronger than more extended ones and, second, because we have data available for all cases in these years. Whenever available, I present the average values for all years under authoritarian rule.

35. If we take all the years of dictatorship for which we have data, the average economic growth during authoritarian regimes for the best performers is 7.42% in Ecuador (1972–79), 5.4 in Paraguay (1961–89), and 6.2 in Brazil (1964–85). The poorest performers were Argentina (1% between 1976 and 1983), and Uruguay (1.1% between 1973 and 1985). We can see that among better and worse performers, there are cases in the delegative and representative categories after their transition to democracy. The average for all authoritarian regimes is 3.9 and 3.2 for all the years of democracy. Representative democracies grew at an average 4.24% for the period; delegative democracies, at 2.98%.

36. Argentina and Brazil received a debt stock equivalent to 51 and 52% of their GNI. These values are similar for Bolivia: 55%. Uruguay got 48% (and if we take four years the value reaches 71%), while Chile got 77% (100% if we consider four years). This variable does not seem to be very supportive of the theoretical argument.

37. The least unequal cases at the time of the transition were Uruguay, with a Gini index of 44 in 1981 (42 in 1989), and Argentina, with a Gini of 45 in 1986. These values can be compared to a much higher 56 for Chile in 1990, 59 for Brazil in 1986, and 50 for Ecuador in 1987 (data at the time of transition to democracy in these cases are available only for these years).

38. Peru had an average unemployment rate of 3% for the two years before the transition to democracy, Brazil's was 4.5, and Argentina's 5%. Chile had 5.5% and Uruguay 12.5% (values are very similar for all cases if we average the last four years of dictatorship).

39. Here, I report the percentage of respondents agreeing with the statement: "Democracy is preferable to any other form of government."

40. I report the percentage of respondents "not being satisfied at all with democracy."

41. I report the percentage of respondents having "no confidence at all" in parties, congress, government, and the president.

42. This can be an acceptable proxy for what O'Donnell referred to as "a strong sense of urgency" differentiating delegative from representative democracies.

43. Concerns over the direction of causality are pertinent here. For obvious reasons, I do not get into the details of these debates here.

44. The Executive Approval Database (managed by Carlin, Hartlyn, and Martínez-Gallardo) compiles this information, but it is still under construction and does not cover all cases and years I study in this work.

45. As a measure of variations in presidential support, the standard deviation in the first group is 17 points, slightly larger than the 15 points in the second group. One difference between the two is that in delegative democracies the minimum value is 7, a bit less than half of the score in representative ones (15%), even when the maximum is similar in both (72 and 78, respectively).

46. I owe this comment to Daniel Brinks.

47. The threshold for the effective number of parties is above 5 and for volatility is around 65; mean values for both variables are 4 and 40, respectively.

48. The number of cases drops to 111, because the first index is not available for Bolivia, while the Pseudo R^2 increases to .22 in the ordinal logit model.

49. The mean value of inflation for the selected cases and years is 131% a year.

50. The lowest value in GDP growth is –11.8 (Peru in 1983; and –11.7 in 1989; Argentina decreased to –10.9 in 2002), and the highest inflation is 12,300% (Bolivia in 1985), followed by Peru (6,837 in 1990), Argentina (3,058 in 1989), and Brazil (2,736 in 1990).

51. Brazil's GDP grew at an average of 2.6% between 1985 and 2002. Its GDP decreased only in three years, at an average of –1.7%. Argentina's GDP grew to half of Brazil's during the period (1.4% between 1983 and 2002), decreasing in nine years out of twenty. The largest falls were a –7.6% in 1985, a –7.5% in 1989, and a –11% collapse in 2002. Brazil never experienced anything similar.

52. We can take for instance two powerful presidents in each country: Carlos Menem and Fernando Henrique Cardoso. Although both of them could reach majorities to pass crucial bills, Menem's party controlled almost four times the share of seats in the Chamber of Deputies that Cardoso's party did.

CHAPTER 12

Accountability Deficits of Delegative Democracy

ENRIQUE PERUZZOTTI

The postconsolidation debate in Latin America revolves around questions of institutional betterment and democratic deepening that drives us to rethink to what extent are inherited notions of democracy useful for framing such an agenda. Once the attention focuses on democratic deficits and the need to democratize existing democracies, the minimalist approach to democracy that influenced the literature on transitions and consolidation loses its conceptual appeal. If the minimalist notion of democracy—understood as a regime based on regular, free, and competitive elections and of a set of constitutional freedoms that make them possible—was useful as a minimum criteria to determine the end of a transition from authoritarianism (the holding of free and competitive elections) as well as the success of the process of regime consolidation (the regular holding of free and competitive elections), it is of limited value when the issue at stake is how to deepen existing democracies. Democratic minimalism establishes too low of a benchmark for evaluating the kind of political and institutional reforms that are the concern of a period that requires a stronger notion of accountability.

The regional debate on democratic deficits was strongly influenced by the work of Guillermo O'Donnell. His concept of delegative democracy inaugurated a fruitful debate about the peculiar nature of some of the new democracies and the troublesome accountability deficits that subtype of polyarchy exhibited. Departing from the notion of delegative democracy, the chapter will describe O'Donnell's arguments about the need to strengthen legal controls on government to improve the overall functioning of the principle of democratic accountability. At the same time, it will argue for a need to address the deficit of political accountability of delegative polyarchies, a deficit that has been largely underconceptualized in the debate on delegative democracy (O'Donnell 1994, 2011). Such underconceptualization is rooted, I argue, in the predominance of a common electoral understanding of political accountability that is shared by delegative and minimalist models of democracy alike. To properly address such deficit, it is necessary to break with the minimalist stress on elections as the quintessential mechanism of accountability to propose a broader notion of democratic accountability that could properly tackle many of the challenges any project of democratic deepening faces. This is done in the last section, which introduces the concept of "mediated politics" as a theoretical framework for analyzing the practice of democratic representation. The idea of mediated politics conceives democratic representation as the product of a multiplicity of interactions that take place in various "partial regimes" that serve as a point of encounter between a plurality of constituencies and the political system. The goal of this conceptual exercise is to highlight another troublesome (vertical) accountability deficit that was not properly addressed by O'Donnell's analyses: the hostility of delegative democracies toward mediated politics.

O'Donnell on Delegative Democracy

The concept of delegative democracy sought to draw attention to the bifurcation of the path toward democratic institutionalization in the continent. On the one hand, there was a set of countries such as Chile and Uruguay in which the democratizing dynamics led to the establishment of representative democracies. On the other hand, there were groups of countries—Argentina, Peru, Brazil in the late 1980s and 1990s; Argentina, Venezuela, and Ecuador nowadays—that exhibited a peculiar form of polyarchy that greatly differs from the latter's classic representative variant. The concept of delegative democracy sought to conceptually delimit this latter subtype of polyarchy. In O'Donnell's eyes, this was characterized by the presence of regular, free, and competitive elections; the existence of basic political freedoms; and a remarkable concentration of power in the executive. Under delegative democracy, the practice of representation becomes a solitary and unconsulted exercise that falls in the shoulders of the presidential figure. The success of that sort of administration depends on the creativity that the president exhibits when confronting the manifold problems that affect society.

The delegative model of polyarchy exempts the executive from the multiple controls that are generally present in its representative variant. Under representative democracy, the act of electoral delegation takes place in an institutional setting characterized by the separation of powers and the presence of multiple mechanisms of checks and balances among state agencies. Accountability mechanisms constitute a safeguard to ensure that representatives properly use the powers that the citizenry has temporarily bestowed on them. Under delegative democracy, instead, the electoral triumph is considered an authorization to act in an unrestricted way: the executive demands from the electorate an act of trust in her political skills and, from the other branches of power, their political subordination to give the presidency the most ample maneuvering margin possible. In this model, the elected president appears as the sole interpreter of the nation's interests: "The core concept of DD is that the election gives the president the right and the duty to make the decisions he deems best for the country, while subjecting him only to the results of the future presidential elections" (O'Donnell 2011: 21; my translation).

The focus of O'Donnell's analysis are the forms of self-understanding and behavior of the executive, forms that at least during the inaugural moments of those administrations are shared by important sectors of the electorate. Those forms of self-understanding presuppose a peculiar notion about the nature of political representation that is predicated on the following assumptions:

- It considers elections the only relevant point of contact between the represented and the representatives.
- The electoral mandate presupposes an act of blind and full delegation of power from the citizenry to the presidency.
- The executive is conceived as the representative actor par excellence (weakening the legitimate claims of the other institutional actors of the representative system that are considered obstacles that conspire against the proper exercise of democratic representation by the president).
- The informal behavior of the executive divorces itself from the formal rules of horizontal accountability that are institutionally set.

The only remaining source of accountability is elections. While delegative democracies share the above features with classical forms of populism, they do not promote the political mobilization of social groups behind a "national-popular" project (Peruzzotti 2013). According to O'Donnell, delegative regimes are inimical to processes of populist polarization; they rely instead on a passive form of political delegation characteristic of depoliticized societies that are confronting a profound economic crisis.

In O'Donnell's view, delegative forms of self-understanding are the product of contexts of crisis (of a socioeconomic, political, or even of a military nature) in which large sectors of the population feel threatened. The presence of a generalized concern with the effects of the crisis in society creates a political conjuncture that prompts the emergence of a delegative leader who sees herself as a stormy-weather pilot (*piloto de tormenta*) who will lead the country out of the storms of economic emergency.[1] Delegative democracy, O'Donnell argues, is born and lives from crisis:

> DDs usually emerge from serious crises. . . . These crises do not necessarily result from objective data. At least regarding their depth and consequences, they also depend on the extent to which the majority of the public opinion deems them as such; to the point of convincing themselves that their worsening will be inevitable unless drastic changes are introduced. Finally, for a crisis to result in a DD, a leader is required, one who is able to solve it and who knows how to solve it. Based on this,

the leader either wins elections or ratifies the position he already holds in government. (O'Donnell 2010c; my translation)

Delegative democracy relies on a negative form of legitimacy like the one that gave birth to bureaucratic-authoritarianism: the diverse crises that affect the institutional edifice or the social fabric of contemporary democracies foment, under specific circumstances, a "ceiling consensus," that is, a social demand for order that is the material from which the delegative leader builds her political legitimacy. Like in any other "ceiling consensus," the legitimacy that emerges from such situations is of a negative nature: social support to an administration is not founded on the presence of a shared normative criterion that serves to validate—simultaneously limiting and strengthening—political authority but fundamentally rest on a temporary demand for order.[2] In this sense, delegative democracies and bureaucratic-authoritarianism face similar problems when confronting the challenge of their institutionalization. In fact, O'Donnell refers to DD as a noninstitutionalized form of polyarchy that—although it presupposes a minimum of democratic institutionalization—is unable to generate processes that could contribute to its institutional strengthening. On the contrary, the dynamics of this subtype of democracy tend to lead to recurrent crises and reproduce a situation of low institutionalization. According to O'Donnell, the political capital bestowed in delegative leaders rapidly erodes once the situation of crisis is overcome. That is, in his view, the sword of Damocles that is always threatening this form of leadership. It is no coincidence that delegative presidents always try to keep the flame of crisis alive:

> the language of crisis—of both past and future crises—, invoking the feelings of fear generated by it, is a constant element of such discourses. Even once the crisis is overcome, DDs try to rekindle a state of permanent emergency, to remind of the abysses and the workings of sinister forces constantly approaching us. This justifies the proclaimed need for extraordinary powers and the hostile attitude toward the "hindrance" posed by representative and accountability institutions. (O'Donnell 2011: 25; my translation)

Once the social sensation of emergency dissipates, O'Donnell argues, the early social support to the executive disappears. Instead, a plurality of demands starts to proliferate in the public realm, including demands for governmental accountability. Styles and behaviors that were celebrated (or tolerated) until recently begin to lose their social appeal, prompting hostile reactions from the media and the citizenry. The high levels of popularity that usually characterize the initial period of this sort of government are followed by an abrupt decline of social support and a "cascade of defections of those who until very recently claimed allegiance to the leader" (O'Donnell

2010c; my translation). This is why he considers that the time span of all delegative experiences is framed by two crises: the original one that fomented the emergence of a delegative leadership and a final one that expresses a shift of social humor that announces the fate of the administration. In O'Donnell's view, the societies in which this form of democracy predominates are trapped in a vicious circle of recurrent crises and chronic institutional weakness.[3]

The Debate on Horizontal and Social Accountability

O'Donnell's emphasis on the institutional deficits of delegative democracy and their consequences for the public life of those regimes opened a very fruitful agenda of research on democratic accountability. He contributed to set the parameters of the debate by proposing an analytical framework to analyze the diverse forms of democratic accountability. Following a spatial metaphor, he argues that accountability initiatives either operate within a horizontal axis of intrastate agencies or on an external vertical actor. The horizontal and vertical planes of O'Donnell's conceptualization of accountability correspond to the distinction between state and civil society (O'Donnell 1999d: 68). *Horizontal accountability* refers to a complex system of intrastate exchanges among a network of agencies and mechanisms. *Vertical mechanisms* instead refer to accountability initiatives that are pushed by citizens, either as voters or as members of civil society. They can be exercised through the institutional mechanism of regular, free, and competitive elections or through the informal influence of civil society and the media in the public sphere (O'Donnell 1999b, 2007a).

In O'Donnell's conception, horizontal accountability does not cover all of the interactions or exchanges that state agencies or powers develop with one another but only those that are exclusively oriented to the punishment of allegedly unlawful behavior, whether on grounds of encroachment or corruption (O'Donnell 1999b: 35). He defines horizontal accountability as the "existence of state agencies that are legally enabled and empowered, and factually willing and able, to take actions that span from routine oversight to criminal sanctions or impeachment in relation to actions or omissions by other agents or agencies of the state that might be qualified as unlawful" (O'Donnell 1999b: 38).

O'Donnell wants to call attention to the linkages between legal and political accountability, arguing that deficits of administrative, legal, and constitutional controls on the Executive respectively weaken the liberal and republican dimension of democratic rule. First, the lack of legal controls undermines the principle of separation of powers and mutual checks and balances, resulting in a subtype of presidential regime characterized by excessive executive dominance. The existence of effective mechanisms to redress encroachments by the executive over the jurisdiction of the legislative or judicial power (or of any other agencies that are part of the intrastate mechanisms of legal oversight) helps maintain a healthy political and institutional equilibrium among state powers, indirectly contributing to the agenda of political accountability. If those mechanisms lack power, then the whole edifice of representative democracy is undermined.

Second, the weakness or absence of institutions capable of enforcing the rule of law affect the autonomy of civil society and the rights of citizens, particularly of those who belong to disadvantaged groups. Mechanisms of legal accountability are crucial to prevent or to sanction unlawful encroachments by state agencies or public officials on citizens. This deficit translates in continuing human rights violations by state agencies under democratic rule and the negation of civic rights to significant sectors of the population (Brinks 2008; Méndez et al. 1999; O'Donnell 2007b; Peruzzotti and Smulovitz 2006; Uildriks and Tello Peon 2010).

Third, agencies of legal accountability contribute to strengthening the autonomy of the democratic state by preventing or sanctioning misuse of public office by unscrupulous elected officials and bureaucrats or its colonization by social groups. The rule of law constitutes the state as a public institution (O'Donnell 2010b: 159). Its absence directly affects the authority and capacities of the democratic state.

The concept of social accountability grew as a specification of O'Donnell's horizontal and vertical typology to emphasize the role civil society and the media played at denouncing and exposing unlawful state behavior to force the activation of horizontal agencies of oversight. It sought to expand what was then a debate that largely focused on formal institutional mechanisms, calling attention to the emergence throughout the continent of a variety of civic initiatives whose common denominator was to expose all sorts of governmental wrongdoing. The politics of social accountability— Smulovitz and I argued (Peruzzotti and Smulovitz 2006)—played a crucial role in calling attention to the legal accountability deficit of current democracies and, as such, introduced a novel and healthy social outcry for the rule of law.

The politics of social accountability should be seen as part of a broader process of cultural and political innovation in Latin America whose goal is to constitutionalize political power. Those developments are the outcome of processes of collective learning that took place after several countries in the region underwent the traumatic experience of political violence and state terrorism. It is in this context that the discourse and politics of human rights made its entrance, exposing the crimes of dictatorships and introducing the novel language of rights. The discourse and politics of human rights introduced a liberal concern for the legal regulation of state and civil society relations to prevent discretional state interventions on the social sphere as experienced under authoritarianism. It values the protective role of constitutional rights as the only institutions that could ensure the formation of a democratic civil society.[4]

The politics of human rights would be soon complemented by the politics of social accountability. The latter introduced a republican concern with the principles of separation of powers and checks and balances. It sought to constitutionalize the state, emphasizing the need for an autonomous judiciary that could ensure the effectiveness of rights and prevent or sanction other acts of unlawfulness committed by public officials. It also sought to force the executive to respect the jurisdiction of the other branches and agencies that integrate the horizontal web of accountability mechanisms.

Both forms of politics represent a key inflection point in the political culture of a region whose democratic tradition has had an ambiguous, if not hostile, relationship with constitutionalism, introducing an accountability model of representation that openly challenges both populist and delegative forms of self-understanding.[5] To what extent are those politics able to promote a process of political change that could break the vicious circle that entraps those societies whose pattern of democratization is dominated by the delegative form of democracy? There is no easy answer to the above question. One can nevertheless suggest two possible outcomes. On the one hand, the strength, constancy, and political skills of all those actors pushing for governmental accountability sets into motion a virtuous circle of "stimulation and induction" between social and horizontal mechanisms that is eventually able to break with the perverse dynamics that helped reproduce delegative democracy. O'Donnell himself suggested this pattern, arguing that, if a scenario emerges where social actors stimulate horizontal agencies to fulfill their mandate and role with responsibility, the latter would necessarily induct more initiatives of social accountability, setting into motion a dynamic that would end in the establishment of a representative form of polyarchy (O'Donnell 2006: 337–39).[6]

On the other hand, the politics of social accountability can provide a presence that is crucial to prevent the fall of delegative democracy into more authoritarian variants. In this scenario, social accountability initiatives are a barrier against the further deterioration of the institutional scenario—and under certain circumstances they accelerate the crisis of delegative leaderships—yet they are not powerful enough to promote the transition to a representative form of democracy. In such a context, the politics of social accountability simply follows—without altering it—the political cycle that characterizes delegative democracies. As Osvaldo Iazzetta rightly argues, delegative democracy is the product of a double and contradictory social impulse in which the society that demands and tolerates the discretional presidential style that characterizes those regimes is the same one that, once the crisis is over, starts to express discomfort and fatigue with the previously celebrated or tolerated behaviors (Iazzetta 2011: 108). One can consequently think of a scenario in which the politics of social accountability simply accompanies the cycle: media expose and social mobilizations become more active and effective during the fatigue period, contributing to the political eclipse of an administration that is losing social support. But they are impotent during the height of the delegative period, that is, in the contexts of crisis that usually gives birth to delegative forms of leadership.

Analyses of social accountability and human rights politics drew attention to specific forms of legal vertical accountability that could improve the performance of democratic regimes in the region by respectively reinforcing the liberal and republican components of the political system. They also serve to expand traditional understandings of legal accountability beyond the horizontal web of state agencies, showing specific ways in which civil society and the independent media contribute to its workings and enforcement. But, in themselves, those forms of civil society politics, even if successful, will only partially address current deficits of delegative democracies.[7] Delegative forms of democracy are not just characterized by the weakness of its liberal and republican dimension but also of its democratic one. This "other" deficit of delegative democracy is the focus of the next section.

The Democratic Deficit of Delegative Democracy

The rich debate that O'Donnell opened with the suggestive concept of delegative democracy served as an important call of attention about the legal dimension of the democratic state, a dimension that had traditionally been relegated from political and academic analyses in Latin America. It was a crucial reminder of the need to develop equilibrium among the republican, liberal, and democratic components that make up contemporary democracies. In this sense, the concept and subsequent analysis of legal accountability broadened and enriched existing understandings about democracy, and, more specifically, about the nature of the democratic state. However, the focus on legal deficits of the state—including works on social accountability—left aside another crucial aspect of the notion of democratic accountability: its political dimension. Not that such dimension was absent in the previous debate; in fact, O'Donnell highlights hostility toward representative mediations as one of the most distinctive aspects of delegative democracy. Delegative leaders are hesitant to subject themselves to legal and constitutional rules that might limit their authority but are also reluctant to share power with other representative institutions like congress and political parties. Presidential leaders in delegative democracy are unwilling to subject their proposals to the filtering mechanisms of structures of political intermediation, privileging instead a closed and secretive pattern of decision making.

O'Donnell also observes the hostility of delegative leaders toward political parties and calls attention to the fact that delegative democracies usually emerge in countries that lack an institutionalized party system (O'Donnell 2011: 24). Yet, this political dimension of accountability is not properly addressed in his typology of diverse accountabilities, which tend to be biased toward the legal dimension of the concept.[8]

The three main forms of accountability that are at the center of his analysis as well as of the literature on social accountability (legal horizontal, vertical electoral, vertical legal) far from exhausting all the dimensions of the concept: the full picture requires further specification, particularly in relation to the vertical political axis.

The lack of an exhaustive conceptualization of the political dimension of accountability is not just a problem of O'Donnell's typology but a more generalized one of the literature on democratization. Such conceptual gap can be explained by the influence that minimalist models exerted on earlier formulations of the concept of democracy. A main premise of such model is that free and competitive elections are the quintessential element of democratic representation. Consequently, the success of any democratizing process is to be measured in relation to the extent that it is able to ensure the regular holding of free and competitive elections and a reasonable degree of public liberties. While such model might have provided a useful yardstick to respectively indicate the closing of the period of transition and consolidation, it is inadequate to evaluate the challenges of a stage where the issue is no longer how to stabilize but rather how to deepen democracy. The most palpable indicator of the limitations of the minimalist model is that the very concept of delegative democracy fulfills the minimum criterion of the minimalist canon.

The main limitation of the minimalist model for thinking an agenda of democratic deepening is its marked skepticism regarding the potentials of democracy. It "realist" vision of democracy requires the disposing of those normative principles that could orient a process of further democratization of existing regimes. The origin of this particular conception of democracy can be traced back to Joseph Schumpeter's critique of classical democratic ideals. His "realist" vision of democracy supposes the abandonment of a crucial feature of any normative conception of democracy: popular sovereignty. Present-day democracies, Schumpeter argues, no longer institutionalize the government of the people but that of politicians. Democracy allows citizens to choose those who will govern them but it is no longer a regime that expresses their will (Schumpeter 1950: 284–85).

Other authors working in that conceptual tradition attempted to moderate some of the aspects of the Schumpeterian model by seeking to introduce a notion of accountability. However, they did not do away with the initial skepticism of the former regarding the potentials of democracy for citizen accountability. The following statement by Adam Przeworski clearly illustrates such skepticism: "Democracy may be the best form of government that was ever invented, but it is congenitally, structurally weak as a mechanism of control over government. This is just the way life is" (Przeworski 2006: 325).

Present versions of democratic minimalism do not completely reject the idea of governmental accountability; rather, they consider unlikely that the latter might be accomplished through elections. The latter are deemed a structurally inadequate tool for the citizens to exert control over governments. This is why authors like Przewor-ski, Stokes, and Manin (1999) consider it more productive to reorient concerns about institutional betterment in a horizontal direction. The demand for greater horizontal controls of democratic minimalism brings that literature close to the concerns of the delegative democracy (and social accountability) argument. This is not surprising, given that the concept of delegative democracy was elaborated by contrasting it with prevailing minimalist models of representative democracy.

There is, to be true to O'Donnell, an additional concern for vertical accountability that is not present in contemporary minimalist authors. Such concern expresses itself in the author's references to the deficit of mediations of delegative democracies that weakens the citizenship principle. This is a point that needs further development if we do not want to constrain the concept of democratic accountability to the limited parameters of democratic minimalism. It redirects attention to another dimension of the original concept of polyarchy that has been largely underplayed by a debate that focused fundamentally on electoral representation: political processes that take place between elections to promote governmental responsiveness (Dahl 1956).

Electoral politics cannot properly address all the challenges posed by democratic representation, particularly those related to the question of political responsiveness to citizen's claims, given the inadequacy of elections as a signaling mechanism of vot-ers' specific preferences. Echoed in recent arguments made by Przeworski, Manin, and Stokes regarding the limitations of elections as a mechanism to signal citizen's preferences over policy, Robert Dahl considered that elections tell us little about the preferences of majorities.

> Strictly speaking—he argues—all an election reveals is the first preferences of some citizens among the candidates standing for office . . . we can rarely interpret a ma-jority of first choices among candidates in a national election as being equivalent to a majority of first choices for a specific policy. Some people evidently vote for a candidate although they are quite indifferent about the issues. Others support a candidate who is opposed to them on some issues. . . . Thus it becomes possible for a resounding majority of the voters to elect a candidate all of whose policies are the first choices only of a minority. (Dahl 1956: 125, 127–28)

Instead of arriving at the pessimist conclusions of Przeworski and other minimalist theorists regarding the potential of democratic institutions as tools for citizen control, Dahl argued for the need to complement elections with other nonelectoral political processes to promote political responsiveness. In his view, the promotion of receptive administrations is more the result of intraelection than of electoral activity. In his view, "the numerical majority is incapable of undertaking any coordinated action, it is the various components of the numerical majority that have the means for action" (Dahl

1956: 146). The effective citizens are, to use Philippe Schmitter's expression, not isolated voters but those who join in an association to advance specific claims (Schmitter 2008).

By introducing the notion of polyarchy, Dahl, as well as other authors who subscribed to pluralism, wanted to emphasize the centrality of those political processes that take place between elections and that in their view constitute a key to understanding how administrations can be held politically accountable. In this rendering, the notion of polyarchy entails not just the existence of an institutional framework that could ensure regular, free, and competitive elections but also the existence of a significant degree of interelection activity by different constituencies that seek to promote governmental responsiveness to their claims and demands (Dahl 1956: 131). Within this perspective, the extent to which a regime is politically responsive to its citizens depends on the nature and dynamics of interelection political processes, for it is then that different minorities seek to influence the policy process to promote public policies that reflect their interests and claims.

Classic pluralism envisioned those processes as a competitive struggle between interest groups (Bentley 1954; Dahl 1956; Latham 1952; Truman 1951). Such vision of the political processes was soon challenged by the literature on corporatism, social movements, and neopluralism that considered that the former's description of political dynamics as competitive failed to address the significant power imbalances that were present among different types of social groups (Schattschneider 1960), the oligarchical tendencies that many policy areas exhibited (McFarland 2004; Offe 1987) and ignored the contribution that new actors such as new social movements and public interest groups make to the contemporary political processes (Berry 1999). Despite their differences, all those authors agreed upon a notion of democratic representation that is not confined to electoral politics. Their emphasis on different sorts of group politics is an important reminder that electoral representation is always partial and incomplete and needs to be complemented with other mechanisms of political accountability.

Seen from this perspective, the problem with delegative democracy is not just the presence of a legally uncontrolled executive (whose behavior needs to be tamed through effective horizontal mechanisms) but the lack of adequate citizen input on the political process as well. Delegative democracies seem to presuppose a passive citizenry that fully delegates political power to elected officials on Election Day and that then recedes to the background during the whole political tenure of the administration (O'Donnell 2010b: 31). If elections are the only legitimate channel of communication between citizens and their representatives, the vote becomes an act of political abdication through which the citizenry forfeits the full control of the political agenda to the elected representatives.[9] A model of democracy that requires a process of complete delegation—such as the one described by O'Donnell—is a problematic one and supposes an unjustified excess of trust in the personal qualities and abilities of the presidency. Absence of citizen input, however, might not be necessarily based on civic apathy but on lack of adequate channels of intermediation between state and society as well. So, even if there are numerous groups in delegative democracies that are reluctant to fully relinquish political agency and promote different sorts of initiatives to influence the policy process, there are no effective channels of vertical political intermediation to canalize, filter, and process their demands. The latter suggests that there are more than horizontal deficits of accountability in delegative democracies: there is a correspondingly vertical deficit in those regimes that expresses itself in the absence of adequate institutional instances of political mediation. The end result is the predominance of a highly personalized and elitist pattern of policy making.

If delegative democracy is characterized by the absence not only of horizontal intrastate controls but also of vertical political mediations, then it is not enough to accomplish a transition from a delegative to a minimalist form of democracy. It is necessary to promote a simultaneous transition toward the establishment of a complex, inclusive, and plural field of mediated politics to improve the political responsiveness of existing regimes.

Representative Democracy as Mediated Politics

If the task of strengthening the democratic legality of the state was accompanied by a sustained effort at theorizing about the crucial constitutive role that constitutional and legal norms play in any democracy (O'Donnell 2010b; Peruzzotti 2012), the chore of elaborating a notion of democratic representation that could orient the agenda to democratic deepening is no less demanding. In this last section, some guidelines are suggested to orient such an agenda.

The first step toward a reconstruction of a notion of democratic representation that could guide the efforts for democratic deepening in contemporary Latin America is to question conceptual models that reduce democratic representation to elections and electoral politics. As Michael Saward (2009) rightly argues, the notion of representative democracy is more exhaustive than that of electoral representation, for it refers to a broader process of formulation and reception of claims that, in great part, takes place between elections and outside electoral channels. From this perspective, the practice of democratic representation is seen as resting on a complex social ecology of actors that develops in different representative "circuits" or "partial regimes" (Schmitter 2008).[10] The electoral circuit, with its mediating structures of political parties and legislatures, certainly represents the central institutional mediation of any democratic regime. However, there are additional circuits that play a relevant role in the political process. First, there is the functional circuit of private interest representation that many consider an informal complement to territorial representation.[11] Second, there is a more recent addition of a circuit of public interest representation organizations that have expanded the traditional understanding of lobbying to include new actors and themes. Third, there is the circuit of newly created policy councils, communal councils, indigenous councils, and other arenas of institutionalized participation.[12] Finally, one should not forget about the crucial role played by an autonomous and pluralistic public sphere as a sounding board of alternative claims and discourses.

It is in such a variety of circuits and arenas and on the interactions that take place among them and the state institutions that the practice of democratic representation occurs between elections. Delegative democracies, by resting solely on a questionable use of the electoral circuit,[13] impoverish the quality of democratic representation, for they deprive the political process of alternative arenas that give expression to a plurality of constituencies and claims during the exercise of political representation.

The concept of mediated politics is meant to encompass the different circuits that allow for the formation, expression, and influence of a plurality of constituencies under representative democracy. The field of mediated politics supposes two things: the existence of a political and institutional framework that encourages the formation of a variety of associational formats that give birth and express different constituencies and the creation of a plurality of formal and informal arenas that serve as points of encounter between those constituencies and different elements of the political system. On the one hand, the concept of mediated politics supposes a variety of organizational forms that give expression to different constituencies that cannot be exhaustively understood by adopting a civil society or pressure group perspective that informs pluralism and corporatism. It presupposes an ecology of groups that is much broader than that assumed by those perspectives, which usually tend to concentrate on one particular form of collective action. The use of an encompassing notion of groups also avoids the usual definitional quarrels that are present in different conceptions of civil society. Theories of civil society are frequently predicated on the relevance of one particular form of collective action for democracy: so, while Habermasian approaches emphasize the role of new social movements operating in the public sphere, those inspired by the neo-Tocquevillean social capital model tend to privilege the role of primary and secondary associations that constitute the prepolitical everyday life world of citizens. In a similar vein, the concept also rejects the narrow conception of pressure groups that informs both pluralism and corporatism. Finally, it incorporates a variety of arenas of a hybrid nature, organized around a notion of cogovernance that can no longer be conceptually understood through the lenses of the literature on civil society, pluralism, or corporatism.

On the other hand, the emphasis on mediating structures breaks with dichotomous conceptions of the political process (state/civil society; representation/participation) to concentrate on the points of contact between them. It is precisely in those mutual interactions that the creative element of democratic representation lies. The conceptual emphasis on state/society linkages should not be read as meaning that any form of linkage or of interaction is legitimate per se or positively contributes to the practice of democratic representation. On the contrary, the emphasis on the need of institutionalizing a broad and plural field of mediated politics should be seen as a call to inquire about the nature and dynamics of the different circuits through which democratic political processes take place to determine to what extent they comply with the demands for openness, inclusiveness, and deliberation emphasized by normative conceptions of democracy.

Normative considerations are crucial when evaluating processes of democratic innovation that result in the creation of new mediating structures, such as the ones that recently took place in different democracies of Latin America. The most relevant innovations are those that promote participatory processes of a different nature than the processes of bargaining that informed the perspective of pluralist or corporatist politics. Under certain conditions, new mediating structures might promote a more dialogical, open, and inclusive pattern of policy making that could lead to more equitable policy outcomes.

Conclusion

The concept of delegative democracy served to open up an important regional debate about the nature and dynamics of contemporary Latin American democracies. Focusing on a number of problematic cases, O'Donnell rightly called attention to how the absence of horizontal controls on the Executive affected the dynamics and quality of democratic representation. In this chapter, I attempted to call attention to another significant deficit of delegative democracy as expressed in the hostility exhibited by that subtype of democracy toward most forms of mediated politics. While the question of the horizontal deficits of accountability received much attention and led to a rich corpus of literature on the contribution of legal mechanisms of accountability to democratic representation, the other deficit of delegative democracy remained underconceptualized. The latter was in part due to the predominance of a purely electoral conception of political accountability that reduced representative democracy to electoral democracy. The concept of mediated politics seeks to expand the theoretical framework of democratic accountability. It does so by calling attention to a set of nonelectoral mediating structures that are relevant for understanding political accountability in contemporary democracies, arguing that when properly designed and/or regulated, an active and independent field of mediated politics can become a crucial asset in the promotion of more inclusive, public, and deliberative political processes. By suggesting an alternative framework to think about representative democracy, the chapter also hopes to contribute to the task that O'Donnell set for himself and us with his studies on accountability: the development of a critical democratic theory that could help us reflect about the pending tasks for democratic deepening in Latin America and elsewhere.

NOTES

1. Lucas González adds another dimension to the economic crisis argument: the existence of low levels of confidence in government. Societies that display higher levels of confidence in the democratic system, he argues, when confronting a serious socioeconomic crisis, might be able to avoid a delegative outcome. See González in chapter 11 of this volume.

2. For the notion of negative legitimacy (to describe Argentine political dynamics in the period of the "impossible game"), see Peruzzotti 1993. There is however a crucial difference between the ceiling consensus that gave rise to the bureaucratic-authoritarian interventions and the one that feeds delegative democracies: in the latter case, the demand for order supposes a minimum respect for some basic democratic criterion (even when under certain circumstances the exercise of delegative leadership might even suppress that agreement, as the case of Fujimori in Peru illustrates). In contrast to the historical context that gave rise to bureaucratic-authoritarianism, delegative democracies take place in societies that have undergone a process of collective learning that contributed to the institutionalization of democracy.

3. It is not completely fair to say that O'Donnell did not explicitly incorporate a dynamic component into the analysis of delegative democracy, as Lucas González states in the previous chapter in this volume. O'Donnell's initial conceptualization of delegative democracy assumes a dynamic model that corresponds to one of the patterns that González delineates in his interesting analysis of the evolution of delegative regimes in the region. O'Donnell thought that societies that adopted the delegative pattern were trapped in a vicious political circle of deinstitutionalization (a "recurring delegativeness" pattern). Lucas González expands O'Donnell's model, adding two other alternative paths to the one he originally envisioned. The first one is the move away from delegative into a representative type of polyarchy ("the eroding of delegative democracy") as exemplified by Brazil and Peru. The other one is what González terms "intensifying delegative democracy," which he employs to refer to the so-called Bolivarian democracies. I do not think that such expression captures some of the recent changes that some countries of the region have experienced. I also do not think that the political projects of Chávez or Correa can be adequately understood as representing a deepening of delegative behaviors. Instead, I tend to side with Sebastián Mazzuca (chapter 4 of this volume) in arguing that a new economic context (which is no longer of crisis but of plenty) made the return of populism into the region possible. This established regimes that— while presenting many of the features present in delegative democracies—departed from the negative form of legitimacy of the former to foster a process of antagonistic political mobilization based on the polarizing discourse of the national-popular political tradition. In some cases, most notably Venezuela, such regimes no longer rely on informal delegative practices but have introduced formal institutional changes that seek to undermine key aspects of the notion of polyarchy, such as the presence of a pluralistic public sphere and of an autonomous judiciary.

4. It is no coincidence that the concept of civil society becomes popularized during processes of democratization. The idea of civil society as a crucial arena for innovation that could promote

the democratization of existing democracies will emerge as a crucial aspect of the radical politics agenda. The project of reconstruction of civil society reoriented radical politics both in a poststatist and a postrevolutionary direction. Jean L. Cohen and Andrew Arato (1992) argued that a politics of civil society should be built around the notion of political self-limitation to avoid the negative experiences of revolutionary and populist politics. For an analysis of the impact of the concept of civil society in the analysis of processes of democratization in Latin America, see Peruzzotti and Plot (2013) and Cohen and Arato (1992).

5. For the challenges that accountability claims pose on delegative democracies, see Peruzzotti 2001. I have also discussed the problems it poses to a populist project of democratic deepening in Peruzzotti 2013.

6. Smulovitz and I also envisioned the possibility of a virtuous circle but also warned about the possibility of social cries for accountability degenerating into a troublesome form of antipolitics. See Peruzzotti and Smulovitz (2006: 349) and particularly Peruzzotti 2005 and 2006.

7. As Lucy Taylor argues, that type of civil society politics serve to protect due process and delimit the jurisdiction that regulated the policy-making process but have no say in the content of those processes and policies (L. Taylor 2010).

8. Undoubtedly, the development of a democratic legal state to ensure the oversight of public authorities, the workings of the system of mutual checks and balances, and the rights of all citizens would represent a major accomplishment for a region like Latin America, characterized by the chronic weaknesses of all institutional checks to the authoritarian tendencies of the presidency. The relevance of such an agenda in any debate on democratic deepening is out of the question. The same can be said regarding the accomplishment of regular, free, and competitive elections. However, those are partial aspects of an agenda on democratic accountability that should include other important dimensions such as the development of adequate linkages between society and the state to ensure political responsiveness to citizen's claims.

9. Again, the latter arguments are not meant to underestimate the relevance of elections or the great accomplishment that the institutionalization of regimes that allowed for regular, free, and competitive elections had in a region like Latin America. But, as O'Donnell's argument of delegative democracy highlights, the existence of regular, free, and competitive elections does not necessarily result in adequate democratic representation.

10. The concept of "partial regimes" is developed in Schmitter (1992: 422). The term "circuits" is taken from Benjamin Arditi, who develops a similar conception in Arditi 2005.

11. This has been the argument of authors like Claus Offe and Philippe Schmitter. See Offe 1984 and Schmitter 1983.

12. Significantly, Brazil—the country that, according to O'Donnell, successfully completed the transition from delegative to representative democracy—is a case that differs from the other examples of delegative democracy in the fact that it consciously expanded the field of mediated politics. It did so not only by adding a new political party that would play a crucial role at democratizing the party system but also by developing a new set of mediating structures oriented to incorporate the poor into the political process. For an analysis of such processes, see Avritzer 2009. For an analysis that seeks to explain the changes across time that led to the weakening of the delegative components of the Brazilian political regime see Lucas González's chapter in this volume.

13. Questionable in the sense that under that form of democracy voting entails an act of political delegation that leaves the isolated citizen powerless until the next election.

PART IV

HUMAN AGENCY AND THE QUALITY OF DEMOCRACY

CHAPTER 13

Democracy, Agency, and the Classification of Political Regimes

JAMES W. MCGUIRE

Guillermo O'Donnell's ideas about democracy are used in this chapter to revisit debates about how to classify political regimes in Latin America. Recognizing that human agency is at the heart of O'Donnell's normative appreciation of democracy, it is argued that protocols for classifying political regimes should take agency more explicitly into account when moving from the conceptualization of democracy to the operationalization of criteria for characterizing a regime as democratic—that is, in formulating criteria to decide whether suffrage is inclusive, whether elections are free and fair, whether basic rights are protected, and whether elected officials can exercise their constitutional authority. In some recent classifications, certain regimes in post-1945 Argentina, Brazil, Chile, and Costa Rica have been designated democratic even though a large share of the adult population has been denied the right to vote; even though electoral competition has been unfree, unfair, or both; even though significant human rights violations have occurred; and even though military officers have constrained the constitutional prerogatives of elected chief executives and legislators. To assess whether a particular regime meets the operational criteria for any of these dimensions of democracy is inevitably a judgment call. Democracy is a value-laden term, however, and to bestow it too broadly is to reduce our ability to discriminate among regimes whose citizens enjoy widely differing levels of rights to participate in the making of the political decisions by which they will be bound.

Schemes for classifying political regimes would be improved, it is argued, by giving more priority to agency in deciding how far a regime can fall short on various dimensions of democracy without becoming a nondemocracy; by recognizing that democracy affects social and political outcomes not just through electoral contestation but also through the freedoms of expression and organization, as well as by altering perceptions of entitlement to state benefits; by using twenty-first-century rather than past standards to characterize regimes; and by classifying regimes into more than three categories. Collier and Adcock (1999: 537) insist that "how scholars understand and operationalize a concept can and should depend in part on what they are going to do with it." By operationalizing democracy in a way more compatible with an agency-centric view of human development, regime classification would depict more validly the degree to which citizens have been empowered in the political realm to lead a thoughtfully chosen life.

Democracy: Conceptualization and Operationalization

Universal agreement on what democracy means is impossible, but that is a good thing. The safest way to improve the polity is to judge it by a variety of contested standards rather than by a single agreed-upon standard. Nonetheless, to communicate research findings effectively, a working definition is needed. Key criteria for democracy, in O'Donnell's view (2010a: 17–23), are "competitive elections for most top governmental positions"; "the positive, participatory rights of voting and eventually trying to be elected"; and "a set of freedoms that surround and are necessary supports for the likelihood of such elections and their related participatory rights." O'Donnell further stipulates that elections—in addition to being competitive, egalitarian, inclusive, and institutionalized—should be decisive. Where elections are decisive, those who get elected actually take office, stay in office until the end of their terms (unless illness or some other uncontroversial circumstance precludes this), and while in office "can actually make the binding decisions that the legal/constitutional framework normally authorizes."

O'Donnell's criteria for a democratic political regime can be reframed as (1) free, fair, and inclusive elections; (2) basic human and civil rights; and (3) authority for those who get elected. The first criterion means that political leaders must be chosen in fair and periodic competitive elections in which almost all adult citizens have the right to vote and to run for office. The second criterion entails that citizens must be granted in principle, and not systematically denied in practice, basic rights like recognition as a person, freedom from physical abuse by agents of the state, freedom of speech and the press, freedom of association and assembly, freedom of religion, and due process of law. The third criterion implies that the decisions of elected officials should not be vetoed or undermined systematically by unelected power holders (e.g., military leaders, local political bosses, criminal gangs, guerrilla groups, or foreign governments).

In O'Donnell's terms "authority for those who get elected" would be evidence of the decisiveness of elections (O'Donnell 2010a: 19–20), and the periodicity of elections would signify their institutionalization (O'Donnell 2004b: 15). In most respects, however, the above definition is consistent with O'Donnell's criteria, as well as with the notion of polyarchy, which Robert Dahl defined as a set of institutions that are necessary to "the highest feasible attainment of the democratic process in the government of a country" (Dahl 1989: 222). Democracy, for Dahl, is a process for making binding decisions: one that is characterized by enlightened understanding, effective participation, voting equality at the decisive stage, control of the agenda, and the inclusion of almost all adult citizens. Some of these criteria are so demanding that full democracy may be unattainable (Dahl 1989: 117). More practicable, Dahl argues (1998: 85–86), is to create a set of institutions in which (1) control of government policy decisions is constitutionally vested in elected officials; (2) officials are elected fairly and periodically; (3) citizenship (including suffrage and the right to run for office) is inclusive of practically all adult permanent residents; (4) citizens have the right to form independent associations like parties and interest groups; (5) there is freedom of expression on political matters, broadly defined; and (6) alternative sources of information exist and citizens have a right to seek them out.

Dahl uses the term polyarchy to describe a regime in which each of these six institutions is present. Two differences are worth noting between Dahl's notion of polyarchy and the shorthand three-part definition of democracy derived from O'Donnell's writings. Whereas Dahl stipulates that in a polyarchy "control of government policy decisions is constitutionally vested in elected officials," the shorthand definition requires that decision-making authority be *actually*, not just constitutionally, vested in elected officials—at least to the extent that the decisions of such officials are not vetoed or undermined systematically by unelected power holders.[1] That is what O'Donnell means by the "decisiveness" of elections. Moreover, whereas Dahl singles out freedom to organize and freedom of expression and information as defining rights in a polyarchy, the notion of "basic human and civil rights" would include rights such as recognition as a human being, freedom from abuse by agents of the state, freedom of religion, and due process of law.

The definition of democracy should be informed by its justification. Democracy may be vindicated instrumentally, by its (hypothesized) beneficial consequences for other desirable outcomes; affirmed intrinsically, as a good thing in itself (or at least as immediately necessary for the exercise of practical reason); or justified constructively, by its role in fostering discussion and interaction in which preferences are formed and modified (Sen 1999: 148). Some recent protocols for classifying political regimes, it will be argued below, have focused heavily on the instrumental role of democracy, to the neglect of its intrinsic and constructive roles.

Democracy and Inclusive Suffrage

In alluding to the positive, participatory right of voting, O'Donnell calls attention to the importance of agency in democracy (see Vargas Cullell's chapter 14 of this volume) and in human development more broadly. Human development may be thought of as the opportunity to lead a thoughtfully chosen life. As Sen points out (1999: 190), "not only are we well or ill, but also we act or refuse to act, and can choose to act in one way rather than another. And thus we . . . must take responsibility for doing things or not doing them." From this perspective, the capability to lead a thought-fully chosen life involves the opportunity to participate in making the decisions that will bind one (or, if the polity is too large, in electing and influencing those who will make such decisions).

From a perspective that values human beings as agents as well as patients, as deliberative doers and makers as well as incarnations of states of well-being, democratic participation is intrinsically important or at least immediately important to the exercise of practical reason. Moreover, as Sen (1999: 148) points out, democratic participation involves not only expanded opportunities to satisfy existing preferences but also discussion and creative interaction in which we discover and rethink those preferences. Democratic participation, including by voting, is part of what O'Donnell (2004b: 39) calls "the positive freedom to decide, with reasonable autonomy, knowledge, and responsibility, the course of one's life—in my terms, to be properly an agent" (see also O'Donnell 2010a: 33, 173; and Vargas Cullell's chapter in this volume).

In a democracy, O'Donnell argues, the right to vote "should be attached to all adults in a territory, irrespective of their social condition and of ascriptive characteristics other than age and nationality." O'Donnell also stipulates that citizenship should be "assigned on the same terms to all adults who meet the nationality criterion" (O'Donnell 2004b: 16, 24). This understanding of inclusiveness parallels that of Robert Dahl, who argues that all adults should be presumed qualified, and roughly equally qualified, to make the decisions that will bind them. Accordingly, Dahl argues that "the demos should include all adults subject to the binding collective decisions of the association" (Dahl 1989: 120), and that "the demos must include all adult members of the association except transients and those proved to be mentally defective" (Dahl 1998: 37–38).

Agency for O'Donnell is not a criterion for democracy in the same sense as, say, the decisiveness of elections. It is rather an assumption or principle with which the criteria for democracy must be consistent. Analogously, Dahl (1989: 31–33, 97–101) stipulates a Strong Principle of Equality, which holds that every adult should be judged to be qualified, and roughly equally qualified, to participate in making the decisions by which he or she will be bound. Dahl justifies democracy as a process for making binding decisions that is consistent with this prior principle. From the standpoint of agency, accordingly, deprivation of the right to vote is inimical to human development both intrinsically and constructively, apart from any consequences it may have for preference satisfaction, social protest, electoral outcomes, or political analysis.

Some classification protocols, however, code regimes democratic even if the right to vote falls short of the "practically all adults" stipulated in Dahl's (1989: 221) definition of inclusive suffrage. In one such scheme, regimes in which women are disenfranchised are judged to be potentially democratic because the struggle for female suffrage never led to major political upheaval and because female enfranchisement "did not significantly change the political spectrum in any country" (Rueschemeyer, Stephens, and Stephens 1992: 48). In another, regimes that deny the vote to women or to illiterate people are coded democratic so as to "capture the considerable cross-country variation in political conditions before World War II" (Boix, Miller, and Rosato 2013: 7). In such protocols, the decision as to whether to classify a particular regime as democratic turns heavily on the degree to which the regime permits contested elections.

Electoral contestation may be worth explaining for its own sake, and it may well affect outcomes of interest regardless of the breadth of the suffrage. Electoral contestation, however, is a perfectly usable concept in its own right. From the perspective shared by O'Donnell and Sen, the label democratic should be reserved for regimes in which women and illiterate people have the right to vote. To designate as democratic regimes that disenfranchise such groups, from their perspective, would be to downplay the intrinsic and constructive importance of democracy and to diminish the centrality of agency in human development.

To regard suffrage as inclusive despite the exclusion of women or illiterates raises additional vexing questions that can be illustrated with reference to literacy restrictions in twentieth-century Chile and Brazil. Chile until 1970 and Brazil until 1985 required voters to pass a literacy test. Nevertheless, several of the major classification schemes code Chile from 1946 to 1969 (the last year when the literacy clause was in effect) and Brazil from 1946 to 1963 (the last year before the 1964–85 military regime) as democratic (Boix, Miller, and Rosato 2013; Cheibub, Gandhi, and Vreeland 2009; Mainwaring, Brinks, and Pérez-Liñán 2001).[2] Boix, Miller, and Rosato (2013), as just noted, label suffrage-restricting regimes democratic in order to maximize variation across regimes in the pre-1945 era. Cheibub, Gandhi, and Vreeland (2010), following Alvarez et al. (1996) and Przeworski et al. (2000), label a regime democratic if its chief executive and legislature are "popularly elected," if elections are contested by more than one party, and if alternation in power has occurred. Mainwaring, Brinks, and Pérez-Liñán (2001, 2007) reject subminimalist definitions of democracy focused on electoral contestation in favor of a multidimensional conceptualization similar to the ones used by Dahl and O'Donnell, but advocate using retrospective (past) rather than contemporary (twenty-first-century) standards, such that the democratic character of a political regime is assessed according to what was viewed as democratic at the time each regime existed, rather than what is viewed as democratic by present-day observers.[3] To choose a contemporary standard, they argue, would invite anachronism, whereby no past regime could possibly live up to a characterization of democracy that includes rights that had not been institutionalized (or possibly even imagined) at the time the regime existed.

Given the normative connotations of the term, a multidimensional conceptualization of democracy seems more valid than a conceptualization focused solely on electoral contestation. Moreover, Mainwaring, Brinks, and Pérez-Liñán (2001, 2007) make an explicit and rigorous case for using past standards to classify political regimes in prior historical eras. A problem with using a past standard of democracy is that it requires the classification team to make another set of (inevitably) contestable judgments. It is not self-evident in what year one should switch from a past to a twenty-first-century standard, and it is debatable whether that year should be the same for all countries. To vary the operational threshold for democracy according to the times, moreover, suggests that it might also be appropriate to vary it according to the culture, such that different standards are applied in Belgium 2010 and in Yemen 2010. Another set of judgments would be needed to establish precisely what the past standard should be in a particular historical era. For example, one would have to decide in what year it became unusual rather than normal to restrict the suffrage to male citizens or to people who are literate. Also, to apply a past standard to the inclusiveness criterion for democracy raises the issue of whether a past standard should also be applied to the basic rights criterion. In 1845, for example, slavery existed in the United States, Native Americans were denied citizenship, and women and many free men lacked the right to vote. Nonetheless, the United States in 1845 was coded democratic by Boix, Miller, and Rosato (2013), and the widely used Polity IV database (Marshall and Jaggers 2010) gave the United States the highest possible democracy score of "10" in 1845 (as well as in 2010). Each of these coding schemes used a "subminimalist" definition of democracy based heavily or entirely on electoral contestation, but a coding scheme that employed a multidimensional definition of democracy that included basic rights would face this issue as well.

Mainwaring, Brinks, and Pérez-Liñán (2001: 40, 46–47; 2007: 157) argue that a literacy qualification for the vote does not violate the criterion of inclusive suffrage if it (1) occurs during a historical era where similar qualifications are common in other countries, (2) fails to generate mass protest, and (3) makes little difference to electoral outcomes. In such cases, they contend, a literacy requirement is simply a cultural artifact. To the extent that suffrage restrictions can be justified in terms of their *consequences* (e.g., for protest or election outcomes) rather than in terms of their *rationales*, it might be equally worth asking (4) what share of the voting-age population is disenfranchised by a literacy test and penalizing the regime in proportion to that share. For example, in assessing the degree of democracy in a country, Arat (1991: 25) discounts one dimension, "inclusiveness of the process," by a factor equal to one minus the proportion of the population that is disenfranchised by the exclusion. Accordingly, if a literacy requirement for voting exists in a country in which 40% of voting-age people are illiterate, Arat discounts the inclusiveness component of the country's democracy score by 40%.

All regimes restrict suffrage. At the end of the twentieth century, no country enfranchised children, and only four granted voting rights to persons adjudicated to have severe mental disabilities. Some countries also denied the vote to prisoners or to expatriates (Blais, Massicotte, and Yoshinaka 2001). Such restrictions, however, are justified by their rationales, not by their consequences. Children and those judged to be mentally incompetent are disenfranchised on the grounds that they are not autonomous agents. Likewise, military personnel are denied the right to vote in ten Latin American countries (Goodwin-Gill 2006: 128 n153), and Buddhist monks are denied the right to vote in Thailand (Chambers 2006: 285). The grounds for these exclusions are not always stated, but soldiers and some clergy are obliged to follow the orders of their superiors and are therefore unable, like children or the mentally ill, to act as autonomous agents. Where prisoners or expatriates are denied the vote, it is on the grounds that they have knowingly acted in ways that compromise their right to membership in the voting-entitled political community.

Let us set aside for a moment the issue of principled versus consequentialist justifications for suffrage restrictions and review some consequences of the literacy qualification for the vote in the cases that concern us here. The literacy requirement for voting in Brazil and Chile generated no mass protest. Moreover, many poor people in pre-1958 Chile and in pre-1985 Brazil were enmeshed in clientelistic networks that predisposed them to vote for conservative candidates (Baland and Robinson 2008: 1747–48; Cohen 1989; Geddes and Zaller 1989), so the literacy requirement probably also did little to change election outcomes. Still, the share of the population affected by the literacy qualification for the vote was not small in either country. As late as 1960, illiteracy in the population aged 15 and older was 39% in Brazil and 16% in Chile (McGuire 2010: 318). Turnout as a percentage of the voting-age population was only 24% in Brazil in 1945 (women had received the right to vote in 1932) and only 28% in Chile in 1952 (female suffrage had been granted in 1949). By comparison, turnout so measured was 67% in Argentina in 1951 (women had received the right to vote in 1947; no literacy clause had ever existed) and 50% in Costa Rica in 1953 (female suffrage was granted in 1949; a literacy requirement was dropped in 1913. Sources: turnout: López Pintor and Gratschew 2002: 158–60; literacy requirements: Engerman and Sokoloff 2005b: 912–13).

Moreover, Brazil and to some extent Chile really were unusual for the length of time when a literacy qualification for the vote was in effect and for the recency of the year in which the qualification was revoked. Brazil was both the last country in Latin America to abolish slavery (in 1888) and the last to abolish its literacy requirement for voting (in 1985), following Peru (1979), Ecuador (1978), Chile (1970), Bolivia (1952), Venezuela (1947), and Guatemala (1946). Among eighteen cases for which information is available, Brazil in 1946 was one of seven Latin American countries to have a literacy requirement for voting; as of 1964 it was one of four (Aidt and Eterovic 2011: 195; Engerman and Sokoloff 2005b: 912–13). In a broader cross-national perspective, the literacy qualification was even more unusual. Reviewing the electoral laws of 187 countries, Przeworski (2009: 298) found that by 1950 only about 10% of countries with any sort of suffrage had literacy, property, or income requirements for voting. Presumably, the share with a literacy qualification specifically was lower.

Let us return now to the issue of principled versus consequentialist justifications for suffrage restrictions. According to the capabilities perspective introduced by Sen (1985, 1999), which O'Donnell in recent years came increasingly to share, the importance of agency in human development, as well as the intrinsic and constructive benefits of democratic participation, mean that the decision to describe a political regime as a democracy, as opposed to something else, should depend neither on the share of the population affected by a violation of a core democratic principle, nor on the consequences of the violation for electoral outcomes or social protest, nor on how common the violation may have been during a particular historical era, nor on analytical convenience. Rather, it should depend on the degree to which a political regime enables people to participate in making the decisions by which they will be bound—that is, to exercise practical reason in politics, and thereby to lead a thoughtfully chosen life.

Such enabling requires that virtually the entire adult citizenry, with very few exceptions (e.g., people who have been legally judged to have severe mental impediments), be enfranchised in a practical as well as legal sense. Discussing the United States, O'Donnell, referring to the era before the Voting Rights Act of 1965, argued that because of "the severe restrictions placed on African Americans and Native Americans, especially in the US South . . . the achievement of inclusive political democracy in the United States must be dated to World War II or as late as the 1960s, in the aftermath of the civil rights movement" (O'Donnell 2004b: 74 n35; see also O'Donnell 2010a: 32 n2). Even the contemporary United States arguably fails to meet a minimal standard for enfranchisement. In 2000 in ten US states, people convicted of serious crimes were denied the right to vote even after serving their sentences. In that year the voting-age population of the United States was 205 million. Among this voting-age population were 4.7 million people who had lost the right to vote owing to a criminal conviction; among them only 1.3 million were currently incarcerated. Had the other 3.4 million been enfranchised, Al Gore would have won the 2000 presidential election and the Democrats would have controlled the senate through the 1990s (Uggen and Manza 2002). These implications, however, involve the practical consequences of disenfranchisement. A separate question is whether it is just, from an agency-centric view of democracy, to deny the right to vote to people who have already served their sentences.

The criteria for polyarchy include not only the right to vote but also the right to run for office (Dahl 1989: 221). It is inconsistent and arguably unjust that the United States constitution should set the minimum age for representatives at 25, senators at 30, and president at 35, while granting the right to vote at age 18 and imposing no limits at all on the minimum age of Supreme Court justices, foreign ambassadors, or members of the cabinet (Seery 2011: 148). If anything, the age limits would seem to be more important for the appointive positions than for the elective positions. The Vietnam War–era rallying cry that contributed to the 1971 constitutional amendment that lowered the voting age from 21 to 18—"old enough to fight, old enough to vote"—should have included "old enough to hold office."

To restrict the right to vote on the basis of race, gender, or literacy status is, from this perspective, unjust both intrinsically, because it denies agency to those in the disenfranchised groups, and constructively, because the disenfranchised people do not have the opportunity to discover or rethink their wants and needs by engaging in a core democratic practice: the right to vote. Imposing a literacy qualification for the vote means denying citizens the intrinsic and constructive benefits of democracy, even in countries in which most people are literate, even if the literacy requirement generates no mass protest, even if enfranchising illiterates would not change election outcomes, and even if many other countries have literacy qualifications. No single vote is likely to change the outcome of an election in a large community, but to exercise the right to vote has intrinsic and constructive value nonetheless. That is after all why people in large communities do vote, even when the information and activity costs of voting greatly exceed the benefits of electing one candidate rather than another, which have to be discounted by the infinitesimal probability that one's vote will tip the election result (Downs 1957: 260–74).

Democracy and Free and Fair Elections

One criterion for democracy upon which virtually all political scientists agree is that elections should be free and fair. Boix, Miller, and Rosato (2013: 1531) "define elections as free if voters are given multiple options on ballots and as fair if electoral fraud is absent and incumbents do not abuse government power to effectively eliminate the chance of opposition victory through peaceful contestation." Having multiple options on ballots is not a very demanding criterion for electoral freeness, however. Among other things, it does not preclude the proscription of particular political parties. Using dichotomous classifications, Boix, Miller, and Rosato (2013), as well as

Cheibub, Gandhi, and Vreeland (2009), coded Argentina "democratic" from 1958 to 1961 and from 1963 to 1965, despite the proscription of orthodox Peronism, as well as of Argentina's Communist Party. The ban on orthodox Peronism gave rise to "neo-Peronist" parties, some of which competed for legislative and gubernatorial offices (McGuire 1997: 18–27, 141–45), but it prevented many Argentines from voting for a presidential candidate associated with their preferred party and thereby (to this extent) from exercising agency in the political realm. Mainwaring, Brinks, and Pérez-Liñán, using a trichotomous coding scheme (democratic versus semi-democratic versus authoritarian), reasonably coded Argentina "semi-democratic" from 1958 to 1961 and from 1963 to 1965, in part because "the military vetoed a few 'unacceptable' but important presidential candidates" (Mainwaring, Brinks, and Pérez-Liñán 2007: quotation 135, rating 157).

Not just in Argentina but also in several other Latin American countries from the late 1940s onward, governments imposed bans on the electoral participation of communist parties. Such bans were in effect in Chile (1948–58), Costa Rica (1949–75), and Brazil (1948–63). In these cases Boix, Miller, and Rosato (2013) and Cheibub, Gandhi, and Vreeland (2009), as well as Mainwaring, Brinks, and Pérez-Liñán (2007), coded the extant political regime democratic.[4] Mainwaring, Brinks, and Pérez-Liñán (2007: 135 n10) explicitly justify this classification. Most of the proscribed communist parties, they argue, were not electorally significant; moreover, the standards of the time permitted the banning of antisystem parties. Munck (2009: 47) takes an intermediate position. He agrees that "the banning of the Communist Party in Chile in the late 1940s and early 1950s was different in scope than the banning of the Peronist party in Argentina" but recommends that a new regime category be established for this case and for similar ones in which the banned party is of limited electoral significance.

Yedo Fiúza, the candidate of Brazil's Communist Party in the 1945 presidential election, won nearly 10% of the popular vote. From a conception of democracy that emphasizes agency, practical reason, and human development, however, the percentage of the vote that a political party obtains is irrelevant to the justness of banning it. To proscribe a party that is likely to win 10% of the vote is no more justifiable than to ban a party that is likely to win 50% of the vote. It is not the vote-getting capacity of the proscribed party, but the rationale behind the ban, that should be decisive in classifying the regime. Some rationales may well be compatible with the persistence of a democratic regime, such as when the banned party is judged likely—after due deliberation by authorities appointed by elected officials and acting in accordance with constitutional guidelines—to destroy the democratic regime itself, should its leaders ever take office (Linz 1978b: 6). This was the rationale by which the West German Constitutional Court outlawed the right-wing Nazi successor Sozialistische Reichspartei (SRP) in 1951 and the communist Kommunistische Partei Deutschlands

(KPD) in 1956. The opinion in the latter case was more than 300 pages long and turned on the argument that the KPD, were it to take power, would not give other political parties an equal chance to do so (Niesen 2002: s. 11).

Such legal decisions to proscribe "antisystem" political parties are always contestable. The bans on Latin American communist parties in the decades after World War II were arguably not justified, however, because such parties were no more "antisystem" than parties that were not proscribed. The Brazilian Communist Party rebelled in 1935, but its leaders subsequently committed themselves to the electoral road (Skidmore 1967: 61–62)—much the same as did the Communist Party of Chile, which allied with Aguirre Cerda in the late 1930s; and the Popular Vanguard Party in Costa Rica, which allied with Calderón in the early 1940s. It seems a stretch to consider most Latin American communist parties from the mid-1930s to the mid-1960s to be distinctively "antisystem parties" or "disloyal oppositions" (Linz 1978b: 28–30). If, as Linz (1978b: 30) contends, "'knocking at the barracks' for armed forces support" also counts as disloyalty, then the communist parties of Argentina, Brazil, Chile, and Costa Rica were no more disloyal than Argentina's People's Radical Civic Union, whose leaders from 1958 to 1962 sent repeated signals that they would welcome a military coup (O'Donnell 1973: 188; Smulovitz 1988: 112).

For O'Donnell, fair elections must be competitive. In each of the cases just discussed one or more political parties was proscribed. The share of the electorate that would have voted for the banned party was higher in Argentina than in Brazil, Chile, or Costa Rica, but the thoroughness of the ban was greater in these other cases than in Argentina, because Peronists had the option of voting for neo-Peronist parties in certain elections. Arguably, moreover, Peronism was more "antisystem" than the communist parties of Brazil, Chile, or Costa Rica. Boix, Miller, and Rosato (2013) as well as Cheibub, Gandhi, and Vreeland (2009) code Argentina "authoritarian" during the entire period of Perón's first presidencies (1946–55); Mainwaring, Brinks, and Pérez-Liñán (2007) code Argentina "semi-democratic" from 1946 to 1950 and "authoritarian" from 1951 to 1954; and Pérez-Liñán and Mainwaring (chapter 1 of this volume) refer to "the authoritarian regime of Juan Perón (1951–55)." If a party established an authoritarian regime the last time it was elected, it might well be expected to do so the next time.

It seems inconsistent, accordingly, that regimes in Brazil, Chile, and Costa Rica should not be penalized for imposing stringent bans on not-very-aggressively antisystem communist parties, whereas the regime in Argentina during the proscription of Peronism should be demoted from a democracy to a semi-democracy for imposing a relatively loose ban on parties associated with the more aggressively antisystem Peronist movement. A higher share of the electorate would have voted for the Peronists in Argentina than for the Communists in Brazil, Chile, or Costa Rica, but, from the standpoint of a conception of democracy that recognizes its intrinsic and constructive merits rather than focusing mainly on its instrumental consequences, the proscription of Peronism in Argentina was arguably more, not less, compatible with a democratic regime than was the ban on the communist parties of Brazil, Chile, or Costa Rica.

The proscription of particular political parties has to do mainly with the freeness of elections, but the fairness of the elections that inaugurated some regimes characterized as democratic is also open to question. Several protocols for classifying political regimes code Brazil under José Sarney (1985–90) as democratic (Boix, Miller, and Rosato 2013; Cheibub, Gandhi, and Vreeland 2010; Mainwaring, Brinks, and Pérez-Liñán 2007). Sarney, however, became president in 1985 because, as vice president, he was next in the line when the indirectly elected president, Tancredo Neves, died before taking office. Neither the indirect character of the election nor the vice-presidential succession would raise an eyebrow had Brazil's 680-member electoral college been chosen fairly by popular vote, but it had not been. Instead, the electoral college comprised all senators and federal deputies plus six representatives appointed by each of twenty-two state legislatures. Each of these electors was in turn elected while the literacy qualification for the vote was still in effect, and after April 1977 electoral reforms shifted voting clout toward the Northeast and toward municipal councils, where the promilitary Partido Democrático Social exerted undue influence through patronage resources (Fleischer 1984: 20–30; Samuels and Abrucio 2000: 52–53).

In a similar fashion, General Pinochet and his allies reformed the Chilean constitution in 1980 to stipulate that, when legislative activity was restored, nine of thirty-eight senators would be appointed rather than elected, two by the president, three by the Supreme Court, and four by a National Security Council composed of military leaders. All former presidents, moreover, would be entitled to stay on as senators-for-life. In 1988 the military regime, anticipating a transition to civilian rule, also created for the lower house a two-seat-per-district electoral system in which a minority party (presumably of the right in most districts) could capture one of the two seats with as little as 33% of the vote. This manipulation did not work as well as General Pinochet and his collaborators had hoped, but it did make the legislative right strong enough after the 1989 elections to block proposals to reform the constitution enacted under military rule (Constable and Valenzuela 1991: 175–76). All of the major classification schemes nevertheless designate Chile democratic from 1990 to 2005, the year in which the constitution was finally amended to do away with the designated senators.

No country has completely fair elections. In various states in the contemporary United States ex-felons are disenfranchised, legislation pushes the limits of voter suppression, single-member districts are gerrymandered by state legislative majorities, and openly partisan officials administer elections and vote counts. It would be useful to have a demarcation line that would tell us when a country's elections were fair enough to qualify as having met the free and fair elections criterion, but no one has yet proposed one. Several schemes for classifying Latin American political regimes seem, however, to have been unduly generous in awarding the designation "democratic" to regimes whose chief executives and legislators have won office in elections that were neither inclusive nor free nor fair.

Democracy and Basic Rights

Political scientists differ on the wisdom of treating basic human and civil rights as constituent elements of democracy. As noted above, O'Donnell (2010a: 23) includes in his definition of democracy "a set of freedoms . . . that are necessary supports for the likelihood of . . . elections and their related participatory rights." Likewise, Dahl (1989: 170) argues that "Freedom of speech . . . is necessary both for effective participation and for enlightened understanding; so too are freedom of the press and freedom of assembly. In large democratic systems the right to form political parties and other political associations is necessary to voting equality, effective participation, enlightenment, and final control over the agenda." Pérez-Liñán and Mainwaring (chapter 1 of this volume) state that "democracies must protect political and civil rights such as freedom of the press, freedom of speech, freedom to organize, and the right to habeas corpus. Even if the government is chosen in free and fair elections with a broad suffrage, in the absence of an effective guarantee of civil and political rights, the regime is not democratic." Other basic rights that might be treated as constituent elements of democracy include freedom from physical abuse by agents of the state, recognition as a person, freedom of religion, freedom to assemble, and due process of law. In some conceptualizations such rights are viewed as necessary conditions for democracy; in others such rights are owed protection in democracies; and in still others such rights are constituent parts of democracy, without which democracy is not just impossible but inconceivable.

If basic rights are both necessary to and protected by the holding of contested elections, then it is most convenient to think of basic rights and contested elections together as constituent parts of democracy rather than treating basic rights as causes, conditions, or consequences of contested elections. To separate basic rights conceptually from contested elections creates a chicken-and-egg problem: basic rights are necessary to have meaningfully contested elections, but meaningfully contested elections are necessary to protect basic rights. Advocates of a minimalist definition of democracy based solely on contested elections, excluding basic rights, argue that, "if democracy requires civil liberties, political rights, freedom of the press, and other freedoms, then inquiries about the connection between democracy and such freedoms are . . . precluded" (Cheibub, Gandhi, and Vreeland 2010: 73). It is not self-evident, however, that treating electoral contestation and basic rights as constituent elements of democracy would block off questions about the connections between them. Several sets of country-year estimates exist for both contested elections and basic rights; it would not be difficult to obtain statistical associations among these estimates. The question would be how to interpret such associations. Would a strong association mean that basic rights were causing contested elections, or that contested elections were causing basic rights, or that both were being caused by a third factor, among which a strong candidate would be a degree of functional interdependence sufficient to characterize basic rights and contested elections as parts of a single whole, democracy?

Some of the major protocols for classifying Latin American political regimes may also have been unduly generous in labeling "democratic" regimes under which widespread, severe, and apparently systematic violations of human rights take place. In Brazil from 1985 to 1990 criminal suspects were routinely tortured by police. In the state of São Paulo in 1989 more than 1,000 prisoners were beaten at a detention center and eighteen prisoners suffocated to death at a police station. From 1985 onward, death squads—often including police officers and operating with apparent impunity—killed hundreds of street children and other suspects. Between 1985 and 1990, some 250 peasants, rural union leaders, or lawyers involved in land disputes were killed in the state of Pará alone, without a single assassin's having been brought to justice. A form of slavery involving confinement and forced unpaid labor (but not commodification) persisted near the Peruvian border. In March 1991, Brazil's Supreme Court finally ruled unconstitutional a law by which men could kill spouses or lovers and win acquittal on the ground of "legitimate defense of honor." These killings were far from rare; 722 men used the "honor killing" defense over a two-year period (1980–81) in the state of São Paulo alone. In August 1991, a local jury in Paraná ignored the Supreme Court's decision and acquitted the man whose case had led to the Supreme Court ruling (*New York Times* 15 May 1989, 19 June 1990, 1 August 1990, 6 September 1990, 13 November 1990, and 29 March 1991; Amnesty International 1991: 46–49; Nelson 1993).

Basic rights violations occur in all countries. The challenge for the researcher is to ascertain how widespread, severe, and systematic they are and to apply the same criteria to each regime. One classification scheme finds that no violation of civil liberties occurred in Brazil from 1983 to 2004 but that massive violations occurred in Argentina from 1951 to 1954, near the end of Perón's presidency (Mainwaring, Brinks, and Pérez-Liñán 2007: 157). The last few years of Perón's presidency were indeed characterized by such antidemocratic practices as the denial of media access to opposition parties, repression of non-Peronist political gatherings, and jailings of opposition candidates (McGuire 1997: 69). These violations of basic civil rights, moreover, may have mattered more directly to the conduct of contested elections than the violations of basic human rights under Sarney. The violations under Sarney, however, were more severe in their immediate consequences for human development, of which an important prerequisite is survival. To live a thoughtfully chosen life, one has to be alive. Given an electoralist conception of democracy, it might be reasonable to conclude that the waning years of Perón's presidency were more authoritarian than the five years during which Sarney held office. From a perspective in which democracy is justified in terms of its ability to encourage human flourishing, however, a quite different conclusion might be warranted.

Democracy and the Decisiveness of Elections

By the decisiveness of elections, O'Donnell means that those who get elected take office, stay in office until the end of their terms (barring some uncontroversial circumstance like a natural death), and while in office are able to make policy in accordance with their constitutional prerogatives. Elections are not decisive when, for example, elected chief executives or legislators find that their policy-making prerogatives are constrained or undermined by military leaders, local political bosses, criminal gangs, guerrilla groups, or foreign governments.

O'Donnell's conviction that the decisiveness of elections is an indispensible dimension of democracy is shared by many other scholars. Coppedge (2012: 26) calls this criterion the scope of democratic authority and argues that "it doesn't matter how a government was chosen if it has no power to carry out its decisions." Valenzuela (1992: 62–70) refers to the absence of tutelary powers and reserved domains as a key criterion for the democracy designation. Pérez-Liñán and Mainwaring (chapter 1 of this volume) insist that a defining criterion for democracy should be that "elected authorities must exercise real governing power, as opposed to a situation in which elected officials are overshadowed by the military or by a non-elected shadow figure."

Agreement on this criterion is not universal, however. Przeworski et al. (2000: 35) write that, "as long as officeholders are elected in elections that someone else has a chance of winning, and as long as they do not use the incumbency to eliminate the opposition, the fact that the chief executive is a general or a lackey of generals does not add any relevant information." Cheibub, Gandhi, and Vreeland (2010: 73) argue that "civilian control of the military, national autonomy with respect to the international system, and bureaucratic responsiveness to executive and legislative authorities, are attributes that vary across political systems, irrespective of the rules they follow to choose who makes decisions for the country. These are attributes of political systems in general, not of a specific type of political regime."

It is true that unelected actors may constrain chief executives and legislators in authoritarian regimes as well as in democracies, but it is equally true that contested elections may take place in authoritarian regimes as well as in democracies (Levitsky and Way 2010). Neither commonality precludes our considering both contested elections and decisive elections to be constitutive elements of democracy. Birds as well as humans have two legs, but this commonality does not preclude our considering bipedalism to be a defining feature of humans.[5] Elections may have important consequences even if they are not decisive, but no regime in which contested elections are *not* decisive can be meaningfully classified as a democracy.

What Stepan (1988) calls military prerogatives and what Garretón (1991) calls authoritarian enclaves are divided by Valenzuela (1992: 62–70) into two types of institutions and practices that allow military leaders to hold sway over civilians elected after transitions from authoritarian rule. The first, *tutelary powers*, has two main embodiments: constitutional clauses that grant the military the right to defend the fundamental interests of the nation (including at times when such "defense" sets the military at odds with the decisions of an elected government), and military-led National Security Councils that claim the right to oversee various aspects of government policy. The second, *reserved domains*, involves specific policy areas that top military officers deem out of bounds for elected officials owing to national security concerns. If one agrees that democracy requires elections that are decisive as well as contested, then the more expansive and efficacious the military's tutelary powers and reserved domains, even in a civilian regime with contested elections, the more dubious it becomes to call such a regime democratic.

In no regime are elected officials completely free to legislate and execute policy without regard to the preferences of unelected elites. Elected officials in capitalist economies are reticent to make or enact policies that undermine business confidence (Block 1977: 16–19). In some cases, however, the influence of such elites expands to the point where elections are arguably no longer decisive. This situation can be illustrated by a comparison of the immediate postmilitary governments in Argentina (1983–89 under Alfonsín), Brazil (1985–90 under Sarney), and Chile (1990–96 under Aylwin). The military in Brazil and in Chile had both of the tutelary powers identified by Valenzuela; the military in Argentina had neither. A similar contrast exists with reserved domains. Whereas Alfonsín took control of military promotions, the military budget, and military-run industries, Brazil's president Sarney and Chile's president Aylwin were compelled to leave these matters in the hands of the armed forces. No military officer served in Alfonsín's cabinet, whereas six of Sarney's twenty-two ministers belonged to security forces. Using these sources of leverage, the army under Sarney exerted enormous influence over the handling of strikes, the nuclear industry, economic integration with Argentina, agrarian reform, and the development of the Amazon (Hagopian 1990: 156; Hunter 1997: 33, 55; Stepan 1988: 103–18; Valenzuela 1992: 62–70). Although military control over elected officials in Brazil and

Chile never reached the height of more extreme military-fist-in-civilian-glove regimes like El Salvador's or Guatemala's (Karl 1986; Mainwaring, Brinks, and Pérez-Liñán 2007: 132), it was high enough to call into question whether either of these countries in its initial postmilitary period surpassed a minimal threshold of democracy. Nevertheless, the major classification schemes code Brazil 1985–90 and Chile 1990–2005 as democratic, and Cheibub, Gandhi, and Vreeland (2009) classify even El Salvador 1984–93 and Guatemala 1986–88 as democratic.

Democracy and the Perils of Electoralism

The preceding review has revealed only one instance—the characterization of Perón's regime from 1951 to 1955—where existing classification protocols may have been too ready to designate a regime authoritarian. In other cases, particularly Brazil under Sarney (1985–90), such schemes appear to have been too generous in awarding the designation democratic, at least from the standpoint of a conceptualization of democracy that emphasizes, as O'Donnell did, the importance of agency, practical reason, and human development as reasons why democracy is worth having. The preponderance of such errors of inclusion (from the standpoint of this agency-centric view) appears to be related to reasoning that applies unduly consequentialist criteria to decide whether suffrage is really inclusive, whether elections are really free and fair, whether basic rights are really being protected, and whether elected officials really exercise their constitutional authority.

The application of such consequentialist criteria (Sen 1999: 58–59, 211–13) may well be related, in turn, to a somewhat restricted view of the processes by which democratic politics affect such outcomes as economic development, macroeconomic stability, income inequality, public goods provision, famine prevention, free-market reform, involvement in trade agreements, and war avoidance or performance. "In all of these areas of research," argue Cheibub, Gandhi, and Vreeland (2010: 73), "the mechanism that links political regimes to outcomes is the presence or absence of contested elections." Even in multidimensional (as opposed to subminimalist) conceptualizations of democracy that explicitly reject "electoralism" from a normative point of view, restrictions on universal adult suffrage are downplayed to the extent that they appear to be inconsequential for election outcomes; the proscription of particular political parties may not count against a regime's democratic credentials if the banned parties seem likely unlikely to win elections in the foreseeable future; and violations of basic rights appear to be given more weight when they interfere with electoral contestation than when they do not.

In fact, however, the mechanisms by which political regime form is likely to affect outcomes of interest go well beyond electoral incentives. The range of such mechanisms can be illustrated by exploring the impact of political regime form on social policies conducive to reducing premature mortality, which is an outcome of particular interest from the human development perspective that O'Donnell in his later writings came increasingly to share. Several studies have concluded that more democracy, as measured by expert ratings from Polity or Freedom House, is associated with lower infant or under-5 mortality or with higher life expectancy at birth, controlling for other factors likely to influence such outcomes (Altman and Castiglioni 2009; Klomp and de Haan 2009; Lake and Baum 2001; Przeworski et al. 2000; Zweifel and Navia 2003; but cf. Ross 2006).

Why might democracies, all else equal, have lower rates of early death than non-democracies? Electoral incentives may well be involved. In democracies, "rulers have the incentive to listen to what people want if they have to face their criticism and seek their support in elections" (Sen 1999: 152). According to the median voter hypothesis, income under majority rule should be redistributed downward to the extent that democratization (e.g., the extension of the franchise) pulls the income of the voter with the median income farther below the mean income of all of the voters (Meltzer and Richard 1981). Analogous forces may influence the provision of basic social services. As democratization enfranchises more people inadequately served by health care, water and sanitation, education, or family planning, vote-maximizing politicians should try to improve the quality, quantity, and accessibility of such services.

The electoral incentives highlighted in the median voter hypothesis are, however, only one mechanism by which democracy affects the proposal, design, approval, and effective implementation of social policies that reduce the rate of early death. The freedoms of association and assembly are another. These freedoms enable community activists, interest groups, and issue networks (informal groups of experts in a particular area of public policy) to pressure for policies that improve services conducive to lower mortality—or, on occasion, for policies that continue to restrict such services to better-off groups. Yet another channel through which democracy affects mortality involves freedom of speech and the press, which enables journalists and others to call attention to social problems, including deficiencies in social performance.

A fourth linkage between democracy and infant mortality is the ratcheting up of legal rights, the empowerment of communities, and the evolution of expectations about who should be eligible for state services, subsidies, and social assistance. The principle that citizens have equal rights—one person, one vote—sets in motion a gradual evolution toward a belief that the state is obliged to provide social services that are sufficient to enable every citizen, no matter how poor, to survive and to live with dignity (Marshall 1950b). The evolution of expectations about state obligations to impoverished (as well as other) citizens should encourage the utilization as well as provision of mortality-reducing social services. Accordingly, long-term democratic experience should be associated more closely than short-term democratic practice with lower premature mortality, which several recent studies suggest is the case (Gerring, Thacker, and Alfaro 2012; McGuire 2010, 2013; Wigley and Akkoyunlu-Wigley 2011).

What is To Be Done?

Protocols for classifying political regimes could be improved, it has been argued, (1) by operationalizing democracy in a way that gives more priority to human agency and thereby to the opportunity to lead a thoughtfully chosen life; (2) by recognizing that democracy affects social and political outcomes not only through electoral contestation but also through the freedoms of expression and organization, as well as through long-term cultural changes; (3) by applying twenty-first-century rather than past standards to decide whether a country meets the operational requisites for democracy; and (4) by adopting less consequentialist and more agency-centric criteria for deciding what degree of shortfall on a particular dimension is compatible with the designation "democratic." It will be argued in this concluding section that regime-classification protocols could also be improved (5) by using more than three categories to classify regimes; (6) by recognizing a trade-off between the likelihood of misclassification and the misleadingness of misclassification; (7) by identifying more explicitly the years in each country when classification judgment calls are the most vexing; and (8) by justifying in narrative form the classification chosen for those years.

Some writers advocate doing research with a continuous measure of democracy, rather than with the dichotomous or trichotomous schemes used in many recent studies. Bollen and Jackman (1989: 618) contend that "democracy is always a matter of degree"; and Collier and Adcock (1999) argue that graded measures of democracy are appropriate for certain research purposes. Others argue that a continuous notion of democracy will lead to absurdities, compelling the analyst "to speak of positive levels of democracy in places like . . . Chile under Pinochet or Brazil during the military dictatorship" (Cheibub, Gandhi, and Vreeland 2010: 78). One way to sidestep this pitfall would be to establish a threshold below which the quality of democracy is zero (Alvarez et al. 1996: 21; Collier and Adcock 1999: 548–50; Sartori 1987: 184–85; Schedler 1998). The Polity IV variable called polity2, which ranges from −10 (most autocratic) to +10 (most democratic; Marshall and Jaggers 2010), is consistent with this recommendation, although the Polity IV coding is open to criticism on other grounds (Bowman, Lehoucq, and Mahoney 2005; Haggard and Kaufman 2012; McGuire 2010: 32–33; Munck and Verkuilen 2002). In Argentina, for example, the 1976–83 military regime received a polity2 score of −9 in 1976–80 and −8 in 1981–82. Democracy stayed at 0 from 1976 to 1982; authoritarianism fell from 9 to 8 in 1981.

In practice, however, for the terms themselves to be meaningful, a democracy does at some point have to slip into authoritarianism, even if it experiences a slow death (O'Donnell 1992) rather than a sudden breakdown. Mainwaring, Brinks, and Pérez-Liñán (2007: 157) argue that this happened under Perón in Argentina in the early 1950s, and Mainwaring (2012: 961) argues that it happened under Chávez in Venezuela in the 2000s. According to the criteria set forth in preceding sections of this chapter, Brazil became a democracy in 1990, Chile in 2005, and Costa Rica in 1975, when the National Assembly amended the constitution to permit the electoral participation of Marxist parties, which had been effectively banned since 1949 (Hernández Valle 2006: 367–68; Martz 1967: 894; Oconitrillo 1981: 210–11). It is reasonable to view such transitions as proceeding at varying paces, and advancing to varying degrees, according to the dimension of democracy analyzed—inclusive franchise, free and fair elections, preservation of basic rights, and authority to those elected. Polity IV, however, sets this zero point almost incidentally, whereas some of the most rigorous attempts to classify regimes according to categories attempt self-consciously to stipulate precisely where the cut-off points should lie, even as they recognize that "even with explicit coding rules, some cases present difficult borderline judgments" (Mainwaring, Brinks, and Pérez-Liñán 2001: 50).

The debate as to whether to characterize democracy according to discrete categories or according to a continuous function is in certain respects misconstrued. As we expand the number of categories into which regimes may be classified, what emerges is not a continuum but a more finely divided polychotomy. Whether a continuum actually underlies this polychotomy is a question that is most prudently left to experts in the humanities. It is inevitably necessary to assign the cases discrete numbers—and thereby to divide them into categories—even if the numbers are carried out to multiple decimal places (they cease to be categories only at the asymptote). In this respect, Sartori (1970: 1038) is correct to assert that human understanding requires categories divided by "cut-off points." The question is how closely to space the cut-off points between the categories. Dichotomous measures are "useful for certain purposes, such as analyzing the duration of democratic regimes. However, [a] dichotomous coding lumps together polities that exhibit quite different regime qualities" (Coppedge, Gerring et al. 2011: 249).

Because of this lumping problem, some of the most transparent and rigorous attempts to classify political regimes in a large number of Latin American countries over a long span of time have elected to place regimes in three categories: democratic, semi-democratic, or authoritarian (Bowman, Lehoucq, and Mahoney 2005; Mainwaring, Brinks, and Pérez-Liñán 2001, 2007). Mainwaring, Brinks, and Pérez-Liñán argue (2001: 37) that their "trichotomy achieves greater differentiation than dichotomous classifications and yet avoids the need for massive information that a fine-grained continuous measure would require." Later, they add the following:

> [W]e may not know whether a country should be scored as a 6 or a 7 on Freedom House's interval scale, but we can be confident it is a semi-democracy. By constructing a trichotomous scale with a modest information demand, we can significantly reduce the number of coding errors and thus achieve greater reliability than would be possible under a more demanding classification scheme. Our scheme has enough categories to avoid forcing cases into classes that violate our common sense understanding, yet has few enough that we do not need to draw fine distinctions among regimes. (2001: 50)

They continue, however, that "of course, even with explicit coding rules, some cases present difficult borderline judgments" and note that Brazil 1946–63, which they decide (with reservations) to code as democratic, serves as a case in point.

Reviewing a remarkable range of societies over the past two thousand years, the philologist Emory Lease concluded that "from time to time in the history of the world various numbers, chiefly those from 1 to 12, have been regarded as possessing a mystical significance, but there can be no doubt that in the extent, variety, and frequency of its use, the number 3 far surpasses all the rest" (Lease 1919: 56). The importance of the Holy Trinity in Christianity is beyond dispute. Berg and Rapaport (1954) found that college students, when asked to design multiple-choice questions with four options, had a strong bias toward placing the correct answer next to the numeral 3, even when asked to sequence the possible answers from 4 to 1 rather than from 1 to 4. For many sports fans, "the third repeat event in a sequence is pivotal to the subjective belief that a streak is occurring" (Carlson and Shu 2007: 113). Achen (2002: 446) concluded that "a statistical specification with more than three explanatory variables is meaningless." Garrison Keillor wrote that "[Ronnie's] ear for multiple-choice tests was good—in Lake Wobegon, the correct answer is usually 'c'" (quoted in Attali and Bar-Hillel 2003: 109).

Trichotomous schemes might thus be expected to have considerable intuitive appeal, and so they do. It is well worth noting that the present analysis utilizes a definition of democracy comprising (1) free, fair, and inclusive elections; (2) basic human and civil rights; and (3) effective authority to those who get elected. Trichotomous regime classifications, however, do not entirely escape the problem of lumping together regimes whose qualities differ significantly. Mainwaring, Brinks, and Pérez-Liñán (2007) coded Argentina authoritarian (the other categories being semi-democratic or democratic) not only during the harsh military dictatorship of General Videla (1976–81) but also in the waning years of Perón's presidency (1951–54). Also, like dichotomous categorizations, trichotomous schemes can be insensitive to major improvements or declines in the quality of democracy. Chile is coded democratic from 1946 to 1973 even though women were denied the vote until 1949, the Communist Party was banned from elections from 1948 to 1958, no secret ballot existed in the countryside until 1958, and voting was restricted by a literacy clause until 1970. Elimination of these democratic defects enabled more Chileans to exercise agency in politics, and some of these reforms had significant consequences for politics and policy. The introduction of the secret ballot in the countryside, for example, shifted votes away from right-wing political parties (Baland and Robinson 2008) and encouraged pro-poor reforms in education, family planning, and health service provision (McGuire 2010).

The more categories a classification scheme has, the greater the *chance* of misclassification; but the fewer categories such a scheme provides, the greater the *consequences* of misclassification for answering research questions. In the Polity IV or Freedom House coding schemes, if a political regime were to receive a democracy score of 7 when it should have received a score of 6, some types of analyses (e.g., large-N time-series cross-sectional analyses) might not be seriously affected. If, however, regimes had to be classified as democratic, semi-democratic, or authoritarian, misclassification might be rarer, but its consequences for analysis would be greater. The fewer the categories (e.g., where classification is dichotomous or trichotomous), the more misclassification changes from a high-probability, low-distortion event to a low-probability, high-distortion event.

Alvarez et al. (1996: 31) contend that dichotomous schemes involve less measurement error than polychotomous schemes, but Elkins (2000: 298–99) shows that the calculations on which this conclusion is founded neglect to compare the error variance with the *total* variance across the observations in each case, and that, if one takes the total variance into account, polychotomous schemes have less overall measurement error. Even when misclassification results from random measurement error (rather than bias), it can be seriously misleading. If regime form is used as a dependent variable, random error in measuring it will reduce the precision of the estimates but will not affect their magnitude. If, however, regime form is used as an independent variable and includes measurement error that is highly correlated with the measurement error in another independent variable, the regression can produce statistically significant estimates with the wrong signs (Achen 1985; Treier and Jackman 2008: 202).

Even a tetrachotomous scheme might therefore be preferable to a trichotomous scheme. Such a classification might involve the categories fully democratic, nearly democratic, nearly authoritarian, and authoritarian (cf. Munck 2009: 42, 45). Three of the four categories would fall below the threshold of democracy, which would be consistent with a stringent definition based on the principles of agency, practical reason, and human development. The principal challenge in applying such a scheme would be to identify qualitative shifts in the severity of authoritarianism, rather than qualitative shifts in the degree of democracy (although that could also be done). Thus we could classify Argentina 1946–50 as nearly democratic and Argentina 1951–54 as nearly authoritarian, without classifying the latter regime as fully authoritarian and thus making it indistinguishable from Argentina 1956–57 or even Argentina 1976–82. A tetrachotomous classification would also enable us to recognize that Brazil 1985–90 went from nearly authoritarian to fully democratic and free us from the need to classify Brazil 1946–53 and 1956–63 as fully democratic, even though the illiterate were disenfranchised, the Communist Party was banned, and the decisions of elected officials were constrained by top military officers. To classify regimes into three categories has a certain undeniable appeal, but at least four and possibly more categories are needed—many of which would fall *below* the minimalist threshold of democracy—to generate a classification scheme that would validly depict to what degree all adult citizens have been empowered in the political realm to lead a thoughtfully chosen life.

The foregoing review of political regimes in Argentina, Brazil, Chile, and Costa Rica in the second half of the twentieth century highlights the complexity of classifying even well-studied regimes. It also underscores, as Mainwaring, Brinks, and Pérez-Liñán (2001: 45) argue, the importance of producing "explicit and sound coding and aggregation rules . . . [that] make it easier for other scholars to assess criteria and actual classifications." Producing and applying rules for classifying political regimes is necessarily a collective enterprise (Coppedge, Gerring et al. 2011: 257–60). One useful expedient might be for each researcher classifying political regimes to indicate which country-years are most vexing to code and to produce a narrative justification for the decisions reached (cf. Haggard, Kaufman, and Teo 2012 for democratic transitions and reversions from 1980 to 2000). To create a valid classification of political regimes, the scholar must inventory a vast range of scholarship, apply contestable coding rules, make precarious judgments about borderline cases, and justify normatively the operationalization as well as the conceptualization of democracy. Guillermo O'Donnell welcomed such challenges and we are richer for his having done so.

NOTES

This chapter was much improved by the comments of Daniel Brinks, Michael Coppedge, Marcelo Leiras, Scott Mainwaring, J. Donald Moon, and Ximena Simpson.

1. As Coppedge points out (2012: 21 n6), Dahl in an earlier work (1971) had required instead that "government policies depend on votes and other expressions of preference." The more demanding formulation in the earlier work (control of government policy decisions should be

actually, not just constitutionally, vested in elected officials) accords better with what O'Donnell intends when he stipulates that elections should be decisive.

2. Mainwaring, Brinks, and Pérez-Liñán subsequently (2007) demote Brazil to "semi-democratic" in 1954 and 1955, but this demotion is due to military intervention in politics; in their disaggregated coding (2007: 157) Brazil in 1954 and 1955 continues to receive a score of "no violation" for "franchise."

3. Mainwaring, Brinks, and Pérez-Liñán (2001, 2007) use the term "contemporary" to refer to what is viewed as democratic by present-day observers and "retrospective" to refer to what was viewed as democratic at the time each regime existed. Because the terms contemporary and retrospective are sometimes misinterpreted, the terms utilized here are "twenty-first-century" (what Mainwaring, Brinks, and Pérez-Liñán intend by "contemporary") and "past" (what Mainwaring, Brinks, and Pérez-Liñán intend by "retrospective").

4. On Brazil, see note 2 above. The legal proscription of the Brazilian Communist Party continued through the military regime implanted in 1964 and was not lifted until 1985.

5. More precisely, all humans are predisposed to be bipedal; a small fraction of people lose, or never acquire, the use of one or both legs.

CHAPTER 14

Democracy and Democratization

Guillermo O'Donnell's Late Attempt to Rework Democratic Theory

JORGE VARGAS CULLELL

In the last ten years of his life, O'Donnell sought to fundamentally revise democratic theory based upon the notion of the citizen as a moral and political agent (O'Donnell 2003b, 2004b, 2007c, 2010b). Citizens, he argued, are not simply voters: they embody a special kind of human agency, one endowed with political rights. They use these rights to elect governments through free and fair elections, the core of democratic politics, but also to enact societal changes in societal power relations. Thus, historically, citizen agency has driven the expansion of the portfolio of rights attached to the original definition of citizenship (T. Marshall 1965); it has set up new ways to hold power holders accountable to the law and to citizen scrutiny, established new institutions for political participation, and installed the "grammar of political rights" in arenas far removed from politics such as corporate governance and families. In short, the willful actions of the diligent vector, the citizen-agent, may alter the ways in which not only regimes but also states and societies organize and function, subjecting them to the purview of democratic politics. Here lies the gist of O'Donnell's critique of procedural democracy, which, in his view, narrowed down democracy too much to the realm of a political regime.

In O'Donnell's view, the citizen-agent gives life to a political regime, but in doing so she may also expand democratic borders by removing previously existing limits to citizen agency stemming from regime, state, and societal institutions. Should we treat these changes as exogenous outcomes of regime democratic politics? O'Donnell's late work suggests otherwise. Once exogenous to core regime politics, these outcomes may later become endogenous to democracy if and when they leave permanent imprints that evolve into entrenched political capabilities and "rules of the game" for citizen agency at subsequent time periods. These consequential imprints led O'Donnell to understand democracy as an open-ended concept and, particularly, to focus on democratization as a broader—and deeper—story than the tale of how a democratic regime comes into being. In this chapter, I address this deeper, more textured idea of democratization by advancing a multidimensional, thick concept of democratization, which in my view opens new avenues of inquiry for comparative politics that shed light on the state and societal foundations upon which citizen agency and democracy rest.

O'Donnell's observation that the individual-level correlate of democracy is citizen agency prompts a more fundamental question: to what extent should we broaden our view of democracy to include all the factors in state and society that limit it? O'Donnell adamantly argued against such possibility. There are infinite things that check agency, from insufficient income to deficient childhood nutrition. Including everything would lead us to conflate democracy with such overarching notions such as justice, equality, or the good society. Democracy, he always stressed, is a political concept. To the end he cautioned against the widely popular viewpoint in Latin America denigrating procedural democracy as "formal democracy" as opposed to a superior "real democracy" defined by social equity and economic development.

However, it is true that O'Donnell understood democracy as an open-ended concept (O'Donnell 2010b). If citizens can expand democracy by virtue of their own agency, how can one set clear political limits to what democracy is? His answer lies on the distinction between the all-encompassing notion of human agency—as described in Amartya Sen's (1999, 2009) human development approach—and the more limited idea of citizen agency, O'Donnell's main concern, which deals with the issues of how people organize the access and use of political power in a democracy. Citizen agency grants individuals the capacity to handle legally enacted rights and freedoms to the purpose of participating in political life. For sure, it is grounded in human agency, but needs not to include individuals' other willful actions in social life at the economic and/or social realms. In sum, the proposition that citizen agency is a special, more restricted kind of human agency enables O'Donnell to keep democracy as a political concept while acknowledging democracy's open-ended nature. In this chapter, I further elaborate on this point.

The idea of a citizen agency enables O'Donnell to criticize procedural democracy for narrowing down democracy exclusively to the realm of the political regime. Procedural democracy leaves aside the interaction between the regime and some institutions of the state that ensure that, once in power, governments govern democratically and do not encroach upon citizen freedom and liberties. Certain—but not all—state norms and institutions delimit, safeguard, and potentiate the capabilities set (rights and freedoms) of citizen agency (O'Donnell 2004b). In this sense, they are not mere "external" prerequisites of political democracy—as many political scientists would easily acknowledge. Once created, they have become part of the core of political democracy because removing them would largely disable modern citizenship. As I argue, O'Donnell's *Estado democrático de derecho* is the case in point, given its centrality for the institutionalization and decisiveness of free and fair elections and, more generally, for the preservation of democratic citizenship. In this sense, O'Donnell allows us to think the concept of democracy in historical terms, allowing room for a subset of consequential outcomes of democracy to become definitional components of it.[1]

To be sure, O'Donnell harbored conflictive views on this topic, as we shall see (O'Donnell 2007c, 2010b). However, his approach helps unearth the concurrent conditions underlying procedural definitions of democracy focusing on electoral democracy and helps us to take heed of nonregime political institutions and power relations that may be of importance in the study of democracy and democratization. At the very least, it helps posit critical questions: does a broader concept of political democracy that best fits the dynamic nature of citizen agency add new insights to the understanding of modern democracy? Is it possible to broaden it without making concessions to substantive views of democracy?

Citizen Agency

All of O'Donnell's last theoretical works on democracy begin acknowledging the centrality of citizen agency for democracy. Citizens are an embodiment of human agency; in addition, they are the individual-level correlate of democracy, its microfoundation or basic unit (O'Donnell 2010b). Moreover, democracy is the "result of an institutionalized wager" (the citizen-agent), who is endowed with rights and has the legal capability to use her rights as she sees fit, within certain parameters also legally set.[2] Democracy, he continues, "is the only kind of regime that is the result of an institutionalized, universalistic, and inclusive wager" (O'Donnell 2004b: 16).

Following Dahl and, more explicitly, Sen, O'Donnell understands agency as the capability to pursue willful and decisive actions based on moral judgments.[3] Agency is universalistic by definition.[4] However, even though citizenship is inherently grounded on human agency, there is a crucial difference between them. Human agency is unboundedly universalistic, an attribute of human beings that knows of no frontiers and can be exerted in all domains of social life. Removing barriers to human agency is the subject matter of human development, an idea that can be best defined as the expansion of human capabilities and the quality of life (Sen 1999).

Citizenship implies "bounded universalism" (O'Donnell 2004b), a more restricted kind of human agency. Certain legal preconditions specify it as political type of agency. On the one hand, although under international law all human beings have the right to a nationality—which nowadays entails a right to a citizenship[5]—actual citizenship is bestowed by nation-states. Hence, citizenship is always a citizenship of a particular state. On the other hand, even if all persons within the territory of a state that contains a regime can potentially become citizens of the said state, citizenship is normally limited to adults who comply with some minimalistic requisites.[6] Finally, citizenship implies a detailed attribution of rights, freedoms, and obligations by the legal system of a state to the purpose of intervening in political life. Only citizens of the said state can fully participate in politics; however, this status is not required for doing business or becoming engaged in all sort of private dealings. In short, all human individuals embody human agency; however, the majority of them are not citizens of a particular state, and only those who fulfill the requisites established by that said state have the right to fully participate in politics.

Given these restrictions, we may understand citizen agency as the mobilizing of political rights and freedoms by individuals so that they can freely participate in the process of selecting those who will govern them and try to influence these elected officials and to participate in all public issues they see fit. Removing the barriers to citizen agency is the subject matter of democratization, a topic to which I return in the following sections. Hence, even though human development and democratization have common philosophical and moral underpinnings, they are two different albeit, in O'Donnell's view, probably reciprocal reinforcing processes.

O'Donnell's distinction between human agency and citizen agency entails important consequences for his theorizing of democracy and democratization. It enables him to keep democracy as a political concept and to reject any attempt to frame it on substantive terms, expanding it to cover issues such as social equity or economic development. The latter are, again, the subject matter of human development. For sure, he extensively wrote about the importance of social requirements for ensuring that individuals can fully enjoy their political rights, freedoms and liberties (O'Donnell 2004b, 2007c). Widespread poverty and inequity diminish the quality of democracy, because they are a hostile environment for political equality: poor people are usually also legally poor (O'Donnell 1999c). However, modern democracy refers to the organization of political power based on free elections, participatory rights, and a set of supportive and necessary freedoms (O'Donnell 2010b: 37).

At the same time, the distinction between human and citizen agency is the basis of O'Donnell's critique of procedural democracy. I deal with this issue more in depth in the last section of the chapter; for the moment, I call attention to the fact that, even if citizen agency is political by definition, it need not be limited to participating in the free selection of rulers. Citizens are not only voters. Their agency also enables them to use their rights and freedoms to bring about change in the polity. To begin with, the exercising of an initially limited pool of rights and freedoms may become a means to acquire new citizen rights, as T. Marshall (1965) first discussed. It can, through legally authorized means, bring about changes in the rules and institutions for selecting governments or create new vertical and/or horizontal accountability mechanisms that expand the opportunities citizens enjoy having a say in the handling of public affairs (O'Donnell 2003a). Last but not least, it also helps preventing governments, once in power, from using their control of state institutions to encroach upon freedoms and liberties.

The main theoretical consequence of positing citizen agency as the individual correlate of political democracy is that the democracy becomes an essentially open-ended concept (O'Donnell 2010b). Not only the idea of democracy has evolved over time but, echoing Dahl, it may evolve in the future due to the dynamic nature of citizen agency (Dahl 1989). At the heart of this openness lies the futility of coming up with definitive and taxonomic lists of citizen rights and freedoms, what O'Donnell labels as the impossibility, from a historical point of view, to set fixed "external and internal limits" to democratic citizenship. This, he acknowledges, may render a less parsimonious theorizing of democracy but may help to understand better the complexities of modern democracy as well as the depth of contemporary processes of democratization.

Thick Democratization

O'Donnell latest works on democratic theory based on the idea of citizen agency contain plenty of insights that provide fertile material for an empirical theory of democratization (O'Donnell 2004b, 2007c, 2010b). The fundamental importance he grants to citizen agency for democracy inevitably leads us to think of the importance of the struggles from below for democratization (Foweraker and Landman 2000), shifting somewhat away from the focus on elite pacts. His reflections on the distinctive historical paths toward democracy in Latin America compared with the "Northwest Quadrant" invite political scientists to pay more attention to history in the long run, in contrast with the focus on rapid political change typical of the transition literature, and questions T. Marshall's (1965) historical account of citizenship. Finally, O'Donnell's essentially open-ended concept of democracy suggests that democratization may not be restricted to the study of regime transitions. In this venue, democratization within democracy—the evolution of democracy after a regime democratizes—may become a subject of empirical studies (Parry and Moran 1994).

Despite these many insights, the fact of the matter is that we don't find a fully developed theory of democratization in O'Donnell's latest works, an unfortunate finding given the important development of cross-national empirical studies of democratization (Acemoglu and Robinson 2006; Boix 2003; Brinks and Coppedge 2006; Coppedge et al. 2008; Coppedge, Gerring, et al. 2011; Coppedge and Reinecke 1991; Gasiorowski 2000; Inglehart and Welzel 2005; Vanhanen 2003; Whitehead 2002). He does not cast a new causal argument specifying previously overlooked driving factors of democratization. In Welzel's recent survey of current democratization theories one would have few hesitations to place a younger O'Donnell within the "elite pacts and mass mobilization" camp (Welzel 2009), however the older O'Donnell would not fit squarely into this category, given the importance he granted to the structure and functioning of the state or his calls to consider the international dimension of domestic democratization (Iazzetta 2011; O'Donnell 2010b).

However, O'Donnell's citizen agency approach may have important consequences for democratization studies, because it leads to the rethinking of the idea of democratization itself. For sure, the idea must necessarily include regime change—setting up free and fair elections and having political rights and freedoms—a necessary condition for the existence of citizen agency. Nonetheless, regime contours, the rules and institutions for accessing political power, are too narrow a limit for the subject matter of democratization studies. Democratization must essentially recount the broader tale of the unfinished journey of citizen agency.

Democratization, thus, refers to the process of removal of barriers for exerting citizen agency. It enables the legal expansion of the set of political rights, freedoms, and obligations attached to the status of citizenship, thus expanding the purview of citizen participation and control over political life. As such, it implies macro changes in the organization of power relations at state and societal levels that impede a fuller exercise of citizen agency (King and Lieberman 2009; Whitehead 2002). Democratization is a vector and entails examining historical trajectories that can have quite different time frames, sequences, and convoluted "rhythms"—as O'Donnell's resistance to cast the Northern Quadrant country trajectories as a general case for the study of democratization may attest. When studying democratization one focuses on change, on how a society goes from point A to point B, for instance, from an authoritarian system to a democratic one. However, the transition from A to B may involve changes not only of regimes but at the state and societal levels as well.

If democratization is fundamentally tied to citizen agency, then the story is broader and runs deeper than the tale of how a democratic regime comes into being. Expanding the capability set attached to citizen agency also expands the ability of individuals to mobilize their political rights in order to instill changes in the structure and functioning of state and societal institutions. From this point of view, states and societies can democratize in ways that are complementary to the ways in which political regimes democratize. This is why I think O'Donnell's citizen agency approach implies a thick concept of democratization.[7] This multidimensional understanding of democratization, I insist, is a logical consequence of O'Donnell's citizen agency point of departure, which is not confined to regime politics. As he would concede, thick democratization is less parsimonious than the narrowing of the *problematique* to regime democratization, but it sheds light on how, in a polity, citizen agency may alter power relations in areas of the state and society not directly related to the issue of selecting government authorities through free and fair elections, thus triggering the diffusion of democratic power relations beyond the regime. By limiting the queries to regime change, scholars may be looking at the proverbial tip of the iceberg and missing out key dimensions of political change.

The expansion of democratization's scope entailed by the idea of citizen agency presents conceptual problems. Scholars have come up with concise definitions of regime democratization, the process by which a minimally democratic political regime comes into being. However, as argued, state and societies are also the subject matter of democratization studies, all of which begs the question: what does state democratization mean? And societal democratization? Comparativists seldom use these concepts.

By state democratization I understand the process through which citizen agency is increasingly able to shape the institutions of the state in order to hold political authority accountable to citizens, making it progressively subject to the democratically approved law and more open to public participation and scrutiny in its everyday dealings with citizens, and most generally, with all the inhabitants living within the state's territory. In principle, one should be able to specify the conditions a state must meet to be classified as a "democratized state" just as contemporary political science does for democratic regimes. In fact, this is what O'Donnell attempted at least since 2003 (O'Donnell 2004b, 2007c, 2010b). His parameters are nontaxonomic in nature, allowing room for accommodating the vast differences existing between regimes and states all over the world.[8] These conditions (or parameters) do not specify a particular organization and functioning of a democratized state, nor do they define the developmental outcomes of a set of public policies a democratic polity must implement. They are general requirements for the exercise of state's political power if and when it has been brought under the purview of citizen agency. In his 2007 piece, O'Donnell lists eleven conditions of a democratic state (O'Donnell 2007c: 51). Some of them are cast in terms of their being "reasonable," "adequate," and "sufficient," which does not help. Nonetheless, a careful scrutiny of his 2004, 2007, and 2010 texts outlines some basic features a democratized state should include (table 14.1).[9]

In turn, by *societal democratization,* I refer to the process by which citizens and their organizations mobilize their bundle of rights and freedoms both to exert societal accountability over the state (Smulovitz and Peruzzotti 2000)[10] as well as to enforce democratic practices in private and social organizations and expand the purview of scrutiny over them. In O'Donnellian terms, the latter encompasses the expansion of citizen agency to market and civil society arenas, realms that in principle are far removed from regime politics but come within the purview of democratic politics as a result of citizens' mobilization of rights and freedoms.

Societal democratization reflects the unintended consequences of granting political rights to the citizenry. It has consequences for markets when "consumers' rights" are enacted and enforced, when stakeholders hold managers accountable on the grounds of transparency, or when firms actively involve themselves in corporate social responsibility because they cast themselves as "responsible citizens." It affects the traditional institution of families when it introduces the grammar of rights into formerly private

TABLE 14.1.
Thick democratization

Result	Description	Requirements
Democratic regime	Broadly inclusive mechanisms allow citizen participation in selecting rulers and guarantee certain freedoms	Free, fair, competitive, decisive and periodic elections Political freedoms and rights Universal citizen enfranchisement
Democratized state	Norms and institutions of the state ensure citizen agency overriding competing sources of power structuring principles	Effective enforcement of rights Subordination of authorities to the law Horizontal accountability[a] Legally enacted instances for citizen participation in policy making and implementation
Democratized society	Mobilization of rights to enforce vertical, non-electoral accountability and to expand the purview of scrutiny over private and social organizations	Citizen support for rights and liberties Societal accountability[b] Societal (private) institutions and groups subject to the law and to the exercise of political rights

[a] For a definition of this concept, see Mainwaring and Welna 2003; O'Donnell 1998a, 2003a.
[b] Smulovitz and Peruzzotti coined this term (Smulovitz and Peruzzotti 2000).

realms. "Children's rights" are enacted and enforced through international conventions and domestic legislation. Even religion does not escape from the outreach of democratization, for example, when church hierarchies are hold accountable to civil law or when public displays of religious beliefs are regulated in the name of republican principles. In sum, societal democratization shapes civil society, because it enables organized citizens to have a voice and to influence policy making and also because it enforces transparency and accountability of social and private organizations. Finally, societal democratization helps the spread of citizen attitudes and beliefs that foster support for democratic practices and respect of rights and dignity of others. Table 14.1 specifies some parameters for specifying societal democratization.

In practice, the scope and breadth of democratization may widely vary across countries and, within them, in different historical periods. Some processes basically consist of changes at the regime level, with little or no state and societal democratization. Let us call this type of process *regime democratization*. In these contexts, democratic regimes cohabitate with largely unreformed authoritarian legacies in the structuring and functioning of a state. One could hypothesize that narrow regime democratization renders hybrid regimes, delegative democracies and the like as prob-

TABLE 14.2.
Types and probable outcomes of thick democratization

Type of democratization	Concomitant conditions	Probable outcome
Regime democratization	Little or no state and societal democratization	Hybrid regimes, delegative democracies, "defective" democracies
Regime and state democratization	Regime democratization	Liberal democracy
Regime, state, and societal democratization	Regime and state democratization	Democratization within democracy (*democracia de ciudadanos*)[a]

[a] The notion is taken from Programa de Naciones Unidas para el Desarrollo's 2004 report on democracy in Latin America, for which O'Donnell was the main theoretical inspiration.

able outcomes inasmuch as the democratic impulse is not strong enough to trigger changes at the level of the state structure. With little horizontal accountability and democratic rule of law, encroachment of the electoral system by an unreformed authoritarian state can be expected.[11] In other cases, democratization encompasses both the establishment of electoral democracy and of robust institutions of the democratic rule of law and horizontal accountability. This is pretty much what one sees in established liberal democracies. Finally, there are cases that finally achieve regime, state, and societal democratization. Here, democratization moves beyond liberal representative democracy toward more participatory varieties—what UNDP ambiguously termed as *democracia de ciudadanos* (PNUD 2004).

In sum, while mainstream political science focuses on regime democratization, thick democratization—based on O'Donnell's idea of citizen agency—unearths new dimensions, thus helping to identify qualitatively different -and previously overlooked- types and outcomes (table 14.2). Moreover, it allows political scientists to think of rapid regime changes, the subject matter of the transition literature, as a special case of democratization but not the historical norm.

New Problems for Democratization Theorizing

It is fair to expect that O'Donnell might have called to task this attempt to build upon his reworking of democratic theory.[12] To begin with, the lack of parsimony of this concept comes with a cost. Multidimensionality implies not only distinctive dimensions, as those above described, but also interactions between regime, state, and societal democratization of which we know very little. Are there any specific patterns of interaction between these dimensions? Is there any sequencing at all? (For example, does regime democratization always come first?) When and why does regime democratization have triggering effects over state and societal democratization? Can state democratization drive regime democratization? Does a democratic regression in one dimension always cause deleterious effects in other dimensions of democratization? The state of our knowledge impedes us from coming up with empirically tested answers to this and other questions. We know very little about how state and/or societal democratization unfolded in established democracies. And the whole dynamic of thick democratization remains to be mapped out before attempting any causal argument of its drivers. However, the issue here is whether thick democratization brings new insights as to previously overlooked dimensions, which may be crucial for gauging the extent to which citizen agency has changed power relations at state and societal levels. From the standpoint of a citizen agency theorizing of democracy, I happen to think it does. Thick democratization helps us tracing the macro consequences of the diligent individual-level correlate of democracy, the agent, whose horizons are not necessarily limited to participating in free and fair elections.

A second problem is the limits of thick democratization. One of the advantages of a narrow understanding of democratization as regime change is the specification of clear-cut outcomes. From a conceptual point of view, the endpoint of regime democratization is a totally democratic regime—one that fully complies with polyarchical requirements. If regime change fails to deliver democracy, some sort of diminished, mixed, or hybrid polity emerges, one that counts as diminished or defective democracy (Collier and Levitsky 1997; Merkel 2004).

When looking at state democratization, things are different. No modern state—even the democratized state—can be organized purely on democratic grounds. In highly complex and diversified societies, such as contemporary ones, monetary, fiscal, telecom, or industrial policies can't be decided by citizen assemblies, by the demos at large (nor should this be and/or is it feasible). Bureaucracy can be subjected to public scrutiny, it can be made accountable, but as such it is organized on hierarchical principles based on expert knowledge. Hierarchy and expert knowledge are not democratic principles (Weber [1922] 1977).[13] In all political systems, imposing order over a territory requires command and control relationships that are not abolished—just tamed—by democracy, what Mann terms "despotic power" (Mann 1984, 2010). Many areas of civil, commercial, international, and/or public law continue functioning with little if any connection to democracy. This is so because the state predates democracy and its workings cover many societal realms (economic, cultural, social).

Strictly speaking, no such thing as a democratic state exists in the sense of a state organized solely on democratic principles. All that one may find is a democratized state, one in which democratic principles for organizing power relations compete, coexist, and conflict with other principles such as bureaucracy and the state's despotic power. In sum, the outcome of state democratization is not a state whose organization and workings solely adhere to democracy but, basically, one that contains norms and institutions that ensure that citizens can act as moral and political agents, keeping in check the nondemocratic power relationships that also organize and crystallize in the state apparatus. However, this underscores the difficulty of tagging a taxonomic set of outcomes to state democratization, which remains an essentially open-ended process.

When thinking of societal democratization one finds analogous problems. Many ways of structuring power coexist in the societal realm: families organize kinship relationship based on patterns of authority that are not democratic in origin; markets organize power relationships between and within firms and consumers based on property rights and the mobilization of economic assets, and so on. Societal democratization does not vanquish these other ways of organizing power and authority between private persons and social groups, although it penetrates and influences them and can prevent these from encroaching on the ability of citizens to act as political and moral agents. However, the outcome of societal democratization remains muddled at best.

So, why complicate matters by introducing a notion such as thick democratization? To be sure, a narrower understanding of democratization renders more easily to comparative empirical studies. The nagging point is that there are good, factual reasons to accept the multidimensionality of democratization. No established advanced democracy is purely a democratic regime: the package also includes—to some extent —democratized states and societies. Political scientists may choose to ignore this basic fact of contemporary democracies at the cost of missing out fundamental parts of its politics. Of course, new empirical data need to be collected in order to systematically study the multiple dimensions of democratization, a task beyond the scope of this chapter. Revisiting country cases will also be required, as well as undertakings to collect new comparative data on previously unresearched issues.[14] Nonetheless, O'Donnell's insistence on the importance of citizen agency for democracy provides a useful theoretical perspective to rethink the connections between regime, state, and society in a broader historical perspective, instead of lumping state and societal changes brought by democracy under the generic label of "outcomes" of democratic politics. As we shall see in the next section, the whole idea of "outcome" of democracy needs to be unbundled.

Toward a Broader Concept of Democracy?

O'Donnell disputed Schumpeter's narrow understanding of democracy as a method to select rulers based on free and fair elections. There is more to democracy than that (O'Donnell 2010b: 24–30). He also argued that Dahl's inclusion of a second dimension of democracy (inclusiveness or participation), though welcomed, still left unexplained a fundamental part of democratic life: how democracy is able to ensure that rulers, once elected, do not abuse their legally authorized power to overrun citizens (Bürhlmann, Merkel, et al. 2007; O'Donnell 2007c, 2010b). There must be a mechanism internal to democracy that prevents rulers from becoming tyrants. Here is where O'Donnell encounters a state, or more precisely, certain institutions of the state, which after much hesitation he finally includes as a component of an expanded definition of a political regime (O'Donnell 2010b).[15]

In O'Donnell's view, some state norms and institutions are inextricably woven into the process of enacting and enforcing the existence of free and fair elections, freedom and political rights, universal enfranchisement, accountability of elected officials—all of which are elements of the regime—to such extent that without them the democratic regime flounders. These institutions—which critically ensure that power is not used against citizen rights and freedoms at electoral and nonelectoral times—are not strictly regime institutions. O'Donnell's *Estado democrático de derecho* is the case in point here. It is a subtype of the rule of law that only exists in democratic polities. In addition to ensuring the effective regulation of social behavior by laws, the norms and institutions of the *Estado democrático de derecho* enact and back citizen rights and freedoms and prevent anyone from being *de legibus solutus*. (O'Donnell 2004b: 33). They critically hinge upon the institutionalization and decisiveness of democratic elections by preventing rulers from forfeiting the democratic game after being elected. At the same time, they protect citizen rights and freedoms from encroachment by state and nonstate actors. However, the *Estado democrático de derecho* is external to the process of freely electing leaders: to be effective, it must uphold its independence and separation from partisan politics. Weakness and lack of independence of the rule of law open the door wide open to threats from state actors to the very existence of a democratic regime, as the recent cases in Nicaragua, Honduras, or Venezuela show (Bejarano 2011; Brewer-Carias 2010; Programa Estado de la Nación 2011b). In short, democratic rule of law institutions are crucial to the subsistence of a regime over time.

In addition, O'Donnell noted, citizen agency has consequences for the structuring of the state: some norms and institutions are (re)shaped by constitutional and/or legal mandates originated in democratic decision making. As a consequence, previously unchecked authorities and bureaucracies are subjected to the purview of citizen scrutiny and participation, and segments of the state are affected by the enactment of new citizen rights and state obligations: as a result of participatory budget laws, public budgeting must make room for citizen decisions (Talpien 2012; Wampler 2007), congress recognizes citizen initiative in the process of law formation, authorities are summoned to call public meetings before taking any decision on public utilities, and so on.[16] All of which is not tied to "a method for selecting authorities" as Schumpeter would like to define democracy, but it is certainly a consequence of citizen agency.

At this point, some fundamental questions emerge: do we need a broader definition of political democracy? Should we turn democratic outcomes (i.e., participatory budgeting) into definitional components of democracy? If so, how to avoid conceptual overstretching, and/or the predictable Tower of Babel of ready-made definitions? Is there any theoretical gain in abandoning a narrow and parsimonious concept of democracy? Why is the framing of the *Estado democrático de derecho* as an external condition to democracy an insufficient theoretical proposition? Answering these questions is beyond the scope of this short chapter. Moreover, in his last books, O'Donnell espoused different and conflicting views on the issue of coming up with a new and broader prescriptive definition of democracy.[17] Nonetheless, at the very least, his reworking of democratic theory demonstrates the limitations of minimalist definitions of democracy, rejects the acritical acceptance of mainstream concepts, and opens up the lid for healthy debates on these issues.

My initial take is that there is room for a cautious broadening of the concept of democracy, one based on a minimal rewrite that requires as little definitional tampering as possible but is significant enough as to amend what is, in my view, the fundamental flaw of minimalist definitions of democracy: the incapacity to explain how democracy is able to ensure that rulers, once elected, do not abuse their legally authorized power to overrun citizens. This basic outcome cannot be attributed to good will on the part of the rulers. Free and fair elections may explain how rulers get to the apex but not what happens thereafter, especially the intriguing fact that they accept participating in new elections in which they may lose and have to surrender power. Nor it seems to me theoretically sound to adjudicate such wonder to a condition exogenous to the democratic mechanism itself. Democracy has to account for the minimal conditions required for its own survival as a method for organizing power relations.

I will briefly elaborate on this point. In all political systems, rulers rule over people —democracy is no exception. However, democracy introduces a crucial change in both the nature and dynamics of the relationship between rulers (the powerful side) and the ruled (the weak side): the invention of citizen agency, which includes the capacity to act as they see fit independently from the will of the powerful, as well as certain rights over them through which the ruled can resist, defeat, or force concessions without destabilizing the political system. In short, democracy creates and institutionalizes the power from below, the power of the ruled.

However, democratic power relations do not abolish the power of the rulers, the power from above. As in all political systems, in a democracy power disparities are protracted, consequential, and systematic. They spring up from substantially asymmetric endowments of assets and capabilities between individuals, organizations, and/or social classes. Moreover, some dimensions of political inequality are legally enacted inasmuch as certain individuals are bestowed with the authority to adopt collectively binding decisions. Although asymmetries are dynamic and not necessarily imply zero-sum games, a democracy without political inequalities has never been seen.

So, in a democracy the weak—citizens—exert (some) power over the powerful, but at the same time, the latter retain the ability to govern. As a consequence, a conflictive and potentially fragile equilibrium inevitably arises that is fueled by the contradiction between the impulse of political equality ("power from below") and of political inequality ("power from above"). Given that the "power from above" is, no doubt, more powerful, in the absence of certain protections that must be effective the impulse for political inequality would easily win. These protections are not exogenous conditions for democracy but an integral part of political democracy: without them, citizen agency (the power from below) would be easily disabled.

All democracies thus enact a complex framework of norms and institutions to ensure that both sides—the rulers and the ruled—preserve their lot but, especially, to protect the weaker side, the community of citizens, from encroachment from above. This framework regulates both the access and the exercise of power and implies careful definitions about its legal and illegal uses as well as about the controls needed to prevent abuses. Please note that the brunt of these rules apply to nonelectoral periods, the time in which democratically elected governments are supposed to govern democratically. This is what O'Donnell calls an *Estado de derecho,* which in a democracy is an *Estado democrático de derecho.* Based on these reasons, I would have theoretical reasons to squarely include the institutions of the *Estado democrático de derecho* as part of the core of democracy's power relations in a way consistent with O'Donnell's citizen-agency approach. Therefore, some broadening of the concept of political democracy may be in order.

Whether in fully established democracies the democratic rule of law norms and institutions emerged in parallel or as an outcome of regime politics, I do not know. "Thick" democratization studies have not been systematically attempted. However, a discussion of sorts is premature and largely misses the point. Even if it were so, the main issue here is the cruciality of the *Estado democrático de derecho* for the very survival of democracy. Why not include all other outcomes of democratic politics that leave imprints in state structuring as definitional components of democracy? Although they may certainly have consequences in terms of citizen agency's capabilities, none is so essential to all modern established democracies as the democratic rule of law. Are participatory budget processes and effective offices of the ombudsman modern democratic outcomes? No question: they are. Can political democracy live and eventually thrive without them? Sure again: not all democracies have incorporated these inventions and yet many of them remain vigorous democratic polities. Can modern democracy live without an *Estado democrático de derecho?* That is a story that has not been told.

In sum, O'Donnell thought that proceduralists excessively narrow political democracy to electoral democracy. For sure, free and fair elections are at the core of modern democracy, they are the privileged arena for exerting citizen rights. On this issue, he squarely sided with proceduralists. However, his careful reading of minimalist definitions of democracy unearths implicit, usually overlooked, additional requirements for the existence of free and fair elections. Minimalist ideas of democracy were not so minimal, he concludes: free and fair elections require a resilient political regime ensuring the institutionalization of the democratic method for selecting rulers and certain concurrent political rights and freedoms, backed by the institutions of an *Estado democrático de derecho*, that enables the fullest possible citizen participation in political life.

One final issue: I am aware that my proposal for discussing a cautious broadening of the concept of democracy runs contrary to mainstream political science, concerned with conceptual parsimony. We have been taught that more parsimony is better than less, especially from the perspective of formal theorizing and empirical studies applying sophisticated methods. I agree, partially. We have to be sure that a fundamental component of democracy is not left out because of methodological concerns for parsimony. As I have tried to briefly show in this section, O'Donnell's idea of the citizen agency as the individual correlate of democracy gives ground for rethinking the crucial role played by the institutional protections against encroachment of agency by authoritative political power. From this standpoint, the *Estado democrático de derecho* is a fundamental albeit insufficiently theorized component of democracy.

Democratization and the Quality of Democracy

A common strand in O'Donnell's latest work is his concern for assessing and comparing the "democraticness" of political systems conventionally judged as democracies (O'Donnell 2003b, 2004b, 2010b). *Democraticness* refers to the quality of democracy, the evaluation of the outcomes of democratization at a given point in time. It is the extent to which, in a polity, citizen agency has been able to remove barriers as a result of democratization struggles. When studying the quality of a democracy, the focus is on the gulf between real outcomes and democratic parameters, how far democratization has closed in into setting up a democratic organization of power relations along different dimensions. These outcomes may vary a lot from place to place and within a given polity. In sum, while democratization implies a diachronic historical approach, the quality of democracy goes for static comparisons of outcomes between polities or within them (Vargas Cullell 2008).

This is a nonnormative way of defining quality of democracy. Although values and principles are woven into the fabric of democratic rules and practices, O'Donnell's *excursi* on the parameters to evaluate the quality of democracy sought to tightly anchor them to a solid theorizing of democracy. For him, democracy, democratization, and the quality of democracy are a closely knit triad (O'Donnell 2004b).

A growing body of literature on the quality of democracy emerged in the past two decades. The seminal works of Beetham and colleagues (Beetham 1994; Klug et al. 1996; Weir and Beetham 1998) opened the way to a spate of works quite disparate in terms of their approaches and outreach (Altman and Pérez-Liñán 2002; IDEA 2001; Programa Estado de la Nación 2001; PNUD 2004; and see works in the edited volume by Diamond and Morlino 2005). In the present decade, there have been attempts to lay out the foundations of the quality of democracy perspective as a theory, concept, and program for empirical research (Alcántara 2008; Gómez Fortes et al. 2010; Hagopian 2005; Levine and Molina 2011; Morlino 2007, 2010; O'Donnell 2004b, 2007c; A. Roberts 2010; Vargas Cullell 2004, 2008). However, authors follow different avenues: some works paid attention to the quality of representation (Alcántara 2008; Hagopian 2005), others to the overall quality of political regimes (Altman and Pérez-Liñán 2002; Levine and Molina 2011), to attitudes and behavior (Gómez Fortes et al 2010; A. Roberts 2010), and others attempted a multidimensional approach in assessing the quality of political life (Morlino 2007, 2010; Vargas Cullell 2004, 2008). Most works have avoided the temptation to devise summary measures of the quality of democracy, the two exceptions being Altman and Pérez-Liñán(2002) and, most recently, Levine and Molina (2011), both of which present composite indexes for Latin American countries.

In such an incipient field as that of the quality of democracy, all these efforts open interesting research possibilities; yet it is clear that some basic agreed-upon theoretical understandings are badly needed. In this respect, O'Donnell's framework provides a useful departure point to avoid both overspecification as well as underspecification of the study of the quality of democracy. If quality of democracy restricts itself to assessing the quality of elections and freedoms, it adds little value to what most empirical work on democratization and democracy already does. It has no distinctive puzzle to offer. However, if the quality of democracy perspective broadens too much to include anything that is good and makes people happy, it loses theoretical coherence. In this sense, Przeworski's recent warning against the excessive expectations placed on the democratic ideal is timely and relevant (Przeworski 2010). O'Donnell's framework connects "thick democratization" (how citizen agency unfolds over time) with the assessment of democratic outcomes (quality of democracy). In consequence, the scope of quality of democracy can be broadened while still anchoring it to the study of politics.

Conclusions

O'Donnell's latest reflections on democratic theory aimed at bridging four distinctive literatures. The core is the modern thinking of procedural democracy, dominant in contemporary political science. According to this strand of literature, democracy is a political regime, a point O'Donnell readily conceded albeit with caveats. Schumpeter and Dahl figure extensively in his reflections on democracy (Dahl 1971, 1989; Przeworski 2010; Schumpeter 1947). The second body of work he brought in was the theories of the state, domination, and legitimacy (Bobbio 1987; Mann 1984, 2010; Raz 1990; Sunstein and Holmes 1999; Weber [1922] 1977). This was necessary for his theorizing of the crucial role of the institutions of the rule of law in democracy and, in particular, of the state capabilities to ensure a democratic order over the territory it claims as his, a *problematique* that grew increasingly important after his observation about the "unrule" of law in fledgling Latin American democracies in the early 1990s (O'Donnell 1993, 1998a, 1999c, 2001, 2007c).[18] O'Donnell thought that theorists of procedural democracy had overlooked the question of state and domination, key to understanding democracy as the rule of the demos. In particular, he objected the conflation of state and "government" made by many American political scientists—which, in his opinion, invisibilized institutions and power relations—and turned his attention to classic legal theorists (O'Donnell 2010b).

The third and more recent strand of literature he relied on for his reworking of democratic theory was human development, notably Sen's (1999, 2009) line of work on human agency, capabilities, and freedom. O'Donnell viewed the citizen as a moral and political agent, not simply a "voter," and democracy as the structuring of societal power relations based on the citizen as agent (Vargas Cullell 2008). Finally, O'Donnell brought explicitly into his reflection the literature on the history of democracy (Dunn 1992, 2005; Skinner 1998). This was important to him, given his contention that modern liberal democracy was a complex composite that married the historically conflictive traditions of liberalism, republicanism, and democracy as such (O'Donnell 1996a, 2007c).

O'Donnell latest line of thinking involved a major departure from earlier positions. On the one hand, for most of his career he adhered to a procedural reading of democracy as a political regime. His earlier contributions to the comparative politics literature (where he excelled as agenda setter for the discipline) such as the bureaucratic-authoritarian state and the transitions from authoritarianism, were fully consistent with Dahl's school of thought. On the other hand, O'Donnell's reworking of democratic theory is also a departure from earlier years because herein he was not concerned with coming up with new types of democracy (such as delegative democracy), with putting forward a new theory of democratization (such as transitions from authoritarianism), or discussing the limits of an existing concept and/or theory.[19] His aim was to lay the foundational groundwork for a new theoretical understanding of democracy that could open fields of inquiry for comparative politics.

Interesting enough, O'Donnell remained reluctant to the end to put forward a new prescriptive definition of democracy substituting for Schumpeter or Dahl's. His

2003–4 and 2010 books contain quite contrasting specifications of the components of democracy as a political regime.[20] One explanation of this reluctance is his assertion that democracy is an open-ended process. One can never fully predict where the journey of the citizen-agent will carry it—as seen, the will and actions of the moral agent constantly reshape democracy's borders. In this sense, O'Donnell seems more concerned with democratization than with democracy as an object. For sure, this theoretical insight sheds light on the importance of the struggles of citizens for democracy and their systemic consequences. However, it begs a question: what do we mean by "democracy" today? From a prescriptive perspective, O'Donnell's answer is paradoxical: it is a political regime—with elections, rights and freedom at its core; at the same time, the concept of political regime needs to be reworked because the very existence of citizen agency requires a polity with a state containing built-in protections against encroachment by authoritative political power. From a normative perspective, the vector of the citizen-agent constantly forges new understandings about what a democracy ought to be.

O'Donnell's critique of procedural comparative theories of democracy outlined in his latest books leads to new avenues of theoretical and empirical research. Instead of rejecting tout court procedural theories, he builds upon them while discussing their inability to grasp, much less explain, real-world events such as state and societal democratization. As we have seen, in his latest reworking of democratic theory, citizen agency, and a democratic regime are two mutually constitutive elements, but the vector is the former. As a consequence, he was interested in democratization more than in prescriptive definitions of democracy. O'Donnell sought to theoretically specify the study of democracy beyond narrow confines of Schumpeterian and Dahlian procedural views by underscoring the close interconnection between regimes and states stemming from the common underlying action of the citizen-agent. In this chapter, I discussed the promise and the shortcomings of his contribution and tried to build upon his ideas to underscore how O'Donnell's closely knit understanding of democracy, democratization, and the quality of democracy open interesting puzzles for comparative research.

NOTES

To Guillermo, my professor and dear friend

1. Given the dearth of comparative research on this topic, one may assume for the time being that, historically, the *Estado democrático de derecho* was a result of regime party politics.

2. The wager is that in political democracy, individuals have the right to participate in selecting who governs but must accept that everyone else who is also a citizen can participate, and must accept the collective outcome even if they oppose it (O'Donnell 2004b, 2010b).

3. In his 1989 book, Dahl talked about the assumption of moral autonomy, which underlies democratic theory. For Sen, agency is "someone [an individual] who acts and brings about change, and whose achievements can be judged in terms of her own values and objectives" (Sen 1999:19).

4. According to Sen, all humans have a "capability set" allowing an individual to choose among various valued functions or affiliations (Sen 2009).

5. Article 15 of the Universal Declaration of Human Rights (UDHR) says: "[e]veryone has the right to a nationality" and that "[n]o one shall be arbitrarily deprived of his nationality nor denied the right to change his nationality" (United Nations 1948).

6. Minimalistic requirements for citizenship include adulthood and some legal requirements that vary from country to country.

7. Mine is an attempt to thicken thin concepts, much along the lines suggested years ago by Coppedge (1999).

8. For example the requirement of "free and fair elections" does not stipulate any electoral system in particular. Instead, it sets up a general parameter that any electoral system claiming to be democratic must meet.

9. Recent comparative research underscores the crucial importance of courts for democratic politics (Gauri and Brinks 2008; Hammergren 2007; Helmke and Ríos Figueroa 2011).

10. Societal accountability encompasses the nonelectoral yet vertical mechanism of control (over state institutions) that rests on the actions of a multiple array of citizens' associations and movements (Smulovitz and Peruzzotti 2000).

11. In the past decade or so, scholars from different disciplines and perspectives have studied the development of the state in Latin America as a hindrance for democratization. See Besley and Persson 2008; Centeno 2002, 2009; Engerman and Sokoloff 1997; Gonzalez and King 2004; Grindle 1996; López-Alves 2000; Sokoloff and Zolt 2006; C. Thies 2005. Other works have alerted about the institutional reforms that have modernized Latin American states in the past decades (Lora and Panizza 2002; Schneider and Heredia 2003). Reflecting on a deviant case (Costa Rica), I highlight the importance of a robust state for Costa Rican regime democratization (Vargas Cullell 2012).

12. By 2002, we had already talked about the consequences for democratization theories of his critique to procedural definitions of democracy, but over the years we did not follow the lead (O'Donnell 2002).

13. For a nice, though dated, compilation on the importance of bureaucracy as an institution, see Dalby and Werthman (1971).

14. There is an ambitious ongoing effort to map the emergence of varieties of democracy in the twentieth century, an acknowledgment that democratization may follow different paths on different dimensions (Coppedge, Gerring, et al. 2011). For example, analyzing how a democratized state was built vis-à-vis the regime transition can shed light on processes we have been missing. King et al.'s (2009) study of US democratization is a case in point. They find that this country's democratization has been an open-ended process that moves "along multiple possible paths toward (or away from) more democracy on multiple dimensions" (King and Lieberman 2009). Take Costa Rica, my home country and one of the oldest and certainly the most stable Latin American democracy. Attention has been paid to how the regime first liberalized and finally democratized over a long period beginning in the late nineteenth century and ending in the 1970s (Lehoucq 1995, 1998; Lehoucq and Molina 2004; Programa Estado de la Nación 2001; Seligson and Booth 1995; Wilson 1998). By contrast, very little is known about how the state democratized. However, there is ample

evidence that the establishment of the judiciary as a fully independent branch of the state roughly happened during the first half of the twentieth century, simultaneous with regime changes, while other horizontal accountability institutions developed well after Costa Rica enjoyed a democratic regime (Jiménez 1974; Programa Estado de la Nación 2001). Most surprising, a robust process of state democratization unfolded in the past thirty years well after the regime transition ended. An activist Constitutional Court has progressively interpreted the scope of citizen rights and state obligations thus expanding the legal definition of citizenship, and multiple vertical and horizontal accountability agencies have been set, thus strengthening citizen oversight over government (Programa Estado de la Nación 2001; Wilson et al. 2004).

15. In his 2010 book, Guillermo added an intriguing final clause to his well-known definition of political regime originally put forward in his 1986 piece with Schmitter—the patterns that determine the channels of access to principal government positions (O'Donnell and Schmitter 1986). He included within the boundaries of a regime the "main" and "more visible" institutions of the state. Unfortunately, this addition is an indeterminate proposition because he did not specify those institutions (O'Donnell 2010b: 33).

16. Congress may create new institutions that do not belong to the political regime but are tightly woven to the exercise of citizen political rights. The ombudsman is exemplary of this process (for a nice analysis of the diffusion of this institution, see Pegram 2011). In addition, congress may create new democratic requirements for policy making that unleash new instances for citizen participation and/or remedy, as well as changes in decision-making processes.

17. In the 2003–4 book, the institutions of the rule of law are viewed as extraregime elements, belonging to the state. He goes on to conclude, in the Spanish version, that "theories of democracy limited to the study of regimes seriously underspecify their subject matter" (O'Donnell 2003b: 73), a clause dropped in the 2004 English version of the book. In his 2007 piece he defines the "democratic state" as an empirical type and narrowly defines political regime in conventional terms (O'Donnell 2007c: 30, 50–51). From this perspective, one could conclude that democracy has extraregime dimensions, the *Estado democrático de derecho* being one of those. However, in the same 2007 piece, O'Donnell introduces the notion of a state that "houses" a democratic regime, an idea that he expands in 2010 by saying that the state is "co-constitutive" of democracy. In this last book he presents an expanded concept of political regime as seen in note 16. Presumptively, the *Estado democrático de derecho* can then be seen as a definitional part of the regime—a contrasting view with that held in his 2003–4 book. This allows him to continue understanding political democracy as a regime albeit in non-Schumpeterian or Dahlian terms.

18. O'Donnell posited a much celebrated metaphor (the infamous "brown areas"), the territories where the state is not capable to ensure the rule of law (O'Donnell 1993).

19. For example, his critique of the democratic consolidation literature (O'Donnell 1996a).

20. "2003–4 books" refers to the Spanish and English versions of the "Democracy, Human Development, and Citizenship" coedited with Osvaldo Iazzetta and Jorge Vargas Cullell (O'Donnell 2003b, 2004b). Here O'Donnell says that a democratic political regime has four distinctive characteristics: clean and institutionalized elections, an inclusive wager, and a legal system that backs up citizen rights and ensures that nobody is above the law. Six years later, in his 2010 book, he identifies three components of political democracy as a regime: elections, positive and participative rights, and a bundle of concomitant freedoms (O'Donnell 2010b).

PART V

GUILLERMO O'DONNELL AND THE STUDY OF POLITICS

CHAPTER 15

"A mí, sí, me importa"

Guillermo O'Donnell's Approach to Theorizing with Normative and Comparative Intent

LAURENCE WHITEHEAD

Since his unexpected and sudden death in November 2011, Guillermo O'Donnell's many colleagues and admirers have begun to produce close-up evaluations of specific features of his manifold contributions to comparative politics and the study of democratization. Some of these revealing studies can be found elsewhere in this volume. It may well be too early for anyone effectively to map the terrain as a whole, but this chapter represents an initial attempt to do so. It is a very extensive landscape, quite diverse, somewhat uneven, and this kind of intellectual reconstruction is still fairly unfashionable.

It is doubtful whether Guillermo was ever entirely at rest with the results of his labors. It is hard to see how he could have been, given their scope. It is also very questionable whether any single colleague can at this stage achieve a balanced overview of all the different aspects that ought to go into a comprehensive overview. However, it does seem an appropriate tribute to his memory to at least open the debate and provisionally to comment both on the unusual breadth and on the unorthodox standpoint of much of his opus.

The first section of this chapter starts at the end of his career. Many of his earlier writings have been widely circulated and discussed. But that is not yet the case as regards his final book *Democracy, Agency, and the State: Theory with Comparative Intent* (2010a), which also appeared in Spanish in the year before his death (2010b). But this was arguably his most ambitious and overarching account of the results of his lifetime of study and involvement in processes of democratization in Latin America and around the world. Not only was it his final and mature assessment of the state of this field at the end of his labors, it was also the most fully integrated statement of his closing beliefs and conclusions. Initially drafted during his sojourns at Oxford, it was extensively revised and improved following his final return to Buenos Aires, as it became more apparent that this was likely to be his ultimate intellectual testament.

It therefore makes sense to start our discussion at the end of the story. If we begin with an interpretative overview of his mature work, it should then be easier to track back through some decisive earlier stages in his extended odyssey. This can help to situate his output in its comparative and historical context and to uncover the genealogy of his underlying preoccupations. This first section also highlights his willingness to theorize in the grand tradition and to revisit foundational assumptions about the nature of modern political life and his concern to link up both "macro-comparative" and "micro" levels of analysis.

Ensuing sections delve into three more thematic aspects of his oeuvre that can be tracked back through the course of his career. These are, first, his desire to connect social theory and observation with the realities of actually lived political practice in the societies he knew and cared about; second, his conviction that "Latin American" experiences and understandings were as important and relevant as those he sometimes associated with the "Northwest" of the world community and that he felt deserved to be put on a parity of esteem with the core Anglo-American points of reference; and, third, his unblushing incorporation of explicitly normative standpoints, and indeed quite personal and vehement moral values, as an integral component of his assessment of how the political world works and what is both possible and desirable.

Successive chapter sections expand on each of these topics, illustrating how they shaped his approach and reflecting on the problems they posed for him as well as the insights they generated. The conclusion offers a provisional assessment of how he tried to fit all these preoccupations together and about the difficulties he inevitably encountered with this vast and in many ways inherently unmanageable project.

Agency and the Microfoundations of a Universalistic Concept of Democracy

Democracy, Agency, and the State is an ambitious exercise in political theory ("theory with comparative intent" is his formulation). It is a demanding text, sometimes condensing complex issues into summary formulations that require careful examination. The synoptic exposition below may serve as a lead into his overall output and the positions he was firm in arguing against.

O'Donnell tells us that, on arriving at Yale (1968–71), he was disconcerted to encounter a literature asserting the incompatibility between "Iberian" culture and the democratic individualism of the Protestant democracies. This line of reasoning suggested that it might be inappropriate or even counterproductive to press Western democracy on societies with unsuitable religious or cultural traditions, and in his view it provided an alibi for those who wished to enjoy the fruits of democracy at home, while benefiting from alliances with authoritarian forces abroad. His "universalism" can thus be understood as a theoretical conception inspired by the need to contest what he saw as both an analytical and also a political error. In a similar vein, his universalism inclined him against the kind of indicator-led comparative statistics that can be used to argue against attempting to democratize in countries below a certain level of income per head or subject to some other apparent impediment, such as ethnic divisions.

He also devoted considerable space to the need to elaborate an expansive conception of democracy. Again, it may help to recall what he was arguing against. He rejected contract theories of democracy, with their starting postulate of the isolated presocial individual, and he was more Aristotelian than Rawlsian in this respect.[1] In contrast, he assumed that all those who enter into the citizenship of a democratic regime arrive carrying with them an already established dense network of social relations (many of them legally defined and backed). Moreover, he took up themes from recent work in the "philosophy of recognition,"[2] which has refined the view that individuality and rights can only be crystallized through lifetimes of mutual interaction with other individuals and other rights bearers. Democratic practices and citizenship identities are therefore socially learned and intersubjectively constructed through long processes of trial, error, and reinforcement. So he reacted strongly against what he termed "a restricted, linear, and unidimensional view of democracy, according to which its individual unit is the voter, not the citizen" (O'Donnell 2010a).

O'Donnell's expansive alternative requires an elaborated view of both agency (the foundation of citizenship) and the state (its guarantor). His extended discussion of agency starts from the origins he detects in the "private" sphere, then traces its expansion into "political" rights and constitutionalism, before turning to the ensuing broadening and proliferation of legally sanctioned "social" rights claims. First in the "Northwest," and now more generally, this has given rise to a political "wager" on inclusive and broad-based citizenship rights, which O'Donnell viewed as always incomplete and uneven. Such claims are "in general . . . a product of contention, often violent contention"[3] and provide moral motives for resistance if "deeply rooted expectations regarding recognition" are violated.[4] This view of agency and citizenship rights implies openness to various kinds of democracy, not just a single abstract end state, and it also envisages democratization as a dynamic process that can follow various paths, that, rather than reaching simple closure, may pave the way to further eventual democratizing potentialities (O'Donnell 2010a: 198).

The book is written with the ambition to work out and substantiate these assertions, to give them firm scholarly authority, and to counter some familiar objections. For example, one oft-repeated observation about the *Transitions from Authoritarian Rule* project had been that, even if it turned out to be more than the "wishful thinking" initially decried by its critics, it was still an exercise in "thoughtful wishing."[5] Whatever Guillermo may have thought about that observation (I never heard him endorse it), it seems clear that he did not intend his final contribution to fall under that rubric; he therefore devoted much of his energies to working out the microfoundations of his claim that an expansive and universalistic conception of democracy is well founded and not merely an arbitrary personal preference.

It would be an injustice to attempt a one paragraph summary of his arguments linking citizenship, agency and the state; and demonstrating that, despite obvious obstacles and setbacks, it is plausible to project an underlying global trend in favor of the universal spread of both human and political rights. The whole book is an extended and sophisticated *plaidoyer* for this position. What perhaps merits emphasis here is that, in contrast to many more naïve enthusiasts for "triumph of democracy," O'Donnell was much more alert to the complexities and pitfalls attending any such project. As his celebrated article criticizing the literature on "consolidation" illustrates, he was never prepared to accept teleological "end-states." Instead, his later work on the "quality of democracy" was very focused on the need for citizenship rights to be made meaningful at the micro level. After all, one of his most remarkable earlier contributions had highlighted the adverse inherited microfoundations for democracy in Argentina and Brazil on the eve of their macro transitions (O'Donnell 1984).

His final book includes a striking passage concerning the Argentine military's attempts to regulate the shortness of hairlines and the length of skirts as an index of authoritarian intolerance (O'Donnell 2010a:134). (Ironically, we now know that, in a different cultural setting, transitions to democracy can also give rise to reinforced dress codes and a microclimate of heightened social discipline and restraint.) More generally, he was also alert to the cross currents on citizenship arising from multiculturalism and legal pluralism, not to mention feminist critiques concerning gender rights.

In order to accommodate such tensions and aporias in his position, O'Donnell had to accept that his expansive conception of democracy would need to be hospitable to different understandings of human agency and that such disagreements would need to be aired and contrasted through dialogical processes. At the same time, he specified indispensable limits within which such questions would need to be channeled. That is why the book also contains a refined account of the role of the modern state, and its law, in underpinning and constraining such democratic deliberations. In the end, however, for him the foundations of democracy reside at the micro level, in the mutual recognition required of rights bearers and in the philosophy of respect that governs his theory of democratic agency.

This brief synopsis of O'Donnell's closing magnum opus may serve to introduce readers both to its richness and also to its complexities. Many of his previous contributions were catchier and easier to assimilate into ongoing research programs. *Democracy, Agency and the State* will probably take longer to filter into the consciousness of his colleagues. As should be apparent from the foregoing, it could not cover all the dimensions of such a vast topic. For example, his refined and illuminating treatment of agency is very focused on political and legal issues. More can be said about the economic aspects of individual agency in a liberalized market economy and how far that reinforces, or competes with, the account of democracy he formulated. So this book was obviously not the last word on these matters; but as it turned out, it was his last word, and it reads as if written for posterity and in the hope that it would stand comparison with other time-hallowed authorities.

Looking back from this end point we can now turn to earlier stages on the journey that got him there. The theoretical positions he developed in his final work were distilled from periods of intense immersion in a wide range of scholarly literatures, but they also derived from a lifelong career of engagement with real-world, especially Latin American, political experiences that challenged many mainstream academic assumptions about political development.

Grounding Theory in Closely Observed Local Practice

O'Donnell's first major contribution was written almost four decades previously and reflected both the quite different academic preoccupation and also the very contrasting political realities of the early 1970s. *Modernization and Bureaucratic-Authoritarianism: Studies in South American Politics* (1973) offered a distinctive South American perspective on the then prevalent "modernization" approach to political development. Many of the conceptual reference points were very recognizable and persisted throughout his career—Weberian angles on the modern state, Marxian intuitions about the economic and class interests that could provide underlying structural determinants of political outcomes, liberal and democratic criticisms of unaccountable policy making and the cumulative injustices it could perpetrate. The bold and original way he combined and synthesized these contrasting theoretical standpoints and used them to account for otherwise puzzling political realities was inspiring, even if the precise conclusions to be drawn from the schema were open to multiple interpretations.

One crucial virtue of this contribution was that it so firmly debunked the Pollyannaish implications of the then-dominant political science orthodoxy: modernization theory. Not all good things automatically flowed together; there was no assured happy ending or convergence around some US-style liberal democratic end point, which the dominant strand in modernization theory assumed would happen, as long as unnatural challenges from ideological communism were seen off.

To the contrary, for O'Donnell, who was schooled in the bitter realities of Peronist and post-Peronist Argentina, it was obvious that the paths to economic modernity could be strewn with pitfalls and structural conflicts. As Gerschenkron and Moore had already demonstrated, if you came from behind you might well have to face very different dilemmas from those who had led the way (Gerschenkron 1962; Moore 1966). And, as the other South American critics of modernization theory, such as his Brazilian counterpart Fernando Henrique Cardoso, were simultaneously arguing through their exposition of dependency theory, if you came from behind then those ahead of you might have a strong propensity to divert your path (or even to block your way; Cardoso and Faletto 1969).

Guillermo O'Donnell was thus taking a leading role in a dominant debate of that time. For late industrializers of the 1960s and 1970s, who governs, how they acquire and protect their power, whether they serve broad external or narrow domestic interests, and whether the economic success they may achieve serves the population as a whole or a privileged and alienated stratum within it were the burning questions of the day in many "third world" societies. The bureaucratic-authoritarian state hypothesis offered a fresh road map for interpreting these issues. In order to challenge such a broad and decontextualized macro standpoint as "modernization theory," it would not be good enough simply to object that it was inapplicable in a particular country; or even in a whole subcontinent in a particular period of time. However well-grounded in Argentine or Brazilian contemporary realities, to make an impact on the academic community the critique would also need to establish its theoretical credentials and its capacity for generalization. This is what the *dependencia* and *estado burocrático autoritario* (EBA) contributions both achieved.

But O'Donnell's bureaucratic-authoritarian framework also posed some severe problems, certainly for area studies and comparativist students. Perhaps the most revealing critique of this approach was provided by José Serra (1979).[6] Serra accepted the framework as one of broader application than merely to a short period in the troubled history of Argentina. Guillermo was, at a minimum, referring to the military regimes of both Argentina and Brazil. But, from Serra's point of view, at least in the case of the Brazilian military dictatorship, this ideal type representation left out too much of the operational reality and therefore pointed in a direction that was not in fact built into the logic of the situation.

As we know from subsequent developments, the trajectories of Argentina and Brazil diverged radically thereafter, thus confirming that Guillermo's attempt at a general framework had not captured all the relevant dimensions. Nevertheless, his determination to provide a generalized, rather than purely national-specific, model of bureaucratic-authoritarianism had the great merit that it elicited recognition and stimulated emulation in a wide variety of other contexts. To take a specific example that Guillermo himself may never have encountered, academics in South Korea who subsequently played a leading role both in that country's democracy movement and in the development of its understanding of comparative politics, were both guided and encouraged by the example of this text.[7]

It is remarkable testimony to the fecundity of his comparative work that the fullest and most convincing example of the phenomenon he was seeking to delineate appears to have arisen—more or less as he was writing—in a remote Asian peninsula about which he could only have had very uncertain and indirect knowledge. Although his analysis was undoubtedly explicitly grounded in contemporary Argentine political experience, it would be a misrepresentation to reduce it to that alone, since doing so would obscure an essential and recurrent aspect of his intellectual achievement: his uncanny capacity to generalize from closely observed realities, thus generating a broader analysis able to "travel" across space and time.

As his subsequent career was to demonstrate, this was not a "one-off" achievement. It applies equally to a succession of other key conceptual innovations that Guillermo also introduced, such as the "transitions" paradigm, "delegative democracy," the notions of "brown areas," horizontal accountability," and to the concepts of human rights and the "quality" of democracy.

The most famous of all his contributions was the fourth volume (the slim green paperback) of *Transitions from Authoritarian Rule*—the concluding essay he coauthored with Philippe Schmitter.[8] This is still constantly quoted, but to my mind not always read with sufficient attention both to text and to context. Here we need focus on just one crucial aspect. One idea that differentiated this contribution from much preexisting literature was that an authoritarian regime could better be viewed as an authoritarian coalition of otherwise nonhomogenous actors and interests. He contributed the idea that under specified conditions, therefore, the coalition might be split (schematically into "hardliners" and "softliners").[9] Where this possibility arose, the prospects for a transition from a liberalized authoritarian regime to a more inclusive and potentially contrasting democratic regime could depend heavily on whether the soft-liners could be reinforced and reassured to the point where the hard-liners would be marginalized and disempowered.

This was a big challenge to the then-prevalent assumption that the more authoritarian a regime became the wider the base of opposition to it, and the more repressive it became the greater the chance of it being overthrown by a fierce and united collective repudiation. The Portuguese Revolution and the overthrow of the Somoza dictatorship by the FSLN appeared to validate the second interpretation, whereas the post-Franco transition in Spain was no doubt the best available instantiation of the O'Donnell and Schmitter alternative. But was Spain a paradigm case or an unrepeatable exception? At the time the work went to press (in 1984) there were still very few empirical cases to draw on, and the roll call was mixed. So what explains the firm embrace of what become known as the "transitions" paradigm (which subsequently also proved so prescient)?

Here again, Guillermo's approach drew both from his theoretical standpoint and his tacit knowledge or background understanding of certain key national political realities: but one might ask again, which ones? It was obvious that, for Juan Linz (1973), the case of Spain almost inescapably ranked foremost. Philippe Schmitter (1975) was broad in his outlook, but no doubt he also was very conscious of what had happened in Portugal and the huge risks that had been run before that transition reached stability. For my part, the cases of Greece (military overreach followed by defeat and collapse) and Bolivia (antidictatorial mobilization that failed to generate a stable democratic alternative) seemed to cloud the picture.

One might have thought that for Guillermo the case of Argentina would once again dominate his model building. But, of course, Argentina in the 1970s had been a thoroughly negative case—not of authoritarian soft-liners building bridges to moderate democratic opponents but, on the contrary, of ever-escalating polarization and the elimination of the "soft middle ground." Perhaps his revulsion at that dynamic in his country of birth was enough to inspire Guillermo to imagine an entirely inverted possibility, what Abe Lowenthal so memorably referred to as the "thoughtful wishing" of the *Transitions* project (Lowenthal 1986: viii). But while clearly differentiating analysis from prediction, O'Donnell intended his analysis of transitions and subsequently of democratization processes more generally, to be grounded on good evidence rather than just good intentions.

Certainly, his profound conviction that not only Argentina but also Chile and Uruguay possessed far richer traditions of political innovation and conflict resolution than were visible at the time must have helped underpin his reasoning. But what he knew at firsthand about the destructive hatreds and fears of the Southern Cone in the 1970s was enough to cast a shadow over any undue cheerfulness about the prospects for a democratic reconciliation. Indeed, strong evidence of the lingering influence of those experiences can be seen in his way of conceptualizing likely transition outcomes (the fear of "authoritarian regression" was always more prominent in his thinking than in that of most of his coauthors) and in his resistance to the subsequent "consolidation" paradigm.

Nevertheless, he did firmly and boldly commit himself to the hard-liner/soft-liner distinction and all its analytical implications. The point to pursue in this section is whether this choice was purely theoretical or whether it could have been shaped to a substantial degree by his understanding of certain exemplary and paradigmatic political experiences. A good case can be made that there was a specific and powerful political process under way that he knew well, and that gave him confidence to make his crucial intellectual move. But arguably this was not Spain (with its civil war, its monarchy, and its inbred commitments to legal formalism); nor was it Argentina, where the soft-liners had been marginalized and the hard-liners had then led the regime to disaster and collapse.

More plausibly, it was Brazil, a country with which he had become far more involved since the mid-1970s. If Onganía represented the EBA then Geisel was the embodiment of a soft-line authoritarian. If violent polarization eliminated the scope for a moderate democratic opposition to build bridges and craft solutions that would marginalize the two extremes, then the tolerated opposition, the Brazilian Democratic Movement (Movimento Democrático Brasileiro, MDB) kept alive a contrasting option, one that became more credible as candidates such as Fernando Henrique Cardoso (key adviser to the "transitions" project) not only stood for election but actually began winning elections of real substance. On this view, even if Guillermo had his head in the densest clouds of social scientific theory, he also had his feet planted firmly on South American soil, with the result that his analytical choices were quite locally grounded, as well as being powerfully transferable.

A personal illustration may be apposite here. I, and perhaps others involved in this kind of analysis during the 1980s—perhaps even O'Donnell—were surprised by the extent to which the transitions insight proved transferable to what seemed to many of us at the time the most inhospitable of territories. I recall lecturing at Oxford in 1989 on this very topic. A distinguished gentleman sitting at the back came forward afterward to tell me that he fully endorsed the transitions paradigm and that moreover he was going to show that it could solve the otherwise intractable political impasse in his own country. Upon learning that he was Frederik Van Zyl Slabbert (soon to become a key negotiator in the South African transition), I wished him well, but told him I could hardly believe that a formula that had brought reconciliation to certain divided republics in South America could be stretched to the point where it applied to the far more absolute deadlock created by White Minority Rule and the apartheid system. He promised to prove me wrong, and in the process he demonstrated for a second time that Guillermo's method of abstraction and generalization from certain very well understood local political realities could create a conceptual framework capable of jumping from one continent to the next and of opening up imaginative possibilities even in far-flung political situations about which he had only the most imperfect sources of information.

Rather than just attempting to "model" or summarize externally existing political realities, O'Donnell's imaginative constructions actually influenced the political actors he was also studying. At best it might have provided them with illumination and reassurance, rather than just empirical validation.

Then there is "delegative" democracy (O'Donnell 1994). More briefly, this surely expresses his reaction to the fact that, although the Peronist Party had the option of learning how to play the conventional role of loyal democratic opposition and of eventually becoming the alternative party in power (it could have chosen Cafiero), in practice it united around Carlos Menem. But Argentina was not Spain, and the Peronist Party opted for a personalist rather than an institutionalist style of electoral politics. So it united around Carlos Menem. The consequences overhang the course of Argentina's democratization to this day. Perhaps there were other secondary influences as well—Collor's brief presidency in Brazil, possibly even the early period of Alfonsín, when he displayed his most "delegative" proclivities.

At any rate the "delegative" insight was also deeply grounded in locally observed realities. Yet it was also tremendously transferrable. I tried to provoke Guillermo into a reaction by observing that Hugo Chávez had provided such a perfect demonstration of the potential of this concept that he must have studied the 1994 article and drawn specific guidance from it. No doubt Chávez has engaged in independent invention, but the crucial point is that Guillermo's insight prefigured yet another most powerful political development in a country that was not in the forefront of his experience. Of course, he knew Venezuela better than South Africa or South Korea, but that was not the empirical base for his conceptualization.

Then there are the "brown areas" (O'Donnell 1993). This notion first arose in a text he wrote in 1992 for the Social Science Research Council project on "economic liberalization and democratic consolidation." Here is the passage that illustrates how he proceeded to build his argument:

> Let us imagine a map of each country in which the areas covered by blue would designate those where there is a high degree of state presence (in terms of a set of reasonably effective bureaucracies and of the effectiveness of properly sanctioned legality) both functionally and territorially; the green color indicates a high degree of territorial penetration and a significantly lower presence in functional-class terms; and the brown color a very low or nil level in both dimensions. In this sense, say, the map of Norway would be dominated by blue; the United States would show a combination of blue and green, with important brown spots in the South and in its big cities; Brazil and Peru would be dominated by brown, and in Argentina the extensiveness of brown would be smaller—but, if we had a temporal series of maps we could see that those brown sections have grown lately. (Quoted from the subsequent version published in chapter 7 of O'Donnell 1999a: 139–40)

From this starting point, Guillermo proceeded to elaborate a comparative and theoretical framework for assessing the rule of law, the effective distribution of rights, and the scope and limitations of the liberalized state in Latin America and some postcommunist countries. Again, my point is the local "groundedness" of this theoretical edifice, rather than its broader implications. As the references to Argentina in particular indicate, he was not theorizing in a vacuum. Rather he was soaking up quite detailed and specific aspects of local political realities that challenged mainstream theorizing (with its simple-minded assumption that a change of national-level political regime would necessarily transform power realities across the relevant jurisdiction) and demanded fresh efforts at reality-based conceptualization. The "brown areas" have been disaggregated and more carefully measured (if not color coded) since then, but the initial insight was his. And it was inspired by tangible specifics, in highland Peru, in the lawless Amazon, and the gang-ridden parts of many cities across the Americas.

It is perhaps otiose to pursue this line of thought much further. But similar observations apply to Guillermo's subsequent theoretical innovations, in such areas as "horizontal accountability" (O'Donnell 1999b; albeit lines of accountability do not necessarily cross at right angles—much empirical evidence seems somewhat diagonal) and the variable and multidimensional aspects of the "quality" of democracy (O'Donnell, Vargas Cullell, and Iazzetta 2004). In every case, the theoretical perspective gave his ideas general and comparative traction. But they were also stimulated, inspired, and checked by well-understood (if not necessarily well-studied) and concretely grounded political practices and power relationships.

"Latin America" as a Source of Universal Theory, as Relevant as the "Northwest"

As demonstrated in the preceding section, O'Donnell drew on his deep understanding of local South American political realities in order to construct concepts and theories that were always comparative and therefore designed to "travel." But he never doubted that it would be possible to find political features resembling his "brown areas," "delegative" democracies, "horizontal" accountabilities, and the rest outside Latin America as well as within it. So he was understandably reluctant to be drawn on the extent and limits of their incidence. Attempts to pin him down on whether he was engaged in the construction of a regionally focused "Latin American" approach to political analysis and comparative politics or whether instead he saw his work as of universal relevance failed to produce an either-or response.

In his 1970s writings he was more inclined to specify "South America" or "Argentina and Brazil," whereas the Transitions project explicitly referred only to Latin America *and* Southern Europe. In fact, after brief discussions it was decided not to include Cuba, Nicaragua, or Poland (it turned out that the "transitions" paradigm would attract interest from Afghanistan to Zimbabwe, but that was not at all foreseen in the early 1980s).[10] But after the mid-1980s, once he moved to Notre Dame and headed up the Kellogg Institute, O'Donnell scaled back the reference to geographically specific locations. Even so, the 1993 article was modestly titled *A Latin American View with*

Glances at Some Postcommunist Countries. In contrast, *Counterpoints* (1999a), the writings on horizontal accountability (1999b), and *The Quality of Democracy* (O'Donnell, Vargas Cullell, and Iazzetta 2004) all presented general arguments, even though they were buttressed by examples nearly all drawn from his region of origin.

Even his final book with its unambiguously abstract and general scope contained one chapter specifically concerned with the subcontinent (chapter 8 offers an overview of Latin America). For him this seemed entirely appropriate even in a volume conceived basically as a dialogue with the great European and Western world thinkers who had aimed to construct universal categories and to uncover underlying truths about the nature of modern mass political praxis without any specific limits of time or space. The focus of that book was not so much on the empirically observable and measurable features of contemporary political behavior but more on the theoretical foundations and imaginative potential of political innovations tailored to the fulfillment of modern human potential. However, his last book was also written with "comparative intent: in it I hope to open avenues for some theoretical discussions, as well as for empirical and comparative research, especially but not exclusively focused on Latin America" (O'Donnell 2010a: 145).[11]

So, as can be seen, Guillermo resisted directly answering my either-or dilemma, because he was committed to keeping both aspects of his work alive and (where possible) in balance. One imperative was to ensure that the Latin American realities he lived so personally were given their due weight—and parity of esteem—in the overall understanding of such abstract general concepts as democratic accountability, human rights, and good government. That required the development of a Latin America–based political science, but one that was confident, outward looking, and insightful about realities beyond the region. The competing objective was therefore to produce "theory with a comparative intent" as his last book title puts it. From this standpoint, universal theory could be reinterrogated and reconstructed in the light of Latin American knowledge, and the results ought to be capable of achieving equal standing with mainstream theory and assumptions, much of which could seem quite as blinkered and parochial in its reference points as any Latin American nationalist discourse.

From this perspective, part of his output could be recognized as a challenge to, and critique of, tendencies in modern political science to neglect the conceptual history and foundational dilemmas on which the discipline had originally been constructed. Of course he was both an insider and an outsider in the American political science profession, so here too it is better to present his position as "both-and" rather than "either-or," but the outsider strand was always present and included some strong views about theories and methods that were not sufficiently comparative or responsive to non–North American realities and analytical perspectives. This accounts for the critical tone that came through on occasions and that was encapsulated in his persistent use of the term "Northwest" as a shorthand version for the false universalism and developed democracy parochialism he had in his sights.

As a parenthesis, it may be worth noting here that, whereas many of his other terminological innovations caught on throughout the entire comparative politics community, his references to the "Northwest" remained personal and were never taken up by the scholarly community. Several explanations for this deserve consideration. At the purely geographical level, while the North American landmass lies somewhat to the west as well as to the north of Buenos Aires, the same is not the case in, say, Mexico City or even Bogota. On a more analytical note, it often seemed as if the old democracies targeted by this label must include at least some located in Western Europe. Indeed it is arguable that O'Donnell's "Northwest" would have to extend at least as far east as Switzerland.

Perhaps there was also a further, more South American, impediment to the adoption of this terminology. Did it not overlap with what previous generations had known as *el imperio*, a pejorative term that Guillermo was bound to eschew? And many social scientists in his cohort made use of another alternative, namely the center-periphery divide. But Guillermo was not a *dependentista,* and his approach was certainly not to accept his region's relegation to a marginal or peripheral position in comparative politics. Instead, by deploying the imagery of the "Northwest," he was trying to relativize the centrality of the core. Another manifestation of the same sentiment was the fierceness with which he opposed US (and therefore international political science) appropriations of the adjective "American."[12]

To some readers, these may seem like minor terminological quibbles, but for O'Donnell quite a lot was at stake here. In his defense it could reasonably be argued that in the course of his career he made remarkable headway in demonstrating that at least some central and universal issues and concepts in comparative politics were more likely to be clarified by taking Latin American instances as paradigmatic cases that by marginalizing his region and theorizing about it on the basis of models derived from without.

At the more practical level, he displayed continuing commitment to the International Political Science Association (IPSA, although he was also prominent in the American Political Science Association, APSA). As President of IPSA at the end of the Cold War, he led the association precisely when the entire world was opening up to his kind of comparative political science. This was not an easy task, and for example he had to contend with the aftermath of Tiananmen Square and with Beijing's efforts to evict Taiwan as a condition for PRC enrolment. He also succeeded in bringing IPSA to Buenos Aires, at a time when many debated its potential status as an international complement (or even challenger) to the "Northwestern mainstream." He thus helped to broaden the geographical base of international political science and to open it to new currents, without necessarily making a judgment that its existing output merited any special intellectual preference.

He was also fully appreciative of the rich creativity and academic leadership that could often be found in North America. He greatly valued the benefits provided by his period of study at Yale. In addition to the obvious influences of Robert Dahl, Juan Linz, and the Yale Latin Americanists, he also paid special tribute to David Apter—whose bold and wide-ranging approach to comparative politics extended the scope of the subject, offering more space for serious consideration of what others might have considered "peripheral" experiences. Outside Yale, one might single out Albert Hirschman as a particularly powerful source of inspiration—a scholar capable of crossing over from economics to history to social theory to extremely vivid and concrete illustrations of how they might be applied and back and a leading US scholar-cum-policymaker who was also deeply aware of European traditions of comparative social analysis. Moreover, Hirschman cared about Latin America, believed its potential could be realized and reasoned from a committed reformist and liberal standpoint. So the "both-and" perspective bears repeating yet again. Guillermo saw himself a building on the best of the North American scholarly tradition, as well as resisting some of its more parochial or ideological features.

Of course the institution-building phase of his career, as founding director of the Kellogg Institute for International Studies at Notre Dame, provided him with an outstanding opportunity both to contribute social science and to enrich it by bringing in Latin American scholars on a basis of parity of esteem. Other chapters in this volume provide more than sufficient testimony on this score. In addition to his leadership roles in Argentina (CEDES), the United States (Kellogg), and IPSA, he was also a major figure in other leading centers. One could mention CEBRAP and IUPERJ, and the Latin American Studies Association. He also played a valuable role toward the end of his life as a regular visiting fellow at Nuffield College, Oxford. In fact, the list could be extended well beyond that (we spent some time together in Taiwan, and he published in the *Taiwan Journal for Democracy*), but even this brief and incomplete inventory is enough to demonstrate that he was a citizen of the scholarly world, a cosmopolitan thinker who was well-qualified to expose partial and parochial assumptions, whether they arose in the "Northwest" or the "Global South" or, indeed, from any other inward-looking local perspective.

An Explicitly Normative Approach to Democratization Studies

Another "either-or" dichotomy that Guillermo always resisted was the choice between descriptive and prescriptive analysis. This was partly a consequence of the subject matter he dealt with. Democratization, citizenship, accountability, and human rights are all ethical as well as empirical topics. They concern how we ought to live as much as how we actually do. But mainstream contemporary social science typically invites us to make a choice—either write normative theory (in which case there can be great latitude to construct ideal worlds and to disregard the evidence of "real existing" trade-offs and practices) or severely limit the scope for subjective commitments to influence or distort the results of dispassionate empirical enquiry.

While normative preferences are still allowed to influence the selection of topics for examination, over the course of Guillermo's career professional social science has become much more insistent about "value free" protocols to guarantee the integrity of the ensuing evidence and research findings. As already mentioned with reference to the "thoughtful wishing" and the "transitions" project, Guillermo was certainly aiming to generate objective knowledge, but he always intended to combine this with some strong and explicit normative commitments. He wanted his findings to be useful, to be influential, to change beliefs about what was possible, and—in particular—to help in uncover ways to overcome authoritarian rule and to enhance the quality of democracy.

This comes across in an interview he gave at the time his last book was launched in Buenos Aires. In response to the question about what the essence of citizen demands was, he responded: "Todas estas demandas de incorporación política, de participación, de derechos, fueron demandas profundamente morales, siempre tuvieron un contenido moral importantísimo: 'Yo soy un ser humano, y usted me debe reconocer como tal. Por eso tengo derecho a votar, a no sufrir violencia doméstica, etcétera.' Este componente moral no siempre es percibido por las teorías políticas y sin embargo, está en el centro de las democracias aun en los períodos en los que uno mira alrededor y dice: acá no pasa nada" (Bruno 2011).

Guillermo had no problem even using quite emotive language when speaking about repulsive aspects of authoritarian rule—a political regime that practiced gross human rights abuses might be referred to as *un monstruo*, reminiscent of the song of his compatriot, León Gieco, "es un monstruo grande y pisa fuerte, toda la pobre inocencia de la gente." He thought this was appropriate because when dealing with torture, mass murder and other forms of cruelty—it would be artificial and distorting to pretend that one was merely a scientist in a white suit disengaged from the objects under scrutiny. This attitude was also a reflection of his ideas about the audience to be addressed and what the consequences might be if promoting a given finding. Perhaps it was also connected to the methods he used (a broad and deep grounding in specific local political realities would require some emotional engagement in conflicts), and it surely helps account for the transferability of his theoretical insights from one connect to another. (He might not know anything about South Korea, but his normative stance about the bureaucratic-authoritarian state, wedded to the acuteness of his analysis, would cause his ideas to resonate for readers in a very distant land.)

At the same time, of course, as a professional academic O'Donnell remained wedded to truthfulness and verifiability. Indeed, his comparative research program was partly inspired by the conviction that a broader range of experiences and a richer theoretical perspective could uncover otherwise neglected truths and expose otherwise concealed assumptions and blind spots. So he was not trying to generate new utopias (on the contrary, his long exposure to Argentine political battles gave him good reason to regard utopian political thinking as in practice destructive); or even to inject "wishful thinking" into contexts where only the most hard-headed of assessments were likely to prove constructive.

As the "brown areas" passage quoted above illustrates, and as many other contributions would confirm, he encouraged the mapping and measurement of the phenomena under study, rather than just the construction of untestable hypotheses about them. It is true that he left much of the detailed work of measurement and verification to others, but he also devoted great energy to organizing and leading teams of scholars who would undertake precisely such work.

That raises two further questions: who the work was for and where the underlying normative commitment came from. Only the briefest and most provisional responses can be suggested here. There have obviously been multiple audiences for the work he produced. From the beginning to the end of his career, one audience was *porteño* and Argentine public opinion, caught up in the passions and distortions of Peronist and anti-Peronist political discourse and conflict. He was still writing Op-Ed pieces and trying to contribute to public debate in his country until the last weeks of his life. These were not necessarily freighted with great learning or theoretical complexity, but they were an integral part of his output, and they derived their authority from his wider scholarly and analytical achievements. Guillermo was a cosmopolitan public intellectual with an exceptionally diverse and multilayered international readership. That made him very sensitive to the inevitable misappropriations and misunderstandings that his work could generate. Some of his readers wanted him to come down clearly on one side or the other of the many "either-or" fences he straddled.

It was not always easy to decide even which language the message should be written in—citizenship has one meaning in English, *ciudadanía* a slightly different resonance in Spanish; similar issues arise with the state, el *estado de derecho*, or the untranslatable "accountability." He tried to express himself clearly (not an aspiration equally shared by all of his celebrated conationals, such as Ernesto Laclau) but his language was sometimes and perhaps necessarily polysemic. And—in contrast to, say, Huntington or Fukuyama—he did not cultivate a single core constituency of readers who might to some extent come to own his output and simplify his messages. It was a rather solitary exercise to write with such impact for a readership that was so diffuse.

A lot of subsequent work was therefore needed to correct misinterpretations and fend off undesired appropriations.

From the evidence, it seems that on the whole O'Donnell handled these inevitable tensions in two ways that could not always be separated out. One audience he had in mind was a quite small circle of close associates and like-minded colleagues, who could situate his output in a shared and well-understood long-run context. But he also tried to write for a much more distant and unspecified readership—thinkers from past and future generations who would grapple with the same kind of problems that troubled him; democratic activists in continents he had yet to visit; and future generations of readers who could not be expected to grasp what it had been like to live through Argentina's "dirty war" or to contribute to the debate over whether there should be a "debtors cartel" to default on South America's obligations to North American banks in the mid-1980s.

These potential audiences would tend to be accepting of normatively inspired but empirically grounded comparative theory. Far from requiring him to write in the constricted idiom of orthodox professional social science, they would respond best and engage most fully with his work if he addressed them directly and from the core of his own convictions (both moral and methodological). Similar issues arose in a more acute form in the parallel career of his Brazilian colleague and partial counterpart, Fernando Henrique Cardoso (Whitehead 2009).

Second, then, there is the issue of the source of his normative commitments. In his "lifetime achievement award" presentation at LASA he gave an unusual amount of biographical background that bears on this question and said more in his interview with Gerardo Munck (Munck and Snyder 2007: 273–304).[13] In the absence of a fuller biographical study, it must suffice just to note such background considerations as his highly political family background; his initial opposition to Peronism; his early, brief, and unhappy direct involvement in Argentine politics during the precarious tenure of the Guido administration (critics would suggest that his hostility to authoritarian politics was partly derived from this early exposure to its temptations); his subsequent political and intellectual responses to increasingly horrific experiences of intolerance and repression; his ideological distance from the radical left, and so on.

On an even more personal level, it could be that a lifelong health disability also colored his outlook. At an early age he suffered from polio, before effective treatment had become available. Throughout his adult life, therefore, he had to bear with fortitude the burdens of a withered leg. Perhaps his ideas about dignity, personal responsibility, respect for difference, and to the use of reason rather than force were all in part informed by the consequences of that unfortunate starting point. In any case, it is possible to observe that his ethical, normative, and psychological outlook was in any case shaped by another basic disposition—he came to detest bullies and bullying. As a strong personality operating in an intensely combative Buenos Aires environment, it could be that that this outlook was also reinforced by his personal awareness of how far *prepotencia* might carry one away.

A single illustration will have to suffice here. As president of the International Political Science Association in 1989, he had every incentive to try to admit the People's Republic of China (PRC) to the world political science community, and many of his colleagues were most anxious for him to do so. It is doubtful whether he had any particular fondness for the regime in Taiwan, which was only just emerging from four decades of harsh authoritarian rule under the still dominant Kuo Ming Tang. Nevertheless, Taiwan was affiliated to IPSA and the PRC was not. While Beijing was encouraging and constructive on all other fronts, one issue was nonnegotiable. The PRC would only allow its fledgling association to enter IPSA if the more developed Taiwan political science association was expelled. There were many elaborate rationales that could be put forward to justify this step. But Guillermo would not be sidetracked on this issue. To him it was straightforward and clear. If the PRC was determined to bully Taiwan, it would have to be resisted. On that he could not be budged. Arguably this episode highlights a recurrent feature of his outlook, one that helps unify the descriptive and prescriptive elements in his scholarly work and that defines his basic outlook on how we ought to live and to organize our political affairs.

By Way of Conclusion

I have sketched out four areas of Guillermo O'Donnell's lifetime of scholarly production, each of which marks him out as at least partially different from mainstream positions in his profession. I have tried to avoid portraying him as a radical outsider. Under each heading he pursued a "both-and" rather than an "either-or" path of differentiation. There are costs associated with trying to reconcile alternative positions. There are also heavy costs involved in pursuing such an ambitious, cosmopolitan, multifaceted, and polysemic agenda. But these four core commitments were pursued with courage and determination. Taken together they constituted a powerful and original contribution that differentiates his output from the social science mainstream and that should continue to speak to us for decades to come.

NOTES

1. In a sense similar to that proposed by Martha Nussbaum (1990).

2. Key exponents include Charles Taylor, notably his 1992 essay, *Multiculturalism and the Politics of Recognition*, also published as *The Politics of Recognition* (1994); Nancy Fraser (2000);

and above all Axel Honneth (1995), which was a particularly important reference for Guillermo O'Donnell.

3. A reference to Charles Tilly, in O'Donnell 2010a: 48.

4. A reference to Honneth, in O'Donnell 2010a: 48.

5. In his foreword to the *Transitions from Authoritarian Rule* volumes (O'Donnell and Schmitter 1986: x), A. Lowenthal wrote: "The project's animus, as I had occasion to say at its first meeting, was never 'wishful thinking', but rather 'thoughtful wishing,' that is, it was guided by a normative orientation that was rigorous and deliberate in its method." As noted below, all of O'Donnell's subsequent output reflected the same spirit, although I never heard him adopt the phrase.

6. The Latin American bureaucratic-authoritarian regimes to which I was most exposed as a student were Banzer's Bolivia, Pinochet's Chile, and PRIista Mexico, and my own solution was, whenever I saw the phrase "bureaucratic-authoritarian state," to substitute the term "Onganía's Argentina." This might sound more of a criticism than intended were it not for the fact that I find it similarly illuminating to substitute "an idealized understanding of US politics" for any universal liberal democratic concepts.

7. Personal communication from Song-Jin Han, Chair of the Joonmin Institute for Social Theory, Seoul, February 2012.

8. O'Donnell and Schmitter 1986, especially chapter 3 on "Opening (and Undermining) Authoritarian Regimes," and O'Donnell, Schmitter, and Whitehead 1986.

9. This insight can be traced back to his more specific work on divisions within the Argentine military following the 1966 coup or perhaps even earlier to the "azul" versus "colorado" split that overshadowed the brief and only semi-democratic Guido administration, in which he briefly served as deputy minister of the interior.

10. We were only cautiously prepared to cast the net as wide as we did then; and as we went to press Samuel Huntington gave a firmly pessimistic response to his question *Will More Countries Become Democratic?* (Huntington 1984).

11. Sadly, the anticipated more specific companion volume eluded him.

12. When he kindly joined me on contributing to the edited volume on *Democratization in America,* it was a source of real discomfort to him that—in deference to Tocqueville—the publisher persuaded the editors to go along with this misnomer, despite his protests (King et al. 2009).

13. The interview took place in March 2002.

Studying Big Political Issues

SCOTT MAINWARING, DANIEL BRINKS, AND MARCELO LEIRAS

In this concluding chapter, we consider five aspects of Guillermo O'Donnell's legacy for the practice of political science, political sociology, and political economy. His work can fruitfully inform and inspire how future generations of scholars and students undertake research in our fields, and it raises fundamental questions for the practice of political science today.[1] We look at the implications of five hallmarks of his scholarship. They are:

1. Addressing macro issues of large relevance in the world;
2. Articulating normative positions as an explicit part of a scholarly agenda;
3. Combining an ambitious theoretical agenda with skepticism about universalizing theories;
4. Using deep knowledge of Argentina, Brazil, and more broadly Latin America to rethink theoretical approaches to politics and to pose new questions; and
5. Rethinking past positions.

We address these issues not primarily to characterize O'Donnell's scholarship but rather to make the argument for approaches to studying politics that his work inspires. All of these issues except for the fifth involve contested questions about social science research.

Addressing Great Issues

O'Donnell always focused on important issues confronting contemporary humanity —such as why democracies break down, how transitions to democracy occur, how to build better democracies, and how to ensure a more effective rule of law and more even citizenship. His focus on questions that are important in the world is part of a grand tradition in comparative politics and political sociology; he was hardly alone in his zeal to study the world's great political questions.

Nevertheless, the future of this grand tradition cannot be taken for granted. Attention to large problems might be sacrificed when it becomes difficult to meet exacting methodological standards or arrive at neat causal identification. There is a potential trade-off between focusing on big questions and methodological rigor for several reasons: (1) It is often more difficult to measure variables that are conceptually wider and more complex. For example, it is more difficult to measure delegative democracy or democracy than many individual-level political behaviors and attitudes. (2) Many important events such as revolutions, transitions to democracy, democratic break-downs, and state failures occur infrequently and are typically less amenable to statistical analysis than more frequent and routine events or to large populations. Because the number of such events is low, and because these events are fairly indeterminate (Almond and Genco 1977; Kuran 1991; Lohmann 1994; O'Donnell and Schmitter 1986), it is challenging to achieve high explanatory leverage through statistical models.[2] (3) The causes and effects of huge macro phenomena do not result from random assignment, so they can rarely be analyzed with experiments, which have become prominent in political science; and (4) many large macro questions involve historical cases, and it is not retrospectively possible to undertake surveys, conduct experiments, or interview deceased leaders and participants. Therefore, important parts of the tool-kit of contemporary social science are not feasible. In addition, important data such as income inequalities and per capita GDP are not available or are less reliable for many countries for years before 1960 and 1945, respectively.

Consequently, as methodological rigor becomes a more important metric for measuring the value of research in political science, the appreciation for O'Donnell's kind of grand theorizing might diminish. Journals might reject articles that do not meet strict empirical and methodological standards; young scholars might be warned away from such work; tenure committees might value rigor over relevance. It is more difficult to shape airtight arguments involving grand macro questions than narrower questions, and as a result, it might be more difficult to publish in many leading journals. Not coincidentally, several pathbreaking scholars who focused on grand macro questions in O'Donnell's generation, including O'Donnell himself, never published in the *American Political Science Review*, the *American Journal of Political Science*, or the *Journal of Politics*—three esteemed journals that typically value methodological rigor. Juan Linz, Philippe Schmitter, and Alfred Stepan are other world renowned scholars who for decades set the agenda for democratization studies without publishing in these journals. To the degree that statistical and experimental methods trump real world importance in defining the agenda for political science, the space for studying big issues will likely diminish.

If we take O'Donnell's legacy seriously, it is critically important that there be ongoing space in the discipline for studying these large macro questions. The suggestion is not to tolerate mediocre work because it purports to speak to important issues but rather to value deep and provocative insights into issues crucial for humanity even when they are grounded in incomplete evidence. Relevance must come first. It should motivate the search for conceptual clarity and methodological feasibility. Rigor and precision do not inherently beget significance.

When O'Donnell published his seminal article on delegative democracy in 1991, it would have been difficult to rigorously test many of his propositions, as Lucas González fruitfully does in chapter 11. There weren't enough observations for quantitative analysis, and there wasn't enough time since redemocratization to gauge how much within-country variance over time would eventually occur. Moreover, even for qualitative analysis, the number of cases and their duration were too limited for definitive empirical study. But our understanding of Latin America and other parts of the world would have been impoverished if we did not have O'Donnell's analysis of delegative democracy. The ensuing debate around the concept and its applicability to particular cases triggered examinations of the relationship between presidents and legislatures that continue to enrich our knowledge of Latin America and other regions.[3]

O'Donnell founded his analyses of these topics on carefully defined concepts and rich empirical knowledge. The main motivation to tackle these intellectual challenges was always significance, not amenability to testing. He believed that the quest for scientific rigor had sometimes led to neglecting great questions.[4] In an interview, he expressed this concern: "I worry that in its current drive toward methodological sophistication, political science has lost the ambition and hubris of writing great books that give an account of big issues" (Munck and Snyder 2007: 303).

We embrace the discipline's quest for methodological rigor, but we share O'Donnell's view that political science should grapple with the most important political realities that confront humanity. On the one hand, scholars who deal with big issues should strive to improve conceptualization, operationalization, measurement, and hypothesis testing. This is a feasible task, and indeed, we point to some notable exemplars later in this section. On the other hand, political science should recognize seminal contributions such as O'Donnell's even when methodological rigor is elusive in the short term. If scholars did not launch important new ideas even if they are not able to rigorously test them, political science would become less interesting and less relevant to understanding big political issues.

Skocpol (2003b) calls this "doubly engaged social science"—social science that aims to understand real world transformations while simultaneously engaging in scholarly debates. Although this doubly engaged tradition enjoys ample space in contemporary US political science, powerful currents focus on disciplinary trends and issues with less concern for real world relevance. In addition, as noted above, there are potential trade-offs between an interest in huge issues and methodological sophistication. Political scientists and political sociologists can create new ways to measure concepts so that the study of big issues becomes methodologically more sophisticated,[5] but empirical measurement and causal analysis is often easier with smaller issues.

Incremental approaches to generating new knowledge are valuable. As social scientists, we must carefully measure variables and concepts and test hypotheses. We applaud major improvements in measurement (e.g., Coppedge, Gerring, et al. 2011) and hypothesis testing (e.g., Przeworski et al. 2000) in O'Donnell's tradition of raising great questions. But one key lesson of O'Donnell's legacy is that social science should not be limited to incremental advances and to testing and refining arguments that have already been presented. It is also crucial to look for major new questions.

From the 1980s on, O'Donnell mostly launched important new ideas without undertaking detailed measurement or doing empirical testing. Part of his legacy through the 1980s involved using methods that were innovative for that time. In the 1970s, he was a pioneer in using a game-theoretic, rational choice analysis to understand the difficulties of building stable democracy in Argentina (O'Donnell 1973). He was also an early user of political economy approaches to understanding regime dynamics (O'Donnell 1982). *Notas para el estudio de procesos de democratización política a partir del estado burocrático autoritario* ("Notes for the Study of Processes of Political Democratization from Bureaucratic Authoritarian States"; 1979a) and *Transitions from Authoritarian Rule: Tentative Conclusions about Uncertain Democracies* (with Philippe Schmitter, 1986) were pioneering game-theoretic analyses of blocs of rational actors. But he viewed methodology as a tool with which to analyze great questions rather than an end in itself.

In today's academic world, in light of journal, hiring, and promotion standards, political scientists must be attentive to the tasks of empirical measurement and testing. The challenge is how to combine these objectives with a focus on great questions about the contemporary political world. We do not analyze this question in the abstract but rather point to three recent exemplars that meet high scholarly standards in empirical measurement and testing while asking important questions about political regimes: Levitsky and Way (2010) on competitive authoritarianism, Darden and Grzymala-Busse (2006) on the electoral fate of communist parties in the post-Soviet region, and Gervasoni (2011a) on subnational democracy in Argentina. All three works have clear connections to O'Donnell's research agenda on post-transition political regimes.

Levitsky and Way (2010) examined the "trajectories of all 35 regimes that were or became competitive authoritarian between 1990 and 1995" (4). Their research question was why some of these countries democratized, others reverted to authoritarian rule, and others remained competitive authoritarian regimes. They carefully defined competitive authoritarianism (5–13) and their explanatory variables. Using qualitative methods, they argued that countries with strong linkages to the West consistently ended up in the democratic camp. Where linkage to the West was weaker, the trajectory of the political regime depended primarily on domestic factors, especially the organizational power of incumbents. Where incumbents were weak, a democratic outcome was more likely if the West had considerable leverage over a country. They employed clear coding rules and procedures to measure the dependent and independent variables, undertook a massive research effort to analyze the thirty-five countries, and carefully entertained alternative hypotheses.

Darden and Grzymala-Busse (2006) analyzed why some communist parties in the countries of the former Soviet Union lost the first free elections and exited power completely, while in other countries the communist parties either won the first free elections and remained a powerful political force or retained power and never allowed free elections. In turn, the electoral fates of communist parties have significantly affected subsequent political regimes and economic outcomes. The countries where communist parties fell by the wayside have established democratic regimes and successful economic reforms. In contrast, the countries where the communist parties have remained a powerful or the dominant political force have had competitive authoritarian regimes or noncompetitive authoritarian regimes.

Darden and Grzymala-Busse's argument focuses on the historical legacy of precommunist schooling. "Where precommunist schooling was firmly established and literacy was widespread, the populations were more likely to vote the communists out of power at the first available opportunity" (90). High literacy before the establishment of communist rule boosted opposition to communism because education created a nationalist sentiment that was implacably opposed to communist rule (98–111). While posing a question related to that of Levitsky and Way, Darden and Grzymala-Busse used quantitative methods. Like Levitsky and Way, they carefully considered alternative explanations.

Gervasoni (2010a, 2011a) analyzed differences in the level of democracy in Argentine provinces under the post-1983 democracy. This issue has become important in the third wave of democracy because many countries including Argentina have combined democracy at the national level with hybrid regimes in some states or provinces (Gibson 2012; McMann 2006). O'Donnell (1993) was a pioneer in studying these issues.

Gervasoni created an innovative new measure of subnational democracy. He showed that provinces that are more dependent on fiscal transfers from the central government are on average less democratic, and he proposed causal mechanisms that might explain why fiscal dependence leads to hybrid subnational regimes. Finally, like the other authors highlighted in this section, he carefully tested for alternative explanations—in his case, in variance in subnational democracy.

The work of Levitsky and Way, Darden and Gryzmala-Busse, and Gervasoni, among others, shows that it is possible to study macro questions about political regimes with attentiveness toward conceptual clarity, reliable measurement, and proper testing. It is essential for political science and political sociology—and for the contributions of these disciplines toward illuminating important problems in the world—to continue focusing on these larger questions (Almond and Genco 1977; Munck and Snyder 2007: 17–22; Skocpol 2003b).

Normative Viewpoints and Scholarly Work

A second defining feature of O'Donnell's work, as Laurence Whitehead observes in chapter 15, was that he believed that scholars could responsibly articulate their own normative positions as part of their work. It is useful to distinguish between the desirability of studying issues about which a scholar has a strong normative viewpoint and the desirability of explicitly communicating that viewpoint in scholarly work. The former is relatively uncontroversial provided that the scholarship is not biased by normative positions. The latter is more controversial; most social scientists do not explicitly advocate for their normative positions although O'Donnell is hardly alone in doing so. Democratic theorists and normative political theorists in general have done that for generations (Dahl 1970; Mackie 2003). But O'Donnell's approach offers one good path for researchers with strong normative commitments.

O'Donnell held deep passions and commitments. He despised military dictatorships, and he had contempt for quotidian abuses of power, as was manifest in his reflections about authoritarianism and daily life in Argentina under the last (1976–83) military dictatorship (O'Donnell 1999a: 51–62) and even before (O'Donnell 1999a: 81–105). He and Schmitter wrote *Transitions from Authoritarian Rule* with an explicitly normative purpose: "The instauration and eventual consolidation of political democracy constitutes per se a desirable goal" (1986: 3). In an interview about his volume with Schmitter, he said, "We were writing politics, not just an academic treatise. . . . We were all very visible intellectuals who were not just writing political science, but we were writing in and about the politics of our countries. And we were sending a message, too: don't despair" (in Munck and Snyder 2007: 292). In the last two decades of his life, he achieved a judicious balance between criticizing the deficiencies of Latin American democracies while not indulging in facile denunciations that could fuel antidemocratic sentiment. He advanced "democratic critiques of democracy"—the subtitle of his 2007 collection of essays (2007b). Somewhat in the spirit of another contemporary giant in the social sciences, Amartya Sen, O'Donnell passionately condemned the "scandal" of poverty and inequality (O'Donnell 1998b: 49) and issued a clarion call for "human decency toward all individuals" (O'Donnell 1998b: 55; see Karl's chapter 6 of this volume).

O'Donnell's combination of normative positions and scholarship was subtle and complex. He was firmly committed to defending human autonomy and equality but was deeply aware of the difficult ethical choices that important political decisions involve. Several of his pieces illustrate the power of social determination and external constraints with sharp, playful descriptions of paradoxes, unavoidable choices, and impossible games (O'Donnell 1993: chap. 4). Yet he always stressed the productive capacity of political action. Because of his commitment to academic excellence, O'Donnell rejected normative scholarship that did not reach high academic standards. He believed that convictions should guide understanding, not replace it.

In explicitly articulating normative positions and following a research agenda driven by them, O'Donnell is hardly alone. But his willingness, indeed eagerness, to explicitly advance normative positions runs counter to what is probably the dominant approach in US social science: Max Weber's position (1946: 129–56; 1949) that, even if the questions we study are linked to our own normative preferences, social science should be value free once scholars have chosen a research question.[6] Some political scientists go much further than Weber and criticize "a science that is heavily committed to dealing with socially and morally relevant problems. . . . For political science to advance, it must shed this professional commitment to solving social and moral problems" (Holt and Richardson 1970: 70–71, quoted in Almond and Genco 1977: 508).[7] O'Donnell was more disposed than Weber was to explicitly articulate his normative viewpoints, but he agreed with Weber that scholars' values should inform their questions, not their answers. O'Donnell and Weber agreed that normative commitments inspire creative research agendas but that these commitments must not distort research findings.

We endorse O'Donnell's and Weber's view that social scientists should study issues of great importance, with academic passion and with a commitment to scientific impartiality, including awareness of inconvenient facts, paradoxes, tradeoffs, and findings that clash with scholars' own normative preferences.[8] In this sense, O'Donnell set a standard worthy of emulation. Other major works in political science that were inspired by a combination of strong normative commitments and high academic standards include Bartels (2008) on inequality in the United States, Huber and Stephens (2012) on social policy in Latin America and their previous book (2001) on the welfare state, Przeworski (1985) and Przeworski and Sprague (1986) on social democracy, and Skocpol (1992) on social policy in the United States, among many others.

Like O'Donnell and Weber, we believe that scholars have a responsibility to scientific impartiality. O'Donnell serves as a model of a scholar who combined that responsibility with a strong commitment to democracy, human dignity and well-being, and decent government.

Theoretically Ambitious Work Skeptical of Universalism

A third defining characteristic of O'Donnell's approach to social science was his combination of theoretical ambition and skepticism about universalistic theories.[9] He used his knowledge of Argentina and Brazil as well as other Latin American countries to rethink great theoretical questions about politics. As Whitehead notes in chapter 15, O'Donnell rejected the universalism of leading theories developed in the United States or Western Europe but that did not fit the realities of Latin America. *Modernization and Bureaucratic-Authoritarianism* and "Reflections on the Patterns of Change in the Bureaucratic-Authoritarian State" (O'Donnell 1978b: 4) eschewed the universalistic pretensions of modernization theory. O'Donnell argued that political trajectories in Latin America differed from those in the developed countries, that the path to democracy was not linear, and that the relationship between modernization and political regimes varied across world regions and over time. When in a prescient work he first reflected at length on the prospects for democratization in the military regimes that dominated Latin America in the late 1970s, he insisted that his analysis was circumscribed to bureaucratic-authoritarian regimes (O'Donnell 1999a: 110) because certain characteristics in these regimes might generate distinctive dynamics.

As he was reworking democratic theory from the vantage point of post-1978 cases of democratization, O'Donnell (2007b: 2) argued that "[e]fforts to analyze new democracies need to recognize how democracies vary across different historical/contextual settings. . . . A theory of general scope should acknowledge how the development of democracy in different settings may generate specific characteristics and that it may be useful to distinguish among subtypes within the universe of relevant cases."

Most previous work on institutions in US political science had focused on formal institutions. O'Donnell recognized that formal institutions did not work in the same way in contexts in which they are weak. Hence, many generalizations implicitly based on the advanced industrial democracies about the effects of institutions did not apply in contexts of weak formal institutions. He spawned a new research agenda on informal institutions and weak formal institutions. He argued that "it is incorrect to believe that there is something called 'democratic theory' that can easily be 'exported,' with only minor adjustments, to settings like Latin America" (Munck and Snyder 2007: 295). For O'Donnell, it was essential to understand the dominant theoretical perspectives but also to realize that they often carried blinders stemming from the US experience. He believed in the value of learning history—of "historicizing the social sciences" (O'Donnell 1978b: 4) and of becoming deeply familiar with one or a small number of countries.[10]

At the same time, O'Donnell did not work narrowly on Argentina and Brazil or even Latin America. He moved from deep knowledge of his own country and Brazil to broader theoretical aspirations and contributions (Munck and Snyder 2007: 293). He was not unique in his effort to move between deep knowledge of some cases and broader theorizing, but he was especially adept at it. This achievement is worthy of emulation as we think of O'Donnell's legacy and the future practice of political science and political sociology. Many chapters in this volume embrace this attempt to build knowledge from empirical realities the authors know well but to generalize beyond a few cases, yielding both an understanding of the cases and contextually informed medium range theories that can be tested in other contexts to see whether they apply and how they need to be modified in the different context.

The degree to which social science should aspire to universal as opposed to partially bounded knowledge is the subject of ongoing debate. Some prominent scholars have claimed that universalistic approaches to social science are more scientific than more bounded approaches (Bates 1997; Ferejohn and Satz 1995). In contrast, Green and Shapiro (1994) criticized rational choice theory for its universalistic aspirations and argued that the search for universal theory sometimes hinders understanding.[11]

Generalizations are important, but social scientists also should be attentive to causal heterogeneity. What causes an outcome in one context might differ from what causes the same outcome in another context; conversely, the same causes might produce different outcomes in different contexts (Hall 2003; Ragin 2000: 88–119). Scholars must be aware of such contextual differences (Adcock and Collier 2001; Bunce 1998, 2000) and of case specificity (Fishman 2007). An awareness of the historically and geographically bounded nature of theories is fully consistent with rigor and can be superior to universalistic claims in advancing understanding of key issues. If a theory or causal mechanism holds in some circumstances but not others, social scientists need to be aware of this fact.

Downs (1957) provides one example of an initial universalistic claim that has subsequently been contextualized. He implicitly presented his theory of party motivation (winning votes) and behavior (adopting ideological positions that enhance the capacity to win votes) in a universalistic way. Subsequent innovations improved on his work but most still retained the idea that all parties focus exclusively on winning votes or seats,[12] thus maximizing their utility in an electoral game. However, in contexts of unstable democracy where some actors might prefer authoritarian rule, parties might sacrifice votes and seats so as to maximize their preferred outcome in a regime game—either to preserve democracy or to thwart it. The parties must play a two-level game, seeking a good electoral outcome *and* a good outcome related to the political regime. In these contexts, it is impossible to understand parties' objectives and behavior through analysis focused exclusively on electoral competition (Mainwaring 2003). The original universalistic theory could conceivably be revised in a more comprehensive manner, but it would have to be a more context-dependent universalistic theory.

Social science should be built on a diversity of research strategies, some stressing generalization above specificities (though all work must also be attentive to some specificities), others paying greater attention to specificities while working within an understanding of broader comparative and theoretical conceptions (Fishman 2007). O'Donnell's effort to generalize and theorize beyond a few cases coupled with an awareness of the dangers of universal theorizing sets a standard for subsequent social science.

Using Knowledge of Latin America to Rethink Theories and Ask New Questions

As Whitehead notes, a fourth O'Donnell trademark (closely linked to the one we have just discussed) was his ability to use his knowledge of Latin America to pose new questions about established theories and to invent new ways of theorizing. O'Donnell's capacity to pose new questions and rethink established theories from the vantage point of Latin America and beyond is one of his most important contributions to social science. His work on modernization and democratic breakdowns, transitions to democracy, delegative democracy, horizontal accountability, green and brown areas, and informal institutions all originated in his knowledge about Latin America but raised important new questions for social science theorizing.

In Chapter 9 of this volume, Levitsky and Murillo epitomize this kind of endeavor by observing that established theory did not adequately describe institutional change in Latin America; it implicitly assumed contexts of solid institutions. They contribute to rethinking theories of institutional change by extending the analysis to contexts of weak formal institutions. Along similar lines, Helmke and Levitsky (2006b) and Levitsky and Murillo (2005b) challenged the previously dominant focus on formal institutions by insisting on the importance of informal ones, especially in contexts of weak formal institutions.

As one example of how Latin Americanists have modified universalistic theories, consider ambition theory, which posits that politicians are motivated exclusively by their desire to win or retain political office—that is, by their own career ambitions (Downs 1957: 24–31; Mayhew 1974; Schlesinger 1991). According to ambition theory, politicians do not have an independent interest in political issues or ideological commitments.

Although ambition theory grew out of the US context, it became the dominant perspective in understanding politicians' motivations and behavior in other contexts. However, as Mayhew (1974: 13–14) presciently recognized, its applicability beyond the US House varies across time and space. Still, many scholars used ambition theory to understand politicians' motivations and behavior in Latin America.

Gradually, some scholars who study Latin America modified the universalistic claims of ambition theory so that it better fits the reality of the region. Carey (1996) argued that in Costa Rica, where consecutive legislative terms are constitutionally banned, scholars need to drop the assumption that reelection is politicians' driving motivation. Samuels (2003) argued that traditional ambition theory focused on re-election as politicians' motivation failed to understand a key aspect of Brazilian poli-tics: politicians frequently sought higher elected office rather than remaining wedded to reelection. In many countries, many members of congress are not interested in reelection. In Mexico, national legislators are not even eligible for immediate reelec-tion because constitutional clauses prohibit it. Carey and Samuels shifted to thinking about broader political career alternatives as motivating factors for legislators. They continued to posit, however, that legislators were self-interested actors who wanted to build political careers.

A more radical challenge to ambition theory came from Guevara Mann (2011), who argued that many Panamanian legislators are motivated not primarily by a quest to build a political career but rather by personal economic gain and by avoiding criminal prosecution. He thus questioned even Carey's and Samuels's significantly modified assumption about legislators' behavior. Panamanian legislators know that their chances for reelection are modest, and most seem not to care. They have few chances for political careers outside the legislature, which sets them apart from politi-cians in Brazil, Costa Rica, or Mexico. If most legislators serve only one term, do not subsequently run for any other political office, and do not accept prominent positions in the public bureaucracy, their motivation in seeking and holding political office is not building a political career. Guevara Mann developed a profound and potentially paradigm-changing insight, with original evidence to support it. A traditional focus on reelection as the fundamental motivation for politicians' behavior obscures more than it illuminates the realities of many countries.

In sum, scholars should not always accept existing theoretical approaches and use them to study realities beyond where these theories were initially conceived. Theoreti-cal approaches about politics are consciously or unconsciously derived in relation to some existing reality. Theories about most aspects of democratic politics were created in the United States and Western Europe, and they usually implicitly reflect the reali-ties of those established democracies. These theories do not always capture the realities of other regions of the world. Scholars should use these different realities to rethink dominant theories.

This is not a plea for highly contextualized, idiographic approaches to political sci-ence. To the degree that theories and generalizations travel across different contexts, social scientists can understand the world in more parsimonious and clearer ways. However, we should not treat as general findings that in the light of new evidence prove to be highly contextual. Social scientists should use their knowledge of some country cases to pose new questions, challenge existing theories, and build new ones. In line with our argument in previous sections of this chapter, this theoretical development should involve an examination of the validity of existing claims to generalization and the elaboration of new claims with explicit geographic and temporal bounds.

One of O'Donnell's greatest gifts was his ability to recognize new questions and problems that had not hitherto been addressed. He always drew upon the antecedent scholarship but often invented new fields of scholarship. For example, at the zenith of the last great wave of authoritarianism in Latin America, in the late 1970s he began his research agenda on the demise of authoritarianism (O'Donnell 1979a, 1979b). This line of work eventually segued into the iconic volume with Schmitter and Whitehead (1986). His work on informal institutions, horizontal accountability, and delegative democracy likewise generated new research fields.

O'Donnell greatly enriched concepts for analyzing what we have called uneven democracies. He created many important new concepts that have endured—bureaucratic-authoritarianism, hard-liners and soft-liners within authoritarian regimes, moderate and maximalist oppositions, horizontal and vertical accountability, delegative democracy, and "brown" and "green" areas within countries (O'Donnell 1993). These concepts were linked to his effort to rework democratic theory and to challenge purportedly universalistic theories. As this volume attests, these concepts sparked major debates and new efforts to empirically test hypotheses and ideas.

Throughout his career, O'Donnell defined and used concepts carefully.[13] He was judicious about creating new concepts, yet when existing concepts did not fit the realities he was grappling with, he was inventive in creating new ones. The proliferation of new concepts can have downsides, as Collier and Levitsky (1997) argued; endless generation of new concepts easily produces conceptual confusion if not chaos. However, O'Donnell showed that creating new concepts is sometimes essential for illuminating key political phenomena. Very few scholars have enriched our conceptual vocabulary as much as O'Donnell. This is another part of his legacy that offers promise for future scholars.

Rethinking Past Positions

O'Donnell often displayed a refreshing capacity to rethink his past positions. Timothy Power's chapter 8 of this volume highlights a striking example. O'Donnell was the pioneer in thinking about democratic consolidation, but later (1996a) he rejected the concept as teleological. *Modernization and Bureaucratic-Authoritarianism* and his work on the political economy of authoritarianism and democracy in Argentina (O'Donnell

1978c, 1982) had structural perspectives; in contrast, *Transitions from Authoritarian Rule* emphasized agency and indeterminacy. The ability to rethink past positions and theoretical perspectives when the evidence so warrants obviously advances social science.

Likewise, O'Donnell's work (1988) on democratic consolidation posited that the mode of transition to democracy was a crucial variable in shaping subsequent outcomes about the political regime. Other distinguished scholars also advanced this claim (Hagopian 1996; Stepan 1986). Although O'Donnell never explicitly recanted this view, beginning with his work on delegative democracy in 1991, he instead focused on other issues, including the solidity of a country's representative institutions and the extent of social exclusion. From this later perspective, countries such as Uruguay and Chile, which underwent somewhat different transitions, had the important shared similarity of more solid democratic institutions than did other new democracies in Latin America. As Hartlyn (1998) has argued, for the Latin American cases, the mode of transition did not ultimately prove to have great medium-term consequences.

In this volume, Philippe Schmitter's chapter 3 captures this spirit of critically reexamining past arguments. Schmitter reflects on where he and O'Donnell were correct in their 1986 analysis and where subsequent events have underscored a need to revise that earlier work.

It should be relatively uncontroversial to claim that we must all be open to rethinking positions that prove to be mistaken in one way or another. And yet the spirit of openness to criticism and the willingness to acknowledge shortcomings in published work that this requires can be scarce. Perhaps a reminder that some of the greatest scholars have revisited earlier positions will give all of us the confidence to do the same.

Conclusion

Those of us who knew Guillermo O'Donnell were constantly surprised by his ability to name concepts and identify problems in a way that set off major research agendas. Not everyone can have Guillermo O'Donnell's creativity. But his ability to frame the great new questions that inspire a whole generation of scholars is due in no small part to the combination of features of his scholarship that we have highlighted here. He focused on great issues out of an explicit normative agenda that inspired his passion and that of others. He combined theoretical ambition with a strong sense of the limits of grand theory, and he was never satisfied to simply rely on his earlier positions. And he did all this out of a deep understanding of the politics, the history, and the social life of Latin America. The combination produced a scholarly output and style that will continue to inspire future generations of scholars.

NOTES

We are grateful to Gabriela Ippolito-O'Donnell, Aníbal Pérez-Liñán, Timothy Power, and Kurt Weyland for helpful comments.

1. Laurence Whitehead's chapter 15 of this volume also contributes to this effort. For more information on O'Donnell's approach to political science, see his lengthy interview in Munck and Snyder (2007: 273–304).

2. Rare events can be studied quantitatively, but as Pérez-Liñán and Mainwaring note in chapter 1, many causal variables of potential interest have not been employed in quantitative studies of these outcomes because of measurement problems. Kuran's (1991) argument about the unpredictable and indeterminate character of revolution applies to democratic transitions and breakdowns.

3. Ippolito-O'Donnell (2011: 54) notes that scholars have analyzed some post-Soviet and Asian cases through the prism of delegative democracy.

4. For a converging opinion, see Almond and Genco (1977), and Stepan and Linz (2011).

5. See Coppedge, Gerring, et al. (2011), who are engaging in a massive effort to improve the historical measurement of democracy over a long time span (1900 to the present) and large number of countries.

6. Fishman (2007: 261) summarized the Weberian perspective as advocating "the pursuit of types of knowledge, and thus the posing of questions, that are meaningful from the value perspective of the investigator . . . alongside the commitment to both impartiality and rigour in addressing those questions so that the answers may be seen as objective."

7. We agree with Holt and Richardson that political scientists should not primarily focus on "*solving* social and moral problems." We are, after all, social scientists, not policy makers or political activists. Where we (and O'Donnell and Weber) perhaps part paths with Holt and Richardson is our view that fundamental political problems with great consequences should be core issues in political science and that social scientists can responsibly analyze issues about which they have strong normative preferences.

8. Weber (1946: 135) wrote that, "[w]ithout this strange intoxication, ridiculed by every outsider; without this passion, . . . without this, you have *no* calling for science and you should do something else."

9. Along related lines, Almond and Genco (1977) cautioned against universal theorizing without awareness of historic and geographic context and specificities.

10. With his intimate knowledge of Spain and interest in and knowledge about a wide range of country cases, Juan Linz was similar in this respect.

11. Parsons (1951) attempted to develop a universal theory of how society functions. His work was hugely influential for decades but has little contemporary resonance, in part, we believe, because his universal aspirations produced a level of generality and abstruseness that is not useful for guiding social science research. Moreover, its accuracy as a way of understanding how societies actually function is suspect. See Mills (1959: 25–49) for a critique of Parsons. Hirschman (1970) similarly argued that searching for general paradigms can hinder understanding.

12. Wittman (1973) is an exception. He argued that parties seek to maximize programmatic goals, not votes.

13. Of course, this is not to claim that his concepts were uncontested.

1936	Born in Buenos Aires, Argentina
1958	Graduates from Law School at the Universidad de Buenos Aires
1968–71	Graduates with MA in political science, Yale University
1973	Publishes *Modernization and Bureaucratic-Authoritarianism: Studies in South American Politics*
1975	Cofounds CEDES (Center for the Study of State and Society) in Argentina
1978	Launches the *Transitions* project, sponsored by the Latin American Program of the Woodrow Wilson International Center for Scholars in Washington, DC
1980–82	Leaves Argentina and moves to Brazil. Works as a researcher at IUPERJ (Instituto Universitario de Pesquisas do Rio de Janeiro) in Rio de Janeiro
1982	Is appointed director of CEBRAP (Centro Brasileiro de Análise e Planejamento) in São Paulo, Brazil
	Publishes *El estado burocrático autoritario. Triunfos, derrotas y crisis* (published in English in 1988 as *Bureaucratic Authoritarianism: Argentina 1966–1973 in Comparative Perspective*)
1982–97	Becomes academic director of the Helen Kellogg Institute for International Studies of the University of Notre Dame
1983–2009	Becomes professor of government at the University of Notre Dame
1986	Publishes *Transitions from Authoritarian Rule: Prospects for Democracy* (four volumes) with Philippe Schmitter and Laurence Whitehead. Volume four is *Tentative Conclusions about Uncertain Democracies,* coauthored by O'Donnell and Schmitter
1987	Receives PhD in political science, Yale University
1988–91	Serves as president of the International Political Science Association (IPSA)
1992	Publishes *Issues in Democratic Consolidation* with Scott Mainwaring and J. Samuel Valenzuela
1993	Introduces the concept of "brown areas" of democracy, in "On the State, Democratization, and Some Conceptual Problems: A Latin American View with Glances at Some Postcommunist Countries."
1994	Publishes "Delegative Democracy" in the *Journal of Democracy*

Note: Full citations of all works are included in the References.

1995	Is elected to the American Academy of Arts and Sciences
1996	Publishes "Illusions about Consolidation" in the *Journal of Democracy*
1998	Publishes *Poverty and Inequality in Latin America* with Víctor Tokman
1999	Publishes "Horizontal Accountability and New Polyarchies"
	Publishes *The (Un)Rule of Law and the Underprivileged in Latin America* with Juan Méndez and Paulo Sérgio Pinheiro
	Publishes *Counterpoints: Selected Essays on Authoritarianism and Democratization*
1999–2000	Serves as vice-president of the American Political Science Association (APSA)
2002–03	Is named Simón Bolívar Distinguished Visiting Professor, University of Cambridge, UK
2004	Publishes *The Quality of Democracy: Theory and Applications* with Osvaldo Iazzetta and Jorge Vargas Cullell
2007	Publishes *Dissonances: Democratic Critiques of Democracy*
2009	Joins the School of Politics and Government at the Universidad Nacional de General San Martín (UNSAM) in Argentina
2010	Publishes *Democracy, Agency and the State: Theory with Comparative Intent* (published in Spanish the same year)
2011	Dies in Buenos Aires

REFERENCES

Acemoglu, Daron, Simon Johnson, and James A. Robinson. 2001. "The Colonial Origins of Comparative Development: An Empirical Investigation." *American Economic Review* 91(5): 1369–1401.

Acemoglu, Daron, Simon Johnson, James Robinson, and Pierre Yared. 2008. "Income and Democracy." *American Economic Review* 98(3): 808–42.

Acemoglu, Daron, and James Robinson. 2001. "A Theory of Political Transitions." *American Economic Review* 91(4): 938–63.

———. 2006. *The Economic Origins of Dictatorship and Democracy*. Cambridge, UK: Cambridge University Press.

Achen, Christopher. 1985. "Proxy Variables and Incorrect Signs on Regression Coefficients." *Political Methodology* 11(3/4): 299–316.

———. 2002. "Toward a New Political Methodology: Microfoundations and ART." *Annual Review of Political Science* 5: 423–50.

Acuña, Carlos. 1995. "Intereses empresarios, dictadura y democracia en la Argentina actual. (O sobre por qué la burguesía abandona estrategias autoritarias y opta por la estabilidad democrática)." In Carlos Acuña, ed., *La nueva matriz política argentina*, pp. 231–84. Buenos Aires: Nueva Visión.

Adcock, Robert N., and David Collier 2001. "Measurement Validity: A Shared Standard for Qualitative and Quantitative Research." *American Political Science Review* 95(3): 529–46.

Adorno, Sérgio. 1994. "Crime, Justiça Penal e Desigualdade Jurídica: as Mortes que se Contam no Tribunal do Júri." *Revista USP* 21: 132–51.

———. 1995. "Discriminação Racial e Justiça Criminal em São Paulo." *Novos Estudos-CEBRAP* 43 (Nov.): 26–44.

Agudelo, Carlos Efrén. 1999. "Política y organización de poblaciones negras en Colombia." In Carlos Agudelo, Odile Hoffmann, and Nelly Yulissa Rivas, eds., *Hacer política en el Pacífico Sur: Algunas aproximaciones*, pp. 2–38. Cali, Colombia: Universidad del Valle.

Agüero, Felipe. 2000. "Institutions, Transitions, and Bargaining: Civilians and the Military in Shaping Postauthoritarian Regimes." In David Pion-Berlin, ed., *Civil-Military Relations in Latin America: New Analytical Perspectives*, pp. 194–222. Chapel Hill: University of North Carolina Press.

Ahlquist, John S., and Erik Wibbels. 2012. "Riding the Wave: World Trade and Factor-Based Models of Democratization." *American Journal of Political Science* 56(2): 447–64.

Ahnen, Ronald E. 2007. "The Politics of Police Violence in Democratic Brazil." *Latin American Politics and Society* 49(1): 141–64.

Aidt, Toke, and Dalibor S. Eterovic. 2011. "Political Competition, Electoral Participation and Public Finance in 20th Century Latin America." *European Journal of Political Economy* 27, no. 1 (March): 181–200.

Alcántara, Manuel. 2008. *Politicians and Politics in Latin America.* Boulder, CO: Lynne Rienner Publishers.

Alesina, Alberto, and Dani Rodrik. 1994. "Distributive Politics and Economic Growth." *Quarterly Journal of Economics* 109(2): 465–90.

Almond, Gabriel A., and Stephen J. Genco. 1977. "Clocks, Clouds, and the Study of Politics." *World Politics* 29(4): 489–522.

Altman, David, and Rossana Castiglioni. 2009. "Democratic Quality and Human Development in Latin America: 1972–2001." *Canadian Journal of Political Science* 42(2): 297–319.

Altman, David, and Aníbal Pérez-Liñán. 2002. "Assessing the Quality of Democracy: Freedom, Competitiveness and Participation in Eighteen Latin American Countries." *Democratization* 9(2): 85–100.

Álvarez, Ángel. 2000. "La democracia delegativa y muerte de la constitución." In Eduardo García de Enterría, ed., *Constitución y constitucionalismo hoy,* pp.743–60. Caracas: Fundación Manuel García Pelayo.

Alvarez, Michael, José Antonio Cheibub, Fernando Limongi, and Adam Przeworski. 1996. "Classifying Political Regimes." *Studies in Comparative International Development* 31(2): 3–36.

American Political Science Association (APSA). 2004. "American Democracy in an Age of Rising Inequality." Washington, DC: American Political Science Association.

Amnesty International. 1991. *Amnesty International Report 1991.* New York: Amnesty International Publications.

Anderson, Leslie. 2006. "The Authoritarian Executive? Horizontal and Vertical Accountability in Nicaragua." *Latin American Politics and Society* 48(2): 141–69.

Anderson, Sarah, Chuck Collins, Scott Klinger, and Sam Pizzigati. 2011. "Executive Excess 2011: The Massive CEO Rewards for Tax Dodging." Institute for Policy Studies. Available at http://www.ips-dc.org/files/3552/Executive-Excess-CEO-Rewards-for-Tax-Dodging.pdf.

Apter, David. 1963. *Ghana in Transition.* Princeton: Princeton University Press.

———. 1965. *The Politics of Modernization.* Chicago: University of Chicago Press.

Arat, Zehra. 1991. *Democracy and Human Rights in Developing Countries.* Boulder, CO: Lynne Rienner.

Archer, Christon, ed. 2000. *Wars of Independence in Spanish America.* Wilmington, DE: Rowman and Littlefield.

Ardanaz, Martin, and Isabela Mares. 2012. "Labor Migration, Rural Inequality and Democratic Reforms." Unpublished manuscript, Columbia University, Department of Political Science.

Arditi, Benjamín, ed. 2005. *¿Democracia post-liberal? El espacio político de las asociaciones.* Barcelona: Editorial Anthropos.

Ashford, Kathryn L. 1986. "The Role of Corporations in the 1980 US Congressional Elections." *Sociological Inquiry* 56(4): 409–31.

Aslaksen, Silje. 2010. "Oil and Democracy: More than a Cross-Country Correlation?" *Journal of Peace Research* 47(4): 421–31.

Assies, Willem, Gemma van der Haar, and André Hoekema, eds. 2000. *El reto de la diversidad: pueblos indígenas y reforma del estado en América Latina* (The Challenge of Diversity: Indigenous Peoples and Reform of the State in Latin America). Amsterdam, Netherlands: Thela Thesis.

Attali, Yigal, and Maya Bar-Hillel. 2003. "Guess Where: The Position of Correct Answers in Multiple-Choice Test Items as a Psychometric Variable." *Journal of Educational Measurement* 40(2): 109–28.

Avritzer, Leonardo. 2000. "Democratization and Changes in the Pattern of Association in Brazil." *Journal of Interamerican Studies and World Affairs* 42(3): 59–76.

———. 2009. *Participatory Institutions in Democratic Brazil*. Baltimore and Washington DC: Johns Hopkins University Press / Woodrow Wilson Press.

Awapara, Omar. 2010. "Despacio se llega lejos: Cambio institucional, instituciones latentes, y el caso de la Presidencia del Consejo de Ministros." *Apuntes* 67(2): 5–36.

Baland, Jean-Marie, and James A. Robinson. 2008. "Land and Power: Theory and Evidence from Chile." *American Economic Review* 98(5): 1737–65.

Barr, Robert. 2009. "Populists, Outsiders and Anti-establishment Politics." *Party Politics* 15(1): 29–48.

Barro, Robert J. 2000. "Rule of Law, Democracy and Economic Performance." In Gerald Driscoll, Kim Holes, and Melanie Kirkpatrick, eds., *Index of Economic Freedom 2000*, pp. 31–49. Washington, DC: Heritage Foundation.

Bartels, Larry M. 2008. *Unequal Democracy: The Political Economy of the New Gilded Age*. Princeton: Princeton University Press.

Bartlett, Bruce. 2012. *The Benefit and the Burden: Tax Reform—Why We Need It and What It Will Take*. New York: Simon and Schuster.

Bates, Robert. 1997. "Area Studies and the Discipline: A Useful Controversy?" *Political Science and Politics* 30(2): 166–69.

Beckford, George L. 1983. *Persistent Poverty: Underdevelopment in Plantation Economies of the Third World*. London: Zed Books.

Beetham, David, ed. 1994. *Defining and Measuring Democracy*. Sage Modern Politics Series. London: Sage Publications.

Bejarano, Ana María. 2011. *Precarious Democracies: Understanding Regime Stability and Change in Colombia and Venezuela*. Notre Dame, IN: University of Notre Dame Press.

Bellin, Eva. 2000. "Contingent Democrats: Industrialists, Labor, and Democratization in Late-Developing Countries." *World Politics* 52(2): 175–205.

Bensusan, Graciela. 2006. *Diseño legal y desempeño real: instituciones laborales en América Latina*. Mexico City: Miguel Angel Porrúa.

Bentley, Arthur. 1954. *The Process of Government*. Chicago: University of Chicago Press.

Berg, Irwin A., and Gerald M. Rapaport. 1954. "Response Bias in an Unstructured Questionnaire." *Journal of Psychology* 38(2): 475–81.

Bergman, Marcelo. 2009. *Tax Evasion and the Rule of Law in Latin America: The Political Culture of Cheating and Compliance in Argentina and Chile*. University Park, PA.: University of Pennsylvania University Press..

Berkowitz, Daniel, Katharina Pistor, and Jean-François Richard. 2003. "Economic Development, Legality and the Transplant Effect." *European Economic Review* 47(1):165–95.

Berman, Sheri. 1998. *The Social Democratic Movement: Ideas and Politics in the Making of Interwar Europe*. Cambridge, MA: Harvard University Press.

Bermeo, Nancy. 1997. "Myths of Moderation: Confrontation and Conflict during Democratic Transitions." *Comparative Politics* 29(3): 305–22.

Bernhard, M., C. Reenock, and T. Nordstrom. 2004. "The Legacy of Western Overseas Colonialism on Democratic Survival." *International Studies Quarterly* 48(1): 225–50.

Berry, Jeffrey. 1999. *The New Liberalism: The Rising Power of Citizen Groups*. Washington, DC: Brookings Institution Press.

Bertelsmann Stiftung. 2012. *Transformation Index BTI 2012: Political Management in International Comparison*. Gütersloh, Germany: Bertelsmann Stiftung.

Besley, Timothy, and Torsten Persson. 2008. "Wars and State Capacity." *Journal of European Economic Association* 6(2–3): 522–30.

Better Markets. 2012. "The Cost of the Wall Street-Caused Financial Collapse and Ongoing Economic Crisis Is More Than $12.8 Trillion," *Better Markets Report*, September 15. Available at http://bettermarkets.com/sites/default/files/Cost%20Of%20The%20Crisis.pdf.

Bill Chávez, Rebecca. 2004. *The Rule of Law in Nascent Democracies: Judicial Politics in Argentina*. Stanford: Stanford University Press.

Birdsall, Nancy, and Frederick Z. Jaspersen. 1997. *Pathways to Growth: Comparing East Asia and Latin America*. Washington, DC: Inter-American Development Bank.

Birdsall, Nancy, Nora Lustig, and Darryl McLeod. 2011. "Declining Inequality in Latin America: Some Economics, Some Politics." Working Paper 251, Center for Global Development.

Birgin, Haydee, and Gabriela Pastorino. 2005. "Violencia contra las mujeres." In Mónica Urrestarazu, ed., *Informe sobre género y derechos humanos. Vigencia y respeto de los derechos de las mujeres en Argentina*, pp. 291–336. Buenos Aires: Biblos/ELA.

Blais, André, Louis Massicotte, and Antoine Yoshinaka. 2001. "Deciding Who Has the Right to Vote: A Comparative Analysis of Election Laws." *Electoral Studies* 20(1): 41–62.

Block, Fred. 1977. "The Ruling Class Does Not Rule: Notes on the Marxist Theory of the State." *Socialist Revolution* 33(May–June): 6–28.

Bobbio, Norberto. 1987. *The Future of Democracy*. Minneapolis, MN: Polity Press.

Boix, Carles. 2003. *Democracy and Redistribution*. Cambridge, UK: Cambridge University Press.

———. 2011. "Democracy, Development, and the International System." *American Political Science Review* 105(4): 809–28.

Boix, Carles, Michael Miller, and Sebastian Rosato. 2013. "A Complete Dataset of Political Regimes, 1800–2007." *Comparative Political Studies* 46(12): 1523–1554.

Boix, Carles, and Susan Stokes. 2003. "Endogenous Democratization." *World Politics* 55(4): 517–49.

Bollen, Kenneth A. 1983. "World System Position, Dependency, and Democracy: The Cross-National Evidence." *American Sociological Review* 48 (4):468–79.

Bollen, Kenneth A., and Robert W. Jackman. 1989. "Democracy, Stability, and Dichotomies." *American Sociological Review* 54(4): 612–21.

Bonilla Maldonado, Daniel, ed. 2013. *Constitutionalism of the Global South: The Activist Tribunals of India, South Africa, and Colombia*. New York: Cambridge University Press.

Bowman, Kirk, Fabrice Lehoucq, and James Mahoney. 2005. "Measuring Political Democracy: Case Expertise, Data Adequacy, and Central America." *Comparative Political Studies* 38(8): 939–70.

Boylan, Delia M. 1996. "Taxation and Transition: The Politics of the 1990 Chilean Tax Reform." *Latin American Research Review* 31(1): 7–31.

Bratton, Michael, and Nicolas van de Walle. 1997. *Democratic Experiments in Africa: Regime Transitions in Comparative Perspective*. New York: Cambridge University Press.

Brewer-Carias, Allan. 2010. *Dismantling Democracy in Venezuela: The Chávez Authoritarian Experiment*. New York: Cambridge University Press.

Brinks, Daniel M. 2006. "The Rule of (Non) Law: Prosecuting Police Killings in Brazil and Argentina." In Gretchen Helmke and Steven Levitsky, eds., *Informal Institutions and Democracy: Lessons from Latin America*, pp. 201–26. Baltimore: Johns Hopkins University Press.

———. 2008. *The Judicial Response to Police Killings in Latin America: Inequality and the Rule of Law*. New York: Cambridge University Press.

———. 2010. "Violencia de estado a treinta años de democracia en América Latina." *Journal of Democracy en Español* 2 (July):10–27.

Brinks, Daniel M., and Abby Blass. 2011. "International Pressures and Potemkin Courts: Real and Apparent Purposes in the Construction of Latin American Courts, 1975–2009." Paper presented at the conference "Ruling Politics: the Formal and Informal Foundations of Power in New Democracies," Harvard University, November 21–22.

Brinks, Daniel M., and Sandra Botero. 2010. "Inequality and the Rule of Law: Ineffective Rights in Latin American Democracies." Paper presented at the American Political Science Association Meeting, Washington, DC, September.

Brinks, Daniel, and Michael Coppedge. 2006. "Diffusion Is No Illusion: Neighbor Emulation in the Third Wave of Democracy." *Comparative Political Studies* 39(4): 463–89.

Brockett, Charles D. 1988. *Land, Power, and Poverty: Agrarian Transformation and Political Conflict in Central America*. Boston: Unwin Hyman.

Brodersohn, Mario. 1973. "'Modernización y autoritarismo' y el estancamiento inflacionario argentino." *Desarrollo Económico* 13(51): 591–605.

Brown, Archie. 2000. "Transnational Influences in the Transition from Communism." *Post-Soviet Affairs* 16(2): 177–200.

Bruno, Fernando. 2011. "La democracia como construcción." Available at http://www.revistae nie.clarin.com/ideas/politica-economia/democracia-construccion-O-Donnell-politica-estado _0_443955784.html.

Bulmer-Thomas, Victor. 1995. *The Economic History of Latin America since Independence*. Cambridge, UK: Cambridge University Press.

Bunce, Valerie. 1998. "Regional Differences in Democratization: The East versus the South." *Post-Soviet Affairs* 14(3): 187–211.

———. 2000. "Comparative Democratization: Big and Bounded Generalizations." *Comparative Political Studies* 33(6/7): 703–34.

Bürhlmann, Marc, Wolfgang Merkel, et al. 2007. "The Quality of Democracy: Democracy Barometer for Established Democracies." Working Paper #10, National Centre of Competence in Research (NCCR), Zurich, Switzerland.

Burke, Paul J., and Andrew Leigh. 2010. "Do Output Contractions Trigger Democratic Change?" *American Economic Journal: Macroeconomics* 2(4): 124–57.

Burris, Val. 2001. "The Two Faces of Capital: Corporations and Individual Capitalists as Political Actors." *American Sociological Review* 66(3): 361–81.

Calvo, Ernesto, and Marcelo Escolar 2005. *La nueva política de partidos en la Argentina*. Buenos Aires: Fundación Pent and Prometeo.

Calvo, Ernesto, and Juan Pablo Micozzi. 2005. "The Governor's Backyard: a Seat-Vote Model of Electoral Reform for Subnational Multiparty Races." *The Journal of Politics* 67(4): 1050–74.

Calvo, Ernesto, and María Victoria Murillo. 2013. "Argentina after the Storm: Democratic Consolidation, Partisan Dealignment, and Institutional Weakness." In Jorge I. Domínguez and Michael Shifter, eds., *Constructing Democratic Governance in Latin America,* 4th ed. Baltimore: Johns Hopkins University Press.

Canache, Damarys, and Michael E. Allison. 2005. "Perceptions of Political Corruption in Latin American Democracies." *Latin American Politics and Society* 47(3): 91–111.

Cantu, Francisco, and Sebastián Saiegh. 2010. "Fraudulent Democracy? An Analysis of Argentina's Infamous Decade using Supervised Machine Learning." Unpublished manuscript, University of California, San Diego.

Cardoso, Fernando H., and Enzo Faletto. 1969. *Dependencia y desarrollo en América Latina.* Mexico City, Mexico: Siglo XXI.

Carey, John M. 1996. *Term Limits and Legislative Representation.* New York: Cambridge University Press.

———. 2000. "Parchment, Equilibria, and Institutions." *Comparative Political Studies* 33 (6/7): 735–61.

Carlson, Kurt A., and Suzanne B. Shu. 2007. "The Rule of Three: How the Third Event Signals the Emergence of a Streak." *Organizational Behavior and Human Decision Processes* 104(1): 113–21.

Carreras, Sergio. 2004. *El reino de los Juárez: medio siglo de miseria, terror y desmesura en Santiago del Estero.* Buenos Aires: Aguilar.

Carter, David B., and Curtis S. Signorino. 2010. "Back to the Future: Modeling Time Dependence in Binary Data." *Political Analysis* 18(3): 271–92.

Cavarozzi, Marcelo. 1987. *Autoritarismo y democracia.* Buenos Aires: Centro Editor de América Latina.

Centeno, Miguel. 2002. *Blood and Debt: War and the Nation-State in Latin America.* University Park, PA: Pennsylvania State University Press.

———. 2009. "El Estado en América Latina." *Revista CIDOB d'Afers Internacionals* 85/86: 11–31.

Cepeda-Espinosa, Manuel J. 2004. "Judicial Activism in a Violent Context: The Origin, Role, and Impact of the Colombian Constitutional Court." *Washington University Global Studies Law Review* 3 (Special Issue): 537–688.

———. 2009. "The Constitutional Protection of IDPs in Colombia." In Rodolfo Arango Rivadeneira, ed., *Judicial Protection of Internally Displaced Persons: The Colombian Experience*, pp. 1–47. Washington, DC: Brookings Institution.

Chambers, Paul. 2006. "Consolidation of Thaksinocracy and Crisis of Democracy: Thailand's 2005 Election." In Aurel Croissant and Beate Martin, eds., *Between Consolidation and Crisis: Elections and Democracy in Five Nations in Southeast Asia*, pp. 277–329. Berlin: Lit Verlag.

Cheibub, José Antonio. 2002. "Minority Governments, Deadlock Situations, and the Survival of Presidential Democracies." *Comparative Political Studies* 35(3): 284–312.

Cheibub, José Antonio, Jennifer Gandhi, and James R. Vreeland. 2009. "Democracy and Dictatorship Revisited." Dataset. Available at https://netfiles.uiuc.edu/cheibub/www/datasets.html.

———. 2010. "Democracy and Dictatorship Revisited." *Public Choice* 143(1–2): 67–101.

Coatsworth, John H. 2005. "Structures, Endowments, and Institutions in the Economic History of Latin America." *Latin American Research Review* 40(3): 126–44.

Cohen, J. L., and A. Arato. 1992. *Civil Society and Political Theory.* Cambridge, MA: MIT Press.

Cohen, Youssef. 1989. *The Manipulation of Consent: The State and Working-Class Consciousness in Brazil.* Pittsburgh, PA: University of Pittsburgh Press.

Collier, David. 1978. "Industrial Modernization and Political Change: A Latin American Perspective." *World Politics* 30(4): 593–614.

Collier, David, and Robert Adcock. 1999. "Democracy and Dichotomies: A Pragmatic Approach to Choices About Concepts." *Annual Review of Political Science* 2: 537–65.

Collier, David, and Steven Levitsky. 1997. "Democracy with Adjectives: Conceptual Innovation in Comparative Research." *World Politics* 49(3): 430–51.

Collier, David, and Deborah L. Norden. 1992. "Strategic Choice Models of Political Change in Latin America." *Comparative Politics* 24(2): 229–43.

Collier, Ruth B. 1999. *Paths toward Democracy: The Working Class and Elites in Western Europe and South America*. Cambridge, UK: Cambridge University Press.

Collier, Ruth B., and David Collier. 1991. *Shaping the Political Arena*. Princeton: Princeton University Press.

Comisión Colombiana de Juristas. 2011. "Informe sobre la situación del derecho al territorio de los pueblos indígenas y las comunidades afrodescendientes en Colombia." Bogotá: CCJ.

Conaghan, Catherine M., James M. Malloy, and Leandro Wolfson. 1997. "Democracia y neoliberalismo en Perú, Ecuador y Bolivia." *Desarrollo Económico* 36(144): 867–90.

Constable, Pamela, and Arturo Valenzuela. 1991. *A Nation of Enemies: Chile under Pinochet*. New York: Norton.

Cook, Maria Lorena. 2007. *The Politics of Labor Reform in Latin America: Between Flexibility and Rights*. University Park, PA: Pennsylvania State University Press.

Coppedge, Michael. 1994. *Strong Parties and Lame Ducks: Presidential Partyarchy and Factionalism in Venezuela*. Stanford: Stanford University Press.

———. 1999. "Thickening Thin Concepts and Theories: Combining Large N and Small in Comparative Politics." *Comparative Politics* 31(4): 465–76.

———. 2007. "Continuity and Change in Latin American Party Systems." *Taiwan Journal of Democracy* 3(2): 119–49.

———. 2012. *Democratization and Research Methods*. Cambridge: Cambridge University Press.

Coppedge, Michael, Ángel Álvarez, and Claudia Maldonado. 2008. "Two Persistent Dimensions of Democracy: Contestation and Inclusiveness." *Journal of Politics* 70(3): 632–47.

Coppedge, Michael, and John Gerring, et al. 2011. "Conceptualizing and Measuring Democracy: A New Approach." *Perspectives on Politics* 9(2): 247–67.

Coppedge, Michael, and Wolfgang Reinecke. 1991. "Measuring Polyarchy." In Alex Inkeles, ed., *On Measuring Democracy: Its Consequences and Concomitants*, pp. 47–68. New Brunswick, NJ: Transaction Publishers.

Corak, Miles. 2006. "Do Poor Children Become Poor Adults? Lessons from a Cross-Country Comparison of Generational Earnings Mobility." *Research on Economic Inequality* 13(1): 143–88.

Cornelius, Wayne. 1999. "Subnational Politics and Democratization: Tensions between Center and Periphery in the Mexican Political System." In Wayne Cornelius, Todd Eisenstadt, and Jane Hindley, eds., *Subnational Politics and Democratization in Mexico*, pp. 3–18. La Jolla: Center for US-Mexican Studies, University of California, San Diego.

Cornia, Giovanni A. 2010. "Income Distribution under Latin America's Left Regimes." *Journal of Human Development and Capabilities* 11(1): 85–114.

Cox, Gary, and Scott Morgenstern. 2001. "Latin America's Reactive Assemblies and Proactive Presidents." *Comparative Politics* 33(2): 171–89.

Cox, Gary, Scott Morgenstern, and Leandro Wolfson. 2001. "Legislaturas reactivas y presidentes proactivos en América Latina." *Desarrollo Económico* 41(163): 373–93.

Crisp, Brian, and Juan Carlos Rey. 2001. "The Sources of Electoral Reform in Venezuela." In Matthew Soberg Shugart and Martin P. Wattenberg, eds., *Mixed-Member Electoral Systems: The Best of Both Worlds?* pp. 173–93. New York: Oxford University Press.

Croissant, Aurel. 2003. "Legislative Powers, Veto Players, and the Emergence of Delegative Democracy: A Comparison of Presidentialism in the Philippines and South Korea." *Democratization* 10(3): 68–98.

Crouch, Colin. 2000. *After the Euro: Shaping Institutions for Governance in the Wake of European Monetary Union*. Oxford: Oxford University Press.

———. 2004. *Post-democracy*. Cambridge, UK: Polity Press.

———. 2011. *The Strange Non-death of Neoliberalism*. Malden, MA: Polity Press.

Crouch, Colin, and Maarten Keune. 2012. "The Governance of Economic Uncertainty: Beyond the 'New Social Risks' Analysis." In Giuliano Bonoli and David Natali, eds., *The Politics of the New Welfare State,* pp. 45–67. Oxford: Oxford University Press..

Dahl, Robert A. 1956. *A Preface to Democratic Theory*. New Haven: Yale University Press.

———. 1970. *After the Revolution? Authority in a Good Society*. New Haven: Yale University Press.

———. 1971. *Polyarchy: Participation and Opposition*. New Haven: Yale University Press.

———. 1989. *Democracy and Its Critics*. New Haven: Yale University Press.

———. 1998. *On Democracy*. New Haven: Yale University Press.

Dalby, Michael, and Michael Werthman, eds. 1971. *Bureaucracy in Historical Perspective*. Glenview, IL: Scott, Foresman.

Darden, Keith, and Anna Grzymala-Busse. 2006. "The Great Divide: Literacy, Nationalism, and the Communist Collapse." *World Politics* 59(1): 83–115.

Dargent, Eduardo. Forthcoming. *Technocracy and Democracy in Latin America: The Experts Running Government*. New York: Cambridge University Press.

Davis, Darien. 1999. *Afro-Brazilians: Time for Recognition*. London: Minority Rights Group International.

Davis, Gerald F. 2009. "The Rise and Fall of Finance and the End of the Society of Organizations." *The Academy of Management Perspectives* 23(3): 27–44.

Deininger, Klaus W., and Pedro Olinto. 2000. *Asset Distribution, Inequality, and Growth*. Washington, DC: World Bank, Development Research Group, Rural Development.

De la Torre, Carlos. 2010. "Movimientos sociales y procesos constituyentes en Ecuador." In Martín Tanaka and Francine Jácome, eds., *Desafíos de la gobernabilidad democrática: reformas político-institucionales y movimientos sociales en la región andina,* pp. 245–76. Lima, Peru: Instituto de Estudios Peruanos.

Diamond, Larry. 1992. "Economic Development and Democracy Reconsidered." In Gary Marks and Larry Diamond, eds., *Reexamining Democracy: Essays in Honor of Seymour Martin Lipset,* pp. 93–139. Newbury Park, CA: Sage.

———. 1996. "Democracy in Latin America: Degrees, Illusions, and Directions for Consolidation." In Tom Farer, ed., *Beyond Sovereignty: Collectively Defending Democracy in the Americas,* pp. 52–104. Baltimore: Johns Hopkins University Press.

———. 1997. "Consolidating Democracy in the Americas." *Annals of the American Academy of Political and Social Science* 550: 12–41.

———. 1999a. *Developing Democracy: Toward Consolidation*. Baltimore: Johns Hopkins University Press.

———, ed. 1999b. *Democracy in Developing Countries: Latin America,* 2nd ed. Boulder, CO: Lynne Rienner.

———. 2008. *The Spirit of Democracy: The Struggle to Build Free Societies throughout the World*. New York: Times Books.

Diamond, Larry, and Juan J. Linz. 1989. "Introduction: Politics, Society, and Democracy in Latin America." In Larry Diamond, Juan J. Linz, and Seymour Martin Lipset, eds., *Democracy in Developing Countries: Latin America*, pp. 1–58. Boulder, CO: Lynne Rienner.

Diamond, Larry, and Leonardo Morlino, eds. 2005. *Assessing the Quality of Democracy*. Baltimore: Johns Hopkins University Press.

Diamond, Larry, and Marc Plattner, eds. 1995. *Economic Reform and Democracy*. Baltimore: Johns Hopkins University Press.

Di Marco, Graciela. 2010. "Women's Movements in Argentina: Tensions and Articulations." In Elizabeth Maier and Nathalie Lebon, eds., *Women's Activism in Latin America and the Caribbean: Engendering Social Justice, Democratizing Citizenship*, pp. 159–74. New Brunswick, NJ: Rutgers University Press.

Di Palma, Giuseppe. 1990. *To Craft Democracies: An Essay on Democratic Transitions*. Berkeley: University of California Press.

Dodson, Michael, and Donald Jackson. 2004. "Horizontal Accountability in Transitional Democracies: The Human Rights Ombudsman in El Salvador and Guatemala." *Latin American Politics and Society* 46(4): 1–27.

Domingo, Pilar, and Rachel Sieder, eds. 2001. *Rule of Law in Latin America: The International Promotion of Judicial Reform*. London: Institute of Latin American Studies.

Dornbusch, Rüdiger. 1992. "Lessons from Experiences with High Inflation." *The World Bank Economic Review* 6(1): 13–31.

Dotsey, Michael, and Peter Ireland. 1996. "The Welfare Cost of Inflation in General Equilibrium." *Journal of Monetary Economics* 37(1): 29–47.

Downs, Anthony. 1957. *An Economic Theory of Democracy*. New York: Harper and Row.

Dunn, John. 1992. *Democracy: The Unfinished Journey, 508 BC to AD 1993*. Oxford: Oxford University Press.

———. 2005. *Setting the People Free: The Story of Democracy*. London: Atlantic Books.

Dunning, Thad. 2008. *Crude Democracy: Natural Resource Wealth and Political Regimes*. Cambridge, UK: Cambridge University Press.

Echebarría, Koldo. 2006. *Informe sobre la situación del servicio civil en América Latina*. Washington, DC: Inter-American Development Bank.

Eckstein, Susan Eva, and Timothy P. Wickham-Crowley, eds. 2003. *What Justice? Whose Justice? Fighting for Fairness in Latin America*. Berkeley: University of California Press.

Economic Commission for Latin America and the Caribbean (ECLAC). 1992. *Preliminary Overview of the Latin American and Caribbean Economy*. Santiago, Chile: United Nations, CEPAL.

———. 1995. *Social Panorama of Latin America*. Available from http://www.eclac.cl/.

———. 2006. *Preliminary Overview of the Economies of Latin America and the Caribbean*. Available from: http://www.eclac.org/cgi-bin/getProd.asp?xml=/publicaciones/xml/3/27543/P27543.xml&xsl=/de/tpl-i/p9f.xsl&base=/tpl-i/top-bottom.xslt.

———. 2009. *Social Panorama of Latin America*. Available from http://www.eclac.cl/.

Edsall, Thomas Byrne. 1989. "The Changing Shape of Power: A Realignment in Public Policy." In Steve Fraser and Gary Gerstle, eds., *The Rise and Fall of the New Deal Order, 1930–1980*, pp. 269–93. Princeton: Princeton University Press.

Eisenstadt, Todd A. 2006. "Mexico's Postelectoral *Concertacesiones*." In Gretchen Helmke and Steven Levitsky, eds., *Informal Institutions and Democracy: Lessons from Latin America*, pp. 227–48. Baltimore: Johns Hopkins University Press.

Elkins, Zachary. 2000. "Gradations of Democracy? Empirical Tests of Alternative Conceptualizations." *American Journal of Political Science* 44 No. 2 (April): 293–300.

Elkins, Zachary, and Tom Ginsburg. 2010. "Nested Jurisdictions and the Case of Human Rights." In *Meeting of the American Political Science Association*, Toronto, Canada, August.

Elkins, Zachary, Tom Ginsburg, and James Melton. 2009. *The Endurance of National Constitutions*. New York: Cambridge University Press.

Ellickson, Robert C. 1991. *Order without Law: How Neighbors Settle Disputes*. Cambridge, MA: Harvard University Press.

Engerman, Stanley, and Kenneth Sokoloff. 1997. "Factor Endowments, Institutions and Differential Paths of Growth among New World Economies: A View from Economic Historians of the United States." In Stephen Haber, ed., *How Latin America Fell Behind: Essays on the Economic Histories of Brazil and Mexico: 1800–1914*, pp. 260–306. Stanford: Stanford University Press.

———. 2005a. "Colonialism, Inequality, and Long-Run Paths of Development." Working Paper #11057, National Bureau of Economic Research, Cambridge, MA.

———. 2005b. "The Evolution of Suffrage Institutions in the New World." *The Journal of Economic History* 65(4): 891–921.

Epp, Charles R. 1998. *The Rights Revolution: Lawyers, Activists, and Supreme Courts in Comparative Perspective*. Chicago: University of Chicago Press.

Epstein, David L., Robert Bates, Jack Goldstone, Ida Kristensen and Sharyn O'Halloran. 2006. "Democratic Transitions." *American Journal of Political Science* 50(3): 551–69.

Equipo Latinoamericano de Justicia y Género (ELA). 2009. *Informe sobre género y derechos humanos en Argentina, 2005–2008*, vol. 2. Buenos Aires: Biblos/ELA.

Esping-Andersen, Gøsta. 1999. *Social Foundations of Postindustrial Economies*. Oxford: Oxford University Press.

Evans, Peter. 1995. *Embedded Autonomy*. Princeton: Princeton University Press.

Fairfield, Tasha. 2010. "Business Power and Tax Reform: Taxing Income and Profits in Chile and Argentina." *Latin American Politics and Society* 52(2): 37–71.

Feldstein, Martin. 1979. "The Welfare Cost of Permanent Inflation and Optimal Short-Run Economic Policy." *Journal of Political Economy* 87(4): 749–68.

Feletti, Roberto. 2011. "Para el Viceministro de Economía, Roberto Feletti, el 'populismo debe radicalizarse,'" *Infobae*, May 5.

Feng, Yi. 1997. "Democracy, Political Stability and Economic Growth." *British Journal of Political Science* 27(3): 391–418.

Ferejohn, John, and Debra Satz. 1995. "Unification, Universalism, and Rational Choice Theory." *Critical Review* 9(1–2): 71–84.

Fernández, Aníbal. 2012. "Aníbal: 'Dura más el ruido de las urnas que el de las cacerolas,'." *El Cronista,* September 17.

Ferreira Rubio, Delia, and Matteo Goretti. 1996. "Cuando el presidente gobierna solo. Menem y los decretos de necesidad y urgencia hasta la reforma constitucional (julio 1989–agosto 1994)." *Desarrollo Económico* 36(141): 443–74.

Ferrie, Joseph P. 2005. "History Lessons: The End of American Exceptionalism? Mobility in the United States since 1850." *Journal of Economic Perspectives* 19(3): 199–215.

Figueiredo, Argelina Cheibub. 1993. *Democracia ou Reformas: Alternativas Democráticas à Crise Política*. Rio de Janeiro: Paz e Terra.

Figueroa, Adolfo. 1996. "The Distributive Issue in Latin America." *International Social Science Journal* 48(148): 231–44.

Finkel, Steven E., Aníbal Pérez-Liñán, and Mitchell A. Seligson. 2007. "The Effects of U.S. Foreign Assistance on Democracy Building, 1990–2003." *World Politics* 59 (3):404–39.

Fish, Steven. 2002. "Islam and Authoritarianism." *World Politics* 55 (1): 4–37.

Fishman, Robert M. 2007. "On Being a Weberian (after Spain's 11–14 March): Notes on the Continuing Relevance of the Methodological Perspective Proposed by Weber." In Laurence McFalls, ed., *Max Weber's "Objectivity" Reconsidered*, pp. 261–89. Toronto: University of Toronto Press.

———. 2010. "Rethinking the Iberian Transformations: How Democratization Scenarios Shaped Labor Market Outcomes." *Studies in Comparative International Development* 45(3): 281–310.

———. 2011a. "Portugal's Unnecessary Bailout." *New York Times*, April 13: A23, national edition.

———. 2011b. "Democratic Practice after the Revolution: The Case of Portugal and Beyond." *Politics & Society* 39(2): 233–67.

———. 2012a. "Anomalies of Spain's Economy and Economic Policy-making." *Contributions to Political Economy* 31(1): 67–76.

———. 2012b. "On the Significance of Public Protest in Spanish Democracy." In Jacint Jordana, Vicenc Navarro, Francesc Pallares, and Ferran Requejo, eds., *Democracia, Politica i Societat: Homenatge a Rosa Viros*. Barcelona: Universitat Pompeu Fabra and Avenc.

Fishman, Robert M., and Omar Lizardo. 2013. "How Macro-Historical Change Shapes Cultural Taste: Legacies of Democratization in Spain and Portugal." *American Sociological Review* 78(2): 213–39.

Fishman, Robert M., and Anthony M. Messina, eds. 2006. *The Year of the Euro: The Cultural, Social and Political Import of Europe's Common Currency*. Notre Dame, IN: University of Notre Dame Press.

Fleischer, David V. 1984. "Constitutional and Electoral Engineering in Brazil: A Double-Edged Sword 1964–1982." *Journal of Inter-American Economic Affairs* 37(4): 3–36.

Fligstein, Neil. 2010. "Politics, the Reorganization of the Economy, and Income Inequality, 1980–2009." *Politics and Society* 38(2): 233–42.

Flores-Macías, Gustavo A. 2010. "Statist vs. Pro-Market: Explaining Leftist Governments' Economic Policies in Latin America." *Comparative Politics* 42(4): 413–33.

Foweraker, Joe, and Roman Krznaric. 2002. "The Uneven Performance of Third Wave Democracies: Electoral Politics and the Imperfect Rule of Law in Latin America." *Latin American Politics and Society* 44(3): 29–60.

Foweraker, Joe, and Todd Landman. 2000. *Citizenship Rights and Social Movements*. Oxford: Oxford University Press.

Fox, Jonathan. 1994. "Latin America's Emerging Local Politics." *Journal of Democracy* 5(2): 105–16.

Fraser, Nancy. 2000. "Rethinking Recognition." *New Left Review* 3 (May–June): 107–20.

Fraser, Steve, and Gary Gerstle, eds. 1989. *The Rise and Fall of the New Deal Order, 1930–1980*. Princeton: Princeton University Press.

Freedom House. 2012a. *Freedom in the World 2012*. Available at http://www.freedomhouse.org.

———. 2012b. *Freedom of the Press 2012. Breakthroughs and Pushback in the Middle East*. Available at http://www.freedomhouse.org/sites/default/files/Booklet%20for%20Website.pdf.

Freeland, Crystia. 2012. *Plutocrats: The Rise of the New Global Super-Rich and Fall of Everyone Else*. New York: Penguin.

Freeman, John, and Dennis Quinn. 2012. "The Economic Origins of Democracy Reconsidered." *American Political Science Review* 106(1): 58–80.

Freeman, Richard. 2011. "Welcome to the World of Inequality." Paper presented at the Organization for Economic Co-operation and Development Ministerial Meeting on Social Policy, Paris, France, May 2–3.

Frey, Bruno, Matthias Benz, and Alois Stutzer. 2004. "Introducing Procedural Utility: Not Only What, but Also How Matters." *Journal of Institutional and Theoretical Economics* 160: 377–401.

Friedman, Elisabeth. 2000. *Unfinished Transitions: Women and the Gendered Development of Democracy in Venezuela, 1936–1996*. Stanford: Stanford University Press.

Fry, Peter. 1999. "Color and the Rule of Law in Brazil." In Juan E. Méndez, Guillermo A. O'Donnell, and Paulo Sérgio Pinheiro, eds., *The (Un)Rule of Law and the Underprivileged in Latin America*, pp. 186–210. Notre Dame, IN: University of Notre Dame Press.

Fukuyama, Francis. 1989. *Have We Reached the End of History?* Santa Monica, CA: Rand Corporation.

———. 1992. *The End of History and the Last Man*. New York: Free Press.

Galston, William A. 2013. "The 2012 Election: What Happened, What Changed, What It Means." Washington, DC: Brookings Governance Studies, Brookings Institution.

Gandhi, Jennifer. 2008. *Political Institutions under Dictatorship*. Cambridge, UK: Cambridge University Press.

Gandhi, Jennifer, and Adam Przeworski. 2007. "Authoritarian Institutions and the Survival of Autocrats." *Comparative Political Studies* 40(11): 1279–1301.

Gangl, Amy. 2003. "Procedural Justice Theory and Evaluations of the Lawmaking Process." *Political Behavior* 25(2): 119–49.

Gargarella, Roberto. 2010. *The Legal Foundations of Inequality: Constitutionalism in the Americas, 1776–1860*. Cambridge, UK: Cambridge University Press.

Garretón, Manuel Antonio. 1991. "La transición chilena: Una evaluación provisoria." Documento de Trabajo, FLACSO—Programa Chile, Serie Estudios Políticos, no. 8, Santiago, Chile.

Gasiorowski, Mark J. 1995. "Economic Crisis and Political Regime Change: An Event History Analysis." *American Political Science Review* 89(4): 882–97.

———. 1998. "Macroeconomic Conditions and Political Instability: An Empirical Analysis." *Studies in Comparative International Development* 33(3): 3–17.

———. 2000. "Democracy and Macroeconomic Performance in Underdeveloped Countries: An Empirical Analysis." *Comparative Political Studies* 33(3): 319–49.

Gasiorowski, Mark J., and Timothy J. Power. 1998. "The Structural Determinants of Democratic Consolidation: Evidence from the Third World." *Comparative Political Studies* 31(6): 740–71.

Gates, Scott, Håvard Hegre, Mark P. Jones, and Håvard Strand. 2006. "Institutional Inconsistency and Political Instability: Polity Duration, 1800–2000." *American Journal of Political Science* 50(4): 893–908.

Gauri, Varun, and Daniel Brinks, eds. 2008. *Courting Social Justice: Judicial Enforcement of Social and Economic Rights in the Developing World*. New York: Cambridge University Press.

Geddes, Barbara. 1999. "What Do We Know about Democratization after Twenty Years?" *Annual Review of Political Science* 2(June): 115–44.

Geddes, Barbara, and John Zaller. 1989. "Sources of Popular Support for Authoritarian Regimes." *American Journal of Political Science* 33(2): 319–47.

Gelli, María Angélica. 2006. "De la delegación excepcional a la reglamentación delegativa. (Acerca de la reforma a la ley de Administración Financiera)." *La Ley: Suplemento Constitucional*, August 22.

Gerring, John. 2008. "The Mechanismic Worldview: Thinking Inside the Box." *British Journal of Political Science* 38(1): 161–79.

Gerring, John, Strom C. Thacker, and Rodrigo Alfaro. 2012. "Democracy and Human Development." *Journal of Politics* 74(1): 1–17.

Gerschenkron, Alexander. 1962. *Economic Backwardness in Historical Perspective*. Cambridge, MA: Belknap Press of Harvard University Press.

Gervasoni, Carlos. 1999. "El Impacto Electoral de las Reformas Económicas en América Latina (1982–1995)." *América Latina Hoy* 22: 93–110.

———. 2010a. "A Rentier Theory of Subnational Regimes: Fiscal Federalism, Democracy, and Authoritarianism in the Argentine Provinces." *World Politics* 62(2): 302–40.

———. 2010b. "Measuring Variance in Subnational Regimes: Results from an Expert-Based Operationalization of Democracy in the Argentine Provinces." *Journal of Politics in Latin America* 2(2): 13–52.

———. 2011a. "A Rentier Theory of Subnational Democracy: The Politically Regressive Effects of Redistributive Fiscal Federalism in Argentina." PhD diss., University of Notre Dame.

———. 2011b. "Democracia, autoritarismo e hibridez en las provincias Argentinas: La medición y causas de los regímenes subnacionales." *Journal of Democracy en Español* 3: 75–93.

Gibson, Edward L. 1996. *Class and Conservative Parties: Argentina in Comparative Perspective*. Baltimore: Johns Hopkins University Press.

———. 2004. "Federalism and Democracy: Theoretical Connections and Cautionary Insights." In Edward L. Gibson, ed., *Federalism and Democracy in Latin America*, pp. 1–28. Baltimore: Johns Hopkins University Press.

———. 2012. *Boundary Control: Subnational Authoritarianism in Federal Democracies*. New York: Cambridge University Press.

Gibson, Edward L., and Tulia G. Falleti. 2004. "Unity by the Stick: Regional Conflict and the Origins of Argentine Federalism." In Edward L. Gibson, ed., *Federalism and Democracy in Latin America*, pp. 226–54. Baltimore: Johns Hopkins University Press.

Gil-Serrate, Ramiro, Julio López-Laborda, and Jesús Mur. 2011. "Revenue Autonomy and Regional Growth: An Analysis of the 25-Year Process of Fiscal Decentralisation in Spain." *Environment and Planning A* 43(11): 2626–48.

Gilson, Dave. 2010. "The Price of Admission to the House and Senate," *Mother Jones*, September/October.

Giraudy, Agustina, and Juan Pablo Luna. 2012. "An Explanatory Typology of State's Territorial Reach: State Actors and Territorial Challengers in Latin America." Paper presented at the American Political Science Association Meeting, New Orleans, August 30–September 2.

Gleditsch, Kristian S. 2002. *All International Politics Is Local: The Diffusion of Conflict, Integration, and Democratization*. Ann Arbor: University of Michigan Press.

Gleditsch, Kristian, and Michael Ward. 2006. "Diffusion and the International Context of Democratization." *International Organization* 60(4): 911–33.

Goett, Jennifer. 2004. "Tenencia de la tierra comunal indígena y afrodescendiente en la RAAS." Primer Informe de Desarrollo Humano de las Regiones Autónomas de Nicaragua, Managua, Programa de las Naciones Unidas para el Desarrollo (PNUD).

Gómez, José María, and Eduardo Viola. 1984. "Transición desde el autoritarismo y potencialidades de invención democrática en la Argentina de 1983." In Oscar Oszlak et al., *"Proceso," crisis y transición democrática*, vol. 2, pp. 29–42. Buenos Aires: Centro Editor de América Latina.

Gómez Fortes, Braulio, et al. 2010. *Calidad de la democracia en España: Una auditoría ciudadana*. Madrid: Ariel.

Goñi, Edwin, J. Humberto López, and Luis Servén. 2011. "Fiscal Redistribution and Income Inequality in Latin America." *World Development* 39(9): 1588–69.

Gonzalez, Francisco, and Desmond King. 2004. "The State and Democratization: The United States in Comparative Perspective." *British Journal of Political Science* 34(2): 193–210.

Goodwin-Gill, Guy. 2006. *Free and Fair Elections: New Expanded Edition*. Geneva: Inter-Parliamentary Union.

Gootenberg, Paul Elliot. 1991. *Between Silver and Guano: Commercial Policy and the State in Post-Independence Peru*. Princeton: Princeton University Press.

Gordon, Edmund T., Galio C. Gurdián, and Charles R. Hale. 2003. "Rights, Resources, and the Social Memory of Struggle: Reflections on a Study of Indigenous and Black Community Land Rights on Nicaragua's Atlantic Coast." *Human Organization* 62(4): 369–81.

Grafe, Regina, and María Alejandra Irigoin. 2006. "The Spanish Empire and its Legacy: Fiscal Redistribution and Political Conflict in Colonial and Post-colonial Spanish America." Working Papers of the Global Economic History Network No. 23/6, May.

Gramsci, Antonio. 1971. *The Modern Prince*. New York: International Publishers.

Granovetter, Mark. 1985. "Economic Action and Social Structure: The Problem of Embeddedness." *American Journal of Sociology* 91(3): 481–510.

Green, Donald P., and Ian Shapiro. 1994. *Pathologies of Rational Choice Theory: A Critique of Applications in Political Science*. New Haven: Yale University Press.

Greif, Avner, and David Laitin. 2004. "A Theory of Endogenous Institutional Change." *American Political Science Review* 98(4): 633–52.

Grindle, Merilee. 1996. *Challenging the State: Crisis and Innovation in Latin America and Africa*. Cambridge: Cambridge University Press.

———. 2010. "Constructing, Deconstructing, and Reconstructing Career Civil Service Systems in Latin America." Harvard Kennedy School Faculty Research Working Paper 10-025 (June).

———. 2012. *Jobs for the Boys: Patronage and the State in Comparative Perspective*. Cambridge, MA: Harvard University Press.

Grzymala-Busse, Anna. 2011. "Time Will Tell? Temporality and the Analysis of Causal Mechanisms and Processes." *Comparative Political Studies* 44(9): 1267–97.

Guerra, François-Xavier. 1994. "The Spanish-American Tradition of Representation and Its European Roots." *Journal of Latin American Studies* 26(1): 1–35.

Guevara Mann, Carlos. 2011. *Political Careers, Corruption, and Impunity: Panama's Assembly, 1984–2009*. Notre Dame, IN: University of Notre Dame Press.

Haber, Stephen, and Victor Menaldo. 2011. "Do Natural Resources Fuel Authoritarianism? A Reappraisal of the Resource Curse." *American Political Science Review* 105(1): 1–26.

Hacker, Jacob S., and Paul Pierson. 2010. "Winner Take-All Politics: Public Policy, Political Organization, and the Precipitous Rise of Top Incomes in the United States." *Politics and Society* 38(2): 152–204.

Haggard, Stephan, and Robert Kaufman. 1992. *The Politics of Economic Adjustment*. Princeton: Princeton University Press.

———. 1995. *The Political Economy of Democratic Transitions*. Princeton: Princeton University Press.

———. 2012. "Inequality and Regime Change: Democratic Transitions and the Stability of Democratic Rule." *American Political Science Review* 106(3): 495–516.

Haggard, Stephan, Robert R. Kaufman, and Terence K. Teo. 2012. "Distributive Conflict and Regime Change: A Qualitative Dataset". Dataset, available at fas-polisci.rutgers.edu/kaufman/ HKT_Dataset_v1.1.pdf.

Hagopian, Frances. 1990. "Democracy by Undemocratic Means: Elites, Political Pacts, and Regime Transition in Brazil." *Comparative Political Studies* 23(2): 147–70.

———. 1996. *Traditional Politics and Regime Change in Brazil*. New York: Cambridge University Press.

———. 2005. "Derechos, representación y la creciente calidad de la democracia en Brasil y Chile." *Política y Gobierno* 12(1): 41–90.

Hagopian, Frances, and Scott Mainwaring, eds. 2005. *The Third Wave of Democratization in Latin America: Advances and Setbacks*. Cambridge, UK: Cambridge University Press.

Hall, Peter. 2003. "Aligning Ontology and Methodology in Comparative Politics." In James Mahoney and Dietrich Rueschemeyer, eds., *Comparative Historical Analysis in the Social Sciences*, pp. 373–404. Cambridge, UK: Cambridge University Press.

Hall, Peter, and Michèle Lamont, eds. 2013. *Social Resilience in the Neoliberal Era*. Cambridge, UK: Cambridge University Press.

Hall, Peter, and Rosemary Taylor. 1996. "Political Science and the Three New Institutionalisms." *Political Studies* 44(5): 936–57.

Halperín Donghi, Tulio. 1992. "Backward Looks and Forward Glimpses from a Quincentennial Vantage Point." *Journal of Latin American Studies* 24: 219–34.

Hammergren, Linn. 2007. *Envisioning Reform: Improving Judicial Performance in Latin America*. University Park: Pennsylvania State University Press.

Hart, Herbert L. A. 1961. *The Concept of Law*. Oxford: Clarendon Press.

Hartlyn, Jonathan. 1998. "Political Continuities, Missed Opportunities, and Institutional Rigidities: Another Look at Democratic Transitions in Latin America." In Scott Mainwaring and Arturo Valenzuela, eds., *Politics, Society, and Democracy: Latin America*, pp. 101–20. Boulder, CO: Westview.

Hayek, Friedrich A. von. 1946. *The Road to Serfdom*. London: G. Routledge & Sons.

Hays, Sharon. 2004. *Flat Broke with Children: Women in the Age of Welfare Reform*. Oxford: Oxford University Press.

Hegel, Georg W. F. (1820) 2002. *Elements of the Philosophy of Right*, trans. by H. B. NIsbet, ed. Allen Wood. Cambridge, UK: Cambridge University Press.

Hegre, Håvard, Carl Knutsen, and Espen Geelmuyden Rod. 2012. "The Determinants of Democracy: A Sensitivity Analysis." University of Oslo, Department of Political Science.

Helfer, Laurence, Karen Alter, and M. Florencia Guerzovich. 2009. "Islands of Effective International Adjudication: Constructing an Intellectual Property Rule of Law in the Andean Community." *American Journal of International Law* 103(1):1–47.

Helmke, Gretchen. 2004. *Courts under Constraints: Judges, Generals, and Presidents in Argentina*. New York: Cambridge University Press.

———. 2007. "The Origins of Institutional Crises in Latin America: A Unified Strategic Model and Test." Paper presented at the Annual Meeting of the Midwest Political Science Association, Chicago, April 12–15.

Helmke, Gretchen, and Steven Levitsky. 2006a. *Informal Institutions and Democracy: Lessons from Latin America*. Baltimore: Johns Hopkins University Press.

———. 2006b. "Introduction." In Gretchen Helmke and Steven Levitsky, eds., *Informal Institutions and Democracy: Lessons from Latin America*, pp. 1–30. Baltimore: Johns Hopkins University Press.

Helmke, Gretchen, and Julio Ríos Figueroa, eds. 2011. *Courts in Latin America*. New York: Cambridge University Press.

Henisz, Witold J., and Bennet A. Zelner. 2005. "Legitimacy, Interest Group Pressures, and Change in Emergent Institutions: The Case of Foreign Investors and Host Country Governments." *Academy of Management Review* 30(2): 361–82.

Henisz, Witold J., Bennet A. Zelner, and Mauro F. Guillén. 2005. "The Worldwide Diffusion of Market-Oriented Infrastructure Reform, 1977–1999." *American Sociological Review* 70(6): 871–97.

Herman, Edward S., and Frank Brodhead. 1984. *Demonstration Elections: U.S.-Staged Elections in the Dominican Republic, Vietnam, and El Salvador*. Boston: South End Press.

Hernández Valle, Rubén. 2006. "Regulación jurídica de los partidos políticos en Costa Rica." In Daniel Zovatto, ed., *Regulación jurídica de los partidos políticos en América Latina*, pp. 367–411. Mexico City, Mexico: Instituto de Investigaciones Jurídicas de la Universidad Nacional Autónoma de México.

Heston, Alan, Robert Summers, and Bettina Aten. 2009. *Penn World Table*, version 6.3, Center for International Comparisons of Production, Income and Prices at the University of Pennsylvania.

Hicks, Alexander. 2003. "Back to the Future? A Review Essay on Income Concentration and Conservatism." *Socio-Economic Review* 1: 271–88.

Hirschman, Albert. 1961. *A Bias for Hope: Essays on Development and Latin America*. New Haven: Yale University Press.

———. 1968. *The Strategy of Economic Development*. New Haven: Yale University Press.

———. 1970. "The Search for Paradigms as a Hindrance to Understanding." *World Politics* 22(3): 329–43.

———. 1971. *A Bias for Hope: Essays on Development and Latin America*. New Haven: Yale University Press

———. 1979. "The Turn to Authoritarianism in Latin America and the Search for Its Economic Determinants." In David Collier, ed., *The New Authoritarianism in Latin America*, pp. 61–98. Princeton: Princeton University Press.

———. 1981. *Exit, Voice, and Loyalty: Responses to Decline in Firms, Organizations, and States*. Cambridge, MA: Harvard University Press

Hochstetler, Kathryn, and Margaret Keck. 2007. *Greening Brazil: Environmental Activism in State and Society*. Durham, NC: Duke University Press.

Hofferbert, Richard I., and Hans-Dieter Klingemann. 1999. "Remembering the Bad Old Days: Human Rights, Economic Conditions, and Democratic Performance in Transitional Regimes." *European Journal of Political Research* 36(2): 155–74.

Hoffman, Kelly, and Miguel Angel Centeno. 2003. "The Lopsided Continent: Inequality in Latin America." *Annual Review of Sociology* 29: 363–90.

Hoffmann, Florian F., and Fernando R.N.M. Bentes. 2008. "Accountability for Social and Economic Rights in Brazil." In Varun Gauri and Daniel M. Brinks, eds., *Courting Social Justice:*

Judicial Enforcement of Social and Economic Rights in the Developing World, pp. 100–145. New York: Cambridge University Press.

Holmes, Stephen. 2003. "Lineages of the Rule of Law." In José M. Maravall and Adam Przeworski, eds., *Democracy and the Rule of Law*, pp. 19–61. Cambridge, UK: Cambridge University Press.

Holt, Robert, and John Richardson Jr. 1970. "Competing Paradigms in Comparative Politics." In Robert Holt and John E. Turner, eds., *The Methodology of Comparative Research*, pp. 21–71. New York: Free Press.

Honneth, Axel. 1995. *The Struggle for Recognition: The Moral Grammar of Social Conflicts*. Cambridge, UK: Polity.

Hooker, Juliet. 2005. "Indigenous Inclusion/Black Exclusion: Race, Ethnicity, and Multicultural Citizenship in Latin America." *Journal of Latin American Studies* 37(2): 285–310.

Htun, Mala. 2003. *Sex and the State*. New York: Cambridge University Press.

———. 2004. "From 'Racial Democracy' to Affirmative Action: Changing State Policy on Race in Brazil." *Latin American Research Review* 39(1): 60–89.

Huber, Evelyne, and John D. Stephens. 2001. *Development and Crisis of the Welfare State: Parties and Policies in Global Markets*. Chicago: University of Chicago Press.

———. 2012. *Democracy and the Left: Social Policy and Inequality in Latin America*. Chicago: University of Chicago Press.

Hungerford, Thomas. 2012. "Taxes and the Economy: An Economic Analysis of the Top Tax Rates Since 1945." Congressional Research Service Report for Congress, Washington, DC.

Hunter, Wendy. 1997. *Eroding Military Influence in Brazil: Politicians against Soldiers*. Chapel Hill: University of North Carolina Press.

Huntington, Samuel. 1968. *Political Order in Changing Societies*. New Haven: Yale University Press.

———. 1984. "Will More Countries Become Democratic?" *Political Science Quarterly* 99(2): 193–218.

———. 1991. *The Third Wave: Democratization in the Late Twentieth Century*. Norman: University of Oklahoma Press.

Iazzetta, Osvaldo. 2011. "La democracia delegativa y su cara estatal. Un abordaje del caso argentino." In Guillermo O'Donnell, Osvaldo Iazzetta, and Hugo Quiroga, eds., *Democracia delegativa*, pp. 79–114. Buenos Aires: Prometeo Editorial.

Institute for Democracy and Electoral Assistance (IDEA). 2001. *The State of Democracy: Democracy Assessments in Eight Nations around the World*. Stockholm, Sweden: Institute for Democracy and Electoral Assistance.

Ilsley, Lucretia L. 1952. "The Argentine Constitutional Revision of 1949." *The Journal of Politics* 14(2): 224–40.

Inglehart, Ronald, and Christian Welzel. 2005. *Modernization, Cultural Change, and Democracy: The Human Development Sequence*. New York: Cambridge University Press.

Instituto Colombiano de Desarrollo Rural. 2010. *Memorias 2006–2010*. Bogotá: INDEPAZ.

Inter-American Development Bank (IADB). 1999. *Facing Up to Inequality in Latin America*. Economic and Social Progress Report, Inter-American Development Bank, Washington, DC.

International Monetary Fund (IMF). 2012. *World Economic Outlook Database*. Available at http://www.imf.org/external/pubs/ft/weo/2012/02/weodata/weoselgr.aspx.

Ippolito-O'Donnell, Gabriela. 2011. "Visiones ciudadanas en torno a la democracia delegativa: Argentina y Brasil." In Guillermo O'Donnell, Osvaldo Iazzetta, and Hugo Quiroga, eds., *Democracia delegativa*, pp. 53–78. Buenos Aires: Prometeo.

Jacobs, Lawrence R., and Robert Y. Shapiro. 2000. *Politicians Don't Pander: Political Manipulation and the Loss of Democratic Responsiveness*. Chicago: University of Chicago Press.

Jacobs, Lawrence R., and Joe Soss. 2010. "The Politics of Inequality in America: A Political Economy Framework." *Annual Review of Political Science* 13: 341–64.

Jensen, Nathan, and Leonard Wantchekon. 2004. "Resource Wealth and Political Regimes in Africa." *Comparative Political Studies* 37(7): 816–41.

Jiménez, Mario Alberto. 1974. *Desarrollo constitucional de Costa Rica*. San José, Costa Rica: Editorial Costa Rica.

Jordana, Jacint, and David Levi-Faur. 2005. "The Diffusion of Regulatory Capitalism in Latin America: Sectoral and National Channels in the Making of New Order." *Annals of the American Academy of Political and Social Science* 598(1): 102–24.

Kaiser, Robert G. 2009. *So Much Damn Money: The Triumph of Lobbying and the Corrosion of American Government*. New York: Vintage Books.

Karl, Terry Lynn. 1986. "Imposing Consent: Electoralism versus Democratization in El Salvador." In Paul Drake and Eduardo Silva, eds., *Elections and Democratization in Latin America, 1980–85*, pp. 9–36. La Jolla: Center for Iberian and Latin American Studies, University of California, San Diego.

———. 1990. "Dilemmas of Democratization in Latin America." *Comparative Politics* 23(1): 1–21.

———. 1995. "The Hybrid Regimes of Central America." *Journal of Democracy* 6(3): 72–86.

———. 1997. *The Paradox of Plenty: Oil Booms and Petro-States*. Berkeley: University of California Press.

———. 2000. "Economic Inequality and Democratic Instability." *Journal of Democracy* 11(1): 149–56.

———. 2003. "The Vicious Cycle of Inequality in Latin America." In Susan Eva Eckstein and Timothy P. Wickham-Crowley, eds., *What Justice? Whose Justice? Fighting for Fairness in Latin America*, pp. 133–57. Berkeley: University of California Press.

Karl, Terry, and Philippe Schmitter. 1991. "Modes of Transition in Latin America, Southern and Eastern Europe." *International Social Science Journal* 128(May): 269–84.

———. Forthcoming. "Dependency and Development Revisited: Their 'Combined and Uneven' Impact upon Inequality." In Patrick Heller, Dietrich Rueschemeyer and Richard Snyder, eds., *Paths of Development in a Globalized World*. Boulder, CO: Lynne Rienner.

Kaufmann, Daniel, Aart Kraay, and Massimo Mastruzzi. 2005. *Governance Matters IV: Governance Indicators for 1996–2004*. New York: World Bank.

Kennedy, Ryan. 2010. "The Contradiction of Modernization: A Conditional Model of Endogenous Democratization." *Journal of Politics* 72(3): 785–98.

Kenney, Charles D. 2003. "Horizontal Accountability: Concepts and Conflicts." In Scott Mainwaring and Christopher Welna, eds., *Democratic Accountability in Latin America*, pp. 55–76. Oxford: Oxford University Press.

Keohane, Robert. 1984. *After Hegemony: Cooperation and Discord in the World Political Economy*. Princeton: Princeton University Press.

Kim, Young Hun, and Donna Bahry. 2008. "Interrupted Presidencies in Third Wave Democracies." *The Journal of Politics* 70(3): 807–22.

King, Desmond, and Robert C. Lieberman. 2009. "American Political Development as a Process of Development." In Desmond King, Robert C. Lieberman, Gretchen Ritter, and Laurence Whitehead, eds., *Democratization in America: A Comparative-Historical Analysis*, pp. 3–27. Baltimore: Johns Hopkins University Press.

King, Desmond, Robert C. Lieberman, Gretchen Ritter, and Laurence Whitehead, eds. 2009. *Democratization in America: A Comparative-Historical Analysis.* Baltimore: Johns Hopkins University Press.

Kleinfeld, Rachel. 2006. "Competing Definitions of the Rule of Law." In T. Carothers, ed., *Promoting the Rule of Law Abroad: In Search of Knowledge*, pp. 31–73. Washington, DC: Carnegie Endowment for International Peace.

Klomp, Jeroen, and Jakob de Haan. 2009. "Is the Political System Really Related to Health?" *Social Science & Medicine* 69(1): 36–46.

Klug, Francesca, Keir Starmer, and Stuart Weir. 1996. *The Three Pillars of Liberty: Political Rights and Freedoms in the United Kingdom.* London: Routledge.

Klug, Heinz. 2000. *Constituting Democracy: Law, Globalism, and South Africa's Political Reconstruction.* Cambridge, UK: Cambridge University Press.

Krasner, Stephen D., ed. 1983. *International Regimes.* Ithaca, NY: Cornell University Press.

————. 1984. "Approaches to the State: Alternative Conceptions and Historical Dynamics." *Comparative Politics* 16, no 2 (Jan.): 223–46.

Kristof, Nicholas. 2010. "Our Banana Republic." *New York Times,* November 6.

Krugman, Paul. 2011. "Oligarchy: American Style." *New York Times,* November 3.

Kubiček, Paul. 1994. "Delegative Democracy in Russia and Ukraine." *Communist and Post-Communist Studies* 27(4): 423–41.

Kuran, Timur. 1991. "Now Out of Never: The Element of Surprise in the East European Revolution of 1989." *World Politics* 44(1): 7–48.

Kuttner, Robert. 2007. *The Squandering of America: How the Failure of Our Politics Undermines Our Prosperity.* New York: Knopf.

Laakso, Markku, and Rein Taagepera. 1979. "'Effective Number of Parties: A Measure with Application to Western Europe." *Comparative Political Studies* 12(1): 3–27.

Lake, David A., and Matthew A. Baum. 2001. "The Invisible Hand of Democracy: Political Control and the Provision of Public Services." *Comparative Political Studies* 34(6): 587–621.

Lamounier, Bolivar. 1981. "Representação Política: A Importância de Certos Formalismos." In Bolivar Lamounier, Francisco C. Weffort, and Maria Victoria Benevides, eds., *Direito, Cidadania e Participação*, pp. 230–57. São Paulo: T. A. Queiroz, Editor.

Lange, Matthew, James Mahoney, and Matthias vom Hau. 2006. "Colonialism and Development: A Comparative Analysis of Spanish and British Colonies" *American Journal of Sociology* 111(5): 1412–62.

Langer, Maximo. 2007. "Revolution in Latin American Criminal Procedure: Diffusion of Legal Ideas from the Periphery." *American Journal of Comparative Law* 55: 617–76.

Langston, Joy. 2006. "The Birth and Transformation of the Dedazo in Mexico." In Gretchen Helmke and Steven Levitsky, eds., *Informal Institutions and Democracy: Lessons from Latin America*, pp. 143–59. Baltimore: Johns Hopkins University Press.

Larkins, Christopher. 1998. "The Judiciary and Delegative Democracy in Argentina." *Comparative Politics* 30(4): 423–42.

Latham, Earl. 1952. *The Group Basis of Politics: A Study in Basing-Point Legislation.* Ithaca, NY: Cornell University Press.

Lease, Emory B. 1919. "The Number Three, Mysterious, Mystic, Magic." *Classical Philology* 14(1): 56–73.

Lehoucq, Fabrice. 1995. "La dinámica política institucional y la construcción de un régimen democrático: Costa Rica en perspectiva latinoamericana." In Arturo Taracena, and Jean Piel, eds., *Identidades nacionales y Estado moderno en Centroamérica*, pp. 151–64. San José: Editorial Universidad de Costa Rica.

————. 1998. *Instituciones democráticas y conflictos políticos en Costa Rica*. Heredia, Costa Rica: Editorial Universidad Nacional Autónoma.

Lehoucq, Fabrice, and Iván Molina. 2004. *Stuffing the Ballot Box: Fraud, Electoral Reform, and Democratization in Costa Rica*. New York: Cambridge University Press.

Lehoucq, Fabrice, and Aníbal Pérez-Liñán. Forthcoming. "Regimes, Competition and Military Coups in Latin America." *Comparative Political Studies*.

Levi, Margaret. 1988. *Of Rule and Revenue*. Berkeley: University of California Press.

Levi, Margaret, and Brad Epperly. 2008. "Principled Principals in the Founding Moments of the Rule of Law." Paper read at World Justice Forum conference, Vienna, Austria, July 2–5.

Levi, Margaret, Audrey Sacks, and Tom Tyler. 2009. "Conceptualizing Legitimacy, Measuring Legitimating Beliefs." *American Behavioral Scientist* 53(3): 354–75.

Levine, Daniel H. 1973. *Conflict and Political Change in Venezuela*. Princeton: Princeton University Press.

Levine, Daniel, and José Enrique Molina. 2011. "Measuring the Quality of Democracy." In Daniel Levine and José Enrique Molina, eds., *The Quality of Democracy in Latin America*, pp. 21–38. Boulder, CO: Lynne Rienner.

Levine, Linda. 2012. "The U.S. Income Distribution and Mobility: Trends and International Comparisons." Washington, DC: Congressional Resource Service Reports.

Levitsky, Steven, and María Victoria Murillo. 2005a. "Conclusion: Theorizing about Weak Institutions: Lessons from the Argentine Case." In Steven Levitsky and María Victoria Murillo, eds., *Argentine Democracy: The Politics of Institutional Weakness*, pp. 269–90. University Park: Pennsylvania State University Press.

————. 2005b. *Argentine Democracy: The Politics of Institutional Weakness*. University Park: Pennsylvania State University Press.

————. 2009. "Variation in Institutional Strength." *Annual Review of Political Science* 12: 115–33.

Levitsky, Stephen, and Kenneth Roberts. 2011a. *The Resurgence of the Latin American Left*. Baltimore: Johns Hopkins University Press.

————. 2011b. "Latin America's 'Left Turn': A Framework for Analysis." In Steven Levitsky and Kenneth M. Roberts, eds., *The Resurgence of the Latin American Left*, pp. 1–28. Baltimore: Johns Hopkins University Press.

Levitsky, Steven, and Lucan Way. 2002. "The Rise of Competitive Authoritarianism." *Journal of Democracy* 13(2): 51–65.

————. 2010. *Competitive Authoritarianism: Hybrid Regimes after the Cold War*. Cambridge, UK: Cambridge University Press.

Levitt, Barry S. 2012. *Power in the Balance: Presidents, Parties, and Legislatures in Peru and Beyond*. Notre Dame: University of Notre Dame Press.

Levy, Frank, and Peter Temin. 2007. "Inequality and Institutions in 20th Century America." Working Paper no. 7/17, Massachusetts Institute of Technology, Department of Economics, Cambridge, MA.

Li, Hongyi, Lyn Squire, and Heng-fu Zou. 1998. "Explaining International and Intertemporal Variations in Income Inequality." *Economic Journal* 108 (446): 26–43.

Lieberman, Evan. 2005. "Nested Analysis as a Mixed-Method Strategy for Comparative Research." *American Political Science* Review 99(3): 435–52.

Lijphart, Arend. 1994. *Electoral Systems and Party Systems: A Study of Twenty-Seven Democracies, 1945–1990.* Oxford: Oxford University Press.

Linhares, Luiz Fernando do Rosário. 2004. "Kilombos of Brazil: Identity and Land Entitlement." *Journal of Black Studies* 34(6): 817–37.

Linz, Juan J. 1973. "Opposition in and under an Authoritarian Regime: The Case of Spain." In Robert Dahl, ed., *Regimes and Oppositions,* pp. 171–259. New Haven: Yale University Press.

———. 1975. "Authoritarian and Totalitarian Regimes." In Fred Greenstein and Nelson Polsby, eds., *Handbook of Political Science,* vol. 3, pp. 259–69. Reading, PA: Addison-Wesley.

———. 1978a. "The Breakdown of Democracy in Spain." In Juan J. Linz and Alfred Stepan, eds, *The Breakdown of Democratic Regimes: Europe,* pp. 142–215. Baltimore: Johns Hopkins University Press.

———. 1978b. *The Breakdown of Democratic Regimes: Crisis, Breakdown, and Reequilibration.* Baltimore: Johns Hopkins University Press.

———. 1994. "Presidential or Parliamentary Democracy: Does It Make a Difference?" In Juan J. Linz and Arturo Valenzuela, eds., *The Failure of Presidential Democracy. The Case of Latin America,* pp. 3–87. Baltimore: Johns Hopkins University Press.

Linz, Juan, and Alfred Stepan. 1978. *The Breakdown of Democratic Regimes.* Baltimore: Johns Hopkins University Press.

———. 1996. *Problems of Democratic Transition and Consolidation: Southern Europe, South America, and Post-communist Europe.* Baltimore: Johns Hopkins University Press.

Lipset, Seymour M. 1959. "Some Social Requisites of Democracy: Economic Development and Political Legitimacy." *American Political Science Review* 53 (1):69–105.

———. 1960. *Political Man: The Social Bases of Politics.* Garden City, NY: Anchor.

Lipset, Seymour Martin, Kyoung Ryung Seong, and John C. Torres. 1993. "A Comparative Analysis of the Social Requisites of Democracy." *International Social Science Journal* 136 (May): 155–75.

Llanos, Mariana. 1998. "El presidente, el congreso y la política de privatizaciones en la Argentina (1989–1997)." *Desarrollo Económico* 38(151): 743–70.

———. 2001. "Understanding Presidential Power in Argentina: A Study of the Policy of Privatisation in the 1990s." *Journal of Latin American Studies* 33(1): 67–99.

Lockhart, James, and Stuart B. Schwartz. 1983. *Early Latin America: A History of Colonial Spanish America and Brazil.* Cambridge, UK: Cambridge University Press.

Lohmann, Susanne. 1994. "The Dynamics of Informational Cascades: The Monday Demonstrations in Leipzig, East Germany, 1989–91." *World Politics* 47(1): 42–101.

Londregan, John, and Keith Poole. 1990. "Poverty, the Coup Trap, and the Seizure of Executive Power." *World Politics* 42(2): 151–83.

Long, J. Scott, and Jeremy Freese. 2001. *Regression Models for Categorical Dependent Variables Using Stata.* College Station, TX: Stata Press Publication.

López-Alves, Fernando. 2000. *State Formation and Democracy in Latin America, 1810–1900.* Durham, NC: Duke University Press.

López-Calva, Luis F., and Nora Lustig. 2010. *Declining Inequality in Latin America: A Decade of Progress?* Washington, DC: Brookings Institution Press and the United Nations Development Programme.

López Pintor, Rafael, and Maria Gratschew. 2002. *Voter Turnout since 1945: A Global Report*. Stockholm: International Institute for Democracy and Electoral Assistance.

Lora, Eduardo, and Ugo Panizza. 2002. "Structural Reforms in Latin America under Scrutiny." Working Paper no. 470, Inter-American Development Bank, Research Department, Washington, DC.

Loveman, Brian. 1993. *The Constitution of Tyranny: Regimes of Exception in Spanish America*. Pittsburgh, PA: University of Pittsburgh Press.

Lowenthal, Abraham F. 1986. Foreword to Guillermo O'Donnell, Philippe C. Schmitter, and Laurence Whitehead, eds., *Transitions from Authoritarian Rule: Comparative Perspectives*. Baltimore: Johns Hopkins University Press.

Lucas, Robert. 2000. "Inflation and Welfare." *Econometrica* 68(2): 247–74.

Luebbert, Gregory M. 1991. *Liberalism, Fascism, or Social Democracy: Social Classes and the Political Origins of Regimes in Interwar Europe*. Oxford: Oxford University Press.

Lustig, Nora, Luis Felipe López-Calva, and Eduardo Ortiz Juárez. 2011. "The Decline in Inequality in Latin America: How Much, Since When and Why." Working Paper no. 211, Society for the Study of Economic Inequality, Verona, Italy.

Lustig, Nora, and Darryl McLeod. 2009. "Are Latin America's New Left Regimes Reducing Inequality Faster?" Washington, DC: Woodrow Wilson Center for International Scholars, Latin American Program.

Lynch, John. 2001. "The Colonial Roots of Latin American Independence." In John Lynch, *Latin America between Colony and Nation: Selected Essays*, pp. 83–86. London: Palgrave.

Machiavelli, Niccolò. (1535) 1985. *The Prince*, trans. Harvey Mansfield. Chicago: University of Chicago Press.

Mackie, Gerry. 2003. *Democracy Defended*. Cambridge, UK: Cambridge University Press.

Madrid, Raúl L. 2012. *The Rise of Ethnic Politics in Latin America*. Cambridge, UK: Cambridge University Press.

Magaloni, Beatriz. 2003. "Authoritarianism, Democracy, and the Supreme Court: Horizontal Exchange and the Rule of Law in Mexico." In Scott Mainwaring and Christopher Welna, eds., *Democratic Accountability in Latin America*, pp. 266–305. Oxford: Oxford University Press.

———. 2005. "The Demise of Mexico's One Party Dominant Regime." In Frances Hagopian and Scott Mainwaring, eds., *The Third Wave of Democratization in Latin America: Advances and Setbacks*, pp. 121–46. New York: Cambridge University Press.

———. 2008. "Credible Power-Sharing and the Longevity of Authoritarian Rule." *Comparative Political Studies* 41(4–5): 715–41.

Mahoney, James, and Kathleen Thelen. 2010. "A Theory of Gradual Institutional Change." In James Mahoney and Kathleen Thelen, eds. *Explaining Institutional Change: Ambiguity, Agency, and Power*, pp. 1–37. New York: Cambridge University Press.

Mainwaring, Scott. 1986. "The Consolidation of Democracy in Latin America: A Rapporteur's Report." Working Paper no. 73, Kellogg Institute for International Studies, University of Notre Dame.

———. 1993. "Presidentialism, Multipartism, and Democracy: The Difficult Combination." *Comparative Political Studies* 26(2):198–228.

———. 2003. "Introduction: Democratic Accountability in Latin America." In Scott Mainwaring and Christopher Welna, eds., *Democratic Accountability in Latin America*, pp. 3–33. Oxford: Oxford University Press.

————. 2012. "From Representative Democracy to Participatory Competitive Authoritarianism: Hugo Chávez and Venezuelan Politics." *Perspectives on Politics* 10(4): 955–67.

Mainwaring, Scott, Daniel Brinks, and Aníbal Pérez-Liñán. 2001. "Classifying Political Regimes in Latin America, 1945–1999." *Studies in Comparative International Development* 36(1): 37–65.

————. 2007. "Classifying Political Regimes in Latin America, 1945–2004." In Gerardo L. Munck, ed. *Regimes and Democracy in Latin America: Theories and Methods*, pp. 123–60. Oxford: Oxford University Press.

Mainwaring, Scott, Carlos Gervasoni, and Annabella España-Nájera. 2010. "The Vote Share of New and Young Parties." Working Paper, no. 368, Kellogg Institute for International Studies, University of Notre Dame.

Mainwaring, Scott, Guillermo O'Donnell, and J. Samuel Valenzuela, eds. 1992. *Issues in Democratic Consolidation: The New South American Democracies in Comparative Perspective*. Notre Dame, IN: University of Notre Dame Press.

Mainwaring, Scott, and Aníbal Pérez-Liñán. 2003. "Level of Development and Democracy. Latin American Exceptionalism, 1945–1996." *Comparative Political Studies* 36(9): 1031–67.

————. 2005. "Latin American Democratization since 1978: Democratic Transitions, Breakdowns, and Erosions." In Frances Hagopian and Scott Mainwaring, eds., *The Third Wave of Democratization in Latin America: Advances and Setbacks*, pp. 14–59. Cambridge, UK: Cambridge University Press.

————. 2007. "Why Regions of the World Are Important? Regional Specificities and Region-Wide Diffusion of Democracy." In Gerardo Munck, ed. *Regimes and Democracy in Latin America: Theories and Methods*, pp. 199–229. Oxford: Oxford University Press.

————. 2013. *Democracies and Dictatorships in Latin America: Emergence, Survival, and Fall*. Cambridge, UK: Cambridge University Press.

Mainwaring, Scott, and Timothy Scully, eds. 1995. *Building Democratic Institutions. Party Systems in Latin America*. Stanford: Stanford University Press.

Mainwaring, Scott, Timothy Scully, and Jorge Vargas Cullell. 2009. "Measuring Success in Democratic Governance." In Scott Mainwaring and Timothy Scully, eds., *Democratic Governance in Latin America*, pp. 11–51. Stanford: Stanford University Press.

Mainwaring, Scott, and Christopher Welna. 2003. *Democratic Accountability in Latin America*. Oxford: Oxford University Press.

Manin, Bernard. 1991. "Métamorphoses du Gouvernement Représentatif." In Daniel Pécaut and Bernardo Sorj, eds., *Les Métamorphoses de la Représentation au Brésil et en Europe*, pp. 48–57. Paris: Editions du CNRS.

Mann, Michael. 1984. "The Autonomous Power of the State: Its Origins, Mechanisms and Results." *European Journal of Sociology* 25(2): 185–213.

————. 2010. *The Sources of Social Power*, 17th ed. Cambridge: Cambridge University Press.

March, James, and Johan Olsen. 1984. "The New Institutionalism: Organizational Factors in Political Life." *American Political Science Review* 78(3): 734–49.

Markoff, John, and Veronica Montecinos. 1993. "The Ubiquitous Rise of Economists." *Journal of Public Policy* 13(1): 37–68.

Marshall, Monty G., and Keith Jaggers. 2010. "Polity IV Project: Political Regime Characteristics and Transitions, 1800–2009." Dataset and associated codebook. Available at http://www.sys temicpeace.org/inscr/inscr.htm.

Marshall, Monty, Keith Jaggers, and Ted Gurr. 2010. "Polity IV Project. Political Regime Characteristics and Transitions, 1800–2010. Dataset Users' Manual." Available at http://www.system icpeace.org/inscr/p4manualv2010.pdf.

Marshall, Thomas H. 1950a. *Citizenship and Social Class, and Other Essays*. Cambridge, UK: Cambridge University Press.

———. 1950b. "Citizenship and Social Class." In Thomas H. Marshall, *Citizenship and Social Class and Other Essays*, pp. 1–85. Cambridge, UK: Cambridge University Press.

———. 1965. *Class, Citizenship, and Social Development: Essays*. Garden City, NY: Doubleday.

Martin, Stacie. 2005. "Labor Obligations in the U.S.-Chile Free Trade Agreement." *Comparative Labor Law and Policy Journal* 25: 201–26.

Martínez Basallo, Sandra P. 2010. "La política de titulación colectiva a las comunidades negras del Pacífico colombiano: Una mirada desde los actores locales." *Boletín de Antropología Universidad de Antioquia* 24(41):13–43.

Martz, John D. 1967. "Costa Rican Electoral Trends, 1953–1966." *Western Political Quarterly* 20(4): 888–909.

Mauceri, Philip. 2006. "An Authoritarian Presidency: How and Why did Presidential Power Run Amok in Fujimori's Peru?" In Julio Carrión, ed., *The Fujimori Legacy: The Rise of Electoral Authoritarianism in Peru*, pp. 39–60. University Park: Pennsylvania State University Press.

Mayhew, David R. 1974. *Congress: The Electoral Connection*. New Haven: Yale University Press.

Mazzuca, Sebastián L. 2010. "Access to Power versus Exercise of Power: Reconceptualizing the Quality of Democracy in Latin America." *Studies in Comparative International Development* 45(3): 334–57.

McCarty, Nolan M., Keith T. Poole, and Howard Rosenthal. 1997. *Income Redistribution and the Realignment of American Politics*. Washington, DC: AEI Press.

McFarland, Andrew F. 2004. *Neopluralism: The Evolution of Political Process Theory*. Lawrence: University Press of Kansas.

McGuire, James. 1997. *Peronism without Perón: Unions, Parties, and Democracy in Argentina*. Stanford: Stanford University Press.

———. 2010. *Wealth, Health, and Democracy in East Asia and Latin America*. New York: Cambridge University Press.

———. 2013. "Political Regime and Social Performance." *Contemporary Politics* 19(1): 55–75.

McKelvey, Richard D., and William Zavoina. 1975. "A Statistical Model for the Analysis of Ordinal Level Dependent Variables." *Journal of Mathematical Sociology* 4(1): 103–20.

McMann, Kelly. 2006. *Economic Autonomy and Democracy: Hybrid Regimes in Russia and Kyrgyzstan*. New York: Cambridge University Press.

McNamara, Kathleen R. 1998. *The Currency of Ideas: Monetary Politics in the European Union*. Ithaca, NY: Cornell University Press.

McNulty, Stephanie. 2011. *Voice and Vote: Decentralization and Participation in Post-Fujimori Peru*. Stanford: Stanford University Press.

Meltzer, Allan H., and Scott F. Richard. 1981. "A Rational Theory of the Size of Government." *Journal of Political Economy* 89(5): 914–27.

Méndez, Juan E., Guillermo A. O'Donnell, and Paulo Sérgio Pinheiro, eds. 1999. *The (Un)Rule of Law and the Underprivileged in Latin America*. Notre Dame, IN: University of Notre Dame Press.

Merkel, Wolfgang. 2004. "Embedded and Defective Democracies." *Democratization* 11(5): 33–58.

Mills, C. Wright. 1959. *The Sociological Imagination*. New York: Oxford University Press.

Moe, Terry. 1995. "The Politics of Structural Choice: Toward a Theory of Public Bureaucracy." In Oliver E. Williamson, ed., *Organization Theory: from Chester Barnard to the Present and Beyond*, pp. 116–53. New York: Oxford University Press.

Montenegro, Nineth. 2002. "The Challenge of Women's Political Participation in Guatemala." In International IDEA, ed, *Mujeres en el Parlamento: Más allá de los números*. Stockholm, Sweden. Available at http://www.idea.int/publications/wip/upload/montenegro-CS-Guatemala.pdf.

Moore, Barrington, Jr. 1966. *Social Origins of Dictatorship and Democracy: Lord and Peasant in the Making of the Modern World*. Boston: Beacon Press.

Morandini, Norma. 1991. *Catamarca*. Buenos Aires: Editorial Planeta.

Moreno, Erika, Brian F. Crisp, and Matthew Soberg Shugart. 2003. "The Accountability Deficit in Latin America." In Scott Mainwaring, and Cristopher Welna, eds., *Democratic Accountability in Latin America*, pp. 79–131. Oxford: Oxford University Press.

Morgan Kelly, Jana. 2003. "Counting on the Past or Investing in the Future? Economic and Political Accountability in Fujimori's Peru." *Journal of Politics* 65(3): 864–80.

Morlino, Leonardo. 2007. " 'Good' and 'Bad' Democracies: How to Conduct Research into the Quality of Democracy". Working Paper no. 85, Universidad Autónoma de Madrid.

———. 2010. "Legitimacy and the Quality of Democracy." *International Social Science Journal* 60(196): 211–22.

Morrison, Kevin. 2009. "Oil, Nontax Revenue, and the Redistributional Foundations of Regime Stability." *International Organization* 63(1): 107–38.

Mukand, Sharun, and Dani Rodrik. 2005. "In Search of the Holy Grail: Policy Convergence, Experimentation, and Economic Performance." *American Economic Review* 95(1): 374–83.

Muller, Edward N. 1988. "Democracy, Economic Development, and Income Inequality." *American Sociological Review* 53 (1): 50–68.

Munck, Gerardo. 2009. *Measuring Democracy: A Bridge between Scholarship and Politics*. Baltimore: Johns Hopkins University Press.

Munck, Gerardo, and Carol Leff. 1997. "Modes of Transition and Democratization: South America and Eastern Europe in Comparative Perspective." *Comparative Politics* 29(3): 343–62.

Munck, Gerardo, and Richard Snyder. 2007. *Passion, Craft, and Method in Comparative Politics*. Baltimore: Johns Hopkins University Press.

Munck, Gerardo, and Jay Verkuilen. 2002. "Conceptualizing and Measuring Democracy: Evaluating Alternative Indices." *Comparative Political Studies* 35 (1): 5–34.

Murillo, María Victoria. 2005. "Partisanship amidst Convergence: Labor Market Reforms in Latin America." *Comparative Politics* 37(4): 441–58.

———. 2011. "La fortaleza institucional argentina en 2003–2011." In Andrés Malamud and Miguel De Luca, eds., *La política en tiempos de Kirchner*, pp. 265–75. Buenos Aires: EUDEBA.

Murillo, María Victoria, Andrew Schrank, and Lucas Ronconi. 2011. "Latin American Labor Reforms: Evaluating Risk and Security." In José Antonio Ocampo and Jaime Ros, eds., *The Oxford Handbook of Latin American Economics*, pp. 790–812. Oxford: Oxford University Press.

Mustapic, Ana María. 2000. " 'Oficialistas y diputados': las relaciones ejecutivo-legislativo en la Argentina." *Desarrollo Económico* 39(156): 571–95.

Narizny, Kevin. 2012. "Anglo-American Primacy and the Global Spread of Democracy: An International Genealogy." *World Politics* 64(2): 341–73.

Negretto, Gabriel L. 2001 "Negociando los poderes del presidente: Reforma y cambio constitucional en la Argentina." *Desarrollo Económico* 41(163): 411–44.

———. 2002. "¿Gobierna solo el presidente? Poderes de decreto y diseño institucional en Brasil y Argentina." *Desarrollo Económico* 42(167): 377–404.

———. 2006. "Minority Presidents and Democratic Performance in Latin America." *Latin American Politics and Society* 48(3): 63–92.

———. 2009. "Political Parties and Institutional Design: Explaining Constitutional Choice in Latin America." *British Journal of Political Science* 39(1): 117–39.

Nel, Philip. 2005. "Democratization and the Dynamics of Income Distribution in Low- and Middle-Income Countries." *Politikon* 32(1): 17–43.

Nelson, Laura Sue. 1993. "The Defense of Honor: Is It Still Honored in Brazil?" *Wisconsin International Law Journal* 11 (spring): 531–56.

Nichter, Simeon. 2011. "Vote Buying in Brazil: From Impunity to Prosecution." Paper presented at the conference, "Ruling Politics: The Formal and Informal Foundations of Power in New Democracies," Harvard University, November 21–22.

Niesen, Peter. 2002. "Anti-Extremism, Negative Republicanism, Civic Society: Three Paradigms for Banning Political Parties, Part 1." *German Law Journal.* Available at http://www.german lawjournal.com/index.php?pageID=11&artID=164.

Nohlen, Dieter. 1984. "Changes and Choices in Electoral Systems." In Arend Lijphart and Bernard Grofman, eds., *Choosing an Electoral System: Issues and Alternatives*, pp. 217–24. New York: Praeger.

North, Douglass C. 1989. "Institutions and Economic Growth: An Historical Introduction." *World Development* 17(9): 1319–32.

———. 1990. *Institutions, Institutional Change, and Economic Performance.* New York: Cambridge University Press.

Nussbaum, Martha. 1990. "Aristotelian Social Democracy." In R. Bruce Douglass, Gerald Mara and Henry Richardson, eds., *Liberalism and the Good*, pp. 203–52. New York: Routledge.

Oconitrillo, Eduardo. 1981. *Un siglo de política costarricense: Crónica de 23 campañas presidenciales.* San José, Costa Rica: Editorial Universidad Estatal a Distancia.

O'Donnell, Guillermo. 1973. *Modernization and Bureaucratic-Authoritarianism: Studies in South American Politics.* Berkeley: Institute for International Studies, University of California.

———. 1977. "Estado y alianzas en la Argentina, 1955–1976." *Desarrollo Económico* 16(64): 523–54.

———. 1978a. "Permanent Crisis and the Failure to Create a Democratic Regime." In Juan J. Linz and Alfred Stepan, eds., *The Breakdown of Democratic Regimes*, vol. 3, *Latin America*, pp. 138–77. Baltimore: Johns Hopkins University Press.

———. 1978b. "Reflections on the Patterns of Change in the Bureaucratic-Authoritarian State." *Latin American Research Review* 13(1): 3–38.

———. 1978c. "State and Alliances in Argentina." *Journal of Development Studies* 15(1): 3–33.

———. 1979a. "Notas para el estudio de procesos de democratización política a partir del estado burocrático autoritario." *Estudios CEDES* 2 No. 5 (Buenos Aires).

———. 1979b. "Tensions in the Bureaucratic-Authoritarian State and the Question of Democracy." In David Collier, ed., *The New Authoritarianism in Latin America*, pp. 285–318. Princeton: Princeton University Press.

———. 1982. *El estado burocrático autoritario.* Buenos Aires: Editorial de Belgrano.

———. 1984. *Y a mí, ¿qué me importa? Notas sobre sociabilidad y política en Argentina y Brasil.* Buenos Aires: Centro de Estudios de Estado y Sociedad (CEDES).

———. 1985. "Notes for the Study of Democratic Consolidation in Contemporary Latin America." Circulated in advance of the working meeting of the project "Dilemmas and Opportunities of Democratic Consolidation in Contemporary Latin America," Centro Brasileiro de Análise e Planejamento (CEBRAP), São Paulo, December 16–17 (mimeo).

———. 1986. "Introduction to the Latin American Cases." In Guillermo O'Donnell, Philippe Schmitter, and Laurence Whitehead, eds., *Transitions from Authoritarian Rule: Latin America*, pp. 3–18. Baltimore: Johns Hopkins University Press.

———. 1988. "Transições, Continuidades e Paradoxos." In Fábio Wanderley Reis and Guillermo O'Donnell, eds. 1988. *A Democracia no Brasil: Dilemas e Perspectivas*, pp. 41–71. São Paulo: Vértice.

———. 1992. "Transitions, Continuities, and Paradoxes." In Scott Mainwaring, Guillermo O'Donnell, and J. Samuel Valenzuela, eds., *Issues in Democratic Consolidation*, pp. 17–56. Notre Dame, IN: University of Notre Dame Press.

———. 1993. "On the State, Democratization, and Some Conceptual Problems: A Latin American View with Glances at Some Postcommunist Countries." *World Development* 21(8): 1355–69.

———. 1994. "Delegative Democracy." *Journal of Democracy* 5 (1): 55–69.

———. 1996a. "Illusions about Consolidation." *Journal of Democracy* 7(2): 34–51.

———. 1996b. "Poverty and Inequality in Latin America: Some Political Reflections." Working Paper no. 225, Kellogg Institute for International Studies, University of Notre Dame, Notre Dame, IN, July.

———. 1997. *Contrapuntos: Ensayos escogidos sobre autoritarismo y democratización*. Buenos Aires: Paidós.

———. 1998a. "Horizontal Accountability in New Democracies." *Journal of Democracy* 9(3): 112–27.

———. 1998b. "Poverty and Inequality in Latin America: Some Political Reflections." In Victor E. Tokman and Guillermo O'Donnell, eds., *Poverty and Inequality in Latin America: Issues and New Challenges*, pp. 49–71. Notre Dame, IN: University of Notre Dame Press.

———. 1999a. *Counterpoints: Selected Essays on Authoritarianism and Democratization*. Notre Dame, IN: University of Notre Dame Press.

———. 1999b. "Horizontal Accountability in New Democracies." In Andreas Schedler, Larry Diamond, and Marc Plattner, eds., *The Self-restraining State: Power and Accountability in New Democracies*, pp. 29–51. Boulder, CO: Lynne Rienner.

———. 1999c. "Polyarchies and the (Un)Rule of Law in Latin America: A Partial Conclusion." In Juan Méndez, Paulo Pinheiro and Guillermo O'Donnell, eds., *The (Un)Rule of Law and the Underprivileged in Latin America*, pp. 303–38. Notre Dame, IN: University of Notre Dame Press.

———. 1999d. "A Response to My Commentators." In Andreas Schedler, L. Diamond, and M. F. Plattner, eds., *The Self-Restraining State. Power and Accountability in New Democracies*, pp. 68–71. Boulder, CO: Lynne Rienner.

———. 2001. "Democracy, Law, and Comparative Politics." *Studies in Comparative International Development* 36(1): 7–36.

———. 2002. "Polyarchy and Democratization." Unpublished Jorge Vargas Cullell notes summarizing O'Donnell's thoughts in a Buenos Aires UNDP-PRODDAL Project Meeting.

———. 2003a. "Horizontal Accountability: The Legal Institutionalization of Mistrust." In Scott Mainwaring and Christopher Welna, eds., *Democratic Accountability in Latin America*, pp. 34–54. Oxford: Oxford University Press.

———. 2003b. "Democracia, desarrollo humano y derechos humanos." In Guillermo O'Donnell,

Osvaldo Iazzetta, and Jorge Vargas Cullell, *Democracia, desarrollo humano y ciudadanía. Reflexiones sobre la calidad de la democracia en América Latina*, pp. 25–147. Rosario, Argentina: PNUD—Homo Sapiens Ediciones.

———. 2004a. "Why the Rule of Law Matters." *Journal of Democracy* 15(4): 32–46.

———. 2004b. "Human Development, Human Rights, and Democracy." In Guillermo O'Donnell, Jorge Vargas Cullell, and Osvaldo M. Iazzetta, eds., *The Quality of Democracy: Theory and Applications*, pp. 9–92. Notre Dame, IN: University of Notre Dame Press.

———. 2006. "Notes on Various Accountabilities and their Interrelations." In Enrique Peruzzotti and Catalina Smulovitz, eds., *Enforcing the Rule of Law: Social Accountability in the New Latin American Democracies*, pp. 334–43. Pittsburgh: University of Pittsburgh Press.

———. 2007a. "Horizontal Accountability: the Legal Institutionalization of Mistrust." In Guillermo O'Donnell, ed., *Dissonances: Democratic Critiques of Democracy*, pp. 77–98. Notre Dame, IN: University of Notre Dame Press.

———, ed. 2007b. *Dissonances: Democratic Critiques of Democracy*. Notre Dame, IN: University of Notre Dame Press.

———. 2007c. "Hacia un Estado de y para la democracia." In Rodolfo Mariani, ed., *Democracia/Estado/Ciudadanía: Hacia un Estado de y para la Democracia en América Latina*, pp. 25–63. Lima, Peru: Programa de Naciones Unidas para el Desarrollo.

———. 2010a. *Democracy, Agency and the State: Theory with Comparative Intent*. Oxford: Oxford University Press.

———. 2010b. *Democracia, agencia y estado. Teoría con intención comparativa*. Buenos Aires: Prometeo Libros.

———. 2010c. "Revisando la Democracia Delegativa." *Revista Escenarios Alternativos*. Available at http://www.escenariosalternativos.org/default.asp?nota=3794.

———. 2011. "Nuevas reflexiones acerca de la democracia delegativa." In Guillermo O'Donnell, Osvaldo Iazzetta, and Hugo Quiroga, eds., *Democracia delegativa*, pp. 19–33. Buenos Aires: Prometeo.

O'Donnell, Guillermo, Osvaldo Iazzetta, and Hugo Quiroga, eds. 2011. *Democracia delegativa*. Buenos Aires: Prometeo.

O'Donnell, Guillermo, and Philippe C. Schmitter. 1986. *Transitions from Authoritarian Rule: Tentative Conclusions about Uncertain Democracies*. Baltimore: Johns Hopkins University Press.

O'Donnell, Guillermo, Philippe C. Schmitter, and Laurence Whitehead. 1986. *Transitions from Authoritarian Rule: Prospects for Democracy*. Baltimore: Johns Hopkins University Press.

O'Donnell, Guillermo, Jorge Vargas Cullell, and Osvaldo M. Iazzetta. 2004. *The Quality of Democracy: Theory and Applications*. Notre Dame, IN: Notre Dame University Press.

Offe, Claus. 1984. *Contradictions of the Welfare State*. Cambridge, MA: MIT Press.

———. 1987. "Challenging the Boundaries of Institutional Politics: Social Movements since the 1960s." In Charles Meier, ed., *Changing Boundaries of the Political: Essays on the Evolving Balance between the State and Society, Public and Private in Europe*, pp. 63–106. Cambridge, UK: Cambridge University Press.

Ollier, María Matilde. 2009. *De la revolución a la democracia: Cambios privados, públicos y políticos de la izquierda argentina*. Buenos Aires: Siglo XXI / Universidad Nacional de San Martín.

———. 2011. "Centralidad presidencial y debilidad institucional en las democracias delegativas." In Guillermo O'Donnell, Osvaldo Iazzetta, and Hugo Quiroga, eds., *Democracia delegativa*, pp. 115–36. Buenos Aires: Prometeo.

O'Neill, Kathleen. 2005. *Decentralizing the State: Elections, Parties, and Local Power in the Andes.* New York: Cambridge University Press.

Organisation for Economic Co-operation and Development (OECD). 2010. "Tax Statistics 2010." Available at http://www.oecd.org/tax/tax-policy/oecdtaxdatabase.htm.

——. 2013a. "Income Distribution and Poverty Database." Available at http://stats.oecd.org/Index.aspx?DatasetCode=POVERTY.

——. 2013b. "Economic Outlook Database." Available at http://www.oecd.org/eco/economic outlook.htm.

——. 2013c. "Trade Union Density Database." Available at http://stats.oecd.org/Index.aspx?DataSetCode=UN_DEN.

Ottaway, Marina. 2003. *Democracy Challenged: The Rise of Semi-Authoritarianism.* Washington, DC: Carnegie Endowment for Peace.

Oxhorn, Philip. 2003. "Social Inequality, Civil Society, and the Limits of Citizenship in Latin America." In Susan Eva Eckstein and Timothy P. Wickham-Crowley, eds., *What Justice? Whose Justice? Fighting for Fairness in Latin America*, pp. 35–63. Berkeley: University of California Press.

Pachano, Simón. 2010. "Gobernabilidad democrática y reformas institucionales y políticas en Ecuador." In Martín Tanaka and Francine Jácome, eds., *Desafíos de la gobernabilidad democrática: Reformas político-institucionales y movimientos sociales en la región andina*, pp. 79–111. Lima, Peru: Instituto de Estudios Peruanos.

Panizza, Francisco. 2000. "Beyond 'Delegative Democracy': 'Old Politics' and 'New Economics' in Latin America." *Journal of Latin American Studies* 32(3): 737–63.

Parker, Sophia, ed. 2013. *The Squeezed Middle: The Pressure on Ordinary Workers in America and Britain.* London: Policy Press.

Parry, Geraint, and Michael Moran. 1994. "Introduction: Problems of Democracy and Democratization." In Geraint Parry and Michael Moran, eds., *Democracy and Democratization*, pp. 1–16. London: Routledge.

Parsons, Talcott. 1951. *The Social System.* Glencoe, IL: Free Press.

Paz, Octavio. 1959. *El laberinto en la soledad,* 2nd ed. Mexico, Fondo de Cultura Economia. add place of pub.

Pegram, Thomas. 2011. "The Global Diffusion of National Human Rights Institutions and Their Political Impact in Latin America." PhD diss., Department of Politics and International Relations, University of Oxford.

Pempel, T. J. 1998. *Regime Shift: Comparative Dynamics of the Japanese Political Economy.* Ithaca, NY: Cornell University Press.

Peruzzotti, Enrique. 1993. "The Weimarization of Argentine Politics and State Autonomy." *Thesis Eleven* 34: 126–40.

——. 2001. "The Nature of the New Argentine Democracy. The Delegative Democracy Argument Revisited." *Journal of Latin American Studies* 33(1): 133–55.

——. 2005. "Demanding Accountable Government: Citizens, Politicians, and the Perils of Representative Democracy in Argentina." In Steven Levitsky and María Victoria Murillo, eds., *The Politics of Institutional Weakness. Argentine Democracy*, pp. 229–249. State College: Pennsylvania State University Press.

——. 2006. "Media Scandals and Social Accountability: Assessing the Role of the Senate Scandal in Argentina." In Enrique Peruzzotti and Catalina Smulovitz, eds., *Enforcing the Rule of*

Law: Social Accountability in the New Latin American Democracies, pp. 249–71. Pittsburgh, PA: University of Pittsburgh Press.

———. 2012. "El derecho a un buen Estado: Reflexiones a partir de 'Democracia, agencia y estado.'" *Temas y debates: Revista universitaria de ciencias sociales* 16(24): 75–83.

———. 2013. "Populism in Democratic Times: Populism, Representative Democracy, and the Debate on Democratic Deepening." In Carlos de la Torre and Cynthia Arnson, eds. *Latin American Populism in The Twenty-First Century*, pp. 61–84. Baltimore and Washington: Johns Hopkins University Press / Woodrow Wilson Center Press.

Peruzzotti, Enrique, and Martín Plot. 2013. "Introduction: The Political and Social Thought of Andrew Arato." In Enrique Peruzzotti, and Martín Plot, eds. *Critical Theory and Democracy. Civil Society, Constitutionalism, and Dictatorship in the Democratic Theory of Andrew Arato*, pp. 1–26. New York: Routledge.

Peruzzotti, Enrique, and Catalina Smulovitz, eds. 2006. *Enforcing the Rule of Law: Social Accountability in the New Latin American Democracies*. Pittsburgh, PA: University of Pittsburgh Press.

Pevehouse, Jon C. 2002. "With a Little Help from My Friends? Regional Organizations and the Consolidation of Democracy." *American Journal of Political Science* 46(3): 611–26.

———. 2005. *Democracy from Above? Regional Organizations and Democratization*. Cambridge, UK: Cambridge University Press.

Pew Research Center. 2012. "Public Views of Inequality, Fairness and Wall Street." Available at http://www.pewresearch.org/daily-number/public-views-of-inequality-fairness-and-wall-street.

Pierson, Paul. 1994. *Dismantling the Welfare State? Reagan, Thatcher, and the Politics of Retrenchment*. New York: Cambridge University Press.

———. 2000. "Increasing Returns, Path Dependence, and the Study of Politics." *American Political Science Review* 94(2): 251–67.

———. 2004. *Politics in Time: History, Institutions, and Social Analysis*. Princeton: Princeton University Press.

Piketty, Thomas, and Emmanuel Saez. 2003. "Economic Inequality in the United States, 1913–1998." *Quarterly Journal of Economics* 118(1): 1–39.

———. 2012. "Top Incomes and the Great Recession: Recent Evolutions and Policy Implications." Paper presented at the thirteenth Jacques Polak Annual Research Conference, Washington, DC, November 8.

Pistor, Katharina, Antara Haldar, and Amrit Amirapu. 2008. "Social Norms, Rule of Law, and Gender Equality." Paper read at World Justice Forum conference, July 2–5, Vienna, Austria.

Poe, Steven C., and C. Neal Tate. 1994. "Repression of Human Rights to Personal Integrity in the 1980s: A Global Analysis." *American Political Science Review* 88(4): 853–72.

Polanyi, Karl. 1944. *The Great Transformation*. New York: Rinehart.

Portantiero, Juan Carlos. 1987. "La transición entre la confrontación y el acuerdo." In José Nun and Juan Carlos Portantiero, eds., *Ensayos sobre la transición democrática en la Argentina*, pp. 257–93. Buenos Aires: Puntosur.

Potter, Anne L. 1981. "The Failure of Democracy in Argentina 1916–1930: An Institutional Perspective." *Journal of Latin American Studies* 13(1): 83–109.

Powell, Jonathan, and Clayton Thyne. 2011. "Global Instances of Coups from 1950 to 2010: A New Dataset." *Journal of Peace Research* 48(2): 249–59.

Power, Timothy J., and Nancy R. Powers. 1988. "Issues in the Consolidation of Democracy in

Latin America and Southern Europe in Comparative Perspective: A Rapporteurs' Report." Working Paper no. 113, Kellogg Institute for International Studies, University of Notre Dame.

Prasad, Naren. 2006. "Privatisation Results: Private Sector Participation in Water Services after 15 Years." *Development Policy Review* 24(6): 669–92.

Pridham, Geoffrey. 1991. "The Politics of the European Community, Transnational Networks and Democratic Transition in Southern Europe." In Geoffrey Pridham, ed., *Encouraging Democracy: The International Context of Regime Transition in Southern Europe*, pp. 212–45. Leicester, UK: Leicester University Press.

Programa de Naciones Unidas para el Desarrollo (PNUD). 2004. *Informe sobre el Desarrollo Democrático en América Latina*. Mexico City, Mexico: Santillana.

Programa Estado de la Nación. 2001. *Auditoría ciudadana de la calidad de la democracia*. San José, Costa Rica: Editorama.

———. 2010. *Decimoséptimo Informe Estado de la Nación en desarrollo humano sostenible*. San José, Costa Rica: El Programa.

———. 2011a. *Cuarto Informe Estado de la Región Centroamericana en desarrollo humano sostenible 2010*. San José, Costa Rica: Estado de la Nación.

———. 2011b. *Cuarto Informe sobre el estado de la región en desarrollo humano en Centroamérica y Panamá*. San José, Costa Rica: Imprenta Gilá.

Przeworski, Adam. 1985. *Capitalism and Social Democracy*. New York: Cambridge University Press.

———. 1986. "Some Problems in the Study of Transitions to Democracy." In Guillermo O'Donnell, Philippe C. Schmitter, and Laurence Whitehead, eds., *Transitions from Authoritarian Rule: Comparative Perspectives*, pp. 47–63. Baltimore: Johns Hopkins University Press.

———. 1991. *Democracy and the Market: Political and Economic Reforms in Eastern Europe and Latin America*. Cambridge, UK: Cambridge University Press.

———. 1999. "Minimalist Conception of Democracy: A Defense." In Ian Shapiro and Casiano Hacker-Cordón, eds., *Democracy's Value*, pp. 23–55. Cambridge, UK: Cambridge University Press.

———. 2003. "Why Do Political Parties Obey Results Of Elections?" In José M. Maravall and Adam Przeworski, eds. *Democracy and the Rule of Law*, pp. 114–44. Cambridge, UK: Cambridge University Press.

———. 2005. "Democracy as an Equilibrium." *Public Choice* 123(3–4): 253–73.

———. 2006. "Social Accountability in Latin America and Beyond." In Enrique Peruzzotti and Catalina Smulovitz, eds., *Enforcing the Rule of Law: Social Accountability in the New Latin American Democracies*, pp. 323–33. Pittsburgh, PA: University of Pittsburgh Press.

———. 2009. "Conquered or Granted? A History of Suffrage Extensions." *British Journal of Political Science* 39(2): 291–321.

———. 2010. *Democracy and the Limits of Self-Government*. New York: Cambridge University Press.

Przeworski, Adam, Michael E. Alvarez, José Antonio Cheibub, and Fernando Limongi. 1996. "What Makes Democracies Endure?" *Journal of Democracy* 7(1): 39–55.

———. 2000. *Democracy and Development: Political Institutions and Well-Being in the World, 1950–1990*. Cambridge, UK: Cambridge University Press.

Przeworski, Adam, and Fernando Limongi. 1997. "Modernization: Theory and Facts." *World Politics* 49(2): 155–83.

Przeworski, Adam, and John Sprague. 1986. *Paper Stones: A History of Electoral Socialism*. Chicago: University of Chicago Press.

Przeworski, Adam, Susan C. Stokes, and Bernard Manin, eds. 1999. *Democracy, Accountability, and Representation*. New York: Cambridge University Press.

Quiroga, Hugo. 2011. "Parecidos de familia. La democracia delegativa y el decisionismo democrático." In Guillermo O'Donnell, Osvaldo Iazzetta, and Hugo Quiroga, eds., *Democracia delegativa*, pp. 35–52. Buenos Aires: Prometeo.

Ragin, Charles C. 1987. *The Comparative Method: Moving Beyond Qualitative and Quantitative Strategies*. Berkeley: University of California Press.

———. 2000. *Fuzzy Set Social Science*. Chicago: University of Chicago Press.

Rapoport Center for Human Rights and Justice. 2007. "Unfulfilled Promises and Persistent Obstacles to the Realization of the Rights of Afro-Colombians." Austin: Bernard and Audre Rapoport Center for Human Rights and Justice, University of Texas School of Law.

———. 2008. "Between the Law and Their Land: Afro-Brazilian Quilombo Communities' Struggle for Land Rights." Austin: Bernard and Audre Rapoport Center for Human Rights and Justice, University of Texas School of Law.

Rawls, John. 1971. *A Theory of Justice*. Cambridge, MA: Belknap Press.

Raz, Joseph. 1979. *The Authority of Law: Essays on Law and Morality*. Oxford: Clarendon Press.

———. 1990. *Authority*. New York: New York University Press.

Reis, Fábio Wanderley, and Guillermo O'Donnell. 1988. *A democracia no Brasil: dilemas e perspectivas*. São Paulo: Vértice.

Remmer, Karen. 1996. "The Sustainability of Political Democracy: Lessons from South America." *Comparative Political Studies* 29(6): 611–34.

———. 2008. "The Politics of Institutional Change: Electoral Reform in Latin America, 1978–2002." *Party Politics* 14(1): 5–30.

Reuter, Ora J., and Jennifer Gandhi. 2011. "Economic Performance and Elite Defection from Hegemonic Parties." *British Journal of Political Science* 41(1): 83–110.

Rich, Frank. 2010. "The Billionaires Bankrolling the Tea Party." *New York Times*, August 28.

Riedl, Rachel Beatty. 2014. *Authoritarian Origins of Democratic Party Systems in Africa*. New York: Cambridge University Press.

Ríos-Figueroa, Julio, and Matthew M. Taylor. 2006. "Institutional Determinants of the Judicialisation of Policy in Brazil and Mexico." *Journal of Latin American Studies* 38(4): 739–66.

Roberts, Andrew. 2010. *The Quality of Democracy in Eastern Europe: Public Preferences and Policy Reforms*. New York: Cambridge University Press.

Roberts, Kenneth M. 1995. "Neoliberalism and the Transformation of Populism in Latin America: The Peruvian Case." *World Politics* 48(1): 82–116.

———. 1998. *Deepening Democracy? The Modern Left and Social Movements in Chile and Peru*. Stanford: Stanford University Press.

———. 2012. "The Politics of Inequality and Redistribution in Latin America's Post-adjustment Era." Working Paper no. 2012/08, United Nations University-World Institute for Development Economics Research (UNU-WIDER) (Jan.).

Roberts, Kenneth M., and Erik Wibbels. 1999. "Party Systems and Electoral Volatility in Latin America: A Test of Economic, Institutional, and Structural Explanations." *American Political Science Review* 93(3): 575–90.

Rodrigues, João. 2012. "Where to Draw the Line between the State and Markets? Institutionalist Elements in Hayek's Neoliberal Political Economy." *Journal of Economic Issues* 46(4): 1007–34.

Romaña Palacios, Nohemy, Claudia Lorena Geovo Bonilla, Francisco José Paz Zapata, and Eliecer Banguero González. 2010. *Titulación colectiva para comunidades negras en Colombia*. Bogotá: Instituto de Estudios para el Desarrollo y la Paz (INDEPAZ).

Rosenbluth, Frances, and Gretchen Helmke. 2009. "The Politics of Judicial Reform." In Margaret Levi, ed., *Annual Review of Political Science*, 12: 345–66.

Ross, Michael L. 2001. "Does Oil Hinder Democracy?" *World Politics* 53(3): 325–61.

———. 2006. "Is Democracy Good for the Poor?" *American Journal of Political Science* 50(4): 860–74.

———. 2012. *The Oil Curse: How Petroleum Wealth Shapes the Development of Nations*. Princeton: Princeton University Press.

Rouquié, Alain. 1982a. *Poder militar y sociedad política en la Argentina, hasta 1943*. Buenos Aires: Emecé.

———. 1982b. *Poder militar y sociedad política en la Argentina, 1943–1973*. Buenos Aires: Emecé.

Rueschemeyer, Dietrich, Evelyne Huber Stephens, and John D. Stephens. 1992. *Capitalist Development and Democracy*. Chicago: University of Chicago Press.

Rustow, Dankwart A. 1970. "Transitions to Democracy: Toward a Dynamic Model." *Comparative Politics* 2 (3): 337–63.

Samuels, David. 2003. *Ambition, Federalism, and Legislative Politics in Brazil*. New York: Cambridge University Press.

———. 2004. "Presidentialism and Accountability for the Economy in Comparative Perspective." *American Political Science Review* 98(3): 425–36.

Samuels, David, and Fernando Luiz Abrucio. 2000. "Federalism and Democratic Transitions: The 'New' Politics of the Governors in Brazil." *Publius: The Journal of Federalism* 30 no. 2 (spring): 43–62.

Samuels, David, and Richard Snyder. 2001. "The Value of a Vote: Malapportionment in Comparative Perspective." *British Journal of Political Science* 31(3): 651–71.

Sanchez, Omar. 2009. "Party Non-systems: A Conceptual Innovation." *Party Politics* 15(4): 487–520.

Santos, Alvaro. 2006. "The World Bank's Uses of the 'Rule of Law' Promise in Economic Development." In David Trubek and Alvaro Santos, eds., *The New Law and Economic Development: A Critical Appraisal*, pp. 253–302. New York: Cambridge University Press.

Santos, Wanderley Guilherme dos. 1986. *Sessenta e Quatro: Anatomia da Crise*. São Paulo: Vértice.

Sartori, Giovanni. 1970. "Concept Misformation in Comparative Politics." *American Political Science Review* 64(4): 1033–53.

———. 1976. *Parties and Party Systems: A Framework for Analysis*. New York: Cambridge University Press.

———. 1987. *The Theory of Democracy Revisited*. Chatham, NJ: Chatham House.

Saward, Michael. 2009. "Authorisation and Authenticity: Representation and the Unelected." *Journal of Political Philosophy* 17(1): 1–22.

Sawhill, Isabel, and John Morton. 2007. "Economic Mobility: Is the American Dream Alive and Well?" Economic Mobility Project. Available at http://www.brookings.edu/papers/2007/05useconomics_morton.aspx.

Schattschneider, Elmer E. 1960. *The Semisovereign People: A Realist's View of Democracy in America*. New York: Holt, Rinehart and Winston.

Schedler, Andreas. 1998. "What Is Democratic Consolidation?" *Journal of Democracy* 9(2): 91–107.

———. 2006. "The Logic of Electoral Authoritarianism." In Andreas Schedler, ed., *Electoral Authoritarianism. The Dynamics of Unfree Competition*, pp. 1–23. Boulder, CO: Lynne Rienner.

Schedler, Andreas, Larry Diamond, and Marc C. Plattner, eds. 1999. *The Self-Restraining State: Power and Accountability in New Democracies*. Boulder, CO: Lynne Rienner.

Schelling, Thomas C. 1978. *Micromotives and Macrobehavior*. New York: Norton.

Schlesinger, Joseph. 1991. *Political Parties and the Winning of Office*. Chicago: University of Chicago Press.

Schmidt, Gregory D. 2000. "Delegative Democracy in Peru? Fujimori's 1995 Landslide and the Prospects for 2000." *Journal of Interamerican Studies and World Affairs* 42(1): 99–132.

Schmitter, Philippe. 1971. *Interest Conflict and Political Change in Brazil*. Stanford: Stanford University Press.

———. 1972. *Autonomy or Dependence as Regional Integration Outcomes*. Berkeley: University of California Press.

———. 1975. "Liberation by Golpe: Retrospective Thoughts on the Demise of Authoritarian Rule in Portugal." *Armed Forces and Society* 2(1): 5–33.

———. 1983. "Democratic Theory and Neo-corporatist Practice." *Social Research* 50(4): 885–928.

———. 1992. "The Consolidation of Democracy and the Representation of Social Groups." *American Behavioral Scientist* 35(4/5): 422–49.

———. 1996. "The Influence of the International Context upon the Choice of National Institutions and Policies in Neo-democracies." In Laurence Whitehead, ed., *The International Dimensions of Democratization: Europe and the Americas*, pp. 26–54. Oxford: Oxford University Press.

———. 1999. "Limits of Horizontal Accountability." In Andreas Schedler, ed., *The Self-Restraining State: Power and Accountability in New Democracies*, pp. 59–62. Boulder, CO: Lynne Rienner.

———. 2000. *How to Democratize the European Union: And Why Bother?* Lanham, MD: Rowman & Littlefield.

———. 2001. "Parties Are Not What They Once Were." In Larry Diamond and Richard Gunther, eds., *Political Parties and Democracy*, pp. 67–89. Baltimore: Johns Hopkins University Press.

———. 2006. "The Political Impact of European Monetary Union upon 'Domestic' and 'Continental' Democracy." In Robert M. Fishman and Anthony M. Messina, eds., *The Year of the Euro: The Cultural, Social, and Political Import of Europe's Common Currency*, pp. 256–71. Notre Dame, IN: University of Notre Dame Press.

———. 2008. "A Crisis of Real Existing Democracy or a Crisis of Representation? Or a Crisis of the Channels of Representation? Or a Crisis of One Channel of Representation?" Paper prepared for the workshop Rethinking Representation: A North-South Dialogue, Bellagio Study and Conference Center, 30 September to 3 October.

———. 2011. "The Future of 'Real-Existing' Democracy." Conference paper, Central European University, January 10. Available at: http://politicalscience.ceu.hu/sites/default/files/field_attachment/event/node-19937/future-of-democracy.pdf.

Schmitter, Philippe, and Imco Brouwer. 1999. "Conceptualizing, Researching and Evaluating Democracy Promotion and Protection." European University Institute Working Paper, SPS no. 99/9. Available at: http://cadmus.eui.eu/bitstream/handle/1814/309/sps99_9.pdf?sequence=1.

Schmitter, Philippe, and Terry L. Karl. 1991. "What Democracy Is... and Is Not." *Journal of Democracy* 2(3): 75–88.

———. 1992. "The Types of Democracy That Are Emerging in Southern and Eastern Europe and South and Central America." In Peter Volten, ed. *Bound to Change: Consolidating Democracy in Central Europe*, pp. 42–68. New York: Institute for East-West Security Studies.

Schmitter, Philippe C., and Alexandre Trechsel. 2004. *The Future of Democracy in Europe. Trends, Analyses and Reforms*. Strasbourg, France: Council of Europe Publishing.

Schneider, Ben, and Blanca Heredia, eds. 2003. *Reinventing Leviathan: The Politics of Administrative Reform in Developing Countries*. Coral Gables, FL: North-South Center Press.

Schrank, Andrew, and Michael Piore. 2007. *Norms, Regulations, and Labor Standards in Central America*. CEPAL, Serie Estudios y Perspectivas No. 77. Mexico City, Mexico: CEPAL.

Schumpeter, Joseph. 1947. *Capitalism, Socialism, and Democracy*. New York: Harper and Brothers.

———. 1950. *Capitalism, Socialism, and Democracy*. New York: Harper and Brothers.

Seawright, Jason. 2012. *Party-System Collapse: The Roots of Crisis in Peru and Venezuela*. Stanford: Stanford University Press.

Seery, John E. 2011. *Too Young to Run? A Proposal for an Age Amendment to the U.S. Constitution*. University Park: Pennsylvania State University Press.

Seligson, Mitchell, and John Booth, eds. 1995. *Elections and Democracy in Central America, Revisited*. Chapel Hill: University of North Carolina Press.

Sen, Amartya. 1985. *Commodities and Capabilities*. Amsterdam: Elsevier Science Publishers.

———. 1999. *Development as Freedom*. New York: Knopf.

———. 2009. *The Idea of Justice*. Cambridge, MA: Belknap Press of Harvard University Press.

Serra, José. 1979. "Three Mistaken Theses Regarding the Connection between Industrialization and Authoritarian Regimes." In David Collier, ed., *The New Authoritarianism in Latin America*, pp. 129–45. Princeton: Princeton University Press.

Shammas, Carole. 1993. "A New Look at Long-Term Trends in Wealth Inequality in the United States." *American Historical Review* 98(2): 412–31.

Shapiro, Ian. 2003. *The State of Democratic Theory*. Princeton: Princeton University Press.

Shaw, Hannah, and Chad Stone. 2010. "Tax Data Show Richest 1 Percent Took a Hit in 2008, but Income Remained Highly Concentrated at the Top: Recent Gains of Bottom 90 Percent Wiped Out." Center on Budget and Policy Priorities, Washington, DC. Available at http://www.cbpp.org/files/10–21–10inc.pdf.

Shugart, Matthew S., and John M. Carey. 1992. *Presidents and Assemblies: Constitutional Design and Electoral Dynamics*. Cambridge, UK: Cambridge University Press.

Sieder, Rachel, ed. 2002. *Multiculturalism in Latin America: Indigenous Rights, Diversity, and Democracy*. Houndmills, UK: Palgrave Macmillan.

Simmons, Beth, Frank Dobbin, and Geoffrey Garrett, eds. 2008. *The Global Diffusion of Markets and Democracy*. Cambridge, UK: Cambridge University Press.

Simmons, Beth, and Zachary Elkins. 2004. "The Globalization of Liberalization: Policy Diffusion in the International Political Economy." *American Political Science Review* 98(1): 171–89.

Skidmore, Thomas. 1967. *Politics in Brazil: An Experiment in Democracy, 1930–1964*. New York: Oxford University Press.

Skinner, Quentin. 1998. *Liberty before Liberalism*. Cambridge, UK: Cambridge University Press.

Skocpol, Theda. 1992. *Protecting Soldiers and Mothers: The Origins of Social Policy in the United States*. Cambridge, MA: Belknap Press of Harvard University Press.

———. 2003a. *Diminished Democracy: From Membership to Management in American Civic Life*. Norman: University of Oklahoma Press.

———. 2003b. "Doubly Engaged Social Science: The Promise of Comparative Historical Analysis." In James Mahoney and Dietrich Rueschemeyer, eds., *Comparative Historical Analysis in the Social Sciences,* pp. 407–28. Cambridge, UK: Cambridge University Press.

Smith, Adam. 1776. *An Inquiry into the Nature and Causes of the Wealth of Nations,* vol. 1. London: Gale, Sabin Americana.

Smith, Alastair. 2008. "The Perils of Unearned Income." *Journal of Politics* 70(3): 780–93.

Smith, Benjamin. 2004. "Oil Wealth and Regime Survival in the Developing World, 1960–1999." *American Journal of Political Science* 48(2): 232–46.

Smith, Peter H. 1978. "The Breakdown of Democracy in Argentina, 1916–30." In Juan J. Linz and Alfred Stepan, eds., *The Breakdown of Democratic Regimes: Latin America,* pp. 3–27. Baltimore: Johns Hopkins University Press.

Smulovitz, Catalina. 1988. *Oposición y gobierno: Los años de Frondizi,* vol. 2. Buenos Aires: Centro Editor de América Latina.

Smulovitz, Catalina, and Enrique Peruzzotti. 2000. "Societal Accountability in Latin America." *Journal of Democracy* 11(4): 147–58.

———. 2003. "Societal and Horizontal Controls: Two Examples of a Fruitful Relationship." In Scott Mainwaring and Christopher Welna, eds., *Democratic Accountability in Latin America,* pp. 309–31. Oxford: Oxford University Press.

Snyder, Richard. 2001. "Scaling Down: The Subnational Comparative Method." *Studies in Comparative International Development* 36(1): 93–110.

Sobrevilla Perea, Natalia. 2010. "The Enduring Power of Patronage in Peruvian Elections: Quispicanchis, 1860." *The Americas* 67(1): 31–55.

Sokoloff, Kenneth, and Eric Zolt. 2006. "Inequality and Taxation: Evidence from the Americas on How Inequality may Influence Tax Institutions." *Tax Law Review* 59(2): 167–241.

Somers, Margaret. 2008. *Genealogies of Citizenship: Markets, Statelessness, and the Right to Have Rights.* Cambridge, UK: Cambridge University Press.

Sousa, Mariana. 2007. "A Brief Overview of Judicial Reform in Latin America: Objectives, Challenges, and Accomplishments." In Eduardo Lora, ed., *The State of State Reform in Latin America,* pp. 87–121. Washington, DC: Inter-American Development Bank.

Spiller, Pablo, and Mariano Tommasi. 2007. *The Institutional Foundations of Public Policy: A Transactions Theory and an Application to Argentina.* Cambridge, UK: Cambridge University Press.

Stanley, Ruth. 2005. "Controlling the Police in Buenos Aires: A Case Study of Horizontal and Social Accountability." *Bulletin of Latin American Research* 24 (1): 71–91.

Starr, Harvey. 1991. "Democratic Dominoes: Diffusion Approaches to the Spread of Democracy in the International System." *Journal of Conflict Resolution* 35(2): 356–81.

Starr, Harvey, and Christina Lindborg. 2003. "Democratic Dominoes Revisited: The Hazards of Governmental Transitions, 1974–1996." *Journal of Conflict Resolution* 47(4): 490–519.

Stein, Ernesto, Mariano Tommasi, Koldo Echebarría, Eduardo Lora, and Mark Payne. 2006. *The Politics of Policies: Economic and Social Progress in Latin America, 2006 Report.* Cambridge, MA: Inter-American Development Bank and David Rockefeller Center for Latin American Studies / Harvard University Press.

Steinmo, Sven, Kathleen Thelen, and Frank Longstreth, eds. 1992. *Historical Institutionalism in Comparative Politics: State, Society, and Economy.* New York: Cambridge University Press.

Stepan, Alfred. 1971. *The Military in Politics: Changing Patterns in Brazil.* Princeton: Princeton University Press.

————. 1978. "Political Leadership and Regime Breakdown: Brazil." In Juan J. Linz and Alfred Stepan, eds., *The Breakdown of Democratic Regimes: Latin America*, pp. 110–37. Baltimore: Johns Hopkins University Press.

————. 1986. "Paths toward Redemocratization: Theoretical and Comparative Considerations." In Guillermo O'Donnell, Philippe C. Schmitter, and Laurence Whitehead, eds., *Transitions from Authoritarian Rule: Prospects for Democracy*, pp. 64–84. Baltimore: Johns Hopkins University Press.

————. 1988. *Rethinking Military Politics: Brazil and the Southern Cone*. Princeton: Princeton University Press.

Stepan, Alfred, and Juan J. Linz. 2011. "Comparative Perspectives on Inequality and the Quality of Democracy in the United States." *Perspectives on Politics* 9(4): 841–56.

Stepan, Alfred, and Cindy Skach. 1994. "Presidentialism and Parliamentarism in Comparative Perspective." In Juan J. Linz and Arturo Valenzuela, eds., *The Failure of Presidential Democracy*, pp. 119–36. Baltimore: Johns Hopkins University Press.

Stiglitz, Joseph. 2009. "Interpreting the Causes of the Great Recession of 2008." BIS Annual Conference, Basel, Switzerland, 25–26 June.

————. 2012. *The Price of Inequality: How Today's Divided Society Endangers Our Future*. New York: Norton.

Stockman, David A. 1987. *The Triumph of Politics: The Inside Story of the Reagan Revolution*. New York: Avon.

————. 2010. "Four Deformations of the Apocalypse," *New York Times,* July 31.

Stokes, Susan C. 1999. "What Do Policy Switches Tell Us about Democracy?" In Adam Przeworski, Susan C. Stokes, and Bernard Manin, eds., *Democracy, Accountability, and Representation*, pp. 98–130. New York: Cambridge University Press.

Streeck, Wolfgang. 2011. "The Crises of Democratic Capitalism." *New Left Review* 71 (Sept.–Oct.): 5–29.

Streeck, Wolfgang, and Kathleen Thelen. 2005. "Introduction: Institutional Change in Advanced Political Economies." In Wolfgang Streeck and Kathleen Thelen, eds. *Beyond Continuity: Institutional Change in Advanced Political Economies*, pp. 1–39. New York: Oxford University Press.

Sunstein, Cass, and Stephen Holmes. 1999. *The Cost of Rights: Why Liberty Depends on Taxes*. New York: Norton.

Svolik, Milan. 2008. "Authoritarian Reversals and Democratic Consolidation." *American Political Science Review* 102(2): 153–68.

————. 2009. "Power Sharing and Leadership Dynamics in Authoritarian Regimes." *American Journal of Political Science* 53(2): 477–94.

Swedberg, Richard. 2003. *Principles of Economic Sociology*. Princeton: Princeton University Press.

Swidler, Ann. 1986. "Culture in Action: Symbols and Strategies." *American Sociological Review* 51(2): 273–86.

Talpien, Julien. 2012. *Schools of Democracy: How Ordinary Citizens (Sometimes) Become Competent in Participatory Budgeting Institutions*. Essex, UK: European Consortium for Political Research.

Taylor, Charles. 1994. "The Politics of Recognition." In Amy Gutmann, ed., *Multiculturalism: Examining the Politics of Recognition*, pp. 25–73. Princeton: Princeton University Press.

Taylor, Lucy. 2010. "Re-founding Representation: Wider, Broader, Closer, Deeper." *Political Studies Review* 8(2): 169–79.

Teixeira, Ruy, and John Halpin. 2012. "The Return of the Obama Coalition." Washington, DC: Center for American Progress. Available at http://www.americanprogress.org/issues/progressive-movement/news/2012/11/08/44348/the-return-of-the-obama-coalition/.

Teorell, Jan. 2010. *Determinants of Democratization. Explaining Regime Change in the World, 1972–2006.* Cambridge, UK: Cambridge University Press.

Teorell, Jan, Nicholas Charron, Marcus Samanni, Sören Holmberg and Bo Rothstein. 2011. "The Quality of Government" Dataset, version 6 April 2011. Gothenburg, Sweden: The Quality of Government Institute, University of Gothenburg. Available at http://www.qog.pol.gu.se.

Thedieck. Franz, and Eduardo Buller. 1995. "Descentralización de la administración en el Perú." In Sociedad Alemana de Cooperación Técnica/Programa de Gestión Urbana, ed., *Descentralizar en América Latina*, pp. 195–236. Quito, Ecuador: Sociedad Alemana de Cooperación Técnica / Programa de Gestión Urbana.

Thelen, Kathleen. 1999. "Historical Institutionalism in Comparative Politics." *Annual Review of Political Science* 2 (June): 369–404.

———. 2004. *How Institutions Evolve: The Political Economy of Skills in Germany, Britain, the United States, and Japan.* New York: Cambridge University Press.

Thelen, Kathleen, and Sven Steinmo. 1992. "Historical Institutionalism in Comparative Politics." In Sven Steinmo, Kathleen Thelen, and Frank Longstreth, eds. *Historical Institutionalism in Comparative Politics: State, Society, and Economy*, pp. 1–32. New York: Cambridge University Press.

Thies, Cameron G. 2005. "War, Rivalry, and State Building in Latin America.*" American Journal of Political Science* 49(3): 451–65.

Thies, Michael. 1998. "When Will Pork Leave the Farm? Institutional Bias in Japan and the United States." *Legislative Studies Quarterly* 23(4): 467–92.

Tilly, Charles. 1975. *The Formation of National States in Western Europe.* Princeton: Princeton University Press.

Tocqueville, Alexis de. 1835. *Democracy in America*, vol. 1., trans. Henry Reeve. London: Saunders and Otley.

Tokman, Victor, and Guillermo O'Donnell, eds. 1998. *Poverty and Inequality in Latin America: Issues and Answers.* Notre Dame, IN: University of Notre Dame Press.

Tomaskovic-Devey, Donald, and Ken-Hou Lin. 2011. "Income Dynamics, Economic Rents and the Financialization of the US Economy." *American Sociological Review* 76(4): 538–59.

Torfason, Magnus T., and Paul Ingram. 2010. "The Global Rise of Democracy: A Network Account." *American Sociological Review* 75(3): 355–77.

Trebilcock, Michael J., and Ronald J. Daniels. 2008. *Rule of Law Reform and Development: Charting the Fragile Path of Progress.* Cheltenham, UK: Edward Elgar.

Treier, Shawn, and Simon Jackman. 2008. "Democracy as a Latent Variable." *American Journal of Political Science* 52(1): 201–17.

Truman, David. 1951. *The Governmental Process: Political Interest and Public Opinion.* New York: Knopf.

Tyler, Tom R. 1990. *Why People Obey the Law.* New Haven: Yale University Press.

Uggen, Christopher, and Jeff Manza. 2002. "Democratic Contraction? Political Consequences of Felon Disenfranchisement in the United States." *American Sociological Review* 67(6): 777–803.

Uildriks, Niels, and Nelia Tello Peon, eds. 2010. *Mexico's Unrule of Law: Implementing Human Rights in Police and Judicial Reform under Democratization.* Lanham, MD: Lexington Books.

Ulfelder, Jay. 2007. "Natural-Resource Wealth and the Survival of Autocracy." *Comparative Political Studies* 40(8): 995–1018.

United Nations. 1948. "Universal Declaration of Human Rights." Available at http://www.un.org/en/documents/udhr/index.shtml.

UN Committee on the Elimination of Racial Discrimination (CERD). 2003. "UN Committee on the Elimination of Racial Discrimination: State Party Report, Brazil." Available at http://www.unhcr.org/refworld/publisher,CERD,,BRA,403e0af14,0.html.

United Nations Development Programme (UNDP). 2004. *Democracy in Latin America: Toward A Citizens' Democracy.* New York: UNDP.

United States Congress Joint Economic Committee. 2010. "Income Inequality and the Great Recession." Report by the U.S. Congress Joint Economic Committee, September.

United States Senate. 2008. "Tax Haven Banks and U.S. Tax Compliance." Staff Report, Permanent Subcommittee on Investigations, July 17.

Useem, Michael. 1984. *The Inner Circle: Large Corporations and the Rise of Business Political Activity in the U.S. and U.K.* New York: Oxford University Press.

Valenzuela, Arturo. 1978. *The Breakdown of Democratic Regimes: Chile.* Baltimore: Johns Hopkins University Press.

Valenzuela, J. Samuel. 1992. "Democratic Consolidation in Post-Transitional Settings: Notion, Process, and Facilitating Conditions." In Scott Mainwaring, Guillermo O'Donnell, and J. Samuel Valenzuela, eds., *Issues in Democratic Consolidation: The New South American Democracies in Comparative Perspective*, pp. 57–104. Notre Dame, IN: University of Notre Dame Press.

Van Cott, Donna. 2005. *From Movements to Parties in Latin America: The Evolution of Ethnic Politics.* Cambridge, UK: Cambridge University Press.

Vanhanen, Tatu. 1997. *Prospects of Democracy: A Study of 172 Countries.* New York: Psychology Press.

———. 2003. *Democratization: A Comparative Analysis of 170 Countries.* New York: Routledge.

Vargas Cullell, Jorge. 2004. "Democracy and the Quality of Democracy: Empirical Findings and Methodological and Theoretical Issues Drawn from the Citizen Audit." In Guillermo O'Donnell, Jorge Vargas Cullell, and Osvaldo Iazzetta, *The Quality of Democracy: Theory and Applications*, pp. 123–190. Notre Dame, IN: University of Notre Dame Press.

———. 2008. "Democratización y calidad de la democracia." In Oscar Ochoa Gómez, ed., *La reforma del Estado y la calidad de la democracia en México*, pp. 11–41. Mexico City. Mexico: Miguel Ángel Porrúa—Instituto Tecnológico y de Estudios Superiores de Monterrey.

———. 2012. *El Leviatán concebido: Ensayo sobre la configuración del Estado en Costa Rica.* San José, Costa Rica: Centro de Investigación y Adiestramiento Político Administrativo.

Véliz, Claudio. 1980. *The Centralist Tradition of Latin America.* Princeton: Princeton University Press.

Viola, Eduardo. 1982. "Democracia e Autoritarismo na Argentina Contemporânea." PhD diss., University of São Paulo.

Vogel, David. 1989. *Fluctuating Fortunes: The Political Power of Business in America.* New York: Basic Books.

Waisman, Carlos H. 1987. *Reversal of Development in Argentina: Postwar Counterrevolutionary Policies and Their Structural Consequences.* Princeton: Princeton University Press.

———. 1989. "Argentina: Autarkic Industrialization and Illegitimacy." In Larry Diamond, Juan J. Linz, and Seymour Martin Lipset, eds., *Democracy in Developing Countries: Latin America*, pp. 59–109. Boulder, CO: Lynne Rienner.

Walker, Ignacio. 1990. *Socialismo y democracia: Chile y Europa en perspectiva comparada.* Santiago, Chile: CIEPLAN/Hachette.

Wallis, John J. 2010. "Lessons from the Political Economy of the New Deal." *Oxford Review of Economic Policy* 26(3): 442–62.

Walsh, Shannon Drysdale. 2008. "Engendering Social Justice: Strengthening State Responses to Violence Against Women in Central America." *Studies in Social Justice* 1(2): 48–66.

Wampler, Brian. 2007. *Participatory Budgeting in Brazil: Contestation, Cooperation, and Accountability.* University Park: Pennsylvania State University Press.

Weber, Max. 1946. *From Max Weber: Essays in Sociology,* ed., H. H. Gerth and C. Wright Mills. New York: Oxford University Press.

———. 1949. *The Methodology of the Social Sciences.* New York: Free Press.

———. (1922) 1977. *Economía y Sociedad.* Mexico City, Mexico: Fondo de Cultura Económica.

Weffort, Francisco C. 1984. *Por Que Democracia?* São Paulo: Brasiliense.

———. 1989. "Why Democracy?" In Alfred Stepan, ed., *Democratizing Brazil: Problems of Transition and Consolidation,* pp. 327–50. Oxford: Oxford University Press.

———. 1993. *¿Cuál Democracia?* San José, Costa Rica: FLACSO.

Weingast, Barry. 2005. "Persuasion, Preference Change, and Critical Junctures: The Microfoundations of Macroscopic Concept." In Ira Katznelson and Barry Weingast, eds. *Preferences and Situations. Points of Intersection between Historical and Rational Choice Institutionalism,* pp. 161–84. New York: Russell Sage Foundation.

———. 2008. "Why Developing Countries Prove So Resistant to the Rule of Law." Paper presented at the University of Texas Comparative Politics Speaker Series, Austin, Texas, December 4.

Weir, Stuart, and David Beetham. 1998. *Political Power and Democratic Control in Britain.* London: Routledge.

Wejnert, Barbara. 2005. "Diffusion, Development, and Democracy, 1800–1999." *American Sociological Review* 70(1): 53–81.

Weldon, Jeffrey. 1997. "The Political Sources of Presidencialismo in Mexico." In Scott Mainwaring and Mathew Shugart, eds., *Presidentialism and Democracy in Latin America,* pp. 225–58. New York: Cambridge University Press.

Welzel, Christian. 2009. "Theories of Democratization." In Christian Haerpfer, Patrick Bernhagen, Ronald Inglehart, and Christian Welzel, eds, *Democratization,* pp. 74–91. Oxford: Oxford University Press.

Weyland, Kurt. 1996. *Democracy without Equity: Failures of Reform in Brazil.* Pittsburgh, PA: University of Pittsburgh Press.

———. 2002. "Limitations of Rational-Choice Institutionalism for the Study of Latin American Politics." *Studies in Comparative International Development* 37(1): 57–85.

———. 2004. "Neoliberalism and Democracy in Latin America: A Mixed Record." *Latin American Politics and Society* 46(1): 135–57.

———. 2005. "The Growing Sustainability of Brazil's Low-Quality Democracy." In Francis Hagopian and Scott Mainwaring, eds., *The Third Wave of Democratization in Latin America: Advances and Setbacks,* pp. 90–120. Cambridge, UK: Cambridge University Press.

———. 2007. *Bounded Rationality and Policy Diffusion: Social Sector Reform in Latin America.* New York: Cambridge University Press.

———. 2008. "Toward a New Theory of Institutional Change." *World Politics* 60(2): 281–314.

Weyland, Kurt, Raúl L. Madrid, and Wendy Hunter, eds. 2010. *Leftist Governments in Latin America: Successes and Shortcomings.* Cambridge, UK: Cambridge University Press.

Whitehead, Laurence. 1986. "International Aspects of Democratization." In Guillermo O'Donnell, Philippe C. Schmitter, and Laurence Whitehead, eds., *Transitions from Authoritarian Rule: Comparative Perspectives,* pp. 3–46. Baltimore: Johns Hopkins University Press.

————, ed. 1996. *The International Dimensions of Democratization: Europe and the Americas.* Oxford: Oxford University Press.

————. 2002. *Democratization: Theory and Experience.* Oxford: Oxford University Press.

————. 2009. "Fernando Henrique Cardoso: The *Astuzia Fortunata* of Brazil's Sociologist-President." *Journal of Politics in Latin America* 1(3): 111–29.

Wigley, Simon, and Arzu Akkoyunlu-Wigley. 2011. "The Impact of Regime Type on Health: Does Redistribution Explain Everything?" *World Politics* 63(4): 647–77.

Wilkinson, Richard, and Kate Pickett. 2009. *The Spirit Level: Why Greater Equality Makes Societies Stronger.* London: Penguin.

Wilson, Bruce. 1998. *Costa Rica: Politics, Economics, and Democracy.* Boulder, CO: Lynne Rienner.

Wilson, Bruce, Juan Carlos Rodríguez Cordero, and Roger Handberg. 2004. "The Best Laid Schemes . . . Gang Aft A-Gley: Judicial Reform in Latin America-Evidence from Costa Rica." *Journal of Latin American Studies* 36(3): 507–31.

Winship, Christopher, and Robert D. Mare. 1984. "Regression Models with Ordinal Variables." *American Sociological Review* 49(4): 512–25.

Wiñazki, Miguel. 1995. *El último feudo: San Luis y el caudillismo de los Rodríguez Saá.* Buenos Aires: Ediciones Temas de Hoy.

————. 2002. *El Adolfo: Crónicas del fascismo mágico en la Argentina.* Buenos Aires: Editorial Planeta.

Wise, Carol. 2003. *Reinventing the State: Economic Strategy and Institutional Change in Peru.* Ann Arbor: University of Michigan Press.

Wittman, Donald A. 1973. "Parties as Utility Maximizers." *American Political Science Review* 67(2): 490–98.

Woodberry, Robert D. 2012. "The Missionary Roots of Liberal Democracy." *American Political Science Review* 106(2): 244–74.

World Bank. 2012. *World Development Indicators.* Available at http://data.worldbank.org/data-catalog/world-development-indicators.

Yashar, Deborah J. 1999. "Democracy, Indigenous Movements, and the Postliberal Challenge in Latin America." *World Politics* 52(1): 76–104.

————. 2005. *Contesting Citizenship in Latin America: The Rise of Indigenous Movements and the Postliberal Challenge.* Cambridge, UK: Cambridge University Press.

Zakaria, Fareed. 1997. "The Rise of Illiberal Democracy." *Foreign Affairs* 76(6): 22–41.

Ziblatt, Daniel. 2006. *Structuring the State: The Formation of Italy and Germany and the Puzzle of Federalism.* Princeton: Princeton University Press.

————. 2008. "Does Landholding Inequality Block Democratization? A Test of the 'Bread and Democracy' Thesis and the Case of Prussia." *World Politics* 60(4): 610–41.

Zweifel, Thomas D., and Patricio Navia. 2003. "Democracy, Dictatorship, and Infant Mortality Revisited." *Journal of Democracy,* 14(3): 90–103.

CONTRIBUTORS

Volume Editors

DANIEL BRINKS is an associate professor of political science at the University of Texas at Austin, specializing in comparative politics and public law. Brinks's research focuses on the role of the law and courts in supporting or extending the rights associated with democracy and constitutional rights more broadly, with a primary regional interest in Latin America. He is currently at work on a project exploring constitutional and judicial transformations in Latin America since the 1970s. Brinks has a PhD in political science from the University of Notre Dame and a JD from the University of Michigan Law School.

MARCELO LEIRAS is an assistant professor of political science at San Andrés University in Buenos Aires and a researcher at the National Council for Scientific and Technical Research (CONICET). Leiras has a PhD in political science from the University of Notre Dame and spent one semester in 2009 as a postdoctoral associate at Yale University. His doctoral dissertation explored the determinants of party system nationalization. His current work explores the causes and consequences of federal and decentralized government arrangements and democratization processes at the subnational level.

SCOTT MAINWARING is the Eugene and Helen Conley Professor of Political Science at the Kellogg Institute for International Studies at Notre Dame. His research interests include democratic institutions and democratization, political parties and party systems, and the Catholic Church in Latin America. His most recent book, co-authored with Aníbal Pérez-Liñán, is *Democracies and Dictatorships in Latin America: Emergence, Survival, and Fall* (Cambridge University Press, 2013). Mainwaring was elected to the American Academy of Arts and Sciences in 2010.

Other Contributors

SANDRA BOTERO is a PhD candidate in the political science department at the University of Notre Dame and a PhD fellow in the Kellogg Institute for International Studies. Her research focuses on comparative judicial politics, particularly courts in new democracies. In her dissertation, she is studying the impact of high-court decisions on socioeconomic rights in Latin America.

ROBERT M. FISHMAN is a Kellogg Institute Fellow and Professor of Sociology at the University of Notre Dame, where he has taught since 1992, working on interdisciplinary approaches to the study of democracy. Fishman is currently writing a book that shows how Portugal and Spain's polar opposite pathways to democracy generated enduring differences in democratic practice and in various societal outcomes. His books include *Democracy's Voices: Social Ties, and the Quality of Public Life in Spain* (Cornell University Press, 2004) and *The Year of the Euro: The Cultural, Social, and Political Import of Europe's Common Currency* (with Anthony Messina; University of Notre Dame Press, 2006). His articles have appeared in the *American Sociological Review*, *World Politics*, *Politics & Society*, *Studies in Comparative International Development*, *Comparative Politics*, and other journals. Fishman earned his PhD in sociology from Yale University in 1985.

CARLOS GERVASONI (MA, Stanford University; PhD, University of Notre Dame) is an assistant professor in the department of political science and international studies at Universidad Torcuato Di Tella. His recent research focuses on the determinants of subnational democracy in Argentina and on developing new indices of subnational regimes that allow for comparisons across countries. He is a regional manager for the Varieties of Democracy Project. His articles have appeared in *Comparative Political Studies*, *Democratization*, *Journal of Democracy en Español*, *Journal of Politics in Latin America*, and *World Politics*.

LUCAS GONZÁLEZ (PhD, University of Notre Dame) is a researcher at the National Council for Scientific and Technical Research (CONICET) and professor at the Universidad Católica Argentina and Universidad Nacional de San Martín. A former Kellogg PhD fellow, he studied with Guillermo O'Donnell, who was his dissertation advisor. He has coauthored two books and numerous articles, most recently in the *Journal of Politics*, *Latin American Research Review*, *Publius: The Journal of Federalism*, and *Desarrollo Económico: Revista de Ciencias Sociales*.

TERRY LYNN KARL is the Gildred Professor of Latin American Studies and Professor of Political Science at Stanford University. She has published widely on comparative politics and international relations, with special emphasis on the politics of oil-exporting countries, transitions to democracy, problems of inequality, the global politics of human rights, and the resolution of civil wars. Her works on oil, human rights and democracy include *The Paradox of Plenty: Oil Booms and Petro-States* (University of California Press, 1997), honored as one of the two best books on Latin America by the Latin American Studies Association. Karl has published extensively on comparative democratization, civil wars in Central America, and political economy. Her work has been translated into fifteen languages. Karl has a strong interest in US foreign policy and has prepared expert testimony for the US Congress, the Supreme Court, and the United Nations. In 1997 she was awarded the Rio Branco Prize by the President of Brazil, Fernando Henrique Cardoso, in recognition for her service in fostering academic relations between the United States and Latin America.

STEVEN LEVITSKY (PhD in political science, University of California at Berkeley) is Harvard College Professor and Professor of Government at Harvard University. His research interests include political parties, political regimes and regime change, and weak and informal institutions, with a focus on Latin America. He is author of *Transforming Labor-Based Parties in Latin America: Argentine Peronism in Comparative Perspective* (Cambridge University Press, 2003), coauthor of *Competitive Authoritarianism: Hybrid Regimes after the Cold War* (Cambridge University Press, 2010), and coeditor of *Argentine Democracy: The Politics of Institutional Weakness* (Pennsylvania State University Press, 2005); *Informal Institutions and Democracy: Lessons from Latin America* (Johns Hopkins University Press, 2006); and *The Resurgence of the Latin American Left in Latin America* (Johns Hopkins University Press, 2011). He is currently writing a book on the durability of revolutionary regimes and coediting a book on the challenges of party-building in contemporary Latin America.

SEBASTIÁN L. MAZZUCA (PhD Political Science, MA Economics, University of California at Berkeley) is a tenured researcher at the National Council for Scientific and Technical Research (CONICET) and an assistant professor of political economy at the Universidad de San Martín (UNSAM) in Buenos Aires. He will start a position as assistant professor of political science at Johns Hopkins University in 2015. He has been a postdoctoral fellow at Harvard University's Academy for International and Area Studies. His work focuses on state-building, regime change, and economic development, and has been published in the *American Journal of Political Science, Comparative Politics, Studies in International Comparative Development, Journal of Democracy, Hispanic American Historical Review*, and the *Oxford Handbook of Political Science*.

JAMES MCGUIRE (PhD, University of California at Berkeley) is professor and chair in the department of government at Wesleyan University. He is the author of *Peronism without Perón* (Stanford University Press, 1997) and of *Wealth, Health, and Democracy in East Asia and Latin America* (Cambridge University Press, 2011). He is a former visiting scholar at two institutions with which Guillermo O'Donnell was closely associated: the Centro de Estudios de Estado y Sociedad in Buenos Aires and the Kellogg Institute of International Studies of the University of Notre Dame. McGuire translated O'Donnell's *El estado burocrático autoritario, 1966–1973: Triunfos, derrotas y crisis*; it appeared in English as *Bureaucratic-Authoritarianism: Argentina, 1966–1973, in Comparative Perspective*.

MARÍA VICTORIA MURILLO (BA Universidad de Buenos Aires, MA and PhD Harvard University) is a professor of political science and international affairs at Columbia University. She published *Labor Unions, Partisan Coalitions, and Market Reforms in Latin America* (Cambridge University Press, 2001) and *Political Competition, Partisanship, and Policymaking in the Reform of Latin American Public Utilities* (Cambridge University Press, 2009), and numerous articles in US and Latin American journals.

ANÍBAL PÉREZ-LIÑÁN (PhD University of Notre Dame, 2001) is associate professor of political science and member of the core faculty at the Center for Latin American Studies at the University of Pittsburgh. His research focuses on constitutional design, political stability, and institutional performance among new democracies. He is the author of *Presidential Impeachment and the New Political Instability in Latin America* (Cambridge University Press 2010) and coauthor with Scott Mainwaring of *Democracies and Dictatorships in Latin America: Emergence, Survival, and Fall* (Cambridge University Press, 2013).

ENRIQUE PERUZZOTTI is Professor of Political Science and International Studies at Torcuato Di Tella University and an independent researcher of CONICET, Argentina. He has published extensively on participatory innovations, democratic representation, and accountability in Latin America. He recently published (with Martin Plot) *Critical Theory and Democracy. Constitutionalism, Civil Society, and Dictatorship in Andrew Arato's Democratic Theory* (Routledge, 2013). Other books include (with Andrew Seele) *Participatory Innovations and Representative Democracy in Latin America* (Johns Hopkins University Press, 2009), (with Carlos de la Torre) *El retorno del pueblo. Populismo y nuevas democracias en América Latina*(FLACSO, 2008), and (with Catalina Smulovitz) *Enforcing the Rule of Law: Social Accountability in Latin America* (University of Pittsburgh Press, 2006) and *Controlando la política Ciudadanos y medios en las nuevas democracias latinoamericanas* (Temas Editorial, 2002).

TIMOTHY J. POWER (Ph.D., University of Notre Dame, 1993) is director of Graduate Studies in Politics and a fellow of St Cross College at the University of Oxford. His research concerns political institutions and democratization in Latin America, especially Brazil. He is currently serving as associate editor of the *Journal of Politics in Latin America* and as treasurer of the Latin American Studies Association (LASA). His most recent books are *Corruption and Democracy in Brazil: The Struggle for Accountability* (with Matthew M. Taylor; University of Notre Dame Press, 2011) and *O Congresso por ele mesmo: Auto-percepções da classe política brasileira* (with Cesar Zucco).

PHILIPPE C. SCHMITTER received his Ph.D. in political science from the University of California at Berkeley and was successively assistant professor, associate professor, and professor at the University of Chicago (1967–81), at the European University Institute (1982–86 and 1996–2004), and at Stanford University (1986–96). He has been the recipient of numerous professional awards and fellowships. He has published books and articles on comparative politics, regional integration in Western Europe and Latin America, the transition from authoritarian rule in Southern Europe and Latin America, and on the intermediation of class, sectoral and professional interests. His current work focuses on the political characteristics of the emerging Euro-polity, on the consolidation of democracy in Southern and Eastern countries, and on the possibility of postliberal democracy in Western Europe and North America.

JORGE VARGAS CULLELL has a PhD in Political Science from the University of Notre Dame. He is director of the Programa Estado de la Nación, a research center based in Costa Rica. He has conducted extensive research on democratization in Central America, the quality of democracy in Costa Rica, and citizen attitudes in Latin America--the last two for UNDP--as well as for the Barometer of the Americas at Vanderbilt University. He has worked as an international consultant for UNDP, IADB, SIDA, and USAID, among others. He led the Citizen Audit on the Quality of Democracy in Costa Rica (2001) and oversaw the preparation of eighteen annual State of the Nation Reports in Costa Rica and four Central American Human Development Reports.

LAURENCE WHITEHEAD is a senior research fellow in politics at Nuffield College, Oxford University, and senior fellow of the College, where he has served as acting warden (2005–6). In 2011–12 he served as senior proctor of the university. His most recent books are *Latin America: A New Interpretation* (Palgrave 2010) and *Democratization: Theory and Experience* (Oxford University Press 2002). His most recent edited publications are *The Obama Administration and the Americas: Shifting the Balance* (Brookings Press 2010), *Democratization in America: A Comparative-Historical Analysis* (Johns Hopkins University Press 2009), and *Citizen Security in Latin America* (Notre Dame University Press 2009). He is editor of the Oxford University Press series "Studies in Democratization" and president of the Conseil Scientifique of the Institut des Ameriques in Paris and belongs to the steering committee of the Red Eurolatinoamericana de Gobernabilidad para el Desarrollo.

Page numbers followed by "t" or "f" refer to tables or figures.